WEB PUBLISHER'S CONSTRUCTION KIT

with **NETSCAPE PLUG-INS**

WAITE GROUP PRESS™
Corte Madera, CA

JONATHAN ANGEL

Publisher • Mitchell Waite
Associate Publisher • Charles Drucker

Acquisitions Manager • Jill Pisoni

Editorial Director • John Crudo
Project Editor • Andrea Rosenberg
Content Editor • Russ Jacobs
Copy Editor • Debi Anker
Technical Reviewer • Alec Plumb

Production Director • Julianne Ososke
Production Manager • Cecile Kaufman
Production Editor • Alice Brzovic
Senior Designer • Sestina Quarequio
Designer • Karen Johnston
Cover Illustration • Anatoly Chernishov
Production • Georgiana Briggs, Cheryl Dietsch, Michael Dietsch, Dana Rhodes, Mark Walchle

Published by Waite Group Press™, 200 Tamal Plaza, Corte Madera, CA 94925.

Waite Group Press™ is a division of Sams Publishing.

Printed in the United States of America
96 97 98 99 • 10 9 8 7 6 5 4 3 2 1

Library of Congress Cataloging in Publication Data
Angel, Jonathan.
Web publisher's construction kit with Netscape plug-ins / Jonathan Angel.
p. cm.
Includes index.
ISBN 1-57169-049-2
1. HTML (Document markup language) 2. Netscape. 3. World Wide Web (Information retrieval system) I. Title.
QA76.76.H94A54 1996
005.3--dc20

96-34734
CIP

ISBN: 1-57169-049-2: $39.99

DEDICATION

To Deborah and William for their patience, and to the memory of Alice Jones John.

Message from the Publisher

Welcome to Our Nervous System

Some people say that the World Wide Web is a graphical extension of the information superhighway, just a network of humans and machines sending each other long lists of the equivalent of digital junk mail.

I think it is much more than that. To me, the Web is nothing less than the nervous system of the entire planet—not just a collection of computer brains connected together, but more like a billion silicon neurons entangled and recirculating electrochemical signals of information and data, each contributing to the birth of another CPU and another Web site.

Think of each person's hard disk connected at once to every other hard disk on earth, driven by human navigators searching like Columbus for the New World. Seen this way the Web is more of a super entity, a growing, living thing, controlled by the universal human will to expand, to be more. Yet, unlike a purposeful business plan with rigid rules, the Web expands in a nonlinear, unpredictable, creative way that echoes natural evolution.

We created our Web site not just to extend the reach of our computer book products but to be part of this synaptic neural network, to experience, like a nerve in the body, the flow of ideas and then to pass those ideas up the food chain of the mind. Your mind. Even more, we wanted to pump some of our own creative juices into this rich wine of technology.

Taste Our Digital Wine

And so we ask you to taste our wine by visiting the body of our business. Begin by understanding the metaphor we have created for our Web site—a universal learning center, situated in outer space in the form of a space station. A place where you can journey to study any topic from the convenience of your own screen. Right now we are focusing on computer topics, but the stars are the limit on the Web.

If you are interested in discussing this Web site or finding out more about the Waite Group, please send me e-mail with your comments, and I will be happy to respond. Being a programmer myself, I love to talk about technology and find out what our readers are looking for.

Sincerely,

Mitchell Waite

Mitchell Waite, C.E.O. and Publisher

200 Tamal Plaza
Corte Madera, CA 94925
415-924-2575
415-924-2576 fax

Website:
http://www.waite.com/waite

Creating the Highest Quality Computer Books in the Industry

Waite Group Press
Waite Group New Media

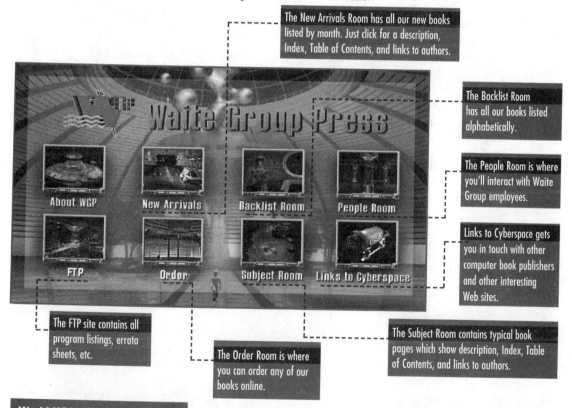

ABOUT THE AUTHOR

Jonathan Angel is a freelance writer in Palo Alto, California. He studied journalism at Stanford University and did graduate work in electronic publishing at the California Publishing Institute (back when CP/M was the business operating system of choice).

He gained early multimedia experience working with 78s, LPs, and even cylinder recordings for the Stanford Archive of Recorded Sound; has a degree from the Aspen Festival Audio-Recording Institute; and started making video tapes back when they were reel-to-reel.

Not *quite* as ancient as all that implies, Angel has worked for twelve years as a columnist, reporter, reviewer, and magazine editor in England and the United States. Publications include articles in *Byte, InfoWorld, LAN Magazine, LAN Times, PC Business World,* and others. Previous books include, with David Kosiur, *A Guide To Local Area Networks* (Prentice-Hall, 1994), and *Virtual Intimacy,* a social history of online relationships.

You can reach him at *http://www.angel.org*.

TABLE OF CONTENTS

CONTENTS

ACKNOWLEDGMENTS

My first debt is to the staff at Waite Group Press—including Mitchell Waite, John Crudo, and Jill Pisoni—for coming up with a great book idea. I am particularly grateful to Charles Drucker, who had the blind faith/dumb luck (select one) to offer the project to me, vast as it was.

The book would never have been completed without Andrea Rosenberg's unique ability to keep all its various elements on schedule. Meantime, Dan Scherf spent days, if not weeks, collecting plug-ins for the CD and—much more difficult—getting permission to include them.

Also essential was the contribution of Alec Plumb at Netscape Communications. Alec not only scrutinized all the chapters for technical accuracy, but also provided vital information about Netscape Navigator 3.0 while it was still on the drawing board.

Netscape Communications' programmers delighted—and, to be honest, often dismayed—me with their ability to obsolete beta releases of Navigator that had only been out for a few days. They regularly update the world's best Web browser, providing proof that there is at least one thing in the world that continues to improve.

I also want to thank my colleague Lawrence J. Magid for his encouragement. Among other things, by loaning a PowerBook 5300c to me while I waited for my own Power Macintosh to arrive, Larry helped me realize my wish that this book be truly cross-platform.

Finally, this must be one of the first books in the world that was completed entirely via the World Wide Web. Nothing—no documentation, no software diskettes, no interview transcripts—physically crossed the door of my office, or needed to. Everything you see and read came to me over the Web via two 28.8K modems—one of which gave its life to the cause. One can only thank the many, many people who have made the Web what it is, and marvel at what it promises to become.

INTRODUCTION

This introduction has a single, not very secret, purpose: to convince you to stop loitering in the bookstore and take the book home. If you're already heading for the cash register, you have my permission to skip directly to Chapter 1. It provides all the "introduction" you're going to need.

If, however, you're still wavering, you might want to read further. If you browse the World Wide Web using Netscape 2.0, 3.0, or future versions, this book should interest you. It should interest you even more if you're already using HTML to create Web pages that have Netscape users in mind. (Since Netscape Navigator has become the most popular personal application of all time—with about 85 percent of the browser market—that's most people.) And you won't want to leave the store without this book if you're planning to incorporate sound, video, or other special data types into your Web pages.

As long as you're running Netscape, it won't matter whether you have a Windows 3.x, Windows 95, Windows NT, or Macintosh computer. This book has been written for users of all these systems. I strongly suggest, though, that you upgrade to Netscape 3.0 and have at least 16MB of Random Access Memory. (As usual with computers, more is better. Faster is better, too.)

If you don't have a connection to the Internet, you don't know what HTML is, and you've never used a Web browser, this book isn't for you. Yet. (That doesn't make you a "Dummy" or an "Idiot," however—you should simply get the background you need by reading some earlier Waite Group Press books, which will treat you like the intelligent and curious person you are.)

However, if you already are familiar with HTML and with Netscape, you should find that everything in this book is easily followed. Rather than going into vast technical depth about any single plug-in, the book was intended to provide as much breadth as possible. You'll read about how to use and create content for more than fifty different plug-ins. You'll learn

- To create the most exciting Web site possible
- To use Netscape to provide access to existing documents over a corporate intranet
- To embed music and movies that users can play almost instantly—even over a dial-up link
- To control exactly how Netscape deals with the information you download
- And plenty more

HOW THIS BOOK IS ORGANIZED

In recognition of the fact that every plug-in user needs to know certain facts, this book starts with the basics in Chapter 1 and moves gradually to a more complex technical level by the time you have reached Chapter 8. Chapters 9-15 may be read in any order you like, since they are devoted to descriptions of, and tutorials about how to use, specific plug-ins. Hence, you can use these chapters to gain an overview of all the plug-ins on the market—or just focus on the one you want to start using right away. Chapter 16 tells how to use the Web to find new plug-ins as they are released.

Chapter 1: What You Need

This chapter introduces the subject of plug-ins, briefly reviewing the sorts of uses to which they can be put. It explains how Netscape has, in effect, become a communications-oriented operating system that runs on different types of computers.

The chapter emphasizes that the book is aimed both at users of plug-in-enabled Web pages and at those who want to learn to *create* such pages. It explains that you need some—though not extensive—HTML experience to use the book and details the hardware and software you need to proceed.

Chapter 2: An Introduction to Plug-Ins

Like most of the chapters that follow, Chapter 2 is divided into lessons. Lesson #1 defines what plug-ins actually are; Lesson #2 provides an overview of how users install plug-ins and how Netscape locates them when it needs to. Lesson #3 shows how Netscape behaves when a Web page calls for a plug-in—but the user has not yet installed that plug-in. Lesson #4 is an overview of plug-ins' technical capabilities. Lesson #5 will help you decide when you should use a plug-in—and when you shouldn't.

Chapter 3: Helper Applications: A Thing of the Past?

Chapter 3 compares and contrasts plug-ins to helper applications, external programs that Netscape and other Web browsers previously used to extend their capabilities. In Lesson #1, it introduces the important concept of MIME types, used by Web servers to tell Netscape what type of data it is dealing with. Lesson #2 shows how helper applications are used to interpret MIME types that Netscape can't handle all by itself. Lesson #3 shows how a plug-in would handle the same situation, greatly improving a Web page's appearance and ease of use. Lesson #4 tells how to configure helper applications. Explaining that helper applications are an obsolete technology—you'll probably prefer to use plug-ins—Lesson #5 lists some of the most common helpers and tells you where to get them if you really want to. Lesson #6 tells you how to remove helper applications from Netscape when you no longer want them.

Chapter 4: What About Java?

Chapter 4 is again one of comparison and contrast. In Lesson #1, it provides you with a brief history of the Java programming language, highlighting its advantages and disadvantages. Lesson #2 will bring you very quickly up to speed on how to find Java applets and incorporate them into your Web pages. Lesson #3 explains the difference between Java applets and JavaScripts, giving some useful examples of the latter. Lesson #4 reviews your choices as a Web developer, positioning plug-ins relative to both Java applets and JavaScripts.

Chapter 5: What Plug-Ins Can Do

The lessons in Chapter 5 give you more detail on how plug-ins operate and what they can do. Lesson #1 explains that plug-ins can use *data streaming* so that, for the first time, sounds can be heard and videos can begin to play even before they have been fully downloaded. Lesson #2 explains that plug-ins can operate visibly—often changing the appearance of Netscape dramatically—or invisibly, as when music is being played. A brief introduction to the plug-ins that come with Netscape 3.0—and those that are sold in the separately available Netscape Power Pack—is also provided.

Chapter 6: Understanding MIME Types

This key chapter explains what MIME (Multipurpose Internet Mail Extensions) are. Lesson #1 tells the history of MIME types, and why they are vital to the Web. Lesson #2 demonstrates how they are handled by Netscape, explaining the difference between the HTTP and FTP file-transfer protocols. It tells why Netscape sometimes seems to pay attention to the extension of files it downloads, while at other times it appears to ignore them. Symptoms of commonly encountered MIME problems are listed side-by-side with their solutions. Lesson #3 addresses the issue of server configuration, explaining how Web servers need to be adjusted before they can successfully host new data types.

Chapter 7: Installing Plug-Ins

A series of lessons in Chapter 7 describes how to add new plug-ins to your copy of Netscape, how to activate and deactivate plug-ins at will, and how to remove plug-ins from your system completely if you no longer want to use them. Like other chapters, this one is extensively illustrated: It features examples for Windows 95/NT, Windows 3.x, and Macintosh.

Chapter 8: Embedding Data in Your Web Pages: An Overview

For would-be authors, this chapter explains everything you need to know to start using plug-ins in your Web pages. Lesson #1 again emphasizes the importance of MIME types, explaining what your ISP (Internet Service Provider) will need to be told. It also tells a "secret" way you can start using plug-ins instantly, even before your ISP has made any changes to server configuration. Lesson #2 provides some quick tips about creating multimedia content. Lesson #3 introduces the all-important <EMBED> tag, plus attributes for it that are used by every plug-in. It also explains how to make it easier for users to download plug-ins they don't already have. Lesson #4 provides ways to make sure your Web page remains intelligible to users who—for some peculiar reason—aren't using Netscape Navigator as their browser. The ActiveX "objects" used by Microsoft's Internet Explorer 3.0 are briefly introduced and contrasted to Netscape plug-ins. You'll learn how to create Web pages that are optimized for Internet Explorer and for Netscape—both at once!

Chapter 9: Audio Plug-Ins

Chapter 9 is devoted to plug-ins that use Netscape Navigator to deliver sound—from simple MIDI synthesis, to speech, to CD-quality audio. It begins by explaining how to use the LiveAudio plug-in that comes with Netscape 3.0. The tutorials continue with coverage of other plug-ins: Crescendo, Echospeech, RapidTransit, RealAudio, Talker, ToolVox, and TrueSpeech.

Chapter 10: Video Plug-Ins

This chapter is about video, probably the most dramatic use of plug-ins. It begins by helping you decide which *type* of video to use in your Web pages, and warns against creating "codec-dependent" videos—those that can be played only if the user's computer has a particular decompression algorithm. The first tutorial is devoted to the LiveVideo and QuickTime plug-ins that come with Netscape 3.0. Others include: Action, CoolFusion, InterVU, MacZilla, MovieStar, VDOLive, and VivoActive.

Chapter 11: Presentation/Animation

In Chapter 11, you'll read about plug-ins that play back content created by specific presentation graphics or animation software programs. They're particularly useful if you have already created content using the relevant authoring program and now wish to "repurpose" it for the Web. Plug-ins surveyed are: ASAP Web Show, Astound, Emblaze, FutureSplash, mBED, Point Plus, Shockwave for Authorware, Shockwave for Director, Sizzler, and WebAnimator.

Chapter 12: VRML Plug-Ins

Virtual Reality Modeling Language (VRML) brings users of a Web page into the three-dimensional world of your choice. Chapter 12 introduces VRML, with simple examples of how VRML worlds are created. It then tells you how to experience VRML on the Web and how to get your own VRML authoring tool. Tutorials begin with a discussion of the Live3D plug-in included with Netscape 3.0. Other plug-ins covered are Topper, V•Realm, VR Scout, and WIRL.

Chapter 13: Graphics Plug-Ins

Chapter 13 is devoted to the large topic of graphics plug-ins, which extend the range of images you can view from within a Web page. Illustrated tutorials include ABC QuickSilver, Corel CMX Viewer, DWG/DXF Plug-in, SVF Plug-in, FIGleaf Inline, Fractal Viewer, LightningStrike, Shockwave for FreeHand, ViewDirector, WebExpresso, and WHIP!

Chapter 14: Document Plug-Ins

Ideal for intranets and other special purposes, these plug-ins let Netscape users view documents created by word processors and spreadsheets—all without modifications to the original source files. They're ideal for making archival information available. This chapter covers Adobe Acrobat Reader, Envoy, Formula/ONE NET, KeyView, and QuickView Plus.

Chapter 15: Other Plug-Ins

This chapter features an overview of plug-ins that are more special-purpose than those in previous chapters. It also includes late-breaking news about plug-ins that were not available in time to be given the full tutorial treatment—but about which you should be aware. Plug-ins covered include

- Argus MapGuide Viewer
- Carbon Copy/Net
- Chime
- CineWeb
- Concerto
- Corel Visual CADD
- CPC View
- CyberAge Raider
- DSM
- EarthTime
- GoScript
- Look@Me
- HindSite
- ichat

- JetForm Web Filler
- Koan
- MIDIPLUG
- Navigate with an Accent
- Neuron
- NET-Install
- PointCast
- PowerMedia
- Project X
- ScriptActive
- SuperCede VM
- Tcl/Tk
- techexplorer
- WebBASIC
- Worldgroup

Chapter 16: Finding New Plug-Ins

This chapter tells how to use the Web to locate newly released plug-ins—during 1996, at least one new plug-in was being released every week. It surveys Netscape's own plug-ins page, the popular BrowserWatch site, and other lists.

Appendixes

Appendix A is for those who may not have a CD-ROM drive always handy. It serves as a reference to what plug-ins are included on disk with the book. Appendix B is for Windows users, decoding the otherwise cryptic names of files in Netscape Navigator's PLUGINS folder.

ABOUT THE CD

If you're a fast reader or you just like hanging out in bookstores—and I plead guilty to both of these myself—you can now dip into any of the chapters to get an even better idea of the book's content.

However, without buying the book, you can't take the CD-ROM home to view its contents. (Not unless you're a consummately evil person, and then, well, you deserve the trouble you're going to have. Most of us find that plastic they seal the CD-ROMs in difficult enough to open when we're at home!)

In order to get around this problem—and because we're proud of its contents—here is a brief preview of the CD.

To run the CD-ROM, you'll need to have upgraded to Netscape 3.0 or above. The HTML shell on the disc was deliberately written to exploit the features of this browser, and it won't work properly with any others. You also need LiveAudio and QuickTime, two of the plug-ins that come with the "standard" edition of Netscape 3.0. If you obtained your browser without these, you can download them separately from *http://www.netscape.com*. You'll also need Apple's QuickTime extensions for Windows or Macintosh if they aren't already on your system.

Once you have the necessary software, access the CD-ROM by using File Manager (Windows 3.x), Explorer (Windows 95 or NT), or the Finder (Macintosh) to locate OPENME.HTM in the root folder. Double-click on this file, and Netscape will open it. (If this fails to happen, because the proper associations have for some reason not been set up on your computer, run Netscape first and then use its File/Open menu to load OPENME.HTM.)

You should now see a screen similar to that shown in Figure A if you have a Windows 95 system. If you have a Windows 3.x computer, it will look more like that shown in Figure B, while Mac users will see a screen similar to the one shown in Figure C.

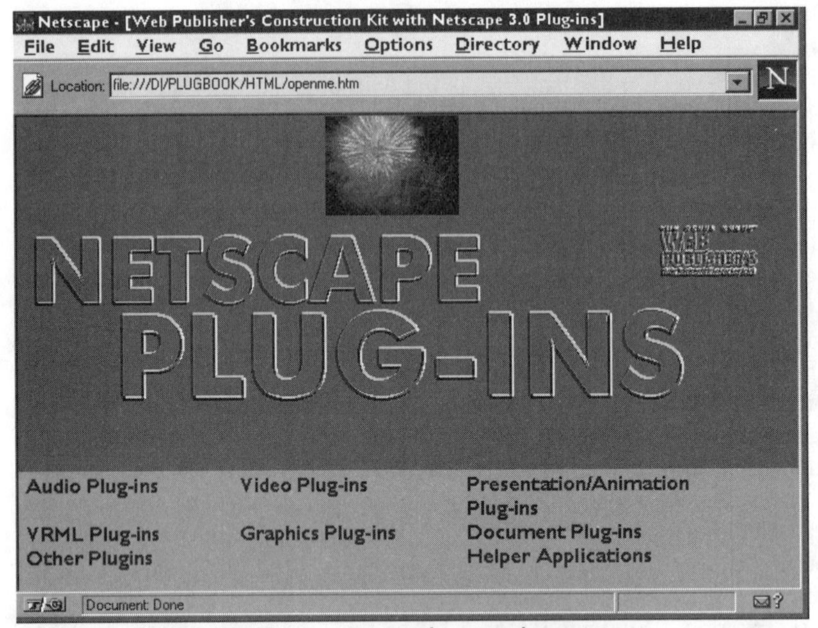

Figure A OPENME.HTM running under Windows 95

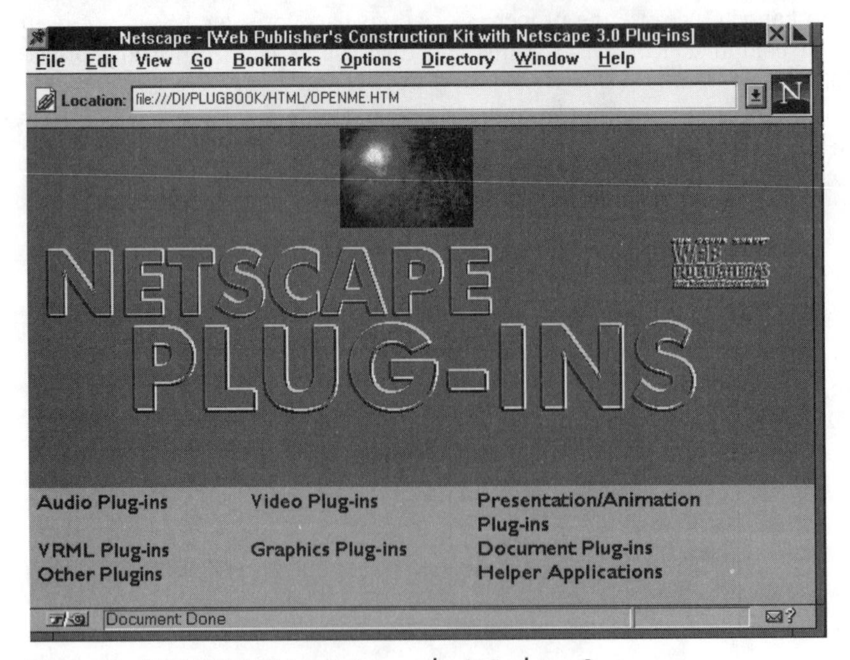

Figure B OPENME.HTM running under Windows 3.x

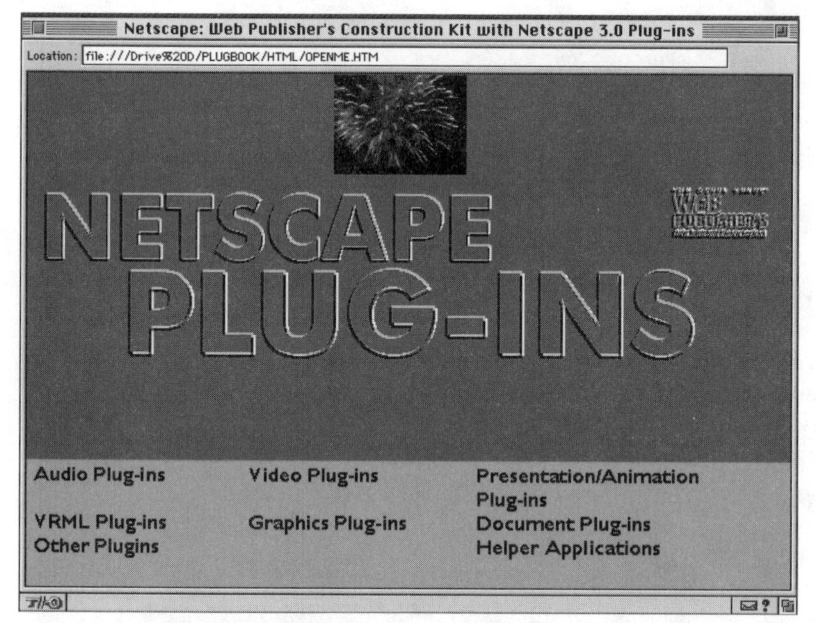

Figure C OPENME.HTM running on a Macintosh

You'll experience a short delay as a QuickTime movie loads from the CD. Once loaded, this will begin playing, providing a visual example of how plug-ins can add "fireworks" to your Web pages. Simultaneously, you'll hear some MIDI music (it's not brilliant, but—hey—MIDI files that are truly public domain aren't easy to find!).

These features not only jazz up our CD-ROM, but also serve to confirm that your installed copy of Netscape is ready to cope with multimedia content. If your computer crashes or has trouble dealing with them, see the section below headed "If You Have Technical Difficulties."

Assuming all is well, you're now ready to make a choice from the menu at the bottom of the screen. The menu entries correspond to book Chapters 9-15 (briefly outlined above); by clicking on any of them, you'll move to a Web page that summarizes the chapter and provides access to each of the plug-ins it mentions.

Figure D shows an example of the page you'll see when you click on the "Graphics Plug-ins" menu entry. To move from one section to another, just make another choice from the menu: Since it is a Netscape frame that always remains on display, navigation is simple.

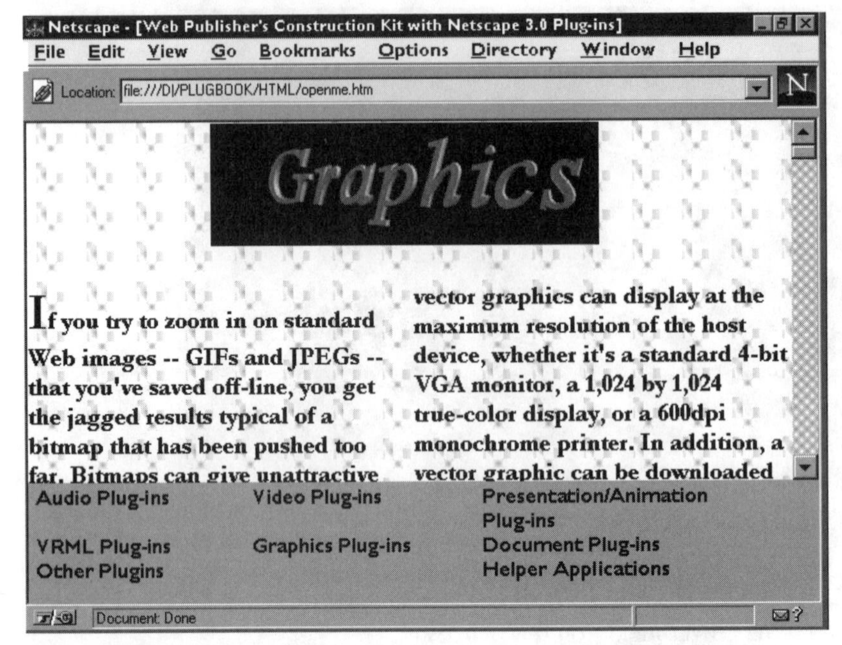

Figure D Each section on the CD-ROM corresponds to a book chapter; this one is for Graphics Plug-ins

To read one of the sections in its entirety, use your PAGE DOWN key or click on the scroll bar at the right. When you have discovered a plug-in that you'd like to install into your copy of Netscape, click on the down arrow that appears in the gray box at the beginning of each write-up. A menu will drop down to indicate which versions of the plug-ins are available on the CD (see Figure E).

Select the version of your choice; then click on the "Click to copy chosen plug-in" button. Netscape will pop up a dialog box that asks you where you want to save the relevant file. Select a location on your hard drive that you usually use for temporary storage (for example, Windows users might want to pick C:\TEMP, and Mac users might want to pick the Desktop). Netscape will use this location to save the setup program that you'll use to install the plug-in. (For more information about installing plug-ins, see Chapter 7.)

If, as in Figure F, the only entry available in the drop-down menu is "Web site," installation files for the plug-in you have chosen are not available on the CD-ROM itself. Not to worry: Simply run the dialer program you normally use to connect your computer to the Internet. (It is not usually necessary to exit Netscape in order to do this.) Then return to Netscape and click on the "Click to go to Web site" button. You'll be taken to the Web site maintained by the authors of the plug-in you're interested in. Follow the links and instructions you'll see there to download the installation program you want.

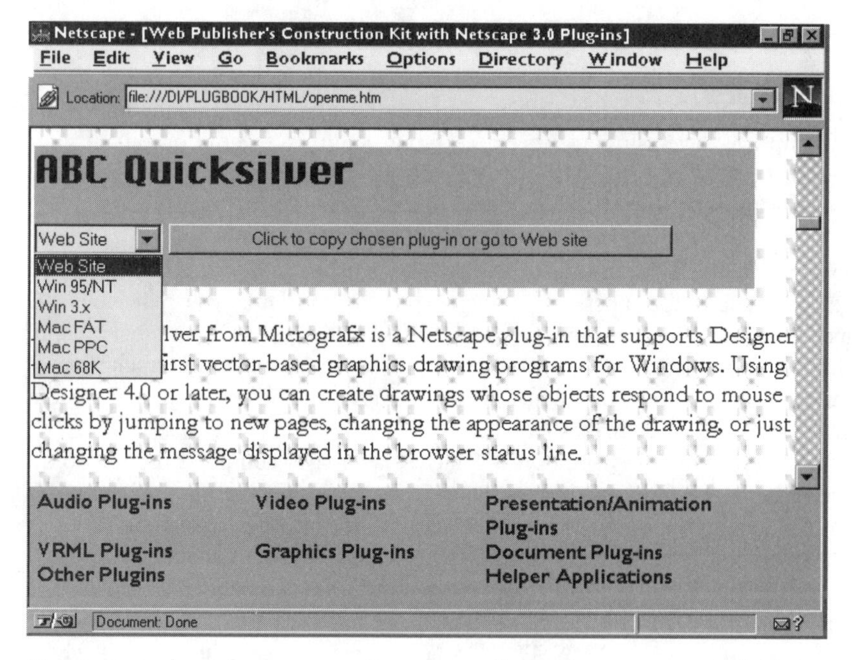

Figure E A drop-down menu shows you which plug-ins are available on the CD

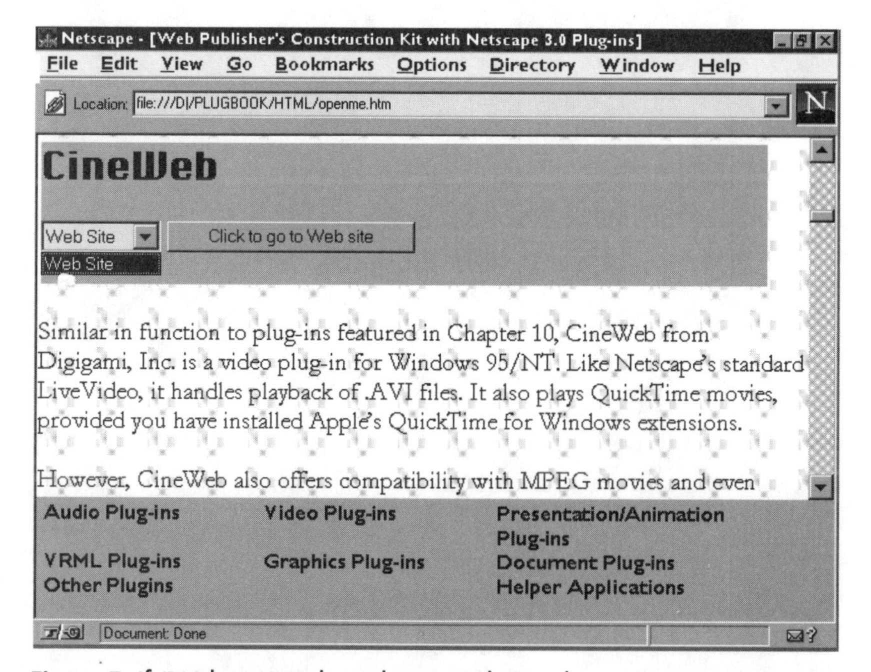

Figure F If "Web site" is the only menu choice shown, you can connect to the Internet to download the plug-in

If You Have Technical Difficulties

If you load OPENME.HTM and do not hear any music, it could be because your computer does not have a MIDI-capable sound board. Or, you may not have amplified speakers or an external amplifier successfully connected to your computer's audio output. If your computer *does* play sound in other Macintosh/Windows applications, but fails to do so here, double-check to make sure that you really installed LiveAudio when you installed Netscape 3.0.

If you load OPENME.HTM and do not see the fireworks video, or if, in the case of Windows 3.x, your computer experiences a general protection fault, you may not have installed QuickTime for Windows—or you may not have the latest QuickTime version. Some graphics display drivers for Windows 3.x may also be unstable with QuickTime. If you persistently get general protection faults, try switching from 256 colors to 16.7 million colors or vice versa to see if that makes any difference.

You may well have difficulties with QuickTime replay if your computer has only 8MB of RAM. In that case, you really need to upgrade your system—most of the other plug-ins mentioned in this book are not going to work either with this amount of memory.

If you have temporary difficulties running QuickTime, but you would like in the meantime to use OPENME.HTM and the files it references, you can do so. Exit Netscape and then disable the QuickTime plug-in as described in Chapters 7 and 10. Then, you can run Netscape again and reload OPENME.HTM. You'll see "missing link" icons where QuickTime movies would have been displayed, but you will still be able to use the menus and files on the CD-ROM as described in the previous section.

1

WHAT YOU NEED

1

Never—except, just maybe, when humans first learned to communicate using words—has the use of a medium changed so rapidly.

Just a couple of years ago, the World Wide Web was being used mostly by computer scientists and other academics to collaborate on projects. Hypertext links within documents were used mostly to annotate sources and elucidate. Graphics were used only when they absolutely had to be in order to clarify a point.

Today? You can't miss the change. While scientific users are still an important part of the Web (and often at the forefront of advancing its technical frontiers), their pages have been engulfed by those dealing with...with...well, let's put it this way: For every activity of humankind—birth, death, sex, work, shopping, left-handed Morris dancing—there is at least one Web site, and usually hundreds more.

And just as the Web has come to reflect what we, the people, think about, it also reflects the *ways* in which we think at the end of the twentieth century. Using video clips, sound bites, photographs, still photographs, music, and more, today's state-of-the-art Web sites positively drip with multimedia.

A WASTE OF BANDWIDTH?

Some people criticize graphics-rich sites for "wasting bandwidth," pandering too much to popular tastes, or becoming too commercial. I agree with them, to a point: We've all encountered sites where elaborate, slow-loading graphics stood in the way of our retrieving the information we needed.

However, I have a couple of responses to this argument. One is that with the advent of technologies such as cable modems, satellite delivery, ADSL, ISDN, and VDSL, any constraints in bandwidth are purely temporary. Another is that the Web—not a single entity, but rather a collection of different computers connected together—is essentially self-regulating. If you, using computer X, choose not to connect to computer Y anymore because of the bloated graphics found on that machine, then the owners of Y have done no damage to anyone but themselves.

In addition, the kind of graphics that most annoy are those that are *extrinsic* to the main purpose of a site. Rather than having informational content, they are there merely to make the site "look better." But, as I hope you'll appreciate by the time you have read a chapter or two of this book, the graphics, sounds, and other media that may be added to a well-designed site using Netscape plug-ins are *intrinsic* to the site. They are not there merely to accompany the information—they *are* the information.

NOTE: In most of this book, the word "Netscape" is used to refer to the Web browser whose full, proper name is "Netscape Navigator," from Netscape Communications Inc. of Mountain View, California. Consider using "Netscape" a small gesture on our part to save paper and ink, keeping the cost of books down.

INFORMATION 'R' US

One of the most exciting aspects of Netscape plug-ins is the opportunity they offer for "repurposing" a company's existing information. Say your company has a wide variety of data sheets that have been written in Microsoft Word, articles that are already laid out in Adobe PageMaker or Quark XPress, presentations that have been prepared in Microsoft PowerPoint, or spreadsheets created via Microsoft Excel. To make these materials available on the Internet for users outside your company—or on an intranet for your own branch offices—once would have meant laboriously converting them to HTML, with inevitable delay and loss of formatting.

Because Netscape plug-ins are nothing more, and nothing less, than program modules that extend the browser's ability to view different types of data, they let the user view those Word, PageMaker, XPress, PowerPoint, Excel, or other documents in their native form. If changes to the source documents were made last night, then the Netscape user with the right plug-in would be able to see those changes. The cost savings and improved timeliness speak for themselves.

WHY NETSCAPE?

Plug-ins are not a new idea. If you've been using personal computers since the mid-1980s, you probably remember "add-ins" for Lotus 1-2-3 that let users spell-check their spreadsheets, access dBase databases, and talk to mainframes. The idea was the same then as it is now: to give the user a tool they already know and understand while extending the capabilities of the tool beyond those conceived of by its original designers.

The combination of DOS and Lotus 1-2-3 became, in effect, a whole new operating system. Similarly, Netscape too has become a new kind of communications-oriented operating system thanks to plug-in technology. Cynics have accused Netscape Communications of trying to lock in customers by turning its Web browser into a bloated user environment that competes with Windows 95. And Microsoft certainly has appeared to be approaching the same market from the opposite direction, adding numerous Internet-specific features to Windows.

No matter what your take is on this battle of the titans, however, you have to agree that users are coming out ahead. Add-ons for Lotus 1-2-3 never worked with any other spreadsheets, but Microsoft, NetManage, and other companies have announced that Netscape plug-ins are, or soon will be, compatible with their Web browsers as well.

Plug-ins have damaged the case of Oracle's Larry Ellison and others trying to popularize the concept of a turnkey "Web computer" or television-based browser. If these "thin clients" have neither the hard disk storage nor the random access memory required to handle plug-ins, their users will be denied access to the full range of media types on the Web. Plug-ins also cause slight harm to those with outdated browsers who have no desire to upgrade them. In this book, though, you'll learn how to employ plug-ins thoughtfully so those who can't access the technology can still interact with your Web pages.

If the industry in general is moving toward plug-in technology, why am I touting Netscape in particular when I don't even own any of the company's stock? Not a bad question. One reason is that Netscape was *there first*. It was the first company to recognize that no browser could be all things to all people, opening its product to third-party extensions. It was the first to publish software development kits for would-be plug-in authors, and the first to make the plug-ins work in its browsers. Today, plug-ins for other browsers are coming into existence, but Netscape has a vast lead.

Another reason is that, like many people, I've tried a lot of Web browsers. Most have some good features, but I keep coming back to Netscape because it simply makes Web pages look better. More important, it seems the fastest—and on the Web, performance is everything.

Best of all, Netscape is agnostic when it comes to operating systems. It runs on Windows 3.x, Windows 95, Macintosh, and UNIX, giving you access to more clients than anyone else. Though Windows 3.x and UNIX versions of Netscape don't have as many plug-ins as the other versions, they are at least *there*. If you develop Web pages with Netscape in mind, you'll have the most potential readers—which can't be bad!

THIS BOOK IS FOR YOU IF . . .

This book is for two different types of readers. No, let me state that more accurately: It's for the *same* type of reader wearing two different hats.

In your passive "couch potato" role, you just want to sit back with your favorite beverage and surf the Web, for both information and entertainment. You want Netscape to be configured with the right plug-ins so you can see all there is to see. This book will help you when you're in couch-potato mode by making sure you have everything you need for "good reception." Along the way, you'll also get clued-in to today's hottest, most scintillating Web sites.

In your active, "workaday role," you want to open your text editor and create a Web site that people will flock to. You want to make Netscape sing and dance—literally. You need to get hold of the plug-ins that are right for your purpose and then quickly learn the HTML extensions they require. This book will help you when you're wearing your workaday hat by providing the information you need all in one place.

WHAT YOU NEED TO KNOW

There are many books on the market that will lead a novice through the procedure of creating his or her own Web pages. However, this is not meant to be one of them. (I can cheerfully refer you to many excellent books on the topic, among them the *HTML Web Publisher's Construction Kit* by David Fox and Troy Downing, which just happens to be a previous volume in this series.)

Rather, so that we can cover new ground together, I need to assume that you already have a basic familiarity with HTML and that, preferably, you've already published your pages on the Internet. Don't worry, however: The level of HTML knowledge this book will require isn't terribly great. If you already know how to place an image on your Web pages using the <IMG SRC> command, then you're but one step away from embedding data that plug-ins can read using the <EMBED SRC> command.

Plug-ins can work well in tandem with advanced HTML techniques such as frames, image maps, and so on, but they do not require them. In fact, you might well discover that plug-ins do so much to spice up your Web pages on their own that you no longer feel the need for so many other programming tricks.

Of course, once you've created Web pages you need to know how to copy them to, and make them available on, a Web server—whether it's located on site at your place of business or at an independent service provider (ISP). Working with plug-ins doesn't change this process any. However, it may eventually require that you contact tech support personnel where the server is located to request that they edit a configuration file or two specifically, those dealing with how the server handles Multipurpose Internet Mail Extension (MIME) types, as explained in Chapter 6, "Understanding MIME Types."

If you already have friends in tech support, send them some good vibes. If, on the other hand, your ISP's tech support is permanently inaccessible, it might be a good time to take your business elsewhere. And if you run your own Web server, then *you* are the tech support. (Fun, isn't it?)

By the way, this book wasn't written for those fine folks who've been busy creating plug-ins (as opposed to the *rest* of us, who just write HTML pages that invoke them). However, any plug-in programmers who've put down their Jolt Cola and C++ documentation to join us are welcome—if only to review what their competition is up to.

WHAT YOU NEED TO HAVE

In order to create and test the Web pages you'll be creating, you need a text editor and a copy of Netscape 3.0. Many plug-ins work with Netscape 2.0 as well (in addition to a few other browsers), but Netscape 3.0 has fixed numerous quirks in how they operate and made configuration easier. You should definitely start work with the latest version of the browser (always available for download from *http://www.netscape.com*) if you can. With Netscape 3.0, you'll get four bundled plug-ins, too: LiveAudio, LiveVideo, Live3D, and QuickTime.

If you're reading this when future versions of Netscape—as I write, nothing more than tentative lists of specifications—have become available, you should find this book just as relevant to your needs. Future versions of Netscape should make installation of plug-ins easier, and they might include a set of bundled plug-ins that's slightly different from Netscape 3.0's. However, they won't affect how third-party plug-ins operate, or change what you need to know to use them in your Web pages—which is 90% of what this book is all about.

In addition to Netscape, your computer should have a full-time or dial-up connection to the Internet. It needs to run either Windows 95, Windows NT, or the MacOS. Windows 95 and NT have the widest availability of plug-ins, but Windows 3.x and the Mac aren't too far behind. (UNIX versions of Netscape will support plug-ins as well, but few are available.)

If you still insist on working with Windows 3.x—because you run OS/2, because you have older machines that just don't run Windows 95 well, or (like me) you just sometimes enjoy a less bloated environment with snappy performance—you can do so. Just be aware that many Windows plug-ins do not come in 3.x versions. Those that do sometimes require the Win32s libraries, which I've found can be slow and unreliable.

Speaking of performance and reliability, 16MB of RAM is a must for Win 95 and Mac users. (If you're running Windows NT, you probably have that much or more already.) I'd love to claim otherwise, but the fact is that 8MB machines are pretty stretched just running Netscape. Plug-ins increase Netscape's memory requirements while they're running, often to beyond 8MB. While you're developing Web pages, you'll also want free memory for your text editor and, probably, some graphics software as well.

Web site development is not the place for platform bigotry. It's fine to be a Windows partisan or Mac evangelist in private, but once you make a Web site public, you don't know who's going to be visiting it. So the more computers you have on hand—with different processor types and screen sizes—to test the Web pages you create, the better.

During the preparation of this book, I used Windows 3.x, Windows 95, and Macintosh computers because that's what I have (in common with most people, I suspect). The Windows 95 and Macintosh machines each had 40MB of RAM—not essential, but jolly nice to have. In order to better share Web pages between platforms in their developmental stages, I used an Ethernet local area network and Miramar Systems' Personal MacLAN Connect (which turns a Windows computer into an AppleShare server and client).

HOW TO USE THIS BOOK (NOT)

When I was young(er) and (even more) foolish, I swore I'd *never* write a book chapter with a section called "How to Use This Book." We've all suffered too many times at the hands of software products that come with a sheaf of giant manuals, plus yet another book that tells us how to *use* them.

So, you *don't* need to read these following paragraphs to use this book! I'd like to mention, however, that you have official permission from on high to read this book in any order you like. If your main reason for getting the book is, for example, because you want to add sound to your Web pages, then feel free to read Chapter 9, "Audio Plug-Ins," first to explore the possibilities, returning to the earlier chapters when you feel you need more information. If, on the other hand, you're getting the book because you've always wanted to know more about MIME types (and this, somehow, I sincerely doubt), you'll get the lowdown on them early on.

You'll find repeated references to Appendix A, which is your key to the files included on the companion CD-ROM. I would have liked to give you, during the course of each chapter, solid information about whether or not a given plug-in is on the CD-ROM—instead of annoying you by making you consult the appendix. However, it's a fact of life in this business that the lead time for the paper portion of a book is longer than for the polycarbonate part.

Rather than artificially restricting the contents of the CD-ROM to fit the contents of chapters that had already been typeset, we decided to arrange matters so that the CD-ROM contains as many plug-ins as possible, in as up-to-date versions as we could get. The disc also contains an online guide to its own contents. Just put the CD-ROM in your computer's drive, run Netscape, and then use the browser's File Open command to open OPENME.HTM in the CD's root folder.

Finally, a few words about the URLs in this book. We've naturally checked and double-checked them, but like everything to do with the Web, these are subject to change monthly, weekly, or even daily. If you enter one of the URLs in this book and Netscape repeatedly tells you the file is not found, the Web page may have been moved or renamed.

Use the trick of progressively backspacing to remove parts of the URL, thereby expanding your search. In other words, if *http://www.aserver.com/plug-in/thingummy.html* gives an error message, try *http://www.aserver.com/plug-in/*. If that doesn't work, try *http://www.aserver.com/*.

2

AN INTRODUCTION TO PLUG-INS

2

Ever since Netscape first burst onto the scene—quickly becoming the world's most popular Web browser—its features have been hyped, publicized, and adopted within (seemingly) minutes by heads-up Web page designers. Anyone who hasn't heard about Netscape innovations, which have included tables, frames, colored backgrounds, Java applets, and (in Netscape Gold) a WYSIWYG HTML editor, probably hasn't read a computer magazine or used a modem for a couple of years.

Plug-ins, however, are one Netscape goody whose debut was almost stealthy. When the plug-in architecture made its debut (in Netscape 2.0), it was overshadowed by some of the above innovations because the company did relatively little to document or publicize it. Additionally, there was only one generally available plug-in, Macromedia's Shockwave for Director (Figure 2-1).

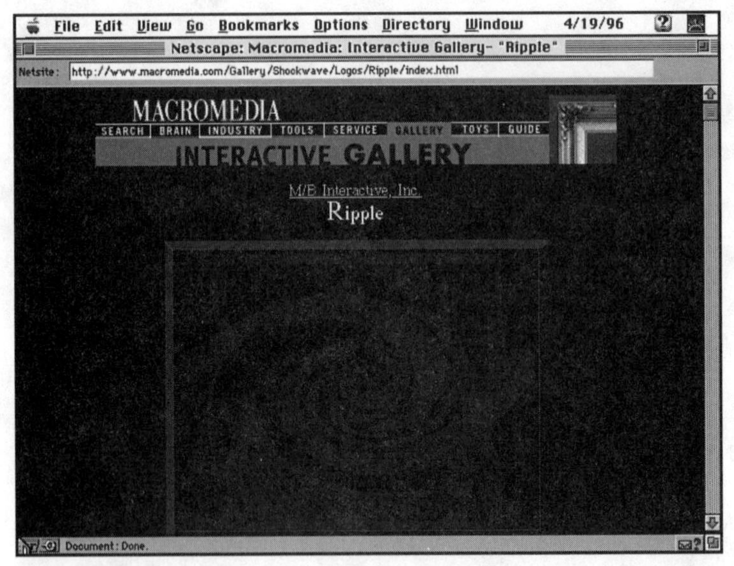

Figure 2-1 Macromedia's Shockwave for Director was the first generally available plug-in

With Netscape 3.0, this has changed. Dozens of plug-ins have already been released, with more appearing daily (or so it seems). Netscape 3.0 also comes with plug-ins of its very own: LiveAudio, LiveVideo, Live3D, and QuickTime. These let you play sounds, view movies, or wander around 3D worlds.

Lesson 1: What Plug-Ins Are

Plug-ins are a way to extend the range of Web pages. They can make a Web page talk to you out loud, sing, or give you a slide show. They can show you a video, hand you a document originally formatted in PostScript, or let you browse through an online file cabinet.

Helper applications and Java applets can perform some of these functions, too. (In Chapter 3, "Helper Applications: A Thing of the Past?," you'll learn more about their similarities to, and differences from, plug-ins.) However, plug-ins are much easier for a user to configure than helper applications. And they're much easier for a Web page author to incorporate than Java applets.

Netscape's plug-in architecture is an API (Application Programming Interface) that lets third-party developers write software programs to extend the capabilities of the browser. These programs—"plug-ins"—are modules written in compiled C or C++ that load themselves when needed and go away when their work is done.

Plug-ins do not change the basic user interface of Netscape. Basic operation such as navigation, history, opening Web pages, and so on, are not changed by any plug-in. Pages without embedded data look no different when plug-ins are installed than they did before. That said, plug-ins can at times make a dramatic difference in the way a Netscape screen looks.

Lesson 2: How Plug-Ins Are Installed

You'll read more about how to install plug-ins in Chapter 7, "Installing Plug-Ins." Briefly, however, the mechanism is as follows: A plug-in is downloaded via the Web (or copied from the CD-ROM included with this book) in a version compatible with the user's machine. Like helper applications (and unlike Java applets), plug-ins have to be designed specifically for the client operating system. There are plug-ins for Windows 3.x, Windows 95, MacOS and UNIX.

Windows 95 and Windows NT plug-ins are identical. However, if you have a machine on which you run both Windows 3.x and Windows 95, or you have a Windows computer and a Mac and you want to use Macromedia Shockwave on both, you would have to obtain versions of the Shockwave plug-in for each machine. Once the plug-in is on the client machine, it is copied—either automatically by an installation program or manually by the user—to a plug-ins folder (or subdirectory, if you insist) within an existing Netscape program folder.

By design, each plug-in is associated with one (or more) MIME data types that Netscape does not support natively (see Chapter 6, "Understanding MIME Types," for more information). In other words, a plug-in might be associated with TIFF graphic images, but there would be no point in creating a plug-in associated with GIF images since Netscape already supports these.

Plug-in programmers create a resource file whose FileExtents entry specifies what file extension the plug-in can deal with, and whose MIME type entry provides more specific information about the MIME data type it handles. For example, a plug-in that plays .WAV files on the Windows version of Netscape would have FileExtents set to WAV and MIME type set to audio/x-wav.

Windows plug-ins can also include a FileOpenName resource. This lets Netscape know that it can open up files containing the new data type directly from within the File/Open dialog box.

When you load Netscape 2.0 or 3.0, it looks in the Plug-ins folder to see what plug-ins are there. Netscape then registers each plug-in for possible future use, recording the information it provides about MIME types, file extensions, and so on.

Before loading even one Web page, you can confirm or deny the presence of plug-ins via the About Plug-ins menu. On Windows machines, it's found under the Help/About Plug-ins menu (Figure 2-2); on the Macintosh, this is found under the Apple menu (Figure 2-3).

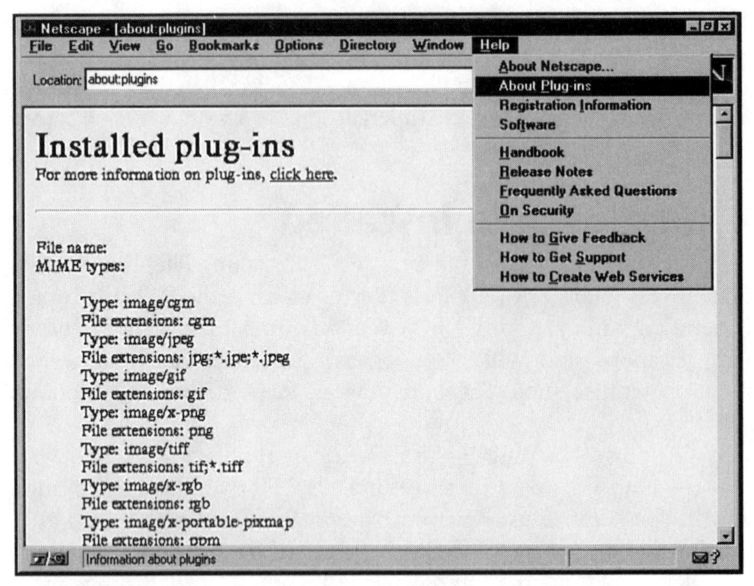

Figure 2–2 You can confirm the presence of plug-ins using the About Plug-ins Menu; above is the Windows version

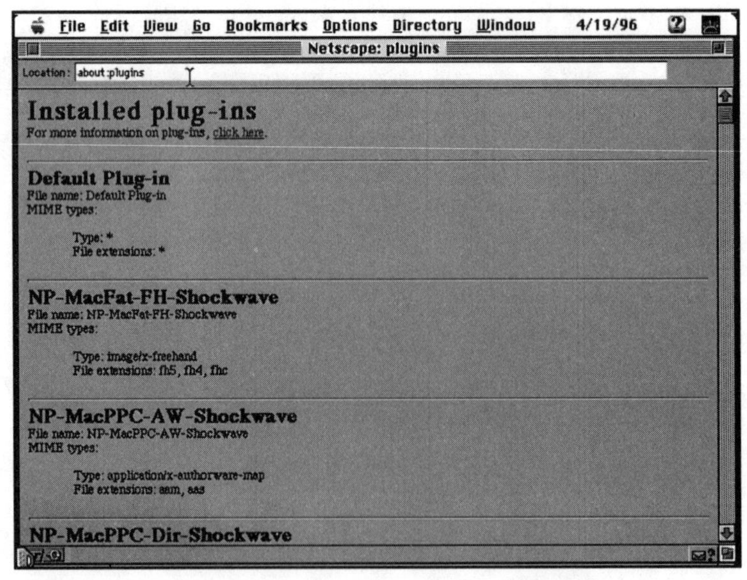

Figure 2–3 The Macintosh version of About Plug-ins

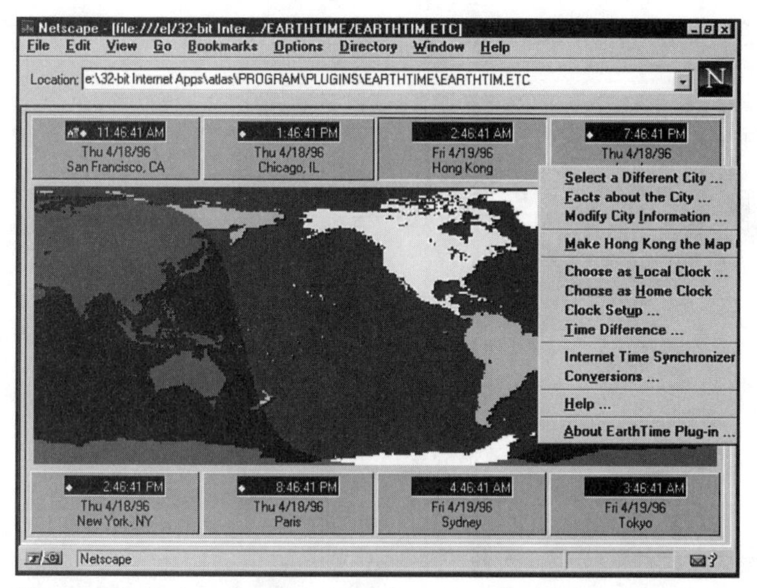

Figure 2–4 Once a plug-in has been installed, Netscape can look dramatically different. This is StarFish Software's EarthTime Plug-in for Windows

NOTE: This book uses a hyphen in the phrase "plug-ins" because, well, because we had to make a choice and this seemed the more frequently used of the two possibilities. Netscape Communications hasn't made a definitive choice: You'll find that the hyphen sometimes appears in program menus and directory names and, at other times, is omitted. Just ignore it.

Later, if Netscape encounters a Web page with a MIME type an installed plug-in can read, it passes the data to that plug-in for interpretation. Once a plug-in loads, the Web page may suddenly look dramatically different (Figure 2-4). Or, you may not even be able to tell that the plug-in is there (Figure 2-5). The area of the screen controlled by a plug-in may look no different from any other part of the Web page—yet an additional software application is there behind the scenes, controlling how the browser responds to mouse clicks, keyboard entries, and other actions.

As mentioned, a cleverly written plug-in integrates with Netscape so well that—on the Windows version—it even adds entries to the program's File/Open dialog box. For example, the LiveAudio plug-in adds the .MID file type to the normal list of those Netscape can open (Figure 2-6).

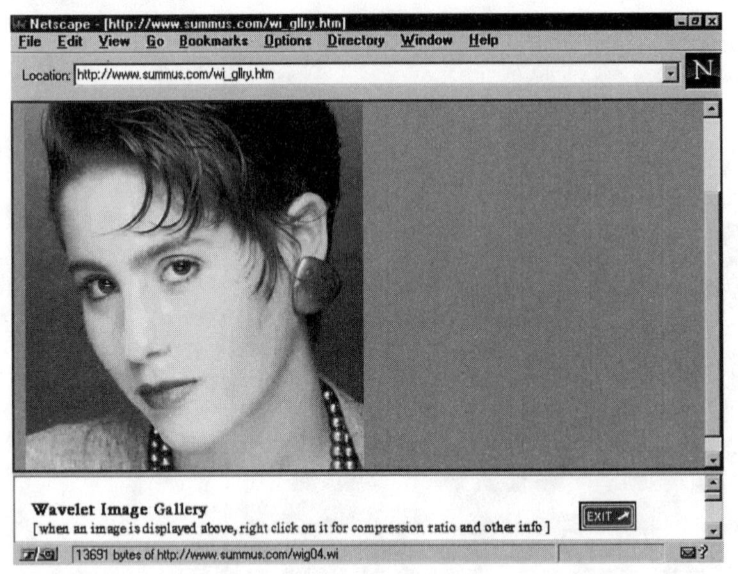

Figure 2–5 Plug-ins can also operate with no immediately visible sign. This Netscape display looks normal, but the graphic is a "wavelet" displayed via a plug-in from Summus Ltd.

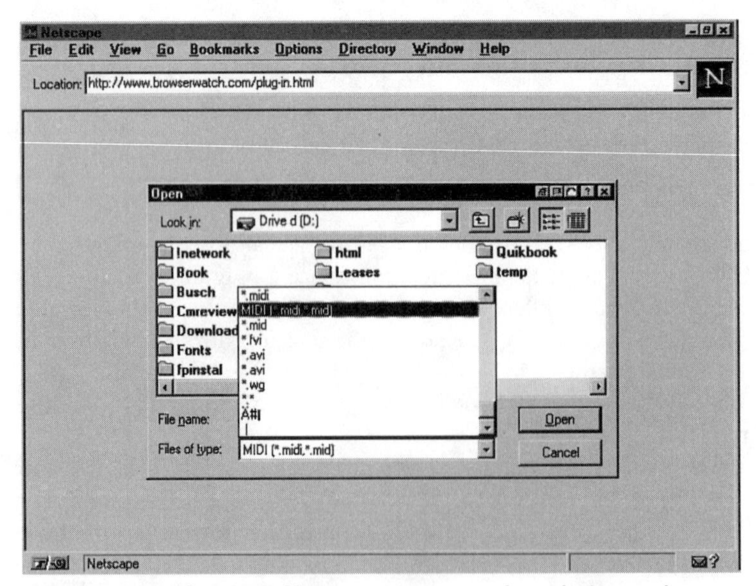

Figure 2–6 The .MID file type appears in this File/Open list courtesy of the NPSOUND plug-in (supplied as standard with Netscape 3.0)

Lesson 3: What Happens If You Don't Have the Right Plug-In

What happens if a Web page incorporates a MIME type—a TIFF image, let's say—for which a plug-in is required, yet the user hasn't yet installed that plug-in into their copy of Netscape? That's a good question.

Figure 2-7 shows the same Web page as Figure 2-5, but *without* the plug-in that helped interpret the embedded TIFF image. As you can see, the TIFF image is not displayed. Netscape instead displays an icon where the image would have been, and pops up a dialog box warning you there is a MIME type it cannot interpret. (This dialog box only pops up by itself once; thereafter the user must click on the mystery icon to invoke it.)

If you click on "Get the Plug-in," Netscape's default behavior is to take you to a list of plug-ins stored on the Netscape Communications server at *http://home.netscape.com/comprod/products/navigator/version_2.0/plugins/index.html.* On that list, it is hoped, you can find a plug-in that will help Netscape interpret the particular type of MIME data involved—whether it's a graphic, a sound, a video, or what have you.

Apart from the fact that the Netscape server is sometimes overloaded and near-unobtainable (especially if a new Netscape version or bug fix was just released), it is awkward and inelegant for users to be bounced to a generic list of plug-ins in this manner. Therefore, Web page developers often arrange things so visitors are taken directly to the source of the one plug-in they need. For more on this technique, and the PLUGINSPAGE attribute that enables it, see Chapter 8, "Embedding Data in Your Web Pages: An Overview."

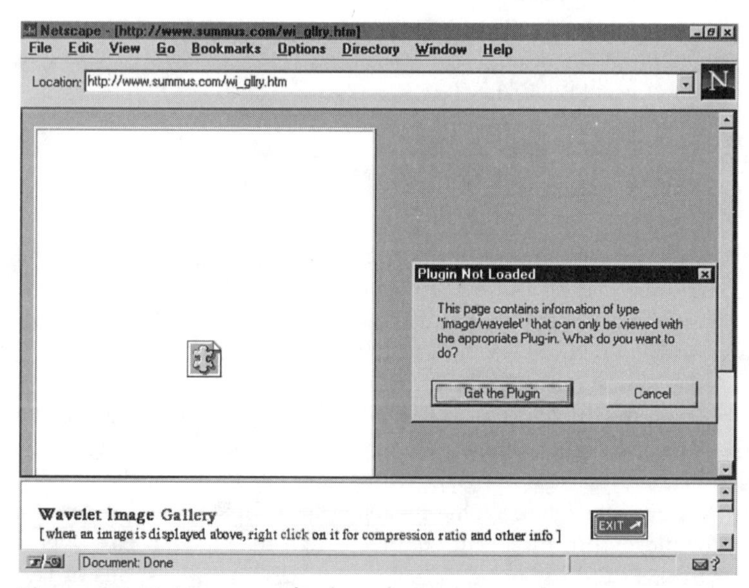

Figure 2-7 Netscape displays this warning when it encounters a MIME type for which no plug-in is already loaded

When you have located the plug-in you need, you download the installation files to the desktop (if you're using a Macintosh) or to a temporary folder/subdirectory (if you're using Windows). Then, as noted above and in Chapter 7, "Installing Plug-Ins," you run an installation program or copy the plug-in to your Netscape Plug-ins folder manually. Netscape must then be exited and restarted so that it can register the new plug-in.

Lesson 4: What Plug-Ins Are Capable Of

Chapter 5, "What Plug-Ins Can Do," contains more information about plug-ins' technical capabilities and the ways in which they can appear—and disappear. From the examples mentioned so far, however, you've already learned that plug-ins can perform most operations associated with any other Windows (or Macintosh, or UNIX) application. They maintain a two-way link with Netscape, using it as the window onto their operations, and they can also communicate with other installed applications on the host machine.

Plug-ins, in fact, have most of the capabilities of separate, stand-alone applications. Although they live within Netscape's browser window, they have the same potential to handle and process events that any other application would.

Plug-ins also support *streaming* technology. Via streaming, large data files are broken into sequential "chunks." In the past, users often had to wait until an entire data file was downloaded before a helper application could play the sound, show the video, or whatever the data might have been. Now, the first chunk of data to arrive suffices to launch the plug-in and, if appropriate, start playing the file. The remaining data can be downloaded in the background. With luck, a fast connection and a strong tailwind—not all of which regularly apply in the real world, of course—information can actually be transferred without any audible gaps or extended delays.

Netscape Communications has proposed an extension to the HyperText Transfer Protocol (HTTP) that lets Navigator request, and a server deliver, information in specified *byte ranges*. This will make random access to large data files (such as a video) quicker and more efficient when Navigator is talking to a Netscape server.

Lesson 5: When to Use Plug-Ins and When Not To

Because they lend themselves to incorporating bloated data types such as video and sound, plug-ins are going to be blamed for increasing congestion on the Internet. This is only partially fair: While plug-ins certainly make it possible to shovel video images inappropriately over a bandwidth-limited modem link—or to attempt to do so, at least—they may also be used to translate desired data for the user quickly and efficiently.

You will read more about the difference between plug-ins and Java applets in Chapter 4, "What About Java?". It's worth noting here, though, that unlike Java applets plug-ins do not require any program code to be sent over the Net (except, of course, for the installation code that places them in your Netscape/Plug-ins folder in the first place). In general, Java applets must be downloaded to the client computer each time a Web page where they lurk is visited. (Netscape 3.0 does, however, support persistent applets, bits of Java code that can be downloaded and then placed in a special folder so they are always available.) Additionally, Java applets are hungrier for CPU cycles since they are generally interpreted on the client computer—plug-ins come already compiled and ready to go.

Plug-ins are also less wasteful of hard disk space on the client computer than the other alternatives. Unlike helper applications, they do not need to be stand-alone programs, instead adding only what is necessary to Netscape to get the job done. So while plug-ins, at worst, may cause larger data files to be sent over the Net, they are more economical on bandwidth and disk space than any of the possible alternatives.

Given that plug-ins *can* make Web pages take longer to load, you can see that they bear the same relationship to good HTML that spices do to good cooking. You'll want them in order to turn out a good product, but a little can go a long way. When planning your Web page, you need to balance your desire to entertain your audience with flashy graphics on the one hand, against the possibility on the other hand that some people will give up waiting for embedded sounds, animations, or videos to load—and simply abandon your Web page for good.

As mentioned in Chapter 1, "What You Need," a good question to ask yourself is, "How intrinsic is the need for this plug-in?" If the purpose of your Web page is to make available (perhaps on a corporate intranet) a library of your company's forms or desktop-published data sheets, the need for a plug-in is intrinsic. With the right plug-in, users can browse your library of information on screen and download or print just the documents they need. The demand for network bandwidth is, if anything, minimized.

If the purpose of your Web page is to provide video clips advertising upcoming releases at a movie theater, the demand for bandwidth might get high. Again, however, the need for the plug-in is intrinsic. With a plug-in that streams video information, users can request a film trailer and then stop it after a few moments if it does not seem to be of interest. No one will be annoyed, since they asked for the information in the first place. This contrasts to the pre-plug-in alternative, where users had to spend many minutes downloading megabytes of video data—only to discover eventually that it wouldn't play or was of no interest to them.

An annoying, extrinsic use of a plug-in, however, might be overuse of inline animations that are merely there to look interesting, adding little or nothing to a Web page's subject area. Still, what to one person might be a total waste of time, might to another person be a reason to revisit your site and introduce it to friends. As always, tastes vary.

The conclusion is that plug-ins take us much further away from the days of just sticking text up on a Web page and hoping someone would read it. They make it necessary that you *know your audience*. Is the Web turning into television, or is television turning into the Web?

WHAT NOW?

You've learned the basic capabilities of plug-ins and are probably eager to try them for yourself. If you would like to start testing plug-ins in your own Web pages right away, you can skip to Chapter 8, which will give you a programming overview. The next two chapters, however, will compare and contrast plug-ins with two other Web technologies: helper applications and Java applets. You'll learn more about which you'd want to use in any given situation. Chapters 6 and 7 then go into more detail about how plug-ins are installed and now MIME types work.

3

HELPER APPLICATIONS: A THING OF THE PAST?

3

The problem is as old as the personal computer itself. You're collaborating on a project with a colleague, you're on deadline, and they mail you a floppy disk that contains the information you need to finish your work. Eagerly, you shove the disk into your computer's floppy disk drive, open up the file, and get…gibberish.

When you call your colleague to complain, he explains that the document is in Word Blitz Pro III format. "I thought everyone was using that these days." Begrudgingly, he agrees to hunt for the Word Blitz documentation that he "must have somewhere" in order to find out how to create a version of the document in simple ASCII so you can read it.

E-mail made the problem even worse. Important documents now get attached to messages in their binary form, sometimes with little or no clue about the application that was originally used to create them. DOS, Windows, and UNIX users—and their software—often try to figure out what a file is by looking at the two- or three-digit extension following the period in the file name. Sometimes this works, sometimes it doesn't—since the extension can easily be wrongly assigned—and indeed today's software developers have long since run out of euphonic three letter codes. (As a result, some extensions have been reused and don't always mean what you might think.) Macintosh users have the luxury of a "resource fork" attached to files that tells their machines what application created them. However, this resource fork is easily damaged or left behind when the data moves over a network or onto another computer type.

Lesson 1: Getting to Know MIME Types

As you can imagine, if figuring out and decoding file types can be difficult with e-mail, it just gets that much worse on the World Wide Web, where a single page can carry as many file types as the author cares to put there. That's why the system of Multimedia Internet Mail Extensions (MIME) was devised. MIME types are discussed more fully in Chapter 6,"Understanding MIME Types." What's important to understand here is that the MIME system makes the process of figuring out what a file is more systematic. It assigns each possible type of data file a MIME type, subtype, and file extension.

Because extensions vary from file server to file server, a file with a MIME type of video and subtype of MPEG might be associated with extensions .MPEG and .MPG. Similarly, a file with a MIME type of video and subtype quicktime might be associated with extensions .QT and .MOV.

In the theoretical example given above, you had to spend a lot of time and frustration figuring out that the data file you needed was in Word Blitz Pro III format. Suppose that, instead, as soon as you put the floppy disk in your computer, the system had popped up a dialog box saying, "I think this is a text document in Word Blitz Pro III format"?

That alone would have been plenty of help. It would've been better still, though, if the computer said, "This seems to be a Word Blitz Pro III file. Microsoft Word, which is on your hard drive, can open it for you. Shall I load the program?" Once the system had your OK, Word—acting as one of the world's larger *helper applications*—would start up and convert the file for you.

In fact this is the kind of convenience that today's computer users *are* accustomed to, although the process of determining the associations—the file extensions, and what file type the computer resolves them into—has never been enjoyable. Windows users are accustomed to having to tinker with .INI files to edit associations or, if they're *really* unlucky, having to edit the registry. Macintosh users who trade files with PC users are accustomed to editing the associations set up by PC File Exchange, or using ResEdit to correct them after the files have already been transferred.

Fortunately, Netscape is deservedly well-known as a sort of "universal client." In addition to turning HTML files into formatted text, it can convert some MIME-formatted files and display them on-screen without users having to do any configuration whatsoever. However, Netscape, even in Version 3.0, can only handle five data types all by itself:

- Unformatted text files

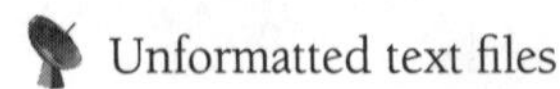

- HTML-formatted text

- X bitmap (.XBM) graphics
- CompuServe GIF graphics
- JPEG images

Lesson 2: Helper Applications and When You Need Them

These data types do account for the vast majority of what you'll encounter on the Web. However, it's inevitable that you will encounter many files on the Web that Netscape can't handle without assistance. These include some types of still image, most animations, sounds, videos, and much more.

It's possible to configure Netscape to save all "mystery files" to your computer's hard disk so that you can attempt to "crack" them offline. Unless you actually want the files stored on your computer—which certainly might be the case if you're downloading something like a movie trailer you want to be able to re-show—this is not terrifically helpful. It takes interactivity away from the Web page, and the chances that you'll remember later what these little files are supposed to be and where you got them aren't very great.

NOTE: You can force Netscape to save files to disk any time you want it to by holding down SHIFT (or COMMAND on a Macintosh) as you click on the relevant links. You'll be prompted as to where on your hard drive the downloaded files ought to be stored.

Here, then, is where helper applications come in. Helper applications are separate programs, external to Netscape, that can be run *at the same time as the browser* in order to manipulate a MIME type Netscape doesn't know about. Thanks to a multitasking operating environment such as Windows, MacOS, or UNIX, a helper application can appear on your computer's screen at the same time Netscape does. (Of course, you have to have enough random access memory (RAM) for both Netscape and the chosen helper application, which means those with less than 8MB of RAM should proceed with care.)

Though the helper application's window may appear above Netscape's window, it is not *part* of Netscape. Figure 3-1 shows a basic example of a helper application at work. An AVI video file has been placed in a Web page using the simple command <IMG SRC="cool.avi"> along with some HEIGHT and WIDTH attributes (not required as far as a helper application is concerned, but suggested in order to keep Netscape running reliably). Netscape could not play the video file itself (at least not in Version 2.0), but—thanks to an association set up via Netscape's Options menu—has started the Windows Media Player application to do so.

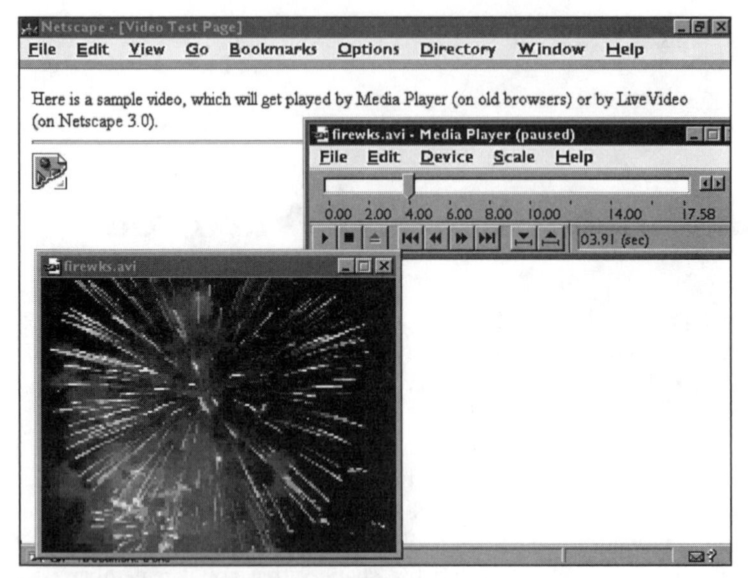

Figure 3–1 A simple helper application in action

If you were to click on the Netscape window behind the Media Player, Netscape would come to the foreground, hiding Media Player. Media Player would still be running—using system resources, and occupying random access memory—even when the video has come to an end. (You would have to return to the Media Player window in order to close it, or at least use the Windows Task Manager to do so.)

Similarly, if you were to log off the Internet and close down Netscape, Media Player would remain in memory as would the AVI file that had been loaded into it. This behavior might be useful (especially if you want to save the video file to disk); more often, however, it is simply an annoyance.

Lesson 3: Helper Applications vs. Plug-Ins

Ironically, for a technology only introduced to browsers in the last couple of years, helper applications are already *obsolete*. Plug-ins do the same job that helper applications do, and they have two big advantages.

First, as you learned in Chapter 2, plug-ins operate within the Netscape browser window. Images are viewed in line; sound plays in the background without another window having to open; even videos and formatted Adobe Acrobat documents appear as an integral part of Netscape.

The second big advantage is convenience. Instead of having to litter your hard drive with helper applications you may never use except when you're browsing the Web, you just store plug-ins neatly within the Netscape folder. While plug-ins might still occupy disk space, they make the Netscape environment much more self-contained and easy to move in its entirety to another computer.

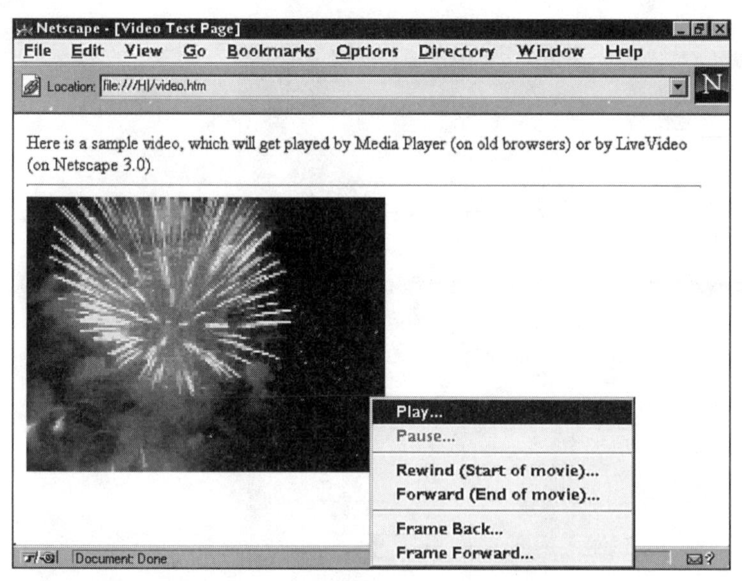

Figure 3–2 An .AVI video file being played by a plug-in

In Figure 3-2, Netscape 3.0 plays the same AVI video file you saw in Figure 3-1, but uses a plug-in this time around. Notice the fact that everything takes place within the browser. A handy pop-up menu lets the user pause or rewind the video at any time by clicking on the image.

In the future, you will want to download, collect, and utilize plug-ins *instead* of helper applications. However, there are still good reasons to know more about the earlier, obsolete technology. Initially, many more visitors to your Web pages will have helper applications than will have plug-ins.

In addition, you might want to keep using, or encourage visitors to your Web site to use, helper applications in some cases because of their fuller functionality. Suppose your company maintains a Web site on an intranet whose purpose is to distribute Word templates and forms for reuse. In this case, a plug-in could preview file contents for users, but this would be an unneeded extra step. It would be better for users to have Word ready-configured as a helper application. Then, when they visited the site and clicked on a file, that file would be automatically loaded into their copy of Word for further editing. Similarly, if you visit Web sites in order to collect and modify graphics you see there—never mind the copyright implications for the moment!—you might want to use an application such as Photoshop as your "helper application." GIFs, TIFFs, and JPEGs would be loaded right into the graphics editing window for you.

Lesson 4: Configuring Helper Applications

Netscape's use of helper applications is controlled by the Options/General Preferences menu. Open this menu, click on the Helpers tab, and you see a window similar to that shown in Figure 3-3. If you're using a Macintosh, the window you see is rather more attractive and easy to use, resembling that shown in Figure 3-4.

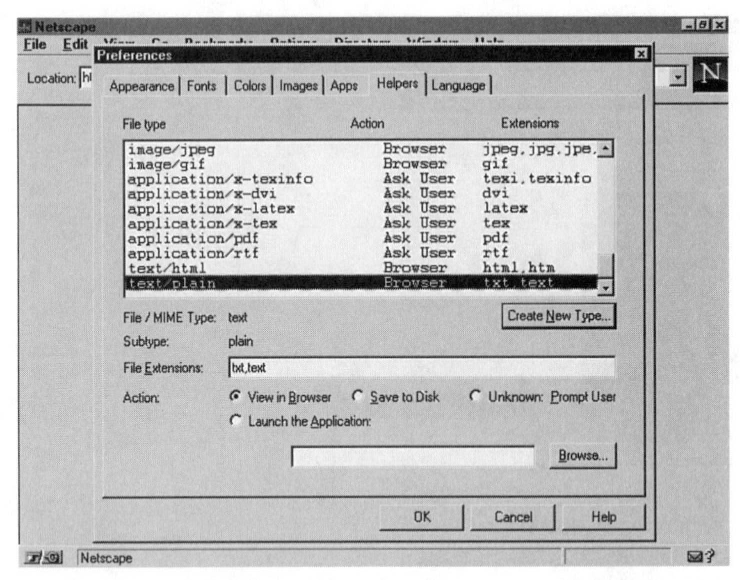

Figure 3–3 The Helpers tab within the Options/General Preferences menu lets you configure helper applications (this is the Windows 95 version)

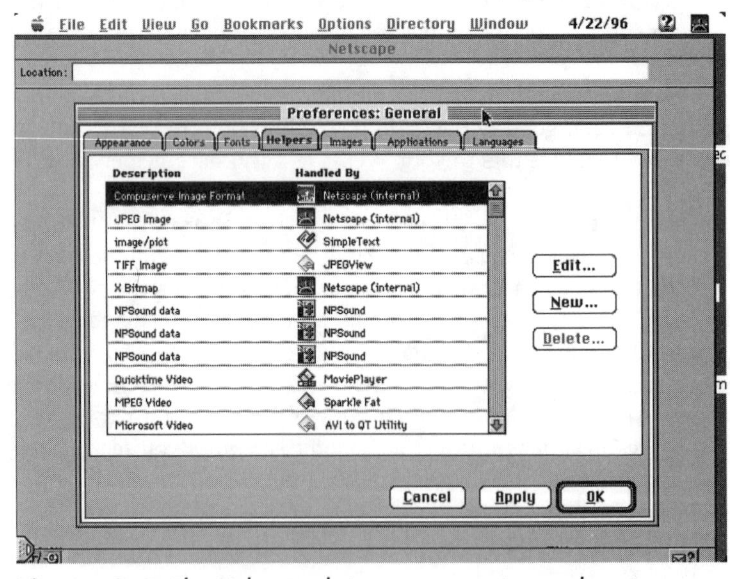

Figure 3–4 The Helpers tab is more attractive and easier to use on the Macintosh version of Netscape

Although this window looks intimidating and detailed, the information within it doesn't yet amount to all that much. Table 3-1 is a listing of MIME types, subtypes, desired actions and associated file extensions copied directly from this window on a newly installed Windows copy of Netscape 3.0. (A Macintosh listing would be functionally similar, although somewhat different in detail.)

Table 3-1 Basic MIME types Netscape can handle (NAPLAYER is a helper application that comes with Windows versions of Netscape)

MIME Type/Subtype	Action	Extension
application/x-qzip	Ask User	qz
application/x-compress	Ask User	Z
application/x-ns-proxy-autoconfig	Browser	pac
application/x-javascript	Ask User	js, ls, mocha
application/x-perl	Ask User	pl
application/x-tcl	Ask User	tcl
application/x-sh	Ask User	sh
application/x-csh	Ask User	csh
application/postscript	Ask User	ai, eps, ps
application/octet-stream	Save	exe, bin
application/x-cpio	Ask User	cpio
application/x-gtar	Ask User	gtar
application/x-tar	Ask User	tar
application/x-shar	Ask User	shar
application/x-zip-compressed	Ask User	zip
application/x-stuffit	Ask User	sit
application/mac-binhex40	Ask User	hqx
video/x-msvideo	Ask User	avi
video/quicktime	Ask User	qt, mov
video/mpeg	Ask User	mpeg, mpg, mpe
audio/x-wav	Ask User	wav
audio/x-aiff	NAPLAYER	aif, aiff, aifc
audio/basic	NAPLAYER	au, snd
application/fractals	Ask User	fif
image/ief	Ask User	ief
image/x-MS-bmp	Ask User	bmp
image/x-rgb	Ask User	rgb
image/x-portable-pixmap	Ask User	ppm

continued on next page

continued from previous page

MIME Type/Subtype	Action	Extension
image/x-portable-graymap	Ask User	pgm
image/x-portable-bitmap	Ask User	pbm
image/x-portable-anymap	Ask User	pnm
image/x-xwindowdump	Ask User	xwd
image/x-pixmap	Ask User	xpm
image/x-bitmap	Browser	xbm
image/x-cmu-raster	Ask User	ras
image/tiff	Ask User	tiff, tif
image/jpeg	Browser	jpeg, jpg, jpe, jfif
image/gif	Browser	gif
application/x-texinfo	Ask User	texi, texinfo
application/x-dvi	Ask User	dvi
application/x-latex	Ask User	latex
application/x-tex	Ask User	tex
application/pdf	Ask User	pdf
application/rtf	Ask User	rtf
text/html	Browser	html, htm
text/plain	Browser	txt, text

As you'll see, the listing confirms that the only MIME types Netscape handles "out of the box"—without the aid of *any* helper applications or plug-ins, that is—are JPEG and GIF graphics plus plain or HTML-formatted text. This is made obvious by the notation "browser" in the second column. For all other MIME types, the default is "Ask User," with the exception of AIFF, AU and SND files—these are handled in this case by NAPLAYER, a rudimentary helper application bundled with Windows copies of Netscape.

NOTE: One reason this book doesn't attempt to cover UNIX versions of Netscape is that the program is available for many different UNIX variants: SunOS, Solaris, DEC OSF, HP/UX, Linux, AIX, and more. Each UNIX version of Netscape has a slightly different look and feel. All present the user with a Helpers tab that, instead of showing a tabular listing, simply points to the user's .mailcap and .mime.types files. The .mailcap file is a text file that identifies the location of a helper application on the system, and the types of files it can read. The .mime.types file associates MIME file types with the file types in the .mailcap file.

The File Type column in the Helpers tab describes a file's MIME type and subtype. The Action column tells Netscape what to do when it encounters the given file type. The Extensions column lists all the file extensions that are associated with a particular file type.

Automatic Configuration

The easiest way to configure Netscape for helper applications is simply to wait until the browser receives a file it doesn't know how to handle. If the file's MIME type doesn't appear in Netscape's default list—or it does appear but the action field is set to "Ask User"—a dialog box asks you whether you want to get more information, to pick a helper application, to save the file to disk, or to cancel the transfer. Figure 3-5 shows an example of this behavior.

If you request more information, you're taken to a generic information page on a Netscape server. Figure 3-6 shows this page, in which the Web address is *http://cgi.netscape.com/eng/mozilla/2.0/extensions/info.cgi?video/mpeg* (the last part of the address is specific to this example).

NOTE: As you can see by looking at the very end of this address, Netscape Navigator "knows" what MIME type you were trying to view, and passes it to Netscape Communications' Web site for processing by a cgi script. This can help users find the type of helper application they need. You can make Netscape's search for a plug-in more specific by using an attribute known as PLUGINSPAGE. You'll read more about how to use it in Chapter 8, "A Programming Overview".

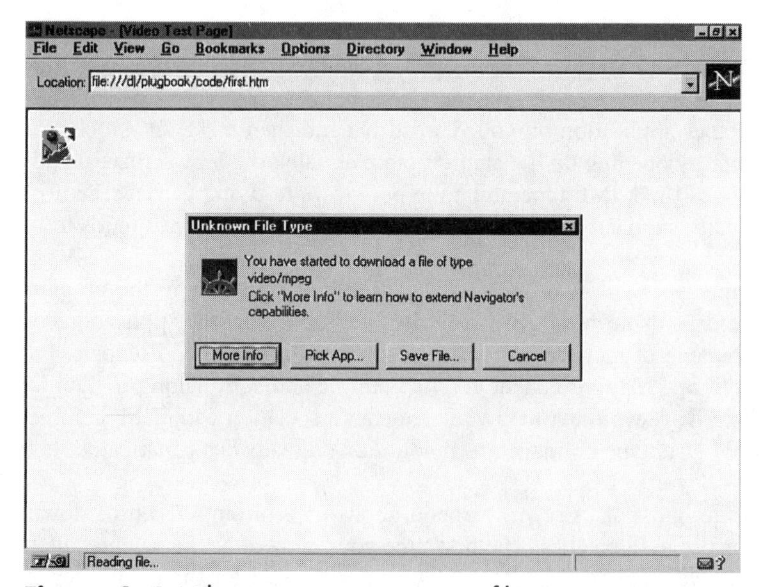

Figure 3-5 When you encounter a new file type, Netscape pops up this dialog box

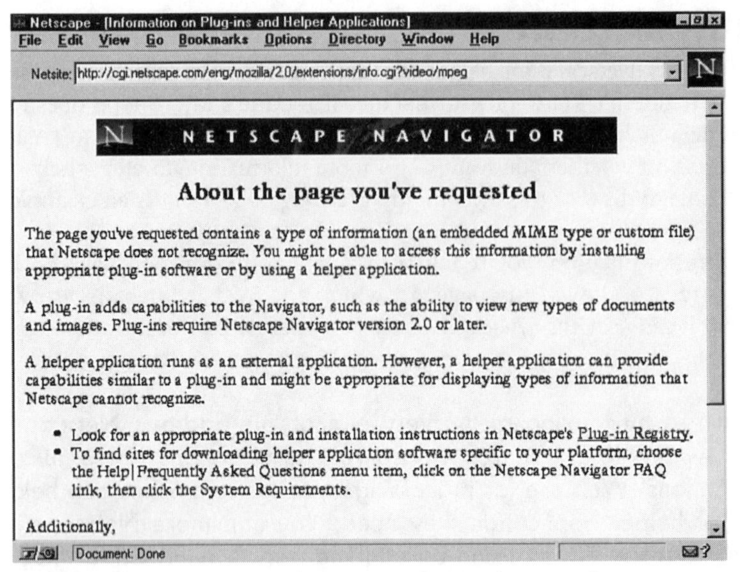

Figure 3–6 Netscape takes you to this Web page if you request more information about helper applications

It is obvious what the Save File and Cancel options can do. If you prefer to configure a helper application, click on the relevant box and Netscape will open a directory browser so you can find the helper application on your hard drive and then make an association. As you can confirm later by opening up the Helpers tab manually, the browser has already made its best guess about the MIME type and subtype you were trying to view. Because this information is usually supplied to Netscape by the remote Web server, it tends to be accurate.

Configuring a helper application automatically is simple if, and only if, the program you want to use is already on your hard drive. You need to know what the applications on your hard drive are capable of and, hence, which of them will make good helpers. For example, having Paint Shop Pro (an excellent graphics editing and conversion program for Windows) on your hard drive wouldn't help you create an association with TIFF graphics (which have a MIME type/subtype of image/tiff) if you didn't already *know* that Paint Shop Pro opens TIFFs.

"Infotainment" aside, most of us seem to spend about 75% of our Web time downloading applications or program patches. The first time your copy of Netscape encounters a .ZIP or Stuffit archive, you can and should configure the browser for the application/x-zip compressed or application/x-stuffit file types and make the default action Save to Disk. Thereafter, you'll be able to avoid the prompt that would otherwise pop up.

NOTE: Sometimes, when Netscape encounters an unknown file type, it won't ask you if you want to configure a viewer. Instead, it will ask you if you want to install a plug-in. This happens when a forward-looking Web author uses the <EMBED SRC> command instead of the <IMG SRC> command in his or her pages. Rest assured that this Web page designer has your best interests at heart, and refer to Chapter 7, "An Overview of Plug-In Installation" for more information on installation of a Netscape plug-in.

Manual Configuration

To configure a helper application manually, start by opening the Options/General Preferences window and clicking on the Helpers tab. You now face one of two instances: Either you want to configure a new helper application to work with a file type that is already listed, or you want to add both a new file type and a new helper application.

The first of these two instances is fairly simple to deal with. Locate the item you wish to work with by scrolling through the list, stopping when you see the file type or extension you're looking for. In Figure 3-7, a Windows user has selected the video/quicktime file type and is about to associate a helper application with it.

To locate the helper application, click in the radio button for Launch the Application, then click on the Browse button. Then, you use the standard Windows (or Macintosh) directory browser to locate the program of your choice. Figure 3-8 shows the former. (Of course, with Windows, if you already know the full path to your program, you can simply type it in directly without using the Browse button at all.)

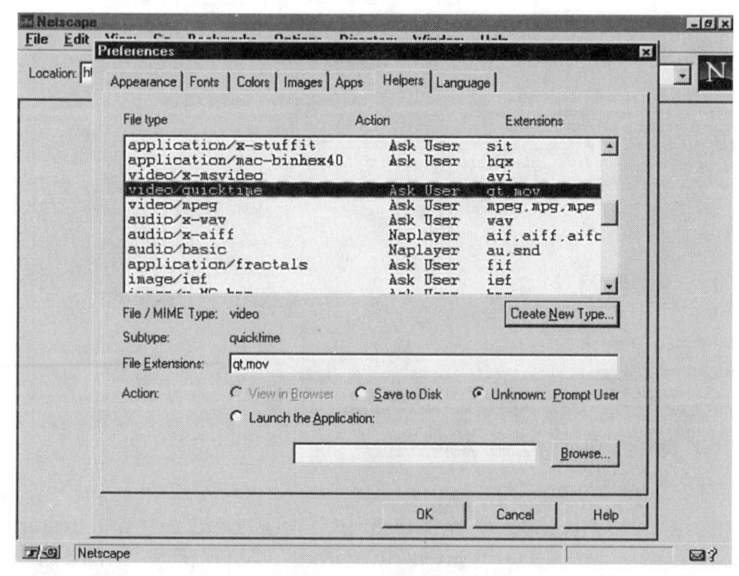

Figure 3–7 To add a helper application, you can select a file type manually and then browse for a program

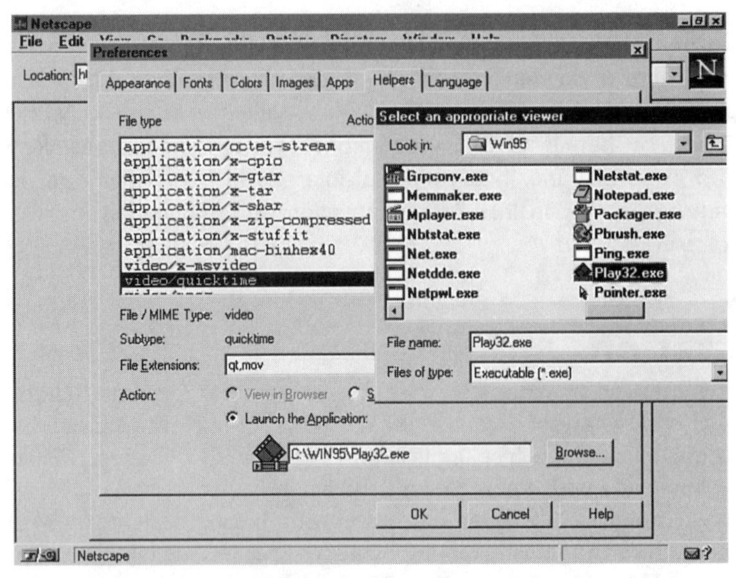

Figure 3–8 The standard Windows directory browser helps you locate a helper application

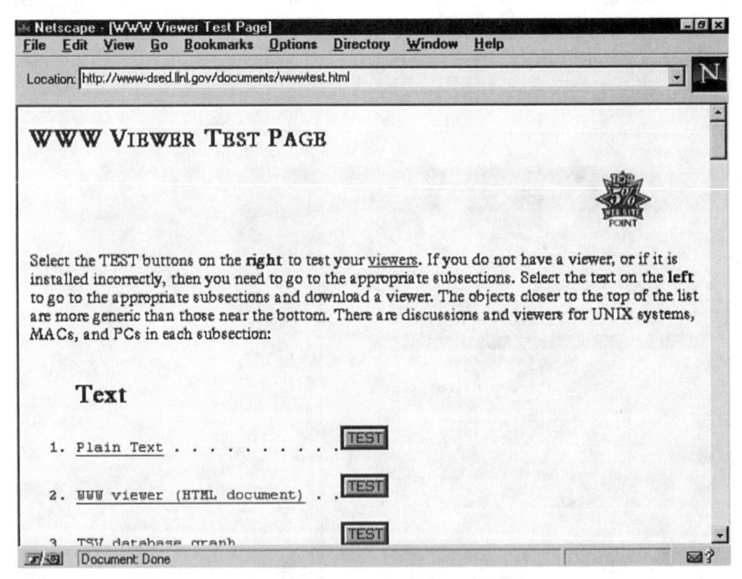

Figure 3–9 A popular helper application test page

Once you have made an association in this fashion, you should exit and restart Netscape. You can then test the helper application by loading a Web page that has the new file type in it. (One popular helper application test page is at Lawrence Livermore Laboratories in California. Shown in Figure 3-9, it's located *at http://www-dsed.llnl.gov/documents/wwtest.html.)*

Figure 3-10, using the Lawrence Livermore test page, shows what you see when downloading a large file that is going to be passed to a helper application. The dialog box should list the chosen "viewer" to which the data will be passed. When the download is complete, the helper application is invoked on top of the browser, as shown in Figure 3-11.

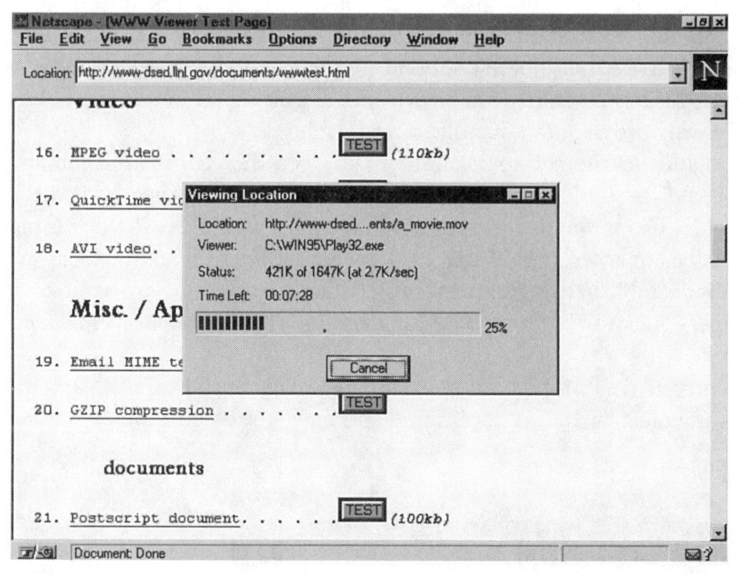

Figure 3–10 Downloading data to a helper application can be tedious, but Netscape at least gives you an indication of progress

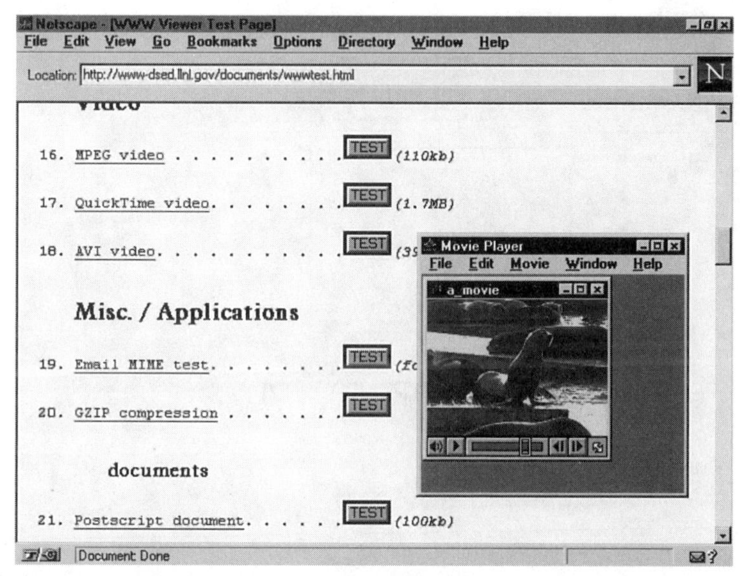

Figure 3–11 The helper application loads, partly obscuring the Netscape window

When you're trying to add a new file type to Netscape's Helpers tab as well as to a new helper application, things get a little more difficult. Are you, perhaps, trying to add a helper app that uses its own special type of files? Something like, for example, Real Audio, with its .RA and .RAM files? If this is what you're up to, *wait.*

Before installing a helper application to handle a new and novel data type, remember that there may be a plug-in you could use instead. In general, the only reason to prefer a helper application over a plug-in is if you have a version of Netscape earlier than 2.0, or if you are using a Brand X browser that doesn't support plug-ins. Approach helper applications with plenty of sales resistance unless you have a special purpose in mind, or a helper application really is the only program that handles a new data type.

Still determined to add that helper application? If so, open the Helper apps tab and click on the Create New Type button. You'll be prompted for a MIME type and MIME subtype (see Figure 3-12). Often, the documentation that comes with a new helper application tells you what values to enter here. If not, or if you're just experimenting, be aware that it's better to follow established hierarchies rather than just making up your own MIME type and subtype. (To see why this is, and for more information about MIME hierarchies, see Chapter 6.)

Once you have entered the MIME type and subtype, click on OK. Then, use the directory browser to find your new helper application and make the association.

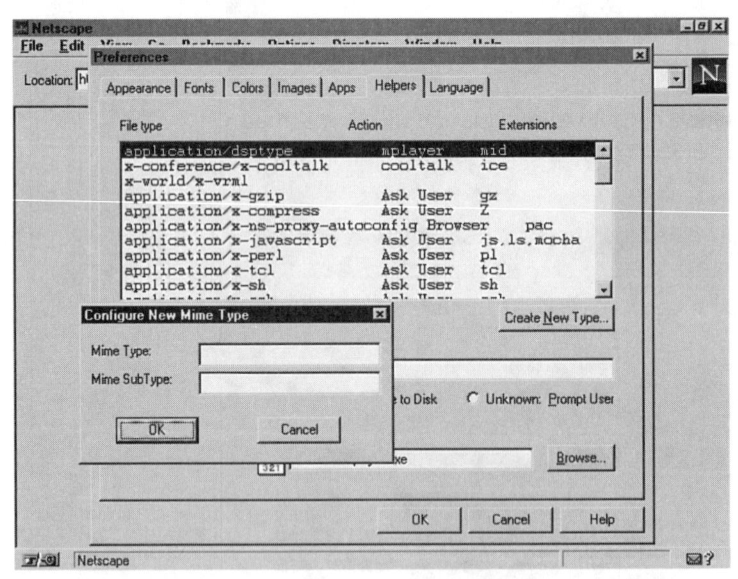

Figure 3-12 Netscape requests a new MIME type and subtype

Lesson 5: How to Find Helper Applications

Helper applications may be obsolescent technology, but they're not going to go away. The simple reason for this is that, while plug-ins must be specially written to the Netscape API in order to operate, any Windows, Mac, or UNIX program can be a helper application.

Chances are that you will continue to need helper applications for some time. Table 3-2 is a guide to some of the most popular helper applications for Windows and Macintosh, many of which you're probably already using. It lists what they're good for and where you can find them. (We only had space to list one URL for each helper application; however, you will often be able to find these popular programs stored in many additional locations on the Internet.)

Table 3–2 Popular helper applications

Application Name	Platform	Description	URL
Audio			
MPEG2 Player	Macintosh	A player for high-compression MPEG2 files	http://www.lpg.fi/audio/MPEG_CD_2.0.5.sea.hqx
Real Audio	Windows/Macintosh	Plays back audio clips and Internet radio stations in real time	http://www.realaudio.com
SoundApp	Macintosh	Sound player/converter that supports AU, AIFF, NeXT, WAVE, QuickTime soundtracks, and more	.http://wwwhost.ots.utexas.edu/mac/pub-mac-sound.html#soundapp-151
SoundMachine	Macintosh	Plays and records SND/AU (mu-law, A-law, linear) and AIFF/AIFC (MACE3, MACE6) sound files	ftp://ftp.ncsa.uiuc.edu/Mosaic/Mac/Helpers/sound-machine 21.hqx
TrueSpeech	Windows	Plays various sound formats including intensively compressed .WAV files	http://www.dspg.com/samples/tsply311.exe
WHAM (Windows Hold and Modify)	Windows	Audio file player/editor	ftp://gatekeeper.dec.com/pub/micro/msdos/win3/sounds/wham133.zip
WPlayAny	Windows	Plays various sound formats	ftp://ftp.cica.indiana.edu/pub/pc/win3/sounds/wplny11.zip

continued on next page

continued from previous page

Application Name	Platform	Description	URL
XingSound Player	Windows	Supports MPEG audio in stereo and mono	ftp://ftp.iuma.com/audio_utils/mpeg_players/Windows/mpgaudio.exe
Graphics			
FIGleaf	Windows	Lets you zoom and pan file formats, including CGM, TIFF, GIF, JPEG, CCITT, Sun Raster, PPM, PGM, PBM, BMP, EPSI, ASCII	http://www.ct.ebt.com/figleaf.html
GIF Converter	Macintosh	Can open and read several file formats, including GIF, TIFF, RIFF, PICT, JPEG (JFIF), MacPaint, and Thunderscan	http://wwwhost.ots.utexas.edu/mac/pub-mac-graphics.html
Graphic Converter	Macintosh	Imports/converts a fast array of graphics file formats, including PICT, Startup-Screen, MacPaint, TIFF, GIF, PCX/SCR, GEM-IMG/-XIMG, BMP, and much more	ftp://ftp.hawaii.edu/mirrors/info-mac/_Graphic_&_Sound_Tool/grf/graphic-converter-24.hqx
Lview Pro	Windows	An image viewer/editor that is capable of displaying a wide variety of formats	ftp://ftp.winsite.com/pub/pc/win3/desktop/lviewp1b.zip
PaintShop Pro	Windows	Extremely versatile image editor that also operates as a screen capture program	http://www.jasc.com
Transparency	Macintosh	Permits creating GIFs with a transparent background	http://wwwhost.ots.utexas.edu/mac/pub-mac-graphics.html
Video			
FastPlayer	Macintosh	A free QuickTime movie player with special options for fast and smooth playback. Includes option to create "flattened" movies for use on non-Mac QuickTime players	ftp://ftp.ncsa.uiuc.edu/Mosaic/Mac/Helpers/fast-player-110.hqx

Application Name	Platform	Description	URL
Movie Viewer	Macintosh	For GL, FLI, FLC, FLX, DL, GIF, JPG, PCX/PIC, and raw PPM files	http://www.umich.edu/~archive/mac/graphics/graphicsutil/macanimviewer1.1.cpt.hqx
MPEG Player for Windows	Windows	Plays MPEG files	ftp://gatekeeper.dec.com/pub/micro/msdos/win3/desktop/mpegwin.zip
MPEGPlay	Windows	Easy-to-use MPEG viewer that comes with one sample file	ftp://ftp.ncsa.uiuc.edu/Mosaic/Windows/viewers/mpegw32h.zip
QuickTime for Windows	Windows	Apple's official QuickTime player for Windows. Can be troublesome on Windows 3.x; works well on Windows 95	http://quicktime.apple.com
QuickTime Viewer for Windows	Windows	Integrates into Windows Media Player to allow playing QuickTime movies	ftp://ftp.ncsa.uiuc.edu/PC/Windows/Mosaic/viewers/qtw11.zip
SmartVid	Windows	Windows QuickTime/AVI converter	ftp://ftp.intel.com/pub/IAL/Indeo_video/smartv.exe
Sparkle	Macintosh	MPEG viewer for the Macintosh. Can convert to and from QuickTime	ftp://ftp.ncsa.uiuc.edu/Mosaic/Mac/Helpers/sparkle-245.hqx
VT Motion Scalable MPEG Player	Windows	Plays MPEG files	ftp://gatekeeper.dec.com/pub/micro/msdos/win3/desktop/mpegxing.zip
Compression			
Stuffit Expander	Macintosh	Will expand Stuffit and CompactPro archives; also decodes the HQX and BIN formats commonly found on the Internet	.ftp:/ftp.utexas.edu/compression/stuffit-expander-352.hqx
WinZip	Windows	Permits uncompressing .ZIP, TAR and gzip files without exiting to the DOS command line	http://www.winzip.com

continued on next page

continued from previous page

Application Name	Platform	Description	URL
Text Viewers			
GhostScript	Windows	Allows displaying and printing PostScript files	ftp://ftp.winsite.com/pub/pc/win3/util/gs261exe.zip
Acrobat Viewer Macintosh, OS/2	Windows	Lets you view and print files in Adobe's PDF format	http://www.adobe.com
Microsoft Word Viewer	Window s	Lets you view and print a Microsoft Word file without having Word on your computer	http://www.microsoft.com/msoffice/
Panorama	Windows	Lets you view SGML files	http://www.sq.com/products/panorama/pan-free.htm

The most up-to-date way to find helper applications is, of course, on the Web itself. Lists of helper apps may be found on countless Web pages. You can locate some of these by using Web search engines such as *http://www.altavista.digital.com* or *http://www.excite.com*, using search strings such as "helper applications AND list." Although specific lists might come and go during the lifetime of this book, you'll always be able to find relevant information by doing a Web search.

Naturally, helper applications are specific to the computer (Windows, Macintosh, UNIX) you're using. One site that helps you home in on the programs your system needs is located at *http://www.shareware.com*. By taking information that your browser makes available to the server, this site is able to determine whether you have a Macintosh or a Windows computer and sets its defaults accordingly (see Figure 3-13). As this is one of the Web's biggest guides to shareware applications, the chances are very good that you'll find the helper application you need.

Some other sites organize their lists according to the functionality that you need. For example, audio helpers can be found on a single page, video helpers on another, and so on. One site that takes this approach is Stroud's Consummate Winsock Applications. As its name implies, this is limited to Windows programs. However, it does an excellent job of listing them either by name or by category, and is always available because it's mirrored on multiple Web servers worldwide. (The address of the main page pictured in Figure 3-14 is *http://www.awinc.com/cwsapps/.)*

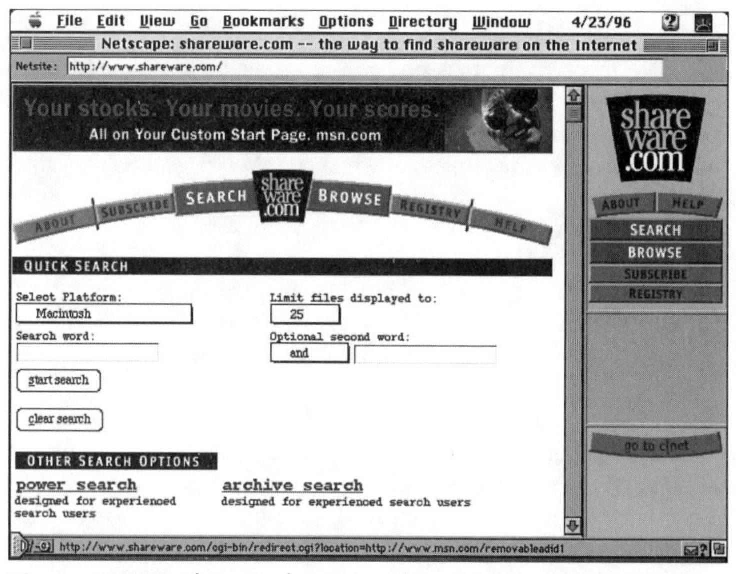

Figure 3–13 The search page at *http://www.shareware.com*

Figure 3–14 Stroud's Consummate Winsock Applications list

Lesson 6: Removing Helper Applications

Apart from the hard disk space involved, there is no harm in keeping a helper application you're no longer using. An unused helper application does not conflict with a plug-in that handles the same MIME type and subtype, because the plug-in automatically takes precedence over the helper app. This happens regardless of whether a Web page uses the <IMG SRC> or <EMBED SRC> HTML tags: Plug-ins simply tap into Netscape at a more fundamental level than helper applications can.

For example, when MovieStar—a plug-in that handles QuickTime video—has been installed, the Lawrence Livermore Labs QuickTime test file (first shown in Figure 3-10) appears within Netscape's own window (see Figure 3-15). This is the case even though the Apple QuickTime Movie Player, installed as a helper application in a prior step, was never removed.

Plug-ins automatically grab data relating to the MIME type(s) they're looking for. Generally, this is exactly what you want: Plug-ins work more conveniently and seamlessly than do helper applications. However, there might be cases when you need special features that are found only in a helper application. Also, plug-ins don't always provide feedback to the user because their designers assume they will be used in combination with the <EMBED SRC> tag, which allows them to appear as part of a Web page. When used with Web pages having only <IMG SRC> tags, they load full-screen, hide the rest of the page and possibly leave the user wondering what's going on.

The only thing you can do to force use of a helper application is to remove the plug-in that's looking for the same MIME type—unless you have a Macintosh, in which case

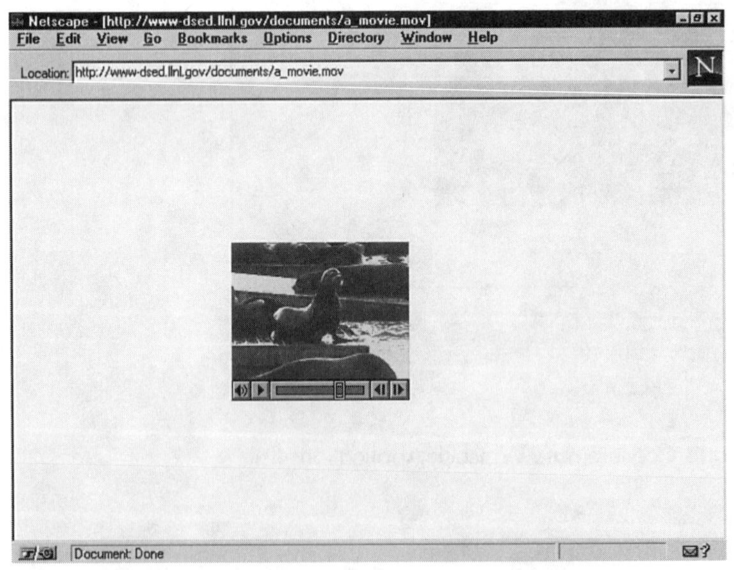

Figure 3-15 When a plug-in is in operation, its output appears inside the Netscape window—contrast this with Figure 3-10

Netscape's Options/General Preferences/Helpers control panel lets you have the final say on how a MIME type will be handled. See Chapter 7 for more information about this topic.

Breaking the association between a helper application and a particular MIME type is easier. Simply select the file type in the Helpers tab, then click on the Save to Disk or Prompt User radio buttons. Netscape does not presently allow you to *remove* a file type from within the Helpers tab. This is an oversight that is not really of any consequence, except that unused file types do tend to clutter this particular configuration screen. If you are determined to eliminate some file type entries, you can do so if you have Windows 3.x by deleting entries in the [Viewers] section of your NETSCAPE.INI file. You can do so in Windows 95 by deleting entries in the system registry at My Computer\HKEY_CURRENT_USER\Software\Netscape\Netscape Navigator\Viewers (see Figure 3-16). However, unless you are experienced at editing .INI files and using the Registry Editor, it is preferable to leave these entries untouched.

WHAT NOW?

You now know the basic difference between plug-ins and helper applications. The next chapter takes a look at Java applets, once again comparing and contrasting them to what you can do with plug-ins. While Java applets definitely have their place, you may find that carefully selected plug-ins pack just as much punch and are much easier to use.

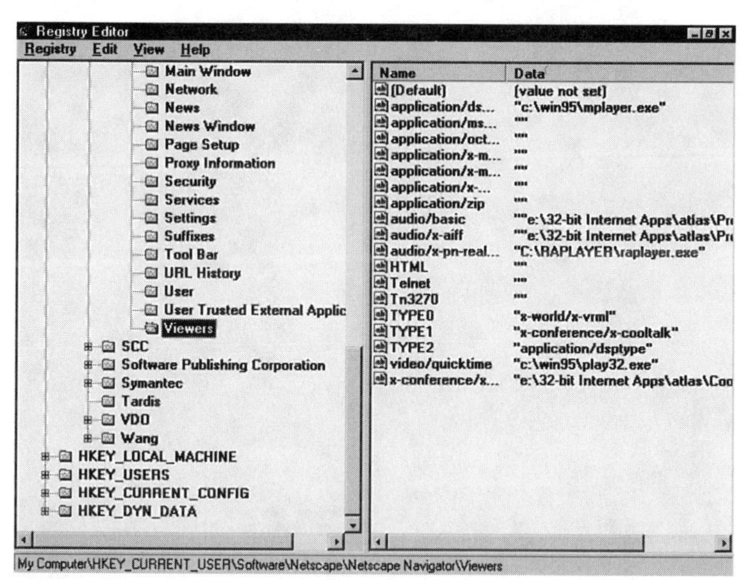

Figure 3–16 In Windows 95, MIME types and associations are hidden in the system registry

4

WHAT ABOUT JAVA?

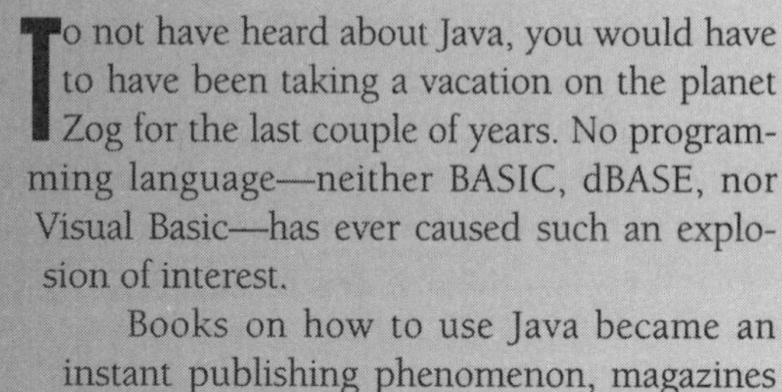

To not have heard about Java, you would have to have been taking a vacation on the planet Zog for the last couple of years. No programming language—neither BASIC, dBASE, nor Visual Basic—has ever caused such an explosion of interest.

Books on how to use Java became an instant publishing phenomenon, magazines about Java were hastily launched, and with it Web pages quickly started wearing Java applets. Java has also been promoted as being the centerpiece of net-centric computers that download all their software via the Web instead of storing it locally.

Merely a fashion phenomenon, flavor of the mid-90s for Web style victims? No—there's a lot more substance to Java than that. Java is already, and will continue to be, an enduring part of the Web scene that, indeed, will play a role in net devices that lack local storage ("thin clients"), but, ironically, will also encourage client computers to take on more and more functions. Tasks such as forms processing that today require server-based scripts, will migrate to "fat clients" with the aid of Java programs.

In this chapter, you will discover that plug-ins are an easier to use, more accessible technology than Java. Furthermore, plug-ins may well replace Java when it comes to some of the functionality—audio, video, moving text, and the like—originally pioneered by Java. But since Java will take on new areas—and can work hand-in-hand with plug-ins in any case—the two are complementary, not competing, technologies.

Lesson 1: What Java Is

It's ironic that some people think of the future of Java as being the language that will drive "Internet appliances" such as smart cable boxes. Ironic, because that's actually Java's *past*. Created at Sun Microsystems in 1990 by developer James Gosling and originally known as Oak, it was to be a key ingredient of a Web browser called WebRunner, which ran on a cut-down SPARCstation jammed into a cable converter.

For better or worse, the deal to produce these boxes fell through. However, Sun found it had a small, incredibly useful computer language on its hands. The company's official description of Java (found at *http://java.sun.com/allabout.html*) is an incredible combination of buzzwords: "a simple, object-oriented, distributed, interpreted, robust, secure, architecture-neutral, portable, high-performance, multithreaded, and dynamic language."

Although this might not be the most graceful description ever written, there is substance to the jargon. Understand the more important terms, and you've gone a long way toward understanding Java. For example:

- *Simple* and *Object-Oriented:* For those who wish to program in it, Java does have a relatively simple, elegant syntax. It's similar to C++, which is used to write many modern computer programs (including Netscape plug-ins), but many esoteric, complicated features were removed to make the language simpler.

- *Distributed:* With built-in TCP/IP and HTTP functionality, Java was designed to be run on a network from Day One.

- *Interpreted:* As with many other programming languages, Java programs are written in source code and then run through a compiler. Instead of being turned into a machine-specific executable, however, these programs are turned into an intermediate format. A Java runtime interpreter, such as that licensed from Sun and built into Netscape, receives these programs from a Web server. It then does the final job of turning them into code that runs on your computer. An interesting aspect of this is that since the Java compiler on a programmer's desk is entirely separate from a user's Java runtime interpreter, a wide variety of development environments is possible. Competing visual programming tools for Java with drag-and-drop features are already available in abundance.

- *Secure:* Java programs are relatively secure because the runtime interpreter examines a program after it has been downloaded. Looking at the Java "bytecodes," it verifies that the code is safe and does not attempt to, for example, erase files. This is not to say that Java is *totally* secure; in March 1996 Netscape and Sun were notified by researchers at Princeton University of a potential vulnerability in Java's bytecode verifier, and alterations had to be made.

NOTE: No rogue Java program has ever been known to cause a problem; the weakness reported to Sun by Princeton researchers was purely theoretical. However, if you are really concerned that a Java program could damage your data, you can disable Java using the switch in Netscape's Security Preferences tab under the Options menu. This switch disables Java programs only, not JavaScript scripts (see Lesson 3) which are inherently much more secure.

- *Architecture-neutral* and *portable:* As suggested, Java programs can be used by many different processors and machines. They do not have a preferred architecture nor do they need to be "ported" from system to system.

- *Dynamic:* Not only are Java programs easy for programmers to change—without a laborious recompile—but they are also easy to distribute to end users. On corporate intranets, for example, program updates may be stored centrally and sent to users at runtime. The advantages for Internet appliances are obvious.

It is technically possible to create a Java application that runs as a stand-alone program without the assistance of a browser. (Still interpreted programs, these applications must call a Java interpreter in order to operate.) The Java programs that are relevant to Web pages, however, are more commonly called "applets": Like plug-ins, these require a Web browser in order to run, and operate within its window.

In an effort to improve applet performance, Netscape Communications continues to enhance the Java interpreter built into Navigator. The Windows 95/NT version of the browser, for instance, includes "just in time" technology licensed from Borland.

Meanwhile, Asymetrix Corporation has released Super Cede VM, a Netscape plug-in that is itself a Java interpreter. Once Web pages have been designed with it in mind, Super Cede VM can run applets five times faster than Navigator could on its own—or so the authors claim. (For more information, see Chapter 15.)

Lesson 2: Using Java Applets

To create Java applets from scratch, a developer needs the Java Developer's Kit (JDK) available from Sun. (You can download it at *http://www.java.sun.com/JDK-1.0/index.html.*) A programmer begins by writing code and saving it to disk with the file extension .java. This is then compiled, using a program called javac, to a binary with the extension .class. Figure 4-1 illustrates how a .class file is sent over the Internet and ultimately interpreted.

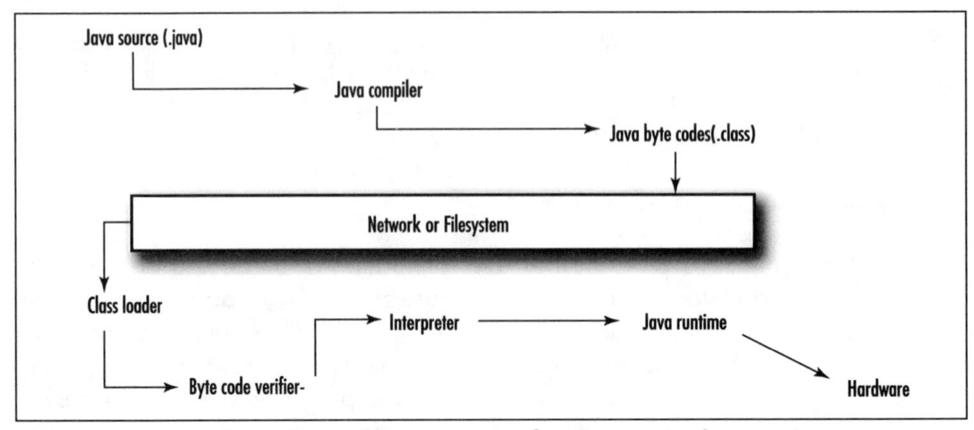

Figure 4–1 How Java source files turn into a functioning applet

A wide variety of programs to help the Java programmer have recently appeared on the market. For example, Symantec offers Java Café, a graphical development environment for Java. This includes a graphical project manager, a professional programmer's editor with "syntax coloring," a debugger, and a compiler that the firm claims is several times faster than javac.

Metrowerks, Inc. of Austin, Texas offers a product called Discover, a Macintosh-based Java compiler and source-level debugger. Roaster is a similar product from Natural Intelligence Inc. of Cambridge, Massachusetts. And of course, there are many other such tools.

Most of us non-programmers will not be writing our own Java code, but instead using applets created by others. Fortunately, many class files have been placed in the public domain for use in anyone's Web pages. One great place to find them is the Web site at *www.gamelan.com* (Figure 4-2), where you'll find hundreds. Although some files found here are Java source aimed at programmers, others are ready-to-use classes.

To use one of these classes in your Web page, you first need to upload it to your Web server (or at least tuck it away on your hard drive for development—but watch out for file name truncation). Next, you write HTML code that invokes the applet using—logically enough–Netscape's <APPLET> tag.

The site pictured in Figure 4-3 uses an applet called Navigator Ticker 2 (the file name is NavigatorTicker11.class) which not only scrolls a message but also lets the user click on sections of that message to be taken to a certain page.

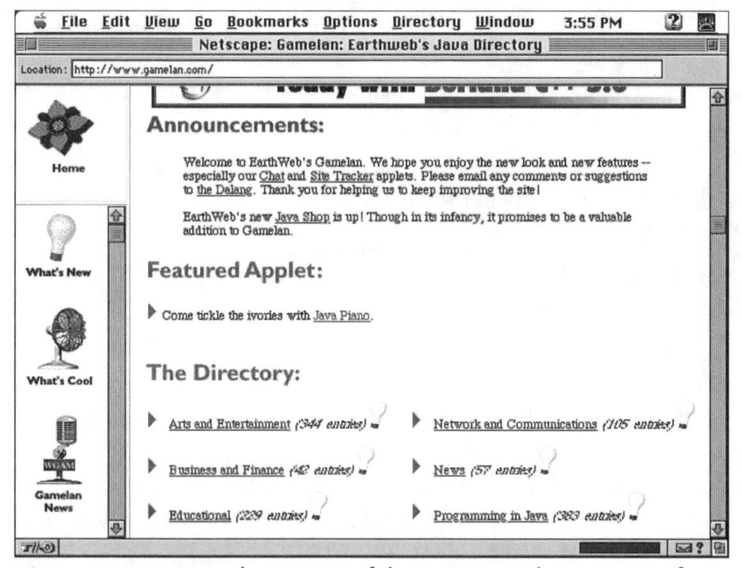

Figure 4–2 Gamelan is one of the most popular sources of Java information

Figure 4–3 This site uses a widely shared Java applet, NavigatorTicker11.class, whose output appears just below the top of the screen

The HTML code that invokes Navigator Ticker 2 appears at the beginning of the body, although it could have been placed anywhere:

```
<applet codebase="http://www.angel.org/classes/" code=NavigatorTicker11.class width=640⇐
height=40>
<param name=count value=3 >
<param name=msg0 value="Welcome to Computer Magazine Review ... \\No Link">
<param name=msg1 value="Click here for our Magazines A-Z ...
\\http://www.angel.org/review/framed.htm">
<param name=msg2 value="   ... and then please let us know what you think ...
\\http://www.angel.org/review/form.htm">
<param name=speed value=10>
<param name=bgco value=255,255,255>
<param name=txtco value=0,0,0>
<param name=linkco value=237,7,60>
If you had Java, you'd see a scrolling ticker here.<p>
</applet>
```

An <APPLET> tag begins the section; its CODEBASE attribute tells the browser where to look to find Java classes, and the CODE attribute names the specific class file to be used. Standard WIDTH and HEIGHT attributes are also required. The parameters in the <PARAM> lines that follow are specific to this particular class, specifying the words that will appear in the ticker and the URLs to which they will take users when clicked on. Finally, the </APPLET> tag concludes the section, and the rest of the page in "normal" HTML follows.

The effect of the paired <APPLET> tags varies according to whether or not the user has a Java-enabled browser. For example, Netscape versions 2.0 and later—which know about Java—are designed to process the first line and any PARAM elements, but to ignore anything else that appears between the tags. Earlier browsers—Netscape 1.22, for example—simply ignore the <APPLET> and <PARAM> tags but process other items normally. Therefore, the ticker doesn't appear at all with these browsers; instead their users see only the line beginning "If you had Java..."

As you can see from this example, using an already written Java applet is simple, provided that you do have access to the class file and you also have documentation for its various parameters. Again, *http://www.gamelan.com* is an excellent source of classes and links related to them.

Although many classes happen to have been released into the public domain, others have become a good vehicle for those creating proprietary programs for forms, etc. they do *not* want others to copy. While anyone can copy an HTML page simply by using File/Save As, there is no analogous way to save an executing class file to disk. Therefore, Java applets have some security advantage.

Unlike C++, Java has no "pointers," so it cannot reference arbitrary locations in memory that might contain sensitive data such as a user password. Applets are restricted from accessing the file system and from performing most I/O routines. They are also restricted from accessing classes that were written in another programming language.

Lesson 3: Java vs. JavaScript

Although Java applets do an outstanding job of pepping up Web pages, they are clearly difficult for anyone but a programmer to modify. In addition, their reliance on server-stored classes means that anyone browsing Web pages off-line will not get the benefit of any Java special effects.

Another problem with Java applets is that it is difficult for them to interact with the HTML of a Web page. Performing operations such as loading different URLs depending on the time of day, modifying information inside a form, or making operations in one frame select another frame to be loaded requires an extensive amount of Java coding—if it is even possible.

For these reasons, Netscape decided to create JavaScript, a simplified programming language that is designed to let objects specified by HTML tags interact with one another. Originally known as LiveScript (and "JavaLite" internally at Netscape), JavaScript was introduced with Netscape 2.0. Although JavaScript is similar to Java, it is not identical. In fact, Macintosh and Windows 3.1 versions of Netscape 2.0 did not support Java, but did support JavaScript. Windows 3.1 is still limited to JavaScript support only.

Instead of relying on external class files, JavaScripts are normally contained within an HTML file. They may be placed anywhere in its body, in a frame or, in fact, in the head (in which case they will be executed before the body of the page is completely downloaded).

To create your first JavaScript, open a text editor and type in the following:

```
<HTML>
<HEAD>
</HEAD>
<TITLE>JavaScript Test Page</TITLE>
<SCRIPT LANGUAGE="JavaScript">
<!-- to hide script contents from old browsers
document.write("This header appears before the body does.<p><hr>");
// End the hiding here -->
</SCRIPT>
</HEAD>
<BODY>
Here's the body of my JavaScript test page.
</BODY>
</HTML>
```

Save your file as TEST.HTM (or whatever name you prefer) and load it into Netscape. You'll see a screen similar to that shown in Figure 4-4.

As you can see, JavaScript employs an HTML tag called <SCRIPT>. Any information between the <SCRIPT> and </SCRIPT> tags is interpreted as JavaScript. The HTML comment tags (<!-- and //-->) are not required, but have been placed in this example to hide the JavaScript code from older browsers that do not understand it and would display it as if it were text.

Unfortunately, some browsers—Microsoft's Internet Explorer, for instance—read the JavaScript regardless, and do not necessarily interpret it in the way you want them to. Another way of hiding the JavaScript code, therefore, is to save it as a separate disk file.

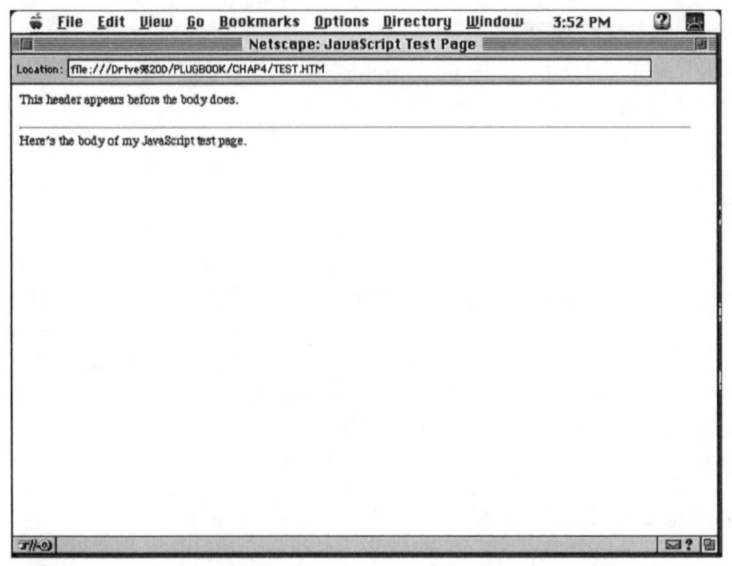

Figure 4–4 The result of a very simple JavaScript—since it's located in the header, it loads before the body of the page does

Return to your TEST.HTM file and highlight only the line beginning with "document.write." Cut it from TEST.HTM and paste it into a new file called TEST.JS. Then edit TEST.HTM so it reads as follows:

```
<HTML>
<HEAD>
<TITLE>JavaScript Test Page</TITLE>
<SCRIPT LANGUAGE="JavaScript" SRC="test.js">
</SCRIPT>
</HEAD>
<BODY>
Here's the body of my JavaScript test page.
</BODY>
</HTML>
```

The output of this code should look exactly the same as Figure 4-4 above. Whether the script really winds up being adequately hidden from every other browser on the market, however, is a matter of trial and error. (If another browser interprets <SCRIPT SRC> the same way Netscape 3.0 does, it may well interpret JavaScripts with pleasingly identical results. However, your mileage may vary!)

JavaScript has event handlers that can respond to events such as a user selecting a text field, clicking the mouse, or even leaving the page. JavaScript functions such as these may be used to verify that a user is entering valid information into a form requesting a telephone number or ZIP code—all without any server intervention or network transmission.

The following code will place a button labeled “Click Here” on a Web page:

```
<FORM>
<INPUT TYPE="button" Value="Click Here"
onClick="alert('Thanks for the Click!')
```

JavaScripts can, of course, quickly become more elaborate. Figure 4-5 shows a Web page with a dialog box for using a search engine of the user’s choice; a drop-down menu allows selecting among several. When the search button is clicked, a new browser window opens to display the chosen search engine’s output (Figure 4-6). This may then be closed if the user wants to go back to the original page.

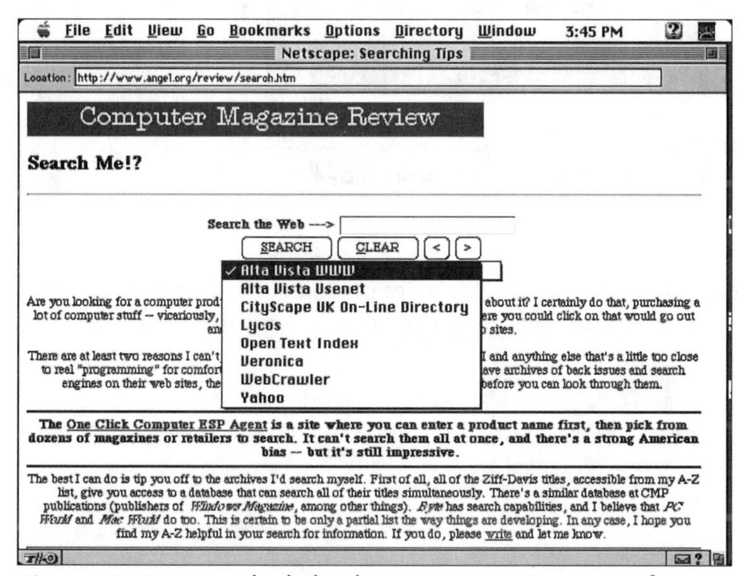

Figure 4–5 A simple dialog box, written in JavaScript, for selecting a search engine

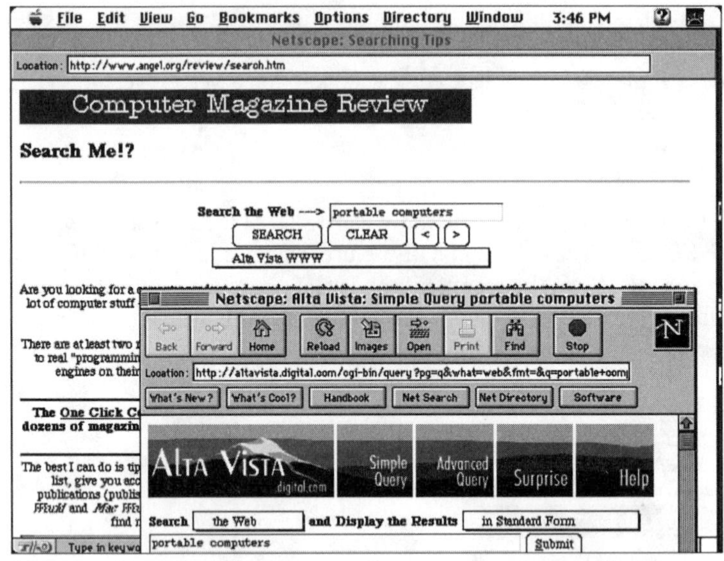

Figure 4–6 The AltaVista search engine, as invoked by the dialog box in Figure 4-5

Here is the beginning of the HTML and JavaScript portion of the Web page in Figure 4-4. Again, much of the script is placed in the header so that it loads first, setting variables and so on:

```
<HTML>
<HEAD>
</HEAD>
<TITLE>Searching Tips</TITLE>
<BODY>
<body bgcolor="FFFFFF">
<IMG SRC="cjrlit.gif">
<H2>Search Me!?</H2>
<HR>
<script language="JavaScript">
<!-- Hiding from old browsers
function plusify(items) {
var plussed = "";
  for (var t = 1 ; t <= items.length ; t++) {
    if (items.substring(t-1,t) == " ") {
    plussed+="+";
    }
    else {
    plussed+=items.substring(t-1,t);
    }
  }
return plussed;
}
```

```
function doSearch() {
      var words;
      words = document.searchforit.query.value;
      var terms;
      terms=plusify(words);
      var index;
      index = document.searchforit.service.selectedIndex;
      var place;
      place = document.searchforit.service.options[index].value;
      place+=terms;
      if (notEmpty(terms))   {
          window.open("","main2");
          window.open(place,"main2");
     }
}
function notEmpty(word)  {
  if (word == "" || word == null) {
   self.status="ENTER SEARCH TERMS";
//   alert("Enter search terms");
   return false;
  }
  else {
   self.status = "SEARCHING FOR:  " + word;
   return true;
  }
}
//-->
</script>
<BASE TARGET="main2">
</head>
<BODY bgcolor="#FFFF00">
<!--
<center>
<FORM NAME="searchforit" ACTION="javascript:doSearch()"
method="GET" TARGET="main2" onSubmit="doSearch()">
<b>Search the Web ---></b>
<input name="query" size=25
onFocus="self.status='Type in keywords to search for, hit enter or select the search⇐
engine.';return true"
onSubmit="doSearch()" onBlur="document.searchforit.query.value=this.value">
<br>
<input type="button" name="formbutton" value="   SEARCH   "
onClick="doSearch()" TARGET="main2">
<input type="button" name="clearbutton" value="   CLEAR   "
onClick="this.form.query.value=''">
<input type="button" value="<" onClick="parent.main2.history.go(-1)">
<input type="button" value=">" onClick="parent.main2.history.go(1)">
<br>
<select name="service" onChange="doSearch()" TARGET="main2">
<option value=
"http://altavista.digital.com/cgi-bin/query?pg=q&what=web&fmt=&q=">
```

continued on next page

continued from previous page

```
Alta Vista WWW
<option value=
"http://altavista.digital.com/cgi-bin/query?pg=q&what=news&fmt=&q=">
Alta Vista Usenet
<option value=
"http://www.cityscape.co.uk/cgi-bin/srch2html?type=Any&field=Any&Location=Any&key=">
CityScape UK On-Line Directory
<option value="http://query2.lycos.cs.cmu.edu/cgi-bin/pursuit?">
Lycos
<option value=
"http://search.opentext.com/omw/simplesearch?mode=phrase&SearchFor=">
Open Text Index
<option value=
"gopher://veronica.uni-koeln.de:2347/7-t1  ?">
Veronica
<option value=
"http://webcrawler.com/cgi-bin/WebQuery?">
WebCrawler
<option value="http://search.yahoo.com/bin/search?p=">
Yahoo
</SELECT>
</FORM>
//-->
```

To delve further into JavaScript would be going beyond the scope of this book. However, the best way to learn how to write your own JavaScripts is to examine, borrow, and adapt examples you find on the Net. You will find that the vast majority of authors are very open to this—if they wanted secrecy, they'd have used a Java *application* instead of a JavaScript.

Again, many JavaScripts are available for you to look at and reuse at *http://www.gamelan.com*. You'll also find a basic introduction to JavaScript at *http://home.netscape.com/eng/mozilla/3.0/handbook/javascript/script.html.*

Lesson 4: Java vs. Plug-Ins

As a terrific scripting language for Netscape, JavaScript is without peer. However, it's relatively light-duty when measured in terms of the probable size of most scripts and the uses they will be put to. Although it adds a new level of ingenuity and control to Web pages, it's not poised to knock anyone's socks off with multimedia content that it single-handedly facilitated.

No, the real contenders are Java applications on the one hand, and plug-ins on the other. In looking at what Java applications and plug-ins are good for, it is difficult to characterize each. Both have become outstanding at delivering features such as animation to the Internet. They just differ in how they do it.

Some people have suggested there is a "left brain, right brain" split in which programmers and technical types prefer Java, while multimedia developers and marketing people prefer plug-ins. This seems hard to understand when the average end user of a Web page cannot tell the difference between a plug-in and a Java application once both are up and running.

One reason for any dichotomy might be that programmers are accustomed to, and in fact often enjoy, having to build tools as part of their work. A Java application, especially one that handles multimedia, is still a much more "from scratch" affair than a plug-in. Plug-ins, in contrast, are more suited to people who just want to use the tools they already know. They're endowed with all the capabilities that any Windows, UNIX, or Macintosh application has to read and write files, so it's easy for them to manipulate your existing data. You'll find that dealing with a plug-in is a cinch—unless, of course, you're actually *writing* one.

Make no mistake, Java applications are great for corporate developers. But if you're working on your own, and just want to put sound, video, animation, and other impressive data types up on your Web pages, plug-ins are the quickest means to the end. There's nothing wrong about cake mix if it's tasty.

Table 4-1 compares Java applications, JavaScripts, and plug-ins. As you'll see, plug-ins have unbeatable simplicity from the Web page developer's point of view. On the other hand, their portability is poor: Plug-ins have to be optimized and recompiled for each type of client computer they run on (though Windows 95 and Windows NT plug-ins are, of course, identical).

If you're the Web page author, you'll find two more major points in favor of plug-ins. While the software developer may have to change things for each computer platform, *you* don't. The HTML code you use doesn't care what type of computer visitors to your Web pages have—not, at least, if they're running Netscape—and data files are compatible from computer to computer if you select the right types.

You've probably heard the debates in the computing community about "thin client" vs. "fat client." Thin clients are those with little or no local storage and relatively little memory. Fat clients are machines with lots of disk space, RAM, and probably more processing power. Some people—Oracle's Larry Ellison is the leading proponent—say that for thin TV-based browsers and small portables to surf the Internet on an equal footing with other machines, more of the Web's intelligence should migrate to servers. That's where Java applications ought to be stored, maintained, and updated, they say. Others (Microsoft's Bill Gates being the prime example) say that Web browsing is already one of the most demanding computer applications, and that more of the intelligence ought to be moved to the client.

As noted in the last row of the table, Java wins out when it comes to "democracy": All clients are the most nearly equal, because as long as they can run Java, the applications will download. Each user will receive an identical experience from any given Web page. Web pages are a less democratic experience with plug-ins because there will always be some users who have the plug-ins and others who don't.

On the other hand, this lack of "democracy" makes plug-ins appropriate for the real world, where most connections to the Internet are bandwidth limited, and even expensive T1 or T3 connections offer lower speed than a CD-ROM drive. Users do not have to repetitively download Java applications in order to interact with Web pages. Instead, they download just the data they want to look at. If they want plug-ins, they can install them with just a single download. Therefore, plug-ins are a solution that scales nicely in accordance with how fast your computer and your Internet connection are.

For the developer, plug-ins are a relatively good choice compared to Java applications if a company already has an existing base of large C applications. Developers can often convert these programs to plug-ins in a matter of days using a "wrapper"—a small amount of conversion code. Plug-ins are also very useful for developers who use programs with existing platform-specific extensions.

There are weaknesses in plug-ins: A separate plug-in must be written for each platform, and security is relatively poor. Plug-ins have full access to users' disk drives and information about their computing environment, meaning that it would not be difficult to write a Trojan horse sort of program. Presently, users must rely on the reputation of the company authoring the plug-in in order to have peace of mind.

LiveConnect

During their short history, JavaScripts, Java applets, and plug-ins have come to be thought of as rival technologies. Competitors they certainly are in that each would like to get your attention—and there is some overlap in the tasks they can take on.

Thanks to Netscape's LiveConnect, however, these "rivals" can work together as equal partners. LiveConnect, introduced with Netscape 3.0, creates connections between HTML elements, Java, JavaScript, and plug-ins. As a result:

- JavaScript programmers can now control plug-ins and Java applet functions.
- Plug-in programmers can now make functions available to JavaScript programmers.
- Objects of different types—Java applets, plug-ins, and HTML (forms, buttons, images, etc.)—can now interact with each other to create live applications.

Two fundamental changes in Netscape 3.0 make this possible. First, its Java and JavaScript environments have been effectively merged. When an applet is downloaded into the browser, it becomes an object that can be referenced from a JavaScript. In other words, JavaScript scripts can now "see" everything a Java applet can see. Second, the so-called Java Runtime Interface (JRI) lets plug-in developers define Java classes. Once the developer has created a Java class for a plug-in, that class is installed each time your plug-in is run. Since all public Java classes in the browser environment are available to JavaScript, any script now automatically has access to a plug-in's Java class—and, therefore, to the plug-in itself.

An example of how this might be used is an online shopping system for a record store. A user could select, start, and stop sample audio tracks via a JavaScript that controls an audio plug-in such as LiveAudio. At the same time, a Java applet could be accepting orders or queries about the availability of any particular recording.

Using LiveConnect requires plug-ins that have been written with this mechanism in mind. Examples include the LiveVideo, LiveAudio, and Live3D plug-ins included with Netscape 3.0 itself.

Unfortunately, LiveConnect was just being completed—and documented—around the time this book went to the typesetters. For more detailed information, therefore, you'll need to resort to the Netscape Web site. You can find a list of plug-ins that work with

LiveConnect in the "LiveConnect Showcase" at *http://home.netscape.com/comprod/products/navigator/version_3.0/connect/lc-showcase.html*. Details on LiveConnect communication appear at *http://home.netscape.com/eng/mozilla/3.0/handbook/javascript/moja.html*. Finally, information aimed at would-be plug-in developers can be found at *http://home.netscape.com/eng/mozilla/3.0/handbook/plugins/index.html*.

Table 4-1 Java applications, JavaScripts and plug-ins compared

	Java Applications	JavaScript	Plug-ins
Simplicity	Moderate for Web page author, fair to poor for applet author	Moderate to fair for Web page author, who may also be the script author	Good to excellent for Web page author, fair to poor for plug-in author
Portability	Outstanding (supports varying browsers, and moves from machine to machine)	Good platform (support of other than Netscape not assured, but moves from machine to machine). Excellent for Web page author, who may not need to modify HTML code	Poor for plug-in developer, requiring separate plug-in development for each
Security	Good	Good	Fair
Dynamism (ease of modifying code)	Excellent for Web page author and above average for applet author	Good	Excellent for Web page author, poor for developer, requires regular updates on the part of the user
Compatibility with existing data ("repurposing")	Low	Low	Excellent
Bandwidth required	Relatively high, requiring download of both applets	Simple Web-page based scripts require little bandwidth	Download of plug-in a chore, but requirements relatively light thereafter
Sizzle factor	Can knock their socks off	Minimalist, but may surprise users with your cleverness	Just as impressive as Java
Democracy (Does each visitor to the site receive the same experience?)	Excellent	Excellent	Poor (there will always be users who don't have or don't want the plug-ins, and they must be downloaded as a separate step)

WHAT NOW?

This chapter set out to increase your familiarity with Java and JavaScript. With any luck it has succeeded, and you now want to seek out further information on Java in order to polish your Web pages further. One good source is Waite Group Press' *Java Primer Plus: Supercharging Web Applications with the Java Programming Language*, by Paul M. Týma, Gabriel Torok, and Troy Downing (ISBN: 1-57169-062-X). This provides a complete, step-by-step guide to Java, plus a CD-ROM containing Java classes, bonus applets, and more.

The rest of *this* book, however, returns to plug-ins, which are—all things considered—the easiest, quickest way to add multimedia content to your Web pages. Chapter 5 provides more detail about plug-ins' capabilities, Chapter 6 adds information about MIME types, and Chapter 7 is devoted to plug-in installation procedures for both Windows and the Macintosh. If you believe you've already learned enough about these topics, feel free to skip directly to Chapter 8, a programming overview that shows how you can add plug-ins to your Web pages.

5

WHAT PLUG-INS CAN DO

5

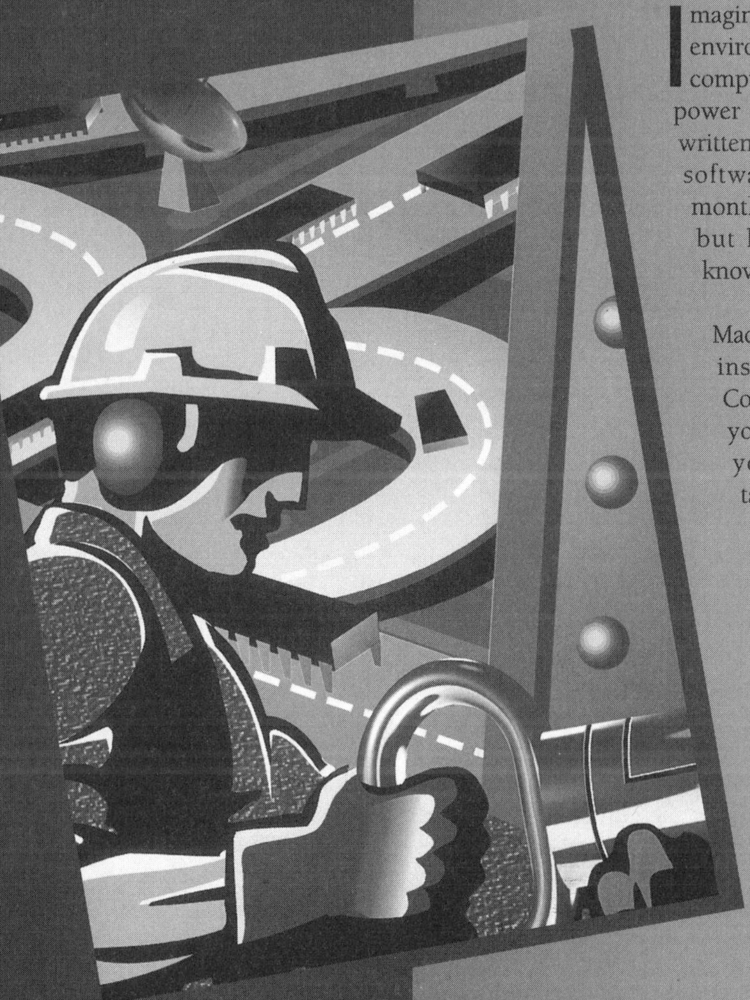

Imagine an easy-to-use, graphical computing environment that's already on your desktop computer. Imagine that you could extend its power and functionality by adding programs written by dozens, or hundreds, of third-party software authors. Imagine that every six months to a year, it gained new features—but kept the user interface you already know.

It sounds like the Windows or Macintosh operating system, doesn't it? But instead of having to go to Egghead or CompuUSA to get the programs you load, you download them over the Web. As you've guessed, it's Netscape we're talking about.

From the technical, programmer's point of view, Netscape isn't an operating system. It has to run on top of Windows, MacOS, UNIX, or whatever; and plug-ins can actually increase its dependence on the host operating system. From the *user*'s point of view, though, Netscape *has* become an operating system...there's no question about it.

So what can plug-ins do? Pretty much anything they want to. To put it another way, plug-ins can do anything that other applications on your computer can do. That includes displaying still or moving images on your screen, printing, using your disk drive, and manipulating your computer's digital sound or MIDI capabilities. (As noted in the previous chapter, that does raise some security concerns, although they're not of severe concern. Provided you get plug-ins from a CD-ROM or from a major company's Web site, you should be all right—just don't download ones you've never heard of before from a local bulletin board.)

Most (though not all) plug-ins can't run without Netscape, since they are dynamic link libraries and rely on it in order to be loaded. However, in other respects they're just like other programs on your computer, most of which, these days, were written in C or C++ themselves.

Lesson 1: Data Streaming

Some people use Netscape because it was provided to them by their companies, because they'd heard the name, or because it is the first Web browser they were able to find on the shelves of their local store. As an active consumer and producer of Web pages, you're probably different. You could have used any browser you want—and you've tried plenty of them—but you settled on Netscape because of its features and its performance.

Netscape established a performance edge over other browsers because it was the first to implement progressive display of GIF and JPEG images. Instead of calling up a Web page and then waiting for large graphics images to load before you can see a thing, you see the graphics being filled in bit by bit as you perform other operations. Most of us now take this for granted, and it's easy to forget how tedious Web browsing could be before the feature was available.

Unfortunately, those same old delays can recur when you try to listen to sound files, view presentations, or look at videos. Using any of these has meant starting a long download, going away to get a cup of coffee, and hoping the file transfer will have completed without an error by the time you've run an errand or two.

As you learned in Chapter 3, "Helper Applications: A Thing of the Past?," playing media types such as sound and video has, in the past, meant having to add helper applications to your computer system. One or two of these, such as the RealAudio player, were able to take data and start playing it before a download had completed. This relied on clever buffering and, in the case of RealAudio, special software that had to be installed on the server in order to send files in the right manner.

Now, plug-in technology brings this "instant-play" capability to all Netscape applications. Although they can't, by themselves, make data travel any faster, plug-ins bring the ability to preview and control what you're going to see and hear. Because they can be designed to download data in the background and cache it on your local hard drive, they can make downloads *seem* faster, too. By the time you request a file, your computer has already got part of it.

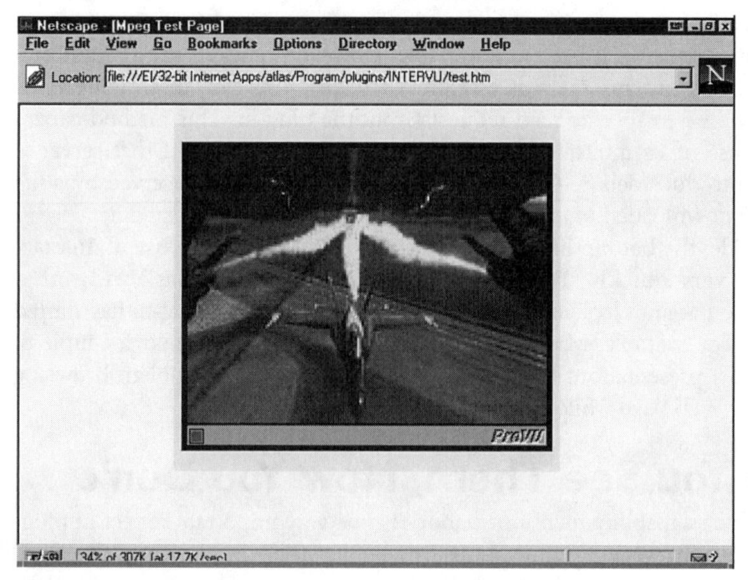

Figure 5-1 The first frames of this video file are available rapidly, thanks to the plug-in's data streaming capabilities

Requesting Their Own URLs

Preceding chapters of this book stressed that the main function of plug-ins is to handle MIME types that Netscape wouldn't know how to handle all by itself. True—but an equally important aspect of plug-ins is that they take on the job of requesting URLs themselves. Netscape fetches the data, but it is passed on directly to the plug-in for its own consumption.

When a plug-in fetches a URL, the data is provided as a stream as it arrives from the network. This lets a plug-in make a decision about how to act on the data without seeing the whole of it.

Instead of waiting for a whole file to download, it can act on a part of it. As a result, it can request the data in the form that its programmer considered best. For example, a video plug-in might fetch the first few frames of each video, display them, then pause the screen to cut down on bandwidth demands (see Figure 5-1). Or it might do the opposite: not show anything to the user immediately, but start a time-consuming download of a video it "knows" the user will want to see in the background.

Streams and Pull Mode

Streams are logical objects representing URLs and the data in them. Netscape creates them in response to a document or user event, or in response to an explicit request from a plug-in. Each stream is associated with a specific instance of a plug-in, and there can be more than one stream per instance. Since a single Web page can have multiple instances of one plug-in, or multiple plug-ins, the potential number of streams is considerable.

Initially streams are served up in the push mode that is normal for Web pages, where data is provided from a server as it becomes available. However, plug-ins can request pull mode (known to plug-in programmers as "seekable streams") instead, in which data is provided only in response to specific read requests from the plug-in. This method carries more overhead because of its multiple instructions to a remote server—if that server is congested, this can introduce delays. (It is ideal, however, if the stream is served by a file that already has been downloaded to local storage.)

Technicalities aside, the bottom line is that plug-ins can often obtain a useful, interactive amount of data very quickly. Furthermore, since plug-ins multitask with other Netscape processes, you are not locked out of a Web page even when a plug-in has started a lengthy download. For example, Macromedia's Shockwave plug-in can take a couple of minutes to download a presentation. However, you'll usually have no problem browsing the rest of the hosting Web page while you wait.

Lesson 2: Now You See Them, Now You Don't

The streaming data fetch capability mentioned above is one very important aspect of plug-ins. Equally important, however, is how plug-ins display that data to you, the user. Working in tandem with Netscape, plug-ins have three different ways of presenting their output:

- Embedded
- Full-screen
- Hidden

Embedded Plug-Ins

An embedded plug-in is part of a larger HTML document. It is visible as a rectangular part of an HTML page just as a GIF or JPEG would be. (Just as with GIFs and JPEGs, a plug-in's output may *appear* to be other than rectangular if part of its background is transparent; logically, however, it can't help but be a rectangle defined by WIDTH and HEIGHT attributes.) However, unlike an ordinary graphic, its working area is often live, and can respond to a user event such as a mouse click.

For example, with a right mouse click (Windows systems) or held-down mouse pointer (Macintosh) a user can pop up a menu that allows controlling the plug-in. Figure 5-2 shows graphics displayed by Iterated Systems' Fractal Viewer plug-in, which hides in the background until the mouse is right-clicked. Then, the plug-in displays the large menu shown in Figure 5-3.

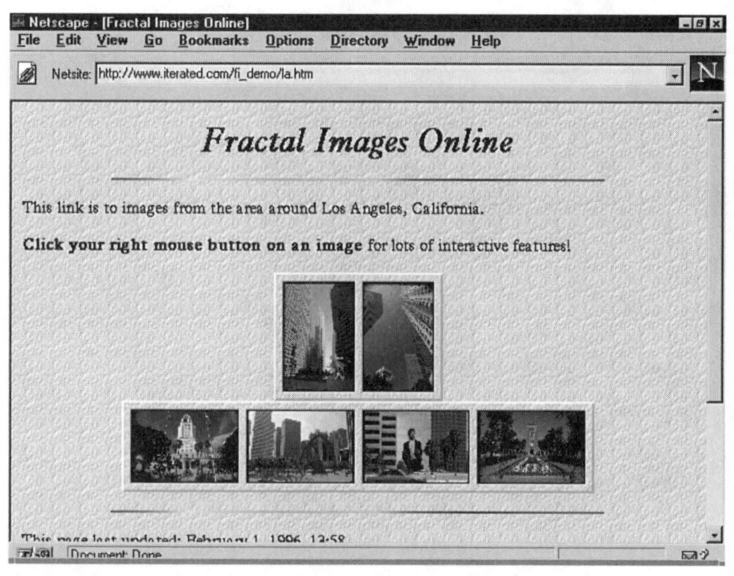

Figure 5–2 This plug-in hides in the background…

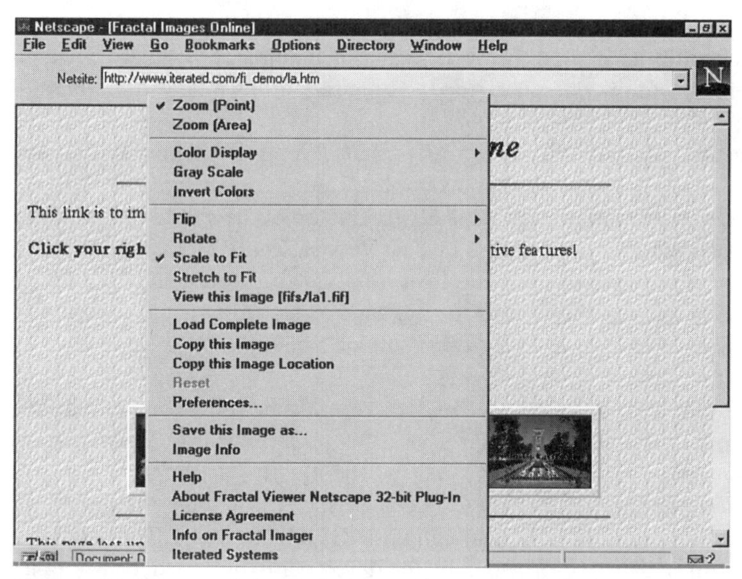

Figure 5–3 …until the right mouse button is clicked

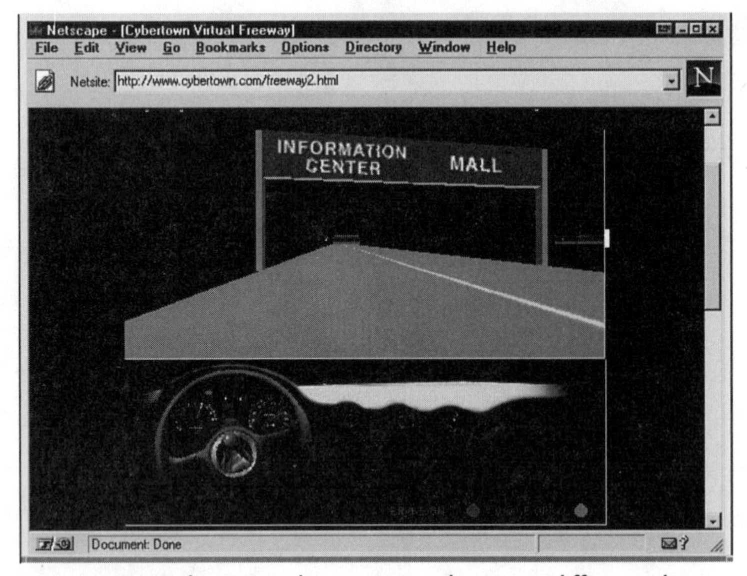

Figure 5-4 The "Virtual Freeway" utilizes two different plug-ins

Though an embedded plug-in may not betray its presence until it is clicked on, it can also display a toolbox within its area on the Web page. For example, a popular choice on the part of video plug-ins is to provide play, stop, and pause buttons modeled on those of a video cassette player.

An interesting aspect of embedded plug-ins is that several of them may be used simultaneously by a single Web page. For example, Figure 5-4 shows the "Virtual Freeway" site *(http://www.cybertown.com/freeway2.html)*. The top of the screen, showing the road, is an environment created by Netscape's Live3D Virtual Reality Modeling Language (VRML) plug-in. You can navigate through the freeway using the mouse and by clicking on various embedded graphics. The bottom of the screen, featuring a dashboard and animated steering wheel effects (and background engine noises, too), is generated by Macromedia's Shockwave plug-in.

When there are multiple plug-ins on one page, there could be some conflict between them when it comes to setting color palettes for 4- or 8-bit graphics boards. When there is more than one plug-in on a page which uses a palette, the plug-ins' authors should have given the Web page designer the opportunity to indicate which of the plug-ins should get the most accurate color (via the PALETTE="foreground" HTML attribute). This attribute, along with others, may or may not be provided by the developer of any particular plug-in. In fact, each plug-in comes with its own specific attributes that get appended to the <EMBED SRC> command.

Of course, plug-ins also respond to generally used attributes such as ALIGN, HEIGHT, and WIDTH (the latter two are required by Netscape for reliable results). These attributes often let you decide, when designing your page, whether or not to show toolboxes (or toolbars, or whatever you want to call them). You'll learn more about these attributes in Chapter 8, "Embedding Data in Your Web Pages: An Overview," and the chapters that follow.

Scroll bars are automatically displayed in most HTML documents that take up more than one screen in a user's copy of Netscape. This is as true of pages that include embedded plug-ins as it is of any other page. However, the screen areas controlled by plug-ins are not set off by scroll bars unless a plug-in's author decided to utilize them.

Full-Screen Plug-Ins

Instead of operating within just a part of the Netscape window, plug-ins can also take over that window entirely. In fact, they can even add toolbars to it that look as if they were part of Netscape all along.

The main reason for using a full-screen plug-in is in the "repurposing" of data that, unlike an HTML page, is already complete in and of itself. For example, a Microsoft Word document might carry all the text and graphics a user could want. The same goes for an Adobe PostScript file as translated into Acrobat format, or a vector graphic in Corel Draw's CMX file format. In these cases, there is intricate detail in the file being translated, so maximal screen area is a good thing.

Though a user should never be aware of it, Netscape does not draw scroll bars around the window for full-page plug-ins. Instead, the plug-in itself is called upon to draw them when necessary—and necessary they usually are unless a page is very small or a user's screen resolution is very high.

Figure 5-5 shows Adobe Acrobat Reader displaying a formatted Acrobat document. (An interesting point about this and other similar documents is that clickable links to other URLs may be placed within them. Although this is not an HTML file, the Acrobat Reader plug-in can be programmed to pass along requests for links just as if it were.)

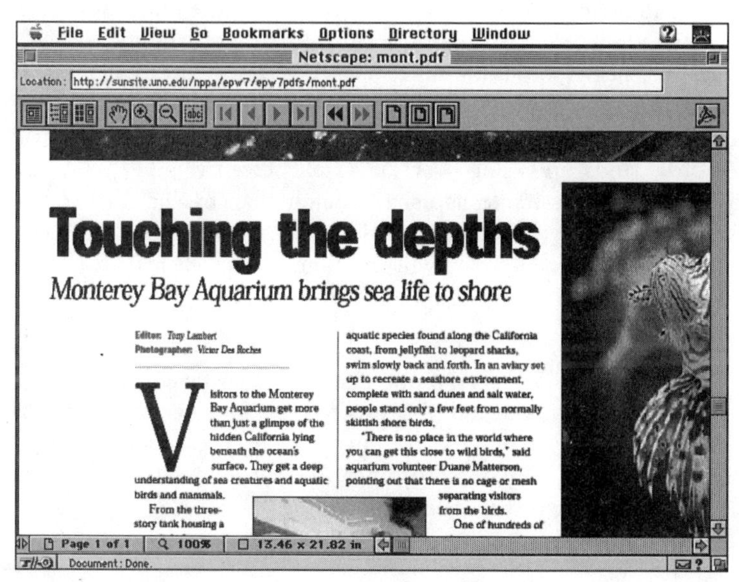

Figure 5–5 Adobe Acrobat Reader displays a document in full-screen mode

Figure 5-6 A Corel graphic displayed by the CMX Viewer

Figure 5-6 shows Corel's CMX Viewer plug-in displaying a graphic. An advantage of the vector graphic format is that it is possible to zoom in it without losing sharpness. Therefore, users can magnify an image without losing detail. The CMX Viewer exploits this fact via the pop-up viewer shown.

Many other plug-ins are designed to run in embedded mode under normal conditions but will also operate full-screen at times. For example, many Web pages include sound or video files that Web page authors have attached to their pages using the <IMG SRC> tag. This tag was the only method to insert such files prior to the release of plug-ins, and it is intended to pass the files to a helper application that opened in a window separate from Netscape. With Netscape 3.0, however, plug-ins have often taken over the relevant MIME type. Instead of passing an .AVI video file to an external player, for example, Netscape will open it with a plug-in that winds up taking over the whole screen (Figure 5-7). This behavior, though not particularly desirable, is usually better than having to invoke a helper application. As more Web page authors exploit plug-ins, changing their HTML tags from <IMG SRC> to <EMBED SRC>, the less you will encounter this problem.

Hidden

Hidden plug-ins are those that run in the background without displaying a window at all. Presently, they are associated mostly with sound files. It is possible for some other types of plug-ins to run in hidden mode by accident if the Web page author forgot to set, or deliberately zeroed out, the WIDTH and HEIGHT attributes. In that inadvertent case, you might have a Netscape plug-in playing you an invisible video.

Figure 5–7 A file attached via <IMG SRC> winds up taking over the screen

NOTE: As we'll reiterate later, setting HEIGHT and WIDTH both to a value of 0 pixels may trigger anomalous behavior in Netscape Navigator. The preferred way of "zeroing out" an image is to set one of these values to 0 pixels and the other to a minimal value such as 4 pixels. Better still, simply use the HIDDEN attribute with your HTML tag.

More typically, plug-ins that default to a hidden state can be made to appear on a Web page if its designer wants them to. By turning on a toolbox and specifying HEIGHT and WIDTH, you can turn a hidden plug-in into one that runs in embedded mode.

Lesson 3: The Plug-Ins You Already Have

Netscape 2.0 users had to spend a long time hunting for the plug-ins they needed—if the plug-ins even existed. You don't need to do that, thanks to the CD-ROM supplied with this book.

The contents of the CD, which has been designed for both Windows 95 and Macintosh users, are described in Appendix A at the back of this book. You'll also find an OPENME.HTM file in the root directory of your CD-ROM: Open this file with Netscape and you'll be able to browse through a visual guide to the plug-ins we've included on the disc.

Even without the CD-ROM, though, you might already have all the plug-ins you need. That's because Netscape 3.0, unlike any previous version of the browser, comes bundled with plug-ins. Together, they let you play digitized sound files in Windows, Macintosh, or UNIX sound formats, let you listen to MIDI tracks, let you see videos in Windows .AVI or QuickTime formats, and even let you explore 3D worlds using VRML.

Netscape used to include a helper application called NAPLAYER in order to play sound files. This worked adequately, but it has been replaced by a new plug-in called LiveAudio. Capable of playing .AU (UNIX), .AIFF (Mac), and .AVI (Windows) sound files, LiveAudio can operate in either embedded or hidden modes.

LiveAudio, which also plays MIDI files with ease, is installed automatically when you install Netscape. You'll find out more about how to control its actions in your Web pages in Chapters 8 and 9.

Netscape also now includes the ability to show videos within any Web page. Its plug-ins interpret .AVI files (on Windows versions of Netscape) or QuickTime files (on both Windows and Macintosh). Again, videos may be embedded within pages or take over the entire screen (though, as you're probably aware, digital videos can look very pixelated when scaled up beyond the original capture size). You'll learn more about how to control LiveVideo in Chapters 8 and 10.

Finally, Netscape now comes with its own VRML client, Live3D. Adapted from WebFX by Paper Software (now a division of Netscape Communications), this lets users browse VRML worlds. You'll learn more about how to use Live3D and control its actions via Web pages in Chapter 12.

The Netscape Power Pack 2.0

A separate product for Windows users is Netscape's Power Pack 2.0, which comes on a CD-ROM. This includes four Internet applications: Netscape SmartMarks, Netscape Chat, CyberSpell for Netscape Mail, and Norton AntiVirus Internet Scanner.

Netscape SmartMarks downloads Web documents for off-line browsing. It automatically manages and tracks favorite sites, downloading documents with new information so you can browse them anytime—even when you're not connected. SmartMarks also helps you organize bookmarks into folders for keeping track of important sites.

New for SmartMarks 2.0 is the useful ability to download Web pages automatically and read them later without an Internet connection. This offline browsing capability means you can download pages over slow dial-up phone lines without having to be there. Later, even on a plane or train, you can browse them at hard disk speeds.

The Windows 95 version of SmartMarks includes support for Windows 95 Shell Extensions and Internet Shortcuts, allowing you to track and manage Internet Shortcuts on your desktop.

Netscape Chat is a graphical client for Internet Relay Chat (IRC) channels. It integrates with Netscape, letting you talk to and collaborate with other chat users. Web sites you select can be automatically sent to other chat users, who can immediately view them.

CyberSpell, by INSO, adds a Spelling menu to all Netscape Mail composition windows. It provides correction for punctuation, formatting, spacing, capitalization errors, and more. Specialized terminology and Internet formatting (URLs, FTP addresses, e-mail addresses, and "emoticons") are handled easily by CyberSpell.

Finally, the Norton AntiVirus Internet Scanner unobtrusively checks every Internet file you download or receive as an e-mail attachment. It may also be launched directly from Windows and used to perform routine scanning of your entire system.

Bundled Plug-Ins

The Netscape Power Pack 2.0 also includes a graphical installation program that helps learn about and install these programs, plus the following Netscape plug-ins:

- ASAP WebShow (Software Publishing Corporation)—This plug-in lets you view business presentations within Web pages. For more information about it, see Chapter 11 "Presentation/Animation."
- Astound Web Player (Gold Disk)—This plug-in lets you play back multimedia presentations created with Astound and Studio M. For more information about it, see Chapter 11, "Presentation/Animation."
- CarbonCopy/Net (Microcom)—This plug-in lets you access and control other PCs over the Internet. For more information about it, see Chapter 15, "Other Plug-Ins."
- EarthTime/Lite (Starfish Software)—This plug-in tells you times around the world using colorful maps. For more information about it, see Chapter 15, "Other Plug-Ins."
- Envoy (Tumbleweed Software)—This plug-in lets you view formatted Envoy documents. For more information about it, see Chapter 14, "Document Plug-Ins."
- FIGleaf Inline Lite (Carberry Technology)—This plug-in lets you view and zoom a wide variety of raster and vector graphics formats. For more information about it, see Chapter 13, "Graphics Plug-Ins."
- FormulaOne/NET (Visual Components)—This plug-in lets you embed and manipulate live spreadsheets and charts. For more information about it, see Chapter 15, "Other Plug-Ins."
- Lightning Strike (InfinitOp)—This plug-in lets you view compressed Web image files. For more information about it, see Chapter 13, "Graphics Plug-Ins."
- Live 3D (Netscape Communications)—This plug-in lets you view 3D VRML documents. For more information about it, see Chapter 12, "VRML Plug-Ins."
- RealAudio (Progressive Networks)—This plug-in lets you listen to live or stored audio on the Internet. For more information about it, see Chapter 9, "Audio Plug-Ins."
- Shockwave for Director (Macromedia)—This plug-in lets you play Macromedia Director animations and presentations. For more information about it, see Chapter 11, "Presentation/Animation."
- VDOLive (VDONet)—This plug-in lets you view real-time video over the Internet. For more information about it, see Chapter 10, "Video Plug-Ins."

- VRScout VR Browser (Chaco Communications)—This plug-in lets you explore 3D VRML environments. For more information about it, see Chapter 12, "VRML Plug-Ins."

- WIRL (VREAM)—This plug-in is another way to access VRML sites . For more information, see Chapter 12, "VRML Plug-Ins."

- Word Viewer (INSO Corporation)—This plug-in lets you view Microsoft Word documents. For more information about it, see Chapter 14, "Document Plug-Ins."

WHAT NOW?

You've learned what plug-ins can do and gotten a feel for how they might be used in your Web pages. Chapters 6 and 7 provide more detail about installing plug-ins and telling Netscape which MIME types you want them to handle.

6

UNDERSTANDING MIME TYPES

In the beginning there was the word. And the word was good—but it didn't go far enough.

To put it another way, when electronic mail—and, later, the World Wide Web—was first devised, it dealt only in simple ASCII text. After all, this was the only type of information that could be shared by many different microcomputers.

There's only so much you can do with the simple numerals, letters, and words of plain ASCII. Users of e-mail soon wanted to send one another formatted documents. Those devising Web pages felt it would be nice if they had a way to include graphics.

For these reasons and more, a system called Multipurpose Internet Mail Extensions (MIME) was devised. MIME attempts to bring order to the panoply of file formats used on the Web, and to a large degree it has succeeded.

Its use is key to Netscape plug-ins and helper applications.

Therefore, in order to understand how these work, you have to have at least a passing knowledge of MIME.

Lesson 1: What MIME Is

Whatever our failings might be, humans are very good at looking at objects and figuring out what type of thing they are. There's no way, for example, that you'd mistake an umbrella for a hat or a hat for an umbrella—unless forced to do the latter by a sudden tropical rainstorm.

Computers, however, have to examine an object painstakingly to figure out what sort of thing it is. They look at its structure, applying a series of tests, or rules, before coming to a conclusion.

The process is relatively slow, as you know if you've used a word processing program that converts documents from "foreign" file formats, or the file viewers built into an operating system shell such as Windows Explorer. And, of course, most software applications don't even have such file parsing routines built in.

Therefore, it makes sense to let a computer know in advance what type of file it's dealing with. As every user knows, this is done in MS-DOS and Windows (not to mention UNIX) via an extension (or suffix)—the characters that follow the period in the file name. On the richer Macintosh System, it's done via the *resource fork,* a special part of each file the operating system uses to ascertain the file type.

Both systems work fairly well. DOS and Windows get confused, however, if a user gives a file an inappropriate extension. They also have problems if the same extension is used by two different software programs. For example, .DOC might mean either a Microsoft Word document or a Word Perfect document.

NOTE: The Windows 95 Explorer defaults to hiding the extensions of files viewed in its directory listings. Since Windows nonetheless requires these extensions, this is a shabby (if minor) trick. For any serious computer work, you should run Explorer, open its View/Options menu, then uncheck the box that appears beside the words "Hide MS-DOS extensions for file types that are registered."

The Mac, for its part, occasionally gets confused if a file was downloaded by, or copied from, another type of computer. In such cases the resource fork can get zapped, resulting in a file that can't be opened until you spend some quality time with ResEdit.

If stand-alone computers can get confused by file types, imagine the potential for chaos offered by the World Wide Web. Users don't know, and don't want to know, what type of computer was used to create the files they're browsing. Web page authors don't know what type of computers their server will be talking to.

Clearly, a better, cross-platform way of specifying file types had to be devised, which is how MIME came about. Evolved in the early 1990s, MIME was a product of collaborative discussions in the Web developer community; though Nathaniel Borenstein and Ned Freed are generally acknowledged as having been the prime movers behind it.

(Dan Connolly, however, is the prime mover who spearheaded MIME's application to the Web. If you want to know more about this significant part of Web history, look at the famous "Request for Comments 1521" describing MIME at *http://ds.internic.net/rfc/rfc1521.txt.* You'll also find animated discussions in the archives of the WWW-Talk mailing list for 1992 and 1993 at *http://www.eit.com/www.lists/.)*

Originally designed with e-mail enclosures in mind (hence its name), MIME places a content header at the top of each data file. The header is hierarchical, with a primary designation, or MIME type, designed to provide an overall classification of the file's content, and a subtype which is more specific. The MIME type and subtype are written with a forward slash between them. For example, a Microsoft Word file might be tagged as application/msword, a PostScript file might be tagged as application/postscript, an HTML file is indicated by text/html, and so on.

A file extension, or suffix, is also associated with each MIME type. For examples of MIME types and suffixes, refer back to Table 3-1 in Chapter 3, "Helper Applications: A Thing of the Past?". Or simply open the Options/General Preferences menu in your copy of Netscape, click on the Helpers tab, and scroll through the menu that appears.

NOTE: Chapter 3 also provides you with a list of the standard MIME types built into Netscape—those it can interpret without the aid of either a helper application or a plug-in. These vary somewhat, however, from Netscape version to Netscape version. Look at the list of MIME types that are the defaults for the UNIX version (it's at *http://home.netscape.com/assist/helper_apps/mimedefault.html)* and you'll see some, such as TROFF documents, that are considered only relevant to that operating environment.

So that they can work in the manner intended, MIME types need to be standardized. When a new software application is written that requires a new type of data file format—and especially if that file format is intended to interact with helper applications or plug-ins on the Web—its author needs to contact the Internet Assigned Numbers Authority (IANA) so that a MIME type can be registered for it.

NOTE: A description of how to get MIME types registered appears at *http://ds.internic.net/rfc/rfc1590.txt.* You'll notice that the official term for what we're calling "MIME type" has been changed to "Media Type." Since "MIME type" is the more distinctive term and is still used by almost everyone, we're sticking with it, too.

As a user of plug-ins, you won't need to be concerned with this process—not unless you take up writing plug-ins, too. However, it is the reason why some plug-ins use a MIME subtype beginning with the prefix "x-". When you see this it means that the subtype, while not "incorrect" in any way, has not yet been officially registered with the IANA.

Some plug-ins are coded to look for more than one subtype associated with the same data file. For example, a plug-in that plays MIDI files might look for them with the MIME type application/midi as well as the MIME type application/x-midi. This is often done when developers anticipate IANA registration of their new MIME type but have not yet actually received it. That way, when the MIME type is approved and servers are updated, the plug-in will continue to work as it should.

Lesson 2: How It Works on the Web

As you learned in Chapter 3, "Helper Applications: A Thing of the Past?," what Netscape does with a file it downloads from the Web depends upon its MIME type. The browser can either interpret and display the file all by itself, or it can hand it off to a helper application or plug-in. (Of course, there are many "decisions" to be made, since a single Web page may well have many different files embedded within it.)

To know what to do, Netscape has to have some way of knowing what the MIME type of the file *is*. You might think that the browser just takes a look at the extension of the file it is downloading and uses that to infer its MIME type. However, it's not that simple. The only time that Netscape uses the extension to guess at the MIME type is when the file is being pulled off a local disk drive or downloaded via FTP. (In this context, "local disk drive" would mean any drive connected to your system using a local area network as well, which would be the case in many intranets.)

If a file is being transferred to your computer by Gopher or by the HyperText Transfer Protocol (HTTP) used on the Web, Netscape *ignores* its extension. Instead, the file's MIME type is passed to Netscape from the Web server directly. The browser doesn't have to guess at the MIME type because that information is integrated into every HTTP file transfer.

In order to send MIME type information to the browser, a Web server obviously has to know that information in the first place. How *does* a Web server know that, for example, every .GIF file stored on it should be sent to browsers with the MIME type image/gif? Ironically, it figures it out by the .GIF file extension. (Some servers are also designed to figure it out by subdirectory. For example, you might configure a server to serve all files in the Images/ directory with the MIME type image/gif.)

In other words, we have Netscape deliberately ignoring file extensions in favor of this MIME type mumbo-jumbo, which is assigned by the Web server to each file it sends by looking at that file's *extension*. Figure 6-1 shows a visual representation of the process.

From a DOS/Windows user's perspective, this doesn't make a heck of a lot of sense. You're probably wondering why the MIME type is used at all when DOS and UNIX systems both require extensions in any case.

The answer is that the designers of the system foresaw the evolution of Web servers that would free their administrators from the tyranny of extensions once and for all. (Advanced Web servers such as—ahem—Macs.)

A Macintosh Web server would be able to determine the type of file being stored on it by looking at its resource fork, then send it out over the Web with the appropriate MIME type. Neither the server nor the browser would, in that case, have to make any recourse to extensions whatsoever.

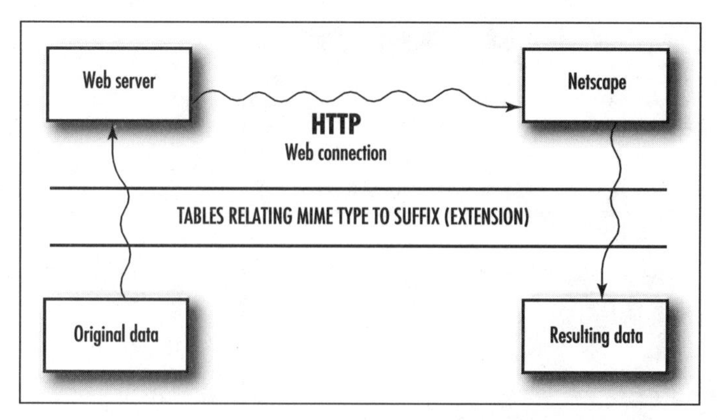

Figure 6–1 A successful HTTP transfer requires translation tables relating file suffixes to MIME types at both ends of a link

For better or worse, most Web servers are not Macs. Furthermore, Macintosh Web server software tends to use the familiar system of suffixes/extensions anyhow. This is because these servers can't assume that everyone uploading files to them will be using Macintosh systems. Still, it was a nice thought…

Table 6-1 lists the most common problems with MIME and some possible solutions.

Table 6–1 MIME problems and some solutions

Symptom	Cause	Solution
If a file appears as gibberish in your Netscape browser window	The Web server was not configured to supply the file's correct MIME type to browsers	Reconfigure the server's MIME types file
Netscape offers to save a file to disk when you really wanted to see it on screen or listen to it	Your copy of Netscape does not "know" about the MIME type the server is sending it	You need to configure a helper application or plug-in to handle this MIME type
Netscape displays a file on screen that you would prefer to save to disk	Netscape is receiving a MIME type it has been set up to display, send to a plug-in, or hand off to a helper application	Before you click on the link, hold down the SHIFT (or OPTION on Macintosh); Netscape will then prompt you for a file name to save it to. If you always want to save this MIME type to disk, adjust Netscape's behavior using the Options/General Preferences/Helpers tab.

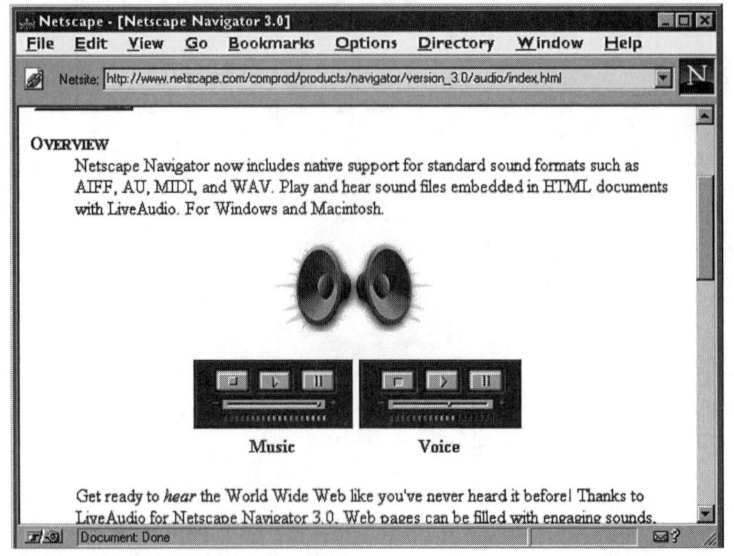

Figure 6–2 A sample Web page advertising LiveAudio

Incidentally, there's a little-known way to get information about any Web page that includes all the files it references *and* their MIME types. Just wait for the entire Web page to load, then select Document Info (or Frame Info, if relevant) from the View menu in Netscape. You'll get a list of all the files referenced by the Web page, and information about whether they were included using the <IMAGE> tag or the <EMBED> tag. Clicking on any individual file then delivers information about whether or not it's in Netscape cache, when it was created, and—most important for our purposes—what its MIME type is.

Figure 6-2 shows the Web page advertising Live Audio at *http://www.netscape.com/comprod/products/navigator/version_3.0/audio/index.html.* Figure 6-3 shows the result of giving the View/Document Info command for that page. As you can see, the first sound sample on the site is an embedded AIF file.

Lesson 3: Configuring Web Servers

Chapters 9–15 of this book deal with installing, configuring, and authoring Web pages for particular plug-ins. In these chapters, you'll read over and over, until you are, alas, heartily sick of it, words like these: "This is the MIME type and suffix you'll need to give the people who run your Web server so they can modify their configuration files."

I got even more tired of composing variations on this sentence than you'll get of reading them! Unfortunately, it had to be repeated: "This MIME typing issue is probably the single most critical hurdle you'll face as you try to develop Web pages that use plug-ins."

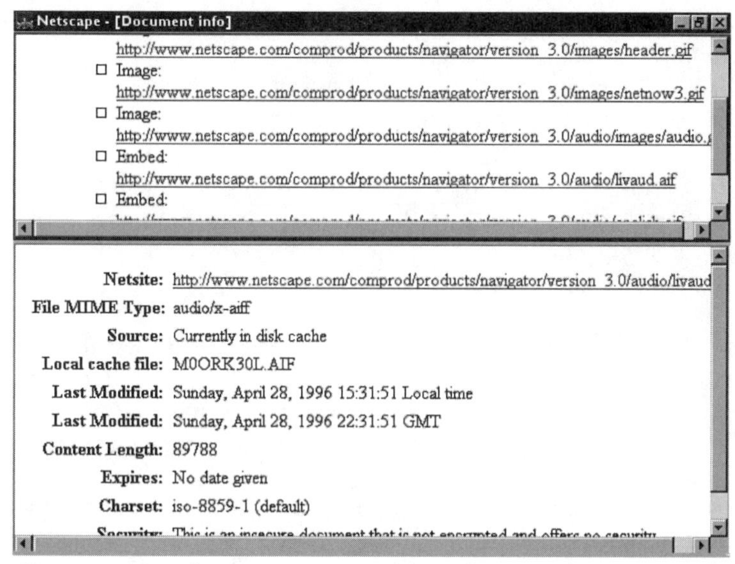

Figure 6–3 Information uncovered via the View/Document Info command

Most Web servers come already set up to associate the most popular file extensions with their equivalent MIME types, which they'll then use when sending the files to users via HTTP. For example, every Web server associates a .GIF file with the image/gif MIME type, just as it obviously associates .HTM and .HTML files with the MIME type text/HTML.

A dozen or more other associations will also have been made by support staff at the Web server, or by the authors of the Web server software itself. These include the MIME types that Netscape can interpret all by itself, plus other popular types such as application/postscript or video/mpeg (to name just two).

However, if a file does not use an extension that appears in the server's configuration files, then it will be sent over the HTTP link using the default text/plain MIME type. This is why new file types often appear as gibberish in Netscape's browser window: Navigator assumes that the files are simple text, since that's what it's been told, and displays them accordingly.

This fact can make impromptu testing of a new plug-in more difficult than it ought to be. Let's suppose you just obtained a great new plug-in that lets you embed animations in Web pages. You create animations using an authoring program that saves them as .ZAP files, which the plug-in expects to receive with the MIME type application/x-zap.

You create Web pages, embed the .ZAP files, and all your testing goes perfectly—until you upload the Web pages to your Web site. When it pulled the pages off your hard drive or your LAN, Netscape used the file suffix to figure out what the .ZAP files were; but now that it's using HTTP, it ignores the suffixes and looks for the MIME type.

Since that MIME type isn't there yet, you and your users get gibberish when you should be getting pretty pictures. Solution? Contact the administrators of the Web server and have them add the MIME type application/x-zap and suffix zap to their configuration files. This usually takes a day or two to get done, but it's a one-time-only fix.

NOTE: Remember, adding a new MIME type to use a new plug-in has to be done for *each* server onto which you upload files. If you have more than one server hosting files for you—or if you move your site from one server to another—you have to have configuration files changed on each system.

There may be times when you want to see how a new plug-in responds over the Web without necessarily disturbing the administrators of your server. Perhaps you're doing comparative tests on three different video plug-ins, each using its own MIME type, and you don't want to cry wolf by having the tech support folks add all three (though there's no real reason they shouldn't).

Or perhaps the people who run your server aren't responsive to your request, either because they don't take customer support seriously, or because they're part of a slow-responding bureaucracy. It stands to reason that it would take CompuServe, America Online, or any other large organization much longer to add new MIME types to its servers than it would a small one- or two-person ISP.

If you can't get the MIME type you want to test added to your server, there is another way you can proceed. It requires that you have, as well as a Web site, an FTP area that users can access. Instead of using this syntax (which will be further explained in Chapter 8, "Embedding Data in Your Web Pages: An Overview"):

```
<EMBED SRC="testfile.zap">
```

or even

```
<EMBED SRC="http://www.myserver.com/testfile.zap>
```

use the syntax:

```
<EMBED SRC="ftp://ftp.myserver.com/pub/testfile.zap>
```

The latter is more awkward, and causes you to have to specify absolute directory paths (instead of the relative path used in the first of the three lines above). However, by using FTP instead of HTTP, you force Netscape to use the file's suffix to determine the MIME type—just as it did when you loaded it from your local disk drive.

If You Run a Server

If you run your own Web server, you already know how to edit its configuration files. This section of the chapter is for the rest of us, so that we'll have some idea of what you go through after we e-mail you to request changes. (If you aren't already familiar with UNIX, don't attempt to follow these directions.)

Adding MIME types to a server generally involves adding an entry to a line in a file called, logically enough, mime.types. The first field in each line holds the MIME type and subtype, while the second field holds the suffix or suffixes pertinent to that MIME type. Since UNIX is case-sensitive, some administrators choose to duplicate suffixes, adding them once in all upper case and once in all lower case. That way the server will perform the way users expect it regardless of the case they use when uploading files.

Editing MIME types on an NCSA HTTPD-based server usually means changing the mime.types file in the SERVER_ROOT/conf subdirectory. Alternatively, a type can be added by inserting an "AddType" line in the srm.conf file.

The NCSA HPPTD server also permits expert users to add their own MIME types by logging on with a shell account and editing .htaccess files that appear in specific directories.

Interestingly, these .htaccess files may also be used to password-protect directories and more. (Netscape servers use .nsconfig files that can accomplish many of the same things.)

Various sites may have different file naming conventions. If you have a shell account on best.com, for example, your access file is called bhtaccess.

To modify your .htaccess file, set file access permission to:

```
user = read and write
group = read
world = read
```

Set the file's privileges to world-readable by typing

```
chmod 644 .htaccess
```

Place the file at the root level of your Web pages (such as the public_HTML directory). Then add a single line for each MIME type you want to add that begins with AddType, and continues with the MIME type/subtype and suffix.

If you are running a Macintosh-based HTTP server, you need to modify the file MacHTTP.config in an analogous fashion.

Servers that use a graphical user interface are slightly easier to configure. For example, to set up a WebSTAR server, you run the application called WebSTAR Admin. Then locate and select your server, which must be running, in the Pick A Server window. Choose Suffix Mapping from the Configure menu; the dialog box that appears will then let you fill in file suffixes, MIME types, and other information.

Adding MIME information to the Microsoft Internet Information Server requires that you edit the registry. Use the registry editor to open the entry HKEY_LOCAL_MACHINE\SYSTEM\ControlSet001\Services\InetInfo\MimeMap. You can then edit MimeMap to add new MIME types and extensions.

The EMWACS HTTP server running on Windows NT lets you add types by opening the HTTP server applet in the Control Panel. Clicking on the button labeled "New Mapping" will let you add a file extension and corresponding MIME type.

Other Web services use similar mechanisms. As you can see, there is nothing particularly complex about adding MIME types. However, the process does require that a server be reinitialized in order for the changes to take effect—which effectively confines the alterations to the wee hours and means that the person making them would rather be at home in bed. You can see why it's best not to make frivolous requests for changes in server configuration.

WHAT NOW?

You should now have a better appreciation of MIME types. Though these can be a thorn in the side, you probably won't have to worry about them as much with plug-ins as you did with using helper applications. If you just want to use plug-ins to use other people's Web pages, you'll find that a plug-in's takeover of specific MIME types happens automatically in almost every case. Server configuration only becomes an issue when you want to embed data in your *own* Web pages.

7

INSTALLING PLUG-INS

7

Now that you have an overall understanding of what plug-ins can do and why you'd want them to do it, it's time to learn how to get some onto your computer. (Well, to be strictly accurate, you already have some plug-ins on your computer—Netscape 3.0 comes with four of them.)

Like the rest of this book, this chapter assumes that you have a copy of Netscape 3.0 for Windows 95, Windows NT, Windows 3.x, or Macintosh. However, much of what is outlined here will work with Netscape 2.0 as well, and should still work with future versions of Netscape—including the forthcoming OS/2 edition—when it appears.

If you're only interested in one type of computer, you can follow the directions at the end of each lesson to skip instructions that relate to other systems. Reading all the lessons, however, will give you an improved understanding of Netscape's architecture and appreciation of how consistent the browser is across platforms.

Lesson 1: Getting Ready (Windows 95 and NT)

In this lesson, you'll learn how to prepare your Netscape environment for successful plug-in installation and management. Our instructions generally assume the use of Windows 95; Windows NT uses the same 32-bit plug-ins, but installation might be slightly different—especially if you have not upgraded to Windows NT Workstation 4.0, which features the Start button, taskbar, and other Windows 95-like features. ***If you're using Windows 3.x or a Mac, you can skip to Lesson 2 or Lesson 3, respectively.***

If you accepted the default choice when Netscape was first installed into Windows, the browser is in the C:\Program Files\Netscape folder. If you did not accept this default, and you have no idea where Netscape is now, there are two ways of finding out.

First, you can right-click on the Start icon, then select Open. Click on the Programs icon that appears within the Start menu folder. Then search through the icons that appear in the programs folder until you locate a Netscape Navigator icon. Double-clicking on this opens a folder with icons that correspond to the Start Menu entries for Netscape Navigator, Netscape Live, and CoolTalk. Locate the icon for Netscape Navigator and right-click on it to view its context menu. Select Properties from this menu, and you'll see the Netscape Navigator Properties window shown in Figure 7-1.

Now click on the Shortcut tab, then read the path listed in the Target field. This shows you the folder where your NETSCAPE.EXE has been installed.

The other way to locate your installed copy of Netscape Navigator is cruder but may be faster. Run Windows Explorer, then select Find from its Tools menu. In the Name & Location tab, enter NETSCAPE.EXE in the Named field, and use the drop-down menu to

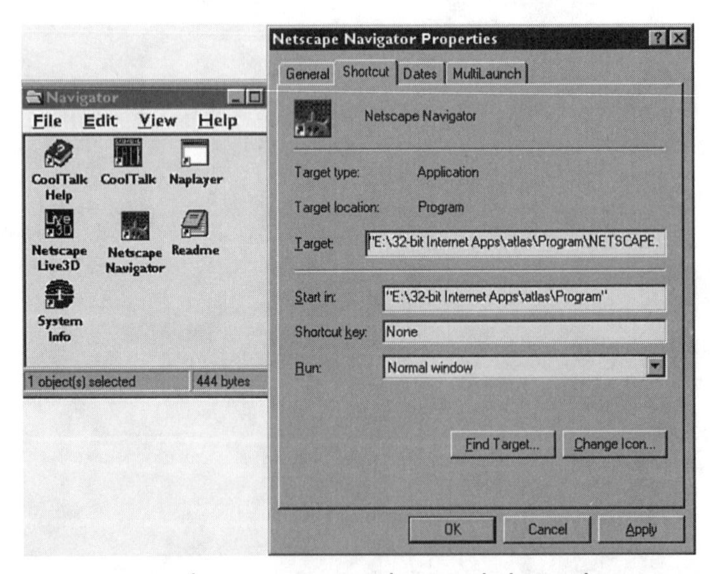

Figure 7-1 This Properties window can help you locate your Netscape Navigator folder

specify the hard drive you wish to search. As Figure 7-2 shows, Explorer will find NETSCAPE.EXE and let you know its path.

Figure 7-2 actually shows two instances of Netscape on the same hard drive. The one at the top of the list is a 16-bit version, for use with Windows 3.x, while the second one listed is the 32-bit version for Windows 95 and NT. There is no problem with keeping two Netscape versions on your hard disk, but you need to remember that plug-ins written for the Windows 95/NT version are *not* compatible with the Windows 3.x version of the program, and *vice versa*. If you or an installation program mixes up the two, Netscape may crash when the plug-in is invoked.

However, Windows 3.x plug-ins are usually labeled via a "16" that appears somewhere in their file name. Windows 95/NT plug-ins have, as you can guess, a "32" in theirs. Therefore, you can avoid mistakes simply by scanning each Netscape version's plug-ins folder and identifying any plug-ins that don't belong.

Once you have identified the path to your version of NETSCAPE.EXE, you should use Explorer (Windows File Manager and Norton File Manager are alternatives) to open its folder. As you can see, the path to the 32-bit version of Netscape on our sample hard drive is e:\32-bit Internet Apps\atlas\Program. ("Atlas" was a code name for beta versions of Netscape 3.0.) Figure 7-3 shows approximately what you'll see when you open the Netscape folder, although your version of the program may have fewer options and folders installed into it than ours—or it may already have more!

The important features to notice are the NETSCAPE.EXE executable and the plug-ins folder that appears beneath it. Click on the plug-ins folder itself, and you'll see a display similar to that in Figure 7-4. As you can see, there are six different files listed: NPAUDIO.DLL, NPAVI32.DLL, NPAVI.ZIP, NPL3D32.DLL, NPNUL32.DLL, and NPQTW32.DLL.

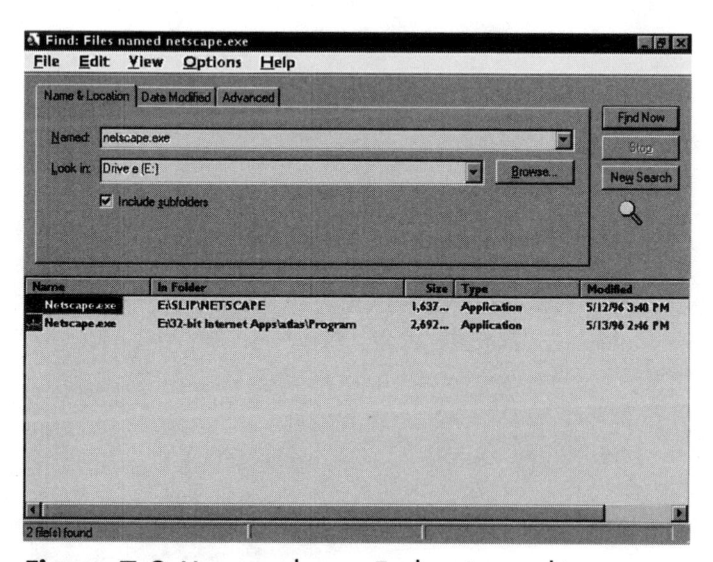

Figure 7–2 You can also use Explorer's searching capabilities to locate Netscape

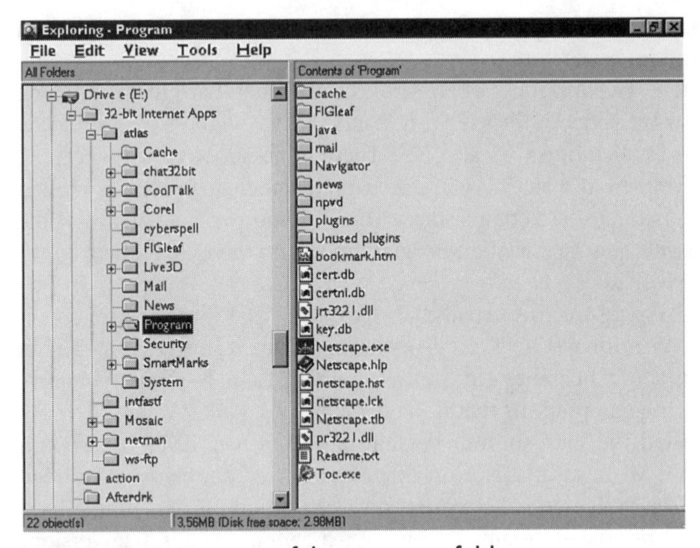

Figure 7–3 Contents of the Netscape folder

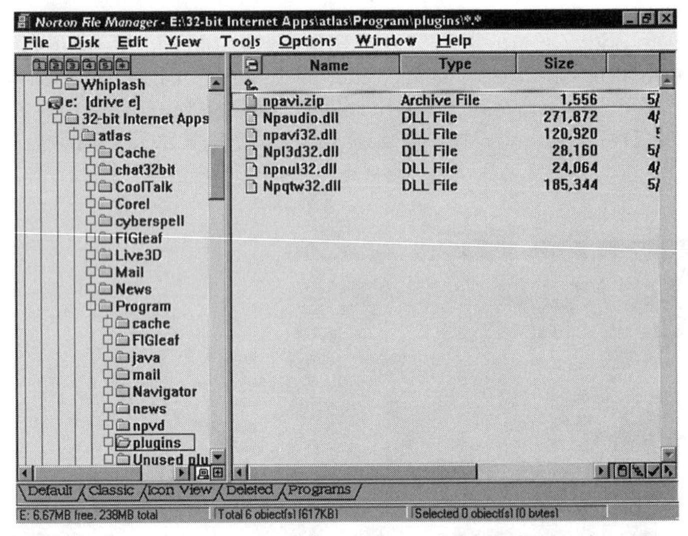

Figure 7–4 This view of the plug-ins folder shows the .DLL files that come with Netscape

Four of these are the default plug-ins that come with the 32-bit version of Netscape 3.0. You'll read below what each of the plug-ins files does. The file extensions stand for Dynamic Link Library, which is what the plug-ins are. (A DLL is a type of Windows program that cannot be started up by a user directly, but is instead invoked by another program that's already running.)

Of the two additional files, NPNUL32.DLL is a "Default plug-in" file that acts as more of a placeholder than anything else—it's required by Netscape, however, so don't erase it. NPAVI.ZIP contains some Java .CLASS files that help the LiveVideo plug-in operate.

If there are more files and folders already listed within the plug-ins folder, it's because you've already installed a third-party plug-in or two. Netscape checks this plug-ins folder each time it starts up, scanning the .DLLs stored there and registering the MIME types they can handle.

When you encounter a Web page that has one of these MIME types embedded within it, Netscape knows it can call on the plug-in that it previously found in the plug-ins folder. Since Netscape only scans the plug-ins folder when it first starts up, successfully installing a plug-in means not only placing its .DLL in that folder, but also restarting the browser so the .DLL will be scanned and registered.

As you'll read in Lesson 7, plug-ins come with installation programs that usually place their .DLLs in the plug-ins folder automatically. Therefore, you may not want to or need to do any further file management. It is very helpful, however, to be able to selectively disable plug-ins for testing purposes.

To make this process simpler, resize the Explorer window so that you can see part of your Windows desktop. Then right-click on the plug-ins folder (which is labeled simply PLUGINS, since Netscape's Windows programmers didn't believe in the hyphen!) and, while you're holding down the mouse button, drag it to the desktop. Release the mouse button and then select "Create Shortcut Here" from the pop-up menu (Figure 7-5).

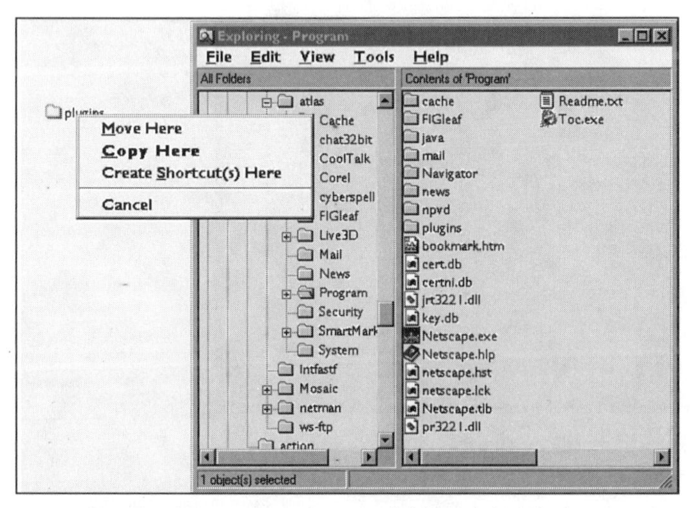

Figure 7–5 Drag your plug-ins folder to the desktop with the right mouse button to create a shortcut

Now, return to the Explorer Window and select File|New Folder to create a new folder in your Netscape program subdirectory. Name this folder something explanatory, such as "Unused plug-ins." Then, using the same method as above, create a shortcut for your Unused plug-ins folder on the Windows desktop.

As Figure 7-6 shows, you now have two shortcuts on your desktop that control plug-in behavior. If you want to examine the contents of your plug-ins folder at any time, just click on its shortcut. If you want to disable any particular plug-ins, just select the relevant .DLLs using Explorer and drag them to the Unused plug-ins shortcut. (Do not remove NPNUL32.DLL.) To enable them, just do the reverse.

Now, skip to Lesson 4.

Lesson 2: Getting Ready (Windows 3.x)

If you accepted the default choice when Netscape was first installed into Windows, the browser may well be in C:\NETSCAPE. If you did not accept this default, and you have no idea where Netscape is now, there are two ways of finding out.

First, you can switch to Program Manager. Select the program group for Netscape and click once on the Netscape icon to highlight it. Then press <ALT>-<ENTER> or select Properties from the File menu. The second item in the Program Item Properties window that appears shows you the command line used to launch Netscape. If you have replaced Program Manager with PC Tools for Windows or Norton Desktop, use the method specific to your shell for discovering the properties of whatever Netscape icon appears.

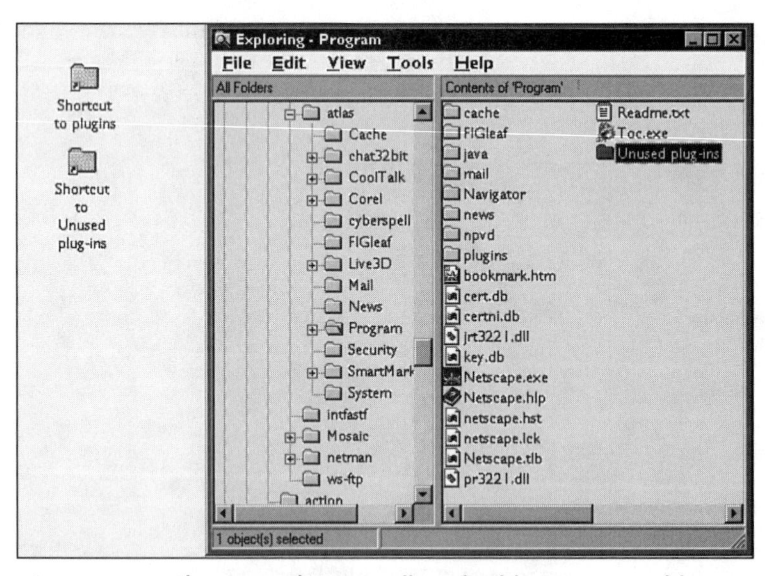

Figure 7-6 These two shortcuts allow disabling or re-enabling plug-ins via drag and drop

The other way to locate your installed copy of Netscape Navigator is by using the search command in File Manager. Run File Manager, then select Search from the File menu. In the Search For field, enter NETSCAPE.EXE. Specify the root directory of whatever hard drive you wish to search in the Start From field. As Figure 7-7 shows, File Manager will locate NETSCAPE.EXE and let you know its path.

Our example actually shows two instances of Netscape on the same hard drive. The one at the top of the list is a 16-bit version, for use with Windows 3.x, while the second one listed is the 32-bit version for Windows 95 and NT. There is no problem with keeping two Netscape versions on your hard drive, but you need to remember that plug-ins written for the Windows 95/NT version are *not* compatible with the Windows 3.x version of the program, and *vice versa*. If you or an installation program mixes up the two, Netscape may crash when the plug-in is invoked.

As mentioned in Lesson 2, however, Windows 3.x plug-ins are usually labeled via a "16" that appears somewhere in their file name. Windows 95/NT plug-ins have, as you can guess, a "32" in theirs. You can avoid mistakes simply by scanning each Netscape version's plug-ins folder and identifying any plug-ins that don't belong.

Once you have identified the path to your version of NETSCAPE.EXE, you should use File Manager to open its folder. As you can see, the path to the 16-bit version of Netscape on our sample hard drive is E:\SLIP\NETSCAPE. Figure 7-8 shows approximately what you'll see when you open this, although your version of the program may have more options and folders installed into it than ours.

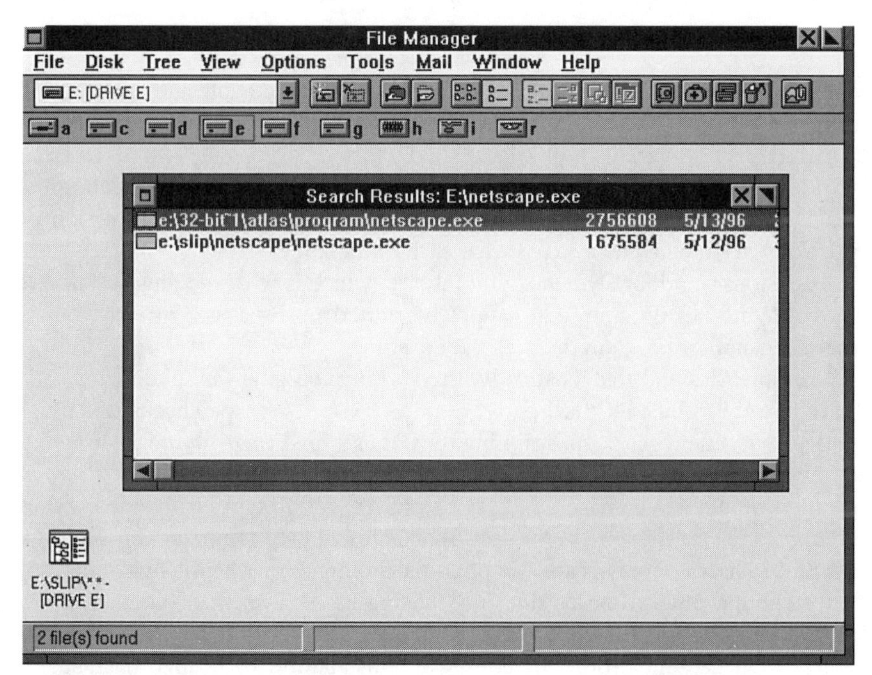

Figure 7–7 File Manager's search capability can find Netscape for you

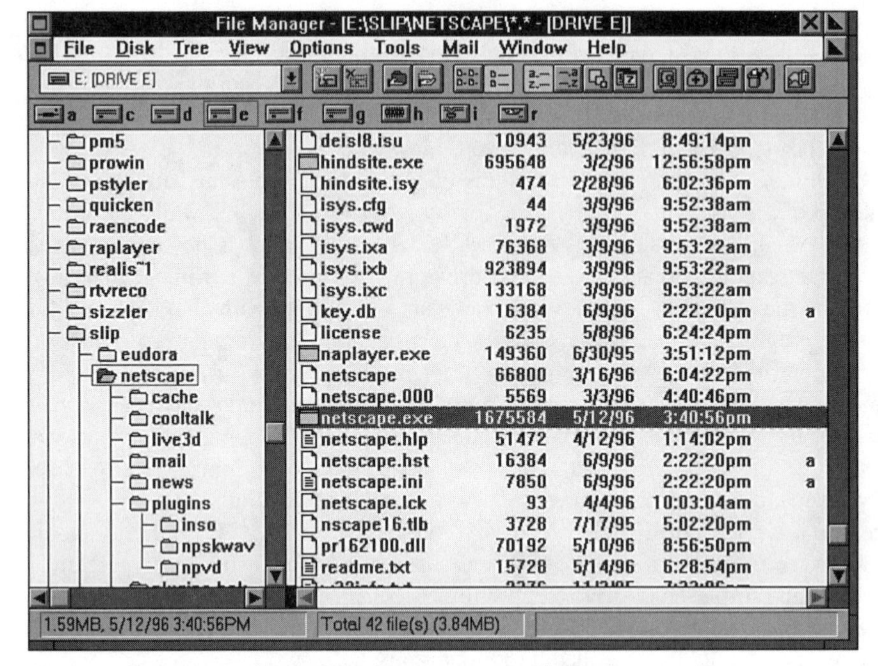

Figure 7–8 Typical contents of a Netscape subdirectory under Windows 3.x

The important features to notice are the NETSCAPE.EXE executable and the plug-ins folder that appears beneath it. Click on the plug-ins folder itself, and you'll see a directory listing that includes five different files: NPAUDIO.DLL, NPAVI16.DLL, NPL3D16.DLL, NPNUL16.DLL, and NPQTW16.DLL. These are the "Default plug-in" placeholder, NPNUL16.DLL, plus the four working plug-ins that come with the 16-bit version of Netscape 3.0. You'll read below how to tell what each of these files is.

The file extensions stand for Dynamic Link Library, which is what the plug-ins are. (A DLL is a type of Windows program that cannot be started up by a user directly, but is instead invoked by another program that's already running.)

If there are more files and folders already listed within the plug-ins subdirectory, it's because you've already installed a third-party plug-in or two. Netscape checks this plug-ins subdirectory each time it starts up, scanning the .DLLs stored there and registering the MIME types they can handle.

When you encounter a Web page that has one of these MIME types embedded within it, Netscape knows it can call on the plug-in that it previously found in the plug-ins subdirectory. Since Netscape only scans the plug-ins subdirectory when it first starts up, successfully installing a plug-in means not only placing its .DLL in that folder, but also restarting the browser so the .DLL will be scanned and registered.

As you'll read in Lesson 7, plug-ins come with installation programs that usually place their .DLLs in the plug-ins subdirectory automatically. Therefore, you may not want to or need to do any further file management. It is very helpful, however, to be able to selectively disable plug-ins for testing purposes.

To make this process slightly simpler, you can create an extra subdirectory to which you will move spare plug-ins. Then, to disable any particular plug-ins, just select the relevant .DLL using File Manager and move it to PLUGINS.BAK (or whatever you've called your extra subdirectory). Do not move NPNUL16.DLL. To re-enable a plug-in, do the reverse.

If you have PC Tools for Windows or Norton Desktop, you can make this process more convenient. Create shortcuts to the PLUGINS and PLUGNS.BAK subdirectories and place them on your desktop. Now, you can control plug-ins using drag and drop just as Windows 95 users do.

Now, skip to Lesson 5.

Lesson 3: Getting Ready (Macintosh)

In this lesson, you'll learn how to prepare your Netscape environment for successful plug-in installation and management. Our instructions were prepared using a Power Macintosh; plug-in installation on a 68K Mac is no different, but you need to make sure that you obtain "fat binaries" or 68K-only code instead of PPC-specific software.

Thanks to long file names and the lack of any ludicrous "Program Files" folders that hide things away, Mac users don't usually have trouble finding their Netscape folders. Yours is probably on your startup drive labeled something like "Netscape 3.0 folder." If you don't see any Netscape folders, you can pull down the File menu and select Find (or just use <COMMAND>-<F>) to search for occurrences of "Netscape Navigator." This should find the correct folder and also alert you to the possibility that you have more than one Netscape folder.

Figure 7-9 shows the result of such a search on a Mac that has both Netscape 2.02 (for lower memory consumption) and Netscape Gold 3.0 (for editing Web pages). In Figure 7-10 you see the result of opening a typical Netscape folder.

The important features to notice are the Netscape Navigator and the plug-ins folder that appears to its right. Click on the plug-ins folder itself, and you'll see a display similar to that in Figure 7-11. As you can see, there are four different files listed: Default Plug-in, Live 3D, LiveAudio, and QuickTime Plug-in. These duplicate the functionality of Windows Netscape, except that Mac users do not get the ability to play .AVI videos.

If there are more files and folders already listed within your plug-ins folder, it's because you've already installed a third-party plug-in or two. Netscape checks this plug-ins folder each time it starts up, scanning the .DLLs stored there and registering the MIME types they can handle.

When you encounter a Web page that has one of these MIME types embedded within it, Netscape knows it can call on the plug-in that it previously found in the plug-ins folder. Since Netscape only scans the plug-ins folder when it first starts up, successfully installing a plug-in means not only placing its file in that folder, but also restarting the browser so that the plug-in will be successfully registered.

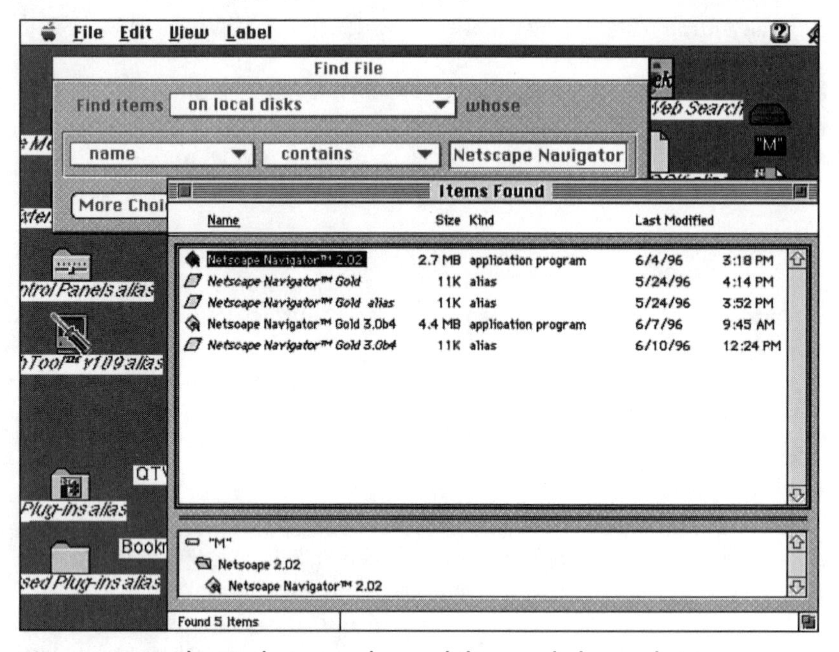

Figure 7–9 The Finder's search capability can help you locate your Netscape folder(s)

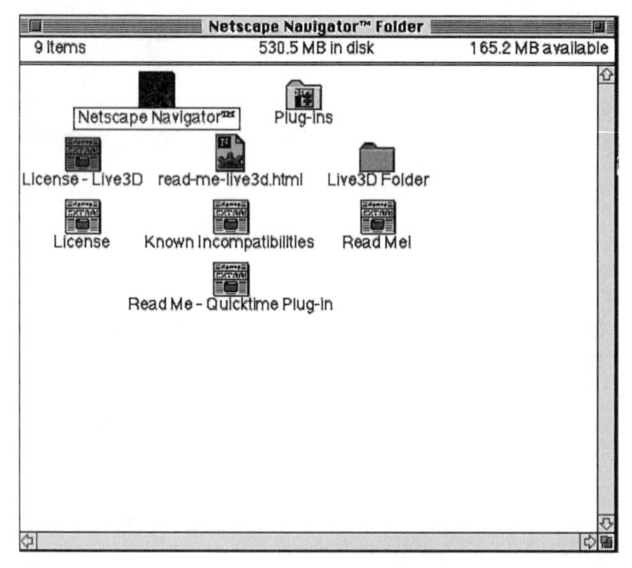

Figure 7–10 This is what a typical Netscape folder looks like on a Mac

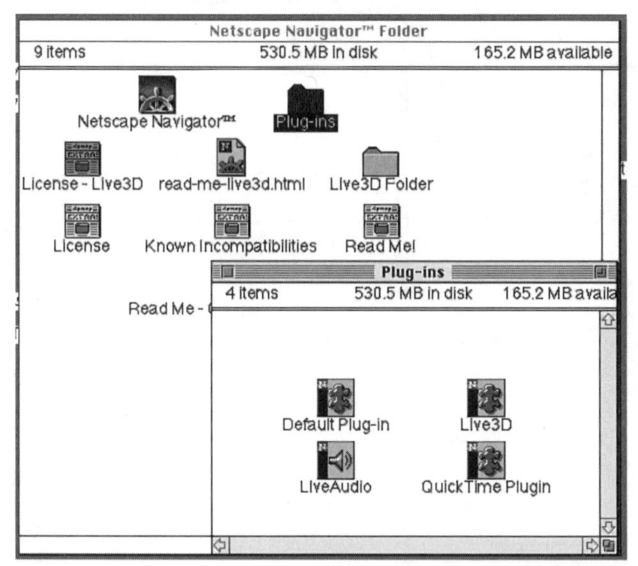

Figure 7–11 Netscape's Macintosh plug-ins folder

As you'll read in Lesson 7, plug-ins come with installation programs that usually place files in the plug-ins folder automatically. Therefore, you may not want to or need to do any further file management. It is very helpful, however, to be able to selectively disable plug-ins for testing purposes.

To make this process simpler, use the Finder's File/New Folder command (or COMMAND-N) to create a new folder within your Netscape folder. Call it "Unused plug-ins" or something similar. Then, you can make aliases to both this folder and the plug-ins folder itself and drag them onto your desktop. Figure 7-12 shows a Mac that has been set up in this way (notice the folder icons in the screen's lower left-hand corner).

You now have two folders on your desktop that control plug-in behavior. If you want to examine the contents of your plug-ins folder at any time, just click on its alias. If you want to disable any particular plug-ins, just select them and drag them to the Unused plug-ins alias. (Do not remove the file called Default Plug-in).

Now, skip to Lesson 6.

Lesson 4: Turning Plug-Ins On and Off (Windows 95 and NT)

You've just set up shortcuts that will help you move the DLLs for various plug-ins around. However, you now need a way to learn what each one of them is.

To find out, start up Netscape (you need not be connected to the Internet). Pull down the Help menu and select About Plug-ins. You'll see a list like that shown in Figure 7-13. For each plug-in, the list tells you its file name and location, where it is stored on your hard drive, plus the MIME types and suffixes it's designed to handle.

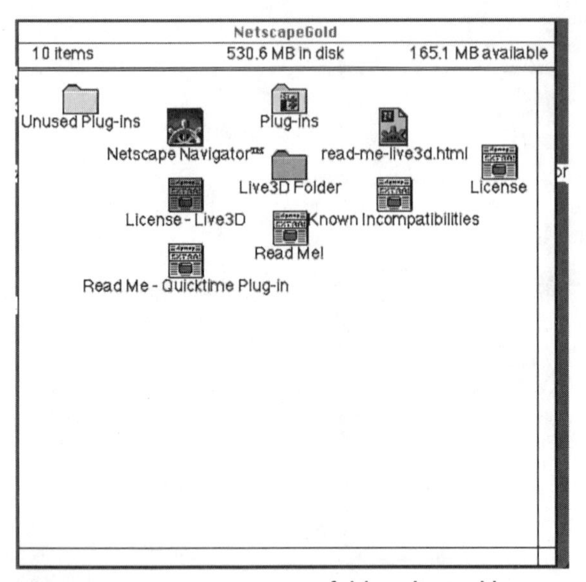

Figure 7–12 You can use folder aliases like those shown at the lower left to turn plug-ins on and off

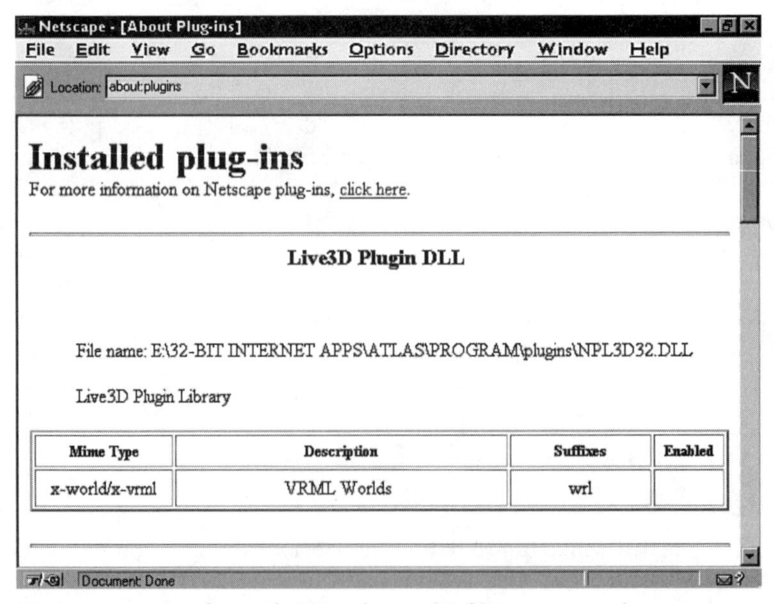

Figure 7–13 About Plug-ins shows the file names and MIME types associated with the plug-ins you've installed

For the moment, we're concerned with the first two pieces of information. Table 7-1 lists the names of the basic Netscape 3.0 plug-ins and the corresponding disk files.

Table 7-1 The default plug-ins for Netscape (Windows 95/NT)

Name of Plug-In	Name of File
Live3D Plug-in	NPL3D32.DLL
Navigator QuickTime Plug-In	NPQTW32.DLL
NPAVI32 Dynamic Link Library	NPAVI32.DLL
LiveAudio	NPAUDIO.DLL
Netscape Default Plug-in	NPNUL32.DLL

You may never want to disable any of these particular plug-ins, unless you want to install a third-party plug-in that handles one of the same MIME types. If you want to turn off a plug-in, do it by moving the relevant DLL to your "Unused Plug-ins" folder for safekeeping, and then restarting Netscape. Select Help|About Plug-ins again and the lines relevant to that particular plug-in no longer appear.

Chapter 3, "Helper Applications: A Thing of the Past?," covered the difference between Netscape helper applications and Netscape plug-ins. As you may recall, Netscape's response to particular MIME types—whether or not it saves them to disk, passes them to a helper application, or pops up a dialog box asking you what to do—defaults to being controlled by the Options/General Preferences menu and its Helpers tab. Once a plug-in has been installed, however, it takes over control from any helper application that may exist.

For example, Netscape 2.0 had a helper application called NAPLAYER that was used to play sound files (identified by their MIME types, such as audio/x-wav, audio/basic, and so on). When you installed Netscape 3.0, you installed the LiveAudio plug-in, which now plays sound files instead of NAPLAYER. It takes precedence over the helper application even though the latter is still on your hard drive and might still be listed in the Helpers tab of Options/General Preferences.

Given that plug-ins have priority over helper applications, the Helpers tab in Options/General Preferences no longer provides complete control over how Netscape will respond to incoming MIME types. The only way to control the behavior of plug-ins is by moving them in and out of the PLUGINS folder as described above.

Future versions of Netscape will feature an Options menu that *is* able to control the behavior of plug-ins. This feature didn't make it into the Windows versions of Netscape, however. If you want a glimpse at what it will look like, take a look at Lesson 6 below, dealing with the Mac version of the program. Macintosh Netscape is a little bit more advanced, since some of the features relating to plug-ins were first developed on the Mac version of the browser and then ported to other editions.

Until this fuller-featured Options menu is a reality, you should avoid installing plug-ins that duplicate one another's handling of MIME types. (For example, since LiveAudio already plays .WAV files, take a deep breath before deciding to install *another* plug-in that plays .WAV files as well.) Dueling plug-ins will not crash Netscape, but they will make the look (and possibly sound) of the Web pages you load somewhat unpredictable.

To learn more about Windows 95/NT plug-in installation, skip to Lesson 7 below.

Lesson 5: Turning Plug-Ins On and Off (Windows 3.x)

You've just set up a PLUGINS.BAK subdirectory in your Netscape folder that will let you temporarily disable plug-ins when you want. However, you now need a way to learn what each plug-in is.

To find out, start up Netscape. (You need not be connected to the Internet, although if you are not, Netscape will gripe that it was "unable to create a Network socket connection".) Pull down the Help menu and select About Plug-ins. You'll see a list like that shown in Figure 7-14. For each plug-in, the list tells you its file name and location, where it is stored on your hard drive, plus the MIME types and suffixes it's designed to handle.

For the moment, we're concerned with the first two pieces of information. Table 7-2 lists the names of the basic Netscape 3.0 plug-ins and the corresponding disk files.

Table 7-2 The default plug-ins for Netscape (Windows 3.x)

Name of Plug-In	Name of File
Live3D Plug-in Library	NPL3D16.DLL
Navigator QuickTime Plug-in	NPQTW16.DLL
Navigator AVI Sample Plug-in	NPAVI16.DLL
LiveAudio for Windows 3.1	NPAUDIO.DLL
Netscape Default Plug-in	NPNUL16.DLL

You may never want to disable any of these particular plug-ins, unless you want to install a third-party plug-in that handles one of the same MIME types. However, if you want to turn off a plug-in, you could accomplish this by moving the relevant DLL to your PLUGINS.BAK folder for safekeeping, and then restarting Netscape. Select Help|About Plug-ins again and the lines relevant to that particular plug-in no longer appear.

Chapter 3 covered the difference between Netscape helper applications and Netscape plug-ins. As you may recall, Netscape's response to particular MIME types—whether or not it saves them to disk, passes them to a helper application, or pops up a dialog box asking you what to do—defaults to being controlled by the Options/General Preferences menu and its Helpers tab. Once a plug-in has been installed, however, it takes over control from any helper application that may exist.

As pointed out in Lesson 4 above, Netscape 2.0 had a helper application called NAPLAYER that was used to play sound files (identified by their MIME types, such as audio/x-wav, audio/basic, and so on). When you installed Netscape 3.0, you installed the LiveAudio plug-in, which now plays sound files instead of NAPLAYER. It takes precedence over the helper application even though the latter is still on your hard drive and might still be listed in the Helpers tab of Options/General Preferences.

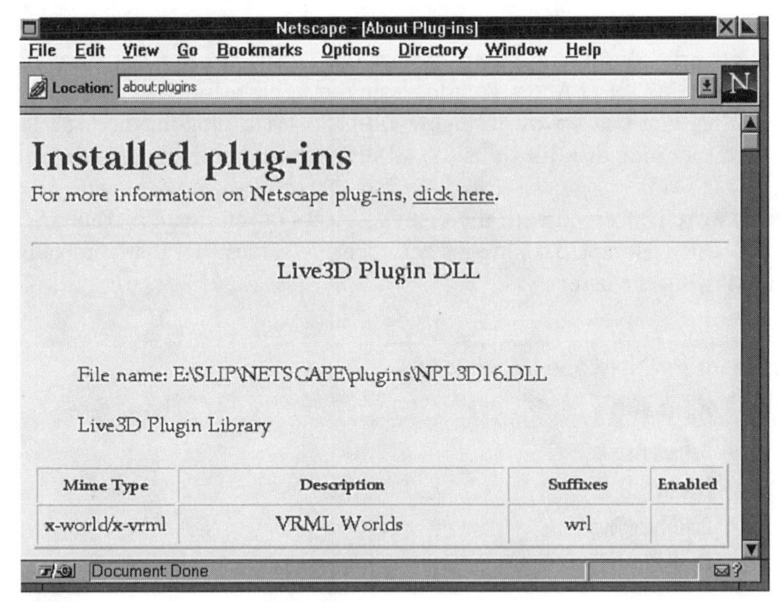

Figure 7–14 About Plug-ins shows you MIME type and file information for all installed plug-ins

Given that plug-ins have priority over helper applications, the Helpers tab in Options/General Preferences no longer provides complete control over how Netscape will respond to incoming MIME types. The only way to control the behavior of plug-ins is by moving them in and out of the PLUGINS.BAK folder as described above.

Future versions of Netscape will feature an Options menu that *is* able to control the behavior of plug-ins. This feature didn't make it into the Windows versions of Netscape, however. If you want a glimpse at what it will look like, take a look at Lesson 6 below, dealing with the Mac version of the program. (Some of the features relating to plug-ins were first developed on the Mac version of the browser and then ported to other editions.)

Until this fuller-featured Options menu is a reality, you should avoid installing plug-ins that duplicate one another's handling of MIME types (for example, since LiveAudio already plays .WAV files, take a deep breath before deciding to install *another* plug-in that plays .WAV files as well). Dueling plug-ins will not crash Netscape, but they will make the look (and possibly sound) of the Web pages you load somewhat unpredictable.

Now, skip to Lesson 7 to learn more about installing plug-ins.

Lesson 6: Turning Plug-Ins On and Off (Macintosh)

You've just set up aliases that will help you turn plug-ins on and off. Better still, unlike Windows users, you don't need any help in figuring out what each of them is. (The Mac's long file names apply to programs as well as data files, unlike Windows 95's.)

However, you still should be familiar with using the About Plug-ins command to determine which Netscape plug-ins are active. Start up Netscape (you need not be connected to the Internet) and select About Plug-ins from the Apple menu.

Now, you'll see a list like that shown in Figure 7-15. For each plug-in, the list tells you its name, the corresponding disk file, plus the MIME types and suffixes it's designed to handle.

For the moment, we're concerned with the first two pieces of information. Table 7-3 lists the names of the basic Netscape 3.0 plug-ins and their file names (not that you really needed any help figuring out the latter).

Table 7-3 The default plug-ins for Netscape (Macintosh)

Name of Plug-In	Name of File
Default Plug-in	Default Plug-in
Live3D	Live3D
QuickTime Plug-in	QuickTime Plug-in
LiveAudio	LiveAudio

You may never want to disable any of these particular plug-ins, unless you want to install a third-party plug-in that handles one of same MIME types. However, you could turn off any plug-in by moving the relevant file to your "Unused Plug-ins" folder for

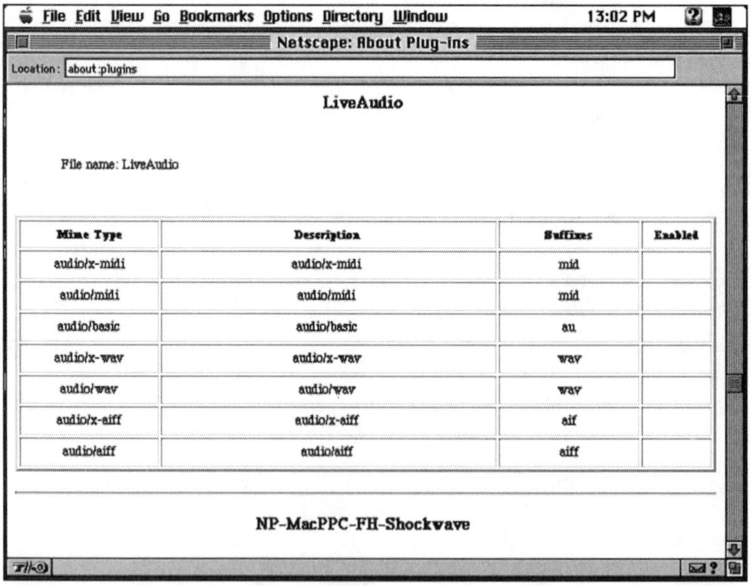

File Edit View Go Bookmarks Options Directory Window 13:02 PM

Netscape: About Plug-ins

Location: about:plugins

LiveAudio

File name: LiveAudio

Mime Type	Description	Suffixes	Enabled
audio/x-midi	audio/x-midi	mid	
audio/midi	audio/midi	mid	
audio/basic	audio/basic	au	
audio/x-wav	audio/x-wav	wav	
audio/wav	audio/wav	wav	
audio/x-aiff	audio/x-aiff	aif	
audio/aiff	audio/aiff	aiff	

NP-MacPPC-FH-Shockwave

Figure 7-15 Once again, About Plug-ins provides MIME type information for your installed plug-ins

safekeeping, and then restarting Netscape. Select Help|About Plug-ins again and the lines relevant to that particular plug-in no longer appear.

Chapter 3 covered the difference between Netscape helper applications and Netscape plug-ins. As you may recall, Netscape's response to particular MIME types—whether or not it saves them to disk, passes them to a helper application, or pops up a dialog box asking you what to do—defaults to being controlled by the Options/General Preferences menu and its Helpers tab. Once a plug-in has been installed, however, it usually takes over control from any helper application that may exist.

Unlike Windows versions of Netscape 3.0, the Mac version has an Options/General Preferences/Helpers tab that is able to control the behavior of plug-ins. In addition to letting you choose whether a given MIME type will be handled by a helper application or by a plug-in, it also lets you arbitrate amongst multiple installed plug-ins.

Figure 7-16 shows the appearance of the Helpers tab. To use it, locate the MIME type in which you're interested in the left hand column, then click on it. Figure 7-17 shows the result of clicking on the MIME type video/quicktime. This copy of Netscape—which has mysteriously had a dozen or so plug-ins added to it since we showed it to you in Figure 7-15!—has both the standard QuickTime plug-in and a plug-in called MacZilla available to it. The Edit Type window lets you select which plug-in you want to have play QuickTime movies (.MOV files).

If you'd prefer to send the movies to a helper application such as MoviePlayer, you can do that, too. Just click on the Application radio button to select it, then use the Browse button to locate the helper application.

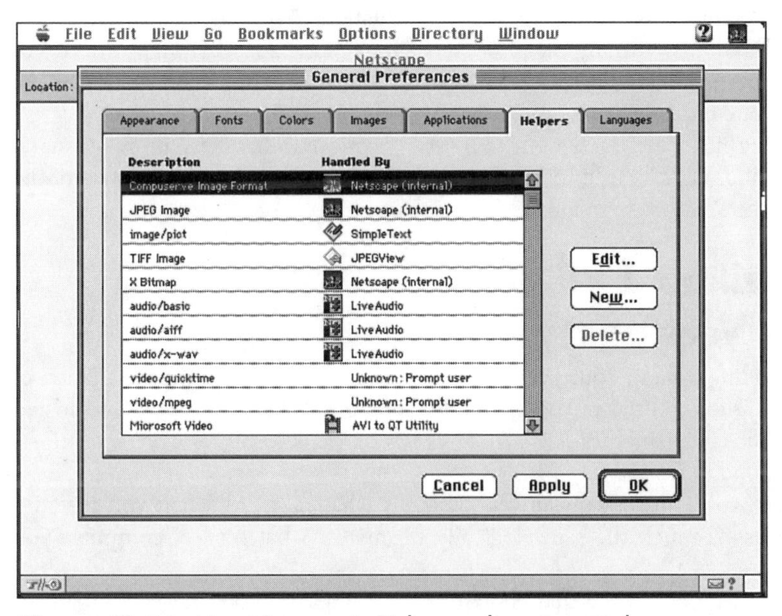

Figure 7-16 Mac Netscape's Helpers tab can control plug-ins as well as helper applications

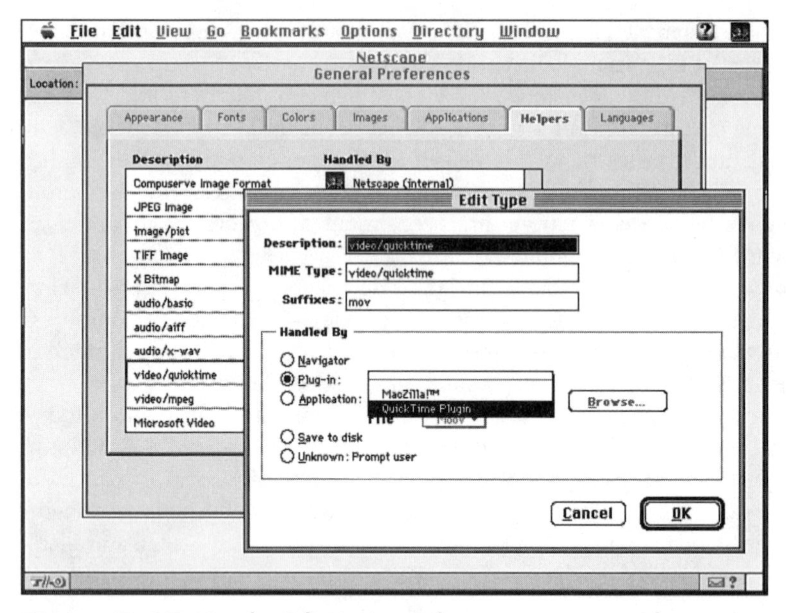

Figure 7-17 Use the Edit Type window to associate a plug-in or helper application with any given MIME type

As you can see, the "Unused Plug-ins" folder we created in Lesson 3 is not nearly as necessary for the Macintosh as it is for Windows installations. You might still want to use it, however, for temporarily turning off plug-ins such as MacZilla, which take control of multiple MIME types. This would save you from having to edit multiple entries in the Options/General Preferences/Helpers tab.

Thanks to plug-ins, combined with the extra configurability its Options/General Preferences menu affords, the Macintosh offers Web browsing that defines the state of the art—at least until the Windows versions of Netscape catch up.

Lesson 7: Installing a Plug-In (All Netscape Versions)

Chapter 8, "Embedding Data in Your Web Pages: An Overview, " covers the installation of one plug-in (PreVU) for tutorial purposes, while Chapters 9–15 tell you how to install other specific plug-ins for Windows 3.x, Windows 95, or Macintosh. We won't, therefore, cover the same ground here.

However, it is worth previewing *in general terms* what happens when you install a plug-in. The process is much the same logically no matter what type of computer you have.

First, you need to locate a file that contains the installer, in compressed format, for the particular plug-in you desire. Many such setup programs are included on the CD-ROM that came with this book. If this doesn't include the installer you want, however, use the author's Web site to locate it.

Then, create a new subdirectory (or folder) on your hard drive. It doesn't matter what you call this folder, since you won't be needing it for long—if you have lots of memory on your computer and have set up a RAM disk, you can put installation files on the RAM disk. Download or copy the installation files to this new location.

Now, double-click on the installer file to uncompress its files and start the setup process. Sometimes—most often with Windows 3.x—this is a two-step process, where you first uncompress installation files, and then have to double-click again on SETUP.EXE. Other times, decompression and setup are accomplished simultaneously.

The installation program locates your Netscape plug-ins folder (just as you did manually in the preceding lessons) and copies the new plug-in into it. Often, it also creates another folder elsewhere on your hard drive that has help files, sample data, or a helper application that works in conjunction with the plug-in you're installing.

NOTE: Some plug-ins are designed to hand off data to a helper application or other supporting program. Therefore, if a plug-in's installation program creates a folder you later decide to erase, make sure that folder contains no application's software before you trash it permanently.

A Windows 95/NT installation program might also add entries to the Start Menu and to the Windows registry. If you're running Windows 3.x instead, changes might be made to Program Manager groups and to .INI files in your Windows subdirectory. These alterations are usually intended to help both you and your operating system locate any helper application that is installed; Netscape itself needs no such help, provided that a plug-in is placed in the plug-ins folder where it ought to be.

Sometimes—especially if you have more than one copy of Netscape on your hard drive—you have to help the installation program select where you want the plug-in to go. If you have two copies of Netscape that can both use the same plug-in (for example, a copy of Netscape 3.0 and a copy of Netscape Gold 3.0), you'll need to install it into just one of them. Later, make a copy of the plug-in, and drag it into the second Netscape's plug-ins folder by hand.

Of course, there are also some plug-ins that come from the authors in compressed form, but whose installation is completely manual. With these, you need to uncompress the plug-in to your temporary installation folder, and then move it to Netscape's plug-ins folder yourself. Before decrying the plug-in's authors as cheapskates who obviously didn't want to make your life convenient by licensing the InstallShield shell, stop to reflect that automatic installation routines exact a toll. For every 500K plug-in downloaded over the Web, 250K or more of that download is accounted for by the menu-driven installer.

By the way, you should always uncompress a plug-in's installation files to a temporary folder, never to the Netscape plug-ins folder itself. Although doing the latter probably won't cause any damage, you can't be sure. Besides, your Netscape plug-ins folder is going to get messy enough on its own!

The last step in installing any plug-in is to restart Netscape. Use the Options/General Preferences menu to clear its disk cache (and memory cache, if relevant). This breaks any outdated MIME type associations that might have been stored in memory, and also helps make the browser more reliable. Now, select About Plug-ins from the Help menu or Apple menu, and the plug-in you just installed should appear in the list.

Lesson 8: Removing a Plug-In

Removing a plug-in is as simple as taking it out of the Netscape Plug-ins folder, restarting Netscape, and then clearing the browser's disk and memory caches. Before engaging in impromptu house-cleaning of your hard disk drive, however, you should be a little patient: Instead of trashing the plug-in completely, move it to the Unused Plug-ins folder for safekeeping.

Then browse the Web as you normally do for a week or so. If the Web pages you use look and sound the same as they did before, then you're fairly safe in erasing the plug-in permanently. If you see Web pages with broken links and pop-up error messages, then this may be a sign that the plug-in was being used more regularly then you realized.

Thorough removal of a plug-in in the Windows environment sometimes also requires deleting helper applications, plus taking away Program Groups or Start Menu entries. In the worst case, it can also involve removing .INI file entries or tinkering with the Windows registry. None of this is stuff that you want to do by hand if you can help it. Therefore, when you take away a plug-in, check in folders associated with it and in the Start Menu to see if there is an Uninstall program you can run.

Some plug-ins use Windows 95's Add/Remove Programs applet in the Control Panel. To be thorough, therefore, open this to see if you notice any entries associated with unused plug-ins.

WHAT NOW?

This chapter has provided you with a general overview of how Netscape plug-ins install. You've also learned how to remove plug-ins, and how to disable them temporarily when you want. In the next chapter, we'll look at a specific plug-in (PreVU, which plays MPEG videos) that is available for Windows 3.x, Windows 95, and Macintosh. You'll learn how to install it and how to modify your Web pages so they can take advantage of it—or any other plug-ins you want to use.

8

EMBEDDING DATA IN YOUR WEB PAGES: AN OVERVIEW

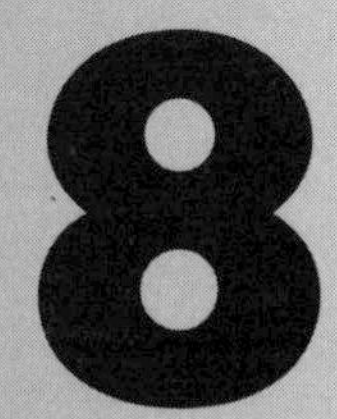

So far, you've learned that plug-ins are program modules written by third parties to extend Netscape's power. Dynamic Link Libraries (on Windows) or Shared Libraries (on Macintosh), lurk within their program folder on your hard drive, waiting to be called into action when Netscape encounters a data type it can't interpret all on its own.

Remember how the aliens on old Star Trek episodes always seemed to be speaking English—thanks to mysterious and invisible "universal translator" technology? Well, plug-ins are translator technology for Netscape. (Although they can't—yet—translate written English into another language on the fly, that day will probably come before we know it.) They translate "alien" file types into data that Netscape can show you on screen or play through your computer's speakers.

Just as the universal translators were almost never visible on Star Trek missions, a properly operating plug-in doesn't have to show itself, either. What you see on your "viewer screen" is merely the Netscape interface you know—with a lot more things popping up in it.

You've also learned: plug-ins' capabilities and modes of operation; how they get their marching orders by waiting for certain MIME types to appear; and how you install them into Netscape or remove them from the browser.

No doubt you've already skipped ahead, installed several plug-ins off the CD-ROM, and gone truffle-hunting on the Net for some cool sample videos, animations, MIDI concerts, or whatever. Now, it's time to learn how to add these goodies into your *own* Web pages.

There are just a couple of potential snags to consider before you start. You don't want to write a Web page that practically qualifies for the Academy Awards only to find out that you can't make it work through no fault of your own. The snags have to do with MIME types and with producing the content your Web pages will be serving up.

Lesson 1: Registering New MIME Types

We've already emphasized the importance of MIME types in preceding chapters, especially Chapter 6. To recap briefly, a MIME (Multipurpose Internet Mail Extensions) type is a standardized method for organizing different binary file formats. When Netscape receives binaries over the Net, it needs to know what to do with them. Does it run one through its HTML interpreter? JPEG? Does it just display it on the screen bit for bit, in binary gibberish? Or does it offer to save it to a disk file?

Ever since Netscape was first released, users have been able to control some of these actions using the General/Helpers panel available from the browser's Options menu. This required you to obtain separate helper applications to interpret each MIME type that Netscape didn't know how to handle. Then, you had to go through the hassle of figuring out how to use the helper programs and configuring Netscape to call them up.

With plug-in technology, all this fuss is in the past. When plug-ins load, they enter MIME type information without any user intervention. As long as the person visiting your Web site has the right plug-in (which you can, of course, help them obtain—as we'll explain below in the "Error Handling" section), they never need worry about MIME types. Future versions of Netscape, which will feature a way to automate installation of plug-ins, will make things easier still for end users.

As a developer of Web pages, you won't be able to forget about MIME types, however, which is why this caution appears up front. The server that hosts your pages, whether it is on site in your home or company, or at the premises of an ISP (Internet Service Provider), needs to provide MIME type information to Netscape when it retrieves files. Otherwise, Netscape—whatever version—will attempt to interpret the files merely by their extension (.AVI, .VOC, or whatever).

The results of this are unpredictable and sometimes not what you want: Files may appear on screen as gibberish, they may get saved to disk, or they may get passed to an old-fashioned helper application when you intended them to appear seamlessly in a Web page. Before you invest much time in writing code for a new plug-in, therefore, you need to send a friendly e-mail to your ISP's technical support representatives asking them if they will add new MIME types for you. The answer is almost always, "Yes, of course," but if you're dealing with a big, slow-responding provider, you may want to get the wheels in motion several days before you start coding.

What providers have to enter in their configuration files varies slightly according to the type of Web server they're using. Chapter 6 briefly reviewed the MIME configuration process for some of the most popular types of Web server.

However, ISPs will *always* need to know a MIME type/subtype and an identifying extension. For example:

MIME Type/Subtype	Extension
application/avi	avi
image/jpeg	jpeg
audio/voxware	vox

For each plug-in covered in Chapters 9–14 of this book, the MIME type/subtype and desired file extension are listed. Pass on this information to your ISP before you upload pages to their server, and you should never have a problem.

One tip mentioned in Chapter 6 bears repeating here: If you are testing a new plug-in and want to see how well it performs over a dial-up connection (as opposed to just loading pages from your local hard drive), you can upload data files to an FTP server. Then, make reference to these files in your test Web pages using FTP instead of HTTP addresses. Since Netscape receives no MIME type information for these files via HTTP, it is forced to use their extensions to decide what they are.

This trick gives you a way to experiment with a new plug-in temporarily before your ISP has made any modfication to the list of MIME types on its server. If you're going to use a particular plug-in permanently, however, you still should get its MIME type registered with your ISP: HTTP is preferable to FTP for use with plug-ins because of its support for data streaming. (Another drawback of FTP is that it doesn't allow the use of relative URLs; each URL must be specified in its absolute form, leading to long tags such as <EMBED SRC="ftp://ftp.scruznet.com/users/johnny/public_html/plugins-test/demo.mpeg">.)

We've all had the experience of doing HTML development on a local hard drive, then finding that some of the links are broken (because we forgot to copy something, or something moved) when we upload the pages to our ISP's server. There's no answer to this problem except intensive testing of all links. Use of plug-ins makes testing even more vital: Pages that tested out OK on your local computer may not run properly from a server if the MIME types they use have not been entered in that server's configuration file.

NOTE: Remember, if you ever move your Web site from one server to another, you'll need to tell the new ISP about the MIME types you need them to register. Never assume that because something worked in one place it will work in another. At times you'll wish you had a server on your premises so you could take care of this all by yourself. That's unless you do have a server, in which case there are days you wouldn't mind having some outside help.

Firewalls

Unfortunately there's another reason that some pages with plug-ins will not work from the server—at least for some users. Firewalls are security devices primarily designed to protect companies from unauthorized access to their servers. They can, however, also block access to some of the functionality on servers outside the company. A *proxy server* can block communication with a particular computer and suppress any unauthorized activity. *Packet filtering* blocks all data that does not fall within a set of logical rules defined by a firewall administrator.

While some plug-ins and associated data types work through firewalls just fine, others (especially the more ambitious audio-video products) do not. For products such as Real Audio and VDOLive, technical assistance from the vendors might be required.

If you're planning to use plug-ins on a corporate server and you know that firewalls are in place, you should talk with your company's network administrators to see if there are any issues involving the products you want to adopt.

Ninety-five percent of us need never worry about firewalls. However, they're a potential pitfall for a few. If everything else has been tried, tested, and debugged, yet your pages have become mysteriously broken, firewalls are worth investigating further.

Lesson 2: Making Sure You Can Create the Content

In the days before plug-ins, it was enough to have something to say. Type it into a computer, convert it into HTML, and you were in business. Add a few scanned graphics and you had decent-looking Web pages.

Since plug-ins can display animations, interactive presentations, video clips, sound files, and much more, they're much more demanding for a Web page's author. Perhaps you just happen to be a crack sound engineer, video camera person, desktop publishing whiz, and announcer par excellence. In that case you might not have trouble producing content for your site. However, most of us can't say the same.

Most plug-ins, like the ones on the CD-ROM included with this book, are distributed at little or no cost to the user. That's because they're a benign, friendly breed of Trojan horse. In other words, while Macromedia's ShockWave for Director might be free, you'll soon need to lay out the money for Director itself if you want to produce any original content. Similarly, if you want to publish documents using the free Adobe Acrobat Reader, you can't do it without purchasing Adobe Acrobat for $150 or so.

Sound recording is a relatively inexpensive area; though you'll need a good microphone, a nice air personality, and a DAT machine, MiniDisc recorder, or at least a good-quality cassette deck for mastering your narrations. Video? Well, you might already have a good camcorder and Microsoft's Video Capture application, but do you have a Windows 95-supported video capture board and preferably a hardware MPEG encoder?

The answer to the problem of content production is to leverage what you already know. If you or a staff member is an artist using Freehand, try Macromedia's Shockwave for Freehand plug-in. If you do a lot of desktop publishing and want classy design to pervade your Web site, try Adobe's Acrobat Reader or Tumbleweed Software's Envoy, and so on. With the right choice of plug-in, you'll be able to reuse your documents, artwork, or videos with little extra work—this is what's meant by "repurposing."

While you're learning to use plug-ins, you can borrow MIDI files, MPEGs, etc., from other sources—not from other people's copyrighted Web sites, please, as there are plenty of public-domain materials on the Web—as you refine your pages. Later on, however, the notion of providing content that isn't uniquely your own will get stale. Fast. So go into the programming and design process thinking about content from day one.

Some plug-ins are quite choosy about how they want data to be sourced. In order to be compressed or otherwise modified so it can be made available over the Web, data has to be in just the right file format. So before you create content in one program, hoping to squeeze it into another, make sure you have all the conversion tools you'll need.

Audio and video plug-ins are some of the most demanding. They want sound to be recorded at just the right sampling rate and video to be sampled at precisely the right size, frame rate, and color bit depth. For example, I tried to record sample video clips for VDOLive, about which you'll read in Chapter 10. Its encoder wanted to receive 16-bit or 24-bit video—fair enough, I thought. But audio (at least in the beta version of the encoder I was using) had to be 16-bit, with a sampling rate of no more and no less than 8KHz. VDOLive offers a Windows 95 video capture application that supports these rates. Problem was, my old video capture board only ran under Windows 3.1, whose Vidicap software doesn't support the required audio sampling rate. Catch-22, and back to silent movies.

Lesson 3: Getting Started with the Embed Tag

Netscape now comes with plug-ins that can read common file types such as MIDI, .WAV and QuickTime. These are extremely useful, and you'll probably want to stick with these for most of your Web pages—after all, it's a great feeling to know that your audience is set up to read your pages without delay.

In this tutorial, however, we're going to utilize a third-party plug-in. This will give you more of a feel for

- Installing a plug-in for yourself
- What visitors to your Web page will see if they don't have the plug-in yet
- How a plug-in extends Netscape's power.

An ideal choice for a tutorial would be a plug-in that handles an interesting data type commonly found on the Internet—one that Netscape can't handle all by itself. We'd want the plug-in to be available for both PC and Macintosh, and to work simply and identically on both. Fortunately I discovered such a plug-in in the form of InterVU from InterVU, Inc. It's designed to play MPEG-compressed videos, which abound in various archives on the Net. While most (not all) MPEGs are silent, they still give a good taste of Netscape's multimedia capabilities.

To install InterVU, switch to the relevant folder on your CD-ROM (Appendix A will help you find it). Hold off on actually installing InterVU for the moment. Instead, just locate the file called DEMO.MPG and copy it to a new folder on your hard drive.

Now, open a text editor and type the following lines into a new file:

```
<HTML>
<TITLE>Embedded MPEG Test Page</TITLE>
<BODY>
Below the horizontal rule is a picture of the Blue Angels.
<HR>
```

Now, we're going to make reference to the MPEG file, DEMO.MPG. As you know, the traditional way to do this in a Web page is to use the <IMG SRC> tag, which in this case would be <IMG SRC="demo.mpg">. In the past, this would have caused Netscape to load a helper application that played MPEG files, if one had been installed.

However, we're using the shiny new plug-ins way to do things, so the next line of our file is:

```
<EMBED SRC="demo.mpg" WIDTH=172 HEIGHT=154>
```

Complete the file with </BODY> and </HTML> tags and save it as EMBED.HTM.

Like the IMG command, the EMBED command is complete in and of itself. It does not need to be followed by an /EMBED tag. It has just three essential attributes:

SRC="url"	**The URL of the source document**
WIDTH=size in pixels	**The WIDTH attribute specifies the width of the window that opens to show the embedded document**
HEIGHT=size in pixels	**The HEIGHT attribute specifies the height of the window that opens to show the embedded document**

Optionally, the ALIGN attribute may be used to let Netscape know how you want text to flow around any image the plug-in might display. It acts similarly to the IMG ALIGN tag (supporting one of TOP, BOTTOM, CENTER, BASELINE, LEFT, RIGHT, TEXTTOP, MIDDLE, ABSMIDDLE, or ABSBOTTOM as possible arguments).

There's another attribute you should be aware of now, even though it isn't relevant to InterVU. This is HIDDEN, which can be used to suppress screen display from a plug-in completely. It's used with audio-only plug-ins that might be set to play a sound automatically when a Web page loads. HIDDEN is new to Netscape 3.0; before it was available, the only way to hide a plug-in was to set either HEIGHT or WIDTH to 0 pixels, and the other dimension to a very low value such as 2 pixels. Sometimes it worked, sometimes it didn't—and setting both HEIGHT and WIDTH to 0 could crash your browser!

If you're designing Web pages for optimal viewing by both Netscape 2.0 and Netscape 3.0—a good idea because of the many copies of 2.0 that are in use—you might be tempted to use both HIDDEN and minimal settings for HEIGHT and WIDTH. This might work OK for you; however, official advice from programmers at Netscape is that HEIGHT and WIDTH settings under 10 pixels ought to be avoided no matter what version of the browser you're using.

An attribute we *will* use on our MPEG Test Page is PLUGINSPAGE. This attribute is considered optional, but you'll probably want to use it on most of your Web pages. Here's why: When Netscape finds an <EMBED SRC> tag, it looks for a plug-in that can handle the relevant MIME type. Netscape will not use any existing helper applications to interpret embedded data; nor, probably, would you want it to. Instead, it searches for a relevant plug-in.

To get an example of this, start Netscape and load EMBED.HTM into it. If your copy of Netscape previously had an MPEG viewer loaded as a helper application, DEMO.MPG could've been played via the <IMG SRC> tag, though it would have loaded into a new window that at least partially obscured Netscape. Since you have used the <EMBED SRC> tag, however, this doesn't happen; what you see instead is a screen like that in Figure 8-1.

Netscape draws a box using the WIDTH and HEIGHT specifications you gave it. Click within the box on the generic file icon, and Netscape pops up a dialog box that cites the image's MIME type and subtype (video/x-mpeg in this case) and asks what you want to do (see Figure 8-2).

The dialog box is intended to alert users that a plug-in is needed. If they click on Cancel, nothing happens. If they click on Get the Plugin, Netscape defaults to a URL that was coded into the browser (currently *http://cgi.netscape.com/eng/mozilla/2.0/extensions/info.cgi?application/x-unknown-content-type*—or didn't you really want to know?). The information found there (see Figure 8-3) tells users: "The page you've requested contains a type of information (an embedded MIME type or custom file) that Netscape does not recognize. You might be able to access this information by installing appropriate plug-in software or by using a helper application."

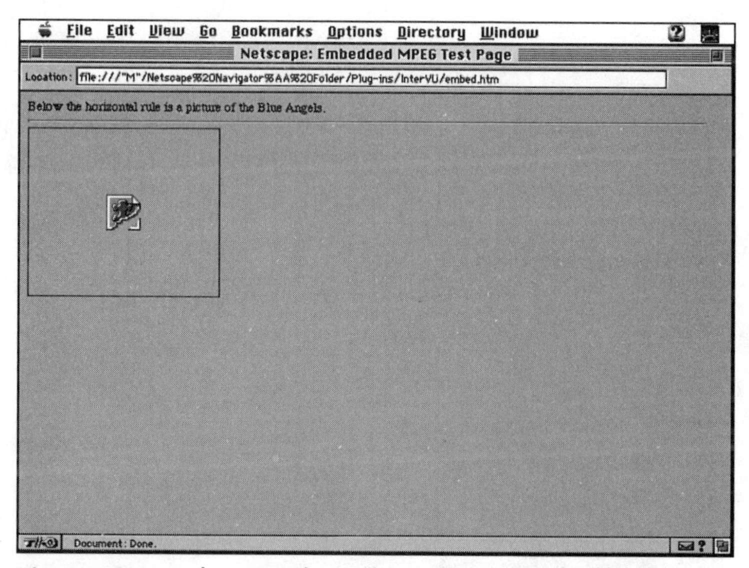

Figure 8-1 When you do not have a plug-in installed to handle the MIME Type Netscape has encountered, a generic file icon appears within a rectangle

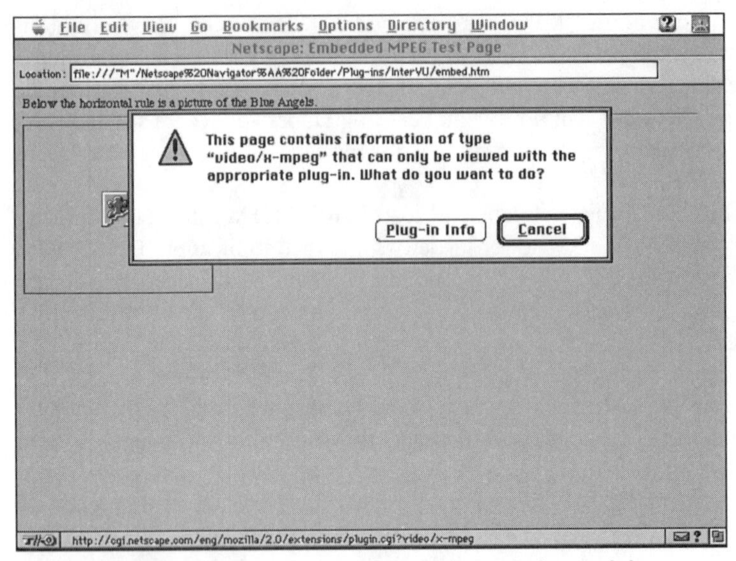

Figure 8-2 Click anywhere within the rectangle, and this dialog box appears

If users then click on the link referring to Netscape's "Plug-In Registry," they're taken to a Netscape-maintained list of currently shipping plug-ins (found at *http://home.netscape.com/comprod/products/navigator/version_2.0/plugins/index.html*). See Figure 8-4.

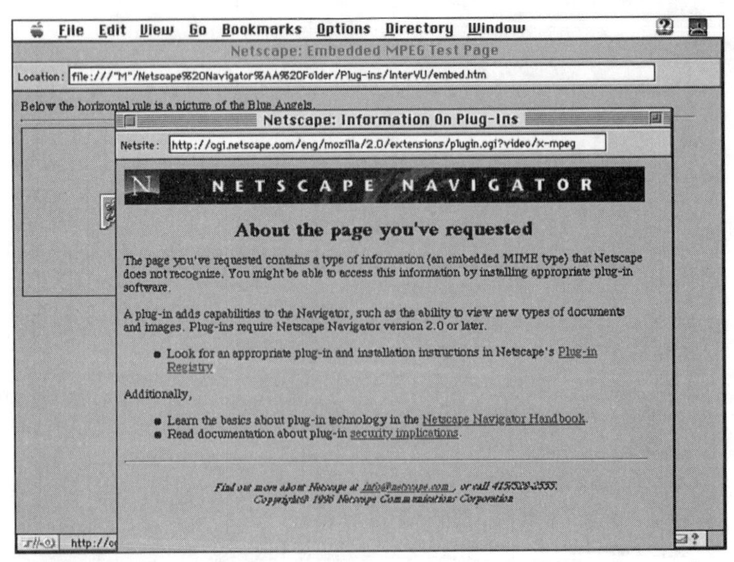

Figure 8-3 Netscape's generic warning that you might need a plug-in

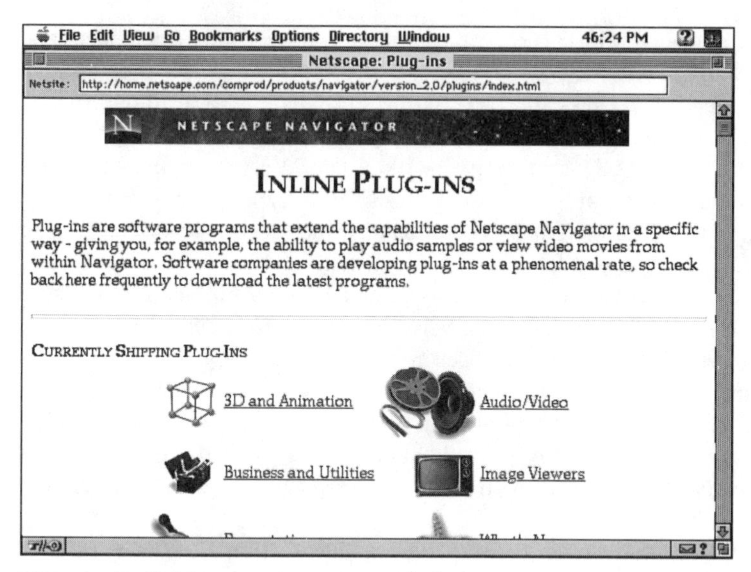

Figure 8–4 Netscape's registry of plug-ins

The problem with this generic list is that a user must wade through it to find a plug-in that might pertain to the information you embedded in your page. There's no guarantee they'll pick the right one, or even that they won't get distracted and forget completely about returning to your Web site.

Taking a User to the Right Plug-In

That's why Netscape's PLUGINSPAGE attribute is so useful. Add it to your <EMBED SRC> statement, and you'll take the user—if need be—to the precise location of the plug-in he or she needs. This can be a page belonging to the plug-in developer, or even another page on your own site (if you've gotten permission to store the plug-in installation program on your server).

Let's see how PLUGINSPACE would work in your tiny little Web page. Once more, open EMBED.HTM, and make the changes you see below to the <EMBED SRC> line:

```
<HTML>
<TITLE>Embedded MPEG Test Page</TITLE>
<BODY>
Below the horizontal rule is a picture of the Blue Angels.
<HR>
<EMBED SRC="demo.mpg" PLUGINSPAGE="http://www.intervu.com/" "WIDTH=172 HEIGHT=154>
</BODY>
</HTML>
```

As you can see, the address for another Web site has been appended to the <EMBED SRC> line. Now, instead of taking the user who needs a plug-in to Netscape's generic pages, you can send them right to the InterVU Web site. After all, you have InterVU already, on your CD-ROM, but they don't. PLUGINSPAGE makes it easy for them to collect what they need.

Load this last version of EMBED.HTM (if you already have it open in a Netscape window, just use Netscape's View/Reload command) and you'll see that Netscape opens a new browser window for the address specified by the PLUGINSPAGE attribute. In this case, it's the download page maintained by InterVU (see Figure 8-5).

Incidentally PLUGINSPAGE not only invokes the Web site you specified (*http://www.intervu.com*, in our example) but also passes a MIME type to that site, ready for processing by a CGI script. This marginally useful feature can let the server on that site know what type of plug-in you are looking for. More often, however, it is harmlessly ignored. To make sure that the CGI information doesn't cause any problems, make sure that you give PLUGINSPAGE a "fully qualified" Web address that ends with a slash.

For example, *http://www.intervu.com/*, as used in our sample, is OK. Netscape turns this into the command *http://www.intervu.com/?video/x-mpeg*, and the InterVU server just ignores the question mark and everything after it with no ill effect. If you had put in *http://www.intervu.com* without the final slash, this would get sent as *http://www.intervu.com?video/x-mpeg*, causing the InterVU server to say it couldn't find any such page.

Perhaps you could get permission to keep plug-in installation files on your own server, using PLUGINSPAGE to specify their local addresses. However, you probably should avoid so doing unless a homogenous look and feel is of such concern that having users open a "foreign" site to download a plug-in offends you. An important reason to leave plug-in installers on the vendor's Web site is that plug-ins are constantly being updated, either to support new platforms, to add functionality, or to correct quirks. By "pluginspaging" right to the source, you automatically ensure that visitors to your Web site get the latest version of whatever plug-in they'll need.

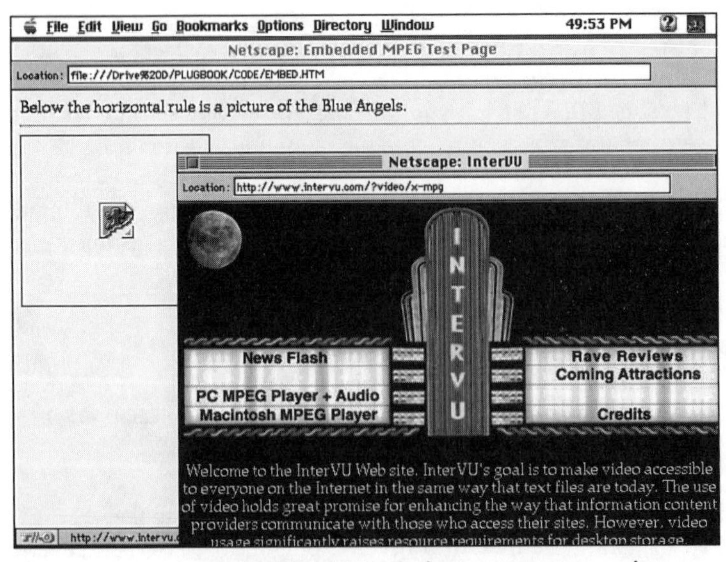

Figure 8-5 The PLUGINSPAGE attribute causes a new browser window to be opened if and when a new plug-in is required

Actually there's an important reason both to use PLUGINSPAGE *and* to document somewhere on your Web page which plug-ins you've used. It is this: The dialog box alerting users they need a plug-in only appears if Netscape does not find any way to handle the relevant MIME type and file extension.

It is possible that a user might have installed a *different* plug-in that already volunteers—like the kid waving her hand to the teacher in a classroom—to handle the MIME type. As a result, your Web page might be rendered, but not in the way you want it to be. This can lead to visual anomalies, or worse.

Take the case of Crescendo, a plug-in for MIDI files that automatically plays files when a Web page is opened (unless you tell it not to). You might have used the HIDDEN attribute in your <EMBED SRC> line, so that instead of seeing the default Crescendo icon, visitors would see an uncluttered Web page and hear music in the background. Other MIDI plug-ins might not automatically play files, instead relying on user controls that appear on screen. Since your use of HIDDEN made these controls invisible, a visitor with the "wrong" plug-in would have no way whatsoever to start the MIDI music.

Installing the Plug-In

Now, make sure your computer is still connected to the Internet, reload EMBED.HTM, and—this time—use the InterVU, Inc. page that appears to download InterVU. (Since you have InterVU on your CD-ROM already, you can obviously bypass this step, though it's always a good practice to find out what visitors to your Web page would have to go through.) Follow the installation instructions that come with the program. If you need more help with installing InterVU, review Chapter 7 and/or refer to the InterVU-specific section in Chapter 10.

The InterVU installer copies an InterVU or InterVU FAT file to Netscape's Plug-Ins folder if you have a Mac. If you have a Windows 95 computer, it copies the file NPIVMPG.DLL to your Plugins folder. On both types of computer, it also copies other files to an InterVU folder that gets stored within your main Plugins folder.

Now, exit Netscape if you haven't already done so and restart the program. Then, reload the EMBED.HTM page using View/Reload (<CTRL>-<R> on the PC, <COMMAND>-<R> on the Mac). You'll see a screen like that in Figure 8-6.

Congratulations. You've just created your first Web page using a Netscape plug-in.

Lesson 4: Making Your Page Browser-Proof

By following the instructions in the previous section, you learned how to create a basic Web page with an embedded MPEG file. Building upon the knowledge of HTML you already have, you'll find it easy to embed other data types in your pages—including video, audio, interactive presentations, and much more.

Chapters 10–15 take a specific look at some of today's hottest plug-ins—many of which are included on the CD-ROM at the back of this book (so don't let anyone steal your disc). You'll learn more about how to source content for these plug-ins, how to install them, and how to implement vendor-specific extensions to the <EMBED SRC> tag. Lead times being what they are, no book could hope to be totally current on what

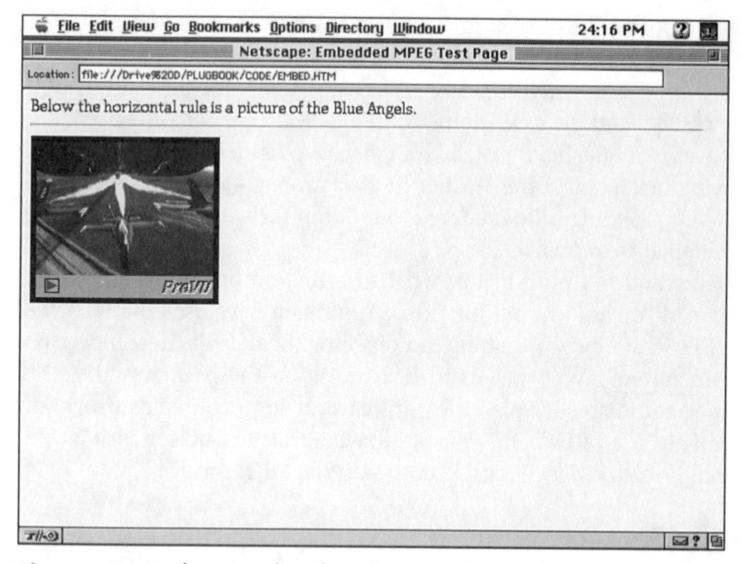

Figure 8–6 The completed Web page shows this MPEG video

plug-ins are available. That's why Chapter 16 is devoted to the ways you can use the Net to discover the latest ones.

Unfortunately, not everyone is using Netscape 2.0 or above. While I am an avowed Netscape bigot—I like the company's competitive scrappiness, and I think their browser is the slickest and fastest—even I have to admit that competitors also have much to offer. I like NCSA Mosaic, for instance, for its presentation mode, which lets you turn off the title and menu bars completely.

Microsoft's Internet Explorer remains something of a dark horse. The hype about the forthcoming version 4.0, and how well it will be integrated into Windows when it is released, has been unrelenting. Version 3.0, recently released, has some promising technical features. For example, it offers ActiveX controls, which are essentially Microsoft's answer to Netscape plug-ins. A limited degree of compatibility with Netscape plug-ins themselves is also offered. These new features complicate matters for Web page designers: For more information, see the section at the end of this lesson.

Other browsers include Apple's Cyberdog, Attachmate's Emissary, and many others. Naturally, many copies of Netscape 1.x are still in circulation too; I use one myself on my aging 486SX subnotebook.

In short, other browsers aren't just going to disappear. With that in mind, let's take a look at how our sample Web page, EMBED.HTM, would be rendered by a couple of "Brand-X" browsers. Figure 8-7 shows the test page as seen by Mosaic 2.1, and Figure 8-8 shows it as seen by the recently replaced Internet Explorer 2.0.

As you can see, something is rotten in Denmark (or wherever the server happens to be). Mosaic and Internet Explorer 2.0 both completely ignore the Netscape-specific <EMBED SRC> tag, displaying nothing except the horizontal rule and the text below it. Actually, this is fortunate: Ignoring the tag is a better response on their part than trying to interpret it and getting hung up.

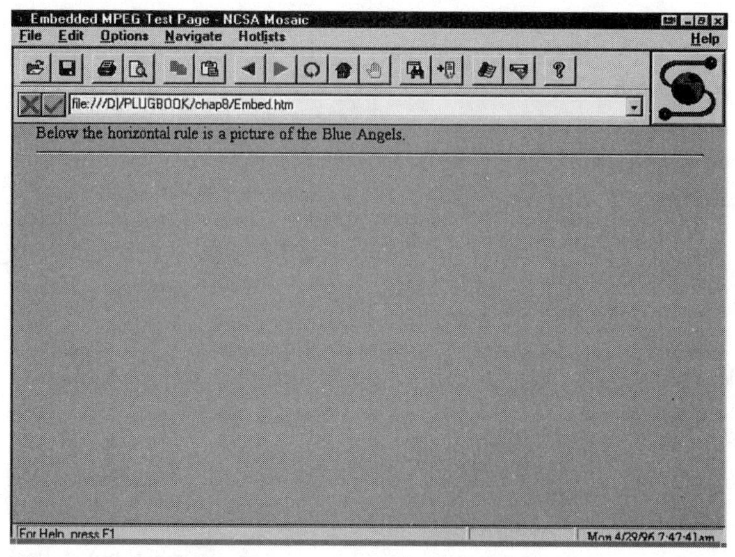

Figure 8–7 The test page as seen by Mosaic

How to cope with this? Well, we can try combining the two versions of EMBED.HTM we created earlier in this chapter. Use the <EMBED SRC> command, but use the <IMG SRC> command, too, calling upon helper applications when necessary so something will display on the screens of those poor unfortunates without Netscape.

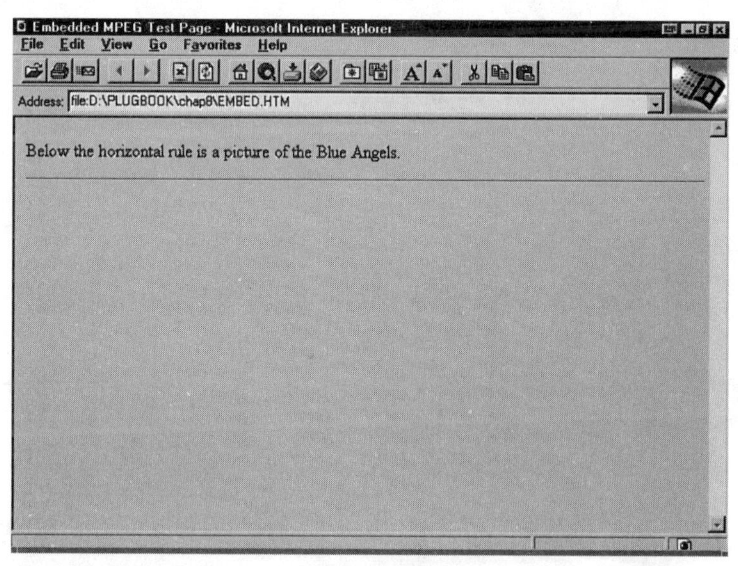

Figure 8–8 The test page as seen by Internet Explorer 2.0

The resulting code might look like this:

```
<HTML>
<TITLE>Embedded MPEG Test Page</TITLE>
<BODY>
Below the horizontal rule is a picture of the Blue Angels.
<HR>
<EMBED SRC="demo.mpg" PLUGINSPAGE="http://www.intervu.com/" "WIDTH=172 HEIGHT=154>
<IMG SRC="demo.mpg">
<HR>
<font jsize=2>Embedded MPEG video optimized for <A
HREF="http://www.intervu.com">InterVU</a>
from InterVU Inc.
</body>
</html>
```

Mosaic and Internet Explorer 2.0 ignore the <EMBED SRC> line, but go on to interpret the <IMG SRC> line, delivering a screen like that in Figure 8-9. So all is well—or is it? A problem now arises for Netscape users, who would see the video, followed by a generic file icon representing the same video all over again (Figure 8-10). Not pretty. Fortunately, the folks at Netscape anticipated this problem, creating a tag called <NOEMBED>.

<NOEMBED> works almost identically to the <NOFRAME> tag, with which you may already be familiar. It is meant to be used in the context of a Web page containing one or more <EMBED SRC> elements. Whereas non-Netscape browsers ignore the <EMBED SRC> tag, Netscape by design ignores the <NOEMBED> and </NOEMBED> tags and anything they enclose.

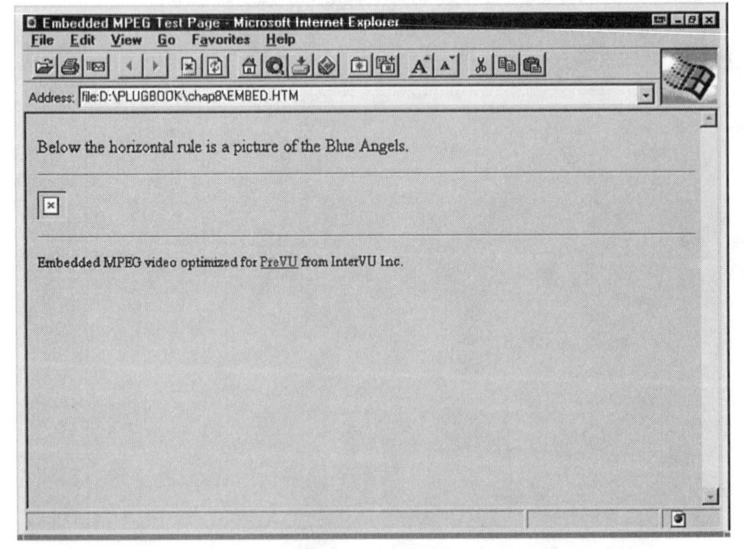

Figure 8-9 Using redundant <EMBED SRC> and <IMG SRC> lines works for both Internet Explorer (pictured) and Mosaic

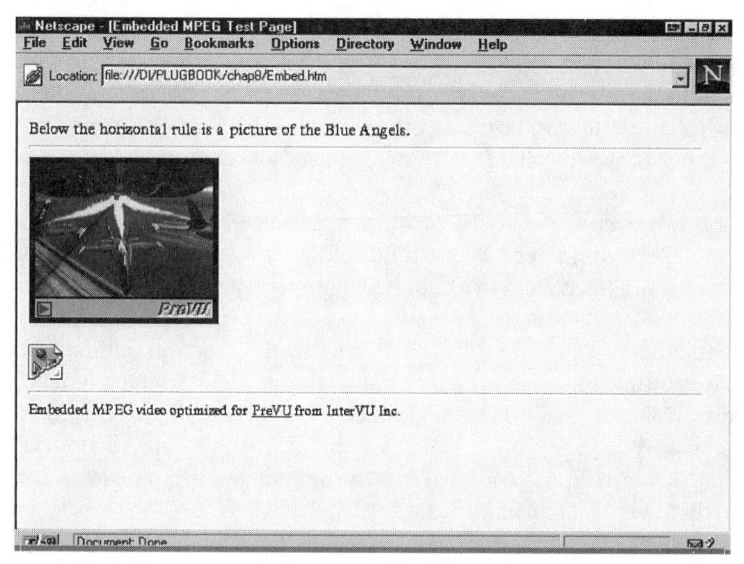

Figure 8–10 Now the page looks odd under Netscape

Here's how you'd use this in EMBED.HTM:

```
<HTML>
<TITLE>Embedded MPEG Test Page</TITLE>
<BODY>
Below the horizontal rule is a picture of the Blue Angels.
<HR>
<EMBED SRC="demo.mpg" PLUGINSPAGE="http://www.intervu.com/" "WIDTH=172 HEIGHT=154>
<NOEMBED>
<IMG SRC="demo.mpg">
</NOEMBED>
<HR>
<font size=2>Embedded MPEG video optimized for <A
HREF="http://www.intervu.com">InterVU</a>
from InterVU Inc.
</body>
</html>
```

Netscape uses its plug-in to view the MPEG video, and then—because of the bracketing <NOEMBED> tags—ignores the <IMG SRC> command entirely. This does away with the problem that was shown in Figure 8-10. Microsoft Internet Explorer and other browsers do the reverse, skipping past the <EMBED SRC> command, but reading what lies between the <NOEMBED> tags just as if they weren't there at all. As a result, you have a page that does its best to cater to all visitors, whether they're running Netscape or not.

There's no limitation on what may be placed between <NOEMBED> tags, so you could use them to add text to the page suggesting that visitors upgrade to Netscape if they want to use plug-ins. (I've found that <NOEMBED> tags can be used to bracket text that only Netscape users will see, even when there's no <EMBED SRC> command on the page. This could also be used to good end on all those sites that urge you to click on a logo to download Netscape: They should use <NOEMBED> to set off the logo—why should you see it when you're already *running* Netscape?)

So far, we've learned how to embed objects that only Netscape will see and interpret. We've also learned how to create images, text, and other links that Netscape users will not see, but those running other browsers will. This gives us a handy way to provide alternatives for the plug-in impaired.

Wouldn't it be nice, however, if we could create text, images, and links on a Web page that only Netscape users could see? This would allow us to create captions, for example, for the window a plug-in creates—without having to worry about users of other browsers getting confused.

There is a somewhat tenuous way to do this. It requires use of JavaScript, but don't be alarmed—you don't have to turn into a C++ coder or something. The trick merely relies upon the fact that a JavaScript "program"—it's too glorified a word for what we're going to do—may be inserted into a Web page via a couple of simple HTML tags. JavaScript can put words on the screen. Better still, the code will not run on some other browsers and may be concealed from them via HTML comment tags.

A script is embedded in HTML with the <SCRIPT> tag:

```
<SCRIPT LANGUAGE="JavaScript">
       ... JavaScript statements ...
</SCRIPT>
```

Here's a simple script:

```
<SCRIPT LANGUAGE="JavaScript">
       document.write ("I just want to say this:")
</SCRIPT>
Hello, world.
```

The output from this program, placed within a Web page, would be:

```
I just want to say this: Hello, world.
```

Another browser, such as NCSA Mosaic, would fail to run the program, but would interpret the line between the <SCRIPT> tags as simple text. The result would be a line reading:

```
document.write ("I just want to say this:") Hello, world
```

Not exactly what we had in mind. But the beauty of this technique is that the JavaScript code may be hidden from many other browsers via HTML comment tags, yet will still run when loaded into Netscape. The tag <!— begins the hiding of comments, and the tag —> ends it.

To understand how this all falls into place, look at this modified version of EMBED.HTM:

```
<HTML>
<TITLE>Embedded MPEG Test Page</TITLE>
<BODY>
Below the horizontal rule is a picture of the Blue Angels.
<HR>
<SCRIPT LANGUAGE="JavaScript">
<!-- The contents of this script will be hidden from most browsers other than Netscape
```

```
        $
document.write ( 'EMBED SRC="demo.mpg"
PLUGINSPAGE="http://www.intervu.com/" WIDTH=172 HEIGHT=154>' )
        document.write ( '<BR>Here is a video that plays just for you, a discerning user of
Netscape plug-ins.<BR>' )
// end hiding script contents from old browsers -->
</SCRIPT>
<NOEMBED>
<IMG SRC="demo.mpg">
<HR>
If you had Netscape, the above video would've played as a snazzy plug-in.
</NOEMBED>
<HR>
<font size=2>Embedded video optimized for <A
HREF="http://www.intervu.com">InterVU</a>
from InterVU, Inc.
</body>
</html>
```

Note the use of the single quotes to begin and end the document.write strings, and also the fact that any HTML commands may be contained in them. You'll notice that I have made the <EMBED SRC> tag part of the script, even though it, at least, would have been ignored by "Brand-X" browsers in any case. It just seems safer and not too much more complicated to give it this double layer of protection.

A Netscape user sees a screen like that in Figure 8-11 (and thus is treated to the video automatically). A Mosaic user sees a screen like that in Figure 8-12, while users of Microsoft's Internet Explorer 2.0 see a screen like Figure 8-13.

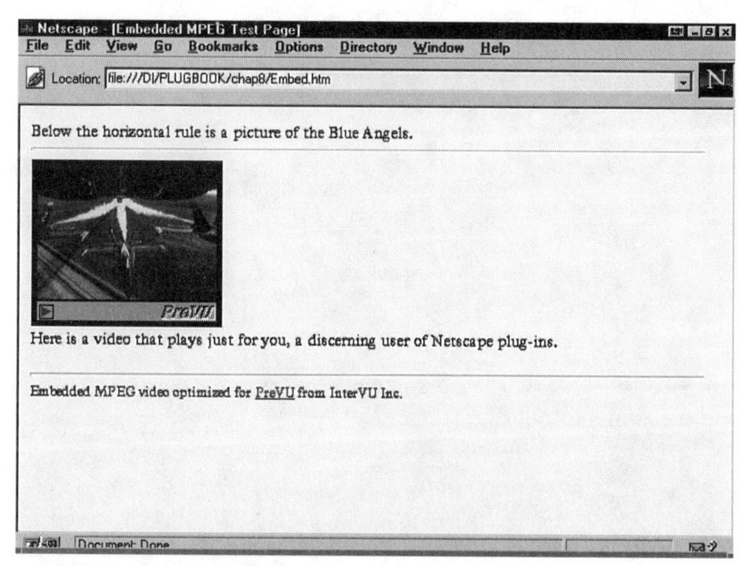

Figure 8–11 The end result in Netscape

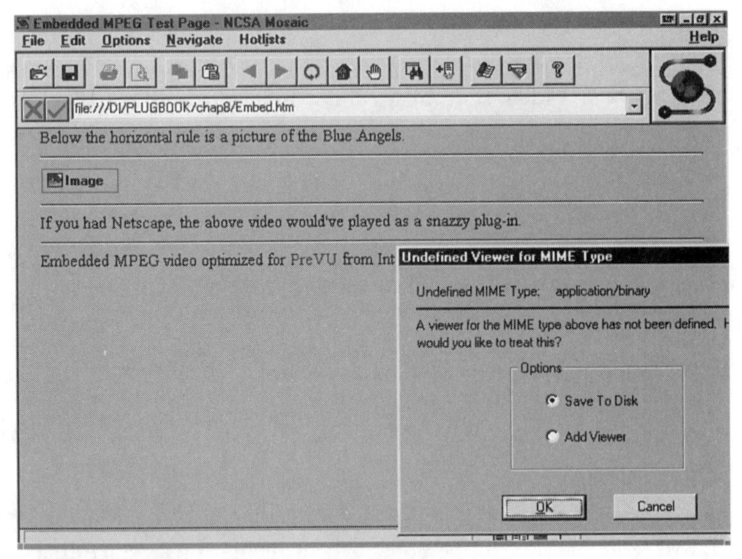

Figure 8–12 The end result in Mosaic

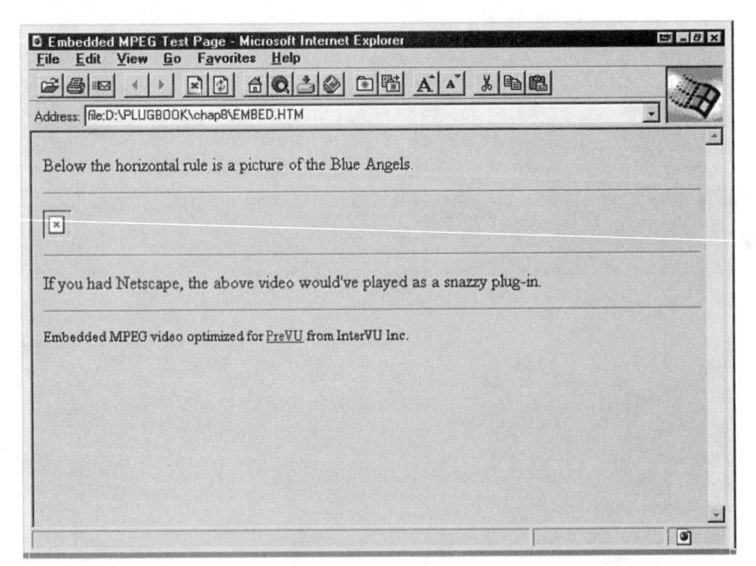

Figure 8–13 The end result in Internet Explorer 2.0

Internet Explorer 3.0

It was inevitable that Microsoft would want to respond to a technology as slick as plug-ins. In August 1996, it did so via the release of Internet Explorer 3.0. This browser supports ActiveX controls, downloadable software components that are very similar to plug-ins in what they can do and how they appear.

Unlike plug-ins—in Netscape 3.0, at least—ActiveX controls can download and install into a user's browser automatically. When the download is finished, the ActiveX program starts, without any need for the browser to be restarted. This may be considered an advantage or a disadvantage, depending upon how much manual control you like to have over your computer.

In addition to offering ActiveX, Internet Explorer 3.0 is also compatible with some Netscape 3.0 plug-ins. In fact, it will even look in your Netscape plug-ins folder to find them, if you have both Netscape and Internet Explorer installed on the same machine.

The HTML code used for ActiveX objects will look very familiar to you if you've used the <APPLET> tag to incorporate Java applets in your Web pages (see Chapter 4). Instead of using a single <EMBED SRC> line, ActiveX uses paired <OBJECT> and </OBJECT> tags with parameters in between.

Here is an example based on the ActiveX version of VivoActive (a plug-in about which you'll read in Chapter 10):

```
<OBJECT CLASSID="clsid:02466323-75ed-11cf-a267-0020af2546ea" WIDTH=176 HEIGHT=144 CODE-
BASE="http://www.vivo.com/ie/vvweb.cab">
<PARAM NAME="URL" VALUE="test.viv">
<PARAM NAME="AUTOSTART" VALUE="true">
<PARAM NAME="VIDEOCONTROLS" VALUE="on">
</OBJECT>
```

The CLASSID attribute is used by Windows to identify the desired program code. The CODEBASE attribute tells Internet Explorer where to get the required ActiveX object if it is not already on the user's hard drive. The <PARAM> elements are analogous to Netscape's <EMBED SRC> attributes, telling the ActiveX object how to display the file previously referenced via <OBJECT SRC>.

None of the code just shown is compatible with Netscape 3.0. However, Internet Explorer 3.0 is compatible with some Netscape plug-ins using the same <EMBED> tag you learned to use earlier in this chapter. Therefore, you might choose to code your Web pages for Netscape using EMBED, and hope for the best when it comes to Internet Explorer 3.0 users. The catch is that Internet Explorer 3.0 is not compatible with *all* plug-ins: The only way to know which will work with it is to test them and see.

If supporting both Netscape 3.0 and Internet Explorer users is important to you, another option is to stick to only plug-ins that are *also* available as Active X controls. VivoActive, mentioned above, is one such. It is not too difficult to code for both browsers, because Netscape 3.0 ignores <OBJECT> , </OBJECT>, and any <PARAM> statements that fall between them; Internet Explorer 3.0, for its part, ignores anything that falls between <OBJECT> and </OBJECT> except for the <PARAM> statements.

To embed a video (or whatever) using a Netscape plug-in for Netscape, and an ActiveX control for Internet Explorer, use code similar to the following:

```
<OBJECT CLASSID="clsid:02466323-75ed-11cf-a267-0020af2546ea" WIDTH=176 HEIGHT=144 CODE-
BASE="http://www.vivo.com/ie/vvweb.cab">
<PARAM NAME="URL" VALUE="test.viv">
<PARAM NAME="AUTOSTART" VALUE="true">
<PARAM NAME="VIDEOCONTROLS" VALUE="on">
<EMBED SRC="test.viv" AUTOSTART=true VIDEOCONTROLS=on WIDTH=176 HEIGHT=144>
</OBJECT>
```

Netscape won't respond to the <OBJECT> tag, while Internet Explorer won't respond to the <EMBED> tag. The similarity between the <EMBED> attributes and the <PARAM> statements ensures that the Web page behaves the same and looks basically identical no matter which of the two browsers you use.

Internet Explorer 3.0 does not support Netscape's LiveConnect mechanism for communication between JavaScripts, applets, and plug-ins. However, it *does* support JavaScript itself (through version 1.0). This means that the trick outlined in the first section of this lesson—using JavaScript to hide <EMBED> tags—will not work.

WHAT NOW?

In this chapter, you created a Web page using a simple plug-in. You also learned how to deal with some of the error conditions that can arise, including the user's not having the desired plug-in or the user not having a copy of Netscape.

Now, you're more than ready to start creating your own sample Web pages. To give you some inspiration, the next chapter starts our survey of available plug-ins with a look at those that handle audio.

AUDIO PLUG-INS

Sound capabilities have been a part of more and more personal computers since the introduction of the first Apple Macintosh. Today, it's a rare desktop or portable computer that doesn't have sound—whether it's a Mac, Windows, or UNIX system.

Outside of multimedia CD-ROMs, however, there have been few effective uses for that sound. Some people—probably those who have spent too long listening to imitation fish tank noises coming from the "talking screen saver" in the next cubicle—still believe computers should be seen and not heard.

But now, Netscape is changing all that. Computer-based sound is no longer just a matter of lighthearted entertainment, it is becoming an integral part of business communication. By building sound right into the Web, Netscape's audio plug-ins offer a new way to provide news and information. They can give Web site visitors an "on demand" way to access radio-like news reports, or they can provide audio narration and instructions that accompany a specific Web page.

Traditional broadcasters are climbing on the bandwagon as well. For example, Virgin Radio in London provides its Virgin Gold pop oldies station 24 hours a day via the Internet. If you prefer classical music, you can tune into Seattle-based KING-FM. These broadcasts are live, compressed, and sent over the Net in real time. Surprisingly, the audio quality is acceptable: Even over a 28.8Kbps modem, they sound comparable to an average AM radio. As you'll read in this chapter, Netscape now comes with LiveAudio, a plug-in that plays audio files digitized in the standard computer formats. These are .WAV (Windows), .AU (UNIX), .AIFF (Macintosh), and MIDI (Musical Instrument Digital Interface).

Because of network bandwidth limitations, however, no one audio plug-in can do it all. While the standard audio file formats above are versatile, they were never designed to minimize transmission time or storage requirements. Therefore, other Net-specific formats have developed to serve special needs. If you want to put extensive narrations on your Web pages, you'll want to try Echospeech, TrueSpeech, or ToolVox. These plug-ins, and their separately available encoders, use compression techniques that have been optimized for speech. With compression ratios of up to 50:1 (relative to a traditionally recorded sound file), they can save vast amounts of transmission time and disk space.

If you want to offer material with a mix of voice, music, and sound effects—as in a radio broadcast—you may prefer RealAudio. Optimized for decent quality plus real-time encoding and decoding, it's the system used by the majority of Web broadcasters (including the two radio stations mentioned previously).

FastMan's RapidTransit plug-in also uses compression, but tries to stay as close to the sound quality of a 16-bit compact disc as it can. Naturally, its files are bigger than RealAudio's. However, RapidTransit is a good way to offer "presentation-quality" audio clips and still save on bandwidth.

Finally, the ultimate way to save on bandwidth is to transmit instructions to a client computer and let *it* do the audio synthesis. That's what MIDI—offered by both LiveAudio and Crescendo—is all about. As always, it's a great way to make a computer play music or sound effects. MVP Solutions' Talker does the same thing for speech: Using a Macintosh computer's voice synthesis capability, it can make a Web page speak to you with little or no increase in download times.

DETAILS TO CHECK BEFORE YOU START

It should go without saying, but before you start to work with audio in the Netscape environment, you need to make sure that your computer is already capable of recording and playing back audio in standard file formats. For PC compatibles this means you usually need to have added a sound board plus an external microphone and powered speakers. Macintosh computers need only a microphone.

If you're planning just to play back sounds from Web pages you browse, it's sufficient to use your computer's sound control panel for testing purposes. Click on one of the sounds that came with your system and make sure it plays back properly. If you're planning to record sounds, dust off your microphone and make sure it can give you clear voice recordings. Or, better still, make test recordings on an external tape recorder and connect it to your computer's line input. That way, you can separate the arduous business of figuring out what you're going to say from the equally arduous business of setting recording levels properly.

NOTE: Though they have not been a great success in the market, Sony's MiniDisc recorders are ideal for mastering short voice clips and sound effects for dubbing to your computer. This is because of their random-access capabilities, which—unlike any other medium's—are a match for a computer's.

It is mercifully beyond the scope of this book to lecture you about copyright law. However, it's worth commenting here that the ease of transferring sound to a computer page may tempt you to copy favorite records, film audio tracks, and so on, to your Web pages. Yes, you've seen it done elsewhere—but don't assume that you can get away with it if your Web site is corporate or otherwise particularly visible.

LIVEAUDIO

Thanks to Netscape's LiveAudio plug-in, the standard digital sound and MIDI file formats may be played from within a Web page. Sounds can be set to play automatically when the user opens a page, or manually by clicking on a control panel.

Because LiveAudio ships with Netscape 3.0, no manual installation is necessary. Technically speaking, however, LiveAudio has been added into Netscape like any other plug-in. You can selectively disable it or choose to remove it entirely.

For Windows 3.1, Windows 95, and Windows NT, LiveAudio functionality resides in the file NPAUDIO.DLL in your Netscape/Plug-ins subdirectory. For Macintosh, the file is LiveAudio in the Netscape Navigator Plug-ins folder.

In all cases, you can check to see if LiveAudio is active by selecting About Plug-ins from the Help menu (Windows 3.x, Windows 95, Windows NT) or Apple menu (Macintosh). As you see from your screen, which will resemble Figure 9-1, LiveAudio is active and is handling the MIME types listed in Table 9-1.

Table 9-1 MIME types handled by LiveAudio

MIME Type/Subtype	Extension (suffix)
Audio/basic	au
Audio/x-aiff	aiff, aif
Audio/aiff	aiff, aif
Audio/wav	wav
Audio/x-wav	wav
Audio/x-midi	midi, mid
Audio/midi	midi, mid

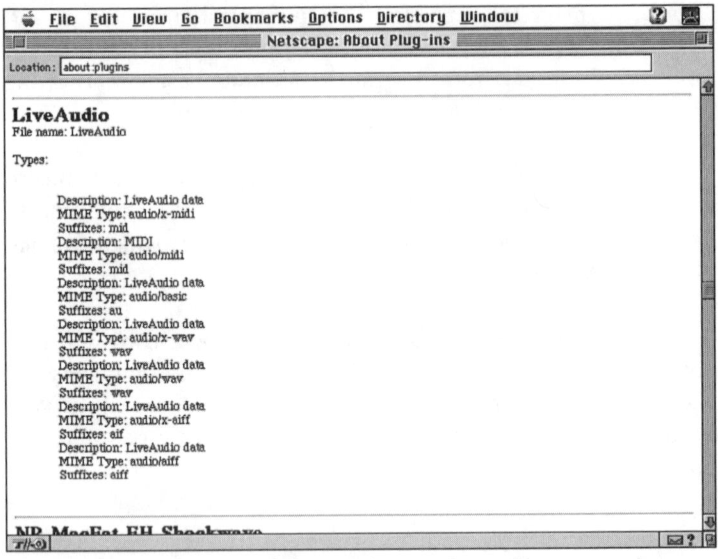

Figure 9–1 The About Plug-ins list confirms that LiveAudio is functioning

If you want to break any of these associations, you can do so by manipulating the Options/General Preferences/Helpers tab as described in Chapter 6. Normally, though, each should remain in place so that Netscape retains its default behavior.

Lesson 1: What It Can Do

Obviously the best way to get a feel for what LiveAudio can do is to load a Web page with embedded sound files. Thanks to the popularity of Netscape, many have already appeared and more are being created even as you read this chapter!

Netscape's home page *(http://www.netscape.com)* offers links to a variety of pages using LiveAudio. One early offering—interesting in that it was developed by the folks at EmeraldNet, who wrote the LiveAudio plug-in for Netscape—is the Verve Pipe page at *http://www.thevervepipe.com/music.html.* As you will see in Figure 9-2, this page offers a menu of sound files in various formats. Click on any of them, and the file will be downloaded and then played in the background.

LiveAudio sound files can take time to load, not being compressed as much as, for instance, JPEG graphics. This is the price to be paid for backward compatibility with the .WAV, .AU, and .AIF file formats, which were never designed with data compression in mind. If minimizing download time is your prime concern, you can either select one of the other audio plug-ins in this chapter, or tap into LiveAudio's capacity to play MIDI files. These files quickly transmit their instructions to a computer's sound board (or, on the Macintosh, to QuickTime), which turns them into music. Once the download of a MIDI file is complete—and it never takes long—there is no further drag on available bandwidth.

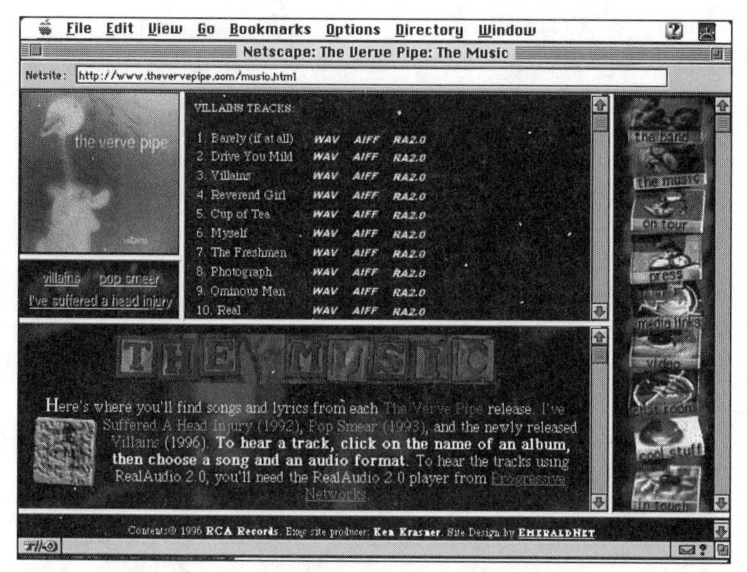

Figure 9–2 The Verve Pipe page was one of the first to use LiveAudio

Lesson 2: Creating Content

Creating content to be played via LiveAudio is easy. If you have Windows, you can record .WAV files (and often other formats) using utilities supplied by your sound board's manufacturer. Usually these are already installed in your computer's Start Menu or Program Manager. If you have a Macintosh, you need to obtain one of the many programs—some are available as shareware—that records sounds and/or converts them from the native format used by the System into one of the formats LiveAudio can understand.

Audio clips should be recorded at a level matching that of those already on your computer. In other words, when you're making a recording, get it to play back at a volume that matches your computer's built-in sounds. Recording level should be ample, but not so loud that there is distortion.

Apart from these general pointers, LiveAudio imposes no special requirements on the sound files you create. Unlike some other plug-ins, it doesn't care whether you save files as 8 bit or 16 bit, and it will play sounds back no matter what sampling rate they were recorded at. Some sound recording utilities let you vary sampling rates from a high of 44KHz (for CD-like sound) to a low of 5KHz (for telephone-like sound). The latter is adequate for voice, and will save on transmission time.

Lesson 3: Embedding Data in Your Own Web Page

Audio files give you a simple, enjoyable way to use the <EMBED> tag you learned in Chapter 8. To embed a sound in a Web page, just insert the tag <EMBED SRC="url">, where *url* is the file name of a .WAV, .AU, .AIF, or .MIDI file. As usual in HTML syntax, you must supply a file name and extension, also including a full path if the sound file is not in the same subdirectory as the Web page itself.

Attributes for the LiveAudio <EMBED> tag are summarized in Table 9-2. The AUTOSTART attribute, with values of TRUE or FALSE, specifies whether or not the sound file will play automatically when the Web page is opened. The LOOP attribute, again with values of TRUE or FALSE, determines whether or not the file will be repeated continuously. The CONTROLS attribute determines what type of control panel, if any, is associated with the sound. The VOLUME attribute determines how loudly the sound will be played relative to others on the same page.

Table 9-2 LiveAudio EMBED attributes

Name	Possible Values	Comments
ALIGN	CENTER|BASELINE|TOP|LEFT|RIGHT	Optional tag that determines how a sound's control panel will be aligned visually.
AUTOSTART	TRUE|FALSE	If set to True, a sound will play automatically when a page is opened. False is the default state if this attribute is not used.
CONTROLS	CONSOLE|SMALLCONSOLE|PLAYBUTTON|PAUSEBUTTON| STOPBUTTON|VOLUMELEVER	Only one of the listed values may be chosen at a time. CONSOLE shows all three types of button and a volume lever. SMALLCONSOLE has only stop, play, and volume controls. PLAYBUTTON, PAUSEBUTTON, STOPBUTTON, and VOLUMELEVER show only the items corresponding to their names. If this attribute is not supplied, CONSOLE is the default.
ENDTIME	Measured in minutes and seconds, e.g., 01:30.	Can specifiy where in a sound file you would like playback to end. The default is to play a file through to the end. Not available in the Windows 3.x version.
HEIGHT	Measured in pixels.	HEIGHT should be set to 60 if CONSOLE is used, 15 if SMALLCONSOLE is used. HEIGHT is 22 for buttons and 20 for VOLUMELEVER
LOOP	TRUE|FALSE or an integer	Determines whether or not a sound will repeat continuously. If an integer is given, the sound will repeat for just the specified number of times.

Name	Possible Values	Comments
NAME	Any character string.	This attribute acts as an identifier to group several embedded controls together so they will operate on a single sound file (see text for explanation).
MASTERSOUND	Takes no values.	If present, tells LiveAudio the file is a genuine sound file that should be started or stopped by any controls sharing the same NAME attribute. See text for further explanation.
STARTTIME	Measured in minutes and seconds, e.g., 01:30.	Can specifiy where in a sound file you would like playback to begin. The default is to begin at the beginning! Not available in the Windows 3.x version.
WIDTH	Measured in pixels.	WIDTH should be set to 144 for CONSOLE or SMALL CONSOLE, 37 for buttons used singly. Can vary for VOLUMELEVER used on its own, but 74 is the suggested value.

Note from the chart that HEIGHT and WIDTH attributes are mandatory. They need to be set according to the proper values for CONSOLE, SMALLCONSOLE, VOLUMELEVER, or for the play, pause, or stop buttons.

If you want to embed a sound that will play automatically when the user opens the Web page, use AUTOSTART=TRUE. Unless you want the user to be able to stop or rewind the sound, you can also use the HIDDEN attribute so it leaves no visual trace on the page. If you're embedding a sound that will take a while to download, place the EMBED command that references it at the *end* of a Web page. This ensures a user will have something to look at during the download.

Listing 9-1 shows you examples of LiveAudio EMBED tags on a simple Web page.

Listing 9–1 This code results in the screen shown in Figure 9-3

```
<HTML>
<TITLE>Sound Test Page</TITLE>
<BODY>
Here is a sample 16-bit Mac file. <EMBED SRC="sound.aif" AUTOSTART=FALSE WIDTH=144⇐
HEIGHT=60 VOLUME=100><p>
Here is a sample 16-bit .WAV file. <EMBED SRC="sound.wav" AUTOSTART=FALSE VOLUME=100⇐
WIDTH=144 HEIGHT=60 CONTROLS=CONSOLE><p>
Here is a sample .WAV file usng the small console. <EMBED SRC="sound.wav" AUTOSTART=FALSE⇐
VOLUME=100 WIDTH=144 HEIGHT=15 CONTROLS=SMALLCONSOLE><p>
Here is a sample .WAV file using the pause button. <EMBED SRC="sound.wav" AUTOSTART=FALSE⇐
VOLUME=100 WIDTH=35 HEIGHT=25 CONTROLS=PAUSEBUTTON><p>
Here is a sample .WAV file using the playbutton. <EMBED SRC="sound.wav" AUTOSTART=FALSE⇐
VOLUME=100 WIDTH=35 HEIGHT=25 CONTROLS=PLAYBUTTON><p>
```

continued on next page

continued from previous page

```
Here is a sample 8-bit .WAV file using the small console. <EMBED SRC="8bit.wav"⇐
AUTOSTART=FALSE VOLUME=100 WIDTH=144 HEIGHT=15 CONTROLS="SMALLCONSOLE"><p>
Here is a sample MIDI file. <EMBED SRC="swngcafe.mid" AUTOSTART=FALSE VOLUME=100 WIDTH=144⇐
HEIGHT=60 CONTROLS=CONSOLE><p>
<HR>
You hear CANYON.MID playing in the background. To stop it, you'll have to exit this page or
play one of the other sounds.<EMBED SRC="canyon.mid" AUTOSTART=TRUE HEIGHT=2 WIDTH=0⇐
LOOP=TRUE>
<HR>
</BODY>
</HTML>
```

The page that results from this code is shown in Figure 9-3 in its Windows version and Figure 9-4 in a similar Mac version.

Table 9-2, above, will help you set the appearance of the control panel for each embedded sound.

Unlike any other plug-in of which I am aware, LiveAudio provides a way for multiple embedded controls to act upon a single sound file. That is, it lets you have play and stop buttons at the very top of your Web page that could start playing a sound; you can then also place pause controls, volume controls, or indeed secondary stop/play buttons, anywhere else on the page—ready and able to operate on that same sound.

You might wonder how this can be possible. After all, LiveAudio is like other plug-ins in that it will not display controls anywhere on a Web page unless it "thinks" they are connected to a data file. And, as with other Netscape plug-ins, you cannot embed the same data file in a single Web page more than once. But you get around this with

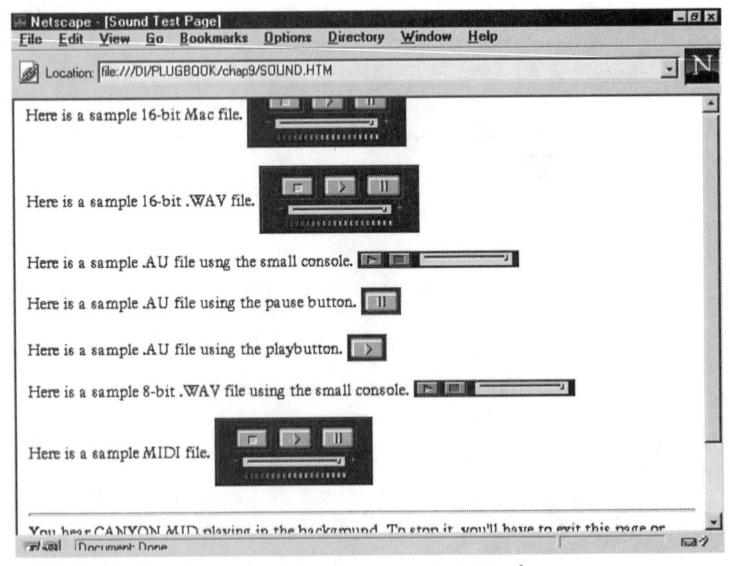

Figure 9-3 The LiveAudio test page in Windows

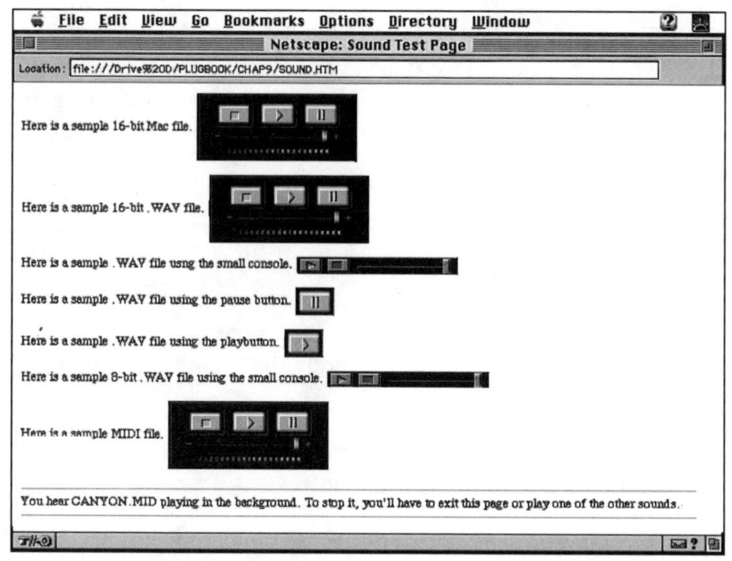

Figure 9–4 The Live Audio test page in Macintosh

LiveAudio by creating *fake* sounds—files that actually contain nothing more than a space or a carriage return. Create these with a text editor, and save them with names such as FAKE1.WAV, FAKE2.WAV, and FAKE3.WAV.

The first time you embed a *real* sound, do so with your choice of controls (whether it's CONSOLE, SMALLCONSOLE, PLAYBUTTON, or whatever). Then append the MASTERSOUND attribute, to tell LiveAudio this is a sound on which you want several different controls to operate, and the NAME attribute to identify it.

For example:

```
<EMBED SRC="any.wav" CONTROLS=CONSOLE WIDTH=144 HEIGHT=60 MASTERSOUND NAME="any">
```

Subsequent controls would be made to appear by embedding tags such as:

```
<EMBED SRC="fake1.wav" CONTROLS=PLAYBUTTON WIDTH=37 HEIGHT=22 WIDTH=37 NAME="any">
```

Each of the subsequent controls, if clicked on by the user, will look for the actual sound file sharing their same NAME value—and will then operate on that sound. Because of the multiple dummy sound files it requires, setting up a MASTERSOUND in this way is not something you'll bother to do often. However, it's nice to know the facility is there.

The control panel for each *genuine* sound file on a Web page has no effect on the playing of any other sounds, except for one exception: Volume control for digital audio under Windows is global. (Incidentally, some sound boards and computers can play MIDI files and digital sound files simultaneously, while others cannot.)

Lesson 4: For Better Performance

As has been mentioned, the big advantage of LiveAudio is its compatibility with the most frequently found sound formats, not its performance. Not that there is anything wrong about the way the plug-in operates—it just takes time to send uncompressed digital audio.

To get good performance from LiveAudio, therefore, you should:

- Keep sampling rates down except when high fidelity is required
- Let the user know in advance how long downloads are likely to take
- Use SoundScript (see below) to defer loading of sounds that may not be required right away

In common with other plug-ins, LiveAudio benefits from Netscape's cache. Therefore, repetitive use of the same sound file will impair performance much less than constantly loading new sounds.

If you wish to embed files using AUTOSTART and make them invisible, place the tags that reference them at the end of a Web page. This ensures that text and graphics will load first, giving users something to read while they are waiting for the sound to load.

Normally all sounds embedded in a Web page download to the client *en masse* whenever that page is opened. Of course, they do not start actually playing unless told to do so by AUTOSTART=TRUE, or until and unless the user clicks on a play button.

Once a Web page and all the sounds it's hosting have downloaded into the browser's cache, any sound may be played instantaneously. As you can imagine, though, a page featuring several different embedded sounds could take quite a while to load—and the user might not realize what was causing the delay.

Fortunately, LiveAudio's designers anticipated this problem. You can use the SoundScript feature to embed a sound in a page, but defer its actual loading until such time as the play button is pressed. To use this feature, create a text file with an editor such as Notepad, WordPad, or BBEdit, and place the following lines in it:

```
<SCRIPT LANGUAGE=SoundScript>
	<OnPlay(http://YourURL/whatever.wav);
</SCRIPT>
```

This file will be a placeholder file that loads the LiveAudio control panel into your Web page where you want it to be, but defers loading the sound until the play button is clicked on. Substitute your actual server name, path, and sound file name for the "YourURL/whatever.wav" in the placeholder file shown; then save the file to disk (and to the server) using an extension it would have if it *were* an actual sound (e.g., .WAV, .MIDI, .AIF, etc.).

In other words, call the placeholder something like STUB.WAV, and then embed it into your Web page. If and when the user clicks on the play button, the script in STUB.WAV will do the job of loading the *real* sound file.

CRESCENDO PLUS

When Netscape already comes with a plug-in that can play MIDI files, is there really a market for another one? Who knows—but LiveUpdate's Crescendo is just that. It will be of interest to those who don't want to upgrade from Netscape 2.x, and it is positioned as being a better choice for MIDI aficionados.

Developed with the assistance of Cakewalk, a well-known author of MIDI software, Crescendo Plus purports to do a superior job of mapping MIDI instruments. It also employs streaming so that extended-length MIDI files can begin playing before they are downloaded fully. Because Crescendo Plus also works with Internet Explorer, you can create pages that work almost identically whether viewed by Netscape or by the Microsoft browser.

Lesson 1: Installation

Crescendo is available in Windows 3.x, Windows 95, and Macintosh versions. To install one of them, download the plug-in from *http://www.liveupdate.com,* or check Appendix A, which lists the plug-ins included on your CD-ROM. Click on the 32-bit installer file if you have Windows 95, the 16-bit version file if you have Windows 3.x. Mac users click on the Crescendo Installer icon.

Each installer creates a test page, CRESTEST.HTM, and a source MIDI file, CRESTEST.MID. It also creates the Crescendo plug-in, NPMIDI32.DLL (for Windows 95 and NT) or NPMIDI16.DLL (for Windows 3.x). If you have a Mac, the plug-in is a file called Crescendo!. Manually drag whichever one of these applies to you into your Netscape/Plug-ins folder and start Netscape.

Crescendo Plus wants control over the four MIME types shown in Table 9-3. Two of them, however, audio/x-midi and audio/midi, are already assigned to LiveAudio. You can resolve this conflict on a Macintosh by opening the Options/General Preferences/Helpers tab. Select these two MIME types and change the association listed from LiveAudio to Crescendo Plus. On a Windows computer, you may need to disable LiveAudio by removing NPAUDIO.DLL from the Netscape plug-ins folder (see Chapter 7 for more information about adding and removing plug-ins).

NOTE: If you adjust Netscape's MIME types for this or any other reason, you may need not only to exit and restart the program, but also to clear the memory and disk caches. Otherwise old settings may tend to linger...

Table 9-3 MIME types handled by Crescendo Plus

MIME Type/Subtype	Extension (suffix)
audio/x-mid	midi, mid
application/x-midi	midi, mid
Audio/x-midi	midi, mid
Audio/midi	midi, mid

Lesson 2: Creating Content

Creating original MIDI files means having your own MIDI keyboard, connected to your computer and MIDI sequencer software—which assigns voices to the different musical lines you lay down. If you're an aspiring composer, you already know this. Most of the rest of us will probably be using MIDI files purchased on a CD-ROM or downloaded from somewhere on the Net.

Fortunately, there is a vast number of Web sites devoting themselves to MIDI files. Many freely offer their files for your reuse. You can find these sites just by putting the phrase "MIDI" into any of the popular Internet search engines. Figure 9-5 shows a typical site.

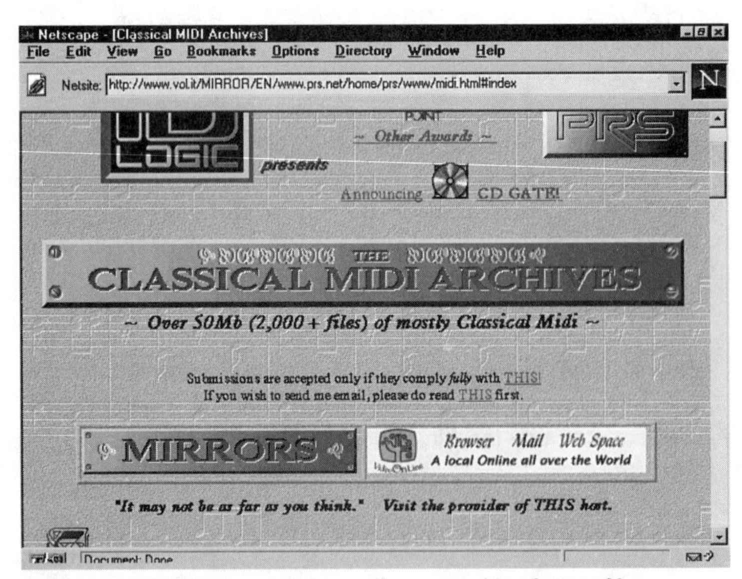

Figure 9–5 Many Web sites offer a wealth of MIDI files

Lesson 3: Embedding Data in Your Own Web Page

To embed a MIDI file in a Web page, insert the tag <EMBED SRC="url">, where *url* is the file name. As usual in HTML syntax, you must supply a file name and extension, also including a full path if the sound file is not in the same subdirectory as the Web page itself.

Attributes for the Crescendo Plus <EMBED> tag are summarized in Table 9-4. The AUTOSTART attribute, with values of TRUE or FALSE, specifies whether or not the sound file will play automatically when the Web page is opened. The LOOP attribute, again with values of TRUE or FALSE, determines whether or not the file will be repeated continuously. The WIDTH and HEIGHT attributes determine what type of control panel, if any, the user will see.

Table 9-4 Crescendo Plus <EMBED> attributes

Name	Possible Values	Comments
AUTOSTART	TRUE|FALSE	Governs whether a MIDI file will play automatically when a page is loaded.
BGCOLOR	#RRGGBB	This attribute can set the background color of Cresendo Plus' control panel to that of your choice. RGB values are notated using the same codes as for Netscape itself.
DELAY	Measured in seconds.	The DELAY attribute can be used to skip the first few seconds of a piece. Enter the number of seconds you want skipped.
HEIGHT	Measured in pixels.	A HEIGHT value of 55, in conjunction with a WIDTH value of 200, shows Crescendo's VCR-like control panel. A height of 50, in conjunction with a width of 46, shows the LiveUpdate logo and link only. A height of 18, in conjunction with a width of 82, shows the Crescendo logo and link. A height of 16 and width of 16 shows only a note graphic.
LOOP	TRUE|FALSE	If the LOOP=TRUE attribute is set, a MIDI file will loop continuously.
TXTCOLOR	#RRGGBB	This attribute can set the text color of Cresendo Plus' control panel to that of your choice. RGB values are notated using the same codes as for Netscape itself.
WIDTH	Measured in pixels.	A WIDTH value of 200, along with a HEIGHT value of 55, shows Crescendo's VCR-like control panel. A width of 46, along with a height of 50, shows the LiveUpdate logo and link only. A width of 82 and height of 18 shows the Crescendo logo and link. A width of 16 and height of 16 shows only a note graphic. For an "invisible" MIDI file, use HIDDEN and AUTOSTART=TRUE.

Listing 9-2 shows you examples of Crescendo Plus <EMBED> tags in the context of a Web page. The page that results from this code is shown in Figure 9-6 in its Windows version. You can rely on excellent uniformity of appearance when using Crescendo Plus to develop Web pages, regardless of platform.

Figure 9–6 Crescendo Plus on Windows, showing the pop-up menu

Listing 9-2 Crescendo Plus <EMBED> tags in a Web page

```
<HTML>
<Head>
<TITLE>MIDI Plugin Tester 2 (Multiple Embedded Files)</TITLE>
</Head>
<BODY BGCOLOR = "#FFFFFF" TEXT = "#000000" LINK = "#0000FF" VLINK =
"#9A0089">
<center>
<font color="red">
<H1>
<HR SIZE=5 WIDTH=88% NOSHADE>
MIDI Plugin Tester 2
<HR SIZE=5 WIDTH=88% NOSHADE>
</H1>
</font>
<h2>3 MIDI Files Embedded in 1 Page</h2>
<p>Bach's Invention #1 (3,864 bytes)<BR>
<EMBED SRC="INVEN1.MID" WIDTH=200 HEIGHT=80 TITLE="Bach's Invention 1">
<P>Now Thank We All Our God (2,256 bytes)<BR>
<EMBED SRC="THANK.MID" WIDTH=200 HEIGHT=80 TITLE="Now Thank We All Our God">
<P>Astley's Hornpipe (5,137 bytes)<BR>
<EMBED SRC="ASTLEY.MID WIDTH=200 HEIGHT=80 TITLE="Astley's Hornpipe">
<center><HR>
<font color="red">Last Update: April 5, 1996</font>
</center>
</body>
</HTML>
```

Unfortunately the differences in desired WIDTH and HEIGHT values mean that a page developed for LiveAudio will look slightly odd for Crescendo Plus, and vice versa. There is no ideal answer to this problem. However, it is a good idea to make a note somewhere on your Web page to the effect that "MIDI playback will be enhanced via Crescendo Plus." Provide a link to LiveUpdate's site at *http://www.liveupdate.com/crescendo.html* so that those currently using LiveAudio can, if they wish, download Crescendo Plus and make the switch.

If visitors to your Web site are using Netscape 2.x, which did not come with LiveAudio, you can arrange for them to be taken to LiveUpdate's Web site automatically when the MIDI MIME types is encountered. Use EMBED SRC's PLUGINSPAGE attribute, as follows:

```
EMBED SRC="whatever.mid" HEIGHT=55 WIDTH=200
PLUGINSPAGE="http://www.liveupdate.com/crescendo.html"
```

Users can also go to LiveUpdate's Web page automatically by clicking on the Crescendo control panel, if visible.

ECHOSPEECH

The Echospeech plug-in uses a codec (compression-decompression algorithm) originally developed for adding speech into software such as Reader Rabbit. Although lacking in flexibility, it has a high degree of simplicity in its favor.

As its name implies, Echospeech is intended for adding speech to your Web pages. The resulting files are highly compressed—hence playable in real time—yet maintain good clarity.

Lesson 1: Installation

Echospeech is available for either Windows 3.x or Windows 95/NT; there are currently no Macintosh or UNIX versions. To install it in your copy of Netscape, visit Echo Speech Corporation's Web page at *http://www.echospeech.com/plugin2.htm,* or consult Appendix A for a guide to the plug-ins contained on your CD-ROM.

Copy the 16-bit installer (if you have Windows 3.x) or 32-bit installer (if you have Windows 95 or NT) to a temporary subdirectory on your hard drive and then run the executable. Either NPECHO16.DLL or NPECHO32.DLL will be created. Copy this file to the PLUGINS folder in your Netscape subdirectory, and then exit and restart Netscape if necessary.

Echospeech is now active, as you can confirm by selecting About Plug-ins from the Help menu. As you will see, a new MIME type/subtype and suffix have been added to those Netscape can handle. The type/subtype are audio/echospeech, and the suffix, or extension, is .ES.

Because neither this suffix nor this MIME type is used by any other plug-in, there is no need to make any manual adjustments. However, if you want to place pages with .ES titles on a Web server, you will need to let your service provider know so it can make the right association in its file of MIME types. Another reason to contact those running your server is that Echo Speech Corporation requires a $99 per-server license fee for the use of Echospeech files. If, after your testing, you want to keep using the plug-in for your Web pages, somebody will need to pay up!

Lesson 2: Creating Original Content

In order to create .ES files, you need the Echospeech voice coder, available at the company's Web site. Download the file EKOCODER.EXE to a temporary subdirectory on your hard drive, then execute it to uncompress files to a subdirectory of your choice. Several sample files, including an HTML page, are included.

The Echospeech Voice Coder (ESCODER.EXE) is designed to accept .WAV voice files sampled in 16-bit mono only, at a rate of 11KHz. If you record other types of .WAV files, they probably will not convert. You can create files of this type using a microphone and the Sound Recorder program provided with Windows.

Once you are happy with the quality, run the Echospeech Voice Coder and use its buttons to select a source .WAV file and output .ES file (see Figure 9-7). The resulting .ES files are less than 1/18th the size of the original .WAVs.

Lesson 3: Embedding Data in Your Own Web Pages

Like other plug-ins, Echospeech relies upon the <EMBED SRC> tag for embedding sounds. To insert a sound in your Web page, simply use the tag <EMBED SRC="anyfile.es">, where *anyfile* is the prefix of the sound file you have chosen. When the Web page is loaded into a user's copy of Netscape, the sound will play automatically.

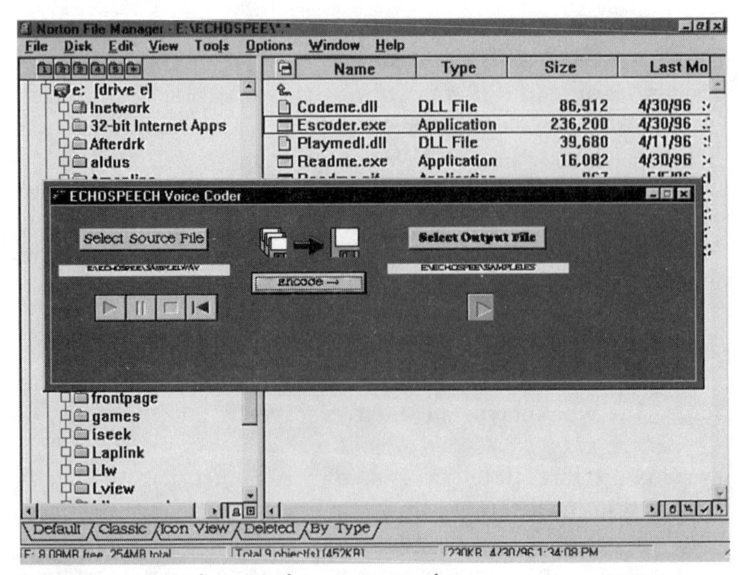

Figure 9-7 Echospeech's Voice Coder compresses 11KHz .WAV file by more than 18:1

Since there is no way to change this behavior, you should stick to one voice file per page. Use the narrations you record as introductions that will lead the user into reading the rest of the page.

Of course, the HEIGHT and WIDTH attributes *are* required, as with any other plug-in. If you want to have the Echospeech logo displayed, you should set WIDTH=120 and HEIGHT=40 to support the plug-in's integral bitmap size. If you would rather have your narration play invisibly—which is probably going to be more often the case—use the HIDDEN attribute. As mentioned previously in this chapter, Netscape behaves unpredictably when height and width are both set to 0, or when one of them is set to 1.

If Echospeech came with every copy of Netscape, it might be an ideal, unobtrusive way of adding spoken introductions to every Web page. However, you have to face the fact that most users will not have a copy. Therefore, their copies of Netscape will complain about not being able to handle the audio/echospeech MIME type. Help users get the Echospeech plug-in by using the PLUGINSPAGE attribute. All you need do is end the first <EMBED SRC> tag that invokes an Echospeech file with the attribute PLUGINSPAGE="http://echospeech.com/plugin2.htm". This will open a new browser window that takes the user to Echo Speech Corporation's Web site.

RAPID TRANSIT

The majority of audio plug-ins are optimized for voice—which is inherently more compressible than music because of its wider frequency and dynamic range. However, Fastman Incorporated has created Rapid Transit, a plug-in that lets Netscape play back high-quality music.

The Rapid Transit encoder accepts CD-quality .WAV files (16-bit, 44KHz sampling rate) and compresses them down to anywhere from 1/10 to 1/70th their original size. Naturally, the less the compression, the greater the quality. The system is ideal for allowing visitors to a Web page to sample a variety of musical tracks.

Lesson 1: Installation

Rapid Transit is available for both Windows 95 and Macintosh. To install it in your copy of Netscape, visit Fastman Corporation's Web page at *http://fastman.com/rapidtransit* (or see Appendix 1 for a list of plug-ins included with this book).

If you're using Windows, run the program RTPLUG.EXE. The installer will prompt you to locate the copy of Netscape you wish to install Rapid Transit into, asking you to click on the actual NETSCAPE.EXE to be sure. (This is a good feature, since some plug-ins install automatically into the "wrong" copy of Netscape when you have more than one on your hard drive.) Then the installer creates a FASTMAN folder within your NETSCAPE\PLUGINS subdirectory and copies some Rapid Transit program files into the new folder. It also copies the plug-in, NPFST32.DLL, into the NETSCAPE\PLUGINS subdirectory.

If you're using Macintosh, click on the Macintosh installer application. This behaves similarly, creating a Fastman folder within your Netscape Plug-ins folder, and also copying a file called FastMan Plug-in into the latter.

Exit and restart Netscape, and you'll see that a new MIME type/subtype has been added, namely application/fastman, associated with the suffix lcc. There is no need to make any adjustments via your Helpers tab. However, if you want to place pages with .LCC files on a Web server, you will need to let your service provider know so it can make the right association in its file of MIME types.

Lesson 2: Creating Original Content

In order to create .LCC files, you'll need the separately available encoder, RAPIDTR.EXE. You can obtain this from Fastman Corporation's Web page. Copy all the files to a subdirectory called RAPID in the root directory of your hard drive (if you place it in another subdirectory, it will *not* work properly).

Figure 9-8 shows the encoder program's menus. These permit selecting a source file in .WAV format and adjusting the compression ratio from 1:1 all the way up to approximately 80:1. While a file is being converted—which can be a lengthy process—graphs illustrate the program's progress. When the program has finished operating, it creates two files in the same subdirectory as the original .WAV file. One is the .LCC file, usually dramatically smaller in size, while the other is an .LCR file. The latter is almost the same size as the original .WAV file; it has been compressed and then decompressed to let you preview the audio quality that Rapid Transit will deliver.

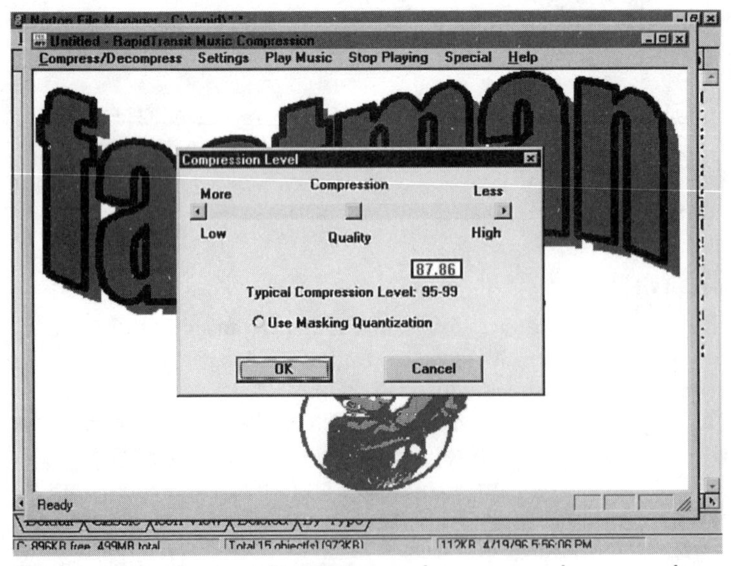

Figure 9-8 The Rapid Transit encoder program lets you adjust the amount of compression

Lesson 3: Inserting Data in Your Own Web Pages

Unlike most other plug-ins, Rapid Transit does not use the <EMBED SRC> tag. Instead, you insert links to .LCC files in your Web page just as you would insert links to other pages. In other words, to provide the user access to a file, you would place instructions like the following in your HTML code:

```
Click <a href="bach.lcc">here</a> to hear a Bach Allegro.
```

If the user clicks on that link, Rapid Transit takes over the screen, displaying a bar graph as it progresses through decompressing the audio information (Figure 9-9). Once done, it shows a Rapid Transit logo, on which the user needs to click (right-click, in the case of Windows) to invoke a pop-up menu (Figure 9-10). Then, the music can be played.

Rapid Transit's design actually provides you with quite a bit of flexibility in creating your Web pages. After all, you can insert links to .LCC files anywhere you like, and associate graphics with them just as you do with any other links. The one drawback is the plug-in's taking over the screen as it decompresses a file. You can alleviate this problem using the time-honored technique of asking Netscape to open a new window as it opens a new link. Do this with code such as:

```
Click <a href="bach.lcc" target="_blank">here</a> to hear a Bach Allegro.
```

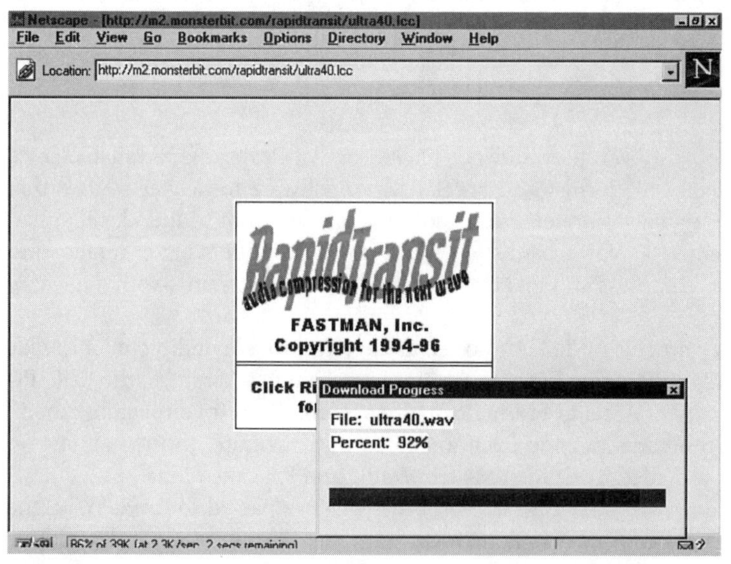

Figure 9-9 Rapid Transit takes over the screen to display its progress at downloading a file

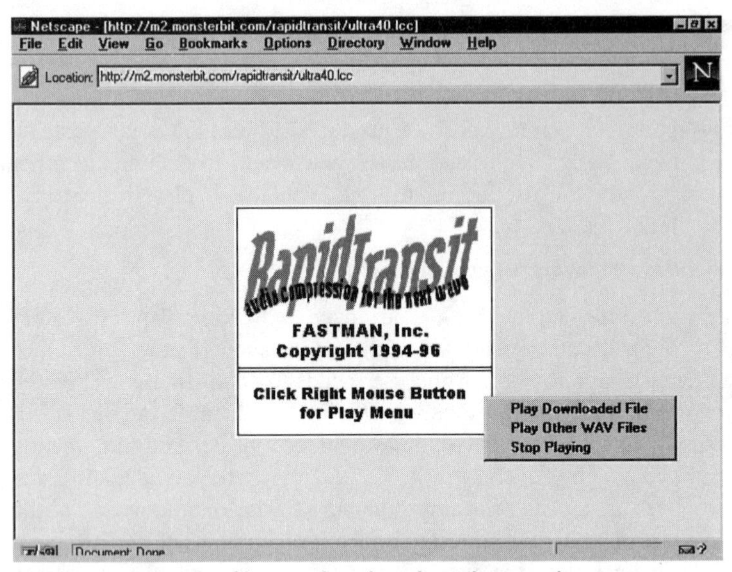

Figure 9–10 The file can then be played using this pop-up menu

Now, your main page can be viewed while the audio file decompresses, and the user need not use the Go Back command to return to it.

REALAUDIO

It would be difficult to be a Web user and not have heard of RealAudio. Available since 1995, it uses a proprietary file format and special server software to deliver sounds that play almost instantly. Originally, it offered AM-radio-like quality from sound files that had taken some time to compress. Now, thanks to several updates, it offers better quality and server software that can compress and make available a live audio stream—with a delay of just five seconds!

A list of companies now using RealAudio technology to provide audio content reads like a Who's Who: ABC, PBS, the CBC, Entertainment Tonight, Virgin Radio UK, PC Week Radio, and a variety of AM and FM radio stations nationwide. If you search Yahoo!, you'll find RealAudio programs ranging from a George Burns tribute, to instructions on how to cook pancakes provided by Golden Malted Waffle and Pancake Flour.

Most RealAudio content is served up as .RAM files that are passed to RAPLAYER, the company's helper application. This program works with any Web browser and performs well. However, with the RealAudio plug-in for Netscape you can listen to or create sounds that are embedded within your Web pages. It makes RealAudio just that much more convenient and accessible.

Lesson 1: Installation

RealAudio is available for Macintosh, Windows 3.x, Windows 95, and Windows NT (as well as for many UNIX variants). To install the RealAudio plug-in, you will need to visit the company's Web site at *http://www.realaudio.com* (or consult Appendix A for CD-ROM details). The RA16_20.EXE file is the installer for Windows 3.x, RA32_20.EXE is for Windows 95 and NT. If you have a Mac, Real Audio Installer is the file you're looking for. Copy your choice of installer to your hard drive, then run it.

If you have Windows 95 or Windows NT, the installer copies NPRA32.DLL to your NETSCAPE\PLUGINS subdirectory, also installing the RealAudio helper application in a subdirectory of your choice. The process is identical for Windows 3.x except that the plug-in is named NPRA16.DLL. On the Macintosh, the procedure is logically the same: A RealAudio Plugin file is placed in the Netscape Plug-ins folder, the RealAudio helper application is placed in a folder of its own, and certain software is also placed in your System folder.

You can confirm that RealAudio has installed by running Netscape (exit and restart if necessary) and using the About Plug-ins menu. You will see that RealAudio has added the following MIME type and file suffix to the list given:

```
MIME Type:  audio/x-pn-realaudio-plugin
Suffixes: rpm
```

Open the General Preferences/Helpers tab and you will see that RealAudio also governs the MIME type audio/x-pn-realaudio, with suffixes ra and ram. This MIME type is associated with the RAPLAYER helper application you also just installed. The obvious (and correct) implication is that RealAudio will open .RA and .RAM files with the helper application, sending only .RPM files to the plug-in. In other words, installing the plug-in doesn't mean that you have seen the last of the helper application.

Real-time delivery of RealAudio files requires that a Web server be running RealAudio Server software, which varies in price according to the number of simultaneous users envisioned. If the server software is not present, RealAudio files must be downloaded to a user's machine in their entirety before they will play. This is not just a ruse by Progressive Networks, Inc. to sell server software—it is because the RealAudio Server and RealAudio Player, by design, communicate more intimately than would be possible using ordinary Internet standards. This improves the performance and controllability of RealAudio files.

The .RAM and .RPM files referenced in Web pages using RealAudio are not sound files themselves. They are "metafiles," small text files that reference one or more .RA files on the server (see Figure 9-11). You'll read more about the implications of this below. Among other things, it means that RealAudio has not adopted a new file format for use with plug-ins, only a slightly modified way of accessing the sound files that are already on a server.

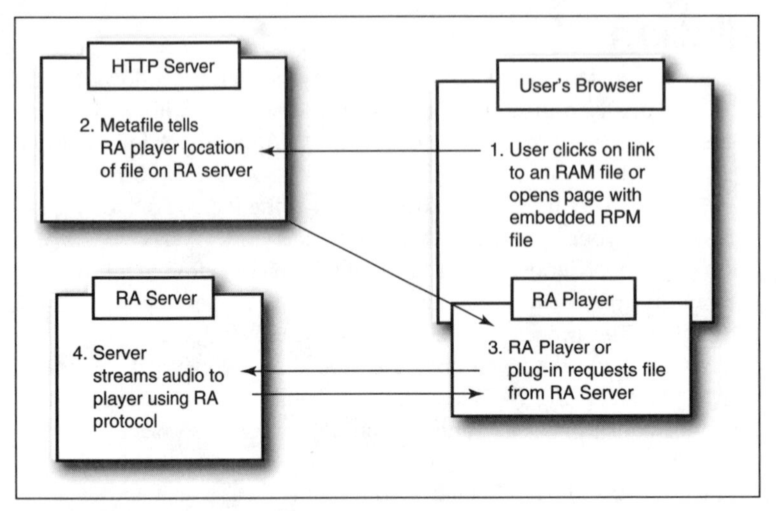

Figure 9–11 RealAudio relies on intermediate "metafiles" to serve up audio files quickly

In any case, a server that is running RealAudio Server software already has the audio/x-pn-realaudio MIME type and ram suffix registered in its configuration files. However, in order to place content on that server that can be accessed by the Real Audio plug-in, you need to ask the administrators to add the rpm suffix and audio/x-pn-realaudio-plugin MIME type as well.

Lesson 2: Creating Original Content

To create sound files for use with RealAudio, you need the RealAudio Encoder, available from the RealAudio Web site. Stand-alone programs are available for Windows 95/NT and for the Macintosh; there is also a RealAudio Encoder Xtra for Macintosh, which allows users of Macromedia's SoundEdit 16 to save files directly in RealAudio format. (Encoding sound in real time, as in live radio broadcasts, requires special hardware and software, and is beyond the scope of this book.)

The encoder requires 16-bit sound files, and a 22KHz sampling rate is suggested for best results. Files sampled at 11KHz and 8KHz are also accepted if you insist. Progressive Networks offers a list of ways to achieve top quality (available at *http://www.realaudio.com/help/content/audiohints.html*) that makes useful reading no matter what company's encoder you're planning to use.

Files may be saved in a form optimized for RealAudio's 14.4Kbps-compatible algorithm, or the newer RealAudio 28.8 format. Source files sampled at 22KHz are reduced from a size of 2.6MB per minute, to 60K or 113K per minute respectively.

Sound files for use with the RealAudio plug-in are no different from those used with the helper application. For technical reasons, each requires a separate metafile, however. The .RAM metafiles are for the helper application, while the .RPM files are for the plug-in.

Each contains a pointer to the .RA file being referenced, in the format pnm://hostname/path. For example, a reference might be

```
pnm://www.realaudio.com/welcome.ra
```

When you have created .RA files, plus .RAM or .RPM metafiles that will reference them, you FTP them to a Web server in the usual fashion. If you are eager to work with RealAudio, yet your service provider does not own the RealAudio server software and has no intention of purchasing it, you still have a couple of options. One is to create hyperlinks to someone else's RealAudio server. Their server holds the .RAM, .RPM, and .RA files and handles the file service. In this case, you will still need to have *your* Web server configured to recognize the .RAM MIME type. Otherwise, the browsers of visitors to your Web site will interpret audio files as unrecognizable text.

Lesson 3: Embedding Data in Your Own Web Pages

RealAudio sound files are traditionally passed to the RAPLAYER helper application by creating a link such as:

```
<A HREF="http://www.realaudio.com/welcome.ram">Click here to hear some words of⇐
welcome.</a>
```

When clicked on, this link uses RAPLAYER to play the sound file WELCOME.RAM (or whatever sound the metafile WELCOME.RAM actually referenced).

To send a sound file to the RealAudio plug-in instead, you use syntax such as:

```
<EMBED SRC="http://www.realaudio.com/welcome.rpm" WIDTH=300 HEIGHT=134>
```

Again, the file pointed to by WELCOME.RPM could be the same as was pointed to by WELCOME.RAM, or it could be something different. You have to do the file name housekeeping. Each <EMBED SRC> tag used in a Web page must have a unique .RPM source; otherwise the second one to appear will be ignored. Nonetheless you can easily embed the same sound file multiple times. Just create multiple metafiles that all point to a single .RA file, then reference each metafile separately.

It is extremely simple to create Web pages that support both the helper application and the plug-in. Simply use Netscape's <NOEMBED> tag as follows:

```
<EMBED SRC="test.rpm" WIDTH=300 HEIGHT=134>
<NOEMBED<A HREF="test.ram">Click here to hear a test sound.</a></NOEMBED>
```

Old browsers would ignore the first line, while Netscape would ignore the second line. Table 9-5 shows the <EMBED> attributes used by RealAudio, while Table 9-6 explains the various possible values of the CONTROLS attribute.

Table 9–5 <EMBED> attributes for RealAudio

Name	Possible Values	Comments
AUTOSTART	TRUE|FALSE	Adding an AUTOSTART=TRUE tag causes a sound to begin playing automatically when the page is visited. Confine this to a single sound per page.
CONSOLE	"_master" or any other character string	Assigning an identical console attribute (character string) to more than one sound links their controls so that one acts upon the other. Specifiying CONSOLE="_master" links the control panel of a sound with this attribute to all others on a page.
CONTROLS	ALL|CONTROLPANEL| INFOVOLUMEPANEL| INFOPANEL|STATUSBAR| PLAYBUTTON|STOPBUTTON| VOLUMESLIDER|POSITIONSLIDER| POSITIONFIELD|STATUSFIELD	Defaults to ALL if no view is specified. See Table 9-6 for descriptions and required HEIGHT/WIDTH settings.
HEIGHT	Measured in pixels or as a percentage of the browser window (as in HEIGHT=75%).	See Table 9-6 for suggested values.
WIDTH	Measured in pixels or as a percentage of the browser window (as in WIDTH=75%).	See Table 9-6 for suggested values.

Table 9–6 The settings for RealAudio's CONTROLS attribute

Value	Results	Required WIDTH/HEIGHT
ALL	Embeds everything including a control panel, information panel, volume control, and status bar. This is the default view.	330/134 (i.e., must use WIDTH=300 and HEIGHT=134 in your tag)
CONTROLPANEL	Embeds just a play/pause button, a stop button, and a position slider.	350/40
INFOVOLUMEPANEL	Embeds just the area showing a sound's title, author, and copyright with a volume slider on the right-hand side.	350/80
INFOPANEL	Embeds the title, author, and copyright information without the volume slider.	320/80

Value	Results	Required WIDTH/HEIGHT
STATUSBAR	Embeds a status bar that shows information about audio clip length and current progress, but cannot initiate playback by itself.	350/22
PLAYBUTTON	Embeds only the play/pause button for a sound.	40/20
STOPBUTTON	Embeds the stop button only.	20/20
VOLUMESLIDER	Embeds the vertically oriented volume slider only.	Either an arbitrary pixel value or a percentage of the overall browser window size
POSITIONSLIDER	Embeds a horizontal position slider only.	Either an arbitrary pixel value or a percentage of the overall browser window size
POSITIONFIELD	Embeds only time position and length information about a sound.	100/25
STATUSFIELD	Embeds only the part of the status bar that displays message	350/25

Figure 9-12 shows a sound embedded using Real Audio's default view, and then using the Play Button and Control Panel views. Listing 9-3 shows the HTML code that produced the page.

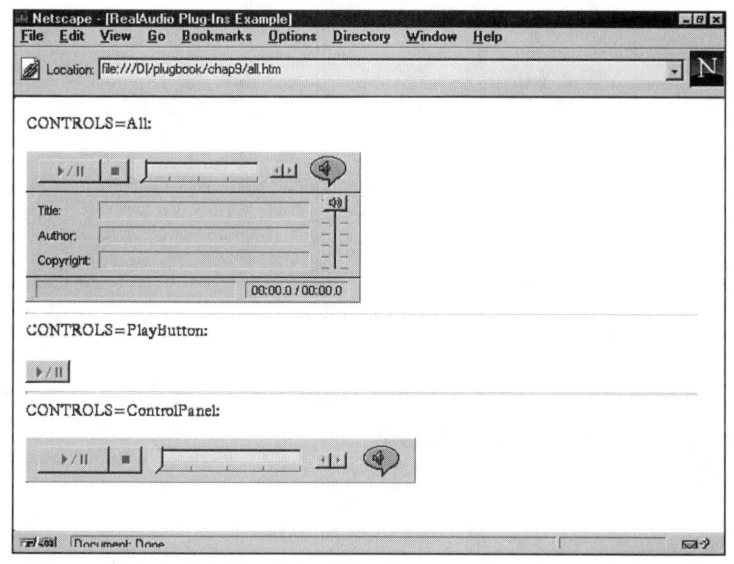

Figure 9–12 RealAudio's default view, plus play and control panel views

Listing 9-3 Code demonstrating RealAudio's default view, plus play and control panel views

```
<html>
<head>
<title>
RealAudio Plug-Ins Example
</title>
</head>
CONTROLS=All:<p>
<EMBED SRC="test.rpm" WIDTH=300 HEIGHT=134>
<HR>
CONTROLS=PlayButton:<p>
<EMBED SRC="test1.rpm" WIDTH=40 HEIGHT=20 CONTROLS=PlayButton>
<HR>
CONTROLS=ControlPanel:<p>
<EMBED SRC="test2.rpm" WIDTH=350 HEIGHT=40 CONTROLS=ControlPanel>
</body>
</html>
```

Figure 9-13 shows how you can link several control panels together to operate on a single sound file. Listing 9-4, which uses the CONSOLE attribute, shows the HTML code that produced it.

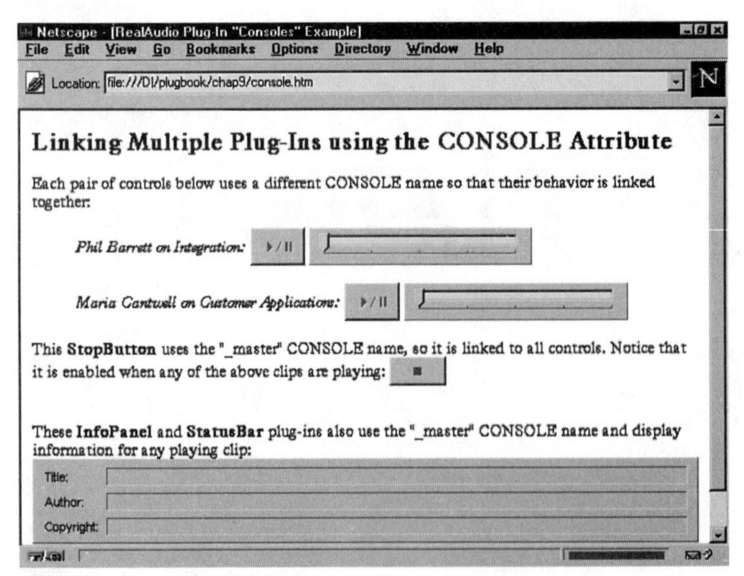

Figure 9-13 By using the CONSOLE attribute, you can link several control panels together

Listing 9-4 This code uses RealAudio's CONSOLE attribute

```
<html>
<head>
<title>
RealAudio Plug-In "Consoles" Example
</title>
</head>

<body background="http://www.realaudio.com/pics/ihn_back.gif">
<H2>Linking Multiple Plug-Ins using the <FONT COLOR=C00000>CONSOLE</FONT> Attribute</H2>
Each pair of controls below uses a different CONSOLE name so that their behavior is linked⇐
together:
<BLOCKQUOTE>
<I>Phil Barrett on Integration: </I>
<EMBED SRC="console2.rpm" WIDTH=50 HEIGHT=33 CONTROLS="PlayButton" CONSOLE=Clip2⇐
ALIGN=absMiddle>
<EMBED SRC="empty2.rpm" WIDTH=200 HEIGHT=33 CONTROLS="PositionSlider" CONSOLE=Clip2⇐
ALIGN=absMiddle>
<P>
<I>Maria Cantwell on Customer Applications: </I>
<EMBED SRC="console3.rpm" WIDTH=50 HEIGHT=33 CONTROLS="PlayButton" CONSOLE=Clip3⇐
ALIGN=absMiddle>
<EMBED SRC="empty3.rpm" WIDTH=200 HEIGHT=33 CONTROLS="PositionSlider" CONSOLE=Clip3⇐
ALIGN=absMiddle>
</BLOCKQUOTE>
This <B>StopButton</B> uses the "_master" CONSOLE name, so it is linked to all controls.
Notice that it is enabled when any of the above clips are playing: <EMBED SRC="empty4.rpm"⇐
WIDTH=50 HEIGHT=25 CONTROLS="StopButton" CONSOLE="_master" ALIGN=absMiddle>
<BR clear=all>
<P>
These <B>InfoPanel</B> and <B>StatusBar</B> plug-ins also use the "_master" CONSOLE name⇐
and display information for any playing clip:
<EMBED SRC="empty5.rpm" WIDTH=100% HEIGHT=75 CONTROLS="InfoPanel" CONSOLE="_master"⇐
ALIGN=LEFT>
<BR CLEAR=ALL>
<EMBED SRC="empty6.rpm" WIDTH=100% HEIGHT=23 CONTROLS="StatusBar" CONSOLE="_master"⇐
ALIGN=LEFT>
</body>
</html>
```

Remember that if you try to experiment with these commands, and any instance of the RealAudio plug-in does not find a unique .RPM file on disk, it will refuse to load—leaving a blank area on-screen. The answer to this problem, assuming you have not already used the encoder to create .RA files that .RPM files can point to, is to save dummy .RPM files that contain a blank line. You can do this with a text editor or, if you're running Windows, by exiting to a DOS prompt and using the COPY CON ????????.rpm command. Just substitute any file prefix for the question marks, type a couple of spaces to give the file some content, and then press CTRL-Z to write the file.

TALKER

Macintosh computers have voice synthesis as a standard feature—one you can test by simply entering text into the Simple Text application and then pressing COMMAND-H. With the Talker plug-in from MVP Solutions, you can tap into Apple's PlainTalk speech synthesis via your Web pages.

In addition to being enjoyable, Talker is extremely economical on network bandwidth. The performance is so speedy that a host Macintosh usually starts speaking text embedded in a Web page before more than a few sentences have been displayed on screen. Obviously, Talker can also be of great use to visually impaired Web users.

Lesson 1: Installing the Plug-In

To install MVP's Talker plug-in, you need a Macintosh, and will get the best results if you have a 68030 machine or newer. You also need Apple's PlainTalk, which comes with recent versions of the System and is also available from the company's FTP site. PowerMacs offer the widest variety of possible reading voices, including "Victoria," "Bruce," and "Agnes" (the highest-quality and most natural-sounding).

Visit the MVP Solutions Web site at *http://www.mvpsolutions.com/PlugInSite/Talker.html* or check Appendix A for details about your CD-ROM. The Talker installer copies the Talker plug-in and some documentation to a Talker folder on your hard drive.

Once the installer has run, copy the Talker plug-in file to the Plug-ins folder within your Netscape folder. Then exit and restart Netscape, if it was previously running. You can now confirm that the Talker plug-in has been installed by selecting About Plug-ins from the Apple menu.

You'll see that a new MIME type/subtype has been installed, text/x-speech, with the suffix talk. As usual for a new plug-in, your service provider will need this information to add the MIME type before you can make .TALK files available to other users. In the meantime, you can experiment by testing .TALK files locally and by listening to those others have created. A list of links to Talker-enabled Web pages is available at the MVP Solutions Web site.

Talker aficionado Colleen Dick offers the Mac doing a Mae West imitation at *http://www.orst.edu/~dickt/aoltalk/sexy.talk* and the "Family Playroom" at *http://www.orst.edu/~dickt/playroom/playroom.html*. The latter site illustrates how a Macintosh could be made to read bedtime stories to your children. Another site at *http://cac.psu.edu/~rmd103/macspeech.html* gives general background in Macintosh speech technology (Figure 9-14).

Lesson 2: Creating Content

The Talker plug-in does not simply read out any and all Web page text as it appears on the screen. (If you are visually impaired and need that kind of functionality, you may want to try the Mac version of NCSA Mosaic, which is the only browser that does this—at least until the Netscape folks get around to adding the function.)

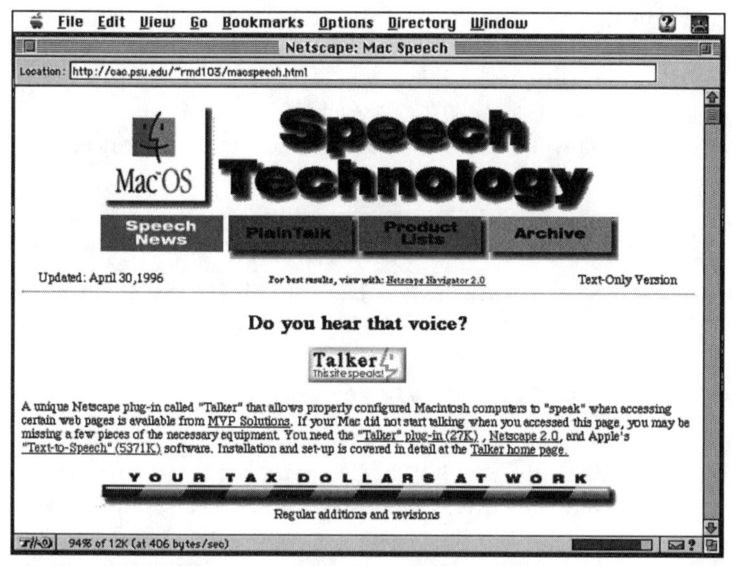

Figure 9–14 This Web site, devoted to Macintosh speech technology, uses Talker

Instead, it reads a separate .TALK file that you embed into your Web page. The contents of this file begin as simple ASCII text, so it's easy to paste all the text on your Web page into it if that's what you want to do. More likely, you'll be using the .TALK file to read a spoken introduction welcoming the user.

Like an HTML file, a .TALK file may be enhanced with embedded commands—they begin and end with double brackets in this case instead of less-than and greater-than signs—to change parameters. You can control many things about the way the text is read, including pitch, rate, emphasis, and which artificial voice is used.

For example, the following commands at the beginning of a .TALK file would cause it to be read in the "Kathy" voice if that is installed and the "Ralph" voice if it is not:

```
[[cmnt talkervoice=Kathy]]
[[cmnt talkervoice=Ralph]]
```

Multiple commands can appear between a set of brackets as long as they are separated by semicolons. For example:

```
[[pmod+1;pbas+1]]Hello![[pmod-1;pbase-1]]This web page can talk.
```

The pmod and pbase commands at the beginning of the above line are direct commands to the PlainTalk synthesizer that set a baseline pitch for the speech and proceed to vary it. Other possible commands adjust volume of the speech, how fast words are spoken, whether numbers are read as a whole or spelled out, and so on. Specialists can also use the [[input PHON]] command to input phonemic symbols directly to make the speech sound more natural.

For more information on these commands, you can refer to the Sound volume of Apple's *Inside Macintosh* manuals. There is also an article on using synthesized speech by Colleen Dick of Orgeon State University. You can link to it via MVP Solutions' pages or go there directly at *http://users.aol.com/AKAMomof4/HCCSpeech.html.*

Chances are, however, that you will find that simple ASCII text meets your needs well enough.

Lesson 3: Embedding Your Speech Files

To embed a .TALK file in a Web page, you use the now-familiar EMBED SRC command as follows:

```
<EMBED SRC="anyfile.talk" HIDDEN
PLUGINSPAGE="http://www.mvpsolutions.com/PlugInSite/Talker.html">
```

The Talker plug-in does not have an icon of its own, nor does it have any user controls. Therefore, there is no reason to make it visible. Files are read as soon as a given Web page is opened; therefore, you should only embed one at a time. Because Talker's performance is so good, it does not matter where in the page the EMBED SRC line falls: Synthesized speech will not cause any delay in loading your page no matter what.

Notice the use of the PLUGINSPAGE attribute. This ensures that Netscape will take a user who does not yet have Talker to the MVP Solutions Web site instead of to Netscape Communications' generic lists of plug-ins.

Unusually, MVP Solutions also permits you to distribute their plug-in directly from your own server. All they ask in return is that you place a link to their site somewhere on your pages, and additionally feature a copyright notice (for its wording, see *http://www.mvpsolutions.com/PlugInSite/TalkerTutor.html*).

Though Apple's FTP servers are notoriously busy, it's also a good idea to link users to a source of the latest PlainTalk English Text-to-Speech software. One source is *ftp://ftp.info.apple.com/Apple.Support.Area/Apple.Software.Updates/US/Macintosh/System.*

TOOLVOX

Yet another plug-in that handles compressed sound is ToolVox from Voxware, Inc. Optimized for voice—incapable of handling music intelligibly, in fact—the system does have some advantages. The first of these is that no special server is required, and the second is that ToolVox consistently achieves compression ratios of 53:1.

Because encoded .VOX files are so compact, they can play with only a small impact on the host Web page. Just 2400bps, out of the typical 14.4Kbps or 28.8Kbps data stream, is utilized, and one minute of speech occupies just 18K.

Lesson 1: Installing the Plug-In

The ToolVox Player is Voxware's Netscape plug-in for replaying .VOX files. The ToolVox Encoder is a separate program that creates .VOX files in the first place. Each of them is available for Windows 95/NT, for Windows 3.x, and for Macintosh.

Access Voxware's Web site at *http://www.voxware.com* (or check Appendix 1 for details of the enclosed CD-ROM). Run the installer identified by "16" in its file name for Windows 3.x systems, or by "32" for Windows 95/NT machines. It will place a help file, helper application, and readme files in a directory you specify, then automatically locate the PLUGINS subdirectory in your Netscape folder and place NP32VOX.DLL within it. (If you're running Windows 3.x, the plug-in is NP16VOX.DLL.)

The .HQX file containing the Macintosh installer decompresses to an application called ToolVox Plugin Installer. When you run the installer, a window will open that asks you to specify the disk drive on which Netscape is stored. Do so, and a file called ToolVox Plug-in will be created in the Plug-ins folder within your Netscape folder. (A folder called Voxware's Web Player is also created; it contains some sample .VOX files and documentation.)

Exit and restart Netscape if it was already running. By selecting About Plug-ins from Netscape's Help menu, you can confirm that ToolVox has been installed, with a MIME type/subtype of audio/voxware and suffix of vox. As you've read so often in this chapter already, your service provider will need this information to add the MIME type before you can make .VOX files available to other users.

Lesson 2: Creating Content for Your Web Pages

The ToolVox encoder, required to create embeddable .VOX files, can either record sound directly or convert .WAV files already stored on your hard drive. To install it, download the version of your choice from the VoxWare Web site.

Figure 9-15 shows the Windows 95 version of the encoder in operation. You can either make a new recording by clicking on the record button, or use the file menu to open a .WAV file for conversion. Source .WAVs need to be in mono, and an 8KHz sampling rate is adequate. If you sample at a higher rate, the encoder will automatically make the conversion.

Take Voxware's advice to stick with voice as a source seriously (I should know—I've tried compressing music!) and you should get good results. As with other voice-only products, you're better off recording your audio clips in a tape recorder far away from your computer's fan and electrical noise. Perfect them on tape, and then dub to the encoder via your sound board's line input later.

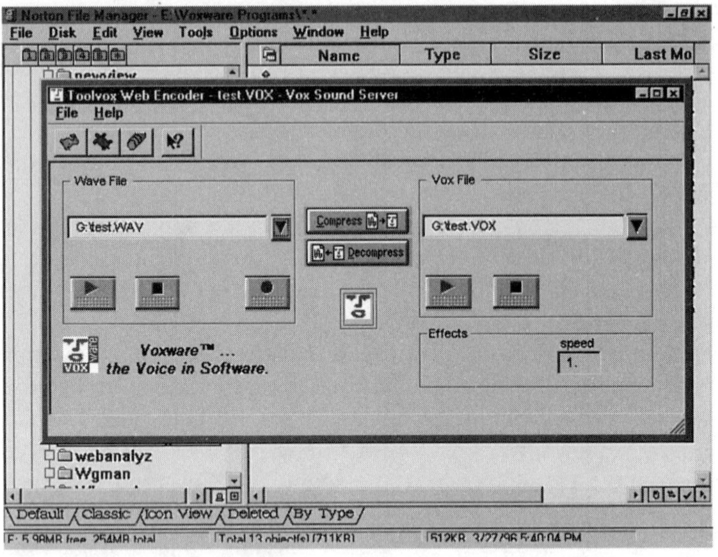

Figure 9–15 The ToolVox encoder shrinks .WAV files to 1/53rd their previous size

Lesson 3: Embedding Your Speech Files

To have the ToolVox plug-in play the voice clips you place in a Web page, simply use the <EMBED SRC="whatever.vox"> tag anywhere on a page. If you have created a clip to be played automatically when a page loads—how to do this will be explained in a moment—you might want to place it at the end of a page so that it does not hinder loading your page's text and graphics. (Voxware files are relatively low-impact, but will slow down a page's loading more than MIDI or Talker files.)

There are only two attributes for ToolVox's <EMBED> tag, PLAYMODE and VISUALMODE. PLAYMODE has three possible values, as follows:

- USER. To start playing the sound, a user must click the VoxWare icon or start button, whichever appears on the Web page.

- AUTO. The sound begins to play automatically when the Web page is displayed in the browser.

- CACHE. The sound is like USER in that it does not play until the user clicks on its icon or start button. However, the sound is downloaded in the background so that subsequent playing will be instantaneous.

VISUALMODE determines how an embedded sound appears (or doesn't appear). VISUALMODE has four possible values:

- ICON. The VoxWare "face" icon appears on the Web page. While the sound is playing, the face changes from white to red. You can try varying the size of this icon, but setting HEIGHT and WIDTH equal to 28 seems to work well. This is the default setting for VISUALMODE.

- BACKGROUND. There is no user interface on the page, and no way to stop the sound from playing.

- EMBED. A player window, which can start, stop and speed up or slow down playback, is embdedded on the Web page.You should set HEIGHT=75 and WIDTH=160 when you use this.

- FLOAT. The player window appears as a floating toobox the user can move around or outside the Netscape window area. This is not too different from what a helper application shows, come to think of it, but it is smaller.

Figure 9-16 shows a Web page in which a voice file was embedded using the following tag:

```
<embed src="publish.vox" playmode=user visualmode=embed vspace=10 height=75 width=160⇐
pluginspage="http://www.voxware.com">
```

Though Voxware does not document the use of the PLUGINSPAGE attribute, this does operate with ToolVox and—as you can see—has been inserted here to take users who don't have the plug-in to the Web page where they can download it.

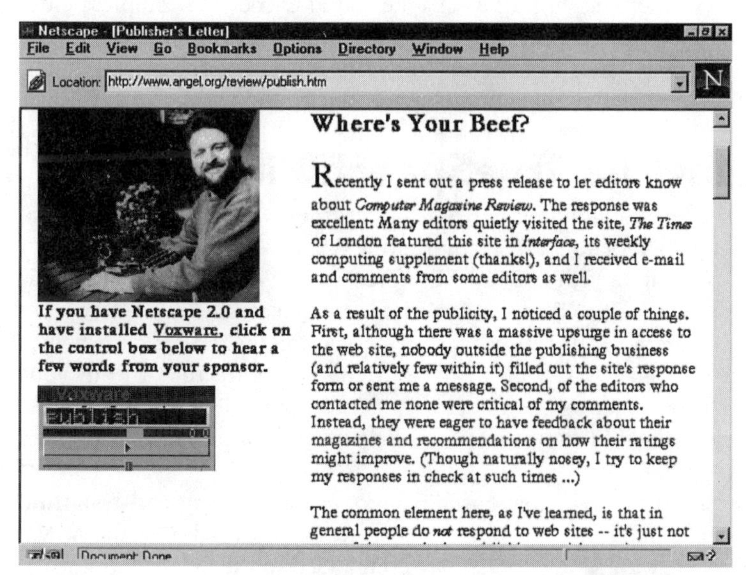

Figure 9–16 A sample of ToolVox's player embedded in a Web page

Since Voxware supplies a helper application for ToolVox sounds, you can also place them on your Web pages using the time-honored <A HREF="whatever.vox"> command, surrounding it by paired <EMBED> and <NOEMBED> tags so that Netscape will ignore the tag.

TRUESPEECH

TrueSpeech is another plug-in vying for the attention of those who want to put audio clips on their Web sites. It offers a middle-of-the-road compression ratio of 15:1, making it suitable for fair-quality music as well as clear speech.

You may be particularly interested in TrueSpeech if you are a Windows 95 aficionado, because Microsoft licensed its compression technology. As a result, the Windows 95 Sound Recorder accessory can save .WAV files directly in TrueSpeech's compressed 8KHz format.

TrueSpeech's native file is .WAV, sort of. In a technique reminiscent of Real Audio—although here, no special server software is required—you first FTP the compressed .WAV files Sound Recorder creates to your server. You then create .TSI files, small ASCII files that tell the TrueSpeech Player plug-in where to find the .WAV files. This design has some performance advantages and also helps your browser figure out whether to use the plug-in to play audio or whether to use the TrueSpeech helper application. (The .WAV file format that both end up using is identical, but this arrangement gives Web page designers some extra control over which will be used.)

Though their product may be closely associated with Windows 95, authors DSP Group, Inc. are supporting Windows 3.x and the Macintosh as well. For Windows 3.x, there is a 16-bit version of the plug-in, plus a separate sound encoder to compress older .WAV file formats. (The company even offers a DOS command-line utility that can convert multiple .WAV files in a batch.) For the Mac, there is a TrueSpeech helper application, though a Macintosh version of the plug-in has not yet appeared.

Lesson 1: Installing the TrueSpeech Plug-In

You can install the TrueSpeech plug-in by downloading it from DSP Group's Web site at *http://www.dspg.com* (or see Appendix A). Copy the file TSPLY95.EXE to a temporary subdirectory on your hard drive (TSPLY311.EXE, if you have Windows 3.x). Run this program, then click on the SETUP.EXE application that is extracted.

The installer will create a subdirectory of your choice for the TrueSpeech helper application. It also installs NPTSP32.DLL in the PLUGINS subdirectory within your Netscape folder. If you have Windows 3.x, the plug-in is called NPTSP16.DLL instead. As a final step, the installer launches the TrueSpeech helper application and plays you a sample greeting.

You can confirm that the plug-in has installed properly by exiting and restarting Netscape, then selecting About Plug-ins from the Help menu. As you'll see, the MIME type/subtype audio/tsplayer, with a suffix of tsi, has been added to the list that appears. If you instead select the Helpers tab within the Options/General Preferences menu, you'll see

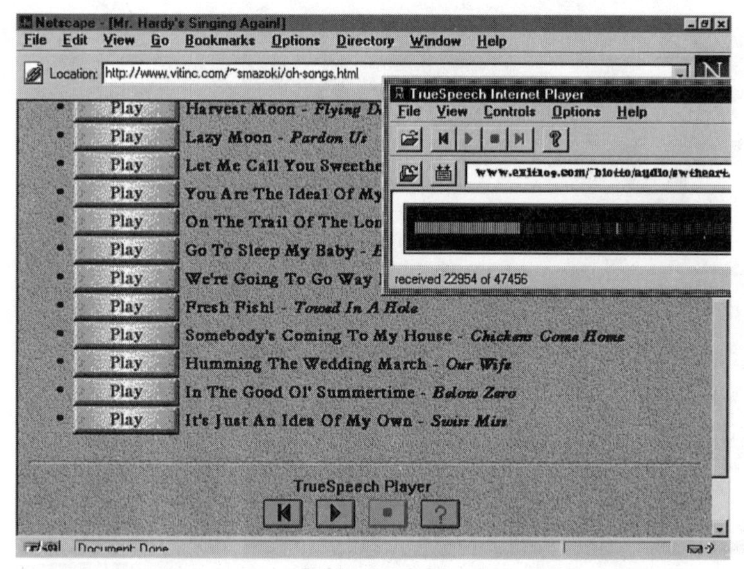

Figure 9–17 TrueSpeech files may be accessed by either the plug-in (below center) or helper application (top right)

that the TrueSpeech installer has *also* installed the MIME type/subtype application/dsptype, with the suffix tsp.

Why the duplication? Because .TSP files may be referenced on Web sites to call the helper application, while .TSI files—using, as mentioned above, the very same compressed .WAV files as their data source—may be referenced to call the plug-in. Some Web sites deliberately use both the plug-in and the helper to deliver content. In Figure 9-17, you see a site using TrueSpeech both ways. You can play a compressed .WAV file by clicking on the embedded control panel at the bottom of the screen or—as a user has done in this case—click on one of the links above to launch the helper application instead.

As previous sections in this chapter have stressed, you need to remember to let the administrators of your Web server know about the MIME types and suffixes TrueSpeech requires. Otherwise, Web pages will work on your local drive but may no longer work when you move them to the server.

Lesson 2: Creating Content for Your Web Pages

As mentioned, the TrueSpeech compression scheme is supported by Windows 95 itself, so creating files for this plug-in is an unusually easy procedure. You'll usually find that the Sound Recorder has been masterfully concealed within the Start Menu: Just work your way up its menus until you've reached Programs/Accessories/Multimedia/Sound Recorder.

Now, you can record or open any .WAV file. For best results, source your file at the 8KHz sampling rate with 16-bit resolution (other rates are supported but there may be

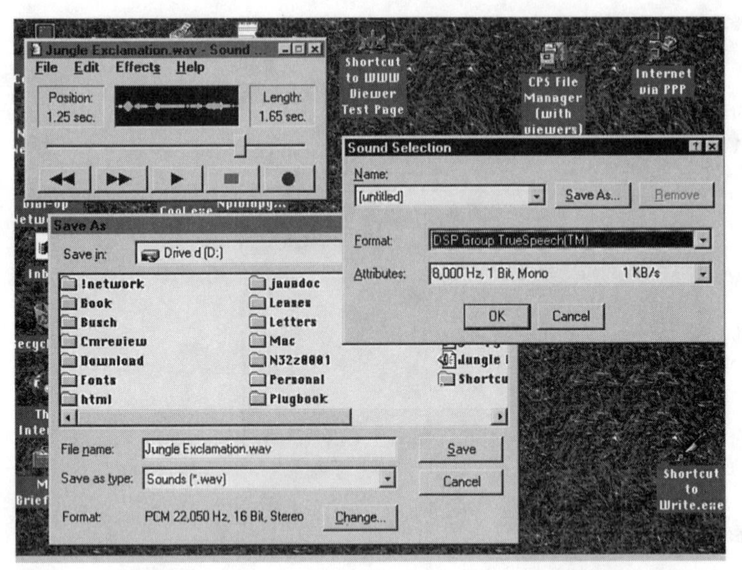

Figure 9–18 Saving a .WAV file in TrueSpeech format

quality losses upon conversion). When you're satisfied with its quality, select Save As, then click on the Change button at the bottom of the dialog box. Once you have done so, the Sound Selection dialog box appears (Figure 9-18). Pull down the menu in its Format field and select "DSP Group TrueSpeech". The correct sampling rate will be chosen for you, and you need only click OK and then save the file.

If you have Windows 3.x, you need to download a TrueSpeech conversion utility from the DSP Group's Web site. This utility, unlike the more accommodating Sound Recorder, accepts .WAV files *only* if they are 16 bit, sampled at 8KHz resolution. The program Cool Edit—found in various libraries of Windows shareware—is particularly useful in performing file conversions; it also permits opening a .WAV file in TrueSpeech format and editing it without any reconversion.

Lesson 3: Embedding Your Sound Files

Placing .WAV files on a server to be played by the TrueSpeech plug-in is a (mercifully simple) two-stage process. You need to FTP the .WAVs to the server. Then, for each .WAV file, create a corresponding .TSI file. This is a one-line file containing the (case-sensitive) characters TSIP>>, followed by the URL of the .WAV file. For example:

```
TSIP>>www.urserver.com/waves/test.wav
```

The TSI line should include only the parts of a URL shown above, not the *http://* characters as well. If you will be using the TrueSpeech helper application as well, you can create similar files that have the extension .TSP instead of .TSI.

Unlike the case with RealAudio, which uses a superficially similar "metafile" mechanism for serving up audio, the .WAV files you point to do not need to be on any particular server. In fact, they do not need to be in TrueSpeech format, since the plug-in supports PCM-standard .WAV files as well (although these naturally take a lot longer to load).

Once .WAVs, .TSIs, and .TSPs (if any) are on the server, you can start creating <EMBED SRC> tags that reference them. A typical tag might be:

```
<EMBED SRC="test.tsi" HEIGHT=60 WIDTH=200>
```

The height and width specifications are those that support TrueSpeech's default control panel. Incidentally this control panel is particularly unobtrusive (as you can see in Figure 9-18 above), since it lets your Web page's background show through behind the rewind, play, and stop buttons.

The only additional documented attributes for this plug-in are AUTOSTART and LOOP, both with possible values of TRUE or FALSE. As you can guess from the names, AUTOSTART sets a sound file to play automatically when a Web page is opened. LOOP forces the sound file to repeat continuously.

If you use AUTOSTART=TRUE, you can try setting HEIGHT to 0 and WIDTH to 2 or *vice versa* in order to hide the control panel. You also can try changing the control panel's placement with ALIGN=LEFT or ALIGN=RIGHT attributes.

WHAT NOW?

In this chapter you learned how to use audio plug-ins to add sound to your Web pages. Sometimes, however, there are times when only a picture will do. Therefore, Chapter 10 ups the multimedia ante—in terms of both required bandwidth and production values—by introducing video plug-ins.

10

VIDEO PLUG-INS

10

One *good* thing about being over 40 is being able to remember when Disney's *Wonderful World of Color* was one of the only TV programs that wasn't broadcast in black-and-white. The excitement upon viewing the fireworks in its title sequence was palpable—if you were visiting the one kid on the block with a color TV set.

Video plug-ins now bring the *Wonderful World of Color*—or any other program you care to create—to your Web pages. If you're under 40, you'll have something to tell your kids, too: "When I was young, Web video meant waiting 25 minutes for a file to download before I could even see if it was something I wanted."

For those of us who have watched computers mature, there is still something amazing about seeing video on part of a computer screen. This fact tends to make video disproportionately compelling—and thus well worth the trouble of using.

Even with video plug-ins, images may still be grainy and postage-stamp-sized. Plug-ins can't improve the quality of the source, although as computers get more powerful videos will improve to reflect their capabilities. (Microsoft and Apple are both working to ensure that computers of the near future handle video as "just another media type.")

But video plug-ins let you integrate videos into a Web page. This is especially vital for videos, since users can view the first frames before deciding whether to download the whole thing. It also means that video isn't some foreign element tacked onto your Web page—it can be an integral part of the whole.

There's no two ways about it: Video files are large, particularly in relation to today's 28.8Kbps modem dial-up links. This problem may soon enough be alleviated by cable "modems" that operate entirely in the digital domain. Motorola's CyberSURFER, one early model, offered downstream transmission speeds of up to 10Mbps (the upstream path, from the user to a server, is a "mere" 786Kbps). Ironically, this speed is more than six times faster than the T1 lines that still connect some ISPs to the Internet backbone.

Although this fact is not directly relevant to your Web pages, it's also possible that Netscape and video plug-ins will be used as an interface for browsing the large amounts of video that come on the DVD disks that are replacing CD-ROM. Why create custom software to find programs when Netscape and its video plug-ins will do the job fine?

WHICH TYPE OF VIDEO?

In order to create videos for the Web, you obviously need a camcorder or video tape deck, plus a video capture board to digitize the analog video onto your computer. (Digital camcorders, just becoming expensively available, may someday bypass the latter requirement—but not just yet.)

Some people argue that a better-than-consumer grade video deck is desirable, Sony's Hi-8 equipment being one example. In homage to this idea, many video capture boards offer a higher-resolution S-video connector in addition to the normal RCA phono jack for composite video. Whether users of your Web pages would actually be able to see a difference is debatable.

The main decision you need to make is whether you're going to encode your videos in:

- Video for Windows (.AVI), Microsoft's standard format for Windows-based digital video;
- QuickTime (.MOV), Apple's pioneering standard for desktop video; or
- MPEG (.MPG, .MPEG), a professional format from the Motion Picture Expert Group that's used internally by DVD and Video CD.

Netscape comes with plug-ins that support .AVI (currently, only in its Windows 95/NT version) and .MOV (in both Windows and Macintosh versions). You might lean towards Video for Windows because every Windows 95 and Windows NT user is already set up to play its .AVI files. Video for Windows generally produces slightly more compact files than QuickTime, too.

On the other hand, QuickTime has become the standard in desktop video for many: Apple counted the number of Web sites using it in April 1996 and came up with a total of more than 20,000. Currently the editing tools for QuickTime, such as Adobe Premiere, are superior to what's available for the other "standards." And unlike Video for Windows, QuickTime is supported by all Macintosh and Windows versions of Netscape 3.0 right out of the box.

The third choice, MPEG, uses files that are smaller than either Video for Windows or QuickTime. (This difference has been made apparently even greater by the fact that many MPEGs available on the Web are silent; MPEG is sound-capable, however.) In that sense, it is ideal for Web use, and we're fortunate to have the several third-party MPEG plug-ins featured in this chapter.

However, MPEG's compactness is not without a price: Encoding MPEG video generally requires hardware assistance in the form of an add-on board that can cost from $500–$5,000. Software-only MPEG encoding solutions do exist, but they are extremely slow.

In an attempt to compete with MPEG on the Web, Intel released its so-called Indeo Video Interactive in September 1995. This added new algorithms for compression and decompression that bring Indeo closer to MPEG in file "compactness"—the word is relative when we're talking about digital video.

LAYING THE SOFTWARE FOUNDATION

Most video plug-ins rely upon other software—which has to have been previously installed on your computer—as a foundation upon which they can build. Before you proceed to work further with video plug-ins, then, you need to make sure you've got the software they require to do their job.

If you want to use a video plug-in with .AVI files, you need Microsoft's Video for Windows software. This comes with Windows 95 and Windows NT, but Windows 3.x users may need to download it from Microsoft's Web site, as mentioned in the previous section. (See the section on MacZilla later in this chapter for details on what you need to play .AVI files on a Macintosh.)

If you want to use a video plug-in with QuickTime files, you need Apple's QuickTime system software. Many people are confused by the distinction between the QuickTime *system software,* on the one hand, and Apple's QuickTime *plug-in* on the other. QuickTime system software is the system software, containing compression/decompression routines and other system extensions, that you need before you can play QuickTime video from within *any* program—whether it's a stand-alone application or a plug-in.

You receive QuickTime system software on your hard drive when you purchase a Macintosh. If you have a Windows computer instead, you need to install the QuickTime system extensions if you haven't done so already. These are available from Apple's Web site at *http://quicktime.apple.com,* either in a 16-bit version for Windows 3.x or in a 32-bit version for Windows 95/NT. The download includes the needed extensions plus a Movie Player applet that will let you load and view .MOV files stored on your hard drive.

You need to have installed QuickTime system extensions before you can use the "other" QuickTime, Apple's QuickTime plug-in for Netscape Navigator. This plug-in, which you'll read more about in the next section of this book, is bundled with

Netscape 3.0. However, like the system software we've already mentioned, it's actually an Apple product, so updates and support are always available from the Apple QuickTime Web (again, *http://quicktime.apple.com*).

Remembering that Apple's QuickTime system software and Apple/Netscape's QuickTime plug-in are separate programs, you'll realize that you don't *have* to use the Apple-sourced plug-in to view QuickTime movies embedded in Web pages. MacZilla and MovieStar, featured later in this chapter, are other plug-ins that do the same job.

Are Your Videos Codec-Dependent?

As if video data files, video system extensions, and video plug-ins weren't enough for you to have to worry about, there's yet another software layer of which you must be aware. If you get this step wrong, you'll unwittingly create Web pages with embedded video plug-ins that work great on your machine, but won't play on most other people's.

This software layer is called a *codec*, short for compression/decompression algorithm. Since video files can be very large, and compressing them down to size is an evolving art, both Microsoft (with Video for Windows) and Apple (with QuickTime) made their system software open: As new, more efficient codecs are written, they can easily be added to an existing software installation and then used to record and play back .AVI or .MOV files.

Codecs can also be found built into the chip set of some video capture boards. In order to use a hardware-based codec—which might feature high speed or superior rates of compression—you need not only the board, but also a software driver that tells QuickTime or Video for Windows to use its special features.

To add codecs to a computer, you place system extensions in your Macintosh's System folder, add drivers using Windows 3.x's Control Panel, or use the Add New Hardware Wizard in the Windows 95 Control Panel (Figure 10-1 shows the latter). This operation is more typically done for you by an installation program for some new piece of software or hardware.

The problem with codecs is that you tend to forget they didn't come with your computer in the first place. Most programs that capture video let you save the resulting files to disk using any of the video codecs on your system. You will naturally be tempted to try each of them in turn and standardize on the one that produces the smallest files.

Unfortunately, when you do this you are unwittingly creating a file that is codec-dependent. For example, Figure 10-2 shows a Mac user about to save a QuickTime video using the Indeo 3.2 codec. This codec can be *added* to a Mac (see later), but most Mac users browsing the Web will not already have it on their computers. Therefore, when users load Web pages into which this codec-dependent video file has been embedded, they will not be able to decompress and view the video.

Codecs wouldn't be so much of a problem if Microsoft and Apple agreed on a standard set of them that would be supplied with Windows and the MacOS, respectively. (But then almost everything *else* to do with computers wouldn't be so much of a problem if Microsoft and Apple...yeah, but don't hold your breath.) The best way to avoid problems with codecs is either to save videos in their "raw" uncompressed state (big, aren't they?) or to let visitors to your Web pages know what codec you're using and where they can get it.

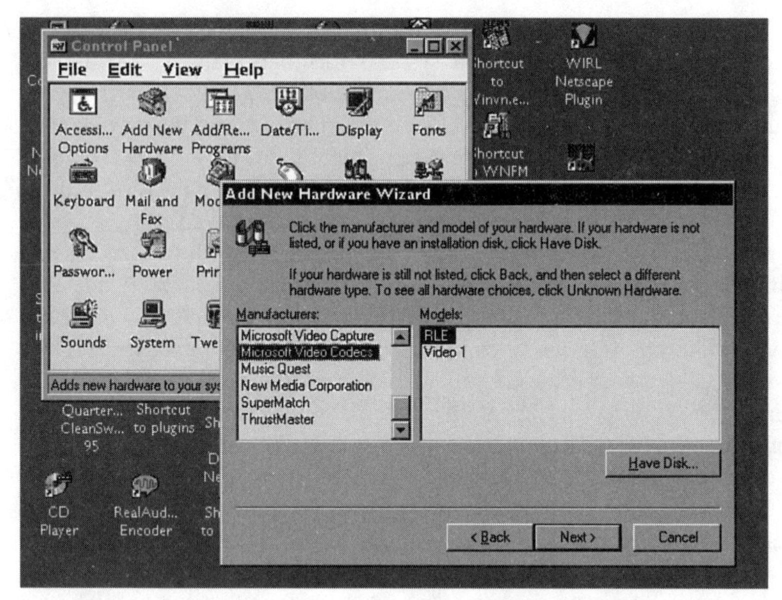

Figure 10–1 The Windows Add New Hardware Wizard lets you add new software codecs—whether or not you're actually installing hardware

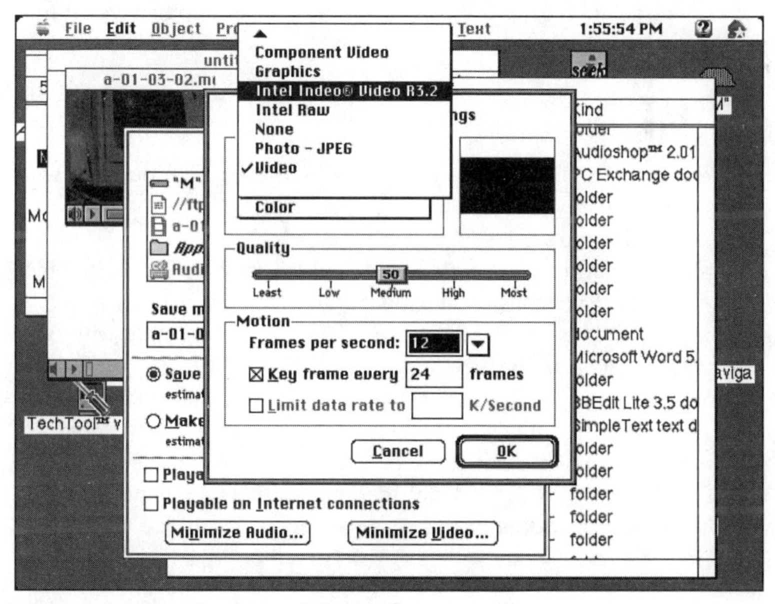

Figure 10–2 The user of this program is about to create a codec-dependent video by mistake

If your machine has an add-on video capture board, check that board's documentation for any codecs it may have added to your system, and then make sure you avoid using them (or find out how you could make them available to people who visit your pages). Be especially wary of proprietary codecs if your video board is no longer manufactured (like my ancient but trusty SuperMac Video Spigot for Windows).

You can read more information about Intel's Indeo codec by pointing a Web browser at *http://www.intel.com/pp-supp/multimed/indeo/index.htm.* The series of Web pages accessed there lets you download updated codecs for both PC and Macintosh. Intel also offers a conversion program, SmartVid for Windows, that does a creditable job of converting .AVI files to .MOV format and *vice versa.* You can find it at *ftp://ftp.intel.com/pub/IAL/multimedia.*

Incidentally, video files not only can be compressed using a variety of codecs, but also can contain different types of sound interleaved within their frames. For example, .AVI files might contain 8- or 16-bit sound in mono or stereo. QuickTime files also vary in terms of their sound contents. This is another reason to subject the video files you wish to embed to intensive testing, preferably on a variety of machines.

The fact that they work with—and require—the standard decoders for digital video is the main thing that distinguishes the plug-ins in this chapter from some of the animation plug-ins featured in the next chapter. Actually, video plug-ins may be used to display animation and, conversely, some programs intended primarily for animation may display "video" if it is sized correctly and divided into the right number of frames.

There is no dividing wall between the two categories of software, so if you want to show moving images on your Web pages but don't find a tool you like in this chapter, be sure to read Chapter 11,"Presentation Plug-Ins," as well. One way or another, you'll find what you're looking for.

LIVEVIDEO/QUICKTIME

LiveVideo and QuickTime are being featured up front because they're both bundled with Netscape 3.0. Therefore, they qualify as "native functionality" you should know about before you look at any other video plug-ins.

LiveVideo is a plug-in designed to play .AVI files embedded in Web pages. It comes with only the Windows 95 and NT versions of Netscape. QuickTime (written by Apple) is a plug-in designed to play QuickTime videos embedded in Web pages. It comes with both the Windows and Macintosh versions of the browser.

Although LiveVideo and QuickTime are both included with Netscape, and both play embedded videos, they don't have any other relationship with one another. You could use one without using the other. You might hear some people describe Netscape's ability to play QuickTime videos as being "part of its LiveVideo capabilities," but never mind. (Anyone putting it in those terms probably hasn't bothered to learn the distinction between Apple's QuickTime system software and its QuickTime plug-in, either.)

LiveVideo

LiveVideo comes with Windows 95/NT versions of Netscape; you don't need to do anything to install it. If you want to verify its presence, select About Plug-ins from the

Help Menu, and you'll see it in the list of active plug-ins that appears. Look for "LiveVideo" or "NPAVI32 Dynamic Link Library."

As the list tells you, the file responsible for LiveVideo is NPAVI32.DLL. This declares an interest in the suffix avi (corresponding, of course, to .AVI files), and the MIME types video/msvideo and video x-msvideo.

To see LiveVideo in action, you can visit demonstration pages at Netscape's own Web site. Check the URL *http://home.netscape.com/comprod/products/navigator/ version_3.0/ video/index.html.* This may be considered the "LiveVideo home page," providing an example of and basic instructions on the plug-in's use. If all is well with your system, you'll see a screen like the one shown in Figure 10-3.

The small video window, a montage of world flags and tourist scenes, loads and plays automatically. Motion is continuous, thanks to looping. Other pages using LiveVideo are shown in Figures 10-4 and 10-5.

Like other plug-ins for the Windows version of Netscape, LiveVideo lets you open local files (those on your hard drive or LAN) using Netscape's File/Open menu. Just pull down the menu, use its drop-down menu to enter "*.avi" in the Files of Type field, and then load any videos that might already be on your hard drive. As you can see from Figure 10-6, they load in the left-hand corner of a browser window, and are paused by default.

To control a video—whether you load it locally, or it appears within a Web page—right-click on it with the mouse. The pop-up context menu lets you play, pause, rewind to the first frame, or advance to the last. You can also move frame by frame.

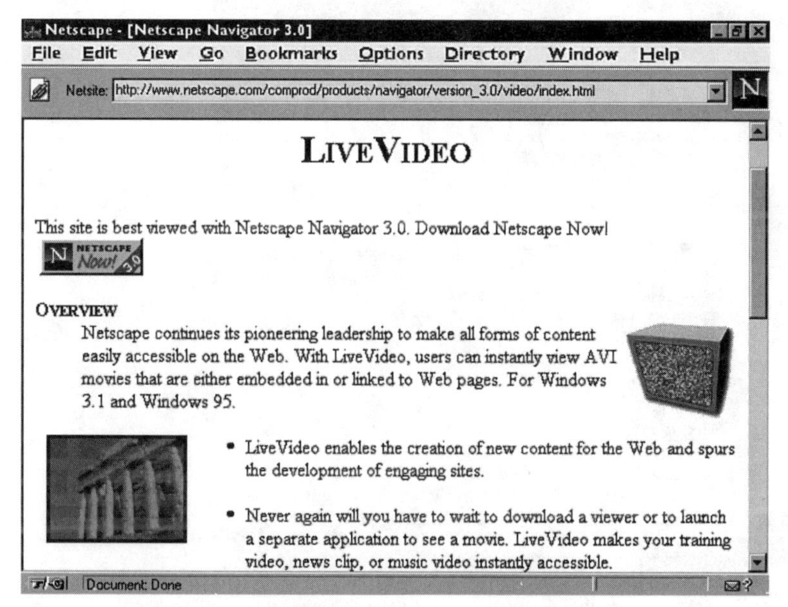

Figure 10–3 The "LiveVideo" home page at Netscape Communications

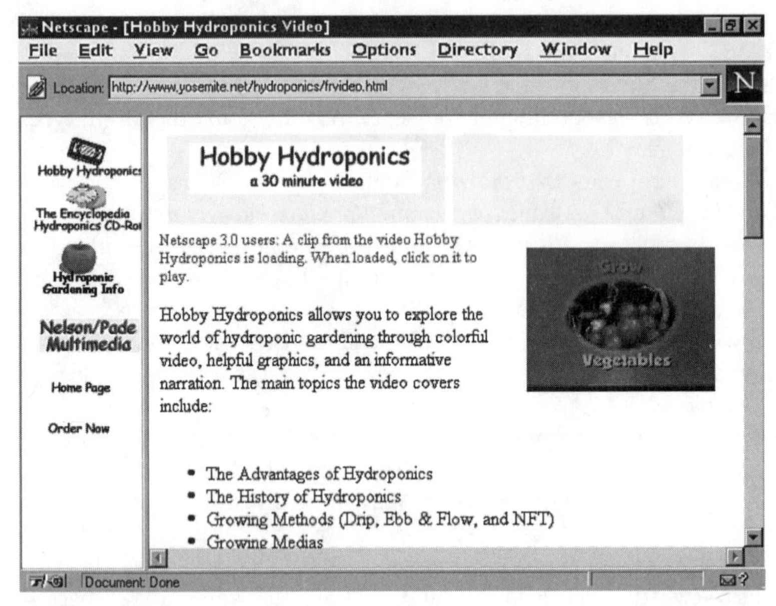

Figure 10-4 This hydroponics video can be demonstrated over the Web, thanks to LiveVideo

Figure 10-5 The "Wandering Italy" Web site incorporates not only LiveVideo, but also a Live3D world with texture-mapped graphics

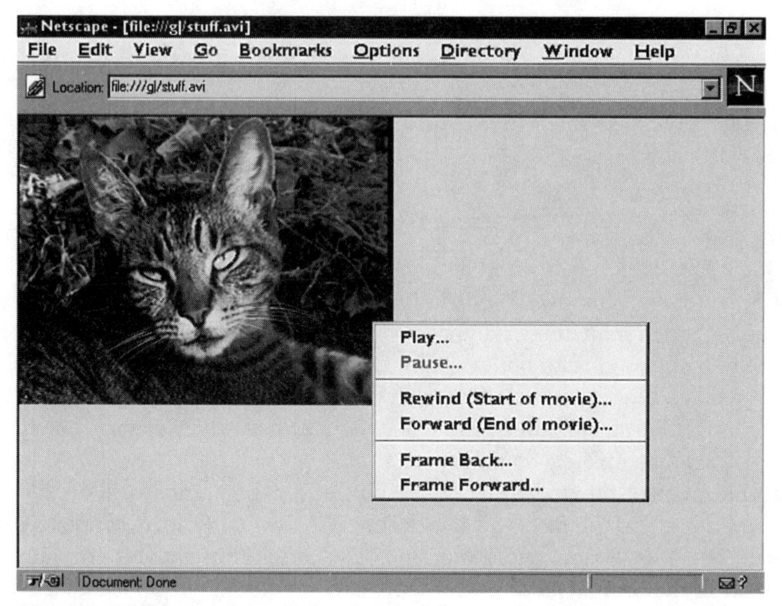

Figure 10-6 An .AVI video loaded from a local drive—note the pop-up menu

Embedding LiveVideo in Your Web Pages

The complicated part about embedding LiveVideo images in your Web pages is creating them, capturing them to disk using a capture board, and using a suitably universal codec while still keeping file size down. Two tips that will help with the latter are minimizing the size of the video window you record and using the lowest number of frames per second you can get away with.

Once you have gotten through *those* hurdles, you'll find it easy to add LiveVideo to your HTML code. The following three <EMBED SRC> lines were responsible for adding video to the Web pages shown in Figures 10-3, 10-4, and 10-5, and are listed in that order:

```
<EMBED SRC="/comprod/products/navigator/version_3.0/video/flagloop.avi"⇐
LOOP=TRUE AUTOSTART=TRUE HEIGHT=90 WIDTH=120 ALIGN=left HSPACE=10>

<EMBED SRC="whobyvhs.avi" HEIGHT="120" WIDTH="160" ALIGN="right"⇐
AUTOSTART="true" LOOP="false" HSPACE="15" VSPACE="15">

<EMBED SRC="title.avi" HEIGHT=90 WIDTH=120 AUTOSTART=TRUE LOOP=FALSE>
```

These have been copied verbatim to show small differences in HTML coding style (quotation marks around the number of pixels for HEIGHT and WIDTH, for instance) that Netscape tolerates without complaint.

As you can guess, LOOP determines whether or not a video will be repeated. AUTOSTART determines whether or not it will begin playing when it has loaded which, remember, will take much longer than loading the rest of the host Web page does. The other attributes are merely those that would work with other Netscape <EMBED> or <IMG> tags as well.

QuickTime

Like LiveVideo, QuickTime is bundled with Netscape 3.0. In this case, however, you get the plug-in whether you have Windows 3.x, Windows 95/NT, or Macintosh versions of the browser, making it a much more universal tool.

The QuickTime plug-in works with both existing QuickTime movies and with movies prepared to take advantage of the plug-in's "fast-start" feature. The fast-start feature will present the first frame of the movie almost immediately, and can begin playing before remaining frames have been completely downloaded.

Because it is able to play movies with text, MIDI, and other kinds of data, the QuickTime plug-in also lets you interact with QuickTime VR (Virtual Reality) Panoramas and Objects. QuickTime VR Objects and Panoramas are QuickTime movies specially photographed so that, as the user steps through them frame by frame, the appearance of moving around an object is given. When VR Panoramas are viewed (either by Apple's Movie Player application or by the QuickTime plug-in), the user can also use the OPTION and CTRL (SHIFT CTRL on Windows) keystrokes in tandem with the mouse to zoom in or zoom out on the movie.

Earlier in this chapter, in "Laying the Software Foundation," I mentioned the need to download QuickTime software if you don't already have it. You need to do this before you can use the QuickTime plug-in. If you want to use QuickTime VR, you need some additional software as well (once again, available from Apple's QuickTime download page at *http://quicktime.apple.com/sw/sw.html*).

QuickTime VR Components for the Mac come in a self-extracting archive file called "vrmac.sea.hqx". Download this file, expand it, and place the resulting file in the Netscape Plug-ins folder. Then exit and restart Netscape.

For Windows, the components are in a file called QTVRW.QTC (for Windows 3.x) or QTVRW32.QTC (for Windows 95/NT). Download the compressed installer file QTVRW.EXE or QTVRW32.EXE and click on it to extract the .QTC file. Then place it in your Windows system folder (usually C:\WINDOWS\SYSTEM, although your installation may be different).

The Macintosh version of the QuickTime plug-in will automatically take you to Apple's QuickTime home page if it detects that you need the QuickTime VR Components. This helpful behavior is coded into the plug-in, and does not require a Web page's author to have set the PLUGINSPAGE attribute accordingly. Look at Figure 10-7 for an example of what you will see when this happens.

If you have installed the QuickTime VR Components, and still get a blank window when trying to view a QuickTime VR file, you may not have enough free memory. Try quitting other open applications, disabling unneeded extensions (if you have a Mac), or adjusting virtual memory settings in the System section of the Control Panel (if you have Windows).

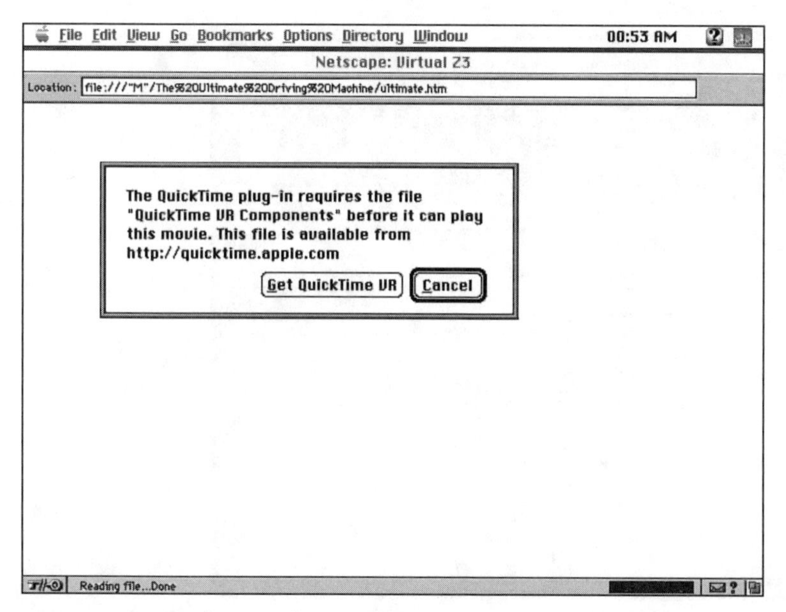

Figure 10–7 The QuickTime plug-in detects when the QuickTime VR Components file is needed and offers to download it

Once you have installed QuickTime and QuickTime VR, you're ready to test the QuickTime plug-in. Start Netscape and select About Plug-ins from the Help or Apple menu. You'll see "QuickTime Plug-in" in the list that appears. As the browser confirms, the plug-in is handling the video/quicktime MIME type with the suffix mov.

The plug-ins list also tells you that QuickTime functionality resides in the file NPQTW32.DLL (for Windows 95 and NT), NPQTW16.DLL (for Windows 3.x), or QuickTime Plug-in (Macintosh). Should you want to use a different QuickTime plug-in—one of the products listed later in this chapter—you could turn off this one by removing the relevant file from your Netscape Plug-ins folder.

To see QuickTime in operation, you can go to Apple's QuickTime "How-To" Web site at *http://www.MediaCity.com/~erweb/.* In addition to giving you general information about QuickTime hardware and software (see Figure 10-8), this site provides sample QuickTime movies. As you can see from Figure 10-9, .MOV files can contain video, audio, or MIDI in various combinations. The "How-To" site gives examples of these and of QuickTime VR.

Figure 10-10 shows a simple Web page with a QuickTime movie embedded in it. The pop-up menu—available via the right mouse button for Windows users, or by holding down the mouse on the Macintosh—lets you play or pause a movie, rewind it, or save it to disk. (To save movies using the Macintosh version of the plug-in, press COMMAND+S.)

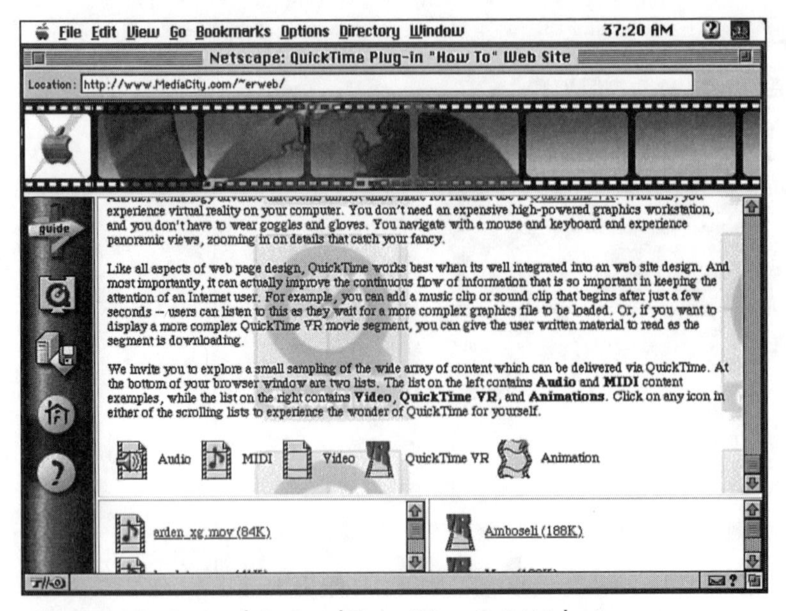

Figure 10–8 Apple's QuickTime "How-To" Web site

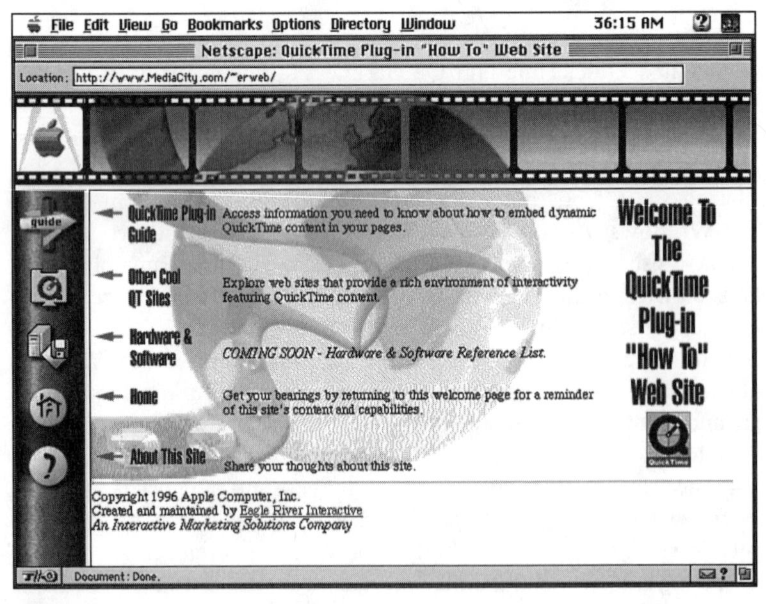

Figure 10–9 The "How-To" site gives examples of the different data types .MOV files can hold

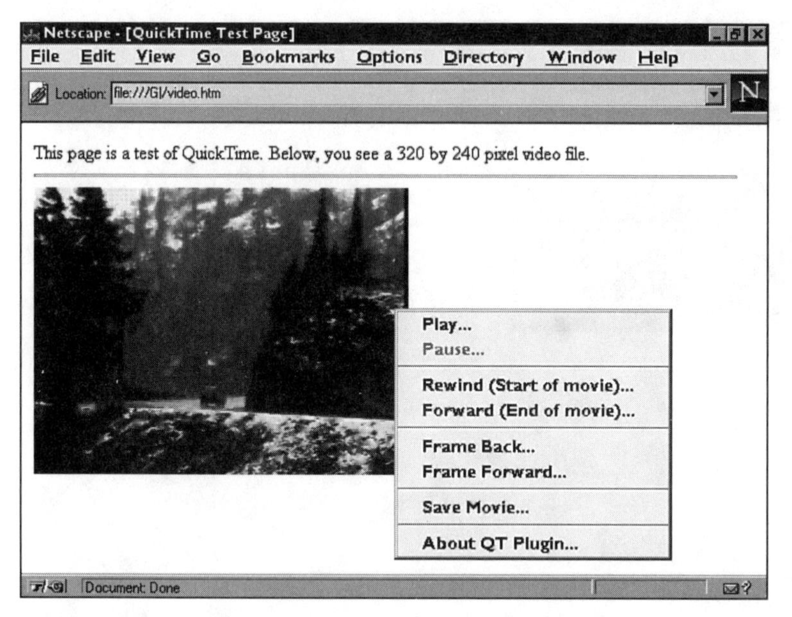

Figure 10–10 The pop-up menu lets you pause a movie, move around it, or save it to disk

QuickTime VR files may be either Objects, which you can move around in a single two-dimensional plane, or Panoramas, which you can not only pan around but also zoom in and out on. When you open a Web page with an embedded VR file, you do not see the controller that is normally displayed below QuickTime windows. Instead, you simply click on the image, then use the mouse (or, on a Mac, arrow keys) to pan either left or right. Use the SHIFT or CTRL keys (OPTION or CONTROL on Macintosh) as modifiers with mouse movements to zoom in or out.

Figure 10-11 shows a QuickTime VR Object file. Users can rotate the car within approximately 270 degrees. The QuickTime VR Panorama shown in Figure 10-12 offers an even wider range of motion.

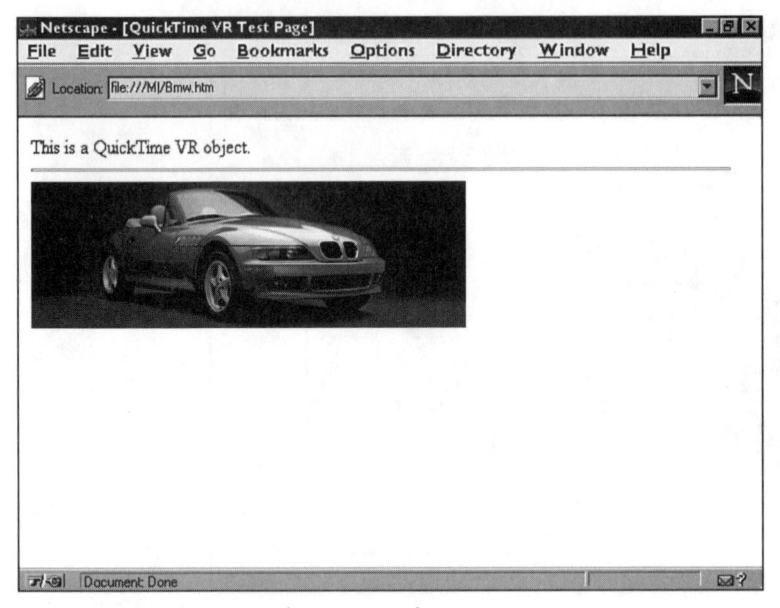

Figure 10–11 A QuickTime VR Object

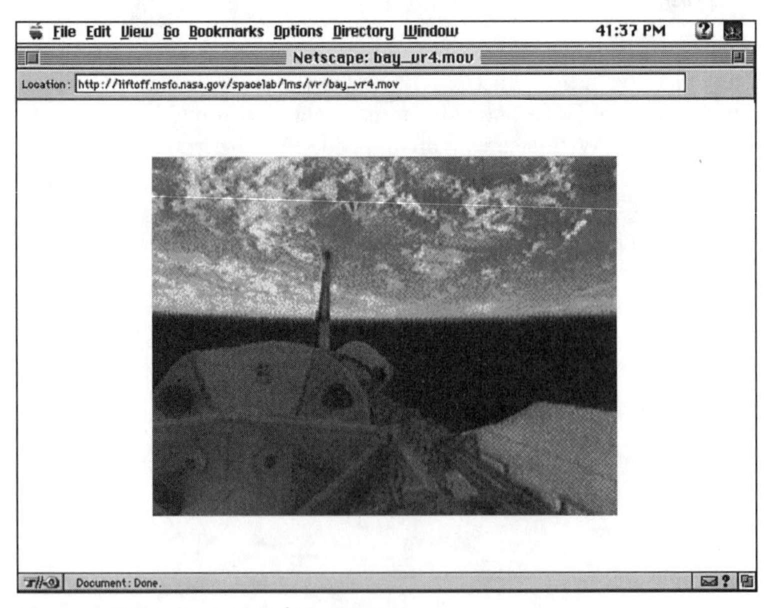

Figure 10–12 A QuickTime VR Panorama

Embedding QuickTime Videos in Your Web Pages

The QuickTime plug-in lets you embed a video in a Web page by using <EMBED> with simple SRC, HEIGHT, and WIDTH attributes. No other attributes are required. However, with optional attributes you can

- Hide the controller that would otherwise appear
- Set a video so that it starts playing as soon as possible
- Choose the initial field of view plus zoom and pan angles from which a QuickTime VR Object or Panorama is initially viewed
- Select a URL that will be opened if the user clicks on the movie, and even define a frame within which that URL will be displayed

Table 10-1 lists these attributes in detail.

Table 10–1 Possible attributes for the QuickTime plug-in

Attribute	Description
AUTOPLAY=*value*	AUTOPLAY is an optional attribute. When set to TRUE, the AUTOPLAY attribute causes the movie to start playing as soon as the QuickTime plug-in estimates that it will be able to play the entire movie without waiting for additional data. The default value of AUTOPLAY is FALSE. This option is not appropriate for QuickTime VR Objects and Panoramas.
CONTROLLER=*value*	CONTROLLER is an optional attribute. The CONTROLLER attribute sets the visibility of the movie controller. Acceptable values for this attribute are TRUE and FALSE. The default value is TRUE for ordinary movies. This option is not appropriate for QuickTime VR Objects and Panoramas since they are controlled by the mouse key.
CORRECTION=*value*	CORRECTION is an optional attribute. Possible values are NONE, PARTIAL, or FULL. This attribute is only appropriate for QuickTime VR Objects and Panoramas.
FOV=*integer*	FOV is an optional attribute that lets you specify the initial field of view angle for a QuickTime VR movie.The range of values for a typical movie would be 5.0 to 85.0 degrees. This attribute has no meaning for a standard QuickTime movie.
HEIGHT=*size in pixels*	The HEIGHT attribute specifies the height of the embedded document, in pixels. This option is appropriate for both QuickTime and QuickTime VR movies, and is required unless you use the HIDDEN attribute (below). If you want to display the movie's controller, add 24 pixels to the HEIGHT. Never specify a height of less than two as this can cause problems. If you want to hide a sound-only movie, use the HIDDEN tag instead.

continued on next page

continued from previous page

HIDDEN	HIDDEN is an optional attribute that can hide a sound-only movie. It is not appropriate for any other types, including QuickTime VR Objects or Panoramas.
HREF=*url*	HREF is an optional attribute. When set, the HREF attribute takes the user to another page when the movie is clicked on. This option would only be appropriate for a movie without a controller. Note: If you are using a relative pathname for the HREF, then it should be relative to the location of the movie specified in the SRC= attribute. This option is not appropriate for QuickTime VR Objects and Panoramas.
LOOP=*value*	LOOP is an optional attribute. When set, the LOOP attribute makes the movie play in a loop. Acceptable values for this attribute are TRUE, FALSE, and PALINDROME. Setting LOOP to PALINDROME causes the movie to play alternately forwards and backwards. The default value of LOOP is FALSE. This option is not appropriate for QuickTime VR Objects and Panoramas.
NODE=*integer*	NODE is an optional attribute. The NODE attribute allows you to specify the initial node for a multi-node QuickTime VR movie.
PAN=*integer*	PAN is an optional attribute. The PAN attribute allows you to specify the initial pan angle for a QuickTime VR movie.The range of values for a typical movie would be 0.0 to 360.0 degrees. This attribute has no meaning for a standard QuickTime movie.
PLAYEVERYFRAME=*value*	PLAYEVERYFRAME is an optional attribute. When set, the PLAYEVERYFRAME attribute causes the movie to play every frame even if to do so it is necessary to play at a slower rate. This attribute is particularly useful to play simple animations. Acceptable values for this attribute are TRUE and FALSE; the default is false. NOTE: PLAYEVERYFRAME=TRUE will turn off any audio tracks your movie may have.
PLUGINSPAGE=*url*	As with other Netscape plug-ins, this attribute lets you specify a URL from which the user can fetch the necessary plug-in if it is not installed. If used here, it should be set to "http://quicktime.apple.com/" which is appropriate for both QuickTime movies and QuickTime VR Objects and Panoramas.
TARGET=*frame*	TARGET is an optional attribute. When set, the TARGET attribute is the name of a valid frame that will be the target of a link (including _self, _top, _parent, _blank, or an explicit frame name). This attribute is for use with the HREF attribute. This option is appropriate for QuickTime movies.
TILT=*integer*	TILT is an optional attribute that lets you specify the initial tilt angle for a QuickTime VR movie. The range of values for a typical movie would be –42.5 to 42.5 degrees. TILT has no meaning for a standard QuickTime movie.
WIDTH=*size in pixels*	The WIDTH attribute specifies the width of the embedded document, in pixels. This option is appropriate for both QuickTime and QuickTime VR movies. The WIDTH attribute is required unless you use the HIDDEN attribute (above). Never specify a width of less than two as this can cause problems.

In order to select the proper HEIGHT and WIDTH attributes for a video, you should find out the height and width of the source file. Otherwise, the movie will be cropped to fit the height and width of the window you specify, or, if that window is larger than the original movie, will be centered within it. Note that if you are using the QuickTime plug-in's controller (which appears by default), you need to add 24 pixels to the height of the window to make room for it.

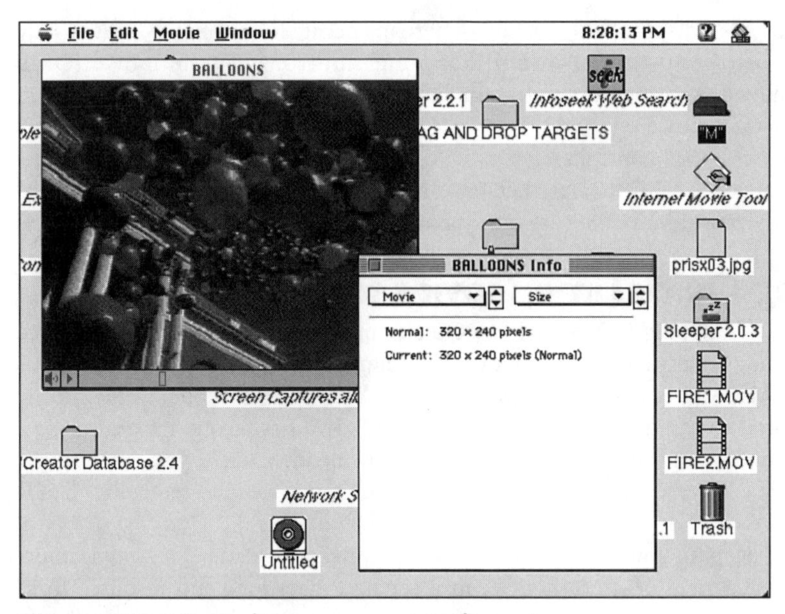

Figure 10–13 Finding out a movie's dimensions

To ascertain a movie's dimensions, open it with the MoviePlayer that comes with QuickTime (PLAYER.EXE or PLAY32.EXE on Windows 3.1) and select Get Info (Get Movie Info under Windows) from the Movie menu. On the Mac version of Movie Player, you will need to select Size from the list of parameters that appears (see Figure 10-13).

NOTE: Like other authors of plug-ins, Apple has done its best to make the QuickTime plug-in work the same on Windows and Macintosh. However, tiny inconsistencies will always linger to bedevil Web page designers. For example, the 24 pixels that must be added to a window's height to make room for the controller comes from Windows (with large fonts turned on, as a user would have done on a high-resolution monitor). On a PC with normal fonts the controller actually turns out to be only 18 pixels high, while on a Mac it's a mere 16 pixels high. What happens to the extra space? As long as you are using a solid color background and not using frames, the plug-in will paint the background color in the unused area below the controller. If you are using frames, the plug-in will paint gray in the unused area. If you are using a background GIF or JPEG, the plug-in will create a slight distraction for Mac users by overlaying this with a strip of the Web page's background color. In this case, you should try to minimize the visual distraction by defining a background color (BGCOLOR) that is as close as possible to the average color of your GIF or JPEG. Apple says the inconsistency of controller heights will be resolved in a future version of QuickTime.

If you choose not to display the controller—perhaps because your movie is set to play automatically and to loop—the user still has some control over the movie. On a Macintosh, if a movie is visible and does not have an <HREF> tag associated with it, double-clicking on the movie will start the movie, and a single click will pause it. (This also works for movies with controllers.) On a PC, a single click toggles the pause/play state. This will not work with movies that have an <HREF> tag associated with them, since clicking on them would in that case take the user to the URL specified by the HREF.

Optimizing QuickTime Movies for the Web

Although the QuickTime plug-in can read any QuickTime movie, there is a big difference between QuickTime movies that work well over the Internet and QuickTime movies optimized for CD-ROMs. After all, many people still have 14.4 or 28.8 modem links to the Internet. A 28.8 modem can download a movie at about 2.5KB per second maximum, so a 20 second, 1MB movie can take several minutes to download. Even if you are creating content for a T1 or T3 connection, or a LAN-based intranet, you need to remember bandwidth limitations.

In addition to keeping a movie's file size down, you need to "flatten" it so that information is no longer stored, Macintosh-style, in a separate data fork and resource fork. Otherwise, Windows computers would have trouble interpreting the movie. To flatten movies, open them with the Macintosh QuickTime Movie Player, then do a File Save As, making sure that the Playable on non-Apple Computers button is checked.

Better still, you can process movies with Apple's Internet Movie Tool, a Macintosh program that is downloadable from the QuickTime Web site *(http://quicktime.apple.com)*. This not only flattens movies but also makes sure that important information is stored at the beginning of the file instead of the end. As a result, the QuickTime plug-in is able to "fast start" the file, playing the movie before all of it has downloaded.

To use the Internet Movie Tool, launch the program and then use it to find the movie you want to convert. Then press the Open button to convert the movie (see Figure 10-14). Alternatively, you can convert movies just by dragging the movies you want to convert from the desktop or Finder window and dropping them on the Internet Movie Tool.

Large movies cannot start playing as soon as a Web page appears, even if they have been optimized with the Internet Movie Tool. The QuickTime plug-in never starts playing any movie until it is sure it can download the rest of a movie before the first part finishes playing. Over a modem, this usually means that almost all of a movie will be transferred before the movie starts to play. Therefore, only movies with a low data- and frame-rate can best take advantage of the Fast-Start feature.

You should design your Web pages and movies with the knowledge that most users will be impatient and click a movie's play button before a download has finished. You should design your movies so the first frames show something interesting (as opposed to a long fade-in from black). If you don't want users to be able to click the start button, use the CONTROLLER=FALSE button and set AUTOPLAY=TRUE.

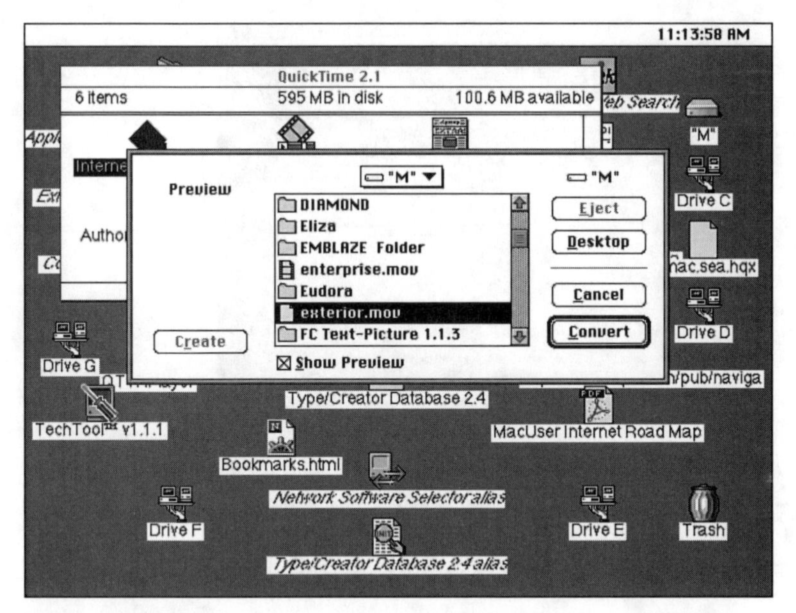

Figure 10–14 The Internet Movie Tool "flattens" movies and moves important information to the beginning

If you want to put a large movie up on your site for download, it's best not to embed the movie directly on the page. Rather, save a frame of the movie as a PICT using Movie Player, convert it to a GIF and use that image as a link to the actual movie. Or make a postage-stamp-sized short clip of the movie, then offer users a "download in full size" link.

A program called Movie Cleaner Pro, available from Terran interactive (*http://www.terran-int.com/*), is a special QuickTime compression utility. It has built-in settings that compress movies for transmitting over the Internet. Features such as adaptive noise reduction make movies look better at low data rates. The program also makes it easy to specify the data rate of a connection and then attempt to optimize a movie for it. Figure 10-15 shows the company's shareware version, Movie Cleaner Lite, which lacks batch processing but offers most of the program's other features.

ACTION

Netscape's standard LiveVideo capabilities may satisfy most users, and the fact that they are available to everyone with version 3.0 of the program provides strong incentive to use them. However, until we all have cable modems or fiber-optic connections, the search for better performance and smaller file size will be unending.

MPEG offers hope here if you have a source of MPEG files or are willing to invest in a hardware encoder. (Need a new video card? You'll find that some companies combine video cards with MPEG encoders using a daughterboard approach.) Action is a

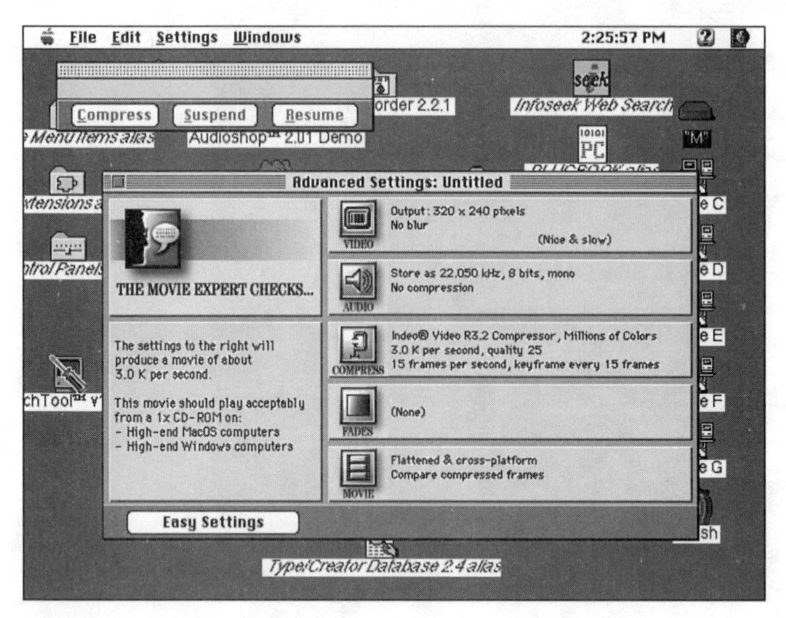

Figure 10–15 Movie Cleaner Lite helps optimize and compress QuickTime movies

straightforward MPEG-1 decoder that offers some visual bonuses, such as letting you automatically double the size of an image or force it to play in gray scale instead of color.

Lesson 1: Installing the Plug-In

Action runs only under Windows 95 or Windows NT. To install it on your system, download the installer from Open2VU's Web pages at *http://www.open2u.com/action/action.html,* or check Appendix 1 for details about your CD-ROM. Copy the installer, ACTION32.EXE, to a temporary subdirectory on your hard drive.

Then run the installer. It will prompt you for a destination directory, which needs to be one already in existence on your hard drive. Then, when you click on OK, the program will create a .DLL file, NPMPG32.DLL, and several files including a demo .MPG and a sample Web page (ACT_DEMO.HTM). Copy the .DLL file to Netscape's plug-ins directory within your Netscape folder (under Windows 95, the default path for this is C:\Program Files\Netscape\Navigator\Program\Plugins, but yours may be different depending on where you installed Netscape).

Now, exit Netscape if it is running and restart. Select About Plug-ins from the Help menu, and you'll see that Action has added a new MIME type/subtype to the list, namely video/mpg with suffixes (extensions) mpe, mpg, and mpeg.

To see Action in...well, er, action, press CTRL+O to use Netscape's File/Open a File function. Then use Windows' file browser to locate the directory where you placed the Action files and load ACT_DEMO.HTM. If everything is working properly, you'll see a screen like the one in Figure 10-16.

Not particularly visual, is it? However, if you left-click on the blank frame, you'll see a pop-up menu that lets you start the movie playing. Figure 10-17 shows the pop-up menu

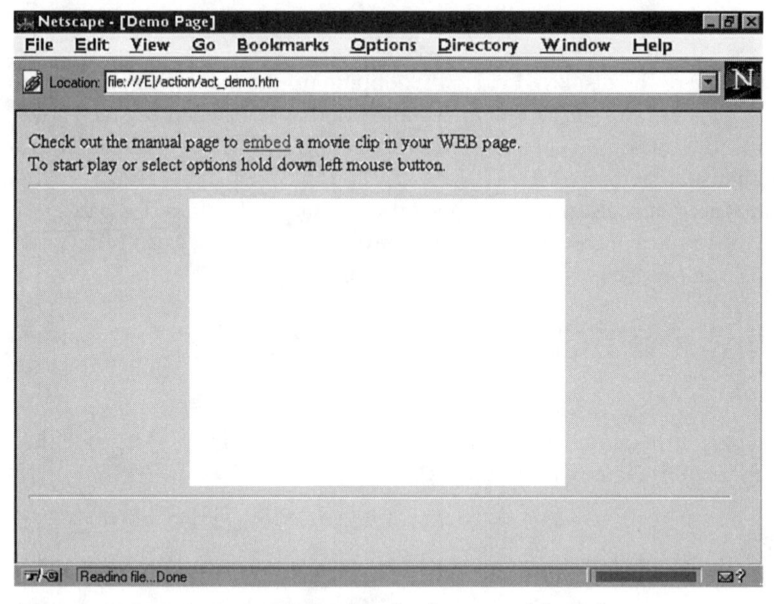

Figure 10–16 Action starts by displaying a blank frame

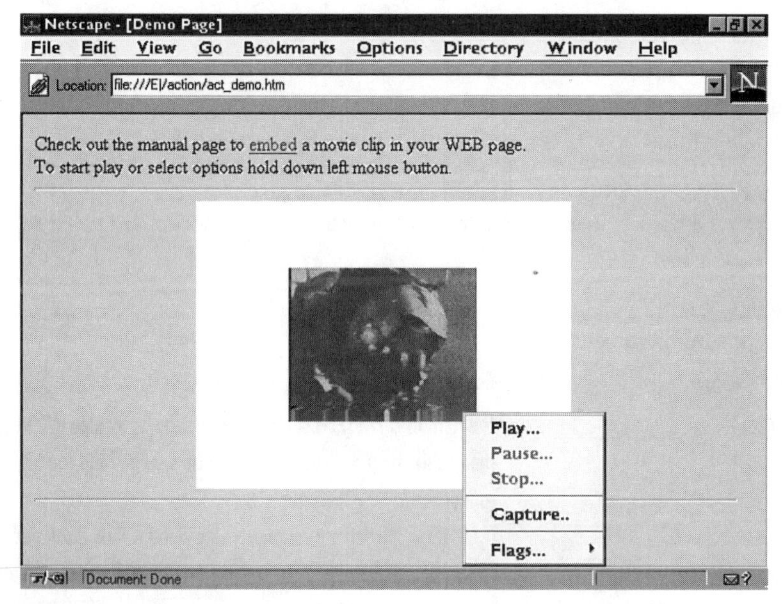

Figure 10–17 You start the action—no pun intended—with this pop-up menu

with the sample movie playing behind it. Here, you see that the frame reserved for video is twice the size of the video itself.

You can alter the size of the displayed video by popping up the menu and clicking on the Flags selection at the bottom. This opens up a submenu that can switch between color and gray scale, double the size of the video, synchronize sound and video, or switch into a debug mode that can display error messages.

As you can see, the menu also has other useful capabilities. It can stop, pause, or replay a video, and the Capture menu choice lets you save a video to disk as an MPEG file. (Since some plug-ins cannot save files, the latter is a welcome bonus.)

Lesson 2: Adding MPEG Images to Your Web Pages

Like other plug-ins, Action relies on the <EMBED SRC> tag. Here is the HTML code that created the Web page seen in Figures 10-16 and 10-17.

```
<HTML>
<TITLE>Demo Page</TITLE>
Check out the manual page to <A HREF="embed.htm">embed</A> a movie clip in your WEB page.
<BR>
To start play or select options hold down left mouse button.
<HR>
<CENTER>
<EMBED SRC="tg_a.mpg" width=320 height=240>
</CENTER>
<HR>
</BODY>
</HTML>
```

Attributes for the <EMBED SRC> tag can control the default size of a video, cause it to play automatically when a page is loaded, and so on. The attributes for Action are listed in Table 10-2.

Table 10–2 EMBED SRC attributes for Action

Attribute	Possible Values	Comments
AUTOSTART	TRUE | FALSE	The default is FALSE. If set to TRUE, display of a video will begin as soon as the page is loaded. Use with care on any but the highest-speed connections.
COLOR	MONO	If COLOR="MONO" is present, a color video will be displayed as gray scale. This can be useful for monochromatic Web pages and other special effects.
DEBUG	ON	Enables DEBUG mode. When this is active, Action stores debug information in a C:\WINDOWS\TEMP\MPEG\MSG file.
HEIGHT	Measured in pixels	This value is mandatory. It should normally be equal to the height of the MPEG file being used.

Attribute	Possible Values	Comments
LOOP	TRUE | FALSE	If set to TRUE, this will continuously replay the movie (from Netscape's cache on second and subsequent playings). The default is FALSE.
PALETTE	FOREGROUND | BACKGROUND	Indicates whether the plug-in has permission to realize its palette as foreground or background in a page with more than one plug-in. The default is BACKGROUND. Set this value to FOREGROUND if you want the appearance of your video to take precedence over other screen areas.
SIZE	DOUBLE	If SIZE="DOUBLE" is used, the video will appear twice its normal size. HEIGHT and WIDTH should be set to match.
SYNC	TRUE | FALSE	Lets you choose to force audio to play in sync with video. This may cause frames to be dropped when Action is behind in displaying the video images. Hence, you can set SYNC to false if video is your priority.
WIDTH	Measured in pixels	This tag is required. Should normally be equal to the width of the source MPEG file.

CLEARFUSION

Iterated Systems' ClearFusion is a plug-in that works with Windows NT or Windows 95 to play embedded .AVI files. You might ask why anyone would want to install another .AVI plug-in when Netscape 3.0 already comes with LiveVideo capabilities.

One market for ClearFusion might be those using Netscape 2.0 who don't want to upgrade, but do want to gain greater functionality through plug-ins. You may also find ClearFusion a good choice if you plan particularly intensive use of .AVI files, such as in a page that offers a collection of movie trailers.

ClearFusion goes way beyond the usual set of EMBED SRC attributes with a system of events, commands, and subcommands that let you vary the size and speed of each individual video clip on a page. You can also decide exactly what happens when a user clicks or double-clicks on an image.

Another distinguishing attribute of ClearFusion is that it is bundled with ClearVideo, a Web-oriented codec (see the section "Are Your Videos Codec-Dependent?" at the beginning of this chapter). Iterated Systems claims this codec—installed into Windows when you run the ClearFusion installation program—creates .AVI files that start playing faster and look better than those produced with other codecs.

Though the ClearVideo codec appeared only as this book was being completed, I was able to sample Web pages created using it—and was indeed impressed by the image clarity. Remember, however, that when you use this or any other nonstandard means of compression, you are forcing users to download and install the codec before they can see the videos on your Web page.

In any case, nothing about the ClearFusion plug-in *forces* you to use the codec. ClearVideo simply becomes an option you can choose when doing a Save As from your Windows video editor or capturing application.

NOTE: ClearFusion is the new name for the plug-in known as CoolFusion until mid-August 1996. This is why you see the CoolFusion name in some of the screens that follow in this section. The functionality and menus remain exactly as shown, except that you will see "ClearVision 2.01" in place of "CoolFusion 2.0".

Lesson 1: Installing the Plug-In

ClearFusion requires Windows 95 or Windows NT. To install it, download the latest version of the plug-in from the Iterated Systems Web page at *http://www.iterated.com,* or check Appendix A, "Where to Get the Plug-Ins Featured in This Book," for details about your CD-ROM.

Copy the installation program to a temporary directory on your hard drive and then run it. You'll be asked to indicate the disk drive that holds your copy of Netscape. The installation program then copies the ClearFusion plug-in, NPCOOL32.DLL, to the PLUGINS subdirectory within your Netscape folder.

To verify that ClearFusion is operating, exit and restart Netscape (if it was running). Then check the Help/About Plug-ins menu. You'll see that ClearFusion has added MIME types/subtypes to the list that appears, as follows:

```
Description: data
MIME Type: video/isivideo
Suffixes: fvi
Description: data
MIME Type: video/msvideo
Suffixes: avi
Description: data
MIME Type: video/x-msvideo
Suffixes: avi
```

The .FVI format that appears first has yet to be seen on the Web. However, it probably will refer to video files specially compressed using fractal technology, since this is another specialty of Iterated Systems, ClearFusion's author.

As you can see, the second two MIME types are those normally handled by the LiveAudio plug-in that ships with Netscape 3.0. ClearFusion has now taken them over, which is presumably what you want. To make sure this happens reliably, you may want to deactivate LiveVideo by removing NPAVI32.DLL from your Netscape Plug-ins folder and then restarting the browser.

Remember that it is important which plug-in you assign to a MIME type. For an example of this, look at Figure 10-18. This shows a sample page written to be viewed with ClearFusion. Three extremely short .AVI files display light bulb images: Initially, their first frames, where the light bulb is "off," are shown. If the user moves the mouse pointer over any of the bulbs, the video advances to the next frame, in which the light bulb is switched "on."

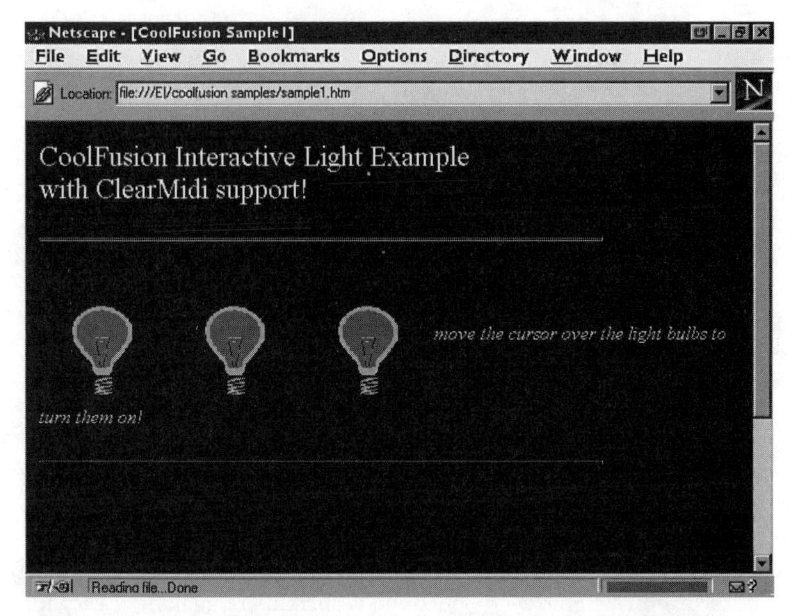

Figure 10–18 A ClearFusion test page shows three light bulbs the user can "switch on"

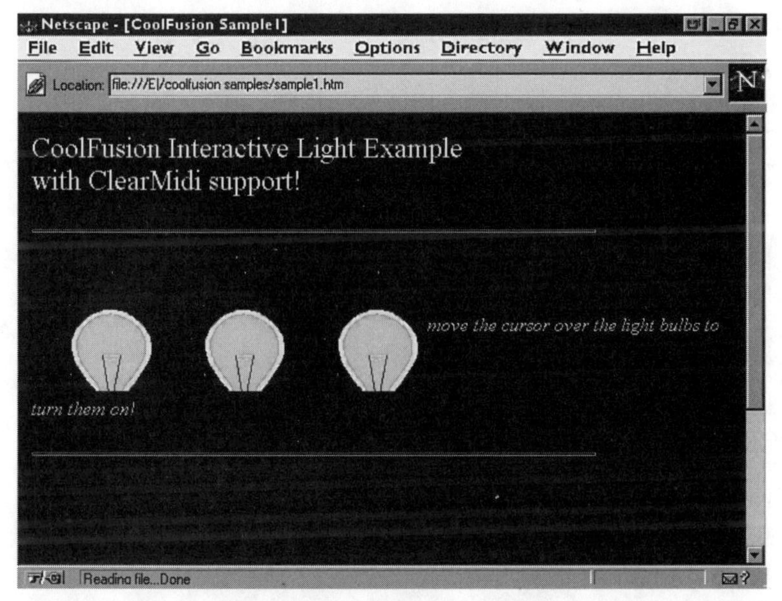

Figure 10–19 When the page is interpreted by LiveVideo instead of ClearFusion, the light bulbs are switched on prematurely

If you remove the NPCOOL32.DLL from Netscape's PLUGINS subdirectory, or deactivate ClearFusion via Netscape's control panel, LiveVideo will interpret the embedded .AVI files instead (if you haven't already deactivated it). This delivers a screen like the one shown in Figure 10-19.

When LiveVideo interprets the embedded videos, each of them is played althrough to the last frame, ruining the joke. This is just a small example of the problems that can arise when a user does not have the plug-in you intended. As has been mentioned elsewhere in this book, if you want to use a plug-in like ClearFusion that takes over functions normally performed by Netscape, you need to let users know that they should install the plug-in in order to view your Web page properly.

Setting the PLUGINSPAGE attribute of any <EMBED SRC> tags, although always a good idea, will not help in this case. Netscape will see that the video/msvideo and video/x-msvideo MIME types are present, but will just pass them to its LiveAudio plug-in instead of popping up a dialog box or going to the Iterated Systems Web page.

Although intended to be used with embedded .AVI files, ClearFusion will, of course, also run when you view a page where videos have been referenced using IMG SRC. In this case, it opens within the Netscape browser window, but draws a window of its own similar to that of a helper application. Figure 10-20 shows what this looks like.

You'll find that ClearFusion streams every video file it encounters, making it easy for you to preview an .AVI file. You can resize the ClearFusion window by dragging its borders, as with any other Windows application. While the mouse pointer is over the ClearFusion window, you can also right-click to open the playback menu, as shown in Figure 10-20. This lets you stop, rewind or play a video, or save it to disk. You can save a

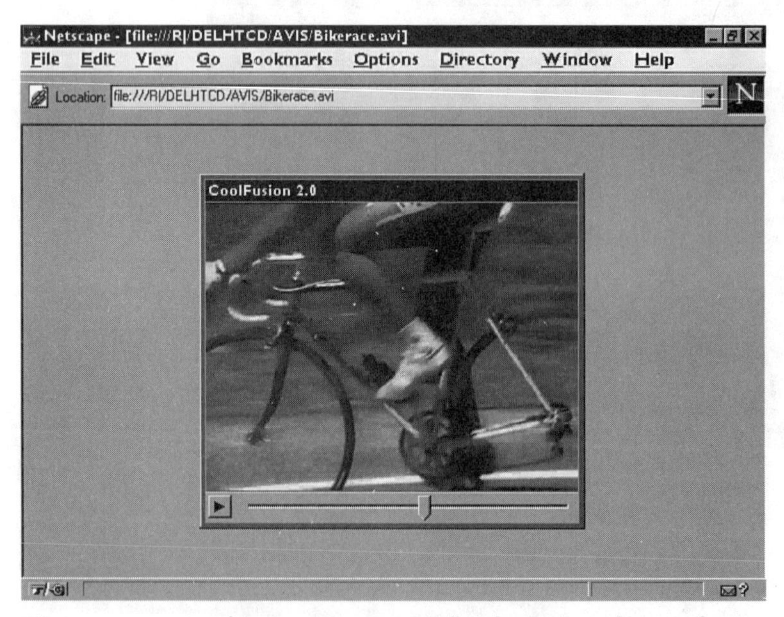

Figure 10–20 ClearFusion streams all videos, even those referenced with the ordinary <IMG SRC> tag

clip at any time during a streaming session, but, obviously, you will only be saving the frames that have thus far been downloaded from a server.

ClearFusion will give you the error message shown in Figure 10-21 if an .AVI file was not saved with a 1:1 interleave of video and sound. In this case, it cannot stream the video correctly but will continue to capture it for you. You can save the video to the Netscape cache without enduring any choppiness by selecting Stop from the pop-up playback menu. By selecting Toggle Menu, you can access other controls that adjust the size, volume, and speed of the video (see Figure 10-22).

Lesson 2: Adding Videos to Your Web Pages

Like almost every other plug-in, ClearFusion relies on the <EMBED SRC> tag. However, it has a number of different attributes that can be used to control the behavior of embedded videos. For example, the light bulbs shown in Figures 10-18 and 10-19 were embedded using these lines:

```
<embed src="light1.avi" oncursor="play" hspace=5 vspace=5 border=0 height=100 width =100 >
<embed src="light2.avi" oncursor="play" hspace=5 vspace=5 border=0 height=100 width =100 >
<embed src="light3.avi" oncursor="play" hspace=5 vspace=5 border=0 height=100 width =100 >
```

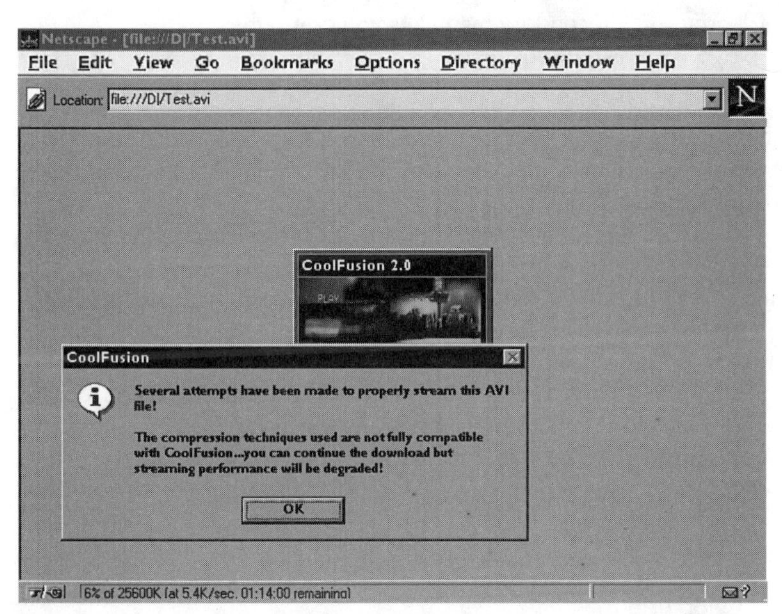

Figure 10-21 ClearFusion warns you if it cannot stream a video properly

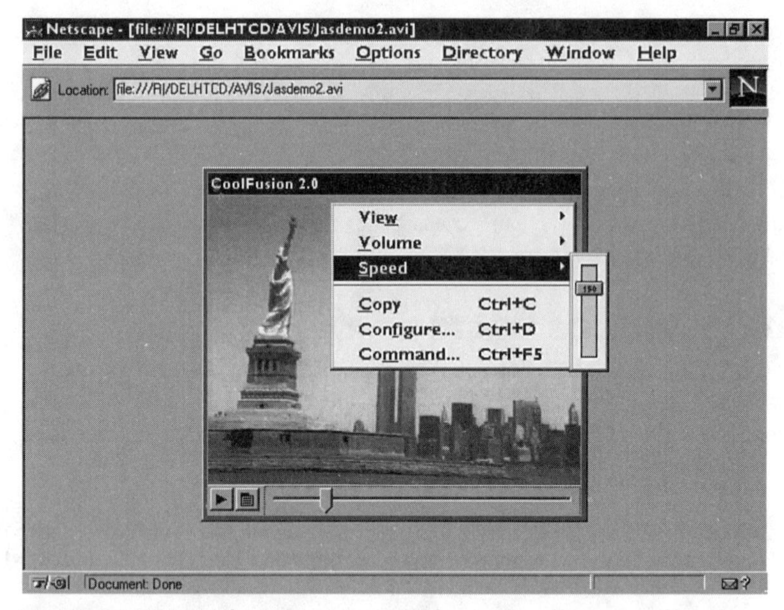

Figure 10–22 ClearFusion's secondary menu lets you adjust the size, volume, and playback speed of any video

As you can guess, the ONCURSOR="PLAY" attribute is responsible for the fact that the videos start playing when the mouse pointer is moved over them. The main attributes for ClearFusion are listed in Table 10-3.

ClearFusion has a special type of attribute known as an *event*. An event is recognizable because it begins with the letters ON. Attached to a given video with the <EMBED SRC> tag, an event attribute waits for a particular event—such as a mouse double-click—to take place. It then performs whatever command had been assigned to that particular event. The commands possible in ClearFusion are listed in Table 10-4.

Clearly, the plethora of events and commands possible in ClearFusion can be confusing. You need to make sure not to assign two different commands to the same event for a given video, and you should also make sure that you associate events and commands consistently on a Web page. For example, a right double-click shouldn't mean one thing for one video, and something different for the next one.

Table 10–3 Attributes for ClearFusion

Attribute	Possible Values	Comments
HEIGHT	Measured in pixels	This required attribute should be set to match the height of the .AVI file you're embedding.
ONBUTTONDOWN	One of the commands listed in Table 10-4	Determines what will happen when the left mouse button is pressed down. For example, ONBUTTONDOWN="STEP BY 1" will advance a video by one frame each time the mouse button is pressed.

Attribute	Possible Values	Comments
ONBUTTONUP	One of the commands listed in Table 10-4	Determines what will happen when the left mouse button was down but is now up. For example, ONEBUTTONUP="STEP BY 1" will advance a video by one frame each time the left mouse button is lifted.
ONCLOSESTREAM	One of the commands listed in Table 10-4	Determines what will happen when a video is through streaming. For example, ONCLOSESTREAM="PAUSE" will leave the video in pause mode.
ONCURSOR	One of the commands listed in Table 10-4	Determines what will happen when the mouse pointer is moved over a video's playback window.
ONDOUBLECLK	One of the commands listed in Table 10-4	Determines what will happen when the left mouse button is double-clicked. For example, ONDOUBLECLK="PLAY" will start a video playing when it is double-clicked on.
ONPAINT	One of the commands listed in Table 10-4	Determines what will happen when the target window is being repainted.
ONPLAY	PAUSE	If set to PAUSE, this attribute causes video playback to be paused until one of the commands in Table 10-4 is executed.
ONRBUTTONDOWN	One of the commands listed in Table 10-4	Determines what will happen if the right mouse button is down. Again, this is not available if the playback menu is in use.
ONRBUTTONUP	One of the commands listed in Table 10-4	Determines what will happen when the right mouse button is up. This event is not available if the playback menu is in use.
ONRDOUBLECLK	One of the commands listed in Table 10-4	Determines what will happen when the right mouse button is double-clicked. This event is not available if the playback menu is in use.
SHOWCONTROLS	TRUE | FALSE	If this attribute is set to TRUE, playback controls are displayed. The default is FALSE.
STREAMONDOUBLECLK	TRUE | FALSE	If this attribute is set to TRUE, the video streams only to its first frame. It then waits for a left-button mouse double-click to resume streaming. The default is FALSE, which tells the plug-in to stream the entire content without user intervention. Once streamed, a file is in Netscape's cache and can begin playing immediately.
WIDTH	Measured in pixels	This required attribute should be set to match the width of the .AVI file you're embedding.

Table 10–4 "Event" commands and subcommands for ClearFusion

Command	Possible Subcommands	Comments
CLOSE	None	This command closes the playback window. For example, attributes of ONRDOUBLECLK="CLOSE" would prime a playback window to be closed when it is right-double-clicked on.
PAUSE	None	Pauses the video when the related "on" event takes place.
PLAY	TO | FROM | FULLSCREEN | REPEAT	Starts playing the video when the related "on" event takes place. The FROM and TO subcommands let you specify frames where playback will begin or end. For example, ONDOUBLECLK="PLAY FROM 10" will begin a video's playback from frame 10 when it is double-clicked on. The FULLSCREEN subcommand lets you specify that full screen mode should be used. The REPEAT subcommand lets you specify that playback should restart from the beginning when the end of the video has been reached.
RESUME	None	This continues playing a video when the related "on" event takes place. Used in combination with the PAUSE command.
SEEK	START | END | frame number	When the related "on" event takes place, SEEK causes a video to seek to START, to END, or to go to a frame number that you specify.
SET	AUDIO | SPEED | VIDEO	Can be used to set audio or video parameters for the playback window. SET AUDIO ALL ON turns sound on, SET AUDIO ALL OFF turns sound off. SPEED sets the relative speed of video playback, where SPEED 1000 is normal, SPEED 500 is half speed, SPEED 2000 Is twice normal, and so on. (Example: ONDOUBLECLK="SET SPEED=2000"). VIDEO OFF disables video output.
STEP	Number of frames	Steps the video ahead one or more frames. Stepping forward by one frame is the default; otherwise, an amount must be specified. For example, ONDOUBLECLK="STEP BY 2".

Figure 10-23 shows a sample Web page designed for ClearFusion. Here is the code that produced it:

```
<html>
<head>
   <title>CoolFusion Test Page</title>
</head>
<p><font SIZE=+2>CoolFusion Test</font> </p>
And now, a couple of words from our sponsor.<p>
<embed src="Test.avi" onplay=pause SHOWCONTROLS=TRUE STREAMONDOUBLECLK=TRUE HEIGHT=200⇐
WIDTH=200 NOMENU=FALSE ALIGN=CENTER>
<embed src="Space.avi" onplay=pause NOMENU=FALSE SHOWCONTROLS=TRUE ONCURSOR="PLAY"⇐
HEIGHT=150 WIDTH=150 VSPACE=20 ALIGN=CENTER>
<embed src="Brunner.avi" SHOWCONTROLS=FALSE ONDOUBLECLK="PLAY" NOMENU="TRUE"⇐
ONRDOUBLECLK=CLOSE HEIGHT=150 WIDTH=200 ALIGN=CENTER><BR CLEAR>
</body>
</html>
```

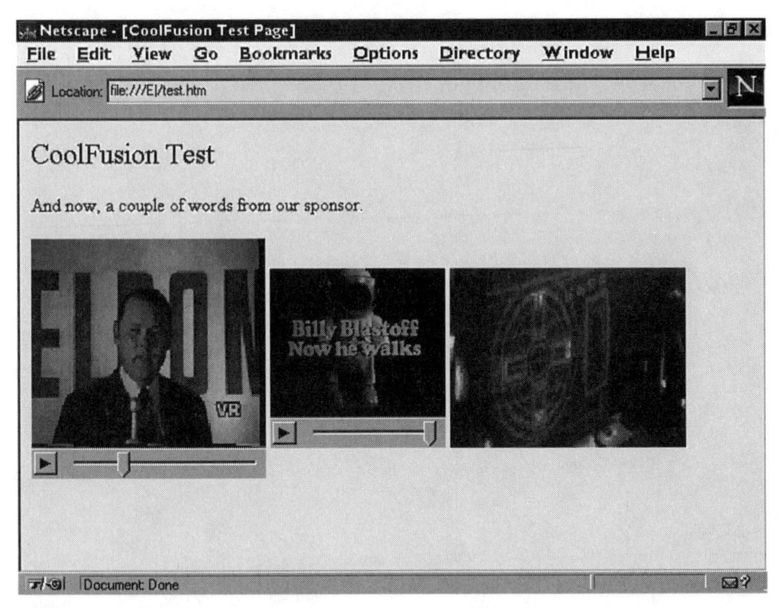

Figure 10–23 This ClearFusion page shows three videos in a row

INTERVU

You may already be familiar with InterVU if you worked though the section "Getting Started with the Embed Tag" in Chapter 8, "A Programming Overview." It's a plug-in designed to handle MPEG video, which makes it similar to Action (previously covered in this chapter). However, InterVU is different in that it is available for both Windows 95 and the Macintosh. This positions it as a widespread solution for reading a MIME type that Netscape cannot handle by itself.

Special features of InterVU include an automatic first frame preview of the MPEG file, streaming video, and full-speed replay from Netscape's disk cache.

Lesson 1: Installing InterVU

If you didn't already install InterVU in the course of Chapter 8, go to the InterVU Web site at *http://www.intervu.com* to download it (or see Appendix A).

The Macintosh InterVU installer requires that you have System 7.5.3 or later. Copy it to your desktop or another convenient location. Expand the relevant installer file using Stuffit Expander, and then just click on it: It will create an InterVU folder on your hard drive and an InterVU plug-in (with a ppc suffix if you installed for a Power PC, or a fat suffix if you installed for both Power PC and 68040 processor types). Copy the InterVU plug-in to the PLUGINS folder in your Netscape subdirectory.

Next, exit Netscape if it was running and restart the program. Select About Plug-ins from the Apple Menu, and you'll now see an entry related to InterVU that looks similar to the following:

```
Description:
InterVuPPC data
MIME Type: video/x-mpeg
Suffixes: mpeg
Description: InterVuPPC data
MIME Type: video/x-mpv
Suffixes: mpv
Description: InterVuPPC data
MIME Type: video/x-mpe
Suffixes: mpe
Description: InterVuPPC data
MIME Type: video/x-mpg
Suffixes: mpg
Description: InterVuPPC data
MIME Type: video/mpeg
Suffixes: mpeg
Description: InterVuPPC data
MIME Type: video/mpv
Suffixes: mpv
Description: InterVuPPC data
MIME Type: video/mpe
Suffixes: mpe
Description: InterVuPPC data
MIME Type: video/mpg
Suffixes: mpg
```

You can now verify the plug-in's operation by using File Open from within Netscape to navigate to the InterVU folder. Open the file DEMO.MPG and you will see the "Blue Angels" image used in Chapter 8. Now you can go to the InterVU Web site to test more images. Figure 10-24 shows the test page found at *http://www.intervu.com/devzone/demolib/todos/todos7.html*. This is the line of code that embedded the travel graphic you see:

```
<EMBED SRC="MPEG/TODOS7.MPG" WIDTH=172 HEIGHT=152 FRAMES=YES>
```

To install the Windows 95 version of InterVU, download the self-extracting installer file to a temporary subdirectory on your hard drive and then run it. This starts a setup program that locates Netscape, installs the plug-in NPIVMPG.DLL in your PLUGINS folder, and creates an INTERVU folder within that. The installer also places an InterVU entry in the Programs section of your Start Menu. Finally, it loads a test page, HELP.HTM, that it created within the INTERVU folder.

After you have inspected this page locally, you can also pick About Plug-ins from the Help menu. This will show you the following list of MIME types:

```
Description: data
MIME Type: video/x-mpeg
Suffixes: mpg;*.mpe;*.mpeg
Description: data
MIME Type: video/mpeg
Suffixes: mpg;*.mpe;*.mpeg
```

Figure 10–24 An InterVU test page running on a Macintosh

You can forward this, or its more exhaustive Mac cousin, to the administrators of your Web server so they can set it to deliver MPEG files with the correct MIME types. However, MPEGs have been common on the Web long enough that this probably will not be necessary. Copy some test Web pages and images to your site and try them out first.

To check how well the Windows version of InterVU can download MPEGs over the Web, you can start with the InterVU Web site. Figure 10-25 shows the undersea page found at *http://www.intervu.com/devzone/demolib/sio/sioiv8.html.*

Like most plug-ins, InterVU has a variety of attributes you can use with the <EMBED SRC> tag. They are pretty much self-explanatory, but you can refer to Table 10-5 for more details.

Table 10–5 EMBED SRC attributes for InterVU

Attribute	Possible Parameters	Comments
WIDTH	Measured in pixels	As usual, this parameter is mandatory. Add ten pixels to the width of the video file if you want to show a frame around the screen
HEIGHT	Measured in pixels	This parameter is required. Add 29 pixels to the height of the frame if you want to show InterVU's controls.
AUTOPLAY	YES|NO	If AUTOPLAY=YES, the video will start playing as soon as the Web page is opened. If AUTOPLAY=NO, InterVU will show the first frame of the video, and the user can then start the video manually.

continued on next page

continued from previous page

Attribute	Possible Parameters	Comments
FRAMERATE	Number from 1 to 20	This attribute can decrease the frame rate for the video being played. The smaller the number you enter, the more the video will be slowed down.
FRAMES	YES	This tag is required if your Web page uses frames.
LOOP	Number	If you want the video to loop, use this attribute and enter the number of times you want it to loop.
DOUBLESIZE	YES	If DOUBLESIZE=YES, InterVU will play the video at double the encoded size. Adjust WIDTH and HEIGHT attributes to match.
HALFSIZE	YES	If HALFSIZE=YES, InterVU will play the video at half the encoded size. Adjust WIDTH and HEIGHT attributes to match.
CONBAR	NO	Using this attribute disables the controls bar of the InterVU player.

Lesson 2: Creating Content for Your Web Pages

Add-on cards that compress data from a video input to the MPEG specification in real time can cost thousands of dollars. Their advantage is video compression ratios of up to 200:1. Additionally, MPEG video captures can be full screen and close to broadcast

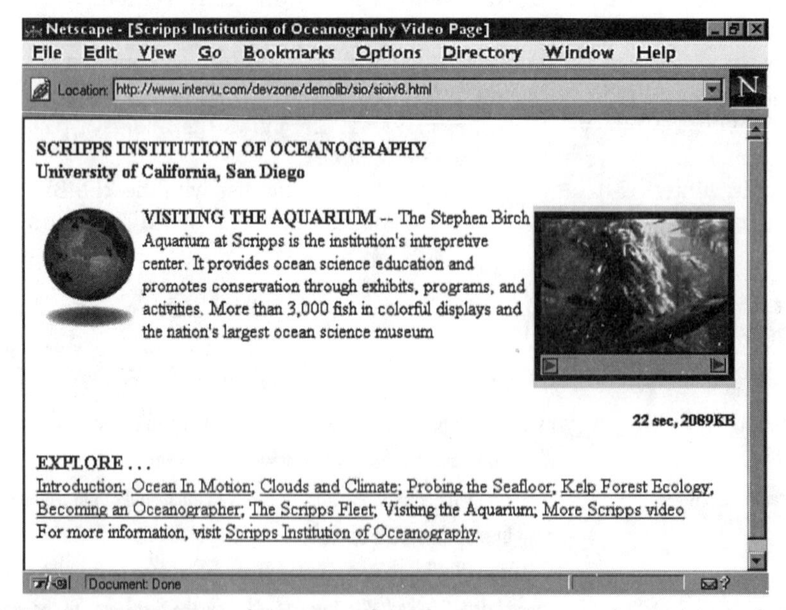

Figure 10-25 A demo page found at InterVU's Web site, viewed via Windows

quality. If you cannot afford an encoder card, however, don't be discouraged: Software-only encoders are available from firms such as Xing Technology and Vitec. The MPEG Plaza at *http://www.visiblelight.com/mpeg.htp* (the "htp" is correct) maintains useful information, including lists of hardware and software encoders.

InterVU, Inc. points out that the "normal" data rate for high-quality MPEG-1 video is around 1.5Mbps per second. A 28.8Kbps modem would be able to download and display only a frame of this every other second. InterVU decreases the video frame to approximately 120 by 160 pixels in order to reduce the bandwidth requirements by about 4:1. This improves raw performance to two frames per second. Data can then be compressed to deliver up to eight frames per second.

A surprising suggestion—to those who are not familiar with MPEG compression—is that you use the highest-quality source video you can get. Video noise, speckles, and other artifacts, because they are random, are hard to compress. Therefore, they can inflate the size of an MPEG video by 100% or even more.

MACZILLA

Some people have criticized the plug-in concept because they think few users will understand how, or take the time, to download and install plug-ins. The fact that Netscape 3.0 is now bundled with major plug-ins is a tribute to this worry.

When future versions of Netscape are released, it will permit automatic installation of plug-ins. (This is also a controversial concept, however. Some people don't want software that they think might put something on their hard drive without asking.) In the meantime, MacZilla, from Knowledge Engineering, looks to be the product of choice if you think visitors to your Web site will only have the patience to install one plug-in.

With just one plug-in, MacZilla handles MPEG, .AVI and QuickTime video, plus all the major sound types including MIDI. If you can get users to install MacZilla, you can probably design your Web site around its capabilities without having to look at any other product. Unfortunately, MacZilla is currently—as its name implies—a Mac-only product. A Windows version is promised.

Lesson 1: Installing MacZilla

To install MacZilla, download it from Knowledge Engineering's Web site at *http://www.maczilla.com* (or check Appendix A for details about your CD-ROM). Run the Maczilla_installer, and a file called MacZilla! will be copied into your Netscape PLUGINS folder.

Exit Netscape if it is running and restart the program. Now select About Plug-ins from the Apple menu. You will see a list of plug-ins that includes the following text:

```
MacZilla!™
File name: MacZilla!™

Types:
Description: MPEG Video
```

continued on next page

continued from previous page

```
MIME Type: video/mpeg
Suffixes: mpg, mpeg, mpe
Description: MacZilla!™ data
MIME Type: video/avi
Suffixes: avi
Description: application/x-macbinary
MIME Type: application/x-macbinary
Suffixes: bin
Description: MacZilla!™ data
MIME Type: application/macbinary
Suffixes: bin
Description: LiveAudio data
MIME Type: audio/x-midi
Suffixes: mid
Description: LiveAudio data
MIME Type: audio/x-wav
Suffixes: wav
Description: LiveAudio data
MIME Type: audio/basic
Suffixes: au
Description: Quicktime Video
MIME Type: video/quicktime
Suffixes: qt, mov
Description: MacZilla!™ data
MIME Type: audio/sfil
Suffixes: sfil
Description: MacZilla!™ data
MIME Type: audio/au
Suffixes: au
Description: LiveAudio data
MIME Type: audio/aiff
Suffixes: aiff
Description: LiveAudio data
MIME Type: audio/x-aiff
Suffixes: aif
Description: MIDI
MIME Type: audio/midi
Suffixes: mid
Description: LiveAudio data
MIME Type: audio/wav
Suffixes: wav
Description: MacZilla!™ data
MIME Type: application/x-maczilla-macres
Suffixes: mzr
Description: MacZilla!™ data
MIME Type: application/x-maczilla-macreslist
Suffixes: mzrl
```

This is an overwhelming number of MIME types for a single 396KB plug-in to take on! Unfortunately, many of them overlap with those handled by Netscape's built-in LiveAudio and LiveVideo plug-ins. For each MIME type, you need to choose which plug-in will handle it.

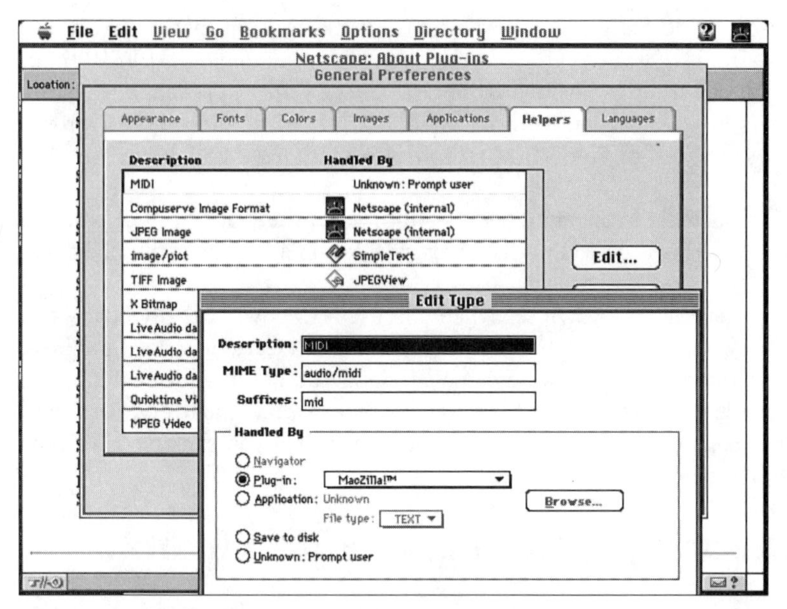

Figure 10–26 Opening the Edit Type window in the Helpers tab is required for each MIME type that two plug-ins might be vying for

Open Netscape's Options/General Preferences menu and select the Helpers tab, as shown in Figure 10-26. For each MIME type that may be disputed, double-click on the Description field in the scrolling list. This opens the Edit Type window shown in the figure. In its "handled by" section, click the plug-in radio button and then select either Live Audio (or LiveVideo, if relevant) or Maczilla.

In order to trust what will happen when Netscape opens Web pages, you need to repeat this procedure for each disputed MIME type in the list. It would be nice to be able to assume a dependable logic to the procedure, whereby MacZilla, being installed after LiveAudio and LiveVideo, automatically defers to them in case of a conflict—only taking over the MIME types that the browser was not already capable of handling. Or, failing that, it would be great for you and users of your Web page to be able to depend on MacZilla to take over every MIME type it could.

Unfortunately, through no fault of MacZilla, Navigator cannot be depended on to organize this consistently. One thing you can count on, at least, is that plug-ins take precedence over helper applications. MacZilla will automatically take over the handling of MIME types you were previously passing to helper applications.

MacZilla's handling of the PC-oriented .WAV and .AVI file types is significant. To get the most out of this feature, you need to download codecs that Microsoft and Intel have separately made available. This should allow you to view .AVI files even if their authors used MS Video or Indeo compression (as is quite likely).

Get the Microsoft Video for Windows extensions for the Mac—if that doesn't sound too contradictory—from *ftp.microsoft.com/developr/drg/Multimedia/jumpstart/VfW11Mac/vfw11.sit*. Get the Intel Indeo extensions from *www.intel.com/pc-supp/ multimed/indeo/i32qtft.htm*. Both sets of codecs come with installers that place the files in their proper locations in your Mac's System Folder. (Microsoft also includes a QuickTime to .AVI conversion utility.)

To confirm that MacZilla is operating as it should, go to the MacZilla Web site and browse the "Zilla Tour." This is basically a list of external Web pages with multimedia files on board.

Maczilla has a unique feature you'll see when you use it to download any binary file. Instead of merely showing Netscape's default bar graph that indicates download progress, it shows a controller that not only indicates how far along you are in a file, but also can play the parts of the file that have already been received. Meanwhile, the overgrown lizard that is the program's namesake roams the screen, emitting roars if you click on it with the mouse. Figure 10-27 is an example of this screen.

Lesson 2: Embedding Sound and Video in Your Own Web Pages

MacZilla is a conservatively designed product that adds few proprietary extensions to the standard EMBED SRC attributes. This somewhat limits your ability to design customized pages, but it also means that your Web site looks fairly normal when it is—inevitably—viewed by those using other plug-ins.

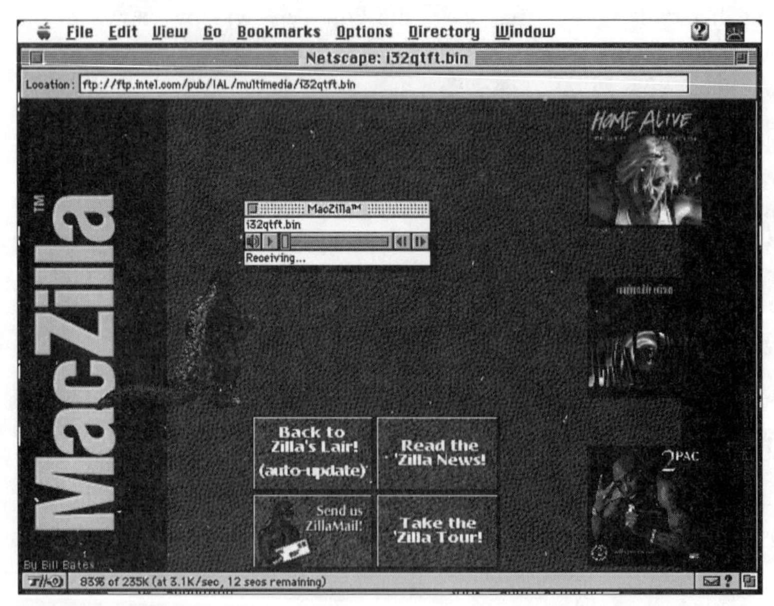

Figure 10-27 Maczilla displays this controller and "game" as it downloads a file

MacZilla uses the <EMBED SRC> tag normally for any of the media types it can embed. HEIGHT and WIDTH are, as usual, required attributes. They should be set to match the size of the video clip, if any, that you are embedding.

If you are embedding a sound and do not want any visual sign of its location, set HEIGHT=0 and WIDTH=2 or *vice versa*. As with other plug-ins, invisible sound or MIDI files should be embedded at the end of a page rather than at the beginning or middle. Otherwise, they may cause not only delays in loading but also unnecessary visual anomalies.

Maczilla also supports a <VISIBLE> tag, which can turn on a controller with stop/play buttons and a slider to indicate its place in a file. AUTOPLAY and LOOPING attributes do what their names imply. For a summary of Maczilla's EMBED SRC attributes, refer to Table 10-6.

Table 10–6 Maczilla's attributes for <EMBED SRC> tags

Attribute	Possible Values	Comments
AUTOPLAY	1|0	If AUTOPLAY is set to 1, the embedded file will be played as soon as the page loads.
HEIGHT	Measured in pixels	This attribute is mandatory.
LOOPING	TRUE|FALSE	Repeats any sound or video. Defaults to FALSE.
VISIBLE	TRUE|FALSE	Toggles display of stop/play buttons and a position slider. Defaults to FALSE.
WIDTH	Measured in pixels	This attribute is mandatory.

MacZilla seems to work well at interpreting most pages. Figure 10-28 shows a site called "The Video Wall," where four video clips have been embedded in a Netscape table. The author of this site used four instances of the following tag to embed the pistons you see:

```
<EMBED SRC="piston.mov" HEIGHT=120 WIDTH=160 CONTROLLER=FALSE AUTOPLAY=TRUE LOOP=TRUE>
```

As you can see, the syntax is not precisely documented for MacZilla. However, the plug-in displays the videos quite effectively.

MOVIESTAR

Where some plug-ins, such as MacZilla, attempt to take on as much as they possibly can, others target themselves at just one function. Such is the case with MovieStar, from Intelligence at Large. This plug-in handles both QuickTime and QuickTime VR movies.

Netscape's own (Apple-sourced) QuickTime plug-in provides substantial competition. However, MovieStar is still worth investigating, as is Intelligence at Large's separate program, MovieStar Maker. This is a useful tool for not only assembling QuickTime movies, but also modifying them so that they stream effectively. The evaluation version is limited to movies 15 seconds or less in duration, but this is sufficient time to test its functions.

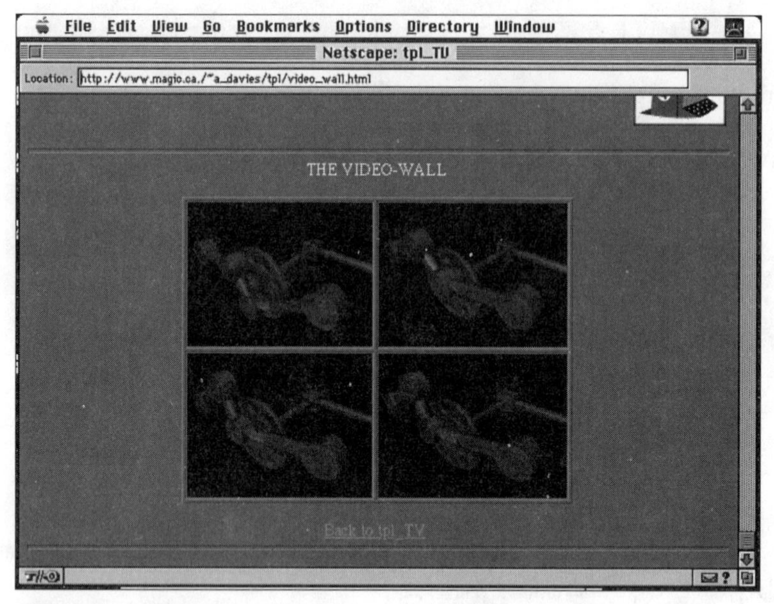

Figure 10-28 MacZilla showing "The Video Wall"

Lesson 1: Installing MovieStar

To install MovieStar, go to the Intelligence at Large Web site at *http://www.beingthere.com*, or check Appendix A for details about your CD-ROM.

If you have Windows 95:

- Copy the file NPSTAR32.ZIP to a temporary subdirectory on your hard drive
- Unzip the file using PKUNZIP, WinZip or a similar utility
- Run the resulting SETUP.EXE, and use its menus to locate the folder that holds NETSCAPE.EXE. The installer will create and install NPSTAR32.DLL to the PLUGINS subdirectory within that folder

If you have Windows 3.1:

- Copy the file NPSTAR16.ZIP to a temporary subdirectory on your hard drive
- Unzip the file using PKUNZIP, WinZip, or a similar utility
- Copy the resulting file, NPSTAR16.DLL to the PLUGINS subdirectory within your Netscape program folder

If you have a Macintosh:

- Run the installer program from your desktop or whatever folder you downloaded it to
- Copy the MovieStar Plug-in file from the MovieStar plug-in folder that is created into your Netscape plug-ins folder (if the MovieStar installer has not already done this automatically)

Since this is a QuickTime plug-in, you also need to install Apple's QuickTime system software if you haven't already. For details about this, refer to "Laying the Software Foundation" earlier in this chapter. Incidentally, Windows 95 users can see whether or not they have QuickTime already by opening the Control Panel: If a QuickTime icon appears there, you can double-click on it to make sure that QuickTime is installed properly. If the icon does not appear, you need to reinstall it.

Once you have installed MovieStar (and QuickTime, if necessary), exit Netscape and restart it. Then, run About Plug-ins from the Apple menu (Macintosh) or Help menu (Windows) and you will see a list that includes the following:

```
MIME Type: application/x-qtc-broadcast
Suffixes: qtc
Description: Quicktime Video
MIME Type: video/quicktime
Suffixes: qt, mov
```

This is the MIME type/subtype information pertaining to MovieStar. On a Mac, you can use Netscape's Options/General Preferences/Helpers tab to work through the MIME types individually to make sure they are now assigned to MovieStar and not some other plug-in. (If you use Windows and want to turn off the Apple QuickTime plug-in so you can test MovieStar, you must move NPQTW32.DLL or NPQTW16.DLL out of your Netscape Plug-ins folder.) Make sure to clear the Netscape cache using the Network Preferences menu selection after you have made any changes.

An advantage of using MovieStar (or the Apple plug-in, for that matter) is that most Web servers have long since been adapted so they serve up .MOV files with the correct MIME type. If the server you use has not, then give its administrators the MIME type/subtype information listed above so they can make adjustments. (Otherwise, QuickTime movies will display fine from your local drive but not when they are loaded from the server.)

To verify that MovieStar is working correctly, you can go to the Intelligence at Large Web site. Their guide to samples is located at *http://www.pair.com/ial/movies/movies.* You'll notice that movies stream to the browser so you can view parts of them before the whole has been downloaded. If MovieStar is installed properly, you initially see its logo in a frame where the video will be displayed. You then see MovieStar's controller strip, and then the first frames of the movie.

Figure 10-29 shows a literal version of "Web surfing," viewed on a Macintosh and courtesy of World Wave Pictures site at *http://www.surftv.com.* Figure 10-30 shows you the same Web page viewed via Windows. As you can see, MovieStar is capable of delivering excellent consistency across platforms.

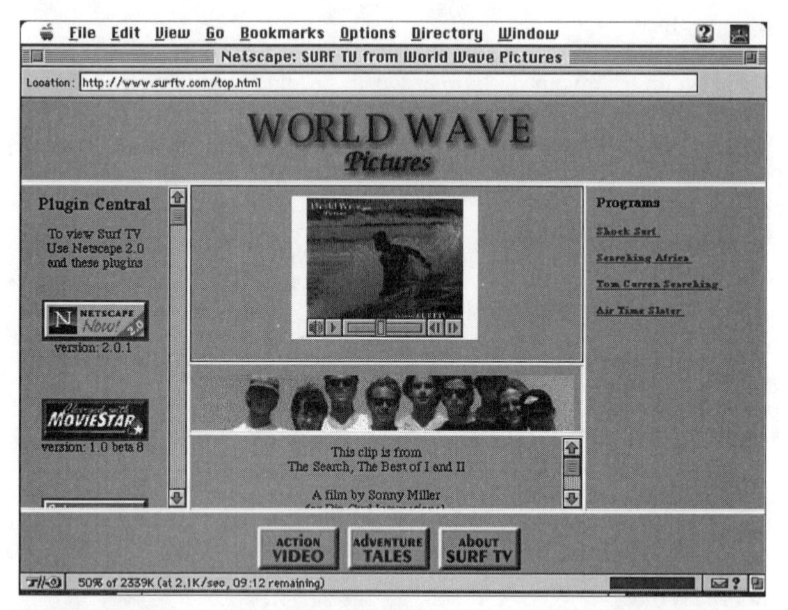

Figure 10–29 "Web Surfing" via the Mac version of MovieStar

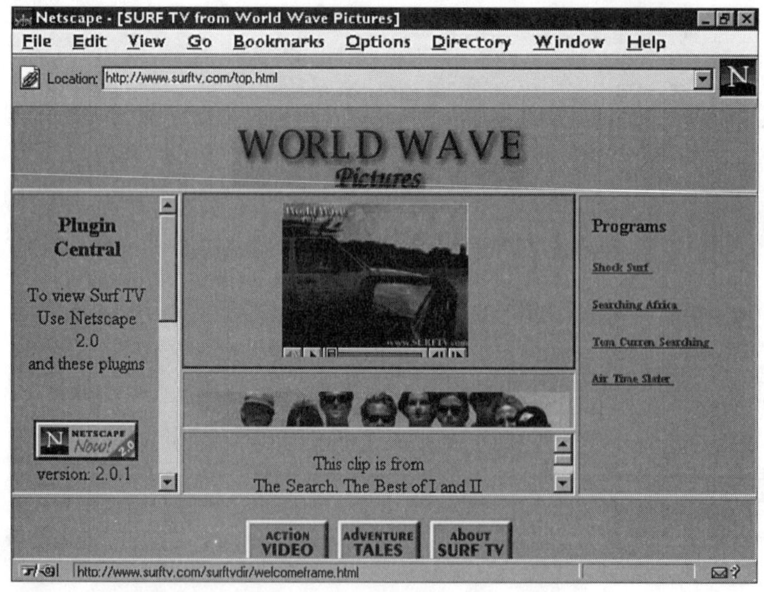

Figure 10–30 The Windows version of MovieStar

Lesson 2: Adding Movies to Your Web Pages

Once again, adding movies to Web pages is performed via the <EMBED SRC> tag. You are already accustomed to the mandatory HEIGHT and WIDTH attributes, as well as the optional LOOP and AUTOSTART attributes—both supported by MovieStar. MovieStar's other special attributes, listed in Table 10-7, have to do with its onscreen appearance and with image map support.

Yes, MovieStar lets you make embedded movies act as image maps the way still Web graphics can. It does so by providing HREF and ISMAP attributes for the <EMBED SRC> tag. You can use HREF with ISMAP to specify the name of a server-side .MAP file that lists coordinates in the video frame and the URLs to which they will take users when clicked on. Or, just use an <HREF> tag by itself and tell users they can move to another Web page by clicking on the video when it's finished playing.

For example, the following line would play a video that takes users to another Web page when they click on it:

```
<EMBED SRC="main.mov" HEIGHT=200 WIDTH=200 AUTOPLAY=TRUE CONTROLLER="false"⇐
HREF="nextpage.htm">
```

Table 10-7 Possible attributes for MovieStar <EMBED SRC> tags

Attribute	Possible Values	Comments
WIDTH	Measured in pixels	The WIDTH should match the preexisting width of your QuickTime file.
HEIGHT	Measured in pixels	The HEIGHT should match the preexisting height of your QuickTime file. Add 16 pixels extra to display MovieStar's controller.
LOOP	TRUE|FALSE|PALINDROME or numerical value	FALSE is the default, causing a movie to stop and wait for action from the user. TRUE will cause the movie to loop up to the number of times the user has set in MovieStar preferences. Using a numerical value causes the movie to loop the specified number of times, unless the user has set a lower number in preferences. The PALINDROME option causes the movie to play backwards from the end to the beginning, then forward, continuing until the user stops the movie or jumps to a different page.
AUTOPLAY	TRUE|FALSE	FALSE is the default for AUTOPLAY, requiring the user to click on the movie or the controller to begin playback. The TRUE option causes a movie to begin playing automatically, thus showing off MovieStar's streaming capabilities. AUTOPLAY only functions if the movie is visible within the browser window.

continued on next page

continued from previous page

Attribute	Possible Values	Comments
AUTOSTART	TRUE|FALSE	Equivalent to AUTOPLAY. Added for improved compatibility with other QuickTime plug-ins. AUTOSTART can be specified on the same line for backward compatibility with earlier versions of the MovieStar plug-in.
HREF	Any URL	The HREF attribute for EMBED SRC lets an embedded movie act like any other Web graphic. A click on the movie will take the user to the URL specified.
HREFABS	Any URL, but must be fully specified with *http://whatever.com* beginning the link	Equivalent to HREF in function, this tag is included for compatibility with the ViewMovie plug-in. Unlike the HREF tag, it requires an "absolute" URL that includes the name of the site. (HREF, in contrast, accepts a relative directory-style path.)
HREFTARGET	The name of a frame or window that has already been declared on the Web page	For sites using frames or multiple windows, this tag will cause the user to be taken to the frame or window specified when they click on the embedded movie.
ISMAP	Requires an <HREF> or <HREFABS> tag to accompany it	This attribute lets you treat a movie as an image map the same way you would a still graphic. Like the ISMAP attribute in an ordinary <A HREF> tag, it requires a server-side image map file to have been created (specifying pixel coordinates in the movie window and the URLs to which they will take users) and a server utility to process it.
PLUGINSPACE	The URL *http://www.beingthere.com/plugn.html#* is suggested	This attribute avoids Netscape's generic list of plug-ins, and will take the first-time user to the Intelligence at Large download page so they can obtain MovieStar.
CONTROLLER	TRUE|FALSE|BADGE	When TRUE, this attribute displays a VCR-style control area under a movie. You should add 16 pixels to the <HEIGHT> tag to leave room for it. FALSE hides the controller; the user can start playback by clicking inside the movie frame. The BADGE option places a tiny picture of a film strip within the movie frame. Clicking on this film strip icon causes the controller to appear at the bottom of the frame.
MCWITHBADGE	TRUE|FALSE	Setting this attribute to TRUE is equivalent to setting CONTROLLER=TRUE and CONTROLLER=BADGE both at once.
MCNOTVISIBLE	TRUE|FALSE	This attribute, provided for compatibility with other QuickTime plug-ins, works in the opposite sense to CONTROLLER. In other words, setting MCNOTVISIBLE=TRUE would be the equivalent of CONTROLLER=FALSE.

Figure 10-31 shows another MovieStar sample page, created by the following HTML code:

```
<HTML>
<HEAD>
<TITLE>Not So Boldly</TITLE>
</HEAD>
<BODY>
This Web page displays a QuickTime movie using MovieStar.<p>
<EMBED SRC="jetland.mov" CONTROLLER=TRUE WIDTH=320 HEIGHT=240 AUTOPLAY=TRUE>
</BODY>
</HTML>
```

Figure 10-32 shows the same page displayed on a Mac.

Lesson 3: Optimizing Movies for the Web

You can use any tools designed for working with QuickTime to prepare your videos for placement on the Web. Intelligence at Large, Inc. offers its own tool, however, called MovieStar Maker.

Streaming QuickTime movies can begin to play while MovieStar is downloading them. They can still be viewed with other QuickTime plug-ins, viewers, and helper applications, although these programs don't support streaming and must download the entire movie file before playing the movie. Changing a conventional QuickTime movie into a streaming QuickTime movie does not increase its file size.

Figure 10-31 A sample MovieStar Web page

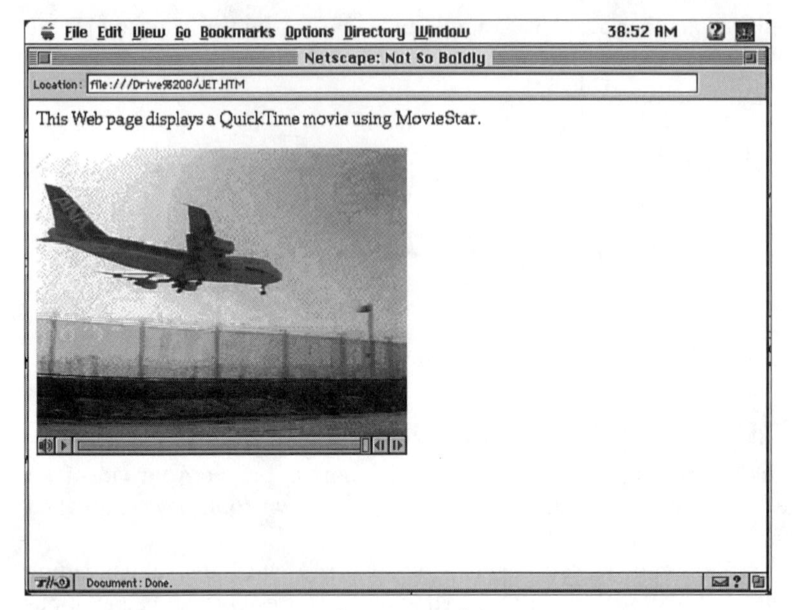

Figure 10–32 A Macintosh version of the same page

To convert a movie with MovieStar Maker (see Figure 10-33), launch the program and open your movie by choosing Open from the File menu. (Or drag-and-drop the movie file onto the MovieStar Maker icon.) From the File menu, choose Save As Movie. Name your movie and select a destination folder, being careful to use a DOS-style file name for compatibility's sake.

Select the checkboxes for the options "Make movie self-contained," "Playable on non-Apple computers," and "Playable on Internet connections." You can also select new compression options by clicking "Minimize Video" or "Minimize Audio." Then click the Save button.

MovieStar and any other streaming plug-in will let users see your movie as it is downloaded. However, there are several options you can consider to speed up download times. The Minimize Audio and Minimize Video options in MovieStar Maker allow you to select a new compression method for your movies.

For example, MovieStar allows you to select JPEG video compression. Sliders let you adjust video quality and change the number of frames per second according to whether your video features fast action or a series of stills.

As pointed out earlier in this chapter, your Macintosh may have codecs on it that are not a standard part of QuickTime. If you use one of these, your movie may not be able to play on other computers. For example, Figure 10-34 shows a file about to be saved using the Indeo codec version 3.2—not necessarily a good idea.

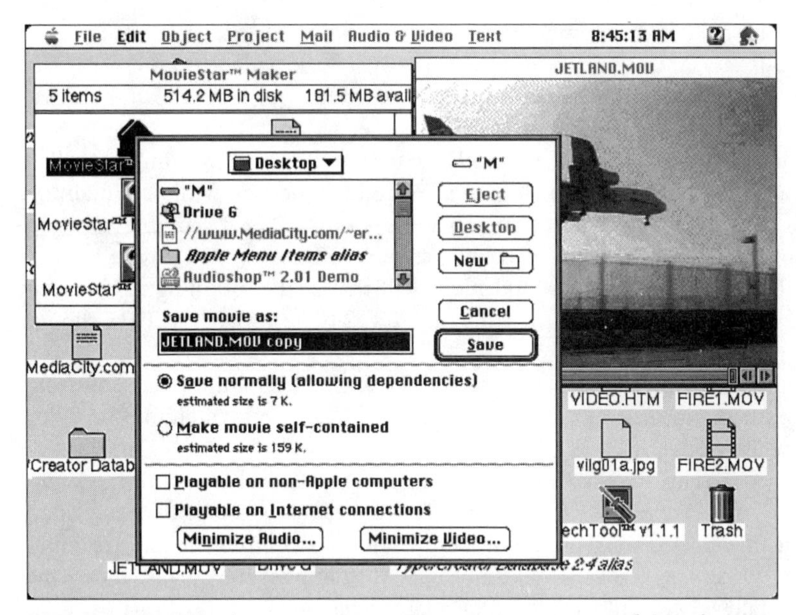

Figure 10–33 The MovieStar Maker program, a useful tool, sums up the parameters you should consider when creating a QuickTime file

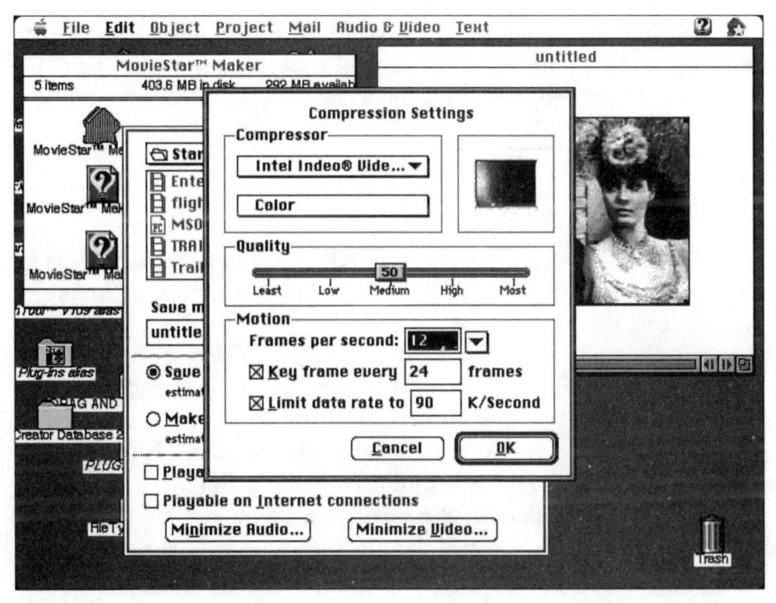

Figure 10–34 Beware of using a nonstandard codec such as Indeo unless you're sure users have it or will download it

Intelligence at Large, Inc. recommends that you use only the "Video," "Animation," "Graphics," "Photo-JPEG," and "Cinepak" settings. The "Cinepak" video compressor is the most useful. It may offer better compression than "Photo-JPEG" for large movie files that are stored at high frame rates (in order to provide smoother action).

To select new audio compression methods, you can click the "Minimize Audio" [Image] button in MovieStar Maker's dialog box. To reduce file size while maintaining acceptable audio quality, you can switch to mono and use the "IMA 4:1" compressor. You can also type in any audio sampling rate you like between 1KHz and 44KHz. The highest frequency that will be audible in your sound file is half that of the sampling rate—given the limitations of the speakers in most multimedia PCs, 24KHz or even 12KHz should usually be ample.

Other compression tips aptly suggested by MovieStar Maker's authors are lowering the frame rate or reducing the size of the video window. You can also switch to 8-bit color or use black-and-white video.

Two options offered by MovieStar Maker are the most vital you'll find in any QuickTime editor. The "Make movie self-contained" choice guarantees that all of the video and sound information is contained in a single movie file, a requirement for streaming QuickTime movies. Otherwise, movie data can be spread among several smaller files. This can happen accidentally when you're editing a QuickTime file.

The "Playable on non-Apple computers" option, also very important, lets your movie play on PCs and UNIX machines. It flattens the movie file into one continuous stream of movie information, rather than dividing the movie into the "resource fork" and "data fork" normally used on a Mac.

Finally, a "playable on Internet connections" choice makes your movie suitable for streaming by moving important movie information to the beginning of the file. This makes sure that the MovieStar plug-in gets the parameters it needs to begin playing a movie.

VDOLIVE

If you've tried video on the Web, you've probably seen VDOLive. This product has been adopted by major content providers such as CBS Television and used to "broadcast" from industry shows such as Internet World.

In many ways, VDOLive occupies the same market position for video that RealAudio (see Chapter 9, "Audio Plug-Ins") does for audio. It streams video (and audio) from a server so that it is viewable in real time over dial-up connections as low as 14.4K (although obviously, faster is better). From the user's point of view, there is less waiting than with even the best of the plug-ins previously discussed in this chapter.

VDOLive uses a wavelet algorithm that divides each video frame into multiple layers, each providing extra detail and image quality. If there is sufficient bandwidth, all layers are transmitted to the user. If not, only some of the layers are transmitted, degrading detail but preserving audio continuity. In fact, VDOLive provides better, less choppy audio than some sound-only products.

The downside, for the amateur Web developer at least, is that server-side software is required to offer up video files. Conceptually similar to RealAudio's, it requires .VDO metafiles—or "video links," as VDONet Corporation simply terms them—that are placed in Web pages. These contain pointers to the actual video files, which use an .AVI format that has been specially compressed.

VDO's server software is able to monitor the actual data transfer to a user and dynamically adjust the amount of information it sends. This customizes video quality for each connection and, unlike RealAudio, eliminates the need for data files optimized for a particular dial-up speed.

If you have a full-time connection to the Internet with its own IP address, you can run VDO's server software. A Personal Server edition is available for Windows 95, Windows NT, and many UNIX versions. If you plan extensive use of the system, however, a dedicated server is advisable—and a license from VDONet (from $1,199 on up) is required.

On the client side, VDOLive was originally a helper application only. It's now available as a plug-in for Windows 3.x, Windows 95, and Windows NT, which lets you embed video clips in your Web pages. A Macintosh plug-in has also been announced but was unavailable during preparation of this book: You should check VDONet's Web site at *http://www.vdolive.com* to see if it has been released. VDOLive tools for capturing and compressing video information, which will be discussed briefly here, are available only for Windows 95.

Lesson 1: Installing the Plug-In

To install the VDOLive plug-in for playing embedded videos, access the VDONet Web site at *http://www.vdolive.com* (also check Appendix A for details of what's included on your CD-ROM). The Windows 3.x installer is in a file called PLGPLY16.EXE, while the Windows 95 installer is in a file called PLGPLY32.EXE.

Run either of these installers, and it will prompt you to locate your Netscape subdirectory. It will also prompt you to specify a directory where you would like to store the VDOLive Player (a helper application), release notes, help file, and several demo pages. Once you have done this, the installer will proceed automatically, installing NPVDO32.DLL or NPVDO16.DLL, whichever is relevant to your Windows version.

You can also take this opportunity to install the VDOLive Personal Tools and Personal Sever software. You should do this if you have any intention of creating original video content; if you just want to view others' Web pages using the plug-in, you can bypass this step. To install the server and compression tools, run PERSSERV. This will prompt you once again for an installation subdirectory, which can be the one you used in the previous step or a new one.

The installer places icons labeled "Install VDOLive Personal Tools Win95" and "Install VDOLive Personal Server NT and 95" in the Programs\VDOLive Personal section of your Start menu. While the server and the tools have been placed on your hard drive, they are not decompressed until you click on these second-stage installers from the Start menu. This saves you disk space until and unless you need to run the software.

Now, you should exit and restart Netscape if it was running. Select About Plug-ins from the Help menu, and you will see that VDOLive has added the following:

```
Description: data
MIME Type: video/vdo
Suffixes: vdo
```

Administrators of your Web server will need this information in order to make video files available to VDOLive users. In this case, of course, the VDOLive Server software is also required.

To see whether or not VDOLive is working, establish your connection to the Internet. Then click on the icon labeled "Local HTML test page" (which the installer placed in the Programs\VDOLive Tools section of your Start menu or Program Manager). If you prefer, run Netscape yourself and then use its File Open capabilities to load TEST.HTM from whichever subdirectory you used for the VDOLive files.

VDOLive draws the video clip displayed on your screen from the company's server in Palo Alto, California, using the following line of code:

```
<embed src=asaf8f20.vdo autostart=true loop=true stretch=true width=160 height=120>
```

The result is shown in Figure 10-35. When you are satisfied that this video plays properly, you can test the links that VDONet provides to other video files. For example, Figure 10-36 shows part of a news broadcast found at *http://www.iguide.com/foxnews/sunday/video/fnsunday.vdo.* Here, the plug-in is running in full-screen mode because the

Figure 10-35 The VDOLive plug-in showing an embedded video clip

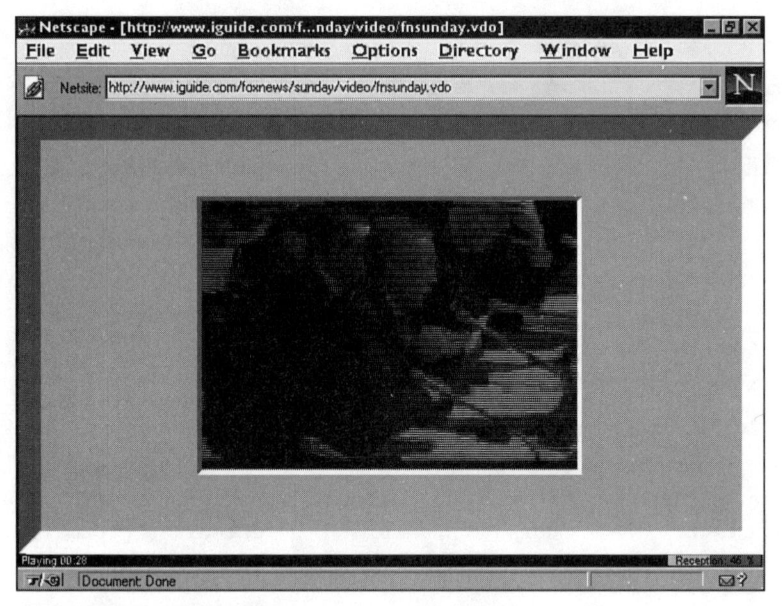

Figure 10–36 VDOLive running in full-screen mode

video was referenced using <IMG SRC> rather than <EMBED SRC>. You can use these and other clips to familiarize yourself with VDOLive's capabilities and user interface.

Lesson 2: Placing VDO Clips on Your Web Pages

Creating links between your Web pages and video clips needs to be done in two steps. First, you need to create a one-line ASCII file with a .VDO extension. This resides on the server and will act as a pointer to the actual video clip your page references.

A .VDO file is in the following format:

```
vdo://server[:TCP port]/filename.avi
```

For "server," substitute either the name of the host where the VDOLive server software is running, or the host's HP address. The optional TCP port value follows after a colon. This is only required if the server is not using the default value of 7000 for its TCP listening port. The file name should include the drive and directory location (if you're running the server on Windows 95 or Windows NT) or the path relative to the root directory (if you're running UNIX).

When you create a link on your Web page, point to a single .VDO file per link. As usual, HEIGHT and WIDTH attributes corresponding to the size of your video file are mandatory. Other attributes pertaining to VDOLive files specifically are listed in Table 10-8.

Table 10-8 EMBED attributes for VDOLive

Attribute	Possible Values	Comments
AUTOSTART	TRUE|FALSE	Can cause the video to play automatically when a user opens the Web page.
STRETCH	TRUE|FALSE	When set to TRUE, this can adjust the size of the video image to fit the assigned size of the plug-in window. This may distort the original image size and aspect ratio. If set to FALSE, ensures that the image is displayed without size distortion. If you set STRETCH=FALSE, make sure that WIDTH and HEIGHT are set to values great enough to show all of the video; otherwise, it will be cut off at the top and right border.

If you have the STRETCH attribute set to FALSE, set WIDTH and HEIGHT so that they are great enough that none of your image is truncated. Also, add 16 pixels at the bottom of the image to leave room for the VDOLive controller and message bar. If you want the frame to be displayed, add eight extra pixels to WIDTH and eight extra pixels to HEIGHT.

Lesson 3: Preparing Video Clips for VDOLive

VDOLive software uses the Video for Windows .AVI format as a "wrapper" around compressed video and audio data created by the VDO codecs. Its compression can achieve some dramatic results. For example, uncompressed video captured from a camera or video tape would occupy 52MB per minute of running time (assuming a frame size of 160 by 120 pixels, 24 bits per pixel, and a frame rate of 15 frames per second). After compression, the same video would require just 180-960KB per minute.

To capture a video, you can use either VDO's own VDO Capture software or the company's VDO Clip utility for converting previously saved video. Obviously, you need a sound card and video capture board that operate under Windows 95. The video board must support capture of uncompressed video in 16-bit or 24-bit color.

Capturing video via VDO Capture is the safest way to ensure it will be compatible with VDOLive. However, if you prefer to use your video board's own capture utility and third-party editing software, you can do so. Make sure that you do not exceed the maximum image size supported by VDO Clip, which is 240 pixels wide and 176 pixels high.

It's preferable to capture at a frame rate between 10 and 15 pixels per second, using 24 bits per pixel if possible. The preferred image size is 160 pixels wide and 120 pixels high.

Perhaps the trickiest aspect of video capture is, ironically, audio. VDO Clip will compress only audio recorded in 16-bit mono with an 8KHz sampling rate. VDO Clip is capable of removing a different-style audio stream from a video clip; you then paste the audio into an external sound editor and convert its sampling rate. Then, you can paste it back into the video file you want to compress. All this, however, is a tricky operation that can result in degradation of audio quality. Therefore, it's much better to stick to the 16-bit/8KHz/mono sampling rate in the first place.

VIVOACTIVE

Of the plug-ins featured so far in this chapter, only one, VDOLive, has come close to providing "video on demand." That's because of the massive amounts of data involved in a video file. Remember, any video simply consists of a series of individual pictures, or frames, displayed rapidly to simulate motion. The higher the frame rate, the smoother the motion.

Natural-looking motion, as on television or in a film, requires a frame rate of about 30 frames per second. This works out to 1,800 frames for a minute of video, which partly explains why video files are so large. Adding audio to a video clip just makes matters worse.

VivoActive is a new plug-in that will let your Web pages approach the elusive goal of video on demand *without* any special server-side software. It uses standard HyperText Transfer Protocol (HTTP), meaning that anyone who can view your Web pages will be able to view your videos as well. It doesn't matter if users are behind firewalls or even connected via SLIP emulation software.

The VivoActive software components consist of:

- The VivoActive Player, a plug-in for Windows 95/NT or Power Macintosh versions of Netscape
- VivoActive Producer Software, a Windows 95/NT program for creating VivoActive files from Video for Windows (AVI) files
- The VivoActive Rehearsal Server, a simple Web server program that emulates various modem speeds, letting you preview how your videos will look to users

VivoActive's image resolution is fixed at 176 × 144 pixels. While you cannot change this resolution, you can control a video's placement on a Web page to some extent. If the .AVI file you use to create a VideoActive (.VIV) file is smaller than 176 × 144 pixels, you may see a border around the VideoActive video when it plays. If the .AVI is larger than 176 × 144 pixels, VivoActive automatically resizes it when converting it to a .VIV file.

The VivoActive Producer program lets you adjust both the bit rate and frame rate of the .VIV files you produce, tuning them for the type of connection (dial-up versus intranet) you expect your users to have. Vivo Software, Inc. claims possible compression of as much as 200:1 relative to uncompressed .AVI files.

An attractive aspect of VivoActive Producer (which it has in common with VDOLive authoring software) is that it uses proprietary codecs that are built into the compression software and the plug-in. This means that, unlike with some other products, you do not have to worry about accidentally using a codec (Indeo, Cinepak, etc.) that users might not have on their computers.

If a video successfully plays and converts on your system, it should play on any Windows 95/NT computer used to view your Web page. The only limitation here is that clients must have 486/66 (or faster) processing speed.

Currently, there is no option for creating audio-only .VIV files, nor is there a way to create .VIV files that contain only video. (To have a silent background, you must deliberately add a silent audio stream to your source .AVI file using video editor software.)

Finally, the VivoActive audio codec is an aggressive one that is optimized for speech, not music. If you produce a video that includes music, the music will sound distorted.

Lesson 1: Installing the VivoActive Plug-In

To install the VivoActive plug-in, go to VivoSoftware's Web site at *http://www.vivo.com* (or check Appendix A for details about your CD-ROM). The VivoActive plug-in is delivered in a self-extracting archive file called VIVOPLAY.EXE, while the VivoActive Producer and Rehearsal Server software is in a file called VIVOPROD.EXE.

When you double-click on VIVOPLAY.EXE, it will run the InstallShield installer, locating your Netscape Plug-ins folder and copying NPVIV32.DLL into it. Double-clicking on VIVOPROD.EXE will prompt you for a folder where you'd like the Producer and Rehearsal Server software to be placed. Once you have made a selection, the installer will copy these programs and some sample files into the folder specified. It also makes a VivoActive entry in the Programs section of your Start Menu. This includes entries for "VivoActive Producer," "VivoActive Rehearsal Server," "Uninstall VivoActive," and more.

The Macintosh version comes in an installer that uncompresses files into a VivoActive folder. This will reside on your desktop or within any folder from which you ran the installer. Open the VivoActive folder and locate the folder within it named "Put in Netscape Plug-ins folder." Opening the latter, you'll see a file called Vivo Plugin. Complete the installation by dragging this file into your Netscape Plug-ins folder. (Like so many things Macintosh, this is all much more difficult to describe in writing than it is to do.)

To test VivoActive, you need to exit and restart Netscape. Select About Plug-ins from the Help menu, and you'll see that VivoActive has installed, taking command of the following MIME types and suffixes:

```
video/vivo      viv
video/vnd.vivo            viv
```

The second of these, video/vnd.vivo, is the one that should be added to a server's list of MIME types, associated with the suffixes viv and vivo. (The video/vivo MIME type has been replaced, and appears only for compatibility with previous VivoActive beta software.)

Now you're ready to try a video. If you installed the VivoActive Producer and Rehearsal software, use Netscape's File Open menu to navigate to the folder where you placed the VivoActive programs. Within that folder, you'll find another folder called HTML. Open the file DEMO.HTM within it, and you'll see a screen like that in Figure 10-37.

The sample video plays automatically after the Web page is opened. If you want to replay it, you can click on the play button you see in the lower-right-hand corner of the video image.

As you can see, this technology really does approach the "video on demand" goal—at least when files are loaded from a hard drive. To test how video performs via a dial-up link (or if you didn't install the VivoActive Producer software), you'll want to return to the VivoActive videos page at *http://www.vivo.com/interview/index.html.* This provides links to third-party material plus videos created by VivoActive itself. Figure 10-38 shows a typical sample.

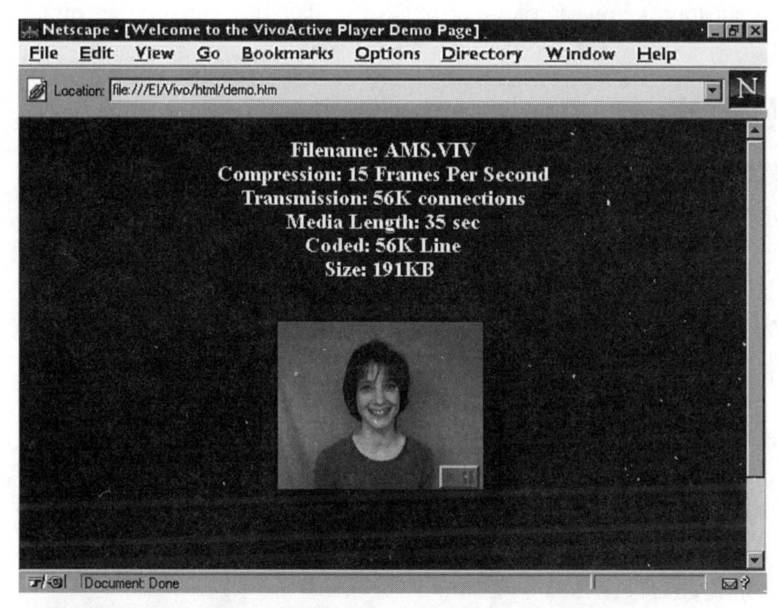

Figure 10–37 This sample video takes up just 191K

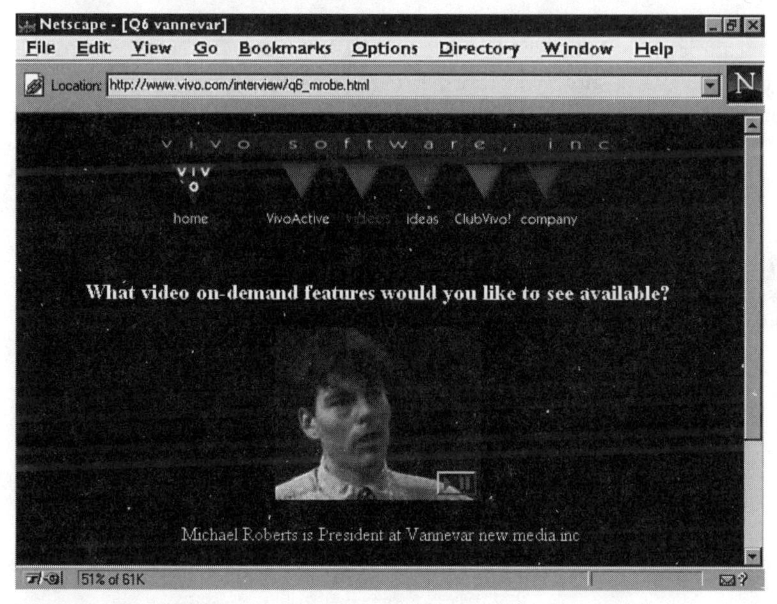

Figure 10–38 Videos may be compressed further for dial-up links—this one is just 61K

You'll notice that while a video loads, its first frame is displayed as a still. The triangular Vivo logo, seen at lower right, rotates to let you know the file is loading. Once enough of the file has loaded, it starts to play (if the Web page's author used the AUTOSTART=TRUE attribute). You can pause or replay the file by clicking on the control button.

Lesson 2: Embedding VivoActive Files in Your Web Pages

Once you have created VivoActive files—about which you'll read more in a moment—embedding them in your Web pages is simple. VivoActive files are always placed in a page using some variation of the following line:

```
<EMBED SRC="test.viv" WIDTH=176 HEIGHT=144>
```

If you want the video to play automatically when the Web page is opened, use the attribute AUTOSTART=TRUE. You can also use Netscape's ALIGN attribute to position the image to the left, right, or center of the Web page. BORDER, followed by a chosen number of pixels, will draw a black frame around the video to set it off from the rest of the page.

As noted, WIDTH and HEIGHT are meant to be fixed with VivoActive. However, I've found that in some cases altering these specifications by a few pixels manually is necessary. You can see that this has been done in Listing 10-1, below.

For the most reliable positioning of an image, Vivo Software recommends embedding it within a table. (In some versions of the VivoActive plug-in, the <ALIGN> tag was not recognized properly.) This not only gives you the best control over positioning, but also can improve the appearance of an image's border. Listing 10-1 shows the code used in the test file DEMO.HTM. This shows how you can use a single-column table to improve the visual presentation.

Listing 10-1 This is the source for DEMO.HTM, using a one-column table to embed a video

```
<html>
<title>Welcome to the VivoActive Player Demo Page</title>
<body bgcolor=0000BB text=ffffff link=ff0000 vlink=ffffff></body>
<p align=center><font size=4><strong>
Filename: AMS.VIV<br>
Compression: 15 Frames Per Second<br>
Transmission: 56K connections<br>
Media Length: 35 sec<br>
Coded: 56K Line<br>
Size: 191KB
</strong>
<br>
<center>
<table border=10>
<tr>
<td>
```

```
<embed src="ams.viv" autostart=true loop=true stretch=true width=175 height=140>
</td>
</tr>
</table>
</center>
<br>
<hr><a href="http://www.vivo.com/">Vivo Software, Inc.</a><br>
<a href="mailto:webmaster@vivo.com">webmaster@vivo.com</a><br>
Waltham, MA, USA</address>
</html>
```

You can test Web pages including .VIV files by loading them from your hard drive or, of course, by FTPing them to a server—once alterations to its MIME types files have been made. Another way to test pages is using the VivoActive Rehearsal Server, which you got a copy of when you downloaded the Producer software.

The Rehearsal Server is not really useful for those of us with a typical part-time, dial-up connection to the Internet. Instead, it's intended for those who have a permanent IP address via an intranet, T1, or other constant connection. A simple Web server program, it's designed to make any Web pages and .VIV files stored in a specified subdirectory available from another machine. A "rate limit" feature lets the server simulate the effect of a 28.8K dial-up connection, even when the actual connection is over a LAN.

To use the Rehearsal Server, run the program from your Start menu. A VivoActive logo now appears to the left of the clock in the Windows 95 task bar. You can configure the server by right-clicking on that logo, where you'll see the tabbed dialog box shown in Figure 10-39. Clicking on its Data Rate tab lets you limit the effective data rate, while clicking on the HTML tab lets you select a subdirectory from which you want files to be served.

To test the connection, switch to another machine and run Netscape. Then enter the URL of the host machine running the VivoActive Rehearsal Server, for example, *http://012.345.67.89*. Netscape will view the preselected subdirectory on the server. You can now retrieve Web pages and .VIVs at whatever data rate had been selected.

Lesson 3: Creating Your Own VivoActive Movies

To create VivoActive movies, you start with .AVI files captured with the use of any camcorder and a video capture card that supports Windows 95 or Windows NT. There are no particular constraints on the kind of video files you can use, but it is unnecessary to capture a frame size larger than 176 × 144 pixels. Since VivoActive Producer currently looks for a sound track when converting .AVI files, you should tell your video capture application to capture with "sound on" even if nothing is connected to your computer's sound input jacks.

(Macintosh users should check the VivoActive Web site to see if the promised Mac version of VivoActive Producer has been made available. As you would hope, this program will be able to convert QuickTime movies directly instead of making you convert them to the .AVI format first.)

Once you have captured an .AVI file and edited it to your satisfaction, convert it by selecting VivoActive Producer from the VivoActive section of your computer's Start menu.

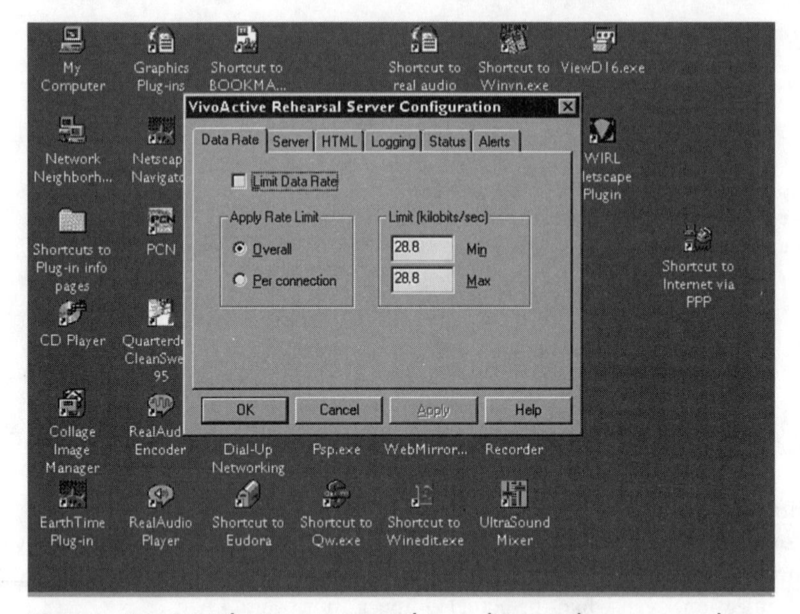

Figure 10–39 The VivoActive Rehearsal Server lets you simulate the data rate of a dial-up connection

The Browse button at the top of the VivoActive Producer window helps you locate the .AVI file you want to convert. Once you have selected a file, its first frame appears in the window to the right (see Figure 10-40).

The sliders at the lower left part of the window let you tune compression to match the type of connection you think most visitors to your Web page will be using. Moving the first slider toward the "Faster Start" end of the scale selects higher compression, compatible with 14.4Kbps or 28.8Kbps dial-up links. As you move the slider toward the "Better Quality" end of the scale, less compression is used, so a faster connection will be required if videos are to start playing quickly. (If you use "Better Quality," the .VIV file still will play via dial-up links—it just will take longer to download.)

The slider marked "Sharper Detail" and "Smoother Motion" actually controls the frame rate of the converted file. If you anticipate that most people looking at your Web pages will have dial-up connections, you may, once again, want to keep the frame rate low.

A common problem with this (and any other) video compressor arises with videos of people talking. If an inadequate number of frames per second is used, poor lip synchronization may result. When creating .VIVs that feature speech, try increasing the frame rate

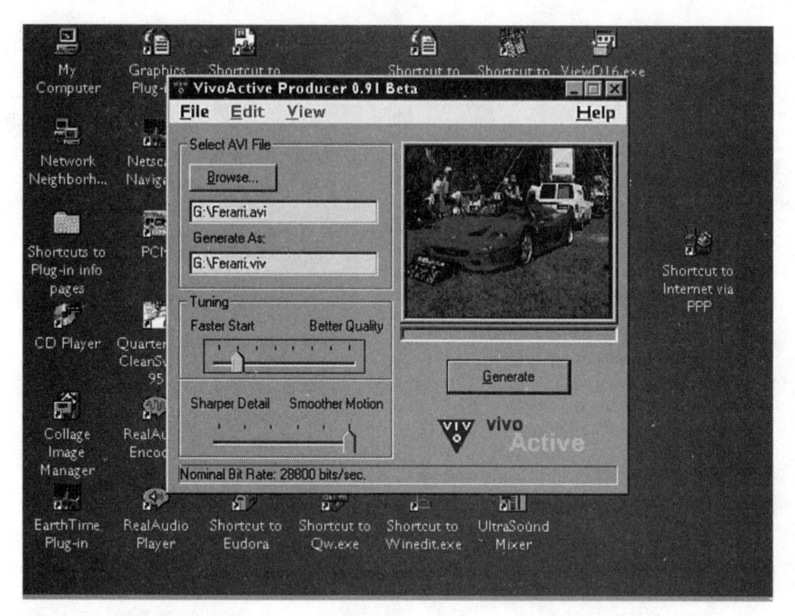

Figure 10–40 VivoActive Producer's browse button lets you select the .AVI file you want to convert—and previews its first frame

as much as possible. Also make sure that the source .AVI file was captured using at least 10 frames per second.

Fortunately, VivoActive Producer not only makes .AVI files drastically smaller, but also does its job rapidly. As Vivo Software says, the compression process only takes about twice as long as it would to play a video—even on a 90MHz Pentium, which most people today consider a low-end system. Once you have started converting a file, Producer lets you watch the conversion frame by frame. It also displays a bar graph to let you know how far it has progressed through a file (see Figure 10-41).

WHAT NOW?

In this chapter, you've read about the leading video plug-ins that work with Netscape, and perhaps chosen which one you're going to use in your own Web pages. If, on the other hand, you are an experienced user of a given animation or presentation graphics program, you probably would rather not have to convert your files to .AVIs, .MOVs, or MPEGs in order to put them on the Web. Fortunately, you don't need to—as you'll read in the next chapter, "Presentation Plug-Ins."

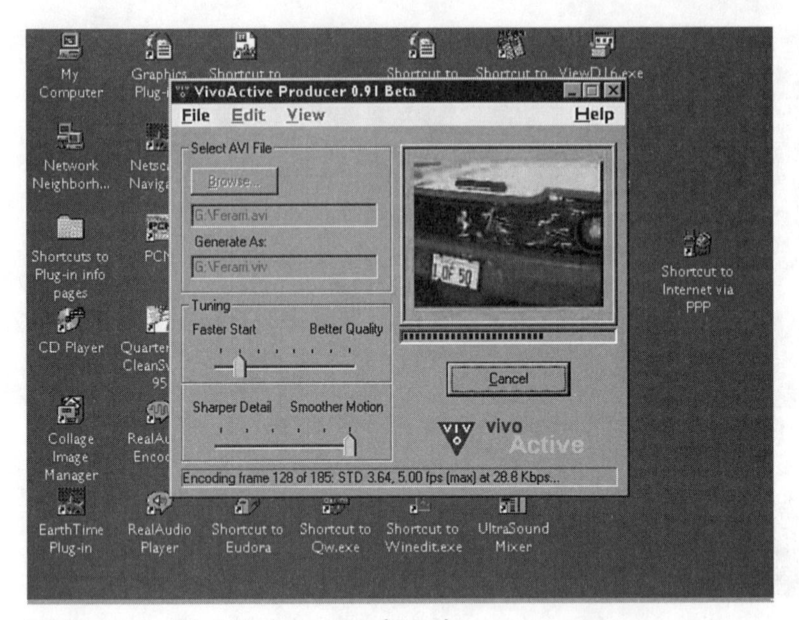

Figure 10–41 VivoActive Producer lets you monitor conversion frame by frame and also displays a bar graph to show its progress

11

PRESENTATION/ANIMATION

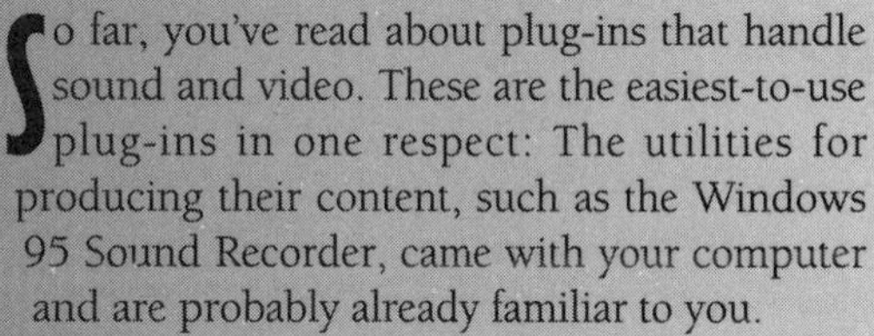

So far, you've read about plug-ins that handle sound and video. These are the easiest-to-use plug-ins in one respect: The utilities for producing their content, such as the Windows 95 Sound Recorder, came with your computer and are probably already familiar to you.

Paradoxically, however, sound/video plug-ins can also be the most *difficult* to use in that creating content for them requires technical expertise and a fresh source of material. If you don't have a sound engineer and announcer or other on-air talent, you'll wish you did. Besides, video and sound files tend to be bulky and time-consuming for users to download.

Audio and video definitely have their place. However, you might find a way around their limitations in this chapter, which covers plug-ins in the presentation and animation field.

There is not a vast difference between audio/video plug-ins and those aimed at the "presentation" market. After all, audio and video are merely a generalized form of presentation, and video is merely a technically demanding type of animation. Furthermore, sound and video can be utilized in presentations, and often are.

Presentation programs, however, tend to be more familiar to the average business user. You may have already learned to use Microsoft PowerPoint, Macromedia Director, ASAP, or other presentation graphics programs. So with presentation plug-ins, you can take the shows you've already created and "repurpose" them, placing them on the Web with minimal extra work.

In addition to presentation plug-ins, this chapter covers several animation plug-ins. These products let you create multimedia files, playing back sounds and video, displaying graphics, or performing other actions in response to user input. In terms of their end result, animation plug-ins can be basically indistinguishable from those that used presentation graphics software as an authoring tool.

ASAP WEB SHOW

Software Publishing Corporation's ASAP Web Show is a plug-in that lets users view, print, and download presentations created with ASAP Word Power (the company's presentation graphics product). Reviewers have complimented ASAP Word Power because of the relative simplicity and small size of the program. For the Web, this is useful in that its data files are also relatively small. Thus, ASAP Web Show is usable with links as slow as 14.4Kbps.

Sound is supported in ASAP Web Show via the RealAudio Player (see Chapter 9). You can link a presentation to RealAudio sound files—as long as you have the RealAudio Server software—and even associate different sounds with individual slides in a presentation. Finally, Microsoft PowerPoint files are supported via ASAP Word Power's ability to import and convert them.

Lesson 1: Installing ASAP Web Show

To install the ASAP Web Show plug-in, you need either Windows 3.x or Windows 95/NT. Point your copy of Netscape at Software Publishing's Web server *(http://www.spco.com)*, or just check Appendix A for details about your CD-ROM.

If you have Windows 3.x, run the 16-bit version of the installer, identifiable by the "16" in its file name. If you have Windows 95 or NT, run the 32-bit installer, identifiable by the (you guessed it) "32" in its file name. The installer locates your Netscape subdirectory and asks you to confirm that this is where you want to install Web Show. It also asks you to specify a location for the ASAP Web Show helper application if desired. Next, it copies the file NPASAP32.DLL (for Windows 95 and NT) or NPASAP16.DLL (Windows 3.x) into the PLUGINS subdirectory of your Netscape folder.

Now, if Netscape is running, exit the program and restart it. As you'll see if you select the About Plug-ins command from the Help menu, ASAP Web Show has added a MIME type/subtype, application/x-asap, to those that Netscape can handle. The suffix asp has been assigned to denote ASAP Web Show files.

As usual, you'll need to supply the MIME type information to the folks who administer your server—whether it's on-site or at an independent service provider. Otherwise, ASAP Web Show files will embed properly on pages you test locally, but may not display on those you place on your server.

To test ASAP Web Show, connect to the Internet and load the page found at *http://www.spco.com/asap/asapgall.htm.* If everything is working properly, you'll see a screen similar to that in Figure 11-1 as the presentation loads, and a screen similar to that in Figure 11-2 after you click on an arrow to start the presentation.

Right-clicking on the presentation area gives you the opportunity to make it full-screen, print it, or go to a particular slide. Figure 11-3 shows the pop-up menu that appears. You can also make a presentation fill the Netscape browser window fully by clicking the "window" icon (third from the right on the embedded navigation bar). Or, you can make it full-screen by clicking the icon with a diagonal arrow at each of its corners. Figure 11-4 shows the result.

Figure 11-1 ASAP Web Show shows this screen while a presentation is loading

Figure 11–2 Once a presentation has loaded, it is embedded within a Web page

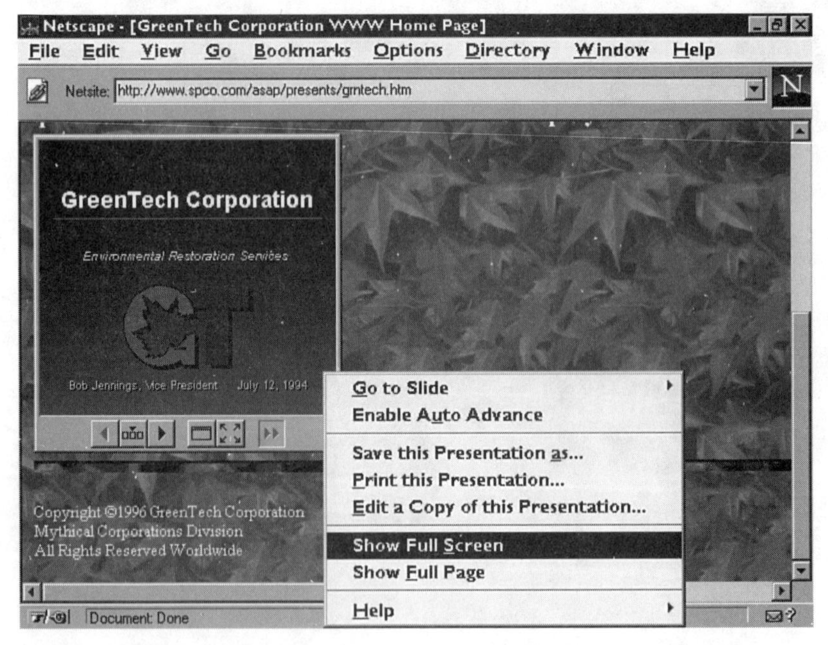

Figure 11–3 ASAP Web Show's pop-up menu appears when you right-click on a presentation

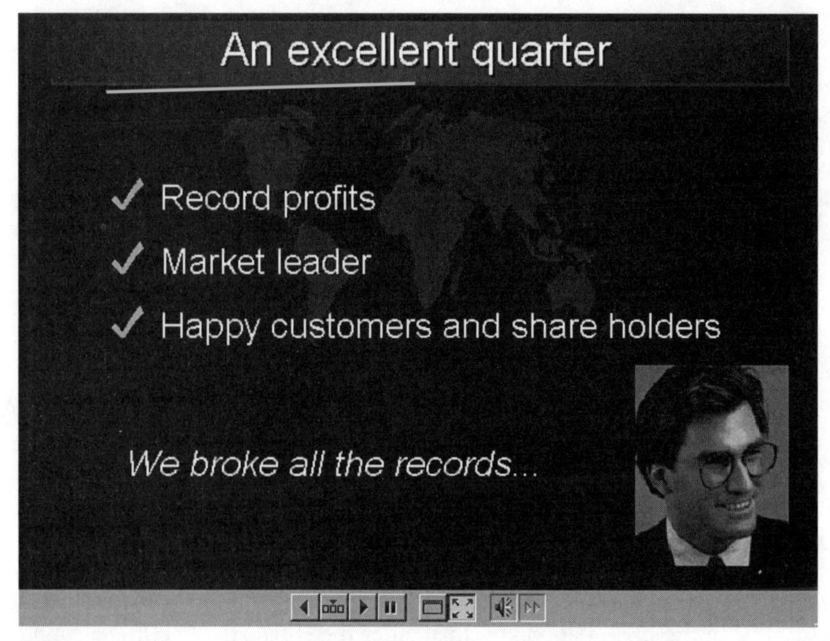

Figure 11–4 An ASAP Web Show presentation zoomed to the full screen

Lesson 2: Embedding Presentations in Your Web Pages

Once you have created an ASAP Word Power presentation—about which more is covered in Lesson 3 below—it is very easy to place it in one of your Web pages. Figure 11-5 shows a Web page with a presentation that automatically runs itself and uses a narration recorded in RealAudio.

This is the HTML code that created the page shown in Figure 11-5:

```
<HTML>
<HEAD>
<TITLE>WebShow And RealAudio</TITLE>
</HEAD>
<BODY>
<BODY BACKGROUND="../../graphics/logo_etc/TILEBKG2.GIF">

<center><IMG ALIGN="center" HSPACE="0" VSPACE="0" BORDER="0"
SRC="../../graphics/headers/WEBAUDIO.gif" WIDTH="580" HEIGHT="100" ALT="ASAP
WebShow header" ></center>
<center><IMG ALIGN="center" HSPACE="0" VSPACE="0" BORDER="0"
SRC="../../graphics/headers/LINEW540.gif" WIDTH="540" HEIGHT="2" ></center>
```

continued on next page

continued from previous page

```
<P>To see and hear this presentation, download the latest version of <A
HREF="../asapbeta.htm">ASAP WebShow</A> and the <A
HREF="http://www.realaudio.com/products/ra2.0">RealAudio 2.0 Player</A>.
Netscape Navigator 2.0 also needs to be installed on your system.
<A HREF="../pubkit/sound.htm">Directions</A> on how to synchronize RealAudio file
with ASAP WordPower are available.</P>

<center>
<EMBED ALIGN="top" VSPACE="3" SRC="DEMO2.ASP" WIDTH="300"
HEIGHT="170" border="WINDOW" dithering="on" navbar="ON"
orientation="freeform" autoadvance="on" delaytime="4" loopback="on"
sound="http://www.spco.com/asap/presents/rasound.txt"><BR>
</center>

<P><BR></P>
</BODY>
</HTML>
```

Look at the EMBED line in this page, and you'll see mostly attributes that will have become familiar to you by now. The only one that is unusual is the SOUND attribute which, as you can see, references a URL ("rasound.txt" in this example).

The sound configuration file this references is a simple text file, in which each line first references a slide in the presentation and then, after the equal sign (=), lists a sound to be played while the slide displays. Sounds need to be recorded in RealAudio .RA format and referenced via an absolute (not relative) URL in RealAudio Server "metafile" syntax. (This is covered in detail in the "RealAudio" section of Chapter 9.)

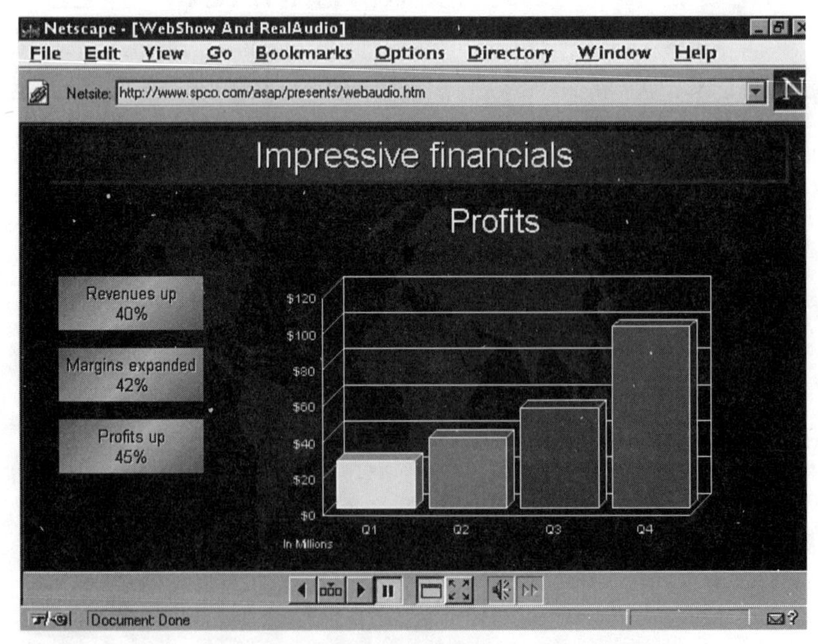

Figure 11-5 This talking ASAP Word Power presentation was embedded via a few simple lines of HTML

For example, the following might be the RASOUND.TXT file for a three-slide presentation, each of which has a sound associated with it:

```
1=pnm://myserver.com/present/slide1.ra
2=pnm://myserver.com/present/slide2.ra
3=pnm://myserver.com/present/slide3.ra
```

Information on the other EMBED attributes possible with ASAP Web Show appears in Table 11-1.

Table 11-1 EMBED attributes for ASAP Web Show

Attribute	Possible Values	Comments
ABOUT	ON|OFF	Specifies whether the About ASAP Web Show menu item appears in the pop-up menu when the user clicks on Help. Defaults to ON.
AUTOADVANCE	ON|OFF	Specifies whether the presentation automatically advances to each slide. If AUTOADVANCE=ON, the user can still stop the presentation via its navigation bar or the pop-up menu. Defaults to OFF.
BGCOLOR	#rrggbb	Specifies a background color for the portion of the embedded window not filled by the presentation if and when a slide is displayed in letter-box format. The color value is in hexadecimal (with notation and possible values identical to that used by Netscape itself).
BORDER	RAISED|RECESSED}SLIDE|SHADOWED|SIMPLE|NONE	Specifies the look of the embedded window. RAISED (the default) shows it with an elevated border. RECESSED shows it with an indented border. SLIDE shows it with a 35mm-style slide border. SHADOWED shows it with a drop shadow border. SIMPLE displays a plain black border. NONE displays no border at all.
DELAYTIME	positive integer	Specifies the number of seconds each slide in a presentation displays before automatically going to the next one when AUTOADVANCE=ON. The default is seven seconds.
DITHERING	EMBED|PAGE|SCREEN|NONE	This attribute controls what color palette ASAP Web Show uses with a 256-color display. When set to EMBED, PAGE, or SCREEN, it uses a distributed color palette that is less prone to conflict with other applications or objects on the same Web page. When set to NONE, ASAP uses its own color palette. This will make presentations look better.

continued on next page

continued from previous page

Attribute	Possible Values	Comments
EFFECT	Name, direction	Used to specify a transition effect and transition direction that will be used when moving from one slide in a presentation to another. For example, EFFECT=SCROLL,RIGHT would scroll right when moving to the next slide. EFFECT defaults to the transition effect that was used in ASAP Word Power when the presentation was created. Other values include BLINDS (with the possible directions left or right, up or down), CLOSE (horizontal or vertical), FADE, IRIS (in or out), NONE, OPEN (horizontal or vertical), RAIN (up or down), REPLACE, SCROLL (up or down, right or left), WIPE (up or down, right or left), PEEL (upper right or lower left, upper left or lower right).
FULLPAGE	ON|OFF	When turned on, makes a presentation fill the Netscape window. When off (the default), places the presentation in an embedded window.
HEIGHT	In pixels or as percentage of the browser window	A mandatory attribute (if it is omitted, Netscape will default to 50, which is too small).
HELP	ON|OFF	Specifies whether the HELP menu item appears on the pop-up menu. The default is ON.
LOOPBACK	ON|OFF	Specifies whether a presentation will loop from end to beginning again repeatedly when AUTOADVANCE is on.
MENU	ON|OFF	Can disable the pop-up menu. The default is ON.
NAVBAR	ON|OFF	Can disable the navigation bar, which is on by default. When it is turned off, the user can still navigate through the presentation by using keys and mouse buttons.
ORIENTATION	LANDSCAPE|PORTRAIT|w:h|FREEFORM	Specifies a presentation's aspect ratio. When set to FREEFORM (the default), no aspect ratio correction is performed, and the slide fills the available window space. When set to LANDSCAPE or PORTRAIT, the proper aspect ratio is maintained via letter-boxing. When set to w:h, where *w* and *h* are values representing relative width and height, the requested aspect ratio will be maintained. For example, for an image twice as wide as it is high, you'd enter 2:1 as values for this attribute.

Attribute	Possible Values	Comments
PALETTE	FOREGROUND|BACKGROUND	Specifies whether an embedded object can use the foreground color palette. Only one object per Web page can do this, so the default is BACKGROUND. When displaying a presentation in an embedded window, set palette to FOREGROUND but use DITHERING=EMBED as well.
PAUSE	ON|OFF	Specifies whether a presentation that can autoadvance begins playing automatically, or only in response to a user action. The default is OFF, meaning that presentations will start autoadvancing as soon as a Web page is opened.
PAUSEBUTTON	ON|OFF	Determines whether the pause button appears on the navigation bar. The default is ON, although a pause button does not appear if a presentation is not set to autoadvance and doesn't have sound.
PLUGINSPAGE	URL	Include this with "*http://www.spco.com*" as its value to link automatically to Software Publishing Corporation's home page if ASAP Web Show hasn't been installed.
PRINTING	ENABLED|DISABLED	Specifies whether a user can print a presentation from the pop-up menu. The default is ENABLED.
SAVEAS	ENABLED|DISABLED	Specifies whether a user can save a presentation to disk as a local file using the pop-up menu. The default is ENABLED.
SOUND	File name of a text file containing the absolute addresses of RealAudio .RA files	Specifies a sound configuration file.
STATUSBUTTONS	ON|OFF	Specifies whether indicators on the status bar show whether a presentation is set to autoadvance or to play sound. The default is ON.
WIDTH	In pixels or as percentage of the browser window	A mandatory attribute (if it is omitted, Netscape will default to 50, which is too small).
ZOOMBUTTONS	ON|OFF	Determines whether the zoom buttons for full page and full screen operation appear on the navigation bar. The default is ON. When ZOOMBUTTONS=OFF, the user can still zoom via the pop-up menu.

Lesson 3: Preparing Content for Your Web Pages

As mentioned above, ASAP Web Show is designed to use the .ASP files created by the ASAP Word Power presentation graphics program. If you don't have that program, you'll need to purchase it from Software Publishing Corporation. Once you've done this, you can save files and upload them to a server directly.

Software Publishing Corporation offers another downloadable program called ASAP Image Compressor. This helps compact .ASP files that include graphics. To obtain it, go to the Web page at *http://www.spco.com/asap/pubkit/compress.htm* and follow the instructions that appear there.

Compression is not available in ASAP version 1.0 for Windows 3.1, but is available in version 1.02 and on Windows 95 versions. For faster transmission time, be sure not to include OLE objects in presentations that you embed in a Web page. OLE objects significantly increase the size of a file and cannot be compressed.

ASTOUND WEB PLAYER

The Astound Web Player from Gold Disk, Inc. is a plug-in that supports presentations created in the company's Astound or Studio M presentation graphics programs. Like them, it is available in versions for Windows, Macintosh, and Power Macintosh (although the Mac versions were not available in time to be tested for this book).

A separate program, the Astound Web Installer, formats Astound presentations for the Web by breaking them into small files that load more quickly. The Web Installer also comes with a Web page template that will help you direct users to your presentations. It does not itself create presentations, however; for that, you need to purchase a copy of Astound.

Lesson 1: Installing the Astound Web Player

To install the Astound Web Player, go to the Gold Disk Web site at *http://www.golddisk.com,* or check Appendix A for details on your CD-ROM. The Windows installer is the file WEBPLAY.EXE; run it and you'll be prompted for a target directory for Web Player files (C:\ASTOUND, or whatever you prefer) and the directory where your NETSCAPE.EXE resides (the installer makes a guess that is usually correct).

The installer places the file NPAWP02.DLL in the PLUGINS subdirectory of your Netscape folder. If you think you may want to play Astound presentations that contain QuickTime movies, you need to install Apple's QuickTime for Windows *(http://quicktime.apple.com)*, as detailed in Chapter 10. You also need to download the file WEBPLAYQ.EXE from the Gold Disk Web site. Extract the QuickTime extensions for

Astound (this file contains a temporary subdirectory), and then copy or move them into the subdirectory where you installed Astound Web player files (C:\ASTOUND, or whatever you called it).

After all this is done, exit and restart Netscape, if it is currently running. You can then use the Help/About Plug-ins menu to confirm that the Astound plug-in has been loaded. As the list shows, this plug-in handles two different MIME type/subtypes and the corresponding suffixes:

```
application/studiom   smp
application/astound   asd
```

To see it in action, load the URL *http://www.golddisk.com/awp/demos.html.* Pick one of the demos listed, and you'll first see a screen like that in Figure 11-6. The Astound Web Player displays this to let you know it is loading a presentation.

The sample file at *http://www.golddisk.com/marshall/webdemo.html* is a particularly good tour. It shows examples of Web pages using Astound, such as Figure 11-7. It also makes the point that static .GIF images grow little in size when they are turned into Astound files.

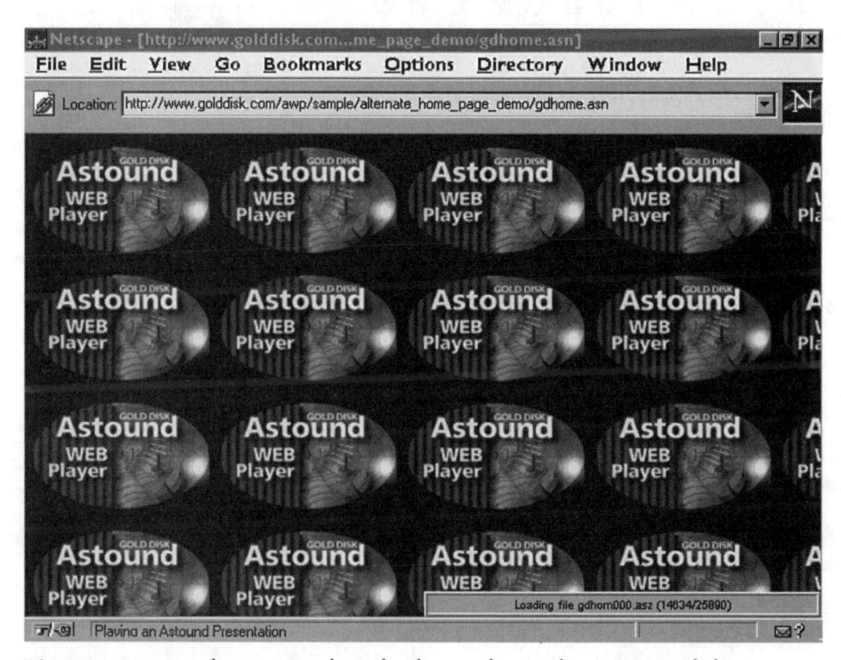

Figure 11–6 The Astound Web Player shows this screen while it is loading a presentation

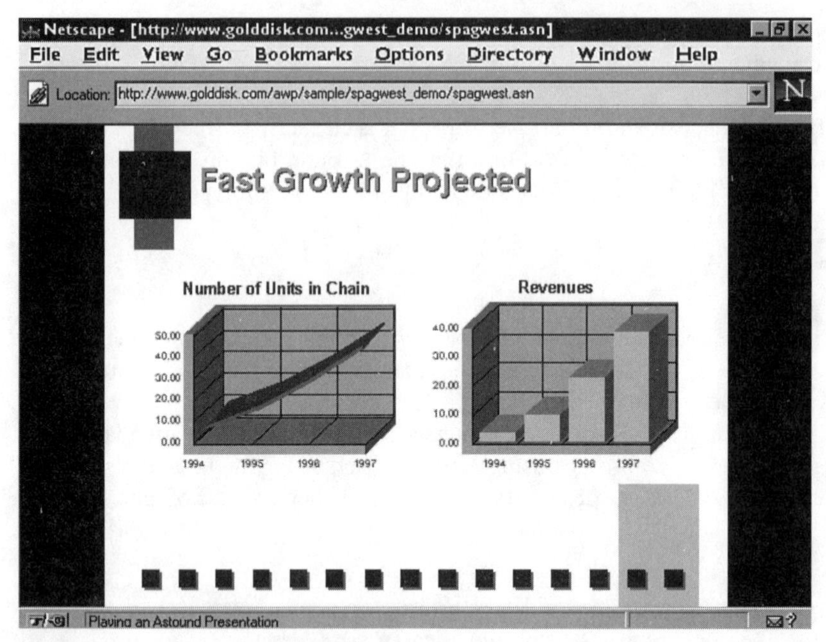

Figure 11-7 This sample Astound presentation advertises a fictional Mexican/Italian restaurant chain

Lesson 2: Embedding Presentations in Your Web Pages

Figure 11-8 shows an animated Web page located at *http://www.golddisk.com/marshall/fridge.html.* This is the HTML code that created it:

```
<HTML>
<HEAD>
   <TITLE>The Fridge Demo</TITLE>
   <META NAME = "GENERATOR" CONTENT = "Astound from Gold Disk Inc.">
   <META NAME = "AUTHOR" CONTENT = "Marshall Goldberg">
</HEAD>
<BODY BACKGROUND="fridgebak.gif">
<H1>Here's the Astound Web Player at Work:</H1>
<P>
<CENTER>
<SCRIPT LANGUAGE="JavaScript">
  <!- Hide from non-Netscape browsers
  document.write( '<EMBED WIDTH=448 HEIGHT=240 PLUGINSPAGE =
"http://www.golddisk.com/awp" SRC="fridge.asn">');
  <!- Done ->
</SCRIPT>
</CENTER>
<CENTER>
<NOEMBED>
```

```
  <IMG WIDTH=319 HEIGHT=171 SRC="fridge.jpg">
</NOEMBED>
</CENTER>
<P>
If you're hungry for more multimedia like this, why not cook up some of your own?<P>
<P>
To download the Astound version of this template, <A HREF =
"ftp://www.golddisk.com/pub/demo/fridge.zip">click here</A>.
<P>
The Astound Web Player Plugin/Viewer can be downloaded from the <A HREF =
"http://www.golddisk.com/awp">Gold Disk Astound Web Player Web Page</A>.<P>
</BODY>
</HTML>
```

This sample uses JavaScript to hide the embedded presentation from non-Netscape browsers, while making sure their users still see something on the page. It also shows that there is little to embedding an Astound presentation: Merely the normal HEIGHT and WIDTH attributes are used.

Gold Disk offers a program called the Astound Web Installer, designed to help you make your presentations available. This is available from their Web site as WEBINST.EXE. Download this file, and then run it, and you'll be prompted for a target directory.

The Astound Web Installer requires that you own Astound or Studio M and have completed a project. It then opens the file and formats it for Web playback by breaking the file into small files. If you wish, the Installer can also create a Web page for you. This

Figure 11–8 This "fridge" presentation is embedded using only the SRC, HEIGHT, and WIDTH attributes

is a customizable template, which allows you to add your own text to direct visitors to your Web project.

By default, the template contains a clickable JPEG image of the first slide of your project, plus a link to the presentation itself. Once the viewer clicks this image, the project's playback begins. The Web page also includes a hyperlink that lets visitors download the Astound Web Player from the Gold Disk Web site. This is convenient for viewers who haven't downloaded the Player yet. You can also provide access to the Web Player by copying the WEBPLAY.EXE file to your Web site and adding a hyperlink.

The installer also simplifies things for you by automatically uploading a project to the Web for you via FTP. (If you don't have FTP access or don't wish to connect, you can save the Web project to your hard drive for subsequent testing and installation.)

If you don't want to use the Installer's Web page template, you can write your own HTML tags instead. To have a presentation take over Netscape's entire window, use a tag like the following:

```
<A HREF="myshow.asn">Click here</A> to see a project play back within the
entire Netscape window.
```

To have the presentation play in just a part of the page, use a tag such as this:

```
<EMBED SRC="myshow.asn" HEIGHT=slide's height in pixels WIDTH=slide's width in pixels>
```

EMBLAZE

Emblaze is a plug-in that focuses squarely on animation. By using aggressive, proprietary compression techniques, it allows animations to be delivered from a server to the user in real time—without any delays or preloading of cache memory.

According to the authors, GEO Interactive Media Group, 256-color animations can be delivered at a rate of 12 to 24 frames per second even over a 14.4Kbps modem. Files are so economical in size that you can store an animation that plays for 30 minutes in only about 4MB.

The Emblaze plug-in is available for both Windows and Macintosh. The authoring tool, called Emblaze Creator, is currently available for Mac only, but a Windows version is planned.

Lesson 1: Installing the Emblaze Plug-In

To install Emblaze, go to Geo Interactive's Web site at *http://www.geo.inter.net/technology/emblaze/*. Installation of the Windows 95 version is simply a matter of downloading or copying the file NPBLZ32.DLL to the PLUGINS subdirectory within your Netscape folder. The Windows 3.x version uses the file NPBLZ16.DLL.

For the Macintosh, a plug-in file called EmblazeFAT supports both Motorola 68K and Power PC-based Macintoshes. Drag it to the Plug-ins folder within your Netscape folder.

Now, for all Netscape versions, exit the program and restart it. Select About Plug-ins from the Help menu or Apple menu, and you will see that Emblaze has adopted the following MIME type/subtype and suffix:

```
video/blz       blz
```

As usual, you need to ask your Internet Service Provider or network administrator to install this MIME type so that Emblaze files will be served properly to client machines.

To test the program, you can load Geo Interactive's animations test page at *http://www.geo.inter.net/technology/emblaze/animations.html*. Figure 11-9 shows the "Netcracker" animation, which is a mere 40K in size but plays for about a minute. Figure 11-10 shows a "Netscape" graphic being overrun by penguins.

Lesson 2: Embedding Animations in Your Web Pages

The code that inserts the animation in Figure 11-10 is simply the following:

```
<EMBED SRC="penguin.blz" HEIGHT=350 WIDTH=500><br>
```

Other than HEIGHT and WIDTH, there are currently no attributes that can be used with Emblaze animations. Animations always play as soon as the Web page hosting them is opened.

Figure 11-9 The Emblaze "Netcracker" animation shown running under Windows

Figure 11-10 The Emblaze "Netscape" animation running on a Mac

In order to create .BLZ files for your Web pages, you need the Emblaze Creator application, a test version of which is available from *http://www.geo.inter.net/technology/emblaze/creator.html*. You can also download sample projects—animations that have not yet been compiled into .BLZs—from *http://www.geo.inter.net/technology/emblaze/sample.html*. Figure 11-11 shows a sample project loaded into the Emblaze Creator.

FUTURESPLASH

FutureSplash is a plug-in that uses vector-based graphics and animations. Via streaming, graphics begin displaying as they are downloaded. You can enlarge images with no loss of quality, while integral anti-aliasing eliminates jagged edges.

FutureSplash is more than just a graphics tool, however. You can embed buttons in its images that start animations or call other URLs. In addition, you can use a system of outline fonts that lets you create large headlines with very small files.

Available for both Windows and Macintosh, FutureSplash requires an authoring tool called CelAnimator (which also runs on both platforms). CelAnimator is a complete, vector-based drawing tool; it can import from and export to file formats including .EPS and AutoCad.

Figure 11-11 An animation being edited in the Emblaze Creator application

Lesson 1: Installing FutureSplash

To install FutureSplash, go to the Web site at *http://futurewave.com* (or check Appendix A for details about your CD-ROM). If you have Windows 95 or Windows NT, run the installer program SPLASH32.EXE. For Windows 3.x, run the installer program SPLASH16.EXE. The installer will locate your Netscape Plug-ins subdirectory and copy either NPSPL32.DLL or NPSPL16.DLL.

The Macintosh plug-ins are FutureSplash PM, for Power Macintoshes, and FutureSplash 68K, for all other systems. Drag whichever version is correct to the Plug-ins folder within your Netscape folder.

Now, for all Netscape versions, exit the program and restart it. Select About Plug-ins from the Help menu or Apple menu, and you will see that FutureSplash has adopted the following MIME type/subtype and suffix:

```
application/futuresplash       spl
```

As you have become accustomed to reading, you need to ask your Internet Service Provider or network administrator to install this MIME type so that FutureSplash files will be served properly to client machines. Obviously, no alterations are necessary to test them on your local hard drive.

To test the program, you can return to the FutureSplash Web pages at *http://www.futurewave.com*. Figure 11-12 shows a Web page that incorporates an animated seal. As you'll discover, animations load rapidly, and motion starts even before files are completely loaded.

Figure 11-13 shows another page incorporating an animated version of an old graphic from the Netscape home page (you'll find it at *http://www.futurewave.com/samples/netscape.htm*).

FutureSplash works automatically, but there are several features that users can take advantage of. For example, a pop-up menu is available when Windows users right-click on a graphic. Macintosh users hold down <COMMAND> and click with the mouse to activate the menu. The menu commands include Zoom, Play, Forward, Back, and About FutureSplash.

To zoom, choose the Zoom In or Zoom Out command from the menu. The Show All command will reset the view to show the entire graphic. When you are zoomed in on a graphic, the cursor will change to a hand that can be used for scrolling. Simply hold down the mouse button and push the graphic to move the view. The view will redraw when you release the mouse or when you pause. Any buttons included in the graphic are still active, so click in the space between buttons for moving around.

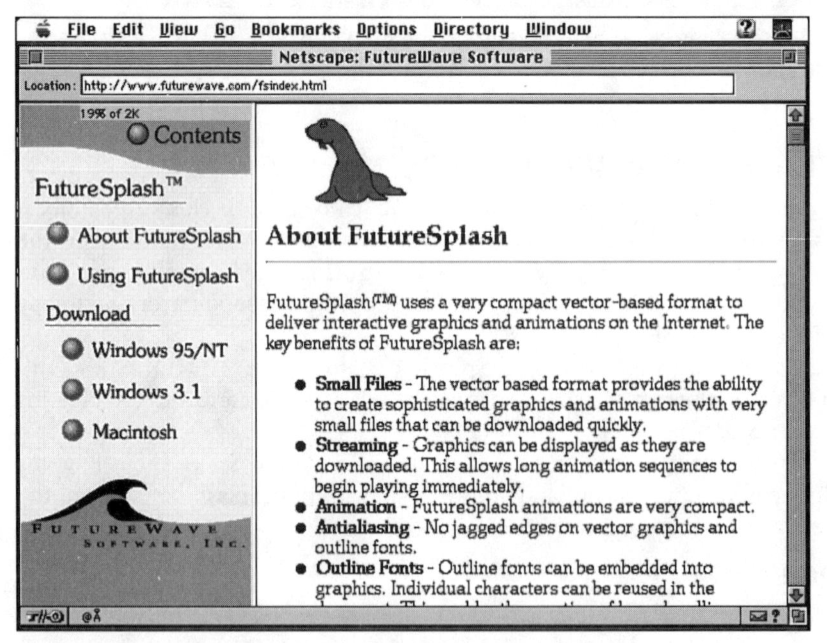

Figure 11-12 This Web page uses a FutureSplash animation to decorate the top of a frame

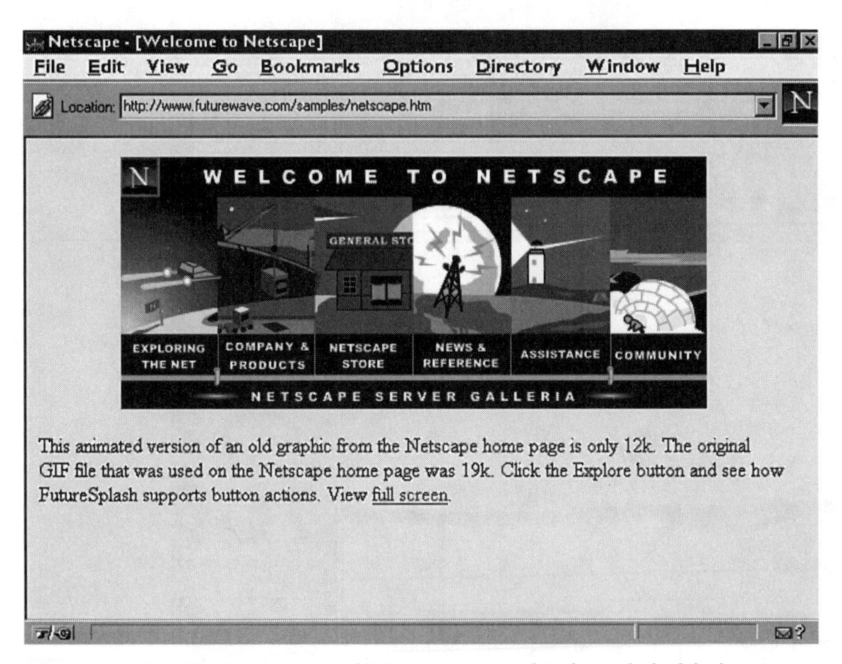

Figure 11–13 An animated Netscape graphic has clickable buttons

To use a FutureSplash button, simply click on a button. The designer of a FutureSplash graphic controls the action of a button. Buttons can perform various actions such as starting or stopping an animation and loading a new page into the browser. Note how the cursor changes to a hand when the mouse is over a button. For buttons that open a new page, you can see the name of the page in the Netscape status bar at the bottom of the window.

Lesson 2: Embedding FutureSplash Graphics in Your Web Pages

To create FutureSplash graphics, you need the CelAnimator application, downloadable (at least in beta form) from *http://www.futurewave.com.* This program is available in both Macintosh and Windows versions. If you download it, the installer will create subdirectories that include sample HTML, sample animations, and documentation.

CelAnimator not only creates FutureSplash animations but also can be used to create animated GIF images. Figure 11-14 shows the Mac version of this useful program.

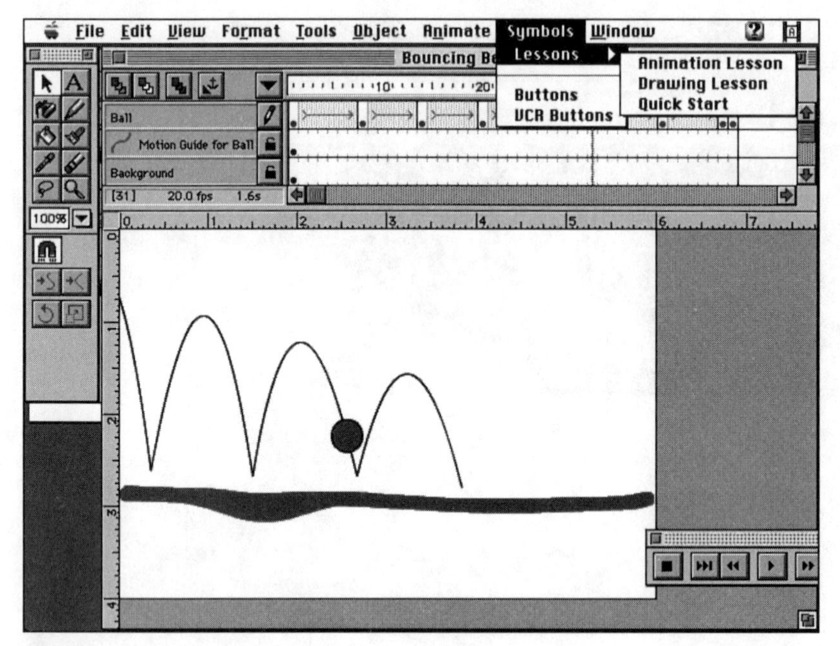

Figure 11–14 CelAnimator is required to create FutureSplash animations

This listing (which happens to be the code that was used to produce Figure 11-13) shows you the basics of embedding a FutureSplash graphic:

```
<html>
<head>
   <title>Welcome to Netscape</title>
</head>
<body>
<center><p><embed SRC="netscape.spl" width=468 height=197 BORDER=0
QUALITY=BEST></p></center>
<p>This animated version of an old graphic from the Netscape home page
is only 12k. The original GIF file that was used on the Netscape home
page was 19k. Click the Explore button and see how FutureSplash supports
button actions. View <a href="netscape.htm" target="_top">full screen</a>.</p>
</body>
</html>
```

Other attributes for the <EMBED> tag are available to provide further control. See Table 11-2 for more details.

Table 11-2 EMBED attributes for the FutureSplash plug-in

Attribute	Possible Values	Comments
WIDTH	Pixel values or percentage of the browser window	A required attribute.
HEIGHT	Pixel values or percentage of the browser window	A required attribute.
QUALITY	LOW|AUTOLOW|AUTOHIGH	AUTOLOW is the default. It means that an animation will begin playing in low quality and switch to better quality if the computer seems to be fast enough. LOW is the fastest mode for animations that need to play quickly. AUTOHIGH starts out in high quality but switches to low if the computer does not seem to be fast enough.
LOOP	TRUE|FALSE	Plays the animation in a continuous loop.
PLAY	TRUE|FALSE	Defaults to TRUE, which starts an animation playing automatically when the Web page is opened.
BGCOLOR	#rrggbb	Can override the background color of the animation. Used to match its background color to the background of your Web page. Takes the same two-digit hex values as Netscape's own BGCOLOR command.
SCALE	SHOWALL|NOBORDER|EXACTFIT	SHOWALL scales an animation so that it fits inside its frame but also uses its original aspect ratio. This may mean it is letter-boxed at the top and bottom, or at the sides, unless your WIDTH and HEIGHT commands match the aspect ratio. NOBORDER will maintain the original aspect ratio by cutting off edges if necessary. EXACTFIT ignores aspect ratio, distorting the animation to fit it in the specified FRAME size.
SALIGN	L or R and T or B	This attribute controls how the animation will be aligned if the SCALE is SHOWALL or NOBORDER but the aspect ratio of the frame does not match the aspect ratio of the animation. L aligns the animation to the left of the frame, R to the right. T aligns it to the top of the frame, and B aligns it to the bottom.

MBED

The mBED plug-in essentially extends HTML to make it more multimedia-oriented. Instead of using a new file format, it operates with .GIF, JPEG, QuickTime, and other standard formats.

mBED's .MBD files—also known as mbedlets—are simple text files that describe various actions that embedded images will perform when a user interacts with them. For example, you can create an icon that becomes animated or plays a sound when the user clicks on it or moves the mouse pointer over it.

Although mBED has made its plug-in an open tool that does not require the purchase of any authoring software, the company offers the "Incredible Mbedable Machine." This is a subscription-based Web site that lets you create mbedlets just by pointing, clicking, and filling in menus. You can then download the mbedlets and incorporate them into your own Web site.

Lesson 1: Installing the mBED Plug-In

To install mBED, go to the mBED Software Web site at *http://www.mbed.com* (or see Appendix A). If you have Windows 95 or Windows NT, run the installer program MBED32.EXE. For Windows 3.x, run the installer program MBED16.EXE. The installer will locate your Netscape Plug-ins subdirectory and copy either NP32MBED.DLL or NP16MBED.DLL.

The Macintosh plug-ins are mBED Plugin PPC for Power Macintoshes, and mBED Plugin for all other systems. Drag whichever version is correct to the Plug-ins folder within your Netscape folder.

Now, for all Netscape versions, exit the program and restart it. Select About Plug-ins from the Help menu or Apple menu, and you will see that mBED has adopted the following MIME type/subtype and suffix:

```
application/mbedlet      mbd
```

Before you place .MBD files on a Web server, you need to ask your Internet Service Provider or network administrator to install this MIME type so that mbedlets will be served properly to client machines. Obviously, no alterations are necessary to test them on your local hard drive.

To test the program, you can return to the mBED Web pages at *http://www.mbed.com.* Figure 11-15 shows *http://www.mbed.com/home.html.* The figure under the "Webcentric Multimedia" legend features spheres that move from left to right and others shooting off into the "sky" behind.

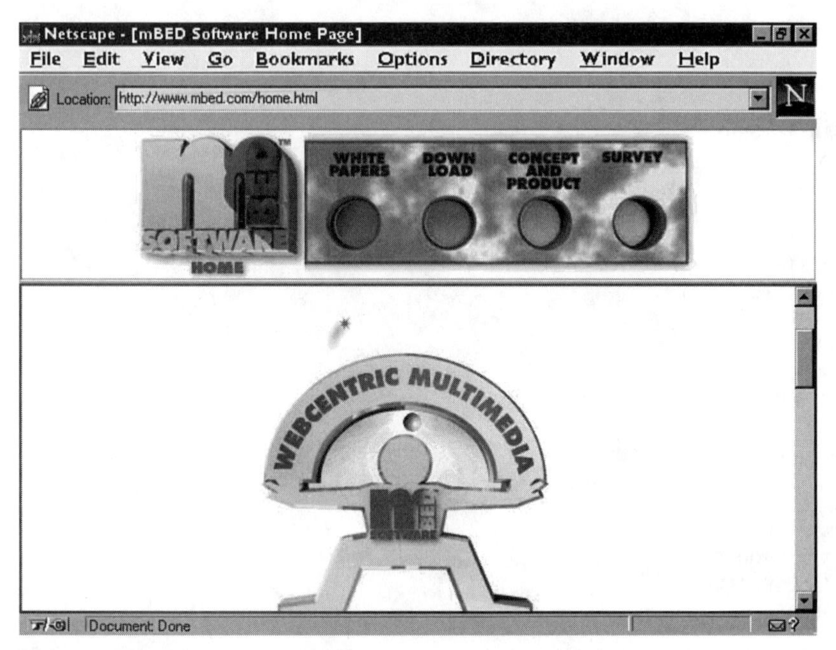

Figure 11–15 An animated greeting appears on this mBED Software Web page

Lesson 2: Embedding Mbedlets in Your Web Pages

mBED makes relatively little use of special attributes for the <EMBED> tag. The HTML code that inserts the figure seen in Figure 11-15 is merely the following:

```
<EMBED SRC="goldguy.mbd" WIDTH=331 HEIGHT=300>
```

The real action takes place inside the mbedlet, a text file that uses an HTML-like command language to bring together graphics, sound, and other elements. A sample is shown in Listing 11-1.

Listing 11-1 This is the text file for the mbedlet GOLDGUY.MBD

```
<MBEDLET>
    <PROTOTYPES>
        <SPRITE NAME=STAR>
            <DATA>
                /images/star.gif
```

continued on next page

continued from previous page

```
            </DATA>
        </SPRITE>
    </PROTOTYPES>
    <PLAYERS>
        <SPRITE NAME=BIGGUY>
            <DATA>
                 /images/bigguy.jpeg
            </DATA>
            <PROPERTIES>
                 VISIBLE
                 LOCATION=0,60
            </PROPERTIES>
            <HANDLERS>
                <MOUSEUP>
                     BIGBEN PLAY
                </MOUSEUP>
                <MOUSEENTER>
                     BROWSER PUT Click me and I do my best Big Ben impression
                </MOUSEENTER>
                <MOUSELEAVE>
                     BROWSER PUT
                </MOUSELEAVE>
            </HANDLERS>
        </SPRITE>
        <SPRITE NAME=BLUE>
            <DATA>
                /images/blue.gif
            </DATA>
            <PROPERTIES>
                 LOCATION=86,121
                 VISIBLE
            </PROPERTIES>
        </SPRITE>
        <SPRITE NAME=YELLOW>
            <DATA>
                 /images/yellow.gif
            </DATA>
            <PROPERTIES>
                 LOCATION=86,121
            </PROPERTIES>
        </SPRITE>
        <SPRITE NAME=BLUEBALL>
            <DATA>
                 /images/blueball.gif
            </DATA>
        </SPRITE>
        <SPRITE NAME=YELLOWBALL>
            <DATA>
                 /images/yellowball.gif
```

```
    </DATA>
</SPRITE>
<STAR NAME=STAR1>
</STAR>
<STAR NAME=STAR2>
</STAR>
<PATH NAME=BALLP1>
    <PROPERTIES>
         STARTPOINT=103,166
         ENDPOINT=158,126
         CURVETYPE=CIRCULAR
         RADIUS=57
         DURATION=1300
    </PROPERTIES>
</PATH>
<PATH NAME=BALLP2>
    <PROPERTIES>
         STARTPOINT=158,126
         ENDPOINT=213,171
         CURVETYPE=CIRCULAR
         RADIUS=57
         DURATION=1300
    </PROPERTIES>
</PATH>
<PATH NAME=STARP1>
    <PROPERTIES>
         STARTPOINT=64,96
         ENDPOINT=164,20
         CURVETYPE=BEZIER
         CONTROLPOINT1=94,50
         CONTROLPOINT2=94,50
         EASEOUT=100
         DURATION=1000
    </PROPERTIES>
</PATH>
<PATH NAME=STARP2>
    <PROPERTIES>
         STARTPOINT=213,60
         ENDPOINT=313,5
         CURVETYPE=BEZIER
         CONTROLPOINT1=253,30
         CONTROLPOINT2=253,30
         EASEOUT=100
         DURATION=1000
    </PROPERTIES>
</PATH>
<EFFECT NAME=WIPEDOWN>
    <PROPERTIES>
         DURATION=1000
```

continued on next page

continued from previous page

```
            TYPE=WIPE
            DIRECTION=DOWN
        </PROPERTIES>
    </EFFECT>
    <EFFECT NAME=WIPEUP>
        <PROPERTIES>
            DURATION=1000
            TYPE=WIPE
            DIRECTION=UP
        </PROPERTIES>
    </EFFECT>
    <SOUND NAME=BIGBEN>
        <DATA>
            /sounds/bigben.wav
        </DATA>
    </SOUND>
    <SCORE NAME=MAINSCORE>
        <DATA>
            0000 STARP2 PLAY STAR2
            0300 MBEDLET LOCK
            0300 YELLOW HIDE
            0300 BLUE SHOW
            0300 MBEDLET UNLOCK WIPEDOWN
            1000 STAR2 HIDE
            1500 BALLP1 PLAY BLUEBALL
            1500 STARP1 PLAY STAR1
            2500 STAR1 HIDE
            3000 STARP2 PLAY STAR2
            3200 BALLP2 PLAY BLUEBALL
            4000 STAR2 HIDE
            4500 STARP1 PLAY STAR1
            4500 BLUEBALL HIDE
            4800 MBEDLET LOCK
            4800 BLUE HIDE
            4800 YELLOW SHOW
            4800 MBEDLET UNLOCK WIPEUP
            5500 STAR1 HIDE
            6000 STARP2 PLAY STAR2
            6000 BALLP1 PLAY YELLOWBALL
            7000 STAR2 HIDE
            7500 STARP1 PLAY STAR1
            7700 BALLP2 PLAY YELLOWBALL
            8500 STAR1 HIDE
            9000 YELLOWBALL HIDE
         </DATA>
         <PROPERTIES>
            PLAYFOREVER=TRUE
         </PROPERTIES>
```

```
        </SCORE>
    </PLAYERS>
    <HANDLERS>
        <STARTUP>
            MAINSCORE PLAY
        </STARTUP>
    </HANDLERS>
</MBEDLET>
```

Clearly, the real trick here is understanding more about what mbedlets are and how to use their command language. Mbedlets are interactive multimedia interfaces within Web pages. They reference graphics, animation, and sound. They access data directly off the Web as needed and can communicate back to the server using standard HTTP methods. Also, they respond to user actions such as mouse clicks and key events.

Each mbedlet consists of players, interacting entities whose behaviors result in the visual, auditory, and feedback characteristics of the mbedlet. Examples of players are sprites that display graphics, effects that show visual transitions, paths that control animation, and scores that control actions over time.

The .MBD file provides a list of players including their type, name, data, properties, and handlers, examples of which you can see in the listing above. It is stored on your Web server in the same directory as the HTML page on which the mbedlet is to run. By specifying data for certain types of players such as sprites and sounds, the .MBD file refers to other resources also located on the server.

The mBED plug-in is invoked by the browser whenever an HTML document refers to an .MBD file. This then proceeds to run the mbedlet, displaying its graphics and playing its sounds, responding to user events such as mouse and key clicks and making requests to the browser to post data to the server or navigate to new locations.

You can create an .MBD file by learning the mbedlet syntax. Alternatively, you can use a point-and-click tool that mBED Software plans to release by Fall 1996. In the meantime, there is another fascinating way to create mbedlets: mBED Software has posted several Web pages with master mbedlets it calls "machines." By interacting with these mbedlets, you can cause others to be created.

Figure 11-16 shows the beginning of a machine that can be used to create animated button bars. The name "Waite Group Press" and the URL *http://www.dnai.com/waite* have been typed right into the mbedlet, specifying that they should be used for the button bar it will create. Scrolling further down this Web page, or machine, if you will, yields other controllers that allow backgrounds, sounds, and animations to be used, and so on. Finally, you can click on a button that creates your new mbedlet (this is seen at the middle right of Figure 11-17). Figure 11-18 shows you the final output, a Web page that demonstrates your new mbedlet—here, an animated button that takes the user to Waite Group's Web site when clicked on—and tells you how to embed it in a page of your own.

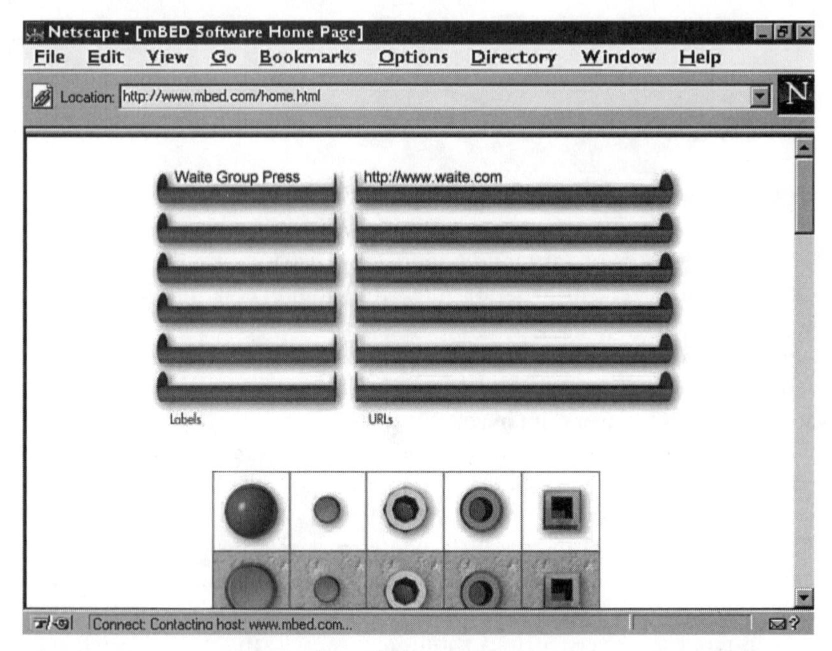

Figure 11-16 This mbedlet, of a type known as a "machine," lets you create other mbedlets that use your own URLs and other specifications

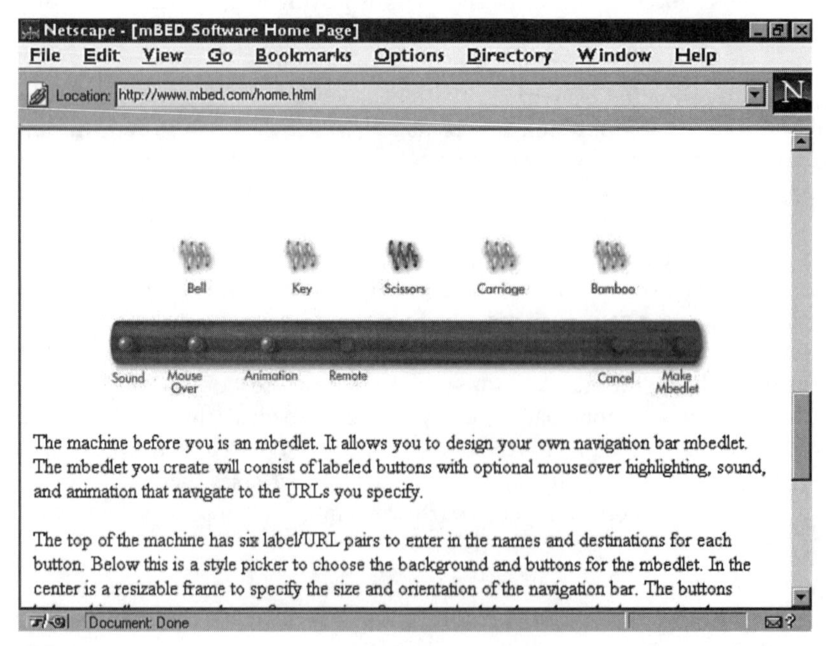

Figure 11-17 Here is the end of the "machine"—you click on the button (middle, right) to create your new mbedlet

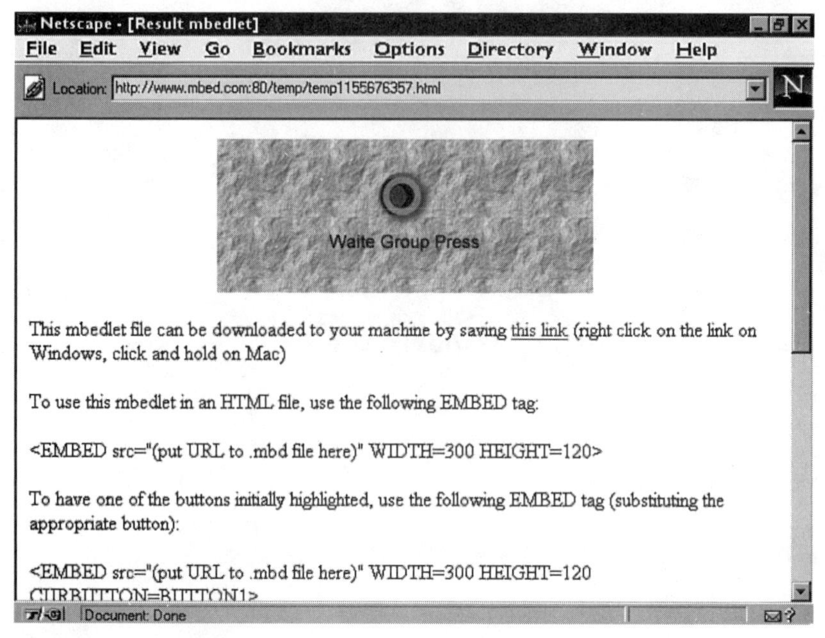

Figure 11–18 The newly created mbedlet can now be placed in your own Web page

Listing 11-2 is the text file comprising WAITE.MBD, the newly created mbedlet shown in Figure 11-18.

Listing 11-2 The text file for the mbedlet shown in Figure 11-18

```
<mbedlet>
    <slots>
         curbutton=button0
    </slots>
    <prototypes>
         <text name=label>
             <properties>
                  visible
                  smooth
                  size=14
                  multiline
                  hjustify=center
                  rect=0,0,300,60
                  regpoint=50,0
                </properties>
         </text>
         <sprite name=hole>
             <data>
```

continued on next page

continued from previous page

```
                /presets/hole4.gif,/presets/holeA4.gif
            </data>
            <properties>
                visible
                rect=0,0,44,44
                regpoint=50,100
             </properties>
        </sprite>
        <button name=menubutton>
            <data>
                empty
                /presets/marker4E.gif,/presets/markerA4.gif
                /presets/hilite4E.gif,/presets/hiliteA4.gif
            </data>
            <properties>
                type=radio
                rect=0,0,44,44
                regpoint=50,100
                visible
                mouseover
            </properties>
        </button>
    </prototypes>
    <players>
        <picture name=bg>
            <data>
                /presets/texE.gif
            </data>
            <properties>
                rect=0,0,300,120
                visible
                tiled
            </properties>
        </picture>
        <sound name=buttonsound>
            <data>
                /presets/sound2.wav
            </data>
        </sound>
        <score name=buttonscore>
            <data>
                0 buttonsound play
                0 me wait buttonsound
                0 browser goto param
            </data>
        </sound>
        <menubutton name=button0>
            <properties>
                visible=false
                location=-44,60
            </properties>
        </menubutton>
        <label name=label1>
```

```
            <properties>
                 value=Waite Group Press
                 location=150,69
            </properties>
        </label>
        <hole name=hole1>
            <properties>
                 location=150,69
            </properties>
        </hole>
        <menubutton name=button1>
            <properties>
                 location=150,69
            </properties>
            <handlers>
                 <toggleon>
                     buttonscore play http://www.dnai.com/waite/,_blank
                 </toggleon>
            </handlers>
        </menubutton>
    </players>
    <handlers>
        <startup>
            $curbutton set value=ON
        </startup>
    </handlers>
</mbedlet>
```

Skim through this, and you'll see where the button's label is stored and where it references the URL for the Waite Group home page. You'll also notice that it references several graphics and sound files—all of which need to be on your server for the mbedlet to work properly.

Although it was mentioned at the beginning of this lesson that mBED makes little use of EMBED attributes, it does use a so-called SLOT mechanism that allows parameters to be passed to mbedlets. Parameters can be added to an <EMBED> tag and then used inside the mbedlet as a SLOT. For example, an HTML file might read

```
<EMBED src="tryme.mbd" WIDTH=200 HEIGHT=110 DAY="Monday">
```

The source for TRYME.MBD reads

```
<MBEDLET>
    <SLOTS>
         DAY=Sunday
    </SLOTS>
    <PLAYERS>
         <TEXT NAME=CAPTION>
             <PROPERTIES>
                  SERIF
                  VISIBLE
                  SMOOTH
                  VALUE=$DAY
```

continued on next page

continued from previous page

```
                    JUSTIFY=CENTER
                    RECT=0,0,200,59
                </PROPERTIES>
            </TEXT>
        </PLAYERS>
</MBEDLET>
```

This mbedlet will display the word "Monday." Note that if no DAY parameter had been sent to the mbedlet, the mbedlet would show the default value Sunday.

POINTPLUS

PointPlus is a plug-in aimed squarely at users of Microsoft PowerPoint. Initially available for Windows, it's intended to put PowerPoint presentations on the Web with a minimum of time and effort.

The "authoring" tool is the PointPlus conversion program, which costs around $300. You simply use it to open any PowerPoint (4.0 or later) presentation and let the program run. Presentations are divided into small packets so that they can be streamed over the Web. When the process is done, you embed the resulting files in your Web pages using the familiar <EMBED SRC> tag.

The PointPlus plug-in, freely available, lets users view the resulting presentations either manually, slide by slide, or automatically. They will hear whatever sound was included in the original PowerPoint file.

Lesson 1: Installing the PointPlus Plug-In

To install PointPlus, go to the Net-Scene Web site at *http://www.net-scene.co.il* (or check Appendix A for details of what's contained on your CD-ROM). If you have Windows 95 or Windows NT, run the installer program PPP3203.EXE. For Windows 3.x, run the installer program PPP1503.EXE. The installer will locate your Netscape Plug-ins subdirectory and copy either NPSLC32.DLL or NPSLC16.DLL.

Now exit Netscape, if it is running, and restart it. Select About Plug-ins from the Help menu, and you will see that the following MIME type/subtype and suffix have been added:

```
application/x-salsa        slc
```

Before you place .SLC files (PowerPoint presentations converted to PointPlus format) on a Web server, you need to ask your Internet Service Provider or network administrator to install this MIME type so that presentations will be served properly to client machines. Obviously, no alterations are necessary to test them on your local hard drive.

To test the program, you can return to the Net-Scene Web pages at *http://www.net-scene.co.il*. Figure 11-19 shows a sample presentation at *http://www.net-scene.co.il/demo2.htm*.

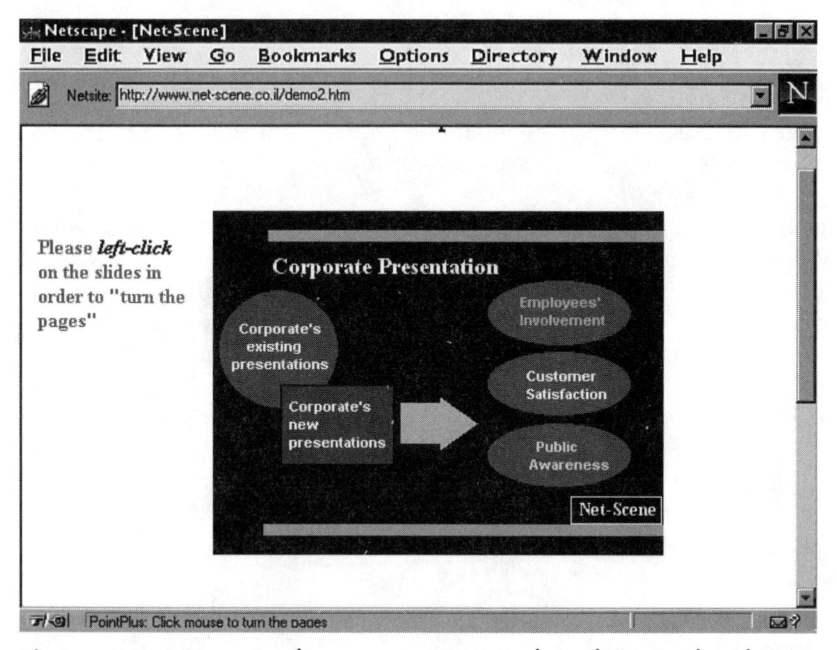

Figure 11–19 A sample presentation viewed via the PointPlus plug-in

Lesson 2: Embedding Presentations in Your Web Pages

The HTML code that embedded the presentation in Figure 11-19 is merely

```
<EMBED SRC="CORPORAT.SLC" WIDTH=360 HEIGHT=269 MOUSE=ON ALIGN=RIGHT>
```

WIDTH and HEIGHT are, of course, standard attributes. The MOUSE attribute determines whether or not the user can page forward through the presentation using the left mouse button and backward using the right mouse button. Setting MOUSE=OFF makes PointPlus ignore the viewer's mouse clicks. Therefore, it should be used only if timings had been assigned to the slides in the original PowerPoint presentation.

Another attribute available with PointPlus, CYCLE, determines whether or not a presentation will loop. If you use the attribute CYCLE=YES, the presentation will run continuously; otherwise, it will run once and then stop.

Winning our prize for what must be the most arcane attribute featured in this book is BGCOLOR—or at least PointPlus's use of it. The background color of a presentation itself is defined when you author it in PowerPoint. However, PointPlus uses the BGCOLOR attribute (whose value is set hexadecimally in the RGB format normally used by HTML) to specify the color of the PointPlus logo that is displayed before a slide show begins!

SHOCKWAVE FOR AUTHORWARE

Introduced in December 1995, Macromedia's Shockwave for Director was the first generally available plug-in. Macromedia now offers plug-ins for Director, FreeHand, and Authorware, all of which use the Shockwave moniker. It plans to make them available for all its other applications as well.

In addition to the plug-ins, Macromedia offers "Afterburners," software tools that compress and optimize standard Macromedia files for use on the Web. The Shockwave plug-ins and Afterburners are available free of charge, but authoring presentations requires purchasing one or more of Macromedia's relatively expensive applications. Of course, if you are already using Macromedia software, Shockwave is ideal.

Because plug-ins serve to advertise and popularize the authoring applications they work with, Macromedia would naturally like you to install all three of its Shockwaves. The design of its Web site encourages this, making it quicker to download an installer for all three than an installer for just one. However, you can install them one at a time, and this might be useful if you have a portable computer or other machine with limited disk space. Shockwave for Freehand is discussed in Chapter 13 because it is purely a graphics application.

Afterburner for Authorware transforms standard Authorware pieces for playback on the Internet. It streams sound, movies, and graphics, compressing information by up to 70 percent. It can also write viewer data back to a Web server, making it a possible vehicle for market surveys, tests and quizzes, or customer service applications.

If you check out Macromedia's Web-based documentation regarding Shockwave for Authorware, you'll notice that it consistently mentions "intranet" instead of "Internet" as being this product's intended platform. While this doesn't mean you can't use Shockwave for Authorware via modem, it might be a tacit admission that the bandwidth required is higher than average. Consider yourself warned.

Lesson 1: Installing the Shockwave for Authorware Plug-In

To install Shockwave for Authorware, go to the Macromedia Web site at *http://www.macromedia.com* (or check Appendix A for details about your CD-ROM).

Macromedia has recently made it extremely difficult to obtain any of its Shockwave plug-ins without getting all of them. In other words, if you want Shockwave for Authorware, you have to install Shockwave for Director and Shockwave for FreeHand as well. There's probably still a way around this, but it's best to go with the flow unless your hard drive is critically overloaded (you can always remove any plug-in you're not using later).

If you have Windows 95, use the compressed, self-extracting installer N32Z005.EXE. If you have Windows 3.x, use N16Z005.EXE. Copy it to a temporary folder on your hard drive and then double-click on it. Temporary files will appear, including another installer program, SETUP.EXE or SETUPEX.EXE. Run the latter, and you'll be asked to locate your Netscape folder using the standard file browser.

The installer then copies a variety of files to the Plug-ins folder within your Netscape folder. Those we're concerned with here are the Shockwave for Authorware plug-in, NP32ASW.DLL (or NP16ASW.DLL for Windows 3.x), and an Authorware folder, NP32ASW (or NP16ASW).

Mac users proceed similarly. Download or copy the installer file to your Desktop or other location and then—if Netscape hasn't already done it for you—use Stuffit Expander, BinHex, or a similar utility to convert and expand them. Then run the installer program, which will locate your copy of Netscape, placing the Authorware plug-in (NP-MacPPC-AW-Shockwave or NP-Mac68K-AW-Shockwave) into its Plug-ins folder.

Now, exit Netscape, if it is running, and restart the program. You can confirm that Shockwave for Authorware is active by selecting About Plug-ins from the Help menu or Apple menu. As you'll see, it has declared a new MIME type/subtype and suffix:

```
application/-x-authorware-map      aam
```

For you to make files available on a Web server, that server's configuration needs to be changed so that it associates this MIME type with the correct file suffix (extension). Because of files called up by some Authorware presentations, the following associations also need to be set up on the Web server:

```
application/x-authorware-seq   aas
application/x-authorware-bin   aab
```

You probably need to contact the people who administer your server so that they can do this. Macromedia does provide do-it-yourself instructions at *http://www-1.macromedia.com/Tools/Shockwave/Authorware/getstart.html* that you can try if you know the platform your Web server is running on.

To test your installation of Shockwave for Authorware, connect to the Internet and go to the Macromedia Web site at *http://www.macromedia.com*. You'll easily find many samples within the "Gallery," although it is not always immediately clear which of the Shockwave plug-ins was used to create them. Look for samples labeled with the Authorware logo (a man with his arms upstretched within the outline of an A). Or use the "Shockwave Vanguard Search" screen located within *http://www.macromedia.com/shockwave/epicenter/vanguard/index.html* (see Figure 11-20).

Figure 11-21 shows part of the "Employee Knowledge Link," written for Pacific Bell employees (and modified slightly for presentation on the Macromedia Web site). This screen shot has not been cropped in any way: The Shockwave for Authorware plug-in was responsible for hiding Netscape's menu and window borders. The Pacific Bell presentation was written for the company's intranet and transfers very slowly over modem links. Go brew some coffee while it loads.

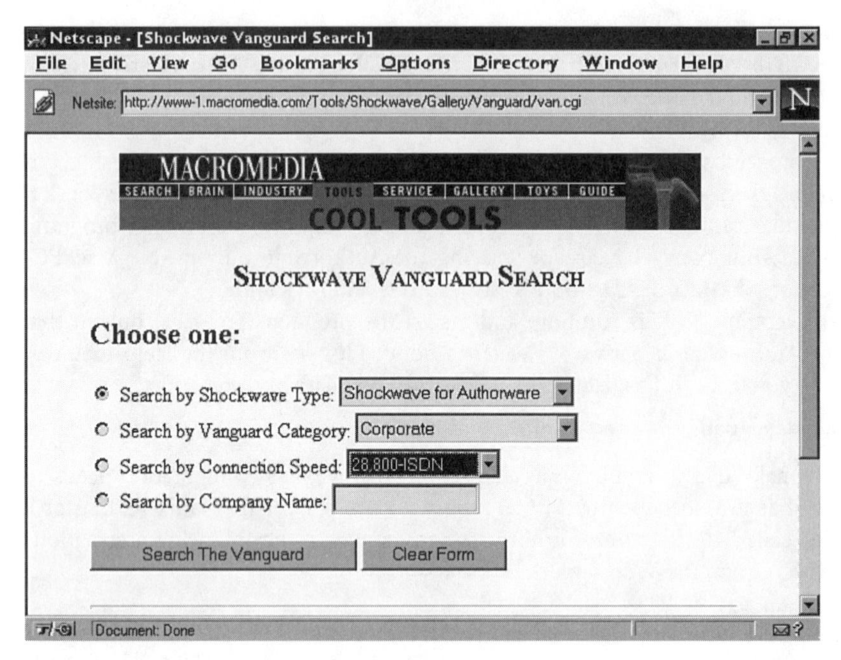

Figure 11–20 This part of the Macromedia Web site helps you search for examples that use Shockwave for Authorware

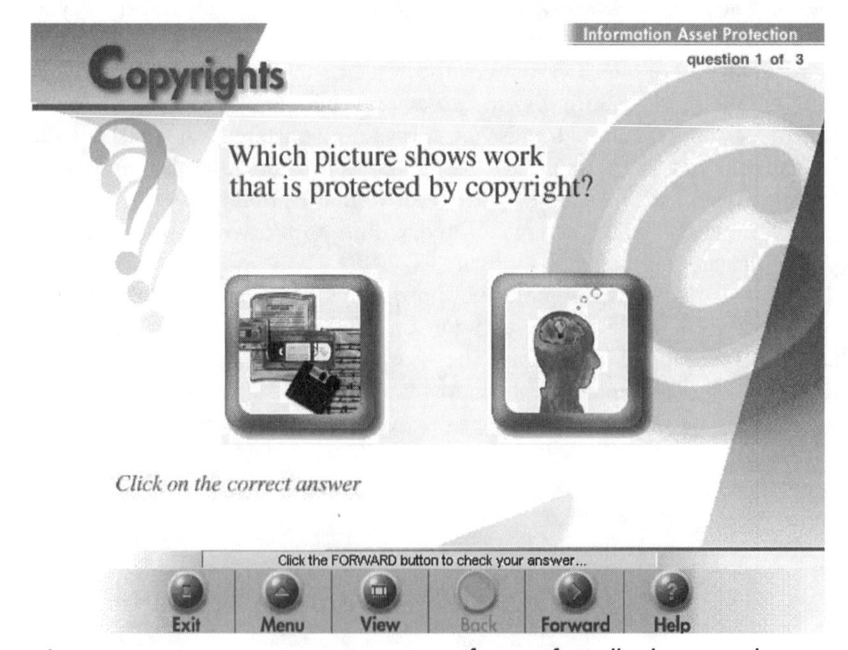

Figure 11–21 A presentation written for Pacific Bell takes over the whole screen

Lesson 2: Embedding Authorware Documents in Your Web Pages

The elaborate screen seen in Figure 11-21, and others like it, is the result of Authorware programming, not fancy HTML. Need proof? Here's the line of code that was used to embed the Pacific Bell presentation in a Web page:

```
<EMBED SRC="pcpb.aam" WIDTH=100 HEIGHT=72 WINDOW=ONTOP>
```

The WIDTH and HEIGHT attributes specify the width and height of the display area in pixels. Netscape crops the image to the size you specify, but it's best to use the size of your presentation window for this setting. WIDTH and HEIGHT settings less than 640 by 480 are preferable. Otherwise, users with their resolution set to 640 by 480 will have to scroll vertically and horizontally to see your whole window.

The WINDOW setting tells how the Authorware piece is displayed in relation to the Netscape browser. WINDOW=INPLACE displays the piece embedded within the HTML page in the browser window. You can use this setting only in Windows. WINDOW=ONTOP displays the piece in a separate window on top of the browser window. This makes your piece look more like a separate application. WINDOW=ONTOPMINIMIZE displays the piece in a separate window and minimizes the browser. This setting makes your piece look the most like a separate, stand-alone application.

If you use WINDOW=INPLACE, don't try to use a title bar on your presentation window. (The Title Bar setting is in Authorware's File Setup dialog box.) The plug-in doesn't allow the display of a title bar. Instead, the height of your presentation window will be reduced by the height of the title bar.

To create Authorware pieces, you need to own and have a working knowledge of Macromedia's Authorware 3.5 or later. While this chapter cannot teach you how to use the program, it is worth noting features that Shockwave for Authorware adds. They include

- Streaming of sound, movies, and graphics to provide rapid startup and playback
- Asynchronous preloading of data
- Compression of 50-70%
- Write-back information via FTP (for customer registration, test answers, or any other type of feedback)
- Embedding documents within a Web page or having them take over the full screen
- Jumping to other URLs from within the Authorware piece

Afterburner for Authorware is an essential tool you can download from the Macromedia server at *http://www-1.macromedia.com/Tools/Shockwave/Authorware/aftrbrnr.html.* It compresses Authorware files and divides them into segments for uploading to a Web server. In addition, it creates a map file used to locate each segment when needed. The map file also identifies any external files used with Authorware, such as Director movies.

On the Macintosh, Afterburner also "flattens" external files such as movies so they can load on PC compatibles. Afterburner creates two different types of file:

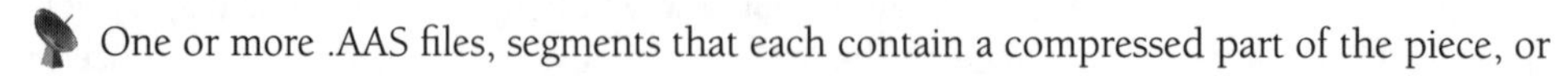

- One or more .AAS files, segments that each contain a compressed part of the piece, or
- One map file (.AAM), containing information that tells the plug-in where to find .AAS files and any external files that are also required

Like an HTML document, an .AAM file is a simple text file. Editing it is relatively simple once you are familiar with the format. Here's what a simple map file looks like, as produced by Afterburner for the file TEST.APP in Windows:

```
ver  0 2
get .
put DOWNLOAD
seg   win     piew0000.aas       0          32931
seg        win     piew0001.aas       32931        30814
seg        win     piew0002.aas       63745        26995
```

The first line gives the version of the map file. The second line (get) tells where the map file is located on the HTTP server. The period after get indicates that the piece is in the same location as the HTML page. (If you store the piece in a different location, you have to edit this line of the map file to show where it is; you can use either relative or absolute URLs.)

The third line (put) specifies a location on the user's computer to which external files such as movies will be downloaded. The default location is a Download folder that's automatically created by the Authorware Plug-In when "put DOWNLOAD" appears in a map file.

The last three lines in the sample map file identify the three segment files that make up TEST.APP. Each line has five columns. The first column specifies the type of entry—in this case, a segment file. The second column tells which platform the piece can run on—in this case, Windows. The third column gives the name of each segment on the HTTP server, including four characters you assigned and four unique digits assigned by Afterburner. The fourth column tells the starting point of each segment (in bytes) in relation to the beginning of the piece. The fifth column gives the size of the segment.

Normally, Afterburner produces all of this information automatically. However, if your piece uses external libraries or other external files, you will have to create additional entries. Also, when you process Mac and Windows versions of a piece with Afterburner, you get two map files and two sets of segment files—which normally require two separate links on an HTML page. Macintosh users and Windows users would have to select the link corresponding to their platform, and labeled as such manually by you. You can make things simpler by providing a single link on the page, which will automatically run the right version of the piece depending on the user's platform. This is done by combining the separate map files into a single file.

Below is an example of a combined map file. This example includes comments, which are lines that begin with the pound sign (#).

```
# Combined Windows/Macintosh map file
ver 0 2
get .
put .
# Windows segment entries.
seg win piew0000.aas 0 32931
seg win piew0001.aas 32931 30814
seg win piew0002.aas 63745 26995
# Macintosh segment entries.
seg mac piem0000.aas 0 32715
seg mac piem0001.aas 32715 33001
seg mac piem0002.aas 65716 30796
# Windows library entries.
lib win winlib1.aam MYLIB1.APR
lib win winlib2.aam MYLIB2.APR
# Macintosh library entries.
lib mac maclib1.aam "MY LIB1"
lib mac maclib2.aam "MY LIB2"
# Shared binary content entries.
bin all movie1.mov MOVIE1.MOV onDemand
bin all movie2.mov MOVIE2.MOV onDemand
```

There is a lot more to this topic. For full details, you should visit the Web page from which this information was extracted, at *http://www.macromedia.com/shockwave/authorware/create.html.*

SHOCKWAVE FOR DIRECTOR

Shockwave for Director compresses and optimizes standard Director files. Therefore, you can use Director to create interactive multimedia for CD-ROM, diskette, or interactive television, and then repurpose those files for the Web with a minimum of extra effort. Links to other URLs are supported, as is Lingo, Director's English-like scripting language.

Macromedia recently updated the Shockwave for Director plug-in so that it works with files created by Director 5. However, it remains backward-compatible with content created via Director 4.

As of this latest version, Shockwave for Director now provides a new way to package and play audio files across the Web, provided that you have Director 5 and, optionally, Macromedia SoundEdit 16 version 2. You can use Shockwave audio streaming and compression technology to add compression to Director movies internally, or create separate audio files that may be invoked as external "cast members."

Shockwave for Director's streaming audio requires no special server-side software, using the standard HTTP protocol for file transfer. Macromedia claims that audio files can be compressed down to 1/176 of their original file size. Settings in either Director 5 or SoundEdit 16 let you choose a sound file's desired bit rate and whether you want it to be stored in stereo or mono.

Lesson 1: Installing the Shockwave for Director Plug-In

To install Shockwave for Director, once again go to the Macromedia Web site at *http://www.macromedia.com* (or see Appendix A for details about your CD-ROM).

As mentioned above in the section on Shockwave for Authorware, Macromedia has recently made it extremely difficult to obtain any of its plug-ins without getting them all. In other words, if you want Shockwave for Director, you have to install Shockwave for Authorware and Shockwave for FreeHand as well. Once again, we'll just go along with this: You can remove the Shockwave for Authorware and FreeHand plug-ins later if you have no use for them.

If you have Windows 95, use the compressed, self-extracting installer, N32Z005.EXE. If you have Windows 3.x, use N16Z005.EXE. Copy it to a temporary folder on your hard drive and then double-click on it. Temporary files will appear, including another installer program, SETUP.EXE or SETUPEX.EXE. Run the latter, and you'll be asked to locate your Netscape folder using the standard file browser.

The installer then copies a variety of files to the Plug-ins folder within your Netscape folder. Those we're concerned with here are the Shockwave for Director plug-in, NP32DSW.DLL (or NP16DSW.DLL for Windows 3.x), and a Director folder, NP32DSW (or NP16DSW).

Mac users proceed similarly. Download or copy the installer file to your Desktop or other location and then—if Netscape hasn't already done it for you—use Stuffit Expander, BinHex, or a similar utility to convert and expand them. Then run the installer program, which will locate your copy of Netscape, placing the Director plug-in (NP-MacPPC-Dir-Shockwave or NP-Mac68K-Dir-Shockwave) into its Plug-ins folder.

Now, exit Netscape, if it is running, and restart the program. You can confirm that Shockwave for Director is active by selecting About Plug-ins from the Help menu or Apple menu. As you'll see, it has declared the following new MIME type/subtype and suffixes:

```
application/x-director    dxr, dcr, dir
```

For you to make files available on a Web server, that server's configuration needs to be changed so that it associates the MIME application/x-director with the file extensions .DXR, .DCR, and .DIR. A .DCR file is a Director movie that has been compressed by Afterburner. A .DIR movie is a standard Director file with no alterations, and a .DXR file is a protected movie that can be played but not edited by Director.

You probably need to contact the people who administer your server so that they can adjust its MIME types. Macromedia does provide do-it-yourself instructions at *http://www-1/macromedia.com/Tools/Shockwave/Director/getstart.html* that you can try if you know the platform your Web server is running on.

To test your installation of Shockwave for Director, connect to the Internet and go to the Macromedia Web site at *http://www.macromedia.com*. You'll easily find dozens, if not hundreds, of samples within the "Gallery," thanks to the "Shockwave Vanguard Search" screen. Figure 11-22 shows part of an interactive children's story at *http://www.cyberkids.com*. Figure 11-23 shows a version of Space Invaders written using Director.

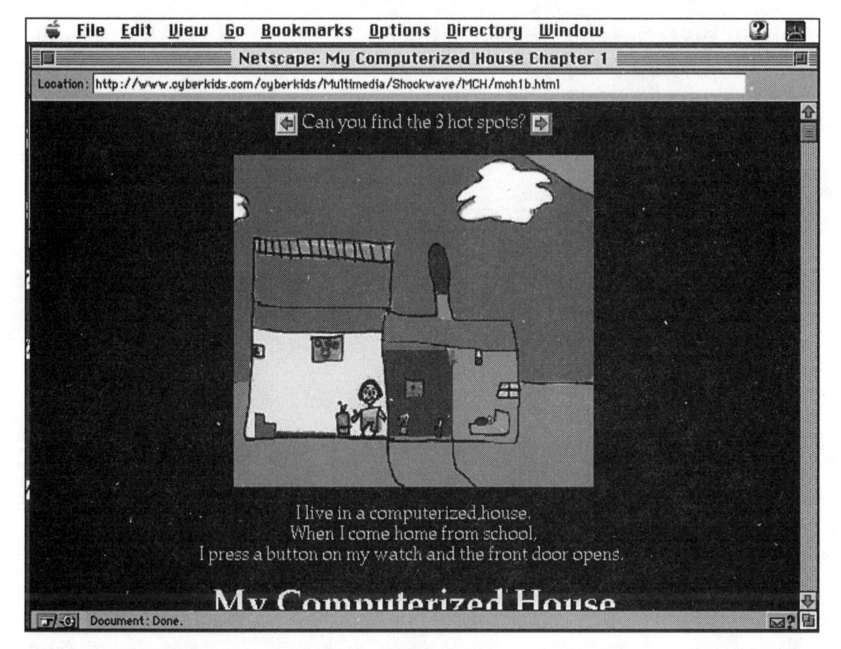

Figure 11–22 An interactive children's story

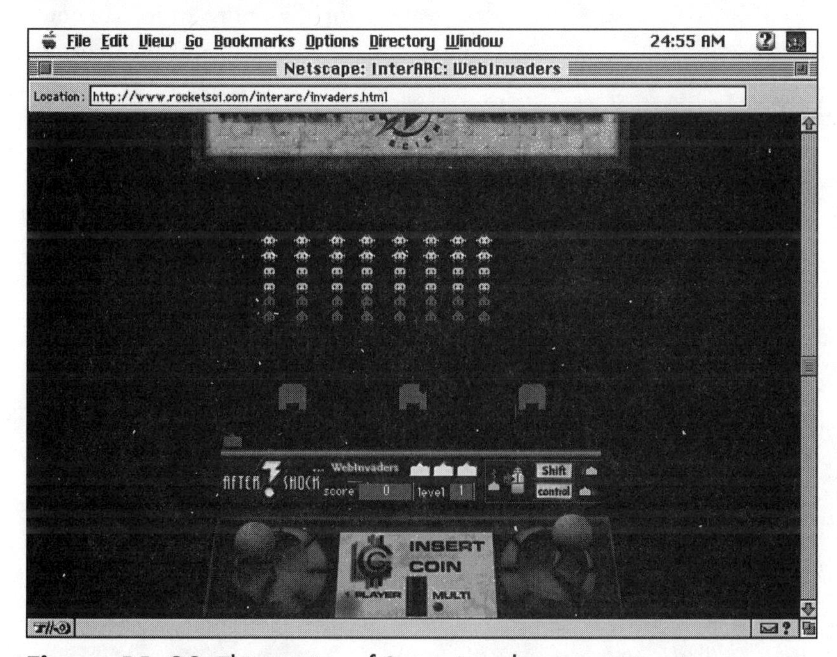

Figure 11–23 This version of Space Invaders was written using Director

You'll find another list of sites using Shockwave for Director at *http://www.teleport.com/~arcana/shockwave*. The sites on this list tend to be less corporate, more expressive of individual interests. For example, Figure 11-24 shows an interactive tour of the London Underground.

NOTE: Some beta-test versions of Netscape 3.0 did not work with some versions of the Shockwave for Director plug-in. If you have problems playing Director presentations, make sure you are using the latest version of both the browser and the plug-in.

Lesson 2: Embedding Director Presentations in Your Web Pages

The `<EMBED>` tag for a Director movie looks like this:

```
<EMBED SRC="path/filename.ext" WIDTH=n HEIGHT=n PALETTE=background>
```

Use the WIDTH and HEIGHT attributes to specify the width and height of the image in pixels. Netscape will crop the image to the size you specify.

The PALETTE attribute allows you control over which palette Netscape uses when it plays a shocked Director movie. If you specify PALETTE=FOREGROUND, the Director movie's palette will be loaded and used as the palette for the entire page. This may

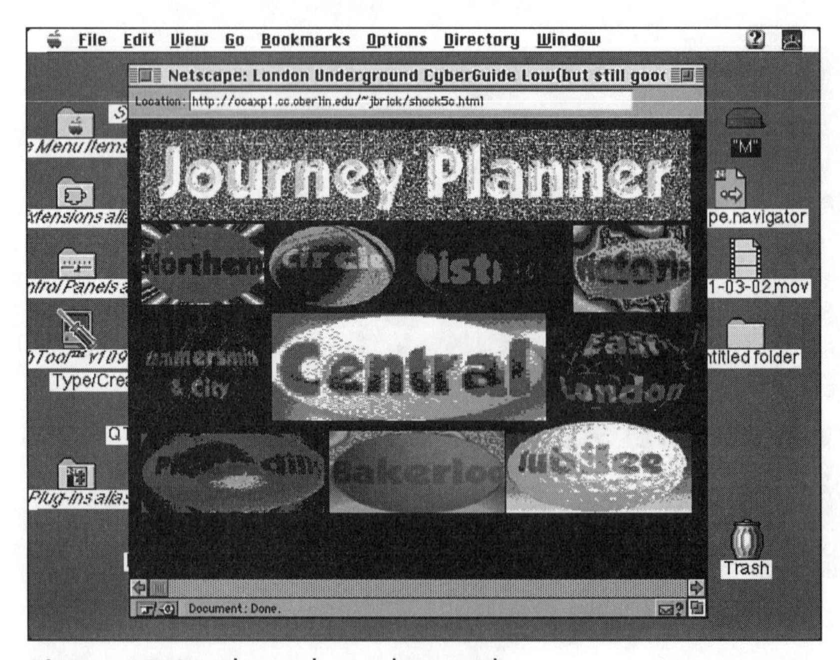

Figure 11-24 The London Underground

adversely affect how other images look. If you set PALETTE=BACKGROUND, the palette of the Director movie will be prevented from loading, and the system palette will be used instead. PALETTE=BACKGROUND is the default when you embed a shocked Director movie in a Web page.

The BGCOLOR attribute is newly available in Shockwave for Director 5. It lets you specify a color that will display while a movie is being downloaded. This helps to make your Web page look like an integrated whole during that awkward period before a movie has arrived.

This example shows how to set up the `<EMBED>` tag for a Director movie named TEST.DCR that is 350 by 245 pixels and that sets the palette for the page.

```
<EMBED SRC="http://www.myserver.com/movies/test.dcr" WIDTH=350 HEIGHT=245
PALETTE=foreground>
```

HTML documents can include more than one movie per page. A user can scroll through the HTML page containing the movie while the movie is playing. The user can interact with the movie and enter text from the keyboard into text fields programmed into the movie. The movie itself, using statements written in Director's Lingo command language, can retrieve information from the network and open additional URLs.

There's no absolute limit to how many movies you can incorporate into a Web page, but it's best to include no more than two or three. When a user leaves a page containing Director movies, the Shockwave Plug-In frees the memory it was using to play the movies.

NOTE: Shockwave for Director's memory requirements can be substantial. You'll want to use it only when you are not running any applications other than Netscape itself. If you have a Macintosh computer with greater than 16MB of memory, you may benefit by increasing the default memory allocation given to Netscape—adjust this using the Finder's Get Info dialog box.

You might have technical problems when Netscape tries to sort out the sound tracks of two movies playing simultaneously. Either use sound in only one movie per page, or program the movies so that the user has to activate the sound tracks by clicking the mouse.

To convert a standard Director movie into a Director movie "shocked" for the Net, use the Afterburner program supplied by Macromedia. This has now been integrated into Director 5 as an Xtra. If you still use Director 4, you can download the Afterburner appropriate to your computer from *http://www.macromedia.com/shockwave/director/aftrbrnr.html.*

When you convert a movie with Afterburner, it looks and works the same as it did before you converted it. However, the movie is compressed and converted to .DCR format.

Macromedia recommends that before you convert a movie with Afterburner, you carefully consider ways to reduce the size of the movie. Also consider whether the user will wait the length of time it takes to download—for a game or other entertainment, they might, but for an advertisement or corporate presentation, they might not!

You should also carefully test your movie on both Macintosh and Windows computers. When the movie is finished, save a copy of it and then drag it to the Afterburner icon (if you have a Macintosh). If you have a Windows computer, open the Afterburner application and use the File Open dialog box to select your movie.

Several new Lingo commands are available to provide a shocked Director movie with access to the network. If you are already familiar with Lingo, refer to Table 11-3 to see some details. (But don't expect these to mean anything to you if you don't have Director and don't know Lingo!) New Lingo commands are also available for precise control over sound playback: See Macromedia's Web site for further details.

Table 11-3 Some of the new Lingo commands support network operations

Command	Possible Content	Comments
getNetText	uri The uri parameter is a universal resource identifier that identifies the HTTP item containing the movie. At present, only HTTP URLs are supported as valid uri parameters. The URL can specify either a file name or an anchor within a file. For example, both of the following URLs are valid: http://www.yourserver.com/movies/movie1.dcr http://www.yourserver.com/movies/buttons.dcr#Contents.	This command starts the retrieval of an HTTP item to be read by Lingo as text. The uri parameter is a universal resource identifier which specifies the HTTP item to be retrieved. Here's an example: on mouseUp getNetText "http://yourserver.com/sample.text" end*** Use netDone to find out when the getNetText operation is completed.
preloadNetThing	uri	This command preloads an HTTP item into the Netscape disk cache so that it can be used later without a download delay. The HTTP item can be anything, including a Director movie, an HTML page, a graphic, and so on. The preloadNetThing command works asynchronously: The current movie continues playing while preloading takes place. You can use netDone to find out when preloading is finished.

Command	Possible Content	Comments
		Keep in mind when you work with preloadNetThing that it's impossible to determine when an item may be removed from the local disk cache.
gotoNetMovie	uri	This command retrieves and goes to a new shocked Director movie from the network. The current movie continues to run until the new movie is available. When the new movie arrives, the plug-in quits the current movie without warning and starts to play the new movie. The new movie occupies the same display area as the calling movie. If a gotoNetMovie operation is in progress and you issue a second gotoNetMovie command before the first is finished, the second command will cancel the first.
gotoNetPage	uri	This command opens a URI, whether it's a shocked Director movie or some other MIME type. Using gotoNetPage opens a new page within the Net browser. You can use netDone to find out when the gotoNetPage operation is completed.

netDone	()	Use this function to test whether getNetText, preloadNetThing, gotoNetMovie, or gotoNetPage is finished. The netDone function defaults to TRUE. It returns FALSE after an asynchronous network operation is started and while the operation is in progress. It returns TRUE when the operation is finished or when the operation has been terminated by a browser error.
		The netDone function must return TRUE before you can place the text in netTextResult into a variable or cast member. Here's an example:
		if netDone() = TRUE then
		put netTextResult() into field "Display Text"
		end if

continued on next page

continued from previous page

Command	Possible Content	Comments
netError	()	This function returns an empty string until the most recently started asynchronous network operation is finished. It returns OK if the operation was completed successfully or None if no asynchronous operation has been started. It returns a string describing the error if the operation failed.
netTextResult	()	This function returns the text result of the operation. For a getNetText operation, this is the text of the HTTP item.
netMIME		This function returns the MIME type of the HTTP item.
netLastModDate		This function returns the date last modified string from the HTTP header for the item.
netAbort		This command cancels a network operation without waiting for a result.

SIZZLER

Sizzler, from Alberta-based Totally Hip Software, Inc., is a relatively simple animation plug-in for your Web pages. Sizzler animations currently cannot perform conditional actions or link to multiple URLs (but clicking on an animation can take the user to a single specified URL).

Thanks to Sizzler's simplicity, however, it can easily support converted PICS or .DIB (Device Independent Bitmap) files. It also supports .AVI and QuickTime files. Many third-party programs, including Macromedia Directory, Gryphon Morph, and Adobe Premiere, can export files that are compatible with the Sizzler converter. However, you can also create animations with Totally Hip's own authoring tool, WebPainter.

Lesson 1: Installing the Sizzler Plug-In

To install Sizzler, go to the Totally Hip Web site at *http://totallyhip.com* (or check Appendix A for details about your CD-ROM). If you have Windows 95 or Windows NT, run the installer program with the "32" in its file name; if you have Windows 3.x, look for the "16" instead. The installer will locate your Netscape Plug-ins subdirectory and copy either NPSPR32.DLL or NPSPR15.DLL.

The Macintosh Sizzler installer automatically locates your Netscape Plug-ins folder and copies the file Sizzler Plug-in into it. If you have two copies of Netscape on your system—for example, a standard version and a copy of Netscape Gold—you may need to check both to see where the Sizzler Plug-in was placed, dragging it to the other Plug-ins folder if necessary.

Now, for all Netscape versions, exit the program and restart it. Select About Plug-ins from the Help menu or Apple menu, and you will see that Sizzler has adopted the following MIME type/subtype and suffix:

```
application/x-sprite    spr
```

You need to ask your Internet Service Provider or network administrator to install this MIME type so that Sizzler will be served properly to client machines. Obviously, no alterations are necessary to test them on your local hard drive.

To test the program, you can return to the Totally Hip Web pages and visit their list of "Sizzling Sites" at *http://www.totallyhip.com/sizzler/6f_sizz.html.* Figure 11-25 shows "The First Fly Caught in the Web," a Sizzler animation located at *http://www.cibernet.it/thebox/english/first_fly.html.* Figure 11-26 shows a home page featuring a rotating logo.

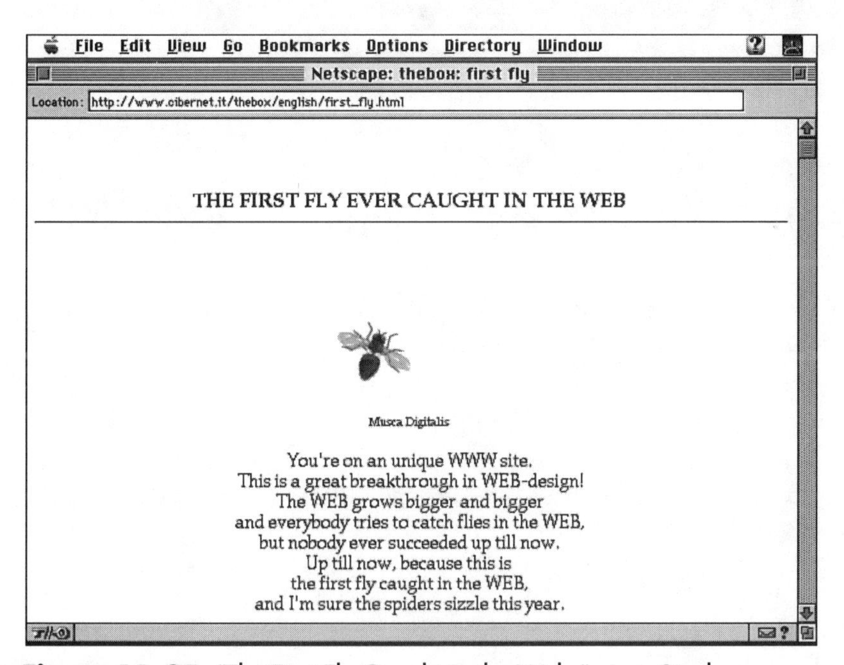

Figure 11-25 "The First Fly Caught in the Web," via a Sizzler animation

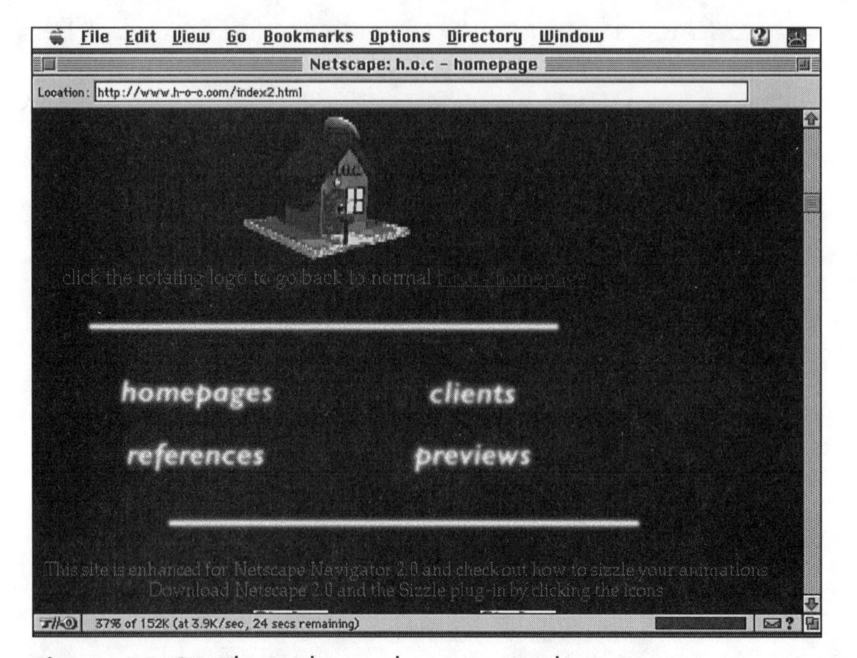

Figure 11-26 This Web page has a rotating logo courtesy of Sizzler

Lesson 2: Embedding Sizzler Images in Your Web Pages

Like some other animation plug-ins, Sizzler doesn't make use of any special EMBED attributes. This makes embedding an animation a simple matter of specifying width and height. For example:

```
<EMBED SRC="FLY_AWAY.SPR" WIDTH=119 HEIGHT=107>
```

In order to create Sizzler animations, known as "sprites," you need Totally Hip's WebPainter application, available for both Windows and Macintosh. Seen in Figure 11-27, this program lets you create animations and then save them as Sizzler sprites, multiple PICTs, or GIF 89a files. The Sizzler Export dialog box lets you specify a URL that will be loaded when the user clicks on the sprite. It also creates an <EMBED SRC> tag with the correct HEIGHT and WIDTH attributes, so you don't have to guess at them later. You can paste this to the clipboard or save it as a text file.

For Windows users, Totally Hip also offers the Sizzler Editor. Downloadable from the company's Web site, this is a bare-bones application with a user interface reminiscent of the Windows 95 Registry Editor. It actually does a good job of letting you create Sprite files by importing from Windows .DIB (Device Independent Bitmap) files and .AVI video clips. Once again, as you see in Figure 11-28, you can specifiy a URL to be included in the sprite—users will be taken to this URL when they click on the animation.

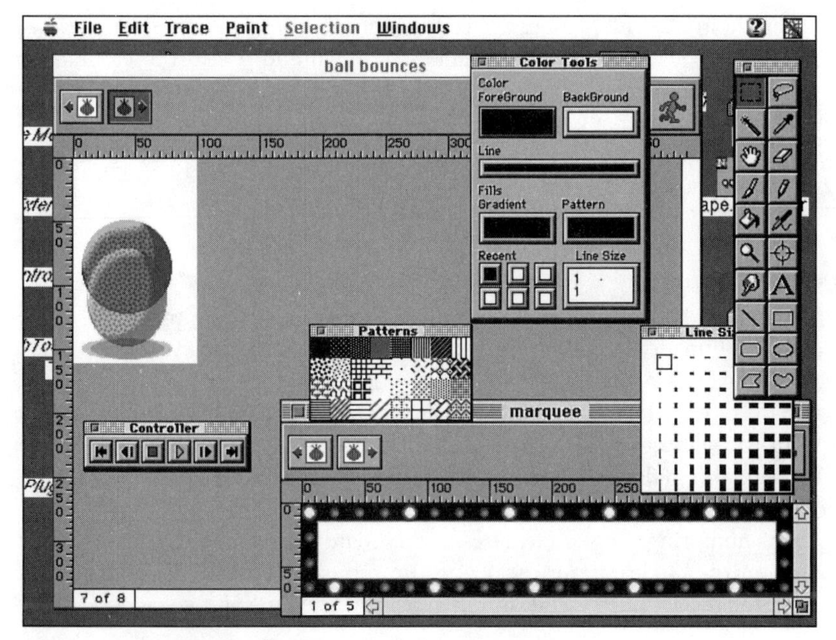

Figure 11–27 Totally Hip's WebPainter can create Sizzler animations

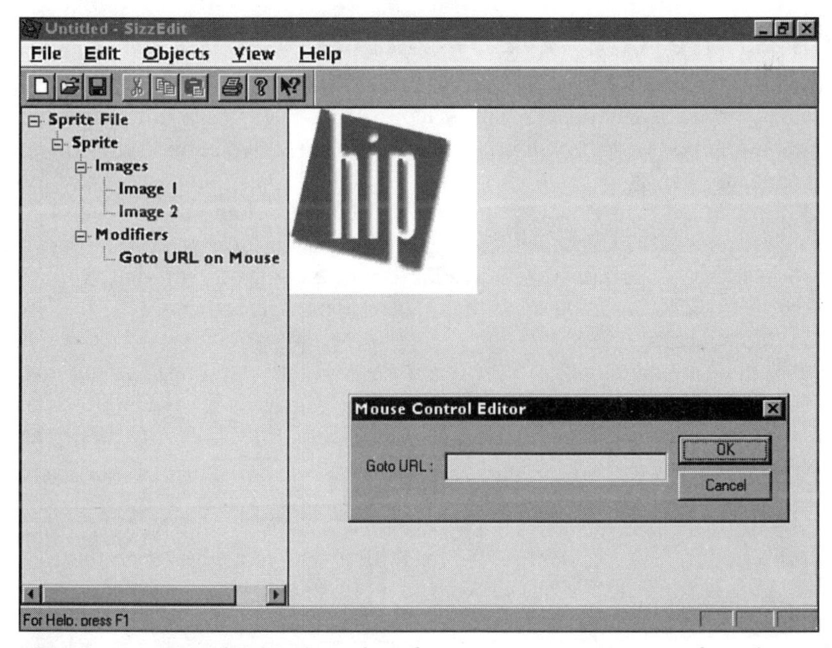

Figure 11–28 The Sizzler Editor features a spare user interface, but can create "sprites" with ease

When you import an .AVI file, you can specify a starting frame and an ending frame. If you want to use a video, it's best to keep frame size down and use just a few frames. Sizzler loads all the frames of any animation into random access memory and could have difficulties with anything other than simple files. The ability to import video files is useful, however—you could create simple animations just by using the screen capture utility that comes with Video for Windows.

WEBANIMATOR

WebAnimator, from DeltaPoint of Monterey, California, is yet another animation plug-in, requiring yet another animation authoring program. What makes it worth your consideration is some interesting technology.

The program keeps down file size by using vector graphics. Nonetheless, other multimedia types—clip art, photographs, movies, and sound—may be imported from other applications. You can also make WebAnimator animations interactive by defining buttons that jump to other parts of an animation or to other URLs.

WebAnimator's authoring program features a storyboard interface that lets you create animations by pointing, clicking, and dragging the mouse. You can maintain direct control over a presentation's timing and speed, synchronizing specific voice and music when desired.

Currently, WebAnimator is Macintosh-only. However, Windows versions of the plug-in, and perhaps eventually the authoring program, are planned.

Lesson 1: Installing the WebAnimator Plug-In

To install the WebAnimator plug-in, go to the DeltaPoint Web site at *http://www.deltapoint.com* (or see Appendix A). The Macintosh installer is a Stuffit Expander archive, WebAnimator.hqx. Netscape will probably expand this for you after it downloads the file; if not, you can open it yourself with Stuffit Expander. Once done, move the file WebAnimator Plug-in to the Plug-ins folder inside your Netscape folder.

WebAnimator requires QuickTime, which is probably already present on your Mac. If you're not sure or want to update the QuickTime you have, you can visit Apple's QuickTime Web site at *http://quicktime.apple.com.* (See "Laying the Software Foundation" in Chapter 10 for more details.)

After all this is done, exit and restart Netscape, if it is currently running. You can then open About Plug-ins from the Apple menu or Help menu to confirm that the WebAnimator plug-in has been loaded. As the list shows, this plug-in handles the following MIME type/subtype and corresponding suffix:

```
plugin/wanimate        wan
```

At the risk of sounding like a broken record (to readers who remember such things!), before you place .WAN files on a Web server, you need to ask your Internet Service Provider or network adminstrator to install this MIME type so that WebAnimator creations will be served properly to client machines. Obviously, there's no such constraint if you're merely testing them on your local hard drive.

In order to see WebAnimator in action, you can load one of the samples found at *http://secure.deltapoint.com/animate*. "Billy's Home Page," shown in Figure 11-29, uses rapid-fire sound and animation and boasts a variety of clickable links.

Lesson 2: Embedding WebAnimator Files in Your Web Pages

You don't need to learn any EMBED attributes to work with WebAnimator. For example, this is the line of code that embedded "Billy's Home Page":

```
<EMBED SRC="newbilly.wan" WIDTH=320 HEIGHT=240
PLUGINSPAGE="http://www.deltapoint.com/animate/index.htm">
```

As usual, PLUGINSPAGE is the optional attribute that takes users to the DeltaPoint site if they don't already have the WebAnimator plug-in.

In order to create and customize .WAN files, you need the WebAnimator authoring program, initially available for Macintosh only. With this program, you can import QuickTime files or create your own animations. WebAnimator comes with predesigned templates for small business, home, or corporate Web sites. These include templates for animated titles, "favorite links" menus, and animated "Jump Bars" to ferry users between the different sections of your site.

Figure 11-30 shows WebAnimator in operation. As you can see, the program provides you with a number of different ways to see your work. These include the storyboard view shown, plus animation, draw, and project windows.

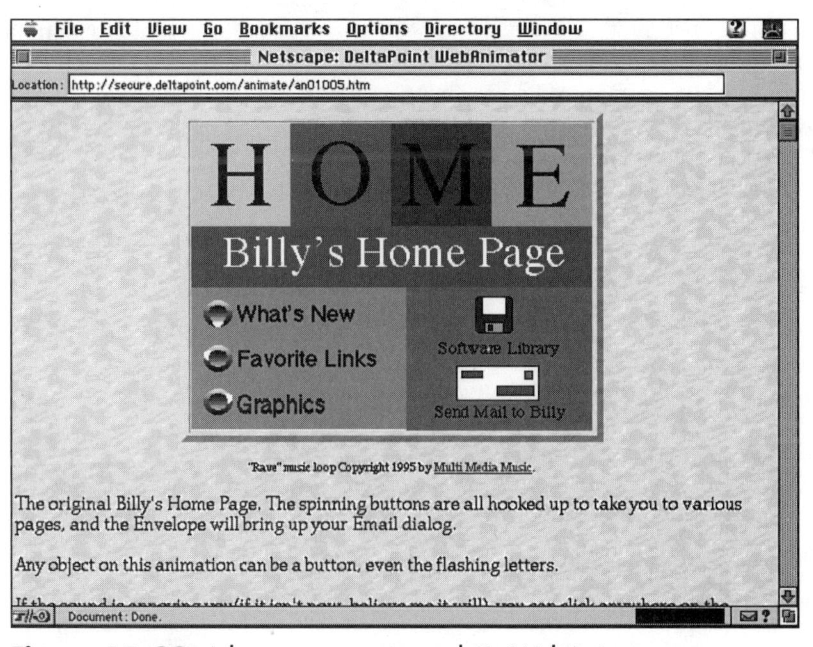

Figure 11–29 A home page animated via WebAnimator

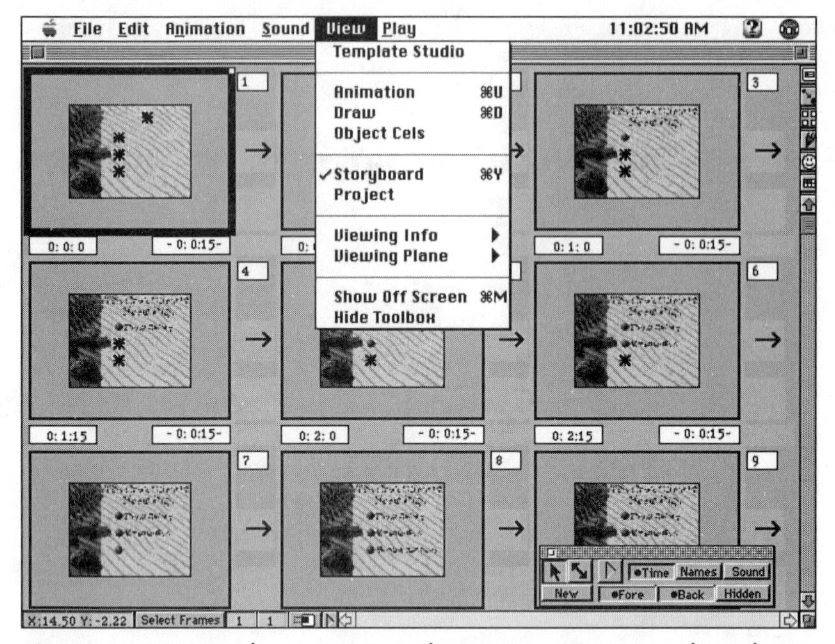

Figure 11-30 WebAnimator's Authoring program in storyboard view

WHAT NOW?

In this chapter, you learned how to use plug-ins with today's most popular presentation and courseware authoring tools. You also discovered animation plug-ins, which can achieve similar results but are more suited to those on a tight budget—some don't even require purchase of new software in order to create content.

The next chapter covers the exotic domain of VRML (Virtual Reality Modeling Language). Then, Chapter 13 returns to the workaday world of two-dimensional graphics.

12

VRML PLUG-INS

12

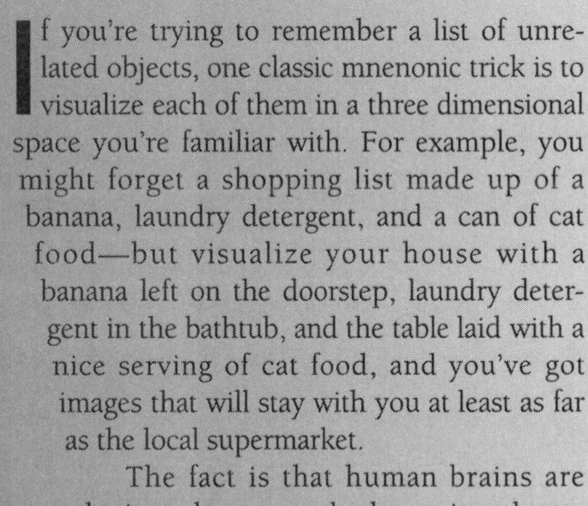

If you're trying to remember a list of unrelated objects, one classic mnenonic trick is to visualize each of them in a three dimensional space you're familiar with. For example, you might forget a shopping list made up of a banana, laundry detergent, and a can of cat food—but visualize your house with a banana left on the doorstep, laundry detergent in the bathtub, and the table laid with a nice serving of cat food, and you've got images that will stay with you at least as far as the local supermarket.

The fact is that human brains are designed to work best in three-dimensional space. Anything that's in 3D will be more engaging, more memorable, and easier to work with than something in two dimensions. The word "flat" doesn't conjure up images of staleness and boredom for nothing.

For many types of projects, then, the idea of 3D Web browsing makes a lot of sense. It took time to come on the scene because, until recently, personal computers just didn't have enough power.

VRML, pronounced "vermil," is slowly becoming a core Web technology as important as HTML itself. Short for "Virtual Reality Modeling Language," it uses simple ASCII files to describe 3D environments the user can navigate in. Because these environments are described mathematically, files can be much smaller than equivalent GIF or JPEG images.

The VRML file format is actually a subset of Open Inventor, a C++ library created at Silicon Graphics to describe three-dimensional objects and their environment. Laudably, Silicon Graphics released both the file format and examples of how to interpret files into the public domain. Mark Pesce and Tony Parisi, considered by many to be the fathers of VRML, created the first VRML Web browser in February 1994.

Subsequently, the VRML 1.0 specification was standardized, enabling 3D worlds that were created on one platform to be browsed by others. VRML browsers and helper applications came to Macs and PCs for the first time. And VRML plug-ins let users navigate 3D worlds without even having to leave Netscape.

One big event of 1996 has been VRML 2.0, which is now being called the Moving Worlds standard. Moving Worlds offers new features such as sound, including both ambient (constant) background sound and "spatialized" audio that changes as the user moves through an environment. Support for more realistic backgrounds and texture mapping has been added, as have "proximity sensors" that let events occur automatically when the user moves to certain parts of the environment.

The other big event of the year has been Netscape's incorporation of Live3D, a leading VRML plug-in, right into the browser. Live3D comes with every copy of Netscape 3.0, making it ready to browse 3D worlds right out of the box.

If Live3D is built into Netscape, why would you want to use one of the *other* VRML plug-ins features in this chapter? That's a reasonable question: The answer is that before the release of Moving Worlds, the VRML language wasn't quite rich enough to do everything people with state-of-the-art VRML sites wanted it to.

The authors of each different VRML plug-in, helper application, or browser therefore came up with their own tweaks. As a result, each VRML Web site wound up being optimized for a different plug-in. Sometimes, this is not a problem. Other times, however, it can mean that users of different VRML plug-ins have very different experiences on the same site. For example, VRML 1.0 did not successfully standardize a client's handling of avatars (virtual selves), the images that are used in multiuser worlds to represent users to one another. Some clients, therefore, gave avatars a standard size and speed, while others related avatars to the overall size of the virtual world.

Moving Worlds may eventually take care of the problem. Today, you still need to know which plug-in the authors of the site you want to visit had in mind—and stick with that plug-in in order to get the best results. One VRML plug-in will often give strange results with a world designed for viewing by another—if it loads it at all. Because it will take time for today's installed base of VRML sites to be recoded, this may continue to be true for a while.

Lesson 1: Getting to Know VRML

VRML files are ASCII text with the extension .WRL (short for "world") that describe the geometry of three-dimensional shapes (or polygons) you want to create. Optionally they can be accompanied by texture map files—like .GIFs encoded into an HTML page—that describe the color, shading, or image that will appear in a certain area.

Geometry is defined by XYZ coordinates and by basic shapes built into VRML. For example: cube, cone, cylinder, sphere, and the IndexedFaceSet. A cube can be comprised of just twelve polygons, since each side is made of two triangles. A sphere, however, can require more than 200 triangular polygons.

The more complex a shape, the more polygons—and hence more computing power—are required. And as more shapes are added to a given scene, the more the polygon count for that world increases. Each time a user's viewpoint changes, the plug-in has to redraw the scene.

Clearly, the more shapes the world contains, the longer the redraw will take. If textures are additionally mapped onto those shapes, redraw times can be significantly slowed—as are intial download times.

Other attributes of a 3D world include lighting, allowing the designer to determine how much light strikes an object or objects, and how much should be reflected. Types of light include spot lights, points of light, directional ("sun") light, diffuse light, and ambient light.

Shading determines how colors are spread across the surface of an object. A designer can use flat shading—where each part of the object has the same color—or Gouraud shading, where a calculation about reflected color is made at each vertex and then smoothly interpolated between them.

VRML files are divided into nodes, or statements that describe the properties of each object in a scene. A node called the WWWAnchor node is the VRML equivalent of the HTML <A HREF> tag, enabling users to be taken to an external Web page when they click on an object. VRML also has a node called the WWWInline node, which allows other .WRL files to be referenced so they can help create a scene.

VRML's Level of Detail (LOD) node determines how far away objects will be visible, within defined ranges of coordinates. This permits making scenes extremely realistic, with many different 3D objects in view, or creating scenes where objects are not visible until "you walk up to them." Thus, you can trade off detail to get better performance on 486 or older Mac computers.

Finally, since VRML files can become lengthy when a scene is detailed, you can compress them to as little as 1/20th their size with the GZIP algorithm (most typically available via the Free Software Foundation's GNU zip tools). VRML plug-ins are designed to recognize GZIP compression and will automatically unzip the file in order to display a scene.

Lesson 2: Writing VRML Code

It would be beyond the scope of this book to teach you how to write VRML—especially since some plug-ins are still using nonstandard extensions, so your code might have to vary. For more information about every aspect of VRML, you should take a look at a previous book in this series. *Web Publisher's Construction Kit with VRML/Live 3D*, by David Fox and Philip Shaddock, was published in 1996 by Waite Group Press (ISBN 1-57169-068-9). It includes VRML editors, modelers, and more than 100 ready-to-use 3D objects.

However, it is worth looking at an extremely simple VRML file here so you have a better idea of what is going on. The beginning of a VRML document is defined by the tag "#VRML V1.0 ascii." (Updated version numbers, such as V2.0, will appear when relevant.)

In Listing 12-1, you see a simple VRML file, annotated so you have a better idea what it's doing. The listing begins by describing a directional light source. It then defines texture to be used for an object: The DiffuseColor is the light color to be reflected off it, specified via R, G, and B percentages in decimals (in other words, they are percentages, with anything less than 100% coming after a decimal point). Here, we use 90% red, 90% green, and 90% blue. Next, a cylinder with a radius of five units and height of ten units is defined.

Next, we define a WWWAnchor node that will call another URL when our next object, a red cube, is clicked on. The cube, moved away from the cylinder by the units specified in the "translation" statement, has width, height, and depth of five units.

Incidentally the units used in a VRML document are not pixels. They are nominally meters, and set relative sizes and distances that are only relevant within the VRML world.

Listing 12–1 A sample VRML file (with explanations at right)

```
#VRML V1.0 ascii                                     Lets your browser (or VRML viewer) know
                                                     this is a VRML file
Separator {
        DirectionLight {                                 Describes a directional light
                                                         source
              direction 0 1 0
        }
        Material {                                       Specifies a color to be used on the
                                                         first object
             diffuseColor .9 .9 .9
        }
        Cylinder {                                       Defines a cylinder, specifying its
                                                         radius and height
             parts ALL
             radius 5
             height 10
        }
       Transform {
              translation 8 0                             Specifies units by which to move
                                                          the object that follows
                                                          away from the cylinder that
                                                          preceded it
       }
       Material {
                diffuseColor .9 .3 .6                     Specifies a color to be used on
                                                          the second object
       }
       DEF Cube WWWAnchor {                               Names the node using the DEF
                                                          command
         name "http://www.urserver.com/another.htm"       Specifies a URL
        description "Click me"                            Specifies text that will label the
                                                          object
```

```
            Cube {                                    Gives dimensions for the cube
                   width 5
                   height 5
                   depth 5
      }
      }
}
```

Figure 12-1 shows the result when this code is passed to Live3D from within a Web page using the simple HTML tag <EMBED SRC="test.wrl" HEIGHT=200 WIDTH=200>. When you change HEIGHT and WIDTH attributes, you change the size of the VRML world within your Web page, all the elements within that world being scaled to match. Figure 12-2 makes the point by changing WIDTH and HEIGHT to 500.

Obviously, VRML is an accessible language. It's easy to start learning it if you really want to. On the other hand, it's enough like "real programming" that you may well want to leave the work to a VRML generator—even if you're one of the people who still do their own HTML painstakingly by hand. Some things to know about VRML are that, unlike HTML, it's case-sensitive. It's also much less tolerant of a misplaced bracket, an unnecessary equal sign, and so on.

As usual, you need to contact the people who administer your Web server to make sure a MIME type/subtype has been set up and associated with the .WRL extension. This is a one-time job no matter what VRML plug-in you use, since all use the same MIME type. (Therefore, only one VRML plug-in can function during a given Netscape session.)

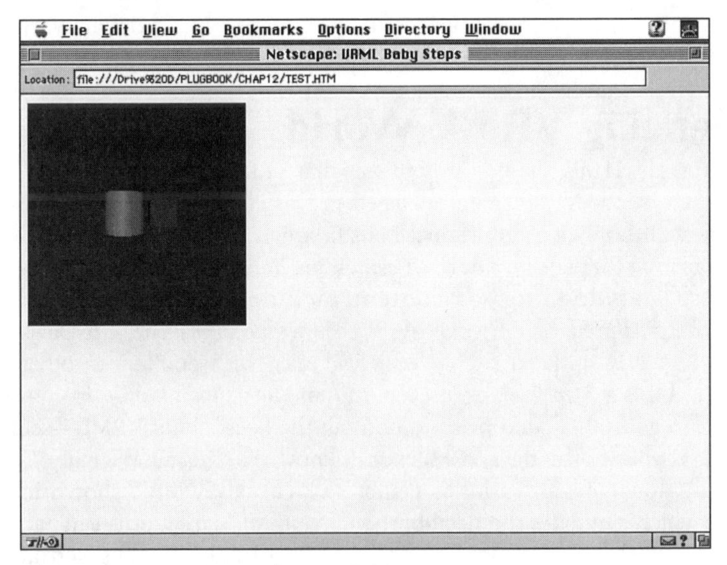

Figure 12-1 A very basic VRML test page

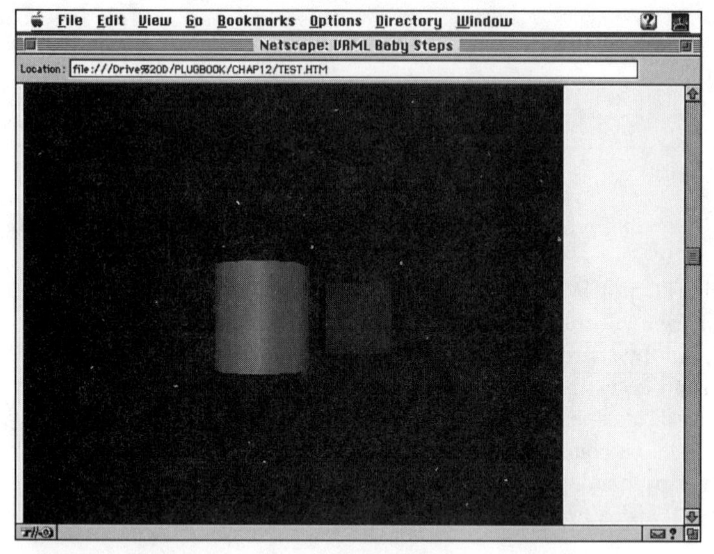

Figure 12-2 The same page with WIDTH and HEIGHT increased

If you are putting up files in compressed form, it is also necessary to add a gzip content encoding line to server configuration files as well. This tells the browser to uncompress .GZ files, turning them into .WRL files in the process. Exact details vary according to your server type.

Lesson 3: Experiencing VRML Worlds

Even more, perhaps, than with HTML, the best way to see what VRML can do is to...well, see it. When you install one of the VRML plug-ins listed in this chapter, you'll find the authors provide links that will show off their product in its best light.

You can find many, many other sites by doing a search via Yahoo! or another search engine. Some places to start looking for content include Netscape's site at *http://home.netscape.com/comprod/products/navigator/live3d/cool_worlds.html.* The Ziff-Davis magazine people have a regularly updated site called VRMLinks, with pointers to other outstanding sites. You'll find this at *http://www.zdnet.com/zdi/vrml/filters/links.html.*

The Ziff-Davis site is, in general, a good place to find out the latest about VRML—see Figure 12-3. In Figure 12-4, you see the site's VRML world, known as "Terminal Reality."

One of the more ambitious virtual worlds is Planet 9's "Virtual SOMA", shown in Figure 12-5. This world, which simulates the neighborhood south of Market Street in San Francisco (where much VRML development has taken place) may be accessed at *http://www.hyperion.com/planet9/worlds/vrsoma.wrl.*

A good collection of models—cars, animals, and so on—is at *http://www.ocnus.com/models/models.html.* Other interesting and elaborate worlds can be found at the Sony CyberPassage site at *http://vs.sony.co.jp/VS-E/Gallery/gallery.html.*

Figure 12–3 This Ziff-Davis site provides up-to-date VRML news

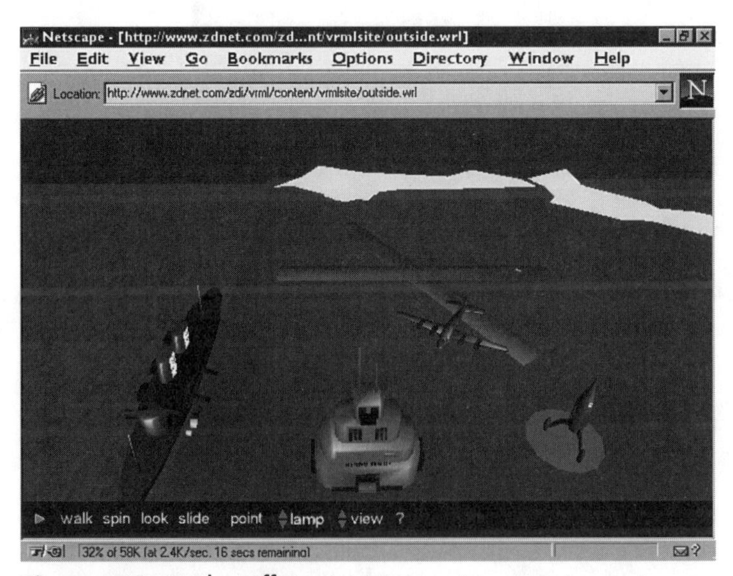

Figure 12–4 The Ziff-Davis VRML environment is an airport nicknamed "Terminal Reality"

All the .WRL files on these pages are GZIP compressed, so they will test the ability of your plug-in to handle this format.

Figure 12-5 Visit San Francisco at the Virtual SOMA site

Lesson 4: Picking a VRML Authoring Tool

If you've made the understandable decision not to do all your VRML by hand, you have two ways to go. You can start the process of creating a virtual world by using a 3D modeling program such as AutoCAD, 3D Studio, or TrueSpace—and then use a converter to change .DXF files to the .WRL format. Or, you can start from scratch with a VRML authoring tool.

Either way, you'll find that VRML has attacted an amazing variety of tools for such a young software category. (A running joke, fairly or unfairly, says that there are more software tools and plug-ins for VRML than there are sites.) You'll find a list of file format converters at *http://www.sdsc.edu/SDSC/Partners/vrml/software/geom_trans.html* (Figure 12-6). A list of authoring tools appears at *http://www.sdsc.edu/SDSC/Partners/vrml/software/modelers.html,* as seen in Figure 12-7.

Different authoring tools suit different types of users. For example, Caligari's Fountain—which is included on the CD-ROM that comes with the *Web Publisher's Construction Kit with VRML/Live3D*—has a reputation as a comprehensive, full-featured editor with a steep learning curve. WalkThrough Pro from Virtus *(http://www.virtus.com)* is somewhat less elaborate, but still versatile. And Virtual Home Space Builder from ParaGraph *(http://www.paragraph.com)* has been called relatively limited, but is also the easiest of these three programs to get started with. To get the latest on these and other modelers, start out by checking the VRML Repository lists mentioned above.

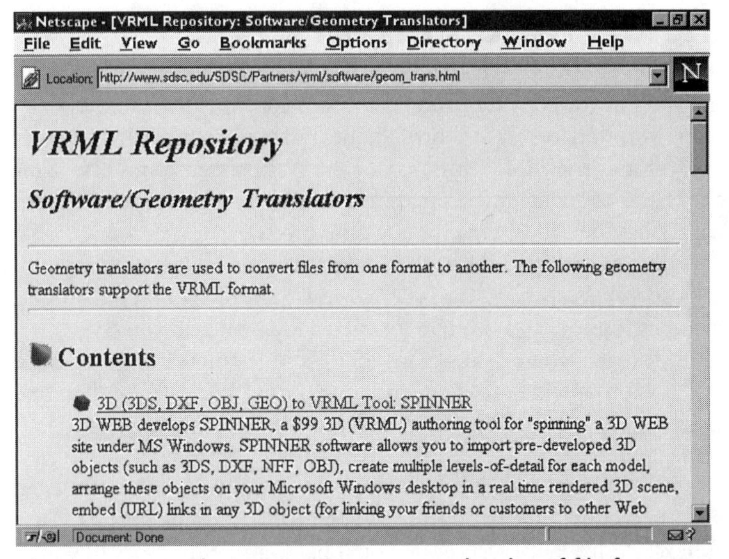

Figure 12–6 The VRML Repository and its list of file format converters

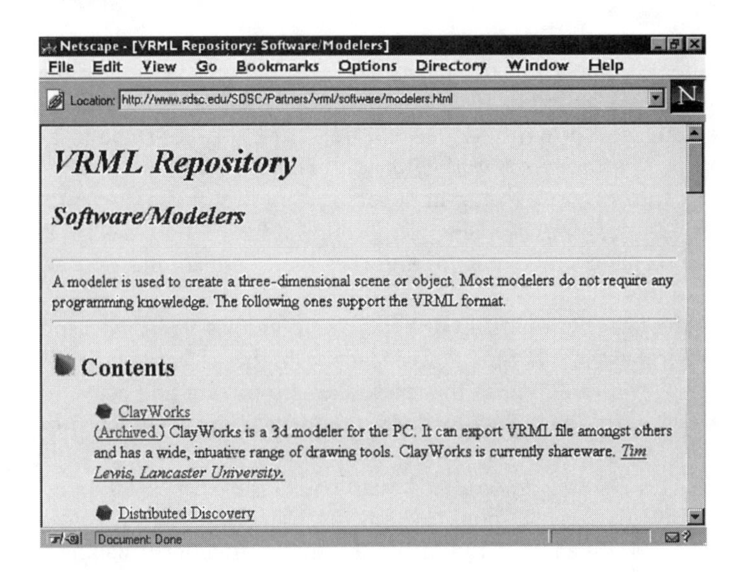

Figure 12–7 The VRML Repository's list of authoring tools

Lesson 5: Installing a VRML Plug-In

Installing a plug-in for VRML is simpler than with most other plug-ins. Though the process of downloading a plug-in (or copying it from your CD-ROM) is the same as ever, there are a couple of things you don't need to worry about. First, since the MIME type is the same—x-world/x-vrml—for every VRML plug-in, and the .WRL extension is also standardized, there may be no need to make any changes at the Web server. (Unless, that is, its administrators never installed the MIME type for any other user.)

Second, since VRML plug-ins all use the same .WRL files, or at least attempt to, there's no need to hunt out fresh Web pages in order to test each of them. Nor do you necessarily need to learn a new authoring technique for each VRML plug-in you try.

Therefore, this chapter describes the process of installing and testing VRML plug-ins a little more briefly than previous chapters have. Remember, you can't install more than one of these VRML plug-ins into your copy of Netscape and have them both work. Instead, you need to make a choice.

However, even if you're deciding to stick with Live3D because that's what Netscape comes with, it's worth familiarizing yourself with how other VRML plug-ins operate. That way, if you design a VRML world for your Web page, you'll be aware of the ways in which users' experiences might differ.

Live3D

Live3D comes with Netscape 3.0 unless you downloaded the "minimum" version of the browser, which comes without any plug-ins. If you didn't get Live3D but want it now, you can obtain it as a separate download. Go to Netscape's Live3D page at *http://home.netscape.com/comprod/mirror/navcomponents_download.html.*

There, you can download the Live3D plug-in separately in any of the currently supported versions. Initially, Live3D was available for Windows 3.x, Windows 95/NT, and Power Macintosh. A version for older 68K Macintoshes was planned and may be available by the time you read this.

The Live3D plug-in is the file NPL3D32.DLL if you have Windows 95 or NT, and NPL3D16.DLL if you have Windows 3.x. For the Power Macintosh, the relevant plug-in is the file clearly labeled Live3D. You can confirm that these files are present and active in your copy of Netscape by selecting About Plug-ins from the Help menu (Windows) or Apple menu (Macintosh).

If you want to deactivate Live3D later in order to install one of the *other* VRML plug-ins in its place, simply remove the Live3D plug-in from the Netscape Plug-ins folder before you start the browser. You'll then need to follow the usual routine for installing a new plug-in into Netscape: Put that plug-in *into* the Netscape Plug-ins folder, start the browser, and make sure to clear its memory and disk caches to help purge any old associations.

You should know—well, you're going to find it out soon enough—that VRML plug-ins can require more memory when they're in operation than just about any other type. They're also relatively hungry for processor speed: Not that you can't run them on a 486 computer if you want to, but you'll find progress through virtual worlds to be slower and jerkier than you'd like it to be.

Anyhow, to test Live3D, just fire up your copy of Netscape and go to *http://home.netscape.com/comprod/products/navigator/live3d/index.html.* If everything is working properly, you'll see a screen like that in Figure 12-8.

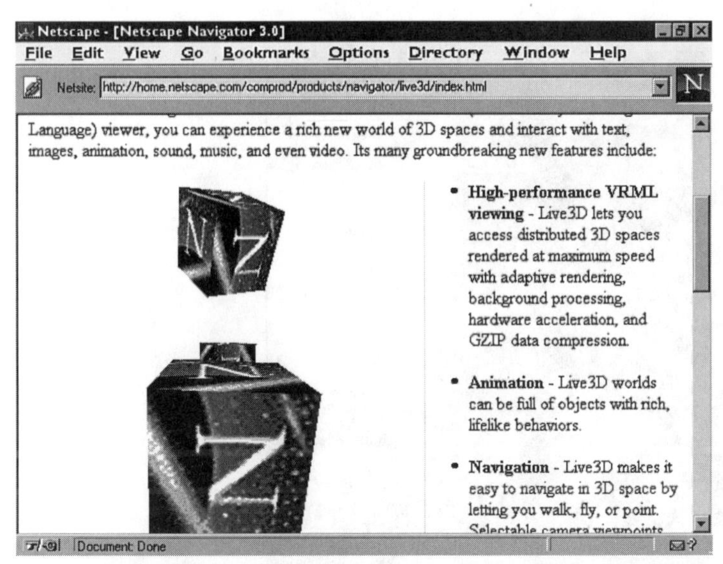

Figure 12-8 This page at the Netscape site is a good starting point for testing Live3D

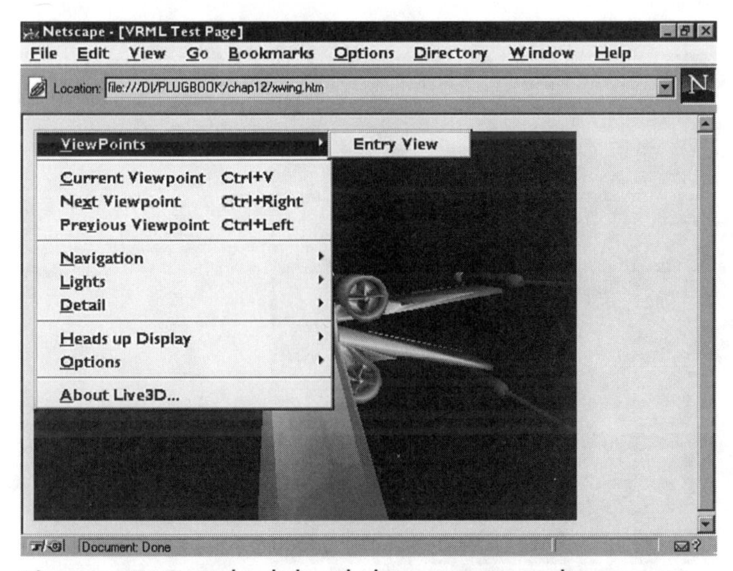

Figure 12-9 Right-click with the mouse to get this menu in Live3D for Windows

Live3D features a pop-up menu you can access by right-clicking on a scene (if you have Windows) or by clicking on the scene and holding the mouse button for a second (if you have a Macintosh). Figure 12-9 shows the Windows version of the menu, while Figure 12-10 shows the Macintosh version.

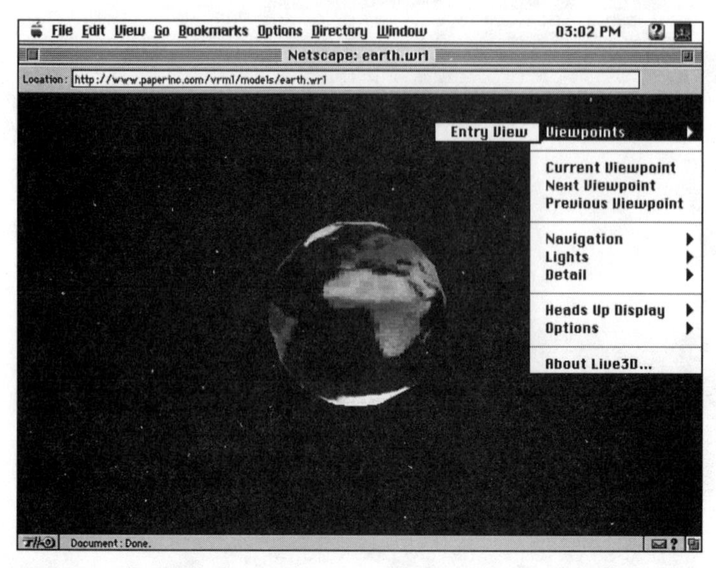

Figure 12-10 On a Mac, you get the menu by holding down the mouse button for a second

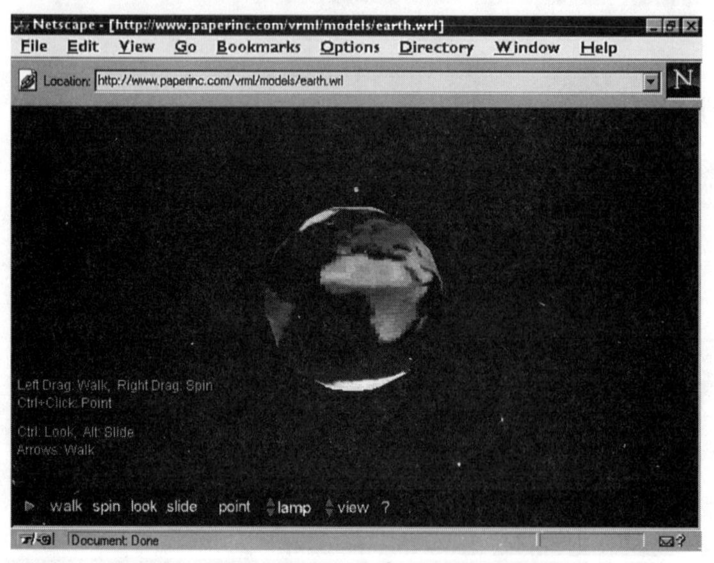

Figure 12-11 You can turn on this Navigation bar at the bottom of the screen as well as the Navigation Help legend

There are three navigation modes in Live3D: walking, flying, and pointing. To switch between modes, use the Navigation selection from the pop-up menu. Or use the "Navigation bar" that appears at the bottom of a scene. Figure 12-11 shows this along with the Navigation Help legend you can turn on using the Heads up Display part of the menu.

You can use either the keyboard or mouse to navigate in each mode. Live3D navigation will probably be the most familiar to those who have misspent hours playing DOOM or Descent! You use the "DOOM" model when walking or pointing, and the "Descent" model when flying. Tables 12-1 through 12-3 summarize the commands Live3D uses for each of its modes.

The right mouse button is, of course, unavailable on a Macintosh, making navigation and switching modes a little more difficult. Table 12-4 summarizes some of the differences in Mac commands.

Table 12–1 Walking mode commands for Live3D

Up/Down Arrows	Move forward/backward
Left/Right Arrows	Turn left/right
A or Z	Tilt head up/down
J	Jump
Mouse Left Drag	Move forward/backward or turn left/right
Mouse Right Drag	Orbit about the entire scene
Mouse+CTRL+Left Click	Automatically walk to the object you CTRL+clicked on
Mouse Right Click	Pop up the menu
SHIFT (with mouse or keys)	Move faster
ALT (with mouse or keys)	Pan left/right or up/down
SPACE	Open doors, manipulate objects

Table 12–2 Flying mode commands for Live3D

Up/Down Arrows	Tilt up/down
Left/Right Arrows	Turn left/right
A or Z	Thrust forward/backward
Q or E	Revolve counter-clockwise/clockwise
Mouse Left Drag	Tilt up/down or turn left/right
Mouse Right Drag	Orbit about the entire scene
Mouse+CTRL+Left Click	Automatically fly to the object you CTRL+clicked on
Mouse Right Click	Pop up the menu
SHIFT (with mouse or keys)	Move faster
ALT (with mouse or keys)	Pan left/right or up/down
SPACE	Open doors, manipulate objects

Table 12–3 Pointing mode commands for Live3D

Keyboard commands	Same as for walking mode
Mouse Left Click	Animates you closer to the point you clicked on
Mouse Left Drag	Move forward/backward or turn left/right
Mouse Right Drag	Orbit about the point currently at the center of the screen
Mouse Right Click	Pop up the menu

Table 12–4 Some Macintosh commands for Live3D

Mouse drag	Walk forward/backward or turn left/right
Up/Down arrows	Walk forward/backward
Left/Right arrows	Turn left/right
CTRL+click	Point: Animate viewpoint toward the object
CTRL+drag	Pan left/right or up/down
COMMAND+drag	Spin (orbit about the entire scene)—to automate the spin, release the mouse button before the command key
Mouse click	Stop spinning
A or Z	Tilt head down/up
SHIFT (with mouse or keys)	Move faster

There are some options you can select to try to improve Live3D performance. They are found on the pop-up menu, and include

- Optimize Window Size: The larger the window, the slower the performance. Turning this option on keeps the VRML viewing area within a reasonable width and height for optimum performance.
- Always Generate Back Faces: Many models assume that the software they are viewed with will display both sides of a polygon. While this is the case on high-end graphics workstations, PC-based 3D rendering engines do not draw the back face of a polygon in order to optimize performance. As a result, Live3D has to assume that every polygon should have a back face, even though that face may not be visible. This slows performance by roughly 50%.
- Heads up Display: The heads up display slows rendering performance. You may wish to leave it off on slower machines.

Topper

Topper, from the Kinetix division of AutoCAD, is a plug-in that not only works with embedded .WRL files, but also supports 3D Studio (.3DS) and AutoCAD (.DXF files directly). In addition, it supports what the company calls VRBL (Virtual Reality Behavior Language).

VRBL is similar to Moving Worlds in that it supports line-of-sight, proximity, and "pick" triggers. This means users can trigger animations and other behaviors based on their location and activity in a 3D world.

To install Topper, you need to have Windows 95 or Windows NT. You'll be replacing Live3D, so you need to locate NPL3D32.DLL. Move it from the Plug-ins folder within your Netscape folder to another folder on your hard drive. (That way, you can always copy it back later if you need to run Live3D again.)

Clear Netscape's memory and disk caches, and then go to the Kinetix Web site at *http://www.ktx.com/products/hyperwire.* (Or check Appendix A for details of the included CD-ROM.) Download or copy the file TOPPER.EXE to a temporary folder on your hard drive. Then run it to extract the installer SETUP.EXE. Exit Netscape and double-click on SETUP.

The installer locates your Netscape subdirectory and asks you to confirm this is the browser you want to use with Topper. It also asks you to specify a folder where Topper files will be installed, including an HTML-based User's Guide. Topper requires that the Microsoft Reality Lab 3D rendering engine be installed on your system, and will install this if it does not find it. (If you have a 80386 or 486SX processor without a math coprocessor, you may have problems using this rendering engine.)

Once the installation procedure is completed, you can restart Netscape. Use the About Plug-ins command from the Help menu to confirm that Topper has been installed. As you'll see, the Topper plug-in is called NPOKNETX.DLL, designed to handle the following MIME types and subtypes:

MIME Type/Subtype	Suffix
x-world/x-vrml	**wrl**
x-world/x-dxf	**dxf**
x-world/x-3ds	**3ds**

You can obtain some outstanding examples of Topper in action by switching to the Kinetix Topper menu item newly placed in your Start Menu. Click on the Examples item and Netscape will show you a variety of possible samples.

Figure 12-12 shows you a walking bird created in 3D Studio, a great example of the animation and quality that can be achieved with Topper. Figure 12-13 shows a plain-vanilla .WRL file.

At the bottom of the window, you see a toolbar with a Kinetix logo at the left. To its right is a button that lets you play animations, if present in the loaded file, or stop any animations that might be currently playing. (The AUTOSTART attribute of the <EMBED> tag determines whether or not a 3D Studio file will "come out swinging.")

To its right on the toolbar you see more icons. The first is for Dolly and Pan mode. Dolly moves the viewpoint forward and backward in the scene, along the line of sight. Pan turns the viewpoint left and right, without changing the viewpoint's position. This is the default navigation mode.

Figure 12-12 This bird began life in 3D Studio

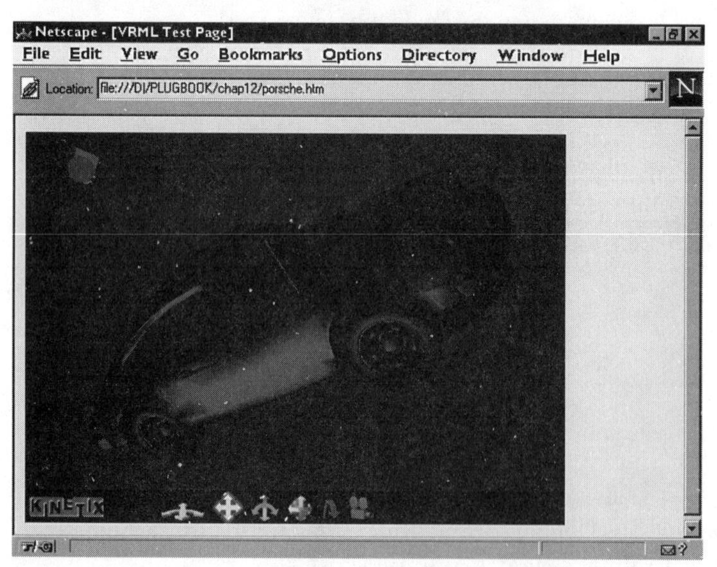

Figure 12-13 Even a "plain" .WRL file sports the Topper toolbar

The next icon is for Truck & Pedestal Mode. This moves the viewpoint up, down, left, and right along the flat plane of the screen. Viewpoint movement continues in the given direction until you release the mouse button. You can access this mode either by clicking on the icon or by holding down CTRL as you move the mouse.

After that comes Pitch & Roll Mode. Pitch circles the viewpoint back to front about the X-axis. Roll circles the viewpoint from left to right about the Z-axis. Viewpoint movement continues in a 360-degree course until you release the mouse button. You can access this mode either by clicking on the icon or by holding down SHIFT as you move the mouse.

Orbit Mode, represented by the next icon, circles the viewpoint about the "pivot point" of the 3D scene. The pivot point is determined by a projection from the scene's center point onto the current line of sight.

With left and right mouse movement, the orbiting continues until you release the mouse button. You can access this mode by holding down ALT as you move the mouse.

Like Live3D, Topper also has a pop-up menu you can access by clicking the right mouse button. You can see part of this menu in Figure 12-14. It can let you switch between "cameras" and viewpoints that may be encoded into a file, toggle "lights" on and off, and more.

Topper lets you specify rendering quality in which to view objects in the 3D scene. The higher the rendering quality, the slower the drawing time. From slowest to fastest, the choices are Smooth, Smooth Performance, Flat, Flat Performance, and Wireframe.

V•Realm

V•Realm is a VRML plug-in specially designed for those who want to explore virtual worlds. As such, it's primarily designed to work full-screen.

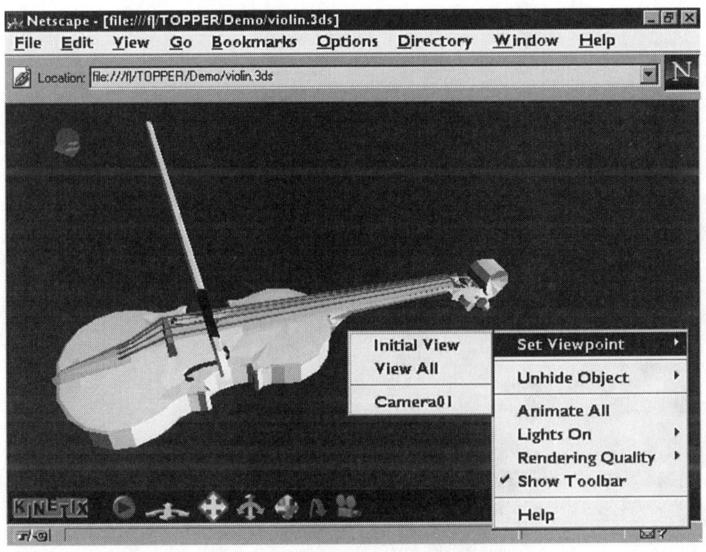

Figure 12–14 Topper's pop-up control menu

This plug-in, for Windows 95 and NT only, features a striking "navigation pad" and sliders that let the user adjust his or her position within the virtual world. It allows you to turn "gravity" on and off and adjust what happens when you collide with an object. You can also save your favorite viewpoints within a virtual world and reuse them the next time you visit that site.

V•Realm Multi-User (which was not available in time for testing in this book) is a new version of this plug-in that uses avatars to represent multiple users. Users can chat to one another via text, or via V•Realm Multi-User's two-way link to LiveAudio.

To install V•Realm, you need to replace Live3D, Topper, or any other VRML plug-in you might have been previously using. Move the .DLL for that program from the Plug-ins folder within your Netscape folder to another folder on your hard drive. Clear Netscape's memory and disk caches, and then go to the V•Realm Web site at *http://www.ids-net.com*. (Or see Appendix A for a guide to your CD-ROM.)

Download or copy the installer file, VRPG.EXE, to a temporary folder on your hard drive. Then, just double-click on it. As usual, the installer locates your Netscape subdirectory and asks you to confirm this is the browser you want to use with V•Realm. It also asks you to specify a folder where V•Realm files will be installed.

Once the installation procedure is completed, you can restart Netscape. Use the About Plug-ins command from the Help menu to confirm that V•Realm has been installed. As you'll see, the V•Realm plug-in is called NPVREALM.DLL, designed to handle the x-world/x-vrml MIME type and .WRL extension. Now, you can open the file TEST.HTM in the V•Realm folder you just created to see a list of interesting examples. One of them, "Street Corner," is pictured in Figure 12-15.

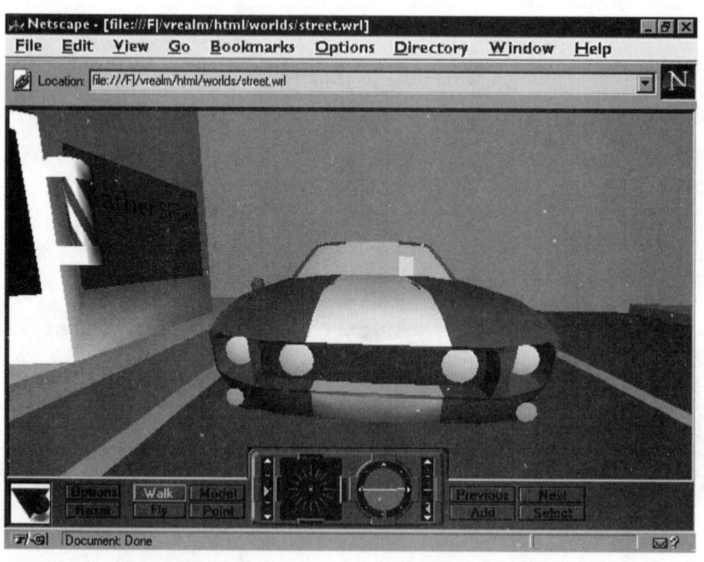

Figure 12-15 V•Realm creates this suburban landscape, complete with traffic signals that change

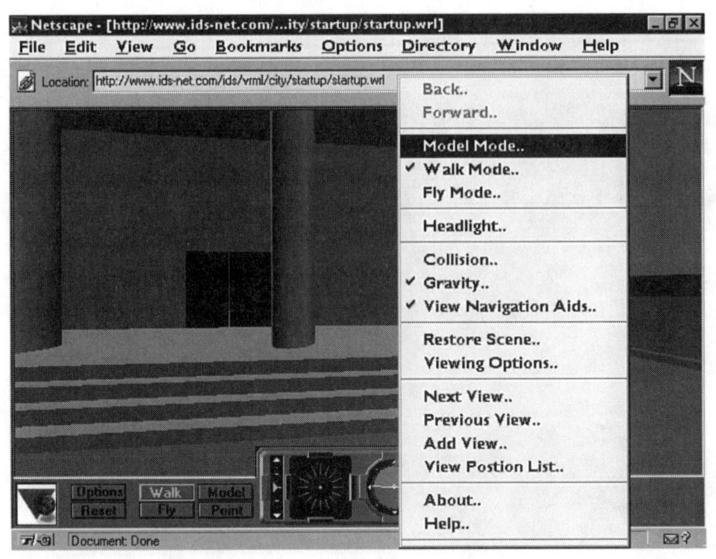

Figure 12–16 Here you can see V•Realm's pop-up menu within a "village" on the IDS-Net Web site

Like so many other plug-ins, V•Realm has a pop-up menu you can call up by right-clicking anywhere within its display area (see Figure 12-16). The Back and Forward choice at the top will move between a currently maintained URL list of views. The Model Mode choice enters a mode that allows the user to inspect objects in the scene. This mode gives users the ability to rotate and move individual objects.

The Walk choice, which can also be made by pressing a button on the control panel at the bottom of the screen, enters the mode that simulates human movement through a world. In this mode the scene is rendered from the perspective of the person walking around in the world. Also, movement in this world is affected by collision detection and gravity.

Setting the mode to Fly will give you the ability to fly around a world like an airplane. The artificial horizon pad and the directional pointer at the bottom of the screen work as they would in an airplane cockpit.

The Headlight option sets a spotlight on the object in the camera's current viewer window. This option can be used to light the entire area that the camera is currently viewing or to beam a narrow focus of light on just a single area that you wish to focus in front of the camera.

The Collision choice turns collision detection on or off in walk and fly modes. With collision detection on you will get a sound to warn you of a collision with an object in the viewing area. On the other hand, V•Realm operates faster when you have collision detection turned off.

The Viewing Options menu choice lets you select from among a wide variety of rendering options (see Figure 12-17). You can adjust the sensitivity of the gravity and collision detection, and you can have texture mapping take place when a scene is in motion or just when it is still.

Figure 12–17 V•Realm provides extensive viewing options

As for the dramatic-looking control area at the bottom of the view screen, some of its buttons duplicate functions in the pop-up menu. Others are unique. For example, the Navigational Movement Pad—the first large dial you see—lets you choose a direction to move in by clicking on that direction in the pad, or by clicking in the pad and dragging the mouse.

"Cruise-controlled" movement can be achieved by double left-clicking on the Navigation Pad. This will start hands-free movement and will cause movement in the view window to track with movement of the mouse in the Navigation Pad area. While in this mode you can move the cursor anywhere within the Navigation Pad area and the scene will track with it. To stop the constant movement, left-click in the Navigation Pad area.

The pad also has a slider bar indicator on its left side of the pad. When you pull the indicator's pointer up it will pan the camera up, when you pull it down it will pan the camera down. The center position is the level position along the horizon.

The second large dial you see, at center right, is the Heading/Artificial Horizon Pad. This displays the current movement direction. You can move the red pointer around the edge of the "compass" to change direction quickly. Also, clicking any of the points of the compass will instantly change the point of view to that heading.

At the right of this pad is a slider bar indicator which is used to increase and decrease the viewing angle in the current world. The center location on this pad translates into the normal (or 0) position. Moving the indicator up will increase the angle and moving it down will decrease the angle.

VR Scout

Chaco Communications' VR Scout is another VRML plug-in, well-respected for its speed and compatibility. Like Topper, it is (currently, at least) available for Windows 95/NT only; it also uses Microsoft's Reality Labs 3D graphics engine.

According to Chaco, VR Scout supports many Open Inventor "nodes"—supersets of VRML, remember—and therefore plays worlds that are not quite compliant with the VRML standard. It also is multi-threading, allowing you to start moving around in a world before all its parts have been loaded.

To install VR Scout, you need—as has already been mentioned for the previous plug-ins—to replace Live3D or any other VRML plug-in you might have been previously using. Move it from the Plug-ins folder within your Netscape folder to another folder on your hard drive. Clear Netscape's memory and disk caches, and then go to the Chaco Communications Web site at *http://www.chaco.com*. (Or check Appendix A for details about your CD-ROM.)

Run the installer file, NPSC.EXE, and it will unzip files to a temporary folder on your hard drive. Setup then begins automatically. After you respond to the license agreement, you need to tell the installer where it can create a VR Scout folder. (The installer says it will "install the VR Scout plug-in in this directory." This is misleading, as the plug-in will actually go in your Netscape Plug-ins folder; the VR Scout folder just holds a help file and a README.WRI document. But never mind.) The installer then asks you where your Netscape subdirectory is.

Once it has all this information, the installer puts the file NPSCOUT.DLL in your Netscape Plug-ins folder, and also installs Microsoft Reality Lab files. When the installation procedure is completed, you can restart Netscape. Use the About Plug-ins command from the Help menu to confirm that VR Scout has been installed. As you'll see, the VR Scout plug-in is, yet again, designed to handle the x-world/x-vrml MIME type and .WRL extension. Now, you can return to the Chaco Communications Web site to view sample files.

One of the links found there is the VR Coffee Gallery, at *http://www.tristero.com/coffee/vrcoffee*. Pictured in Figure 12-18, this is a VRML model of the Coffee Gallery in San Antonio, Texas, complete with texture maps that look especially impressive via VR Scout.

You see VR Scout's toolbar at the bottom of the screen. By right-clicking anywhere in the scene, you can invoke the pop-up menu shown in Figure 12-19.

To use VR Scout's walk mode, click on the scene and move the mouse in the direction you want to walk. Normally, dragging the mouse "walks" you around in the world. When CTRL is pressed, you can use the mouse to look up and down. When SHIFT is pressed, your position is shifted from where you are standing, but your orientation isn't changed. You can also drag diagonally to combine movements.

The further you move away from where you originally clicked, the faster you will move. The 3D Graphics preferences dialog box allows you to degrade the quality of the image while moving so that you move faster.

Figure 12–18 VR Scout provides good support for texture maps, such as the bricks on the wall and the "public-access Web browser" shown

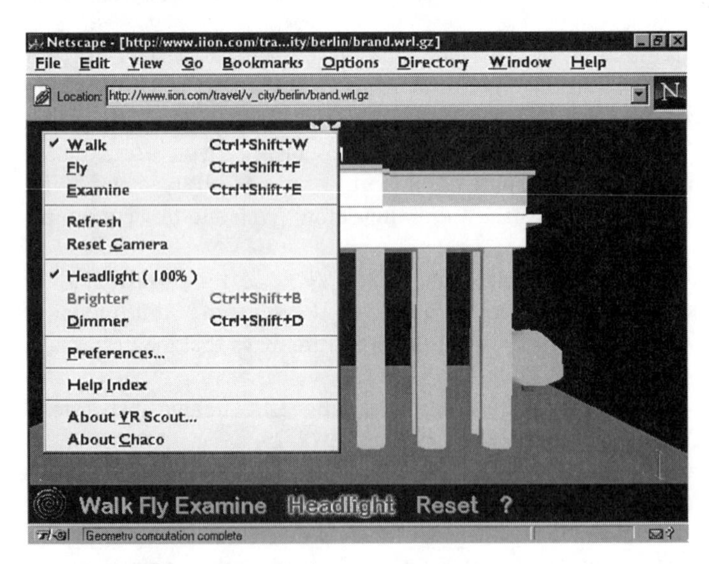

Figure 12–19 VR Scout's pop-up menu

Using VR Scout's fly mode—whose function ought to be familiar to you by now, since it's similiar to the other plug-ins'—operates similarly to walk mode. Examine mode, on the other hand, doesn't move you around a scene: It takes you outside the scene and turns it so you can examine it carefully. Probably the best way of using the examine mode is to rotate an object by grabbing it and rotating it using the mouse. Then, use the up and down arrow keys to move into or away from the object.

WIRL

To install WIRL, you need to have Windows 95 or NT. You might want to replace Live3D or any other VRML plug-in you might have been previously using. Move it from the Plug-ins folder within your Netscape folder to another folder on your hard drive. Clear Netscape's memory and disk caches, and then go to the WIRL Web site at *http://www.vream.com.* (Or see Appendix A.)

Run the installer, WIRL.EXE, and files will be copied to a temporary folder on your hard drive. The setup program then runs automatically. After you assent to a license agreement, this program locates your Netscape subdirectory and asks you to confirm this is the browser you want to use with WIRL. It also asks you to specify a folder where WIRL files will be installed.

A screen asking if you want a Typical, Compact, or Custom Installation then appears. "Typical" installs the plug-in and sample files, "Compact" installs only the plug-in, "Custom" is merely a redundant way of choosing between these two.

The installer also asks if you want to make WIRL the default VRML plug-in. If not, Netscape will use Live3D or any other VRML plug-in you wish—assuming you didn't deinstall it in the steps above—but will still read Vream worlds and VRML files that use a .VRW extension.

Once the installation procedure is completed, you need to restart your computer. This is because the installer has modified the CLASSPATH environment variable in your AUTOEXEC.BAT file so that WIRL can find Java programs (classes) it uses. You could ignore the installer's advice to restart, but some WIRL functions might not work.

Once you have restarted your PC and loaded Netscape, use the About Plug-ins command from the Help menu to confirm that WIRL has been installed. As you'll see, the WIRL plug-in is called NPWIRL.DLL, designed to handle the x-world/x-vream MIME type and .VRW extension. (The installation program copied both this DLL and another, VRCJAVAI.DLL, to the Plug-ins subdirectory within your Netscape folder.) If you told the installer you wanted WIRL to handle x-world/x-vrml, it does that as well.

To test WIRL, use Netscape's File/Open command to open COOL.HTM in the WIRL folder you installed previously. (You can also open COOL.HTM by selecting "Cool WIRL 3D Worlds" from the WIRL section newly added to the Programs section of your Windows start menu.) You'll see a list of demonstration files in the left-hand frame and a rotating, texture-mapped WIRL logo in the right-hand frame. Figure 12-20 shows the Virtual Man demo: Here, the man is in the middle of a flip started by clicking with the left mouse button.

Figure 12-21 shows an example of how a Vream virtual world can be embedded within a Web page (the tag used here is merely the familiar <EMBED SRC>, with height and width specifications). The legends with arrows telling the user what to do are .GIF files; the buttons above on the "remote controller" within the WIRL window control the helicopter's motion.

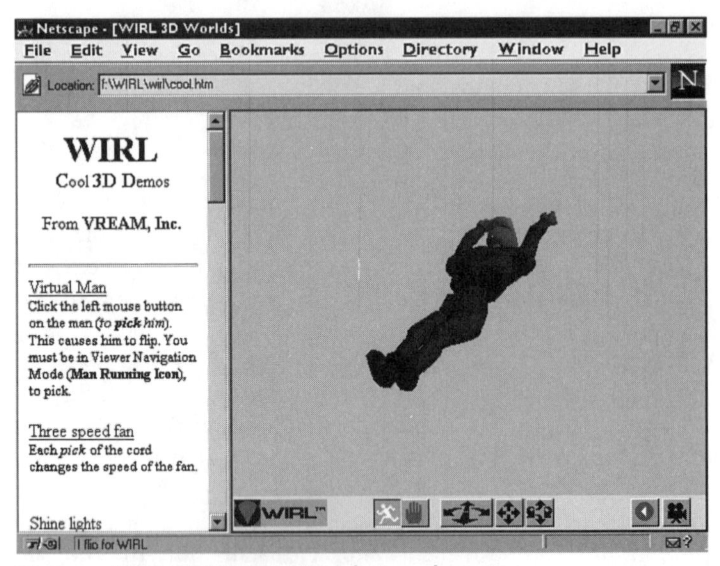

Figure 12–20 WIRL's Virtual Man demo

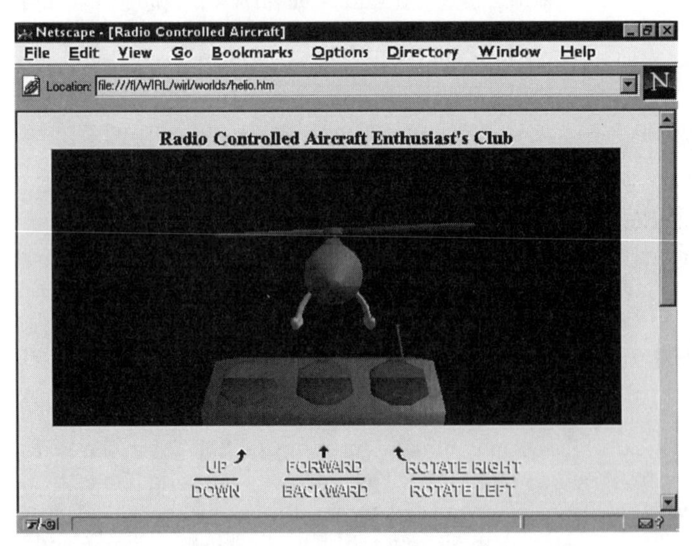

Figure 12–21 This remote-controlled helicopter is an interactive world embedded into a Web page

WIRL provides two modes in which to experience virtual worlds, Viewer Navigation mode, and Object Manipulation mode. You can select the Viewer Navigation mode by clicking the image of a person running that appears on the WIRL control panel. You can select Object Manipulation mode by clicking on the hand.

Within each mode, you can interact with the world by clicking on the arrow buttons within the WIRL Control Panel, or by clicking the mouse buttons within the virtual world. Some ways to interact with the virtual worlds are listed in Table 12-5.

Table 12-5 WIRL navigation commands

Vream WIRL Logo	Displays About WIRL Message
Moving Person Button	Viewer Navigation Mode
Hand Button	Switches to Object Manipulation Mode
First Button with Direction Arrows	Viewer Move forward/backward and Yaw left/right
Second Button with Direction Arrows	Viewer Move up/down and Move left/right
Third Button with Direction Arrows	Viewer Pitch up/down and Roll left/right
Reset Button	Resets the Viewer to Original Position
Camera Button	Sets a New Viewer Position
Mouse Left Click on an Object with a URL	Jumps to the URL Site
Mouse Left Click on an Object with Logic	Executes the Logic Associated with the Object
CTRL +Mouse Left Click on an Object	Automatically Moves to the Object
Mouse Left Drag	Viewer Move forward/backward and Yaw left/right
CTRL +Mouse Left Drag	Viewer Move up/down and Move left/right
SHIFT +Mouse Left Drag	Viewer Pitch up/down and Roll left/right
Mouse Right Drag on an Object	Object Move forward/backward and Yaw left/right
CTRL +Mouse Right Drag	Object Move up/down and Move left/right
SHIFT +Mouse Right Drag	Object Pitch up/down and Roll left/right

While it supports standard 3D files in the VRML 1.0 format (VRML 2.0 support is pending), WIRL also supports fully interactive virtual reality worlds in Vream's Virtual Reality World format (file extension .VRW). In addition, it lets you give standard 3D VRML files to be given true virtual reality capabilities by creating a Virtual Reality Extensions file (file extension .VRE) that contains Vream's scripting language commands. This should let you create files that will not break ordinary VRML plug-ins, but will provide WIRL users with an enhanced experience. Vream Inc. offers VR Creator, a world builder with a drag and drop user interface.

Uniquely, the WIRL plug-in gives you some authoring capabilities all on its own. You can access these using the World Attributes menu, as shown in Figure 12-22.

The "Virtual Office" world you see in this figure features a Windows 95 desktop that was captured as a .GIF image. It was then texture-mapped to the background via WIRL's World Attributes menu. This menu is unable to save changes, however, in the version of WIRL that is freely distributed over the Net. If you want to be able to save changes, you need the commercial version of WIRL (priced around $29).

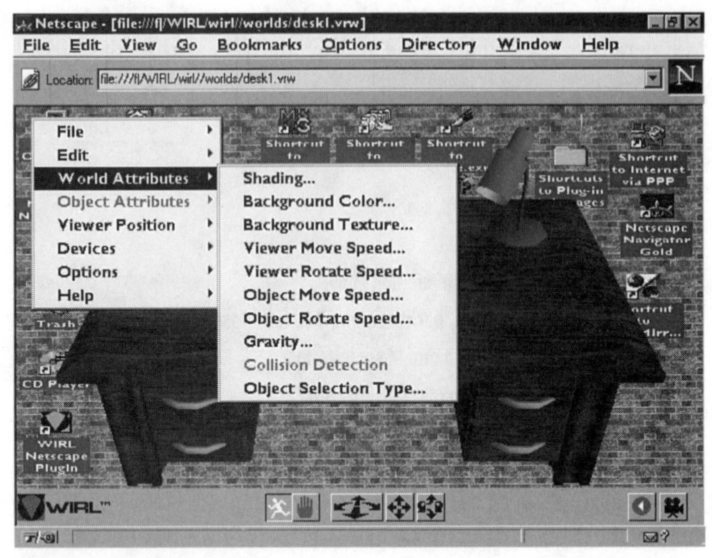

Figure 12–22 WIRL's World Attributes menu lets you apply texture mapping to existing scenes

WHAT NOW?

This chapter explored the exciting, vertiginous world of VRML plug-ins. As it has shown, VRML plug-ins are fascinating for what they do, but perhaps less interesting as plug-ins *per se*. In other words, because users interact with VRML worlds in full-screen mode most of the time, they won't often see the benefit of using a VRML plug-in as opposed to a VRML browser or helper application. If you already know VRML, however, these plug-ins will let you embed virtual worlds in your Web pages with a minimum of effort.

The next chapter returns to the more everyday world of two-dimensional graphics. It features plug-ins that extend Netscape's power to integrate images into your Web pages.

13

GRAPHICS PLUG-INS

13

Ask anyone what he or she likes *least* about surfing the Web, and one of the first answers you get is likely to have something to do with…graphics. What was once just a communication medium for scientists and academics has become a major vehicle for corporate America to communicate with its customers, and a television substitute for just about everybody.

These trends mean graphics—lots of them, oozing off almost every Web page. People with slow dial-up connections can have a particularly difficult time with graphics. Though Netscape is excellent at letting you get on with your browsing while images load, many Web pages are no longer intelligible and usable until all the graphics are filled in. And all too often—from the user's point of view, if not from the Webmaster's—those graphics are *advertising*. A new product called Internet Fast Forward (available at `http://www.privnet.com`) works with Netscape to strip ads from Web pages you commonly view. It also lets you right-click on any image to prevent it from being downloaded in the future. Well worth trying, this program is sure to annoy Web advertisers—or at least get them to change their graphics more frequently.

Faster connections via cable or satellite will do away with a lot of the waiting. However, they won't take away some of the *other* problems you commonly encounter with Web graphics. For example, if you like to print Web pages for future reference, you've found that the graphics don't print well: They're tied to a typical screen resolution of 96 or even 72 dots per inch and can't get the best out of any printer.

If you try to zoom in on standard Web images—GIFs and JPEGs—that you've saved offline, you get the jagged results typical of a bitmap that has been pushed too far. Bitmaps can give unattractive results when they are scaled. Therefore, designers of Web sites where a single image (such as a logo or button) is used in many different sizes have to create multiple versions of that image.

A more esoteric complaint about standard Web images is that their photorealism is almost too seductive. Designers reason that since any graphics are going to take time to load, they might as well use the most realistic ones available. The result is a bias toward photographs and away from other types of images. Next time you read a really well-designed, enjoyable magazine, take a conscientious look at the illustrations: You'll probably see a careful mix of photographs with line art and other types of graphics.

Unless you just fell off the proverbial turnip truck, you probably already know the answer to some of the above problems: vector graphics. Vector graphics have been around for many years, and in fact were employed in the first graphical computer game, the legendary Space War. Instead of being based on a resolution-specific bitmap, they contain a mathematical description of the lines, curves, patterns, and fills needed to draw an image.

Unlike raster (bitmap) graphics, vector graphics can display at the maximum resolution of the host device, whether it's a standard 4-bit VGA monitor, a 1,024 by 1,024 true-color display, or a 600dpi monochrome printer. In addition, a vector graphic can be downloaded once, cached, and then displayed at different sizes wherever it needs to occur on a Web page. This makes vector graphics ideal for the logos and button bars that clog the Net. Because of their quality and detail, they're also great for technical illustrations and manuals, whether distributed over the Internet or just made available to local users on an intranet.

Another interesting advantage of vector graphics is that their authoring tools often let you associate URLs with particular objects in an image. Unlike with raster graphics, you do not have to create separate image maps. What's more, you're not limited to predefined hot-spot shapes such as circles or rectangles.

Alas—there never has been anything approaching a standard when it comes to graphics file formats. Instead, software authors have created their own formats customized for the task at hand. Some of the better-known vector file formats are CorelDraw, AutoCAD, and Aldus (now Macromedia) FreeHand.

While it's a pity that no single format has reached critical mass, you can use any of the popular types of vector graphics in your Web pages, thanks to plug-ins. As long as users download and install the correct plug-in—which you, of course, encourage them to do via a notice and use of the PLUGINSPAGE attribute—they'll be able to zoom in on your graphics and print them at high resolution.

This chapter primarily features plug-ins that handle vector graphics. However, you'll also learn to install some plug-ins that improve Netscape's handling of raster graphics. With these plug-ins, you can

- View additional industry-standard raster formats (such as .TIF and .BMP), or
- Use formats employing new, superior types of compression for faster downloading

ABC QUICKSILVER

ABC QuickSilver from Micrografx is a Netscape plug-in that supports Designer—one of the first vector-based graphics drawing programs for Windows. Using Designer 4.0 or later, you can create drawings whose objects respond to mouse clicks by jumping to new pages, changing the appearance of the drawing, or just changing the message displayed in the browser status line.

Since ABC QuickSilver can change graphics on the fly, you can also collect data locally or off the Net and use it to update an image. One very slick aspect of Designer authoring is that any properties—such as a hotlink—you assign to an object within a drawing stay with that object wherever it is used. You can copy an object from one drawing to another using the Windows clipboard. This can make interactive graphics substantially easier to produce.

Lesson 1: Installing ABC QuickSilver

To install ABC QuickSilver, you need to be running Windows 95 or NT. Go to the Micrografx Web site at *http://www.micrografx.com* (or check Appendix A, "Where to Get the Plug-Ins Featured in This Book," for details on your CD-ROM). Once you have downloaded or copied the file ABCQS.EXE to a temporary subdirectory on your hard drive, exit Netscape.

Now start the installer by double-clicking on it. The setup program will list the copy of Netscape into which it thinks you want to install the plug-in. If the choice is correct, just click on the Next button. Otherwise, click on Browse and locate the copy of Netscape you wish to use with ABC QuickSilver.

NOTE: Some versions of ABC QuickSilver do not work with some copies of Netscape Gold. If you have problems with this combination, contact Micrografx for advice.

The installer copies several files, placing the plug-in NPDSGNET.DLL in your Netscape Plug-ins folder. You can verify its operation by restarting Netscape. From the Options menu, use the Network Preferences menu to clear the browser's disk and memory caches. Now, select About Plug-ins from the Help menu. As you'll see, QuickSilver now asserts its interest in the following MIME types and suffixes:

MIME Type/Subtype	Suffix
image/x-mgx-drw	drw
image/x-mgx-ds4	ds4
image/x-mgx-dsf	dsf

As usual, these are the values you'll need to give the people who run your Web server, ensuring that it will handle these file types as ABC QuickSilver documents instead of plain text. You probably have already guessed that the extensions correspond to file types used by Micrografx Designer, which you'll need to author graphics for ABC QuickSilver.

To test the ABC QuickSilver plug-in, return to the Micrografx Web site. Open the ABC QuickSilver Gallery at *http://www.micrografx.com/gallery/abcqsgallery*. (Avoid the other "galleries" at this Web site: Even when they feature Designer graphics, the images have been converted to GIFs or JPEGs so users without QuickSilver can see them.) Figure 13-1 shows the chessboard graphic found at *http://www.micrografx.com/gallery/abcqsgallery/chess.htm*.

Figure 13-1 An embedded chess game courtesy of ABC Quicksilver

Lesson 2: Embedding Designer Graphics in Your Web Pages

As you realize if you've clicked on the chess board sample pictured in Figure 13-1, there's a little more to it than meets the eye. Yet the HTML code that placed it there is completely ordinary:

```
<EMBED SRC="CHESS.DSF" WIDTH=500 HEIGHT=406>
```

The chessboard contains Designer objects that can detect events such as mouse movements and respond to them by executing commands that the graphic's author specified. The following is a list of ABC QuickSilver event names and when they occur:

Event	Action
OnMouseEnter	Moves the mouse pointer over the object
OnMouseLeave	Moves the pointer away from the object
OnMouseDown	Presses the left mouse button while over the object
OnMouseUp	Releases the left mouse button while over the object
OnLoad	First opens the Web page containing the document

If you like to play chess, you can work through the following steps—as suggested by Micrografx—with the chessboard example to better understand ABC QuickSilver events:

- Move your cursor over the words BEGIN GAME and notice the cursor change to a hand. This is an example of an OnMouseEnter event calling a CursorShape Hand command.

- Click BEGIN GAME. This text is an object in the Designer file named "Begin" which has three event properties and command values associated with it which control its actions. When you clicked on BEGIN GAME, the RESET BOARD object changed colors from gray to black, the text object E2-E4 and a red arrow were displayed, and the BEGIN GAME object changed from black to gray. These actions were performed instantly, without the screen redrawing or a new HTML file opening.

- Click E2-E4. You have made your first move. The pawn object moved from E2 to E4, the first move changed to gray, and the red arrow displayed next to the second move. Once again, these objects moved and changed on the fly.

- Click E7-E5 and then finish the chess match by clicking on the remaining moves. In each instance, objects interact through simple property events and corresponding command values.

- Click on RESET BOARD after the word CHECKMATE displays. You are ready to replay the chess match again.

As noted, to create an ABC QuickSilver graphic and tie events to its various objects, you need a copy of Designer—making this discussion somewhat academic for those of us who don't have one. If you do own Designer, you can tie an event and resulting command to any object in an image by using the Properties command from the program's Objects menu.

Table 13-1 shows the commands that can be tied to each event for processing by ABC QuickSilver.

Table 13-1 Possible Designer commands and their effect in ABC QuickSilver

Command	Effect
Jump *localURL*	Instructs the browser to load and display the new URL *LocalURL*. *LocalURL* must be an absolute or relative URL reference. Since this closes the current page and, therefore, the current plug-in, any additional commands for the event are ignored.
InplaceJump *URLstring*	Instructs the plug-in to discard its current contents and display the new drawing located at *URLstring*. *URLstring* must refer to a Designer drawing. The new drawing assumes the dimensions of the discarded drawing. Since the current file is discarded, any additional commands for the event are ignored.
StatusLine *text*	Displays the text string *text* in the browser's status bar. To clear the status bar, omit the *text* parameter.
CursorShape *shape*	Sets the shape of the mouse pointer. A *shape* of "Link" or "Hand" displays the hand pointer. To restore the normal arrow pointer, use any other value for *shape* or omit *shape*.
ObjectColor *color*	Sets the object's interior-fill color to the value represented by *color*. The *color* parameter must be either a predefined Netscape color name or a Netscape-style "#rrggbb" color specification.
ObjectText *text*	Sets the object's text to *text*. To clear the text, omit the *text* parameter.
MoveOver *objectname*	Moves the object and centers it to the position of the object named *objectname*.
HideObject ShowObject	Hides or shows the object. These commands do not use any parameters. A hidden object does not detect events, but you can use another object's event to show (reactivate) a hidden object.
FlashObject *flashrate/count* EndFlashObject	Flashes an object, whether the object is hidden or not. Enter the flash rate in milliseconds. To flash once a second, use 1000. To flash every half-second, use 500. The maximum flash rate is 50ms, and the minimum flash rate is 30,000ms. Enter the flash count to set how many times to flash the symbol. To flash until an EndFlashObject command is received, use –1 (infinite flashing). Separate parameters with a space.
SpinObjectCW *steptime/steps/revolution* EndSpinObject	Spins an object about its center in a clockwise direction. Enter the steptime in milliseconds. To rotate an object one step every second, use 1000. You must set the steptime between 10 and 60,000ms. Enter the number of rotation steps it takes to complete a revolution. For example, a value of 8 steps would cause the object to rotate 45 degrees every step. Enter the number of revolutions you want the object to make. To rotate until an EndSpinObject command is received, use –1 (infinite spinning).

Command	Effect
SpinObjectCCW *steptime/steps/revolution*	Spins an object abouts its center in a counterclockwise direction. Otherwise, this is identical to the SpinObjectCW command.
Beep *beeprate/count* EndBeep	Causes a system beep using the default sound. Enter the rate between beeps in milliseconds. To beep once a second, use 1000. To beep once every half-second, use 500. The maximum beeprate is 100ms, and the minimum beeprate is 30,000ms. Enter the beepcount to set how many times to beep. To beep until an EndBeep command is received, use –1 (infinite beeping). Separate parameters with a space.
Bring Object ToFront SendObjectToBack	Moves the currently selected object in front or behind all others on the current layer. These commands do not use any parameters. A hidden object does not detect events, but you can use another object's event to show (reactivate) a hidden object.
BringObject Forward SendObjectBackward	Moves the currently selected object one level toward the front or back. These commands do not use any parameters.

Although control of ABC QuickSilver is mostly ceded to Designer, there are a couple of EMBED attributes specific to the program. One is the ANTIALIAS attribute, which can be added to an <EMBED SRC> tag. It smooths jagged edges in an image by blending them with the surrounding pixels. However, it is ignored if the user's display is set to 256 colors or fewer. Also, you should avoid it with objects you have programmed to move or change color in response to an event.

The second special attribute may be any character string, and a value for that string, that you care to specify. That string can then be inserted as a Designer command, and its value will be resolved later. For example, you might embed a graphic into a page with this line:

```
<EMBED SRC="drawing.dsf" WIDTH=200 HEIGHT=300 ANTIALIAS MYSTRING="itsvalue">
```

DRAWING.DSF could then contain an object with an event whose associated command is

```
ObjectText    %mystring
```

When the graphic is opened, the percent sign tells ABC QuickSilver to resolve mystring into the value you specified in the <EMBED SRC> tag. Therefore, the character string "itsvalue" appears as the relevant object's text. You could use this technique as an easy way to reuse graphics, varying text without having to make any other modifications.

CMX VIEWER

With 2.5 million users, CorelDRAW comes closer to being a standard for vector graphics than almost any other product (the overall leader, of course, is AutoCAD). Not only that, but hundreds of ready-made images have shipped with CorelDRAW, Corel GALLERY, and other products.

If you're a CorelDRAW user, you can export images in the .CMX format used by CMX Viewer from within the program. If you don't use CorelDRAW, you can download sample images from Corel's Web site or purchase them economically on one of the company's CD-ROMs. Like other vector formats, .CMX is particularly efficient for logos, gradient fills, and any image that will be repeatedly used in different sizes.

Lesson 1: Installing the CMX Viewer

Corel's CMX Viewer is available only for Windows 95 and NT. To install the plug-in, visit the company's Web site at *http://www.corel.com/corelcmx/* (or refer to Appendix A). Once you have downloaded or copied the file CORELCMX.EXE to a temporary subdirectory on your hard drive, exit Netscape.

Now start the installer by double-clicking on it. The setup program will first ask you where you want sample CMX files to be installed. Select the folder C:\COREL or any other location that will be memorable to you. Next, the installer prompts you to, if you wish, rename the entry it will place in your Start menu. The default is "CorelCMX Viewer."

After the sample files have been copied, the setup program continues installation by copying the file NPCMX32.DLL into your Netscape Plug-ins folder. Unlike some other installers, it does not pause to ask you where your copy of Netscape is or which copy to use. Instead, it looks in your Windows registry, checking the value of the HKEY_CURRENT_USER/Netscape/Navigator/Main/Installation directory. If this value (which you can check using REGEDIT) does not match the location of the Netscape you want to use with the CMX Viewer, simply move NPCMX32.DLL accordingly.

Now, restart Netscape. Then use the Network Preferences menu to clear the browser's disk and memory caches. After selecting About Plug-ins from the Help menu, you'll see that CMX viewer has installed the following MIME type and suffix:

```
image/x-cmx     cmx
```

As always, supply this information to your Web server's administrators before you embed CMX graphics in your Web pages.

To test the CMX viewer, you can simply use Netscape's File Open command to navigate to the directory where you installed sample files. Open SAMPLES.HTM and you'll see a list of test images. Figure 13-2 shows a "Presentation Slide" example taken from this collection. You can also visit the Corel Web site for a variety of other samples.

As you can see, Corel CMX has a pop-up menu (invoked, as usual, by the right mouse button) that lets you flip, rotate, or zoom in on an embedded graphic. The menu also lets you save the graphic as a local .CMX file. Selecting "Pop Up" lets you view the graphic in a separate window.

To zoom in, you select the relevant menu choice, changing the mouse cursor to a magnifying glass. Figure 13-3 shows the result of zooming an image—demonstrating the flexibility of vector graphics—while Figure 13-4 shows the image in the Popup window.

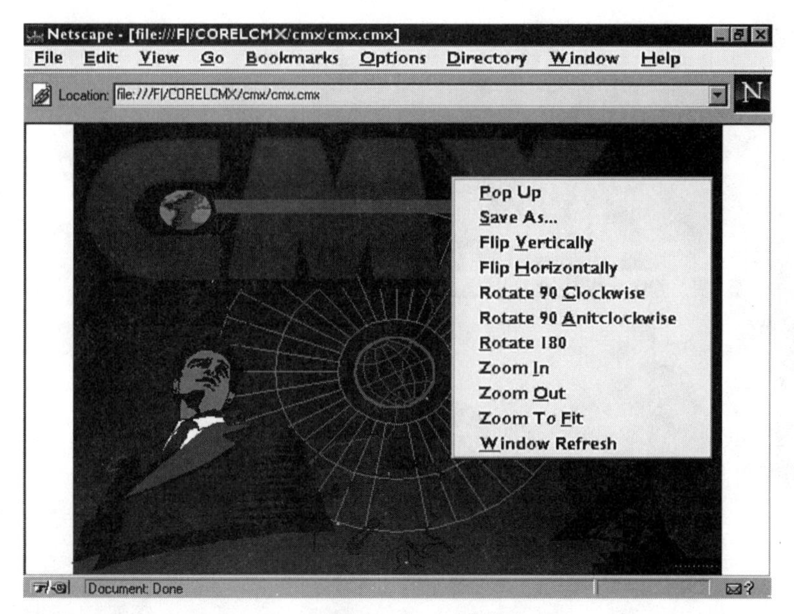

Figure 13–2 A CMX image displayed full-screen within the browser

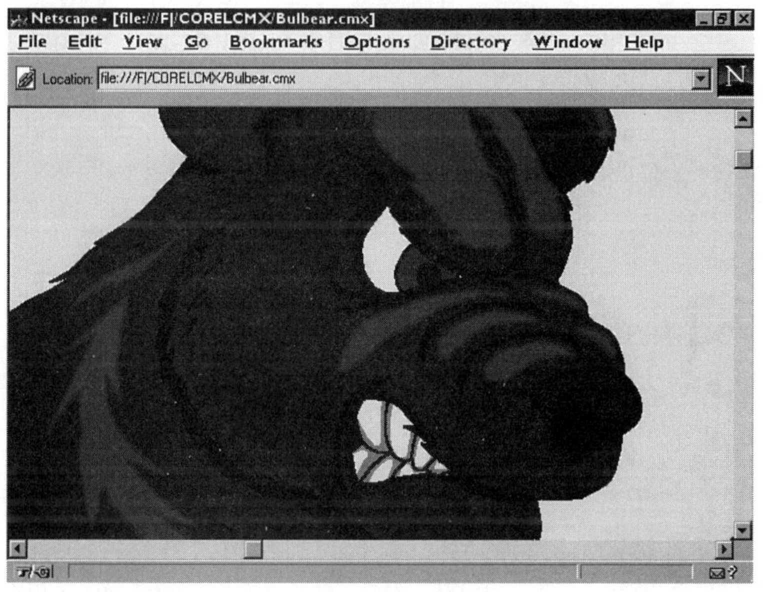

Figure 13–3 The result of a zoom

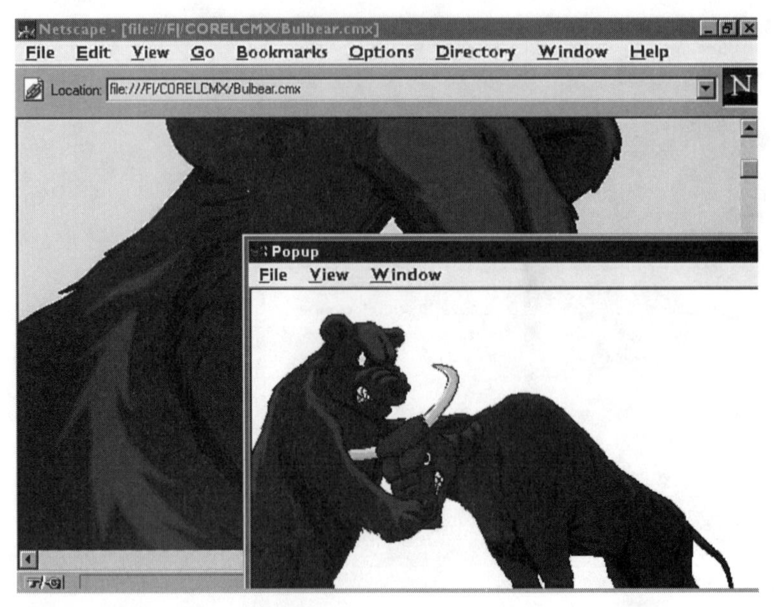

Figure 13–4 Corel CMX can view any embedded graphic in a window that is separate from the host Web page

There are two other interesting aspects of the Corel CMX plug-in. First, embedded graphics can have a transparent background; the color behind the bear and the bull in Figures 13-3 and 13-4 is merely Netscape's default. Second, like many other plug-ins, Corel CMX adds its file type to those viewable in Netscape's File Open menu. If you have not yet embedded a .CMX file in a Web page, you can still preview it by loading it directly from disk. When you do this, the graphic is sized automatically to fit Netscape's current window. Figure 13-5 shows what happens when an instance of Netscape that is not running full-screen loads a graphic from disk.

Lesson 2: Embedding CMX Graphics in Your Web Pages

To create .CMX files, you need a copy of CorelDRAW. Simply use the program's export facility once you have created a drawing. The only thing you need to know is that any fonts in the graphic should be converted to curves before exporting the file to the .CMX format. Otherwise, their appearance may tend to vary when they're viewed by the plug-in.

In order to embed images in your Web pages, you just employ the standard <EMBED SRC> tag. The only attributes you need are WIDTH and HEIGHT which, as usual, are required for reliable results. Of course, you can also use PLUGINSPAGE="http://www.corel.com/" to make sure that the user who doesn't yet have the Corel CMX plug-in knows where to get it.

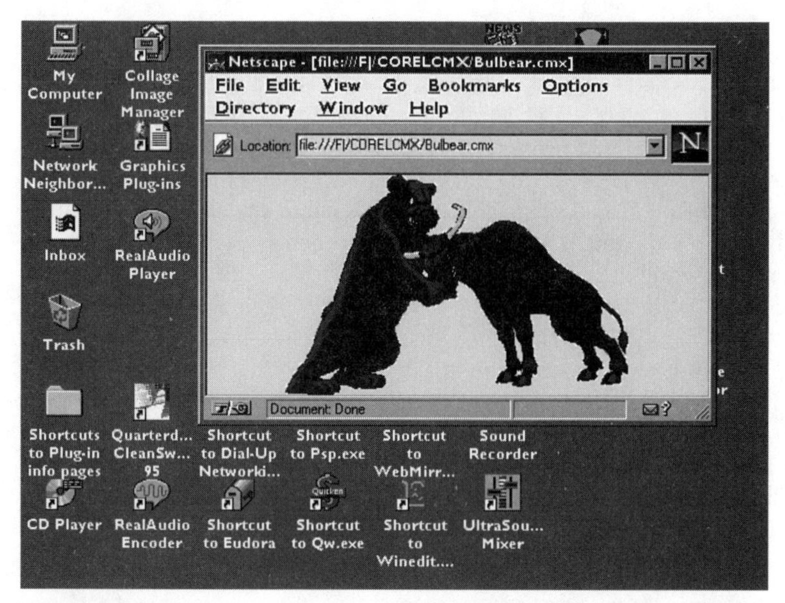

Figure 13–5 If you are not running Netscape full-screen, CMX graphics can scale themselves to whatever space is available

DXG/DXF AND SVF

Autodesk says it gets more new customers each year for AutoCAD than other companies have as a total installed base for their vector graphics formats. We'll look at the company's own plug-in, WHIP!, later in this chapter. Meanwhile, here is proof of AutoCAD's status as a standard in the form of a third-party plug-in from SoftSource, Inc.

SoftSource's DWG/DXF plug-in may not be catchily named, but it does what it says. You can use it to view AutoCAD drawing (.DWG) and .DXF files, from AutoCAD version 2.5 through release 12. (Release 13 is not supported, however.) These files can be generated by almost any CAD program, including SoftSource's own Virtual Drafter program.

Once a drawing has been downloaded to a user's copy of Netscape, he or she can zoom, pan, or magnify portions. He or she can also toggle visibility of different layers without re-downloading.

SoftSource's separate SVF plug-in works with the Simple Vector Format the company jointly developed with NCSA. This operates similarly to the DWG/DXF plug-in, with an added feature: Hot links may be associated with any object in a drawing.

SVF also features "notifications," links that get activated automatically when the user zooms in past a certain magnification level. This lets you create drawings such as maps, which can start by providing an overall view and then load more detailed information about the area a user wants to visit.

Lesson 1: Installing the DWG/DXF Plug-In

SoftSource's plug-ins are available only for Windows 95 and NT. To install the DWG/DXF plug-in, visit the company's Web site at *http://www.softsource.com/softsource/plugins/* (or check Appendix A for details on your CD-ROM). Download or copy the file NPDWG32.EXE to a temporary subdirectory on your hard drive, and then exit Netscape.

Now double-click on the installer file. This extracts component files and then automatically starts the setup program. This first asks you to name a folder where it will "install the program"—actually, the folder will hold sample files, not the plug-in itself. Select the folder C:\DWGDXF or any other location that will be memorable to you. Next, the program asks you to specify the location of your browser. Once you have done this, it copies NPDWG32.DLL into your Netscape Plug-ins folder.

Now, restart Netscape. After selecting About Plug-ins from the Help menu, you'll see that a small host of MIME types and suffixes have been added to the browser. These are intended to cater for the various ways in which Web servers may already be offering up .DXF and .DWG files. As usual, however, if your Web server has never been used to host AutoCAD files, you should give its support staff the following list:

MIME Type/Subtype	Suffix
image/vnd.dxf	dxf
image/vnd.dwg	dwg
image/x-dxf	dxf
image/x-dwg	dwg
vector/x-dxf	dxf
vector/x-dwg	dwg

To test the plug-in, use Netscape's File Open command to navigate to the directory where you installed sample files. Open the file HELP-DWG.HTM to view some test images.

Figure 13-6 shows one of the images in this file; as you can see, the DXG/DXF plug-in features a pop-up menu. This lets you zoom in or zoom out. The Zoom Window command lets you control the zoom area more precisely: After selecting this from the menu, just click the mouse on the upper left-hand corner of a rectangle, drag it to the lower right-hand corner, and click again. The viewing area zooms to the area you defined. To zoom out, use the Zoom Extents command.

The Layers command allows you to access any layers that were created in the source file, so you can focus on just the information you're interested in. Figure 13-7 shows a sample of its use.

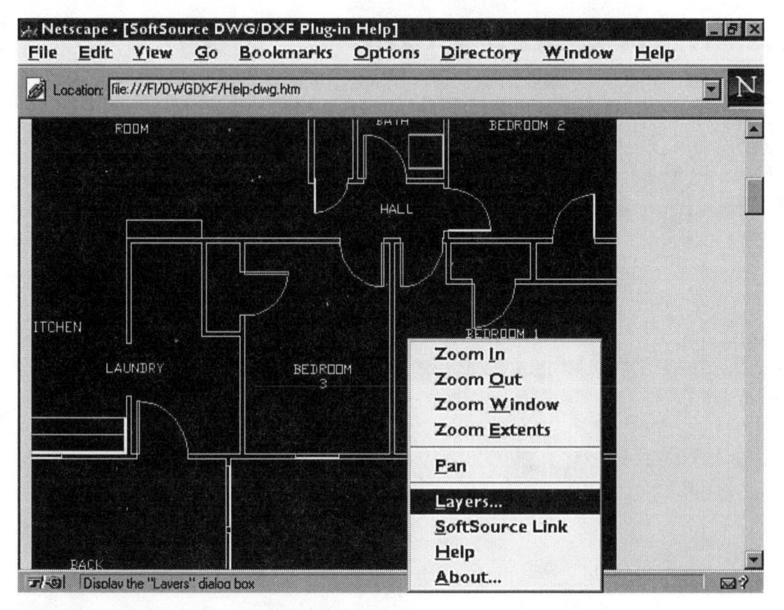

Figure 13–6 The DWG/DXF plug-in

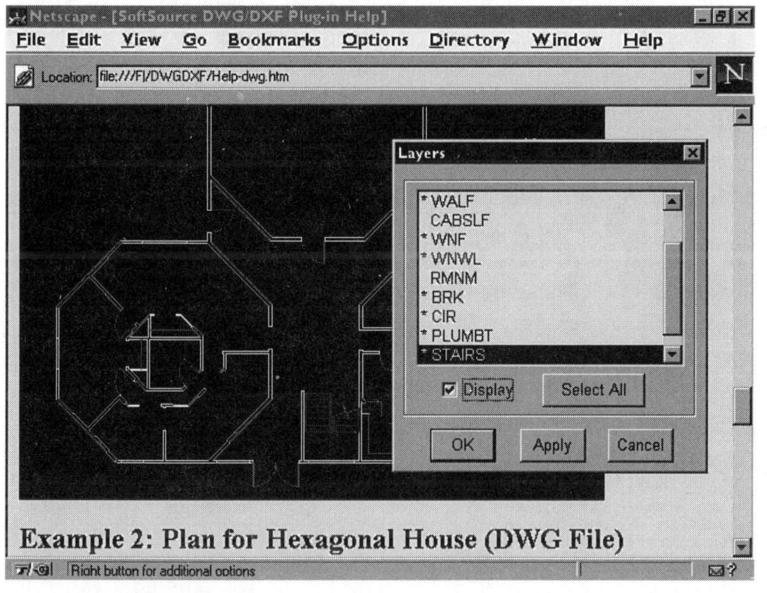

Figure 13–7 Using the Layers menu

Lesson 2: Installing the SVF Plug-In

To install the SVF plug-in, revisit the SoftSource Web site (or Appendix A). Download or copy the file NPSVF32.EXE to a temporary subdirectory on your hard drive, and then exit Netscape.

Now double-click on the installer file. This extracts installation files and then automatically starts the setup program. This first asks you to name a folder where sample files will be placed. Choose the folder C:\SVF or any other location you'll remember. Next, the program asks you to specify the location of your browser. Once you have done this, it copies NPSVF32.DLL into your Netscape Plug-ins folder.

Now, restart Netscape. After selecting About Plug-ins from the Help menu, you'll see that the following MIME types and suffixes have been added to the browser.

MIME Type/Subtype	Suffix
image/vnd.svf	svf
image/x-svf	svf
vector/x-svf	svf

To test the plug-in, use Netscape's File Open command to navigate to the directory where you installed sample files. Open the file HELP-SVF.HTM to view some test images. As you'll see, .SVF files contain layers just like DWG and DXF files do. They also add additional information, changing the Netscape status line to display messages that vary according to where your mouse pointer is.

The status line in Figure 13-8 indicates that North State Street in Bellingham, Washington (home of SoftSource) is a one-way street. The rectangle at upper left represents SoftSource's offices: This object has been hot-linked so that double-clicking on it will take you to the URL for their home page.

Like other Windows versions of Netscape plug-ins, the SVF Plug-ins can also load files from your local hard drive via Netscape's File Open command. Files loaded this way appear full-screen instead of being subject to WIDTH and HEIGHT attributes.

No matter how files have been loaded, a pop-up menu is once again featured. This lets you zoom in or zoom out and select your choice of layers to view.

Lesson 3: Embedding CAD Images in Your Web Pages

You can use a variety of CAD programs to create .DWG or .DXF files. To create .SVF files, you can use SoftSource's own program, Virtual Drafter, or pick from among a variety of translators.

Embedding an image is accomplished using the usual <EMBED SRC> tag. You can specify HEIGHT and WIDTH in pixels or in percentages of the available browser window. (For example, to have an image take up one-half of the window's width and three-quarters of its height, use the attributes WIDTH=50% and HEIGHT=75%.)

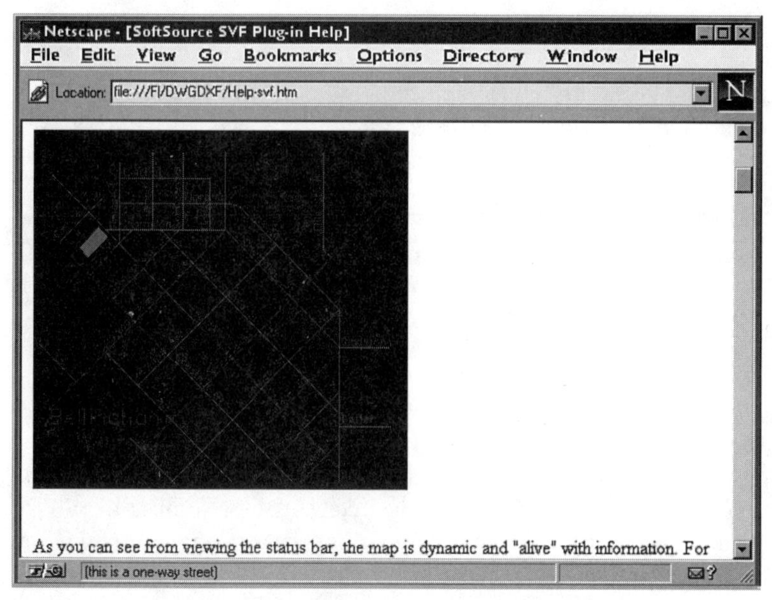

Figure 13–8 An embedded SVF file can change the status line (see the bottom of the screen) according to the cursor position

Additional attributes let you selectively turn on or off access to particular layers in the drawing. Use the attribute LAYERON to turn on layers, and LAYEROFF to turn them off. For example:

```
LAYERON=NAME1, NAME2, NAME3
LAYEROFF=NAME 1
```

If you're using the DWG/DXF plug-in, you can also specify a default view that has been named and saved in the drawing. Use the attribute as follows:

```
NAMEDVIEW=viewname
```

Other attributes let you selectively disable features in the pop-up menu. If you wanted to turn zoom, pan, and the list of layers off, you would add these attributes to the end of your EMBED SRC line:

```
ZOOM=FALSE PAN=FALSE LAYERS=FALSE
```

With the SVF plug-in, the left mouse button usually activates a link. If you would like to disable links for a particular instance of a drawing, add the attribute LINKS=FALSE.

The text in a SVF link can be a URL or merely any of the above attributes. It can even contain both. For example, to have a hyperlink take the user to another drawing which has some layers turned off, you would use instructions similar to the following:

```
HTTP://MYSERVER.COM/ANOTHER.SVF LAYEROFF=WIRES, GIRDERS LAYERON=PIPES
```

FIGLEAF INLINE

FIGleaf Inline is the Swiss Army knife of graphics plug-ins. Once installed, it greatly expands the range of graphics file types Netscape can view. Embedded within a Web page, these graphics can be magnified for closer inspection using the mouse or a pop-up menu.

The list of formats handled by FIGleaf Inline is pretty overwhelming. For a start, it accepts two vector-based formats, .CGM (Computer Graphics Metafile) and .WMF (Windows Metafile). .CGM files may be zoomed without losing quality, although this is not the case with .WMF files (since some contain bitmaps).

Encapsulated PostScript (.EPS) files are also supported if they have bitmapped headers. However, as anyone who has ever worked with .EPS files knows, they come in many flavors—you'll need to try the ones you want to include in your pages carefully to make sure they work.

FIGleaf Inline also adds support for two major raster graphics formats: TIFF and .BMP. Though it is hard to see why you wouldn't just convert these formats to .GIF or .JPG before using them in a Web page, FIGleaf's support for them might be useful if you have a library of dozens or hundreds—on an intranet, perhaps.

You can also configure your browser so that FIGleaf takes over from Netscape when it comes to handling GIF and JPEG images. The advantage here is merely the ability to zoom, if desired.

You don't have to embed graphics files in a Web page for FIGleaf Inline to view them. Like other plug-ins, it also lets you open the files it handles using Netscape's File Open menu. Therefore, FIGleaf Inline handily converts Netscape into a graphics viewer for files stored on your local hard drive.

The other formats handled by FIGleaf Inline are CCITT Group 4 fax Type I (.G4), CCITT Group 4 fax Type II (.TG4), Portable Bitmap (.PBM), Portable Network Graphics (.PNG), Portable Pixmap (.PPM), Portable Graymap (.PGM), Sun raster file (.SUN), and Silicon Graphics RGB (.RGB).

Lesson 1: Installing FIGleaf Inline

To install FIGleaf Inline, access Carberry Technology's Web site at *http://www.ct.ebt.com/figinline/* (or check Appendix A for details on your CD-ROM). To proceed, you'll need to have Windows 95 or Windows NT. Download or copy the file FINL10.EXE to a temporary subdirectory on your hard drive, and then exit Netscape.

Now double-click on the installer file. This starts the setup program, which first asks you to specify a folder for FIGleaf sample files (it defaults to creating a folder called FIGleaf in your Netscape Program subdirectory). Next, it copies the file NPFIGLF.DLL into your Netscape Plug-ins folder.

Now, restart Netscape and clear its disk and memory caches. Select About Plug-ins from the About Plug-ins menu, and you'll see that a massive collection of MIME types and suffixes has been added to the browser (see Table 13-2). These represent the types of graphics FIGleaf Inline can handle.

Generally speaking, this extensive range of capabilities is welcome. However, if you already had another plug-in that handled one of these MIME types, you would need to disable it in order to ensure that Netscape's behavior would be predictable. Also, instead of deciding to fill your pages with different types of graphics, you still should standardize on one or two—that way, the list of MIME types and suffixes you have to provide the administrators of your Web server will be kept reasonable.

Table 13-2 The graphics—and corresponding MIME types—that FIGleaf Inline can handle

MIME Type/Subtype	Suffix
image/cgm	cgm
image/jpeg	jpg;*.jpe;*.jpeg
image/gif	gif
image/x-png	png
image/tiff	tif;*.tiff
image/x-rgb	rgb
image/x-portable-pixmap	ppm
image/x-portable-graymap	pgm
image/x-portable-bitmap	pbm
image/x-MS-bmp	bmp
image/x-eps	eps;*.epsi;*.epsf
image/x-g4	g4
image/x-tg4	tg4
image/x-cmu-raster	ras;*.sun
image/x-wmf	wmf
image/x-cgm	cgm

Looking over the table, you might wonder what happens when the Netscape/FIGleaf combination encounters a graphic (.GIF or JPEG, for example) that the browser already handles natively. The answer is that Netscape displays the graphic in its usual way if that graphic was included in a Web page using the <IMG SRC> tag. If the graphic was instead referenced using the <EMBED SRC> tag, FIGleaf will start up, making its special features available.

Figure 13-9 shows a GIF file displayed two ways: In the first instance, it has been placed in the Web page using the <IMG SRC> tag (with no attributes), appearing in its original size with no assistance from FIGleaf. In the second instance, it has been included in the page via the <EMBED SRC> tag (with mandatory HEIGHT and WIDTH attributes) and scaled by FIGleaf Inline.

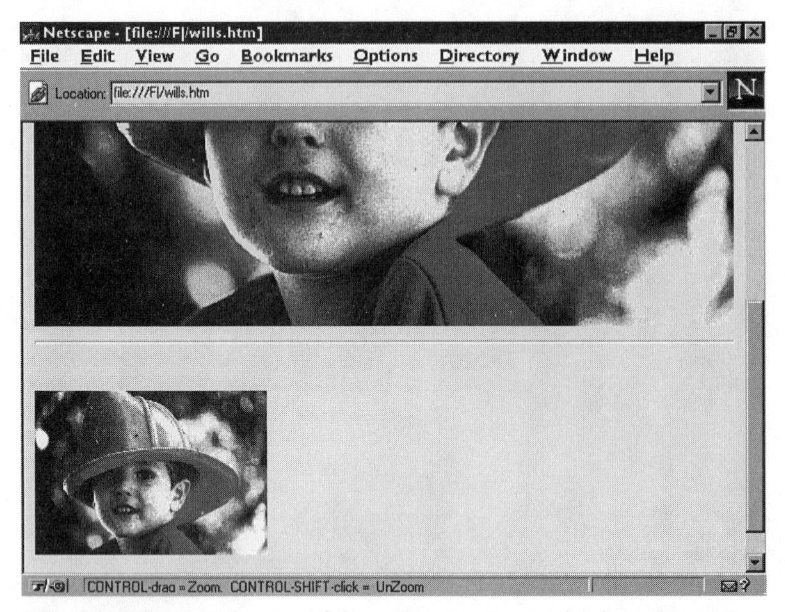

Figure 13–9 At the top of the page, Netscape displays this GIF file by itself; at the bottom, it's scaled with the help of FIGleaf Inline

To get a demonstration of FIGleaf Inline, go to the Carberry Technology Web site at *http://www.ct.ebt.com/figinline/demofrm.html*. Figure 13-10 shows one of the test pages you'll find there. FIGleaf Inline lets you zoom in on an image by holding down the <CTRL> key and dragging the mouse to define a rectangle within that image. In this figure, the image has been zoomed—making scroll bars appear at its borders.

The next illustration, Figure 13-11, shows FIGleaf Inline's pop-up menu. You can use this to rotate or scale an image, turn dithering on or off, save it to disk, and more. Images appear full-screen, as seen here, when you load them from a local disk drive using Netscape's File/Open command, or when you right-click on a link and ask Netscape to open it in a new browser window.

Lesson 2: Embedding FIGleaf Inline Graphics in Your Web Pages

Provided that you have arranged for the relevant MIME information to be placed on your Web server, there is little trick to embedding graphics in your Web pages. However, you have to bear in mind that the user without FIGleaf may not be able to view them. Or, Netscape may offer to launch helper applications when it encounters your page, ruining its carefully crafted effect.

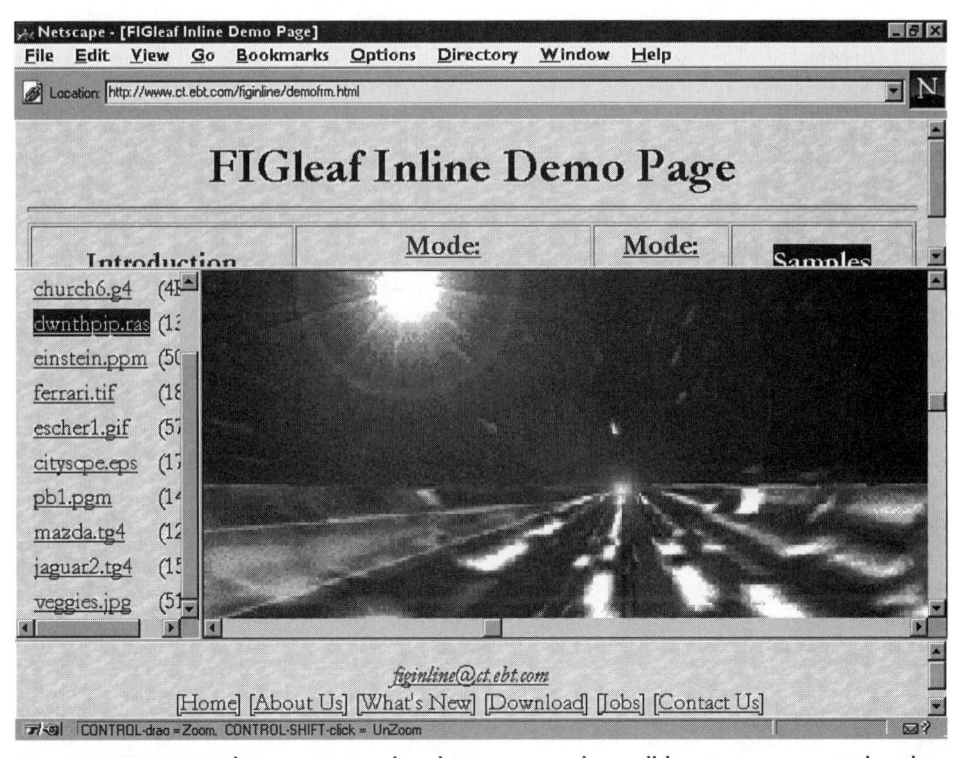

Figure 13–10 When an image has been zoomed, scroll bars appear at its borders

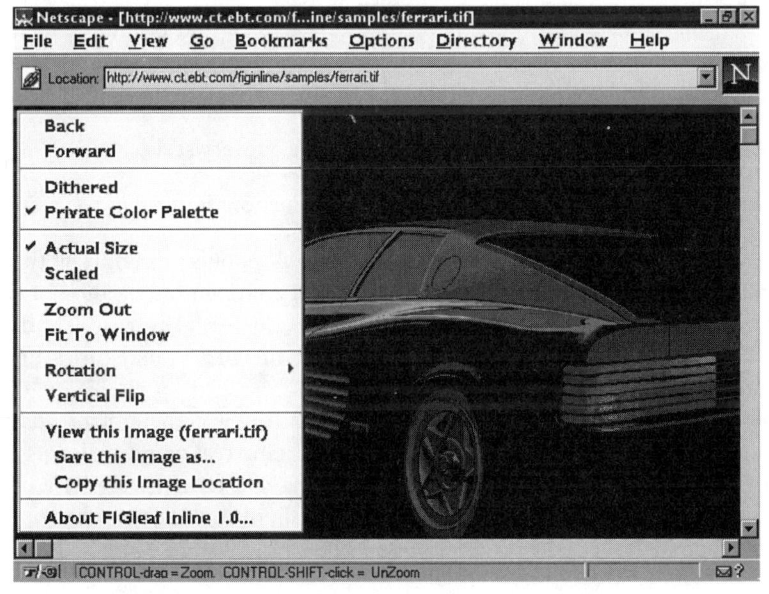

Figure 13–11 FIGleaf Inline's pop-up menu

Thus, as is so often the case, you need a way to let users know about the plug-in they need. You should also use the PLUGINSPAGE attribute in your <EMBED> tag so that users can be taken to the Carberry Technology Web site automatically.

The only other things you need to remember are the usual HEIGHT and WIDTH, which are required. FIGleaf Inline also supports the usual BORDER attribute, to which you can assign pixel values to draw boxes around your images. The available COLORMAP=DITHERED attribute can improve the appearance of Web pages containing multiple embedded images.

Carberry Technology also points out some limitations in FIGleaf Inline. Their plug-in isn't less capable than others; they're just being more candid than some other companies:

- Scrolling is only available using the mouse.
- The Forward and Back menu items are never dimmed. This functionality isn't provided in the Netscape Plug-in API.
- Print Preview does not work with FIGleaf Inline. If you are viewing an image in EMBED or FULL mode, then you will not be able to use the Print Preview option.
- Printing while FIGleaf Inline is within a frame and partially obscured sometimes distorts the image.

FRACTAL VIEWER

The term *fractal* was coined by Benoit Mandelbrot (see his book, *The Fractal Geometry of Nature*) to describe a structure possessing similar-looking forms of many different sizes. A basic explanation of fractals—adapted from lengthier materials you'll find on the Iterated Systems Web site at *http://www.iterated.com*—is that they are extensions of classical Euclidean shapes (lines, squares, circles, and so on) with the following two properties:

- When viewed, they are infinitely magnifiable with structure at every scale.
- They can be generated by typically small, finite sets of instructions and data.

The first widely known fractals all looked very abstract. A popular example is the Mandelbrot set. Fractal images like these, when viewed with a computer application, are infinitely magnifiable. They can be zoomed to any extent to reveal new levels of complexity. Fractal patterns can be manipulated to generate imaginary landscapes for flight simulators, movies, illustrations, and other applications.

Michael Barnsley discovered that it was also possible to control the content of a fractal picture precisely and to make it look incredibly similar to a specific real-world image. An early example of a fractal picture generated in this way was that of a fern. The entire fern looks like each of the fronds in it, each frond resembles the smaller fronds in it, and so on. The more the fern is magnified, the more levels of these fronds are visible.

Since real-world objects, such as this fern, have fractal properties, Barnsley reasoned that any real-world image could be expressed mathematically. The process that he developed to express a real-world image in terms of its fractal properties is the Fractal Transform. This now makes it possible to create computer images that look photo-realistic (as do raster graphics) yet are created using mathematics (as are vector graphics).

The fractal model of images represents an image entirely in terms of its fractal properties. Rather than a set of values for every pixel, a Fractal Image Format (FIF) file contains a record of repeated patterns that exist in the image. This not only makes fractal images substantially smaller than bitmaps but also makes them resolution-independent. Iterated Systems' Fractal Viewer is a plug-in that makes mathematics fun, letting you view bitmaps compressed using the company's proprietary algorithms.

With Fractal Viewer, currently available for Windows 95 and Windows 3.x, you can download images progressively, starting with a thumbnail that grows to full screen. You can instantly zoom any part of the image, copy it to the clipboard, or save it as a bitmap for use in other applications.

Lesson 1: Installing the Fractal Viewer Plug-In

To install the plug-in version of Fractal Viewer, you need Windows 95/NT or a Macintosh. Go to the Iterated Systems Web site at *http://www.iterated.com/fracview/info/fv-info.htm,* or check Appendix A for details about your CD-ROM.

To install the Windows version, download or copy the installer file. Run this installer to extract approximately ten files, including the SETUP.EXE program you need. Click on SETUP, and you'll be asked which copy of Netscape you wish to install Fractal Viewer into. Pick the correct Program folder and then click on Next. The installer copies NPFIF.DLL into your Netscape Plug-ins folder. It then prompts you to select another subdirectory where sample files will be installed. Choose any name, such as C:\FRACTAL, that you'll be able to remember.

To install the Macintosh version, once again download or copy the installer file, a self-extracting archive called Fractal Viewer for Netscape.sea. Click on this file, and a folder will be created that's called—no surprise here—Fractal Viewer for Netscape. Within this folder are a Read Me file, a sample file called SKIER.FIF, and another file called ViewFIF. This last file is the actual plug-in, so move it to the Plug-ins folder within your Netscape folder.

Now exit Netscape (if it is running) and restart, being sure to clear the program's disk and memory caches. Select About Plug-ins from the Help or Apple menu—it shows you that Fractal Imager has been installed with the MIME type image/fif and the suffix fif. (Yes, you guessed it—these are the values you'll need to supply to administrators of your Web server if you want to make embedded fractal graphics available to others.)

To test the program, return to the Iterated Systems Web site, where you'll find the "Fractal Image Gallery" at *http://www.iterated.com/fi_demo/images/gallery.htm.* You'll notice that images load as thumbnails and gradually grow larger as they decompress.

Figure 13-12 shows an image partially obscured by Fractal Viewer's huge pop-up menu (a resolution greater than the 640 by 480 pixels shown would work better). This

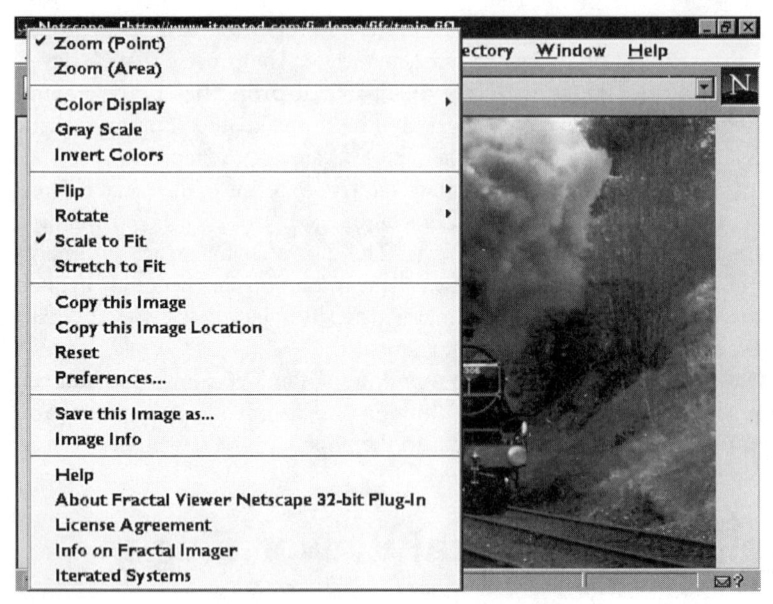

Figure 13–12 Fractal Viewer's comprehensive pop-up menu is available on both Windows and Macintosh versions.

menu lets you zoom, change color depth, adjust an image's size or alignment, copy an image, or save it as an ordinary bitmap file, and more.

On a Windows computer, you can use the menu—invoked by clicking on an image with the right mouse button—to save any .FIF image as a standard Windows .BMP file. On a Mac, you can use the menu—invoked by clicking on an image and holding the mouse button down—to save any .FIF image in PICT format.

Lesson 2: Embedding Fractal Images in Your Web Pages

You can download the Iterated Systems encoder, Fractal Imager, to create your own .FIF images with fractal compression. Fractal Imager requires either Windows 95/NT or Windows 3.x with the Win32s extensions; there is presently no Macintosh version of the program.

Go to the company's Web site at *http://www.iterated.com/fractimg/download/fi-loadp.htm* and download the compressed installer. Run this program to create files in a temporary subdirectory; then run SETUP.EXE to extract Fractal Imager into the folder of your choice.

To convert an image, you can use the program's File Open command to select an image in GIF, JPEG, PhotoCD, .PCX, Windows bitmap (.BMP), TIFF, Targa, or Sun Raster formats. If you do not want to select files individually, there is also a batch mode for unattended processing of groups of files. Fractal Imager can also save graphics in any of the formats it reads, making it a useful conversion tool.

Figure 13-13 shows Fractal Imager about to compress a graphic. As you can see, a slider in the Fractal Compression Options window lets you tinker with the image quality. A high quality factor (up to 100) will give you a sharper image, a larger file (with a lower compression ratio), and a longer processing time. A low quality factor (down to 1) will give you a less detailed image, a smaller file (with a higher compression ratio), and a shorter processing time.

The actual quality, file size (compression ratio), and processing time that you achieve depend not only upon the size of your image, but on its fractal qualities. Test your images with the preset quality factors to find the best results for your needs. In the case of the graphic shown in the screen, you can see from Figure 13-14 that it compressed from an original 709K size down to just 20K, a 37:1 compression ratio. Although it may be hard for you to see in this reduced, grayscale screen capture, the compressed image looks better than the original in some ways because it eliminates grain and other random noise. You really need to try this for yourself!

Under Fractal Imager's Options menu you'll find Set Progressive Display that lets you preview the way your images will download from the Web. Normal Decompression is the instant, nonprogressive display you get when loading files from a hard drive. Progressive Focus lets you watch images come gradually into focus as they do when downloaded via the Web. Progressive Expansion causes images to gradually increase in size from a thumbnail. Simulated baud rate governs how fast the previewing takes place, from an apparent 9600bps to 115Kbps.

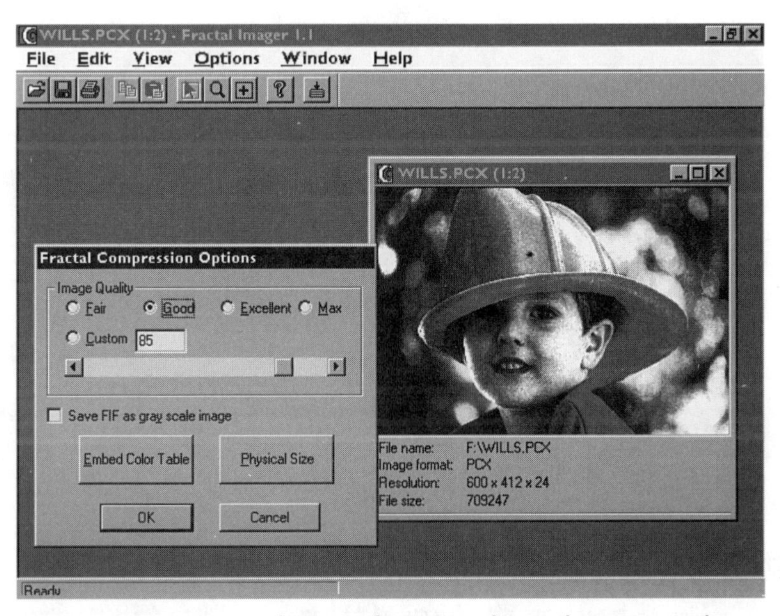

Figure 13–13 Fractal Imager lets you tinker with image quality using this slider

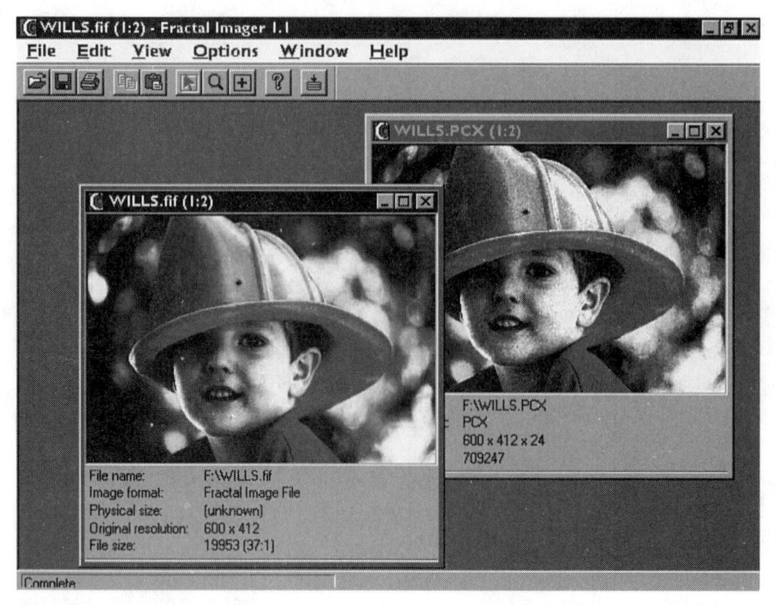

Figure 13–14 A compressed image can be less than 1/30 the size of the original

Once you are satisfied with the .FIF files you have created, you can embed them in your Web pages using a command such as:

```
EMBED SRC="test.fif" WIDTH=200 HEIGHT=200
```

As always, WIDTH and HEIGHT need to be specified in pixels. Fractal Viewer has a wide range of other attributes in addition, listed in Table 13-3. These attributes let you exert precise control over how an image is aligned and how it appears while decompressing.

You'll be pleased to learn that one of the attributes is MAP, which you can use to specify the URL of an NCSA or CERN-compatible imagemap. In other words, you can use Fractal Viewer to create and display a large imagemap that works just as if it were a GIF or JPEG—but takes much less time to download.

Table 13–3 EMBED attributes for Fractal Viewer

Attribute	Function
BOTTOMCENTER	Aligns the image in the bottom, center area of the frame.
BOTTOMLEFT	Aligns the image in the bottom, left area of the frame.
BOTTOMRIGHT	Aligns the image in the bottom, right area of the frame.
CENTERCENTER	The default. Aligns the image evenly in the center area of the frame.
CENTERLEFT	Aligns the image in the center, left area of the frame.
CENTERRIGHT	Aligns the image in the center, right area of the frame.

Attribute	Function
CROPHEIGHT = value	The height of a cropped image.
CROPWIDTH = value	The width of a cropped image.
CROPX = value	The distance along the x-axis (from the left) to begin cropping.
CROPY = value	The distance along the y-axis (from the top) to begin cropping.
DITHER	When set to TRUE, enhances colors by approximating the true color values with available colors so that colormapped values appear more accurate.
EXPANDPROGRESSIVE	The image is displayed in focus, but gradually increases from a miniature size to full embed window size as it downloads.
FLIPHORIZONTAL	When set to TRUE, the image appears flipped horizantally once it is downloaded.
FLIPVERTICAL	When set to TRUE, the image appears flipped vertically once it is downloaded.
FOCUSPROGRESSIVE	The image is displayed in full size, but gradually increases in focus as it downloads.
GRAYSCALE	When set to TRUE, displays the image in grayscale instead of color.
INTERNALPALETTE	Applies a unique colormap that is embedded with the FIF.
INVERTCOLORS	When set to TRUE, displays the RGB compliment.
MAP = value	The URL name of the Map file (either CERN or NCSA format).
NOPROGRESSIVE	The image is displayed with no progressive steps.
OPTIMIZEDPALETTE	Applies a colormap that best enhances a single image.
ROTATE180	The image displayed is rotated 180 degrees clockwise once it is downloaded.
ROTATE90CCW	The image displayed is rotated 90 degrees counterclockwise once it is downloaded.
ROTATE90CW	The image displayed is rotated 90 degrees clockwise once it is downloaded.
STANDARDPALETTE	Applies a colormap that is optimal when multiple images appear on the same page.
STEP1	Displays only the first progressive step of an image as it downloads.
STEP2	Displays only the first two progressive steps of an image as it downloads.
STEP3	Displays only the first three progressive steps of an image as it downloads.
STEP4	Displays only the first four progressive steps of an image as it downloads.
STEP5	Displays all five progressive steps of an image as it downloads.
TOPCENTER	Aligns the image in the top, center area of the frame.
TOPLEFT	Aligns the image in the top, left area of the frame.
TOPRIGHT	Aligns the image in the top, right area of the frame.

LIGHTNINGSTRIKE

Wavelets are mathematical functions that cut up data into different frequency components and then study each component with a resolution matched to its scale. They were developed independently in the fields of mathematics, quantum physics, electrical engineering, and seismic geology. New applications are being developed that range from image compression—the FBI is interested in wavelets as a way to compress its database of fingerprints—to radar and earthquake prediction.

One plug-in using wavelet technology to read highly compressed images is Lightning-Strike from Infinop, Inc. This runs on Windows 3.x, Windows 95/NT, or a Macintosh (68040 or faster). The LightningStrike compressor, for converting source graphics, runs on Windows 95/NT. It is free to private individuals, nonprofits, or educational organizations, and costs approximately $100 for others.

On the Infinop Web page at *http://www.inifinop.com* you can view images that have been compressed using LightningStrike and then reconverted to the .GIF format so that you can evaluate their quality before you take the time to install the plug-in.

If you're interested in wavelet compression, you should also check out a plug-in called WI Decompressor, from Summus Ltd. *(htttp://www.summus.com)*. Summus Ltd. is led by Bjorn Jawerth, one of the early contributors to wavelet theory. The company recently licensed its video compression technology to Corel for inclusion in future products, and Magnavox is working on a hardware compression product that incorporates it. The WI (Wavelet Image) decompressor plug-in works in Windows 3.x, Windows 95/NT, or Macintosh. It is not covered here in more depth because, unlike with LightningStrike, the compression program is not (currently) available for downloading.

Lesson 1: Installing the LightningStrike Plug-In

To install the LightningStrike plug-in, call up the Infinop Web page or check Appendix A for details on your CD-ROM. The Windows installer is called LSTPLUG.EXE, while the Mac installer is called LightningStrike.

Windows users need to download or copy LSTPLUG.EXE to a temporary subdirectory on their hard drive. Then exit Netscape and double-click on the installer. It locates copies of Netscape that may be on your hard drive, asking you to choose between 16 bit and 32 bit if you have both versions. For the typical Windows 95 or NT installation, just click on the 32-bit box to continue. You're then offered the choice of whether to install just the plug-in or whether to also install a readme file and some samples. (Since the latter only occupy an additional 100K, if you don't have room for them it's time to go shopping for a new hard drive.)

Now, you need to manually select the Plug-ins folder of your copy of Netscape. Do so using the typical Windows directory browser that appears, and then select a folder for sample graphics. Next, the plug-in NPCOD32.DLL is installed if you have Windows 95, and NPCOD16.DLL if you have Windows 3.x. The Macintosh installer places the LightningStrike plug-in file on your hard drive, but you might have to move it to your Netscape Plug-ins folder manually.

Next, restart your copy of Netscape and clear its memory and disk caches using the Options/Network Settings menu. Then pick About Plug-ins from Netscape's Help menu or the Apple menu, and you'll see that LightningStrike has installed with the MIME type image/cis-cod and suffix cod.

Windows users can use Netscape's File Open command to browse the samples. Mac users do not get the samples as part of their installer—or didn't, when this book was being written—but can access sample pages at *http://www.infinop.com/html/ls_images.html.*

As Figure 13-15 shows, the Windows version of LightningStrike has a minimalist pop-up menu. This lets you save images to disk as bitmaps or just see statistics comparing their original size to their present, compressed size.

Figure 13–15 LightningStrike's pop-up menu lets you save an image to disk as a bitmap

The Macintosh LightningStrike currently has no pop-up menu, but does let you view .COD files. Figure 13-16 shows an image that has been compressed to 1/60 its original size.

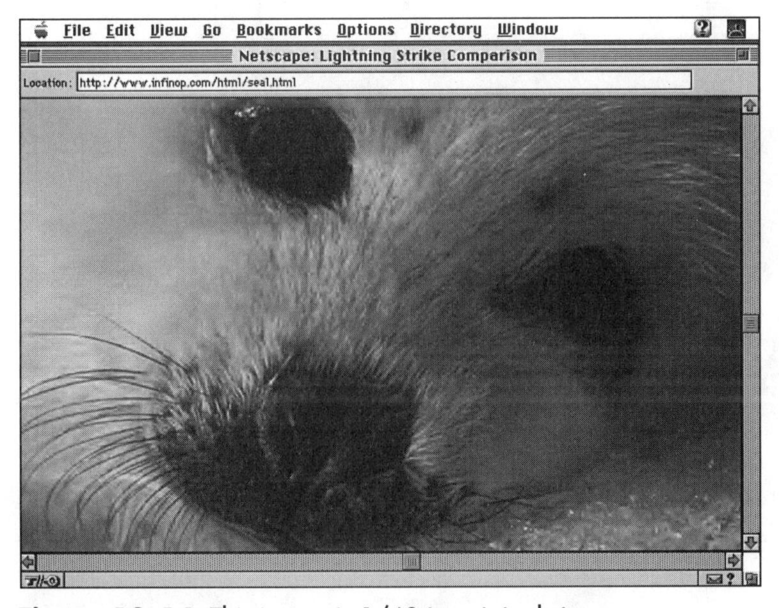

Figure 13–16 This image is 1/60 its original size

At *http://www.infinop/html/comptable.html* (see Figure 13-17) you can access original GIF files plus their LightningStrike and JPEG equivalents. Compare their quality and load times and draw your own conclusions. As the table shows, compression ratios of up to 170:1 are feasible!

Lesson 2: Embedding LightningStrike Images in Your Web Pages

You can create your own LightningStrike .COD files by obtaining Infinop's compression engine from *http://www.infinop/html/compressor.html*. Unzip ISIC25.ZIP to a directory of your choice. You can then run the program, ISIC25.EXE, using it to open either .TGA or .BMP files. (Bitmaps must be saved as uncompressed files, not RLE encoded.)

Select Compress from the File menu, and the currently open file will be compressed quite rapidly. (A good thing, because the compressor currently lacks a batch mode—although you'll find this in an available command-line version of the utility.)

The compressed image in the upper left-hand corner of Figure 13-18 takes up just 1/117th the storage of the original (shown at lower right). In addition to being much smaller, the compressed version is freer of grain and random noise (although some blotchiness has been introduced).

Once you have created .COD files, you can embed them in your Web pages as you would any other image. As usual, HEIGHT and WIDTH are mandatory attributes, and PLUGINSPAGE is strongly suggested.

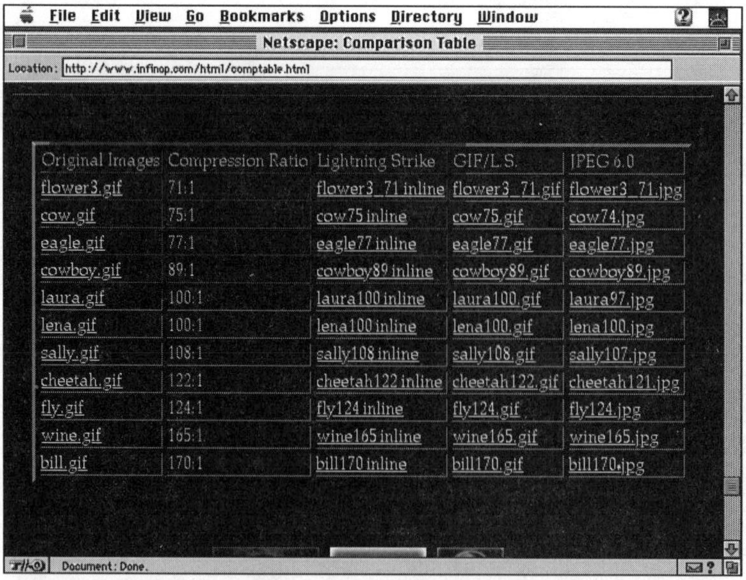

Original Images	Compression Ratio	Lightning Strike	GIF/L.S.	JPEG 6.0
flower3.gif	71:1	flower3_71 inline	flower3_71.gif	flower3_71.jpg
cow.gif	75:1	cow75 inline	cow75.gif	cow74.jpg
eagle.gif	77:1	eagle77 inline	eagle77.gif	eagle77.jpg
cowboy.gif	89:1	cowboy89 inline	cowboy89.gif	cowboy89.jpg
laura.gif	100:1	laura100 inline	laura100.gif	laura97.jpg
lena.gif	100:1	lena100 inline	lena100.gif	lena100.jpg
sally.gif	108:1	sally108 inline	sally108.gif	sally107.jpg
cheetah.gif	122:1	cheetah122 inline	cheetah122.gif	cheetah121.jpg
fly.gif	124:1	fly124 inline	fly124.gif	fly124.jpg
wine.gif	165:1	wine165 inline	wine165.gif	wine165.jpg
bill.gif	170:1	bill170 inline	bill170.gif	bill170.jpg

Figure 13-17 A table that compares LightningStrike compression ratios to JPEG

Figure 13–18 The compressor can produce images (upper left) that occupy less than 1/100th the storage of the original (lower right)

LightningStrike's few specific attributes have to do with image quality and loading method. The COLORMAP attribute, which takes either TRUE or FALSE as an argument, defaults to TRUE. This setting makes all images look as good as possible on an 8-bit monitor without degrading other images. If you have several images that use similar colors, you can set COLORMAP to FALSE. This improves the quality of 24-bit images but degrades other images on the page—even the Netscape logo will change colors because of the forced custom palette. The INCREMENTAL attribute, which, again, can be either TRUE or FALSE, governs whether an image is seen while loading or waits to be displayed all at once.

SHOCKWAVE FOR FREEHAND

Another plug-in that brings object-oriented graphics to the Web is Macromedia's Shockwave for FreeHand. Ironically, getting the most out of this tool means not only adding a program to Netscape's Plug-ins folder, but also adding modules to FreeHand's conceptually similar Xtras folder.

The Afterburner and URLs Xtras add Web functionality to FreeHand itself. With Afterburner, you can import and export compressed FreeHand files; with URL Manager, you can add URL hot spots to FreeHand graphics of any shape.

Lesson 1: Installing the Shockwave for FreeHand Plug-In

To install Shockwave for FreeHand, go to the Macromedia Web site at *http://www.macromedia.com* (or check Appendix A for details on your CD-ROM). The site uses drop-down menus to help you locate the correct version of the plug-in for your machine. (It also tends to encourage acquisition of Shockwave for Director, Shockwave for Authorware, and Shockwave for FreeHand all at once—but the choice is yours.)

If you have Windows 95 or NT, be sure to obtain the 32-bit installer for Shockwave for FreeHand; use the 16-bit installer if you have Windows 3.x. Copy the installer to a temporary folder on your hard drive and then double-click on it. Approximately ten files appear in the folder, including SETUP.EXE. When you run the latter, you'll be asked to locate your Netscape folder using the standard file browser. The installer then copies NP32FSW.DLL (or NP16FSW.DLL) to the Plug-ins folder within your Netscape folder.

Mac users follow a similar procedure, selecting an installer for 68K, Power PC, or both types of Mac. Download or copy the installer to the Desktop or other location and use Stuffit Expander, BinHex, or a similar utility to convert and expand it. The end result will be a folder containing the FreeHand plug-in. Drag this into the Plug-ins folder within your Netscape folder.

Now, you should exit Netscape, if it is running, and restart the program. Clear the program's disk and memory caches. You can confirm that Shockwave for FreeHand is active by selecting About Plug-ins from the Help menu or Apple menu. As you'll see, it has declared a new MIME type/subtype and suffix:

```
image/-x-freehand            fhc (fh5 and fh4 may also appear)
```

For you to make files available on a Web server, that server's configuration needs to be changed so that it associates this MIME type with the correct file suffixes. Ask the administrators to connect the image/x-freehand MIME type with the fhc, fh4, and fh5 suffixes. Macromedia provides do-it-yourself instructions for server configuration at *http://www-1/macromedia.com/Tools/Shockwave/Freehand/getstart.html* that you can try if you know the platform your Web server is running on.

To test your installation of Shockwave for FreeHand, connect to the Internet and go to the Macromedia Web site at *http://www.macromedia.com*. You'll easily find many samples within the "Gallery," although it is not always immediately clear which of the Shockwave plug-ins was used to create them. To find FreeHand-specific files, use the "Shockwave Vanguard Search" screen located within *http://www.macromedia.com/Tools/*.

While a drawing is loading, you'll see the "made with Macromedia" logo in its place. Figure 13-19 shows a clickable, zoomable FreeHand map of the different products in the Netscape software family. Figure 13-20 shows custom printer fonts, FreeHand having been used as a way to create characters a user can zoom in on.

When you're viewing a FreeHand document in Netscape, the pointer cursor will change into a "pointing finger" cursor any time it is moved over a FreeHand object with an attached URL. To go to that URL, simply click the object while the "pointing finger" cursor is visible.

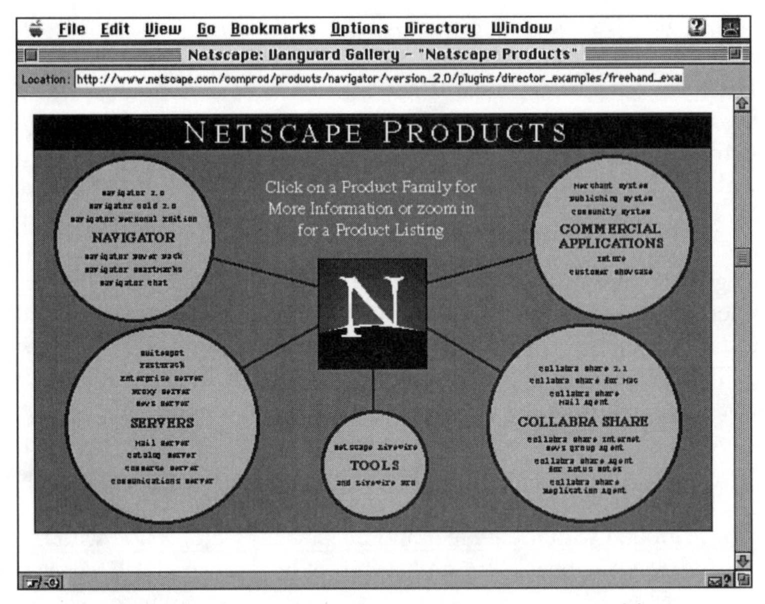

Figure 13–19 This FreeHand-sourced map is zoomable and clickable

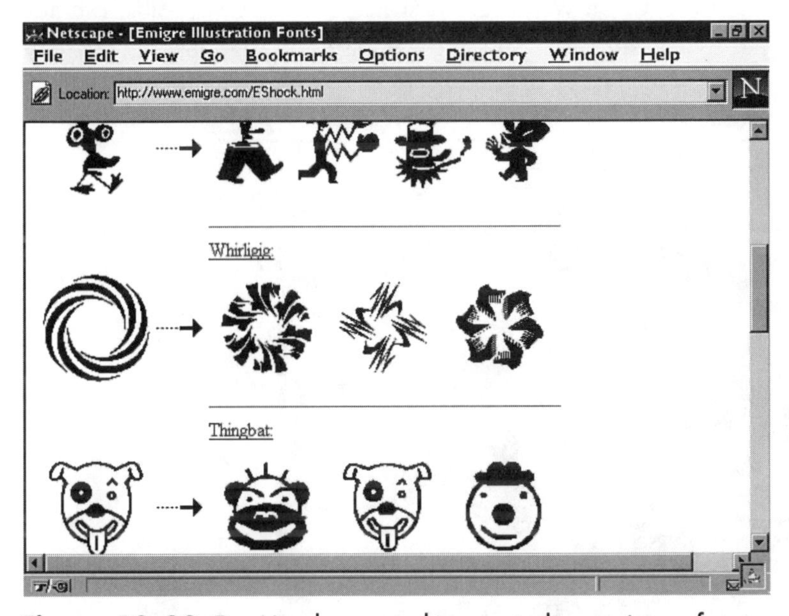

Figure 13–20 FreeHand was used to create the previews of these fancy fonts

Shockwave for FreeHand uses zoom tools similar to those found in FreeHand itself. When you have opened a FreeHand document in Netscape, you may zoom in and out (up to 26,500 percent!) or zoom to a defined area. When active, the zoom tool looks like a small magnifying glass with a "+" or "–" in it, showing whether you are about to zoom in or zoom out. To activate the zoom tool in the Mac version of Netscape, hold down <COMMAND> and click the mouse button to zoom in on the desired area. Holding down <COMMAND>+<OPTION> on the Mac will zoom out. If you hold down <COMMAND>+<SHIFT> and click, the view will return to its original magnification.

To zoom in using the Windows version of Netscape, just click your right mouse button over the portion of the document you want to zoom in on. To zoom out, hold down <ALT> as you click. You can also hold down <CTRL> while clicking the left mouse button to zoom in; <CTRL>+<ALT> with the left button to zoom out. <SHIFT>+<CTRL> or <SHIFT>+right-click will return the view to its original magnification. You can also define a rectangular zoom area using the zoom tool. With the zoom tool active, just click and drag the mouse to draw the area you want to magnify. That area will zoom to fill the entire space of the original FreeHand document.

You can pan or move around within the FreeHand document by dragging it with the "Grabber Hand" tool. To use the Grabber Hand on Macintosh, hold down <CTRL> as you click and drag with your mouse. To activate the Grabber Hand tool in Windows, hold down <SPACE BAR> as you click and drag. The FreeHand document will be moved in the direction you drag.

If—but only if—specified by a Web page's designer, a Shockwave toolbar can also appear at the top or bottom of an embedded FreeHand document (see Figure 13-21). The

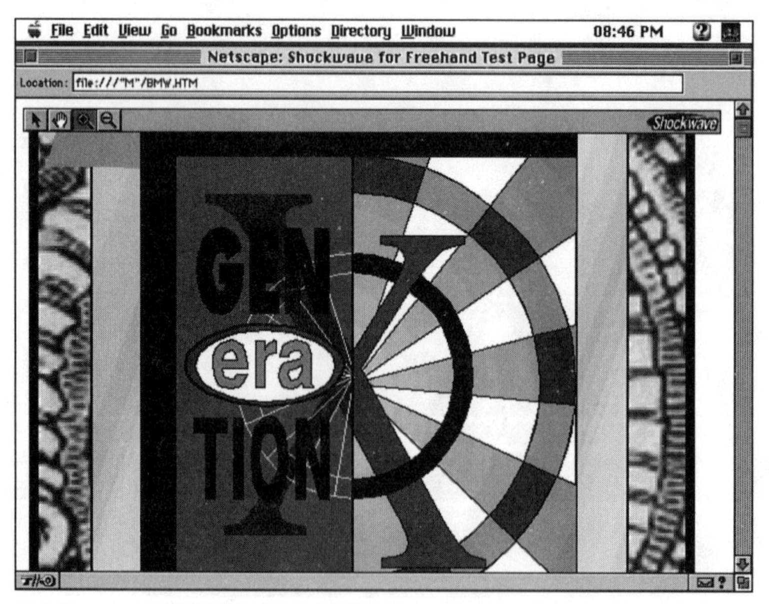

Figure 13-21 A toolbar appears at the top of this embedded FreeHand image

toolbar displays Arrow, Grabber Hand, Zoom in and out tools, and a Shockwave logo. Clicking on the tools provides access to the same hot-linking, panning, and zooming features that are available through keyboard commands.

To return an image to its original state after panning or zooming, you can click on the Shockwave logo. Images must be at least 85 pixels wide for the toolbar to be displayed. If there is no toolbar visible, you have to use the keyboard commands.

Lesson 2: Embedding FreeHand Graphics in Your Web Pages

To create FreeHand graphics for your Web pages, you obviously need a copy of FreeHand. You also need two FreeHand add-ons, or Xtras, to use the company's term. Get these from the Web page at *http://www.macromedia.com/Tools/Shockwave/Freehand/aftrbrnr.html.*

Pull-down menus help you obtain the Xtras you need for either a Macintosh or a Windows machine. By downloading, uncompressing, and running the Mac installer, you'll create a folder called Shockwave for FH Xtras. Within, you'll find files called URLs and Afterburner. Drag these into the Xtras folder located in your FreeHand folder.

For Windows, download the installer to a temporary subdirectory. Double-click on the file to uncompress it, and then run SETUP.EXE. This will install the two Xtras, URLS.FHX and AFTERBURN.FHX, into the XTRAS directory within your FreeHand directory.

Now, next time you run FreeHand, a "URLs palette" will be found under "Other" in FreeHand's Windows menu. The Afterburner Xtra will be found within the Xtras menu.

The URLs palette works similarly to FreeHand's Color List. It supports drag and drop for linking URLs to your FreeHand objects. To add a URL to the URLs palette, select "New" from the Options pop-up menu on the URLs palette. Type or paste the URL text into the New URL dialog box which appears and then press <ENTER>.

To change a URL that has been added to the URLs palette, click that URL and select "Edit" from the Options menu of the URLs palette. In the Edit URL dialog box which appears, you may make any changes you wish to the URL. Press <ENTER> when you're done.

After the URL has been added to the URLs palette, you can drag the desired URL selection to the FreeHand object in the same manner as you apply colors in FreeHand. You may also apply a URL to several objects at once by selecting multiple objects on the pasteboard and then clicking the desired URL in the URLs palette. To remove a URL from an object that has already been tagged, either drag the "none" entry to the object or select the object from which you want to move the URL and click "none" on the URLs palette.

The URLs palette's Find button can determine what objects have been linked to a specific URL. For best results, deselect all FreeHand objects on the pasteboard by pressing <TAB>; then click a URL and select Find from the Options menu of the URL Links Manager. FreeHand will then display selection handles on all objects on the pasteboard that are linked to the selected URL.

URLs may not be added to grouped objects. However, you can add URLs to individual objects in groups. To select an object within a group, hold down <OPTION> as you click on that object. Then, with the object selected, add a URL as you normally would.

Shockwave for FreeHand supports the standard FreeHand file format, so it can read .FH5 or .FH4 files directly if you place them on a server. However, it's better to use the Afterburner Xtra to compress your documents. You do this by using the Export option found within the Compression section of the Xtras menu. Click on the Locked option in the dialog box if you don't want any Web users to be able to open and edit the FreeHand file.

You may use TIFFs and custom fonts in FreeHand files before you Afterburn them, but be aware that TIFFs will become pixelated when users zoom in. If you want the look of custom fonts to be preserved, you should use the "Text to Paths" option within FreeHand to convert your fonts to path outlines.

After all this, you'll be glad to hear that embedding the resulting files in Web pages requires learning no new EMBED attributes. WIDTH and HEIGHT are all you need. You can specify these either in pixels or as a percentage of the available browser window.

To make it easier for users to zoom in on or pan around an image, you can add a toolbar to it by adding the attribute TOOLBAR=TOP or TOOLBAR=BOTTOM. The toolbar is 20 pixels high, so you must add that number of pixels to the HEIGHT specification you would have used previously.

An image must be at least 85 pixels wide to use the toolbar at all. The toolbar will expand to fit the width of larger images. If an image is less than 149 pixels wide, however, the Shockwave logo on the toolbar will not be visible. Clicking on this logo is what returns an image to its original view after having been panned or zoomed. When they cannot see the logo, users will have to use the keyboard command (<COMMAND>+<SHIFT> with a click for Macintosh, or <CTRL>+<SHIFT> with a click for Windows) to return to original view.

VIEWDIRECTOR

ViewDirector, like FIGleaf Inline, is a multipurpose imaging plug-in that supports more graphics file formats than most of us knew existed. Available for Windows 3.x and Windows NT, it supports TIFF in a variety of flavors (uncompressed, modified Huffman, G3 1&2D, and G4). It also supports JPEG, BMP, CALS Type 1 and Type 2 (TRIF), NIRS/NIFF, EDMICS/C4, and the PCX format.

You can manipulate images using pan and zoom, display images in a full window, and enhance image quality by turning on scale-to-gray and color smoothing functions. Unlike some other graphics plug-ins, ViewDirector can also print the images it displays.

Lesson 1: Installing the ViewDirector Plug-In

To install the ViewDirector plug-in, call up the TMS Web page site at *http://www.tmsinc.com/plugin/download.htm.* Or, check Appendix A for details on your CD-ROM. The plug-in runs under Windows 3.x, whose installation program is VIEWD16.EXE, or Windows 95 and NT, where the installer—you guessed it—is VIEWD32.EXE.

Download or copy the relevant installer to a temporary subdirectory on your hard drive. Then exit Netscape and run the installer. Normally able to locate your installed Netscape without assistance, it installs NPVD32.DLL or NPVD16.DLL in your Netscape Plug-ins folder.

Restart your copy of Netscape and clear its memory and disk caches using the Options/Network Settings menu. Then pick About Plug-ins from Netscape's Help menu. You'll see that ViewDirector has installed, declaring its interest in the following MIME types and file suffixes:

MIME Type/Subtype	Suffix
image/x-cals	mil, cal
image/x-pda	pda
image/x-dcx	dcx
image/x-MS-bmp	bmp
image/x-pcx	pcx
image/x-tif	tif
image/jpeg	jpg

Since some of these duplicate assignments were made by FIGleaf Inline, you should exit Netscape and move NPFIGLF.DLL out of your Netscape plug-ins folder. Then restart Netscape and again clear its caches. This will prevent any conflicts during your testing.

TMS does not supply any sample graphics or sample HTML with ViewDirector. That's not much of a problem. Although it's unlikely that you already have a Web page with one of these file types embedded in it, it's equally *likely*—dead certain, in fact—that you have graphics like this on your hard drive. Windows comes with .BMP files that are installed in the Windows subdirectory.

To get an initial idea of how ViewDirector works, you can use Netscape's File Open command to browse the .BMP files on your drive. Most of these, of course, are designed to be tiled as screen backgrounds. You'll find that ViewDirector, like other plug-ins, opens them using the full browser window, which can lead to silly-looking results.

Figure 13-22 shows a Web page that was quickly assembled from one .PCX file and one .TIF. As you can see, ViewDirector features a pop-up menu you can summon via the right mouse button. Before this menu was called up, the Web page looked exactly the same as it would have if the graphics were .GIF or .JPG files referenced using the <IMG SRC> tag.

The menu lets you zoom in and out on an image, view it full screen, save it, "smooth its colors," or print it. The Advanced Features section of the menu is inoperative on this freeware copy of ViewDirector, but you can upgrade to a version that lets you (among other things) select partial areas out of embedded graphics and copy them to the clipboard.

If you want to print just a graphic, use the print command from the pop-up menu rather than Netscape's File Print command. ViewDirector does a superior job of printing

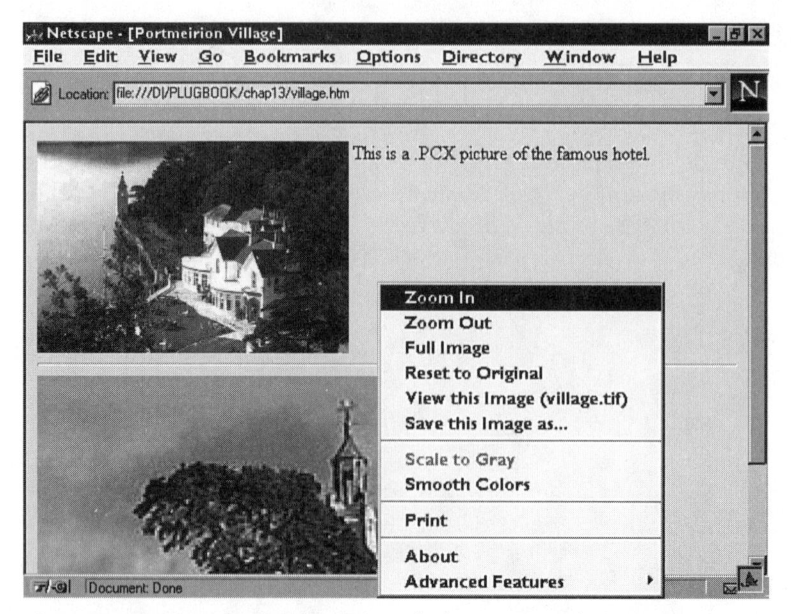

Figure 13–22 This Web page includes .PCX and .TIF images

images and can spread them over the full width of the page. Also, should you print using Netscape's File menu, the browser will no longer send mouse actions to the ViewDirector plug-in (such as the right mouse click that brings up the plug-in's menu). To work around this problem, select Reload from Netscape's View menu, which will restore the plug-in's functionality.

Lesson 2: Embedding Graphics in Your Web Pages

Actually, it's so simple to put graphics into your Web pages using ViewDirector that the topic hardly merits a "lesson." The images seen in Figure 13-22 were embedded using the <EMBED SRC> tag: Its required WIDTH and HEIGHT attributes were set to the size of the source graphics. The only other attribute used was ALIGN=TOP, which aligned the caption flush with the top of the first image.

Thoughtful use of the ViewDirector plug-in would also suggest adding the PLUGINSPAGE attribute, and a note to let users know what plug-in was used and where they can get it. This raises the main question regarding products such as ViewDirector: Is the convenience of not having to convert every raster graphic to .GIF or .JPG, plus the better print quality, worth asking all your users to download and install a plug-in? Only you can say for sure.

WEBXPRESSO

WebXpresso, from DataViews Corporation, is a plug-in that lets you embed 2D and 3D vector graphics files in your Web pages. Users can interact with the graphics using a variety of "widgets" such as sliders, buttons, and switches. In addition, graphics may be revised by data fed into them from a server, allowing applications such as a stock market graph that is continuously updated.

Beyond this, WebXpresso has interesting potential for those who want to develop graphical control or monitoring applications that run both within Netscape and in selected UNIX environments. It is closely related to the company's DV-Xpresso tool for adding graphics to X and Motif applications.

To create animations for WebXpresso, you'll need DataViews' WebXpresso Graphics Editor, which lets you edit the layout and appearance of widgets. Ready-made widget packages are also available, including those for 2D graphs, 3D graphs, controls, and tables.

Also required is the WebXpresso Drawing Server, which runs on a Web server and is responsible for translating drawing files into the WebXpresso plug-in format. It requires CGI-BIN support.

Lesson 1: Installing WebXpresso

Given all the above, WebXpresso seems more suited for specific, customized corporate requirements than for the average Web page designer. Still, it's worth installing and testing to get a feel for what it can do.

To install the plug-in, you need Windows 95 or Windows NT. Go to DataViews' Web site at *http://www.dvcorp.com* (or check Appendix A for details about your CD-ROM) and download the installer to a temporary subdirectory. This is available in two versions, either as a setup program that automatically finds your copy of Netscape and installs the plug-in, or—a quicker download—as a .DLL file you decompress and install manually.

By now, you're pretty accustomed to performing either kind of installation. Whether done automatically or manually, installation consists of copying the file NPXPL32.DLL into your Netscape Plug-ins folder. Once you've done this, exit Netscape and restart it. Then select About Plug-ins from the Help menu, and you'll see that WebXpresso has added the following MIME types and associated suffixes to the list that appears:

```
xpd/x-xpresso      xpd
xpg/x-xpresso      xpg
```

The .XPG extension corresponds to files that hold drawing information, providing the animation, interaction, and navigational capabilities of WebXpresso. The .XPD extension corresponds to files that have no visual representation but can feed information to .XPG files. As usual, you'll need to inform administrators of your Web server so they can make these associations in the system's MIME types file.

To see WebXpresso in operation, you can return to the DataViews Web site. Follow the links to the WebXpresso sample page, and then click on one of the six links provided. (Please note: This company's server will return a "not found" error if you enter any URL longer than just *http://www.dvcorp.com;* to drill down to the examples, you'll just have to use the links on their Web pages.)

Figure 13-23 shows a 3D WebXpresso graphic (.XPG file) that represents the DataViews Web site in graphical format. You can use the sliders at the left and top of the image to rotate the image or change the viewing angle. Additionally, clicking on one of the blocks will take you to the Web page it represents.

Figure 13-24, the "Multiple Graph Drawing," demonstrates the multiple graph types—optionally live—the program can create. Figure 13-25, the "Multiple Control Drawing," shows sliders, gauges, and controls.

Lesson 2: Embedding WebXpresso Graphics in Your Web Pages

Since most of the "heavy lifting" is done by the WebXpresso authoring software, the plug-in itself uses fairly simple EMBED attributes. For example, here is the line of HTML code that embedded the controls in the Web page shown in Figure 13-25:

```
<EMBED SRC=CONTROLS.XPG WIDTH=500 HEIGHT=500>
```

As noted, WebXpresso also allows an image to be continuously updated by a data file stored on the Web server. The attribute DATASOURCE is used to reference a CGI-style URL that will be used to provide the data stream.

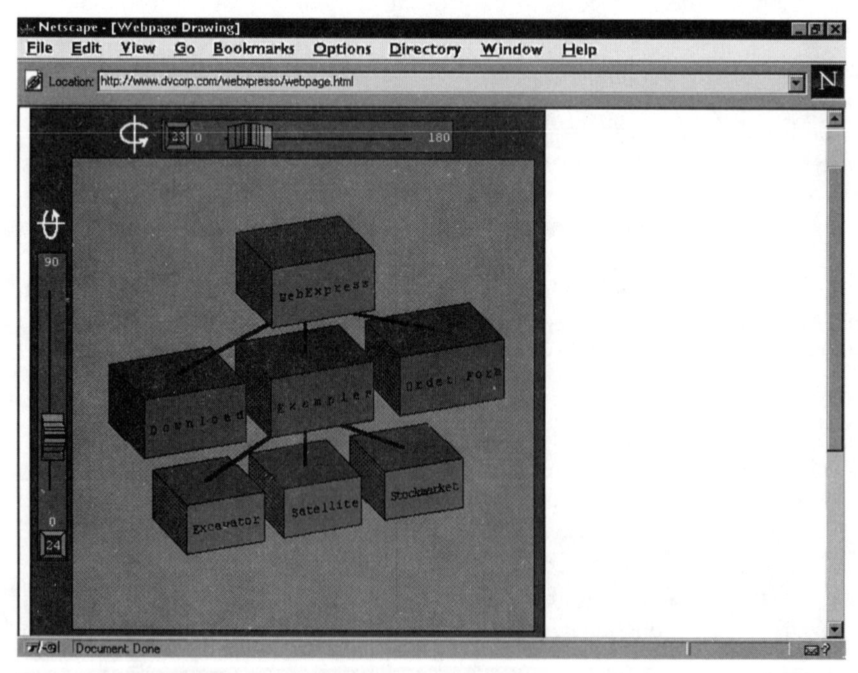

Figure 13-23 This WebXpresso graphic represents the structure of the company's Web site—and can be moved, rotated, or clicked on

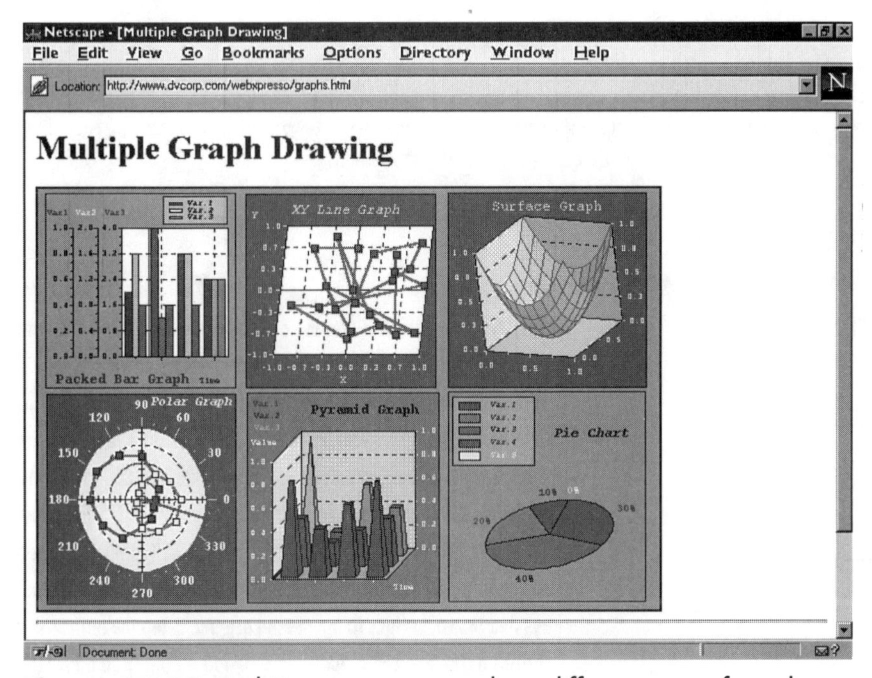

Figure 13–24 WebXpresso can create these different types of graph—here, it incorporates them all into one embedded image

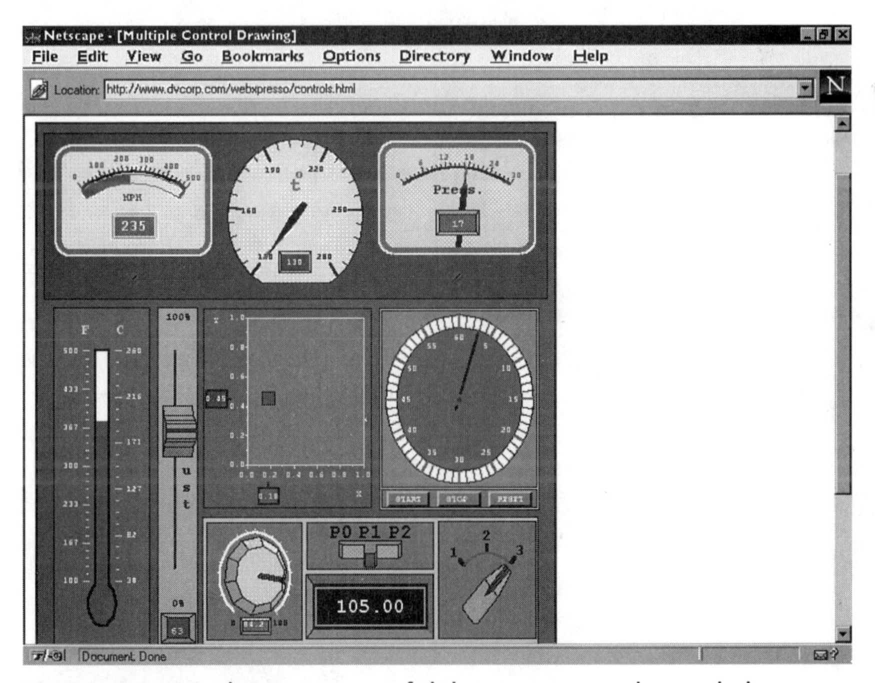

Figure 13–25 These are types of sliders, gauges, and controls that can be used to control WebXpresso graphics

Table 13-4 lists EMBED attributes relevant to WebXpresso. Please note, however, that the attributes indicated with an asterisk were not enabled when this book was prepared, and that the operation of some others (SERVERNAME, for instance) is hard to fathom without experience with WebXpresso authoring. The table is provided here merely for your future reference and as another example of life's rich tapestry.

Table 13–4 EMBED attributes for WebXpresso

Attribute	Values	Action
AUTOSTART= *	TRUE|FALSE	If AUTOSTART=TRUE, the drawing automatically connects to the data stream specified by the DATASOURCE attribute and begins updating graphics based on information arriving from the server. To stop dynamic updating, click the pause button on the navigation bar or select the Pause AutoStart menu item from the right mouse button menu. You can then use the navigation buttons to step forward and backward through the data stream. Click the pause button again, or select AutoStart from the right mouse button menu to resume continuous updating of the current page. If AUTOSTART=FALSE (the default), use keys and mouse buttons to update the graphics from the data stream.
DATASOURCE=	URL	Specifies a URL that will provide the continuous data stream for update graphics.
FULLPAGE= *	ON|OFF	If FULLPAGE=OFF (the default), the presentation is embedded in the HTML document. If FULLPAGE=ON, the presentation uses the entire page area of the browser.
HEIGHT=	Height in pixels or as a percentage	Sets the height of the embedded window in pixels or as a percentage of the page height. For example, HEIGHT=300 sets the window 300 pixels high, while HEIGHT=50% sets the window height to half the current page height.
LOOP= *	TRUE|FALSE	With LOOP=TRUE, dynamic updating from this script file begins again after the file is exhausted. With LOOP=FALSE (the default), dynamic updating terminates when the end of the script file is reached.
MENU= *	ON|OFF	If MENU=ON (the default), the right mouse button menu is available. If MENU=OFF, the right mouse button menu will not appear. There are very few situations where it is appropriate to completely block access to menu, but examples might include scrolling messages where no user input is required or intended.
NAVBAR= *	ON|OFF	With NAVBAR=ON (the default), the navigation bar will appear. If NAVBAR=OFF, use keys and mouse buttons to move through the on-screen presentation.

Attribute	Values	Action
PALETTE=	FOREGROUND|BACKGROUND	Sets whether the plug-in is allowed to take control over the color palette in order to optimize its display. Only one plug-in in an HTML document should use a foreground palette. For pages with multiple plug-ins, all others should use background palettes. Plug-ins default to using background palettes when this attribute is not set explicitly.
SERVERNAME=	String	A plug-in of MIME type xpg/x-xpresso can be a "server" that receives its data from a "client" plug-in of MIME type xpd/x-xpresso. The SERVERNAME string links the two. For embedded .XPG files, it is used to name the server, while for embedded .XPD files it is used to specify the server data should be sent to.
WIDTH=	Width in pixels or as a percentage	Sets the width of the embedded window in pixels or as a percentage of the page width. For example, WIDTH=400 sets the window 400 pixels wide, while WIDTH=50% sets the window to half the current page width.

* Indicates features that were unavailable in the beta release

WHIP!

As mentioned earlier in this chapter, the AutoCAD .DWG and .DXF formats for storing 2D vector graphics are the world's most popular. This is true particularly, of course, in the design and engineering community.

Until now, however, there has been some reluctance on the part of designers to make drawings available on the Net. Since .DWG and .DXF are editable formats, their use poses potential intellectual property and liability pitfalls.

Therefore, Autodesk has created a new file format known as .DWF, short for Drawing Web Format. Autodesk's WHIP! plug-in is a .DWF viewer for Windows 95/NT versions of Netscape.

Whereas .DWG files are full-fledged CAD drawings containing arcs, vectors, splines annotation, and extended entity data, .DWF files are more secure and more highly compressed. They contain just vector data, text, and (optionally) URL hot links.

At the user's discretion, complete .DWG data can be embedded in a .DWF file. Appropriate for intranets and other secure situations, this permits users to drag and drop the data file right into an AutoCAD session.

Lesson 1: Installing the WHIP! Plug-In

To install WHIP! you need to be running Windows 95 or Windows NT. (Additionally, using the plug-in, at least in beta form, requires that your graphics board be switched to 256-color mode.) Visit the Autodesk Web site at *http://www.autodesk.com/products/products.htm* (or check Appendix A for details about your CD-ROM).

Download or copy the compressed, self-extracting installer WHIP02.EXE to a temporary subdirectory on your hard drive. Then double-click on it. You see the familiar "InstallShield wizard," which prompts you for a folder where it will "install the WHIP! Netscape plug-in." As you realize by now, the plug-in isn't going to be stored here—it's going into the Netscape Plug-ins folder. Instead, this folder will be just for readme files (and perhaps samples, in an updated version of the installer). Supply a name and location, such as C:\WHIP!, that you'll remember.

Once installation is complete, you should exit and restart Netscape, if it is still running. Clear the browser's disk and memory caches if you wish, to be on the safe side—although here there is no previous plug-in that conflicts with WHIP!'s MIME type and suffix. Open the Help/About Plug-ins menu, and you'll find that the WHIP! plug-in, NPWHP32.DLL, has been installed, governing a MIME type of drawing/x-whip and a suffix of whp.

To see sample files, you'll need to log on to the Net. Go to the Autodesk Web site and take a look at *http://www.autodesk.com/products/autocad/whip/whip.htm*. This page includes a number of samples based on fictitious companies. In Figure 13-26, you see plans for a new office complex. Figure 13-27 shows a property developer's Web page, using a map with clickable hyperlinks.

When looking at a drawing, you can click the right mouse button to use WHIP!'s pop-up menu. By default you are in pan mode, and your mouse pointer is a "pan" icon, a cross with arrowheads pointing in various directions. If you click the left mouse button and drag, you can pan around a drawing. If you select Zoom from the pop-up menu, as shown in Figure 13-28, the cursor changes to a magnifying glass, and you can now click with the left mouse button and drag (up and down the screen) to zoom in/out.

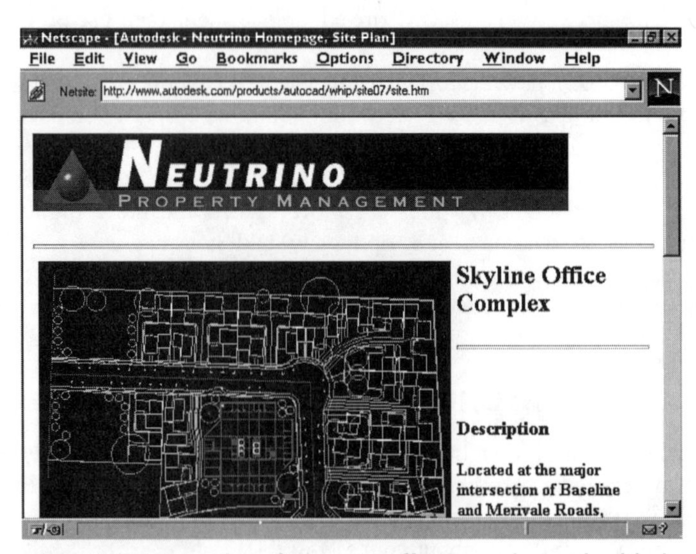

Figure 13-26 Plans for a new office complex embedded via WHIP!

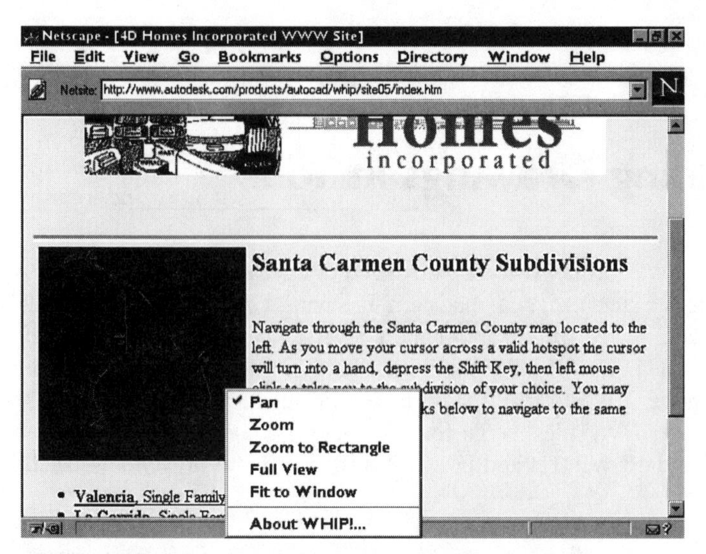

Figure 13–27 Clicking on this map will take the user to other URLs

If you select Zoom to Rectangle from the pop-up menu, the cursor changes to a cross. This lets you click the left mouse button and drag a rectangle over the area you want to zoom to. If you right-click and select Full View, the drawing fills the browser window entirely.

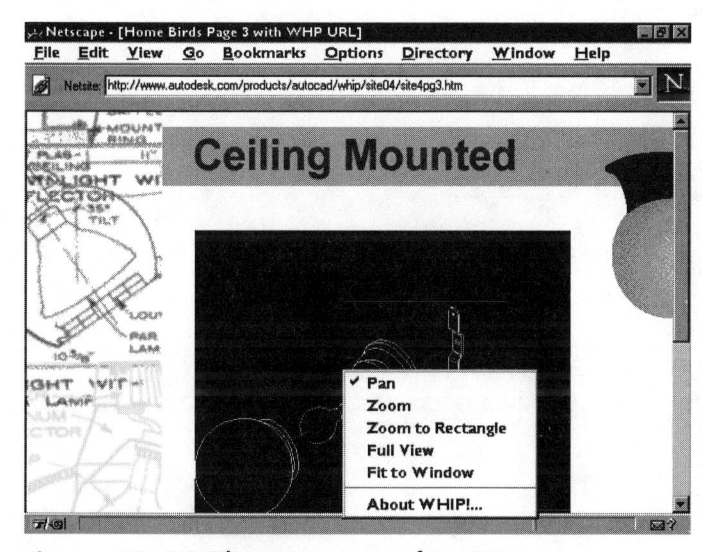

Figure 13–28 The pop-up menu for WHIP!

If your mouse is positioned over a hot link, your cursor changes to a pointing hand icon. Also, the Netscape status bar at the bottom of the page shows the URL of the link. To go to that URL, hold down <SHIFT> while you click on the link.

Lesson 2: Embedding Drawings in Your Web Pages

In order to create files in .DWF format, you currently need to have AutoCAD release 13. A WHIP! driver is available for that program that permits saving CAD files in the proper format. Autodesk also plans to release a stand-alone conversion utility that can convert existing release 12 .DWG or .DXF files. The company says that third-party CAD vendors should also be supporting the .DWF format, thanks to an available developer's toolkit.

If you are able to create .DWF files, you'll find no trick to embedding them in Web pages. WHIP! uses the standard WIDTH and HEIGHT attributes, with no vendor-specific additions.

WHAT NOW?

In this chapter, you learned how to extend Netscape's power into the area of vector graphics. You also discovered ways to compress bitmap graphics more than ever, making downloads faster and getting more out of the limited storage space on your server.

The next chapter covers "document" plug-ins. These let you publish—or "repurpose," as the trendy catch phrase would have it—your existing collection of documents, spreadsheets, and the like without necessarily changing a single byte.

14

DOCUMENT PLUG-INS

14

You might be wondering what the title of this chapter means by "Document Plug-Ins." After all, you say, *every* HTML Web page is a document, isn't it? And surely the graphics, presentation, and other plug-ins you've already read about comprise part of those documents?

You're right, and right again. But the plug-ins in this chapter are ones whose main aim is to supplant HTML. Instead of accepting its limitations as a page description language, they take over from it and use a richer format. Adobe's Acrobat Reader, for example, uses a modified version of the PostScript format. It lets you view documents that look every bit as elegant as they did within the desktop publishing programs that originally created them.

Even word processors have richer file formats—at least when it comes to displaying multiple fonts and other text-oriented fillips—than HTML does. So INSO Corporation's QuickView Plus and FTP Software's KeyView let you view files from Microsoft Word and other word processors, without leaving Netscape. Visual Components' Formula One/NET does the same for Excel spreadsheets.

Richer in appearance than most HTML documents, the files used by the plug-ins in this chapter have some other technical advantages. For one, they're usually complete entities in and of themselves. Unlike a Web page created in HTML, they don't depend on links that could get broken or on graphics files that could go missing. Also, they can often contain vector graphics as well as raster (bitmap) graphics. The resulting space savings means these documents don't have to be larger than the equivalent HTML.

The plug-ins you've read about in the previous chapters generally, though not exclusively, display their output as a mere part of an overall Web page. You might see an animation or video, but you also see HTML text and hyperlinks above, below, and around it. (After all, it's precisely that kind of integration that gives plug-ins their biggest advantage.)

The document plug-ins featured here, in contrast, generally take over Netscape's entire browser window. There'd be no point, after all, in viewing a PostScript-formatted document with multiple fonts, if it only appeared on a Web page looking like a postage stamp. These plug-ins make only limited use of EMBED attributes.

Therefore, you might be wondering if there's any real difference between these document plug-ins and the separate helper applications that are in every case a possible alternative. (For example, Adobe Acrobat is available as a helper application; Microsoft offers a Word viewer as a helper app; and, for that matter, any word processor on your hard drive could be configured to run as a helper.)

In fact, document plug-ins have some big advantages. First, like other plug-ins they centralize the software you need for Web browsing in your Netscape folder. Configuration, hard disk maintenance, even transfer of your Web browsing environment from your desktop computer to your portable—all are much easier than if you had scads of helper apps to worry about. Second, because they run within Netscape, document plug-ins are easier to use and are integrated with it technically.

Plug-ins, unlike helper applications, can use Netscape's disk and RAM caches. They also let you use Netscape's File/Open command to open documents that have been stored locally: You'll find yourself using Netscape to browse your own hard drive!

ACROBAT READER

Acrobat Reader is a plug-in for inline viewing of documents in Adobe's Portable Document Format (.PDF). These documents, with color graphics, elaborate formatting, and the possibility of multiple embedded fonts, can look as though they just rolled out of a PostScript printer—except that they're displayed on screen within your copy of Netscape.

Instead of waiting for an entire .PDF file to download before it can be displayed—as is necessary with Adobe's Acrobat helper application—you can view the document one page at a time. Files download progressively so that you see text first and images next. Text is first displayed using substitute fonts you already have on your system, but, as a final part of a download, embedded font outlines are retrieved and "blitted" on screen for absolute fidelity to the original design.

Boasting text that is automatically anti-aliased so that it's easier to read on screen, Acrobat Reader also lets you print documents using Netscape's usual File/Print command. This makes it easy to get a permanent copy of data sheets, company newsletters, or whatever you're using Acrobat Reader to view.

NOTE: In beta versions Adobe's Acrobat Reader was known as Amber. Acrobat Reader and Amber are actually one and the same product.

Lesson 1: Installing the Acrobat Reader Plug-In

The Acrobat Reader plug-in is available for Windows 3.1, Windows 95/NT, and Macintosh. To obtain it, either go to the Adobe Web site at *http://www.adobe.com/acrobat* or check Appendix A for details on your CD-ROM.

The Windows 95/NT version of the Acrobat Reader installer is READ32.EXE. For Windows 3.x, it's READ16.EXE. Download or copy the appropriate program to a temporary subdirectory on your hard drive. Double-click on it, and you'll start the familiar InstallShield setup program, which asks you to accept the license agreement and then requests a subdirectory where it can install Acrobat Reader. The subdirectory (or folder, call it what you will) needed here will hold a helper application and the supporting files, not the plug-in itself. Give the installer a name such as C:\ACROBAT or something else you'll remember.

The setup program then copies the reader and some font outlines into the subdirectory you just defined. For Windows 95/NT, it checks the system registry to locate your copy of Netscape and copies NPPDF32.DLL to your Netscape Plug-ins folder. For Windows 3.x, it checks NETSCAPE.INI to locate your copy of Netscape and copies NPPDF16.DLL to your Netscape Plug-ins subdirectory.

Occasionally the Windows 95 installation process places the DLL other than where it should be. If, in the steps below, the Acrobat Reader plug-in does not seem to be working for you, use the Find command from the Tools menu of Windows Explorer to locate NPPDF32.DLL, and then move it to the Plug-ins folder manually.

Mac users should download or copy ReaderInstaller3.0.hqx or Reader Installer3.0b.bin. Both files contain the Reader 3.0 Installer; one has merely been compressed by Stuffit Expander while the other has been BinHexed. Select an installer according to whether you have Stuffit or BinHex on your computer.

Next, exit *all* currently running applications and double-click on the Reader 3.0b1 Installer file. After showing you a license agreement and asking you to confirm which drive to use for installation, the installer will copy files to a newly created Adobe Acrobat 3.0 folder. It will also place the plug-in, called PDF Viewer, into your Netscape Plug-ins folder.

Should you have more than one version of Netscape—easier to do on a Mac than with Windows 95, since there isn't a system registry that's constantly getting confused—you'll find that Adobe has included an extra copy of the plug-in to make things easier for you. Just open the folder Web Browser Plug-in, which you'll find within your Adobe Acrobat folder, and move the spare PDF Viewer file to the Plug-ins folder of your second Netscape.

Now, for all versions of Netscape, you need to exit the browser if it is running. Restart Netscape and then select About Plug-ins from the Help or Apple menus. As you'll see from the list Netscape displays, the Acrobat Reader claims the MIME type application/pdf with the suffix pdf. (Give this information to the people who run your Web server before you place .PDF files on it.)

You're ready to log on to the Net and return to Adobe's Web site to check out some sample Acrobat files. The many interesting sites available include the auto brochure shown in Figure 14–1.

Acrobat normally loads .PDF files using Netscape's full browser window, especially if the files were referenced in the Web page with an <A HREF> tag. This makes sense because most Acrobat files *are* full-page, mimicking the look of a document that just rolled out of some kind of color laser printer. You can magnify the page on screen or shrink pages down to thumbnails by clicking on the buttons Acrobat has integrated with Netscape's horizontal scroll bar, as shown in Figure 14–2. These buttons also let you select which page out of a long document you want to look at.

The Windows version of Adobe Acrobat can additionally load .PDF files that already reside on your hard drive. Figure 14–3 demonstrates this fact in a rather cheeky way. What you see is a very elaborate .PDF created by *MacUser* magazine. An "Internet Road Map," it originally came on a Mac CD-ROM and contains links to hundreds of sites. I renamed it using a short file name and .PDF extension on the Mac, and then copied it

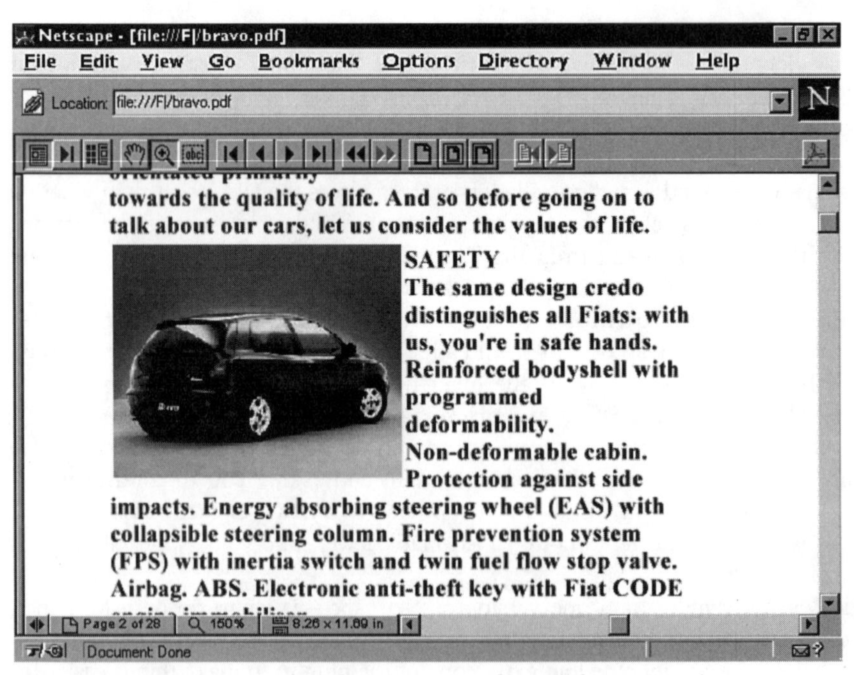

Figure 14–1 This auto brochure was sent from Italy via Acrobat

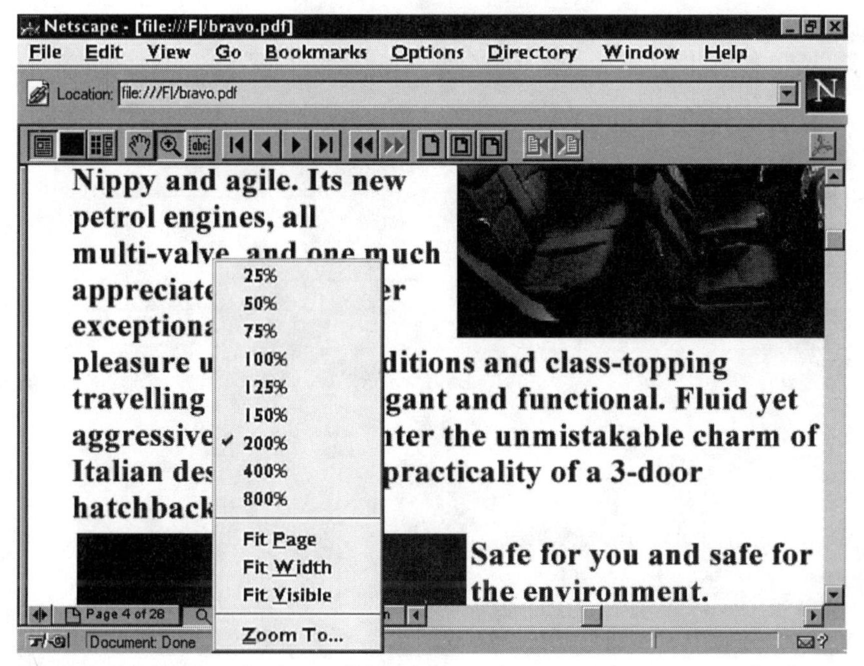

Figure 14–2 Acrobat's scroll bar buttons let you pick a page and adjust magnification levels

over to a Windows machine. Then, it was loaded with no problem using Netscape's File | Open command. As you can see, the Acrobat Reader easily handles cross-platform files.

Figure 14–3 also shows the task bar at the bottom of the Windows display in order to make a point. When Netscape loads a .PDF file, the plug-in calls the Acrobat Reader file that you installed in a separate subdirectory as VIEWER16.EXE or VIEWER32.EXE—the task bar confirms that this program is running. But, instead of displaying its output in a separate window, the Acrobat Reader sends pages to Netscape's window. In other words, Acrobat is an example of a plug-in that needs more than just the program code in the Netscape Plug-ins folder to run.

Lesson 2: Embedding Acrobat Documents in Your Web Pages

To create .PDF files you can use in your Web pages, you need the Acrobat Exchange program (about $200) for Windows or Macintosh. This includes special printer drivers that write .PDFs to disk, Adobe Type Manager, and a utility that performs full-text searching of .PDF files that were indexed by Adobe Catalog software. The Acrobat Pro package (about $300) gives you all the preceding, plus Adobe Catalog and Adobe Distiller, a utility that converts existing PostScript files.

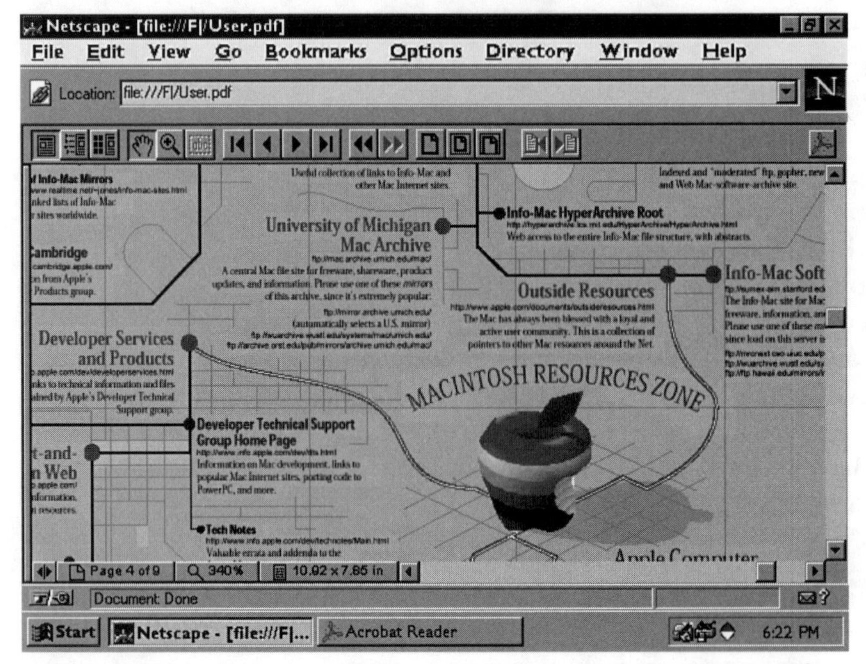

Figure 14–3 Because Acrobat is cross-platform, this map—designed for Mac users—was easy to heist into a Windows computer

Once you have the .PDF files, you'll find it often suits your purpose to reference them in Web pages using the <A HREF> command. After all, you want them to load full-screen anyhow, and using this tag means you do not have to write any additional code to support users who don't have the plug-in—or who, perish the thought, are using a different browser. Provided that they have configured their systems to use Adobe Acrobat as a helper application, they'll see your documents as intended.

Since Acrobat Reader *is* a plug-in for Netscape users, however, you can take advantage of its special behavior if you really want to. Figure 14–4 shows a .PDF document embedded in a Web page as a thumbnail. The screen shows the first page of the document; to view the rest of it, users can right-click on the thumbnail to open it full-screen.

Unfortunately the Mac version of Acrobat Reader has no way—none that I could discover, at least—to open such thumbnails. Therefore, if you use this form of presentation you should also create an alternative link to your document using <A HREF> so that Mac users can view it too.

Here is the HTML that created this simple page:

```
<HTML>
<TITLE>Fiat Bravo</TITLE>
<BODY>
<EMBED SRC="bravo.pdf" WIDTH=320 HEIGHT=400 ALIGN=TOP BORDER=2 HSPACE=10
><b>Here is our 1997 model sales sheet.</b>
</BODY>
</HTML>
```

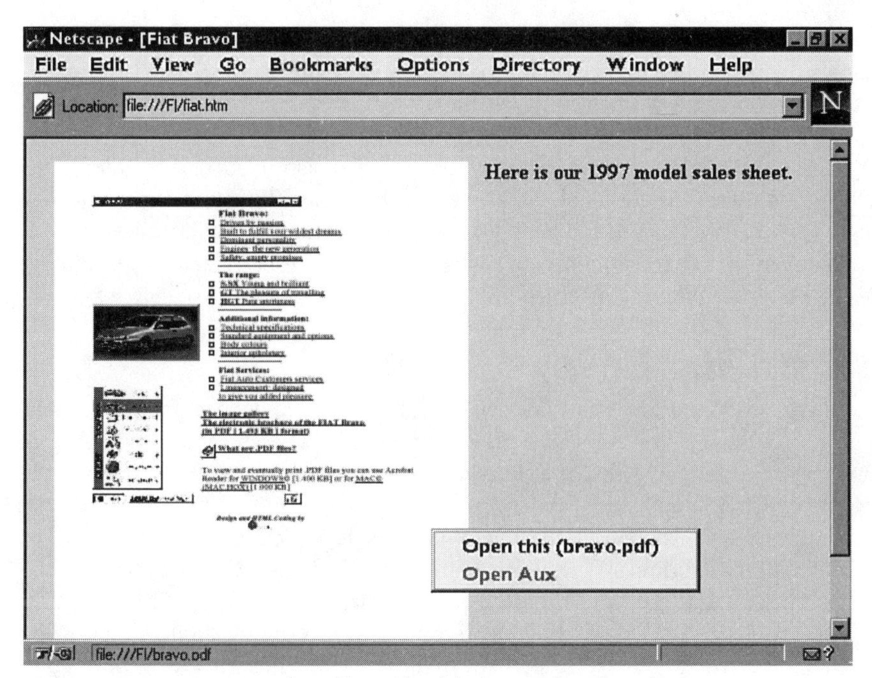

Figure 14–4 An Acrobat file embedded as a thumbnail

As you can see, WIDTH and HEIGHT are required attributes. You can also use ALIGN, BORDER, HSPACE, and VSPACE to adjust the appearance of a thumbnail in the same way you'd use them for any other image in a Web page.

Note that some Web servers do not support Acrobat's page-at-a-time downloading of large .PDF files. This feature requires a server to "byte serve" files, implementing the "Byte Range Retrieval Extensions to HTTP" protocol. (See *ftp://ds.internic.net/internet-drafts/draft-ietf-http-range-retrieval-00.txt* for more information.) Adobe has written a script that can enable byte serving on many servers that support Perl CGI scripts. You may want to refer the administrators of your Web server to information about it at *http://www.adobe.com/acrobat/3beta/byteserve.html.*

ENVOY

Tumbleweed Software's Envoy is very similar to Acrobat Reader in intent. You create Envoy documents using either the company's printer driver (around $80 for Windows or Macintosh) or by saving batches of PostScript files to disk and then processing them with Tumbleweed Publisher (around $200). The Tumbleweed Publishing Essentials package (approximately $700) gives you a ten-user license to the printer driver, plus the ability to insert links in documents, build indexes, create outlines, and more.

(Incidentally, the Envoy printer driver is included with Corel's WordPerfect Suite 7 upgrade package, which is available for around $100 to anyone who currently owns a

Windows word processor or spreadsheet. WordPerfect Suite 7 comes with not only Envoy, but also with a full version of the INSO QuickView product covered later in this chapter. It's a significant bargain, even if you have no interest in WordPerfect or Quattro Pro.)

Envoy files can contain raster or vector graphics. They also include embedded fonts that use Bitstream's TrueDoc technology. Reviewers have said Envoy is faster and less RAM-hungry than Acrobat, while the latter—being fundamentally PostScript-based—can do better at converting extremely complex PostScript files. (Acrobat files also outnumber Envoy files, as far as the Web is concerned.)

Lesson 1: Installing Envoy

Envoy is available for Windows 3.1, Windows 95/NT, for the Power Mac, for 68K Macs, and even as a "FAT binary" that runs on both PPC and 68K Macs. To get a copy, either go to the Tumbleweed Software Web site at *http://www.twcorp.com,* or check Appendix A for details about your CD-ROM.

The Windows 95/NT version of the Envoy installer is SETUP32.EXE. Download or copy it to a temporary subdirectory on your hard drive. Double-click on it, agree to the licensing agreement you'll see, and then tell the installer where your NETSCAPE.EXE lives. Click on the Browse button to find the location using Windows' File Open dialog box, if you haven't learned your Netscape path by heart now! Then click on Continue to complete installation. The Envoy plug-in, NPEVY7.DLL, is copied to your Netscape Plug-ins subdirectory.

For Windows 3.1, the installation process is the same, except the installation program you run is (you guessed it) SETUP16.EXE. When this runs, it copies the plug-in NPEVY7S.DLL.

If you have a Power Macintosh, you need the file envoy-pm-plugin-hqx. Download this or copy it to your desktop, and then use Stuffit Expander, BinHex, or a similar program to turn the program into a Mac executable. Then run the installation program you've extracted, Envoy-PM-Plugin. This copies the file EnvoyPM.plg to your Netscape Plug-ins folder.

For the Macintosh FAT binary, which you want if you need to support both 68K and PPC Macs, copy envoy-plugin.hqx. The installer for 68K Macs only is envoy-68k-plugin.hqx. Follow the same procedures as in the last paragraph, and the Envoy plug-in will be copied to your Netscape Plug-ins folder. If you have more than one copy of Netscape on your Mac, make sure you have put the plug-in in the right place.

Now, whatever type of machine you have, exit the browser if it is running. Restart Netscape and then select About Plug-ins from the Help or Apple menus. As you'll see from the list Netscape displays, Envoy claims the following MIME types and suffixes:

MIME Types/Subtypes	Suffixes
application/x-envoy	evy
application/envoy	evy

You'll need to pass this information on to administrators of your Web server if you want to place Envoy files on it.

Now, return to *http://www.twcorp.com* to see some Envoy samples. Figures 14–5 and 14–6 show a newsletter and a book chapter, respectively, loaded full-screen. Figure 14–7 shows a magazine layout reduced so that two pages appear in the browser window.

Envoy's pop-up menu—available via the right mouse button on Windows and by holding down COMMAND while you click on Macintosh—lets you zoom an embedded image to occupy the whole screen. As shown in Figure 14–8, it also lets you call up online help or save an .EVY file to disk. On the Mac version of Envoy, you can even use the pop-up menu to search the .EVY file for a text string you specify.

The toolbar seen at the top of the screen lets you zoom in and out on an image, change magnification levels, and move from page to page on a multipage document. Two useful buttons (sixth and seventh from the left) let you fit the image you're looking at within the browser window's width or height, respectively.

Figure 14–5 A newsletter created by Envoy

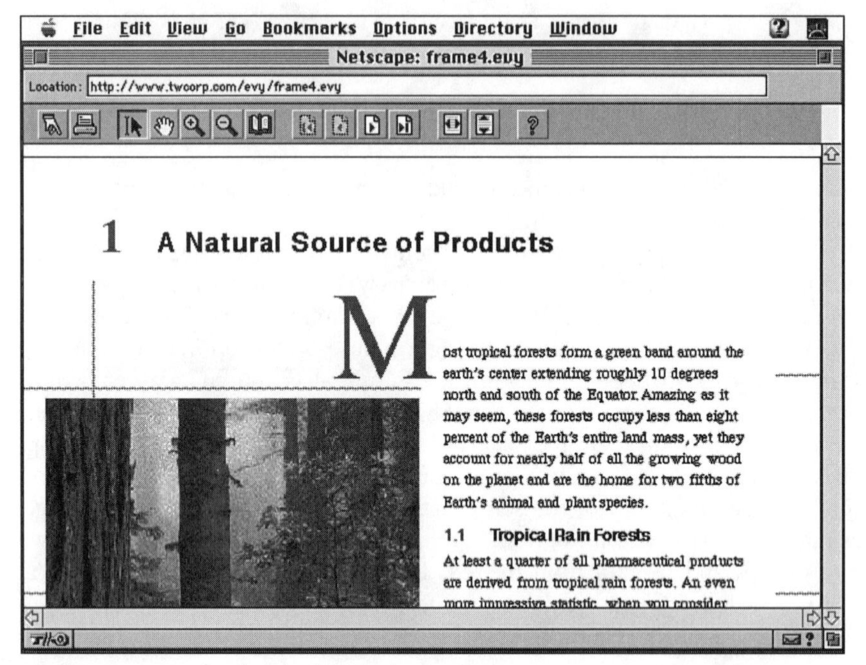

Figure 14-6 This book chapter looks the same on a Mac as it does in Windows

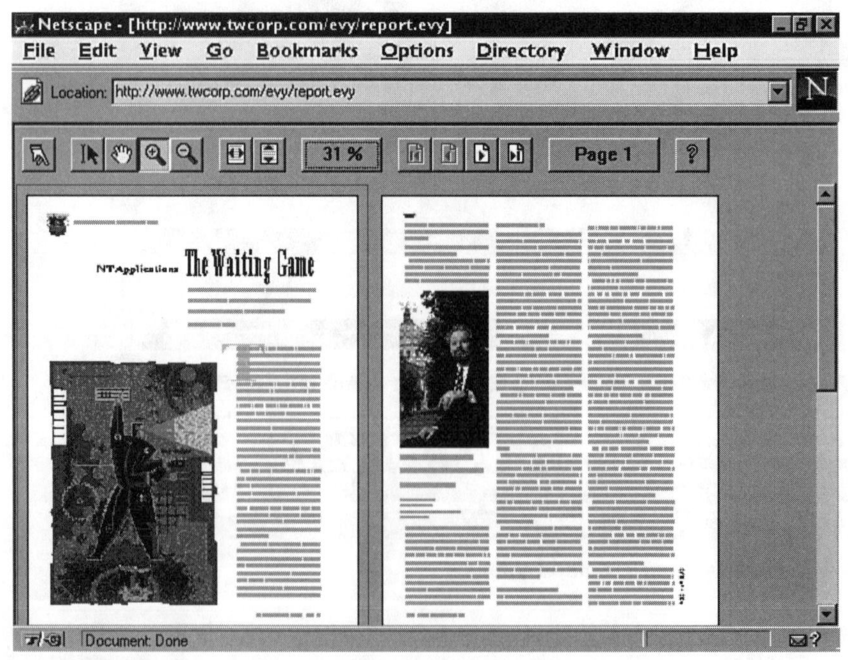

Figure 14-7 You can easily show two pages side-by-side in reduced view

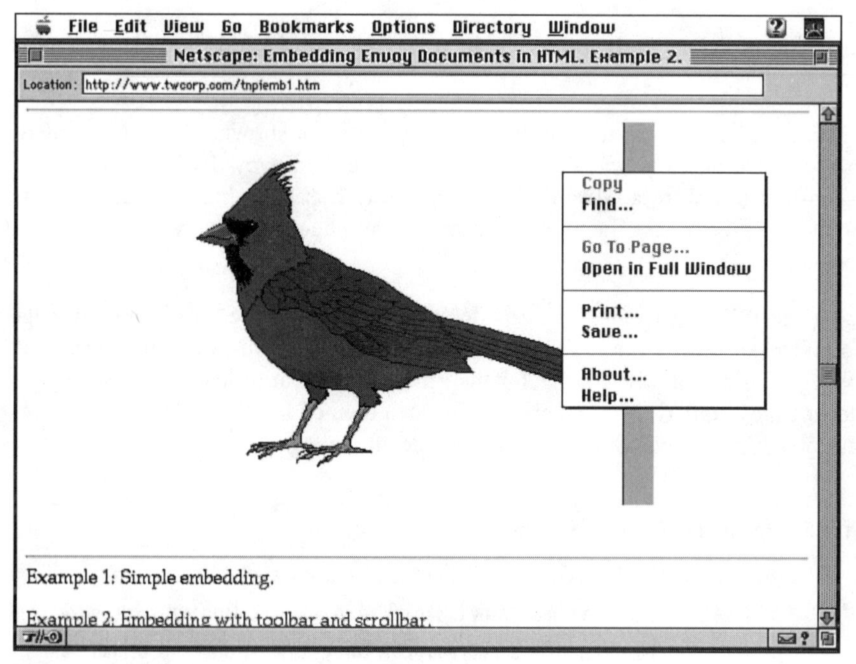

Figure 14–8 Envoy's pop-up menu

Lesson 2: Embedding Envoy Documents in Your Web Pages

As with Acrobat, you can use the <A HREF> tag to reference .EVY files if you want to support users with other browsers without any extra programming effort. If you do decide to use <EMBED SRC> instead—retain the <A HREF> tag, bracketed by <EMBED> and </NOEMBED> commands, to support users of Brand X browsers—then you have added control over how your Web page will appear.

The basic syntax is familiar, requiring only a line like the following:

```
<embed src="whatever.evy" width=100 height=200>
```

You can add the PLUGINSPAGE attribute to let users who don't have the Envoy plug-in instantly access the Tumbleweed download page:

```
<embed src="another.evy" pluginspage="http://www.twcorp.com/" width=300 height=400>
```

The embedded file will load into the window you define using HEIGHT and WIDTH, without any toolbar or scroll bar (Figure 14–8 is an example of this). Another attribute you can add is INTERFACE, which has three possible values, FULL, SCROLL, or STATIC:

- INTERFACE=FULL. The toolbar and scroll bar are shown, and the full right-click menu is enabled.

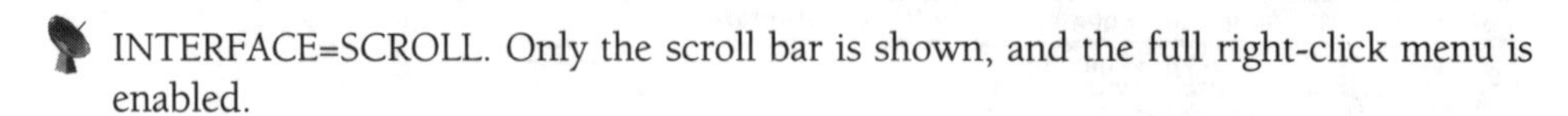

- INTERFACE=SCROLL. Only the scroll bar is shown, and the full right-click menu is enabled.

- INTERFACE=STATIC. The toolbar and scroll bars are not shown, and only a scaled-down right-click menu is available. This lets you use the Envoy document as a static image, just as if it were a GIF or JPEG image. Any hypertext links included in the Envoy file are functional. Therefore, this setting can effectively give you a client-side image map.

By using the RECT attribute, you can define a rectangular area of the Envoy page you've chosen to load (using the PAGE attribute). For example, you can define a heading, graphic, or logo. Then, you can arrange for the Envoy document to load into a Web page with its viewing area limited to or centered on the area defined by RECT. Table 14–1 gives more details of RECT, along with other attributes specific to Envoy.

Table 14–1 Attributes for embedding Envoy files

<table>
<tr><th>Attribute</th><th>Result</th></tr>
<tr><td>BOOKMARK=name</td><td>Goes to a named Envoy bookmark when opening a document. A bookmark, which has to have been created using one of the Envoy authoring programs, defines the way the document should be positioned and zoomed.</td></tr>
<tr><td>HORI=FIT|LEFT|CENTER|RIGHT,PAGE|RECT</td><td>Selects how the Envoy page or rectangle should be located and fitted to the view rectangle on the horizontal axis. FIT fits the border of the page or the rectangle to the view rectangle (this keyword affects the zoom). LEFT aligns the left border of the page or rectangle with the left border of the view rectangle. CENTER centers the border of the page or the rectangle to the view rectangle. RIGHT aligns the right border of the page or rectangle with the right border of the view rectangle. After selecting either FIT, CENTER, TOP, or BOTTOM, you enter either PAGE or RECT after the comma. Valid examples include "HORI=FIT,RECT," "HORI=TOP,PAGE," and so on.</td></tr>
<tr><td>PAGE=n</td><td>Set this attribute to the page number of the page you want to show first.</td></tr>
<tr><td>RECT=left, top, right, bottom</td><td>This attribute can be used to define a rectangle on the destination page in typographic points (1/72nd of an inch). Enter numerical values for left, right, top, and bottom. This rectangle can then be used by the HORI and VERT keywords.</td></tr>
<tr><td>VERT=FIT|CENTER|TOP|BOTTOM,PAGE|RECT</td><td>Selects how the Envoy page or rectangle should be located and fitted to the view rectangle on the vertical axis. FIT fits the border of the page or the rectangle to the view rectangle (this keyword affects the zoom). TOP aligns the top border of the page or rectangle with the top border of the view rectangle. CENTER centers the border of the page or the rectangle to the view rectangle. BOTTOM aligns the bottom border of the page or rectangle with the bottom border of the view rectangle. After selecting either FIT, CENTER, TOP, or BOTTOM, you enter either PAGE or RECT after the comma. Valid examples include "VERT=FIT,RECT," "VERT=TOP,PAGE," and so on.</td></tr>
</table>

Attribute	Result
ZOOM=FITWIDTH|FITHEIGHT|FITPAGE|%	Selects how the Envoy page should be fitted to the HTML embedded rectangle. If you want to specify the zoom factor explicitly as a percentage, substitute a number for the percent sign.

FORMULA ONE/NET

If you can publish documents on the Web, how about spreadsheets? That was the thinking behind Formula One/NET from Visual Components (a division of Sybase). This plug-in lets Excel-compatible spreadsheets appear in all, or part of, Netscape's browser window.

Within the Formula One/NET work area, users who are familiar with Excel can view worksheet data, format and edit text, perform calculations, and even save files. If you upgrade to the Formula One/NET Pro plug-in, which costs $79, you can create charts, place buttons on worksheets that reference URLs, and more.

The Formula One/NET Pro edition is also required for authoring, since only it can read and write Excel files. Version 4.0 worksheets and Version 5.0/7.0 workbooks are all supported.

Lesson 1: Installing Formula One/NET

Formula One/NET is available only for Windows 3.x or Windows 95/NT. To install it, go to the Visual Components Web site at *http://www.visualcomp.com*. Or, check Appendix 1 for details on your CD-ROM.

If you're downloading from the Web site, you'll find that Visual Components makes two different versions of the download available. One includes the ubiquitous InstallShield installation program, while the other just includes a compressed version of the plug-in itself. This is interesting in that you save from 800K to 1MB if you are willing to install manually. (Clearly, convenience has its price.)

To install the plug-in manually, download F1NET16P.EXE (for Windows 3.x) or F1NET32P.EXE (for Windows 95 or NT). Run either of these installers to extract the DLL and some sample files. Copy the sample files to a location you'll remember; then move NPF116.DLL and WCF1DL16.DLL (Windows 3.x) or NPF132.DLL and WCF1DL32.DLL (Windows 95 and NT) into your Netscape Plug-ins folder.

The automatic installers are F1NET16S.EXE for Windows 3.x and F1NET32S.EXE for Windows 95 and NT. When you run these programs, they'll extract the plug-in files and copy them into the relevant folder for you. They also copy sample files into a folder you specify.

Now, exit and restart Netscape. Select About Plug-ins from the Help menu, and you'll see that Formula One has installed. It uses the MIME type workbook/formulaone and the suffix vts. (And—you guessed it—you'll need to give that information to the folks who run your Web server before you try to place .VTS files on it.)

To view samples of Formula One in operation, use Netscape's File | Open command to locate the folder where you installed sample files. Then open the file LIVE.HTM. It provides examples of five different embedded worksheets.

Figure 14–9 shows a basic empty worksheet and Formula One's pop-up menu. This menu lets you read and write .VTS files (and Excel files on Formula One/NET Pro) or print them. You can also cut, copy, or paste cells into other applications.

Figure 14–10 shows a interactive worksheet with embedded URLs. Clicking on any of the fund names in this example transfers you to the corresponding page on Fidelity Investments' Web site. Figure 14–11 shows an embedded chart.

Lesson 2: Embedding Worksheets in Your Web Pages

To create your own worksheets and embed them, you need the $79 Formula One/NET Pro plug-in, as mentioned above. The standard Formula One/NET will give you an error message when you try to import Excel files, whereas Formula One/NET Pro not only reads and writes Excel files but also comes with a separate Workbook Designer program.

Workbook Designer, which is a 32-bit application that requires Windows 95 or Windows NT, lets you interactively format and design embedded worksheets. You can also create worksheet-based applications using Visual Components' Formula One, an OLE control for visual development environments. This lets you employ Visual Basic 4.0, Delphi 2.0, or PowerBuilder 5.0 to create spreadsheets.

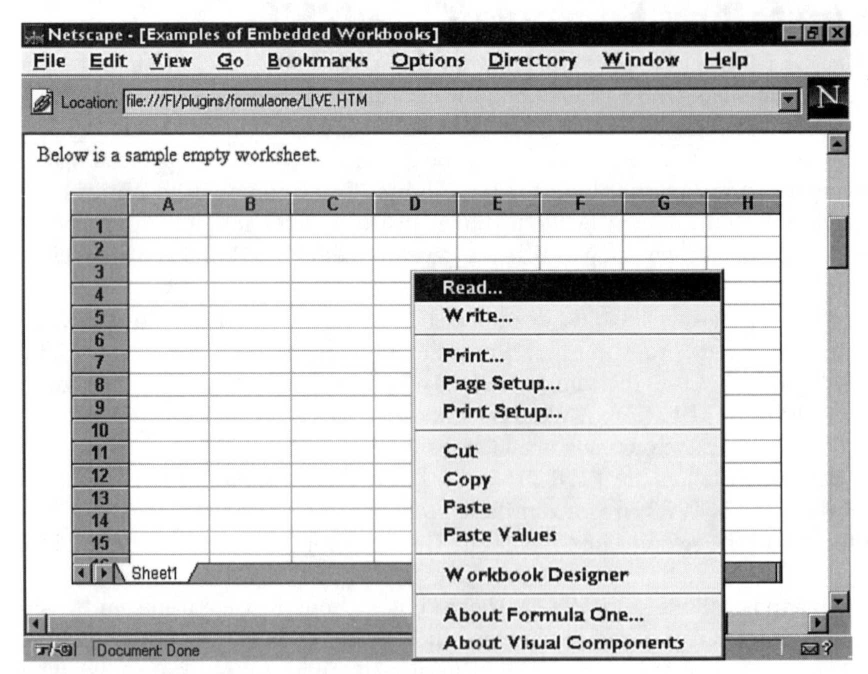

Figure 14–9 Formula One's pop-up menu

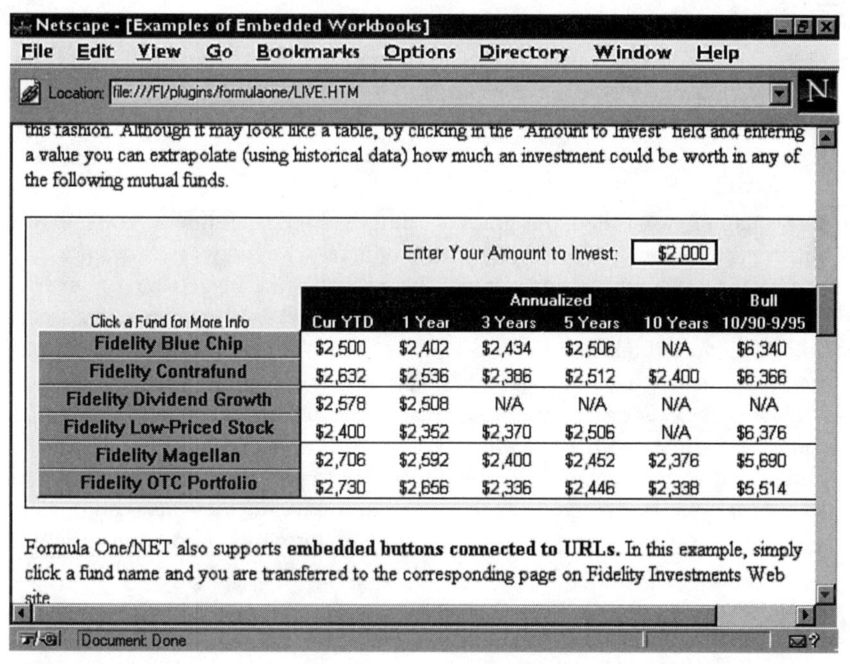

Click a Fund for More Info	Cur YTD	Annualized 1 Year	3 Years	5 Years	10 Years	Bull 10/90-9/95
Fidelity Blue Chip	$2,500	$2,402	$2,434	$2,506	N/A	$6,340
Fidelity Contrafund	$2,632	$2,536	$2,386	$2,512	$2,400	$6,366
Fidelity Dividend Growth	$2,578	$2,508	N/A	N/A	N/A	N/A
Fidelity Low-Priced Stock	$2,400	$2,352	$2,370	$2,506	N/A	$6,376
Fidelity Magellan	$2,706	$2,592	$2,400	$2,452	$2,376	$5,690
Fidelity OTC Portfolio	$2,730	$2,656	$2,336	$2,446	$2,338	$5,514

Figure 14–10 An interactive worksheet that features embedded URLs

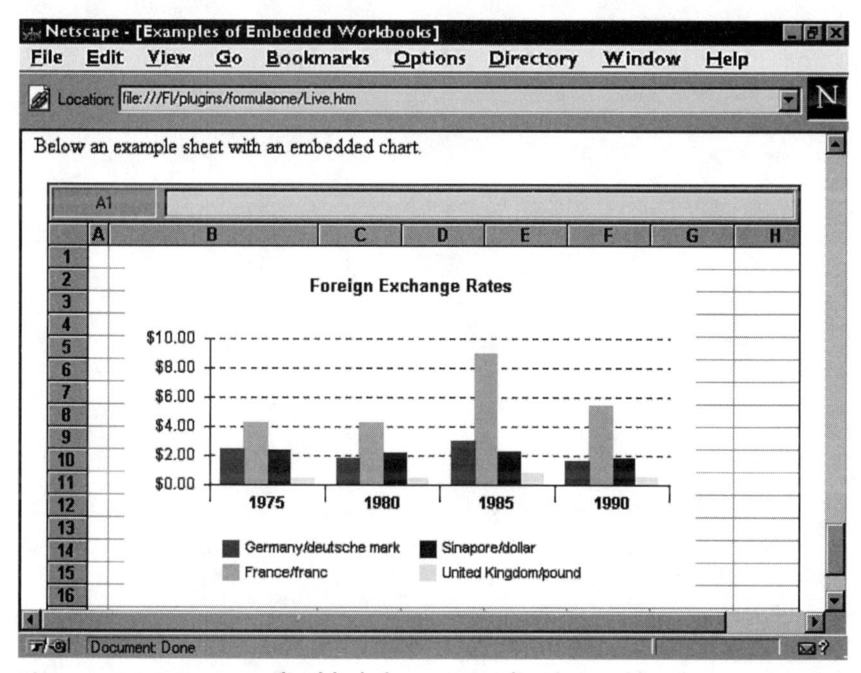

Figure 14–11 An embedded chart created with Workbook Designer

Once worksheets have been created, the only EMBED attributes that are required are HEIGHT and WIDTH. You can verify this by examining the source for LIVE.HTM, the sample Web page you loaded in the previous lesson.

KEYVIEW

In the previous chapter, we called the graphics plug-in FIGleaf Inline a "Swiss Army knife." It seemed to make sense at the time—but now here is KeyView, a program whose abilities make it more like a set of Ginzu knives. It's probably the biggest plug-in ever in terms of program size (uncompressing from a 3.7MB installer), and it is unsurpassed in the number of MIME types it takes on.

For a complete list of what FTP Software's KeyView can do, you'll have to refer to Table 14–2 below. It begins by being able to read more than eighteen different word processor formats, continues with fourteen different raster and vector graphics formats, adds spreadsheet compatiblity, and—oh yeah—the ability to play .AVI and MPEG movies plus .WAV sound files. But that's not all, as the ads used to say: KeyView also can uncompress files in PKZip, Z, GZ, UUencode, TAR, and BinHex formats. In addition to letting you view different formats from within Netscape, KeyView also lets you *save* them to the format of your choice.

Freely downloadable in beta format, KeyView will time out after thirty days' use. You'll need to purchase the commercial version if you want to keep using it.

Table 14–2 File types KeyView can view or convert

VIEWERS
Word Processing Formats
Aplix Asterix
ASCII
Cliq Word
DECdx
Executables
HTML
Lotus AMI Pro
MS RTF
MS Word for Mac
MS Word for Windows
MS Word 6.0/7.0
MS Works WP
MS Write/Word PC
Uniplex II Plus
Wang Wita
WordPerfect 5.0

VIEWERS
WordPerfect 6.0
WordPerfect Mac
Wordstar
Picture/Graphics Formats
AMIDraw Graphics
CGM
Corel Draw!
DCX FAX
EPS
GIF
JPEG
MacPicture
MacPaint
PC PaintBrush
PNG
TIFF
Windows Bitmap
Windows Cursor/Icon Graphics
WMF
WordPerfect Graphics
WordPerfect Graphics 2
Spreadsheet Formats
Lotus 123
MS Excel
MS Works
Quattro Pro
Multimedia
AVI
MPEG
WAV
Compression/Encapsulation Formats
BinHex
GZ
PKZip
TAR
UUencode
Z

continued on next page

continued from previous page

CONVERSIONS
Word Processing Formats
ASCII (source and target)
HTML (target)
Lotus AMI Pro (source and target)
MS RTF (target)
MS Word 6.0/7.0 (source)
MS Word for Mac (source)
MS Word for Windows (source)
WordPerfect Mac (source)
Picture/Graphics Formats
AMIDraw Graphics (source)
CGM (source)
Corel Draw! (source)
DCX FAX (source)
EPS (source)
GIF (source and target)
JPEG (source and target)
MacPaint (source)
MacPicture (source)
PC PaintBrush (source and target)
PNG (source)
TIFF (source and target)
Windows Bitmap (source and target)
Windows Icon/Cursor Graphics (source)
WMF (source and target)
WordPerfect Graphics (source and target)
WordPerfect Graphics 2 (source)

Lesson 1: Installing KeyView

To install KeyView, you'll need Windows 3.x or Windows 95/NT. Go to the FTP software Web site at *http://www.ftp.com*, or check Appendix A for details on your CD-ROM.

The setup program is K516DH.EXE for Windows 3.x users and K532DH.EXE for Windows 95 users. Copy either one to a temporary subdirectory and then run it.

NOTE: If you're on a Windows 3.x or NT system, you might want to retain this "temporary" subdirectory so that you can run the installer contained therein if you need to. Under Windows 95, you should deinstall the program via the Add/Remove programs feature, which undoes the changes it made to the Windows 95 start menu and registry. Thus, Windows 95 users don't need to retain the separate installation program.

The installer will ask you to enter your name. It then requests you to name a folder where it will install KeyView files (this should not be your Netscape Plug-ins folder, but rather another folder whose name you'll remember).

This installs the KeyView helper application and supporting files. Next, the Windows registry is modified, and the installer asks you which browsers you want KeyView to integrate with. Unless you're using Mosaic and Internet Explorer as well as Netscape, use the arrow keys to highlight these entries and the space bar to deselect them. Then click on Next.

The installer copies the KeyView plug-ins NPXV.DLL, NPKVX.DLL, and NPKVX2DLL to your Netscape Plug-ins folder. When setup is complete, KeyView loads a readme file in its own HTML viewer (see Figure 14–12).

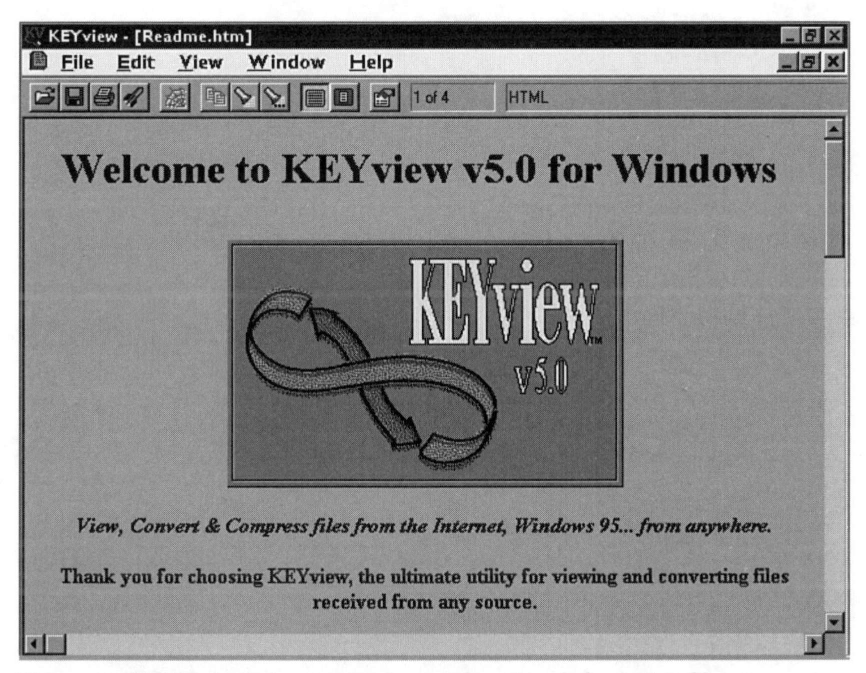

Figure 14–12 KeyView incorporates this viewer for HTML files, into which it loads this README file as the last step in setup

Since KeyView Plus takes over some of the same MIME types as plug-ins that came with Netscape 3.0, you might want to retire the standard plug-ins for safekeeping while you perform your tests. If this concerns you, use File Manager or Explorer to create a backup directory somewhere on your hard disk, with a name such as "PLUGINS.BAK" if you have Windows 3.x or "Unused Plug-ins" (if you have Windows 95 or NT). Then locate your Plug-ins subdirectory within the Netscape folder and move NPAUDIO.DLL and NPAVI32.DLL (or NPAVI16.DLL) to the backup directory. This disables Netscape's standard audio and video plug-ins so that KeyView can take over from them.

Now, restart Netscape and clear its disk and memory caches. If you select About Plug-ins from the Help menu, you'll see the vast list of MIME types and suffixes that KeyView has taken on (Table 14–3). The correlation between these and the file types listed in Table 14–2 will be obvious.

Table 14–3 KeyView handles this incredible list of MIME types

MIME Type	Description	Suffix
application/dca-rft	IBM DCA-RFT	dca
application/dec-dx	DECdx	dx
application/mac-binhex40	BinHex	hqx
application/msword	Microsoft Word	doc
application/octet-string	Binary Data	*
application/rtf	Rich Text Format	rtf
application/wita	Wang WITA	wta
application/wordperfect5.1	WordPerfect	wpd
application/x-compress	Compressed Files	z
application/x-gtar	GTAR Files	gta
application/x-gzip	GZIP Files	gz
application/x-msexcel	Microsoft Excel	xls
application/x-tar	TAR Archives	tar
audio/wav	Microsoft Wave Audio	wav
audio/x-wav	Microsoft Wave Audio	wav
image/cgm	CGM Image	cgm
image/png	Portable Network Graphics	png
image/tiff	TIFF Image	tiff;*.tif
image/x-MS-bmp	Windows Bitmap	bmp
image/x-png	Portable Network Graphics	png
text/plain	Text	txt
text/richtext	Rich Text	rtx
text/tab-separated-values	Tab Separated Values	tsv
text/x-setext	Extended Text	etx

MIME Type	Description	Suffix
video/mpeg	MPEG Video	mpeg;*.mpg;*.mpe
video/quicktime	QuickTime Video	mov;*.qt
video/x-msvideo	Video for Windows	avi

Whether or not you removed Netscape's standard audio and video plug-ins, you'll find that you experience some problems because of the fact that KeyView handles the same MIME types. That's because some Web pages—like, of course, Netscape's own—expect LiveAudio and LiveVideo to be there and give strange results when they're not. When I tried leaving LiveAudio and LiveVideo in place and installing KeyView on top of them, in effect, the result was that LiveAudio tried to play sounds but KeyView tried to play videos. The results, as Figure 14–13 shows you, are not always a pretty sight.

The fact that this happens isn't an indictment of KeyView, nor does it mean the program is badly behaved. It's just that FTP Software created the plug-in as an interface to its file translation/conversion software without knowing what plug-ins Netscape would later bundle with the browser itself.

Netscape Navigator should offer you the ability to look at the list of installed plug-ins and MIME types they handle, and then assign any duplicate MIME types to a particular plug-in. This would be a logical extension of how it presently handles helper applications.

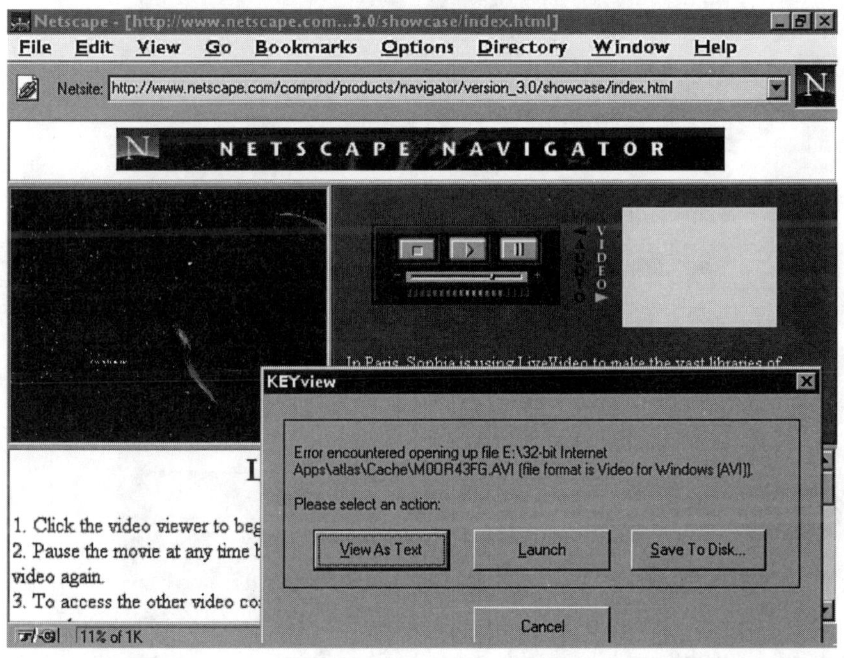

Figure 14–13 KeyView can conflict with the standard Netscape plug-ins, giving awkward results

Unfortunately, this didn't make it into the Windows release of Netscape 3.0. The Macintosh version does have such a mechanism (see Chapter 7), but that won't help you out with KeyView!

Even if you could turn KeyView's MIME types on and off individually, as a Web page author you would have no way of knowing how other people have configured the program. Therefore, it's probably best *not* to incorporate images or other types of data in your Web pages for deliberate use with KeyView. Rather, it's best to use KeyView as it was no doubt meant to be used—as a general-purpose viewer for intranets and as a viewer and conversion tool for your own hard drive.

Figure 14–14 shows KeyView being used to access a local .BMP file via Netscape's File Open command. You'll notice both the pop-up menu—which permits saving this file as a .GIF, JPEG, .PCX, .WMF, or TIFF file—and the toolbar.

In Figure 14–15, you see an Excel 4.0 spreadsheet that KeyView has opened. The foreground shows KeyView's tabbed dialog box, which you can use to control its behavior for the various file types it reads.

Incidentally, you don't have to have Netscape running to use KeyView. You can also start it from the Windows 95/NT Start menu or from the Program Group (Windows 3.x) the installation program created.

When you're through testing KeyView, remember to reinstall LiveAudio and LiveAudio plug-ins if you moved them in the course of this lesson.

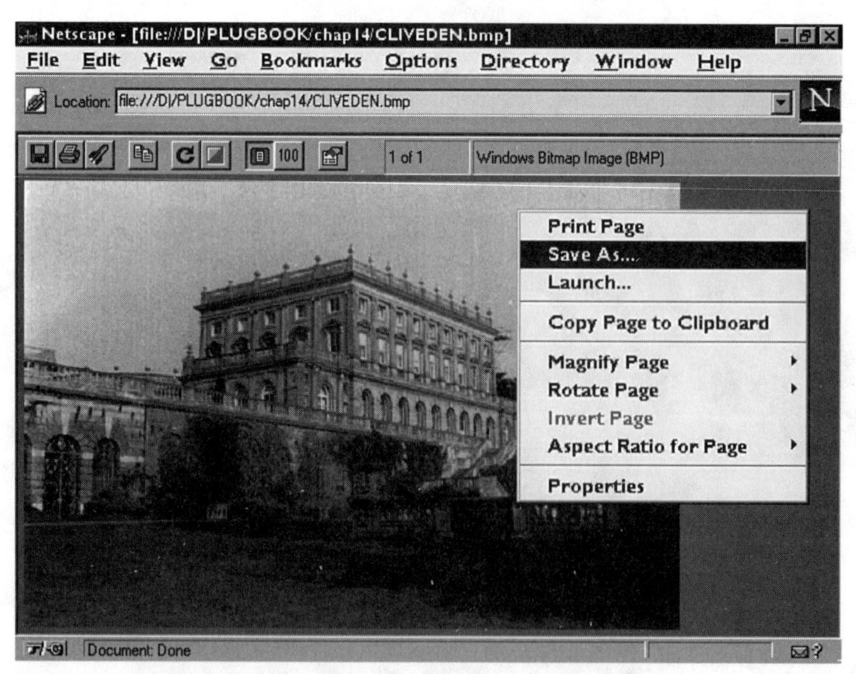

Figure 14–14 A Windows bitmap as viewed by KeyView

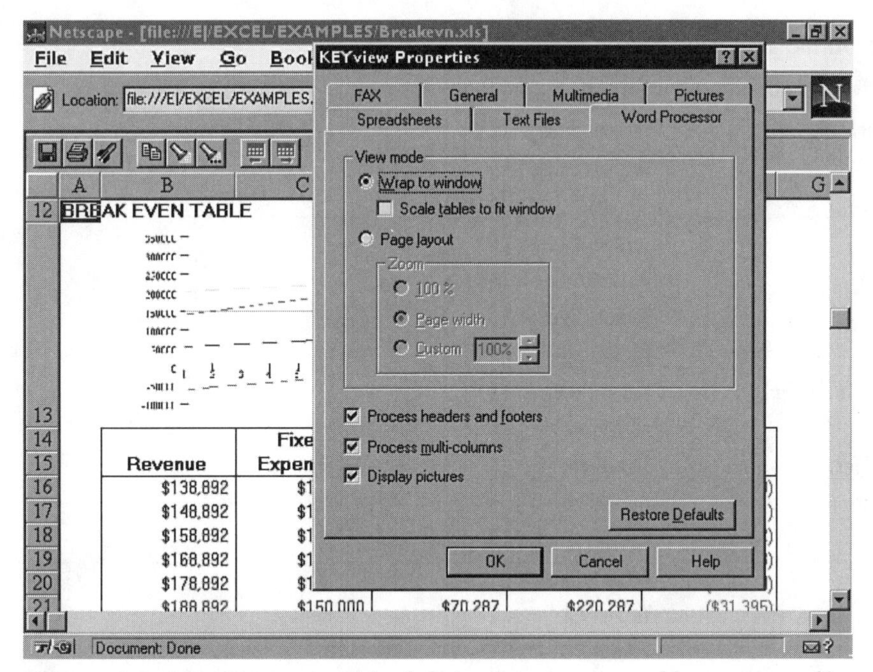

Figure 14–15 KeyView's tabbed dialog box can control how various file types are viewed

QUICKVIEW PLUS

INSO Corporation is known to software developers for its spell-check technology, and to consumers for its Outside In file viewer. The company's first plug-in was Word Viewer, which focused on letting you view Word documents from within Netscape.

Word Viewer is still available as a free download, but now there's QuickView Plus, which includes the viewer for Word files plus a *lot* more. Alas, this QuickView Plus "trial-ware edition" software will self-destruct 30 days after installation. Don't be surprised if, once you've seen what it can do, you find yourself filling out an order form. (As noted earlier in this chapter, the most economical way to get the product is with Corel's WordPerfect Suite 7 update.)

QuickView probably handles even more file formats than KeyView—but who's counting (and who wants to)? A complete list appears in Table 14–4. This table was compiled from information supplied by INSO Corporation, not from actual testing on my part—otherwise you wouldn't have been able to read this book for, oh, about six months. If there is one particular format you're concerned with, be sure to test how it behaves in QuickView Plus before you go further.

Table 14–4 File formats handled by QuickView

Document Formats	Versions
Ami/Ami Professional	Versions through 3.1
DEC WPS Plus (DX)	Versions through 4.1
DisplayWrite 2 & 3 (TXT)	All versions
DisplayWrite 4 & 5	Versions through 2.0
Enable	Versions 3.0, 4.0, and 4.5
First Choice	Versions through 3.0
Framework	Version 3.0
HTML (Internet World Wide Web)	Versions through 3.0
IBM FFT	All versions
IBM Revisable Form Text	All versions
IBM Writing Assistant	Version 1.01
JustWrite	Versions through 3.0
Legacy	Versions through 1.1
MacWrite II	Version 1.1
Manuscript	Version 2.0
MASS11	Versions through 8.0
Microsoft Rich Text Format	Versions through 2.0
Microsoft Windows Write	Versions through 3.0
Microsoft Word for DOS	Versions through 6.0
Microsoft Word for Macintosh	Versions 4.0 through 6.0
Microsoft Word for Windows	Versions through 7.0
Microsoft Works for DOS	Versions through 2.0
Microsoft Works for Macintosh	Versions through 2.0
Microsoft Works for Windows	Versions through 4.0
MultiMate	Versions through 4.0
Navy DIF	All versions
Nota Bene	Version 3.0
Office Writer	Version 4.0 to 6.0
PC-File Letter	Versions through 5.0
PC-File+ Letter	Versions through 3.0
PFS:Write	Versions A, B, and C
Plain Text (including ASCII, ANSI, Unicode)	n/a
Plain Text with UUEncoded objects	n/a
Professional Write	Versions through 2.1
Professional Write Plus	Version 1.0
Q&A	Version 2.0

Document Formats	Versions
Q&A Write for Windows	Version 3.0
Samna Word	Versions through Samna Word IV+
SmartWare II	Version 1.02
Sprint	Versions through 1.0
Total Word	Version 1.2
Volkswriter 3 & 4	Versions through 1.0
Wang PC (IWP)	Versions through 2.6
WordMARC	Versions through Composer Plus
WordPerfect	Versions through 6.1
WordPerfect for Macintosh	Versions 1.02 through 3.0
WordPerfect for Windows	Versions through 6.1
WordStar	Versions through 7.0
WordStar 2000	Versions through 3.0
WordStar for Windows	Version 1.0
XyWrite	Versions through III Plus
Spreadsheet Formats	
Enable	Versions 3.0, 4.0, and 4.5
First Choice	Versions through 3.0
Framework	Version 3.0
Lotus 1-2-3 Charts for DOS & Windows	Versions through 5.0
Lotus 1-2-3 Charts for OS/2	Versions through 2.0
Lotus 1-2-3 for DOS & Windows	Versions through 5.0
Lotus 1-2-3 for OS/2	Versions through 2.0
Lotus Symphony	Versions 1.0,1.1, and 2.0
Microsoft Excel Charts	Versions 3.0 through 7.0
Microsoft Excel for Macintosh	Versions 3.0 through 4.0
Microsoft Excel for Windows	Versions 2.2 through 7.0
Microsoft Multiplan	Version 4.0
Microsoft Works for DOS	Versions through 2.0
Microsoft Works for Macintosh	Versions through 2.0
Microsoft Works for Windows	Versions through 4.0
Mosaic Twin	Version 2.5
PFS:Professional Plan	Version 1.0
QuattroPro for DOS	Versions through 5.0
QuattroPro for Windows	Versions through 6.0
SmartWare II	Version 1.02

continued on next page

continued from previous page

Document Formats	Versions
SuperCalc 5	Version 4.0
VP Planner 3D	Version 1.0
Database Formats	
Access	Versions through 2.0
DataEase	Version 4.0
dBASE	Versions through 5.0
dBXL	Version 1.3
Enable	Versions 3.0, 4.0, and 4.5
First Choice	Versions through 3.0
FoxBase	Version 2.1
Framework	Version 3.0
Microsoft Works for DOS	Versions through 2.0
Microsoft Works for Macintosh	Versions through 2.0
Microsoft Works for Windows	Versions through 4.0
Paradox for DOS	Versions through 4.0
Paradox for Windows	Versions through 1.0
Personal R:BASE	Version 1.0
Q&A	Versions through 2.0
R:BASE	Versions through 3.1
R:BASE System V	Version 1.0
Reflex	Version 2.0
SmartWare II	Version 1.02
Graphic Formats	
Ami Draw (SDW)	n/a
AutoCAD DXF (Binary and ASCII)	Versions 12 and 13
Binary Group 3 Fax	All versions
CompuServe GIF	All versions
Computer Graphics Metafile	n/a
Corel Draw! (TIFF header only)	Versions 2.0 through 5.0
DCX (multipage PCX)	n/a
Encapsulated PostScript (TIFF header only)	n/a
GEM Paint (IMG)	n/a
HPGL Hewlett Packard Graphics Language	Version 2
JPEG	All versions
Lotus PIC	n/a
Lotus Snapshot	All versions

Document Formats	Versions
Macintosh PICT1 & PICT2 (Bitmap only)	n/a
MacPaint	n/a
Micrografx Designer and Draw (DRW)	Versions through 4.0
OS/2 Bitmap	All versions
PCX (Paintbrush)	All versions
TIFF	Versions through 6
TIFF CCITT Group 3 & 4	Verisons through 6
Truevision TGA (TARGA)	Version 2.0
Windows Bitmap	All versions
Windows Cursor	All versions
Windows Icon	All versions
Windows Metafile	Versions through 3.1
WordPerfect Graphics (WPG and WPG2)	Versions through 2.0
Presentation Formats	
Freelance for OS/2	Versions through 2.0
Freelance for Windows	Version 2.0
Harvard Graphics for DOS	Versions 2.x and 3.x
Microsoft PowerPoint for Macintosh	Version 4.0
Microsoft PowerPoint for Windows	Versions through 7.0
Compressed and Collection Formats	
Microsoft Binder	Version 7.0
Unix Compress	n/a
Unix TAR	n/a
ZIP	PKWARE versions through 2.04g
Other Formats	
DOS EXE	All versions
Windows 16-bit EXE or DLL	All versions
Windows 32-bit EXE or DLL	All versions

Lesson 1: Installing QuickView Plus

To install QuickView Plus, you need either Windows 95 or NT. Go to the INSO Corporation Web site at *http://www.inso.com,* or check Appendix A for details on your CD-ROM. Download the installation file QVPTRW32.EXE for Windows 95/NT or QVPTRW32.EXE for Windows 3.x to a temporary subdirectory on your hard drive.

Run the installer, and you'll be prompted for a subdirectory where QuickView Plus will be installed. (This should not be the same as your Netscape Plug-ins folder; only the

Plug-in component of the program will go there.) Then the installer will ask whether you want to install the QuickView Plus viewers plus help and sample files, or just the viewers (for a savings of about 1.4MB).

QuickView Plus makes changes in the Windows 95 registry and other configuration files so that it can appear on the context menu (available when you right-click on any file in Explorer, Exchange, Find, and Open and Save dialog boxes). Next, it asks if you want to integrate its operations into Norton Navigator or any Web browsers; just click on the Next button to continue.

The installer now scans to see if any of the programs it can integrate with can be found. It will find Netscape Navigator, and perhaps others, on your computer (see Figure 14–16). Next, it asks if you want to install QuickView Plus as a plug-in or as a helper application (see Figure 14–17). Make sure "plug-in" is checked and continue.

Once the installer finishes running, you can restart Netscape. Then open About Plug-ins from the Help menu, or just use File Manager or Explorer to look in your Netscape Plug-ins subdirectory. At first glance, it will seem as though QuickView made a real mess in there: It has installed 43 different Dynamic Link Libraries, numbered NPQ00032.DLL through NPQ04232.DLL. (If you have Windows 3.x, the file prefixes end in 16 rather than 32.)

As the About Plug-ins list reveals, however, each of these DLLs is associated with a different MIME type. What this means is that you can choose just the ones you need.

Figure 14–16 Here the QuickView installer has found two Navigators, Norton and Netscape

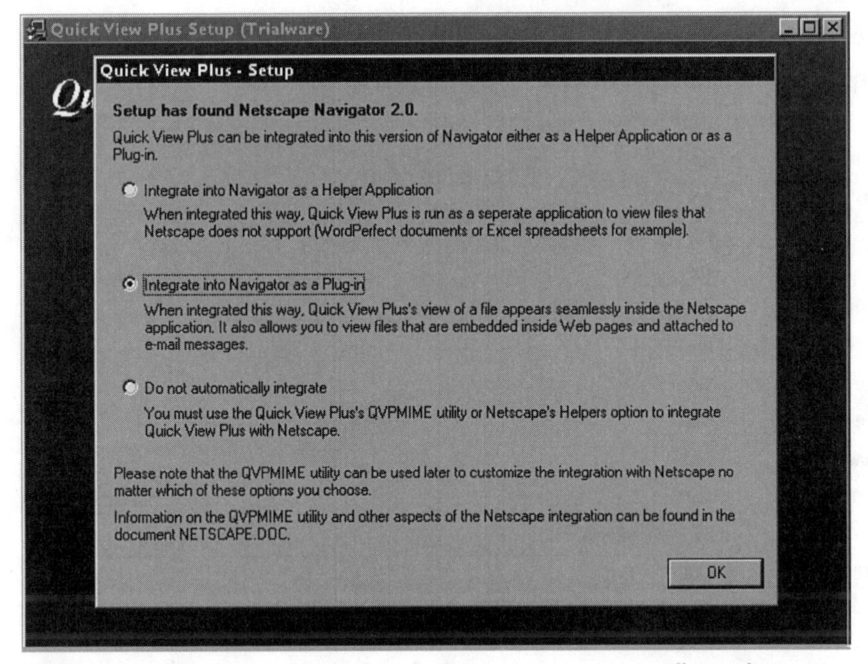

Figure 14–17 This screen asks whether you want to install QuickView Plus as a plug-in or a helper application

How? By deleting them manually from your Plug-ins folder, if that's how you want to do it. But INSO, anticipating the release of such a tool by Netscape itself, has created a program called QVPMIME. Installed in the SUPPORT folder within the QuickView Plus subdirectory, it's a utility that lets you view all the MIME types currently being handled by Netscape plug-ins.

NOTE: If you're using the Windows 3.1 version of QuickView Plus, the QVPMIME program is in a subdirectory called ADDONS, again within the QuickView Plus subdirectory.

A further explanation of QVPMIME appears in a file called NETSCAPE.DOC in your QuickView Plus subdirectory. Well worth reading, this file is a concise, lucid discussion of MIME types and how they impact the Netscape user. My debt to it in the paragraphs that follow is gratefully acknowledged.

When QuickView Plus is installed, it sets itself up to be the plug-in for MIME types and extensions listed in Table 14–5. You can readily see the correlation between this list and Table 14–4.

Table 14–5 The MIME types and suffixes QuickView Plus can handle

MIME Type/Subtype	Extension (suffix)
application/dca-rft	rft,fft
application/dec-dx	dx
application/msword	doc
application/rtf	rtf
application/x-ami	sam
application/x-compress	z,taz
application/x-dbase	dbf
application/x-enable-spreadsheet	ssf
application/x-enable-wp	wpf
application/x-framework	fw3
application/x-freelance	pre
application/x-lotus123	wks,wk3,wk4,wg2
application/x-msaccess	mdb
application/x-msbinder	odb
application/x-msexcel	xls,xlc
application/x-mspowerpoint	ppt
application/x-msworks-db	wdb
application/x-msworks-wp	wps
application/x-mswrite	wri
application/x-multiplan	mod
application/x-paradox	db
application/x-quattro-dos	wq1,wq2
application/x-quattro-win	wb1,wb2
application/x-quickviewplus	qvp
application/x-supercalc5	cal
application/x-tar	tar
application/x-wordperfect6	wpd
application/zip	zip
image/tiff	tif,tiff
image/x-amidraw	sdw
image/x-autocad	dxf
image/x-cgm	cgm
image/x-gem	img
image/x-harvard-graphics	sy3,ch3
image/x-hpgl	pgl

MIME Type/Subtype	Extension (suffix)
image/x-lotus-pic	pic
image/x-micrografx	drw
image/x-pc-paintbrush	pcx,dcx
image/x-targa	tga,targa
image/x-win-bitmap	bmp,ico,cur,rle,dib
image/x-win-metafile	wmf
image/x-wordperfect-graphics	wpg

While these types cover the needs of most users, they might not be right for you. For example, you might have a utility for uncompressing ZIP files you like better than the support in QuickView Plus. In such a case, you might wish to remove QuickView Plus's support for the application/zip MIME type, allowing you to install your favorite ZIP utility as a helper application. Alternatively, you might have MIME types that your corporation uses internally or were unknown to INSO Corporation that you want QuickView Plus to handle. For instance, your corporate intranet might use application/wordperfect instead of application/x-wordperfect6 as a MIME type for WordPerfect documents.

The QVPMIME utility can get around these problems. It differs from the Helpers tab within Netscape's Options/General Preferences menu in that it doesn't include many default MIME types. The authors reasoned that since many of these are hard-coded into Netscape Navigator and cannot be changed, they might as well make the control panel more readable.

Additionally, QVPMIME shows you all the MIME types on your system that are being supported by plug-ins. For each, you can find out which .DLL file is providing the support. Although the list in About Plug-ins does this, QVPMIME has the added ability to control the MIME types that are related to QuickView. For each one, you can determine whether it will be sent to the QuickView plug-in, to a helper application, or just saved to disk.

Run QVPMIME.EXE as you would any other Windows application. If you are going to use it often, you might create an icon for it in Program Manager under Windows 3.1 or add it to your Start/Programs menu under Windows 95.

QVPMIME consists of a single dialog box, as shown in Figure 14–18. If, as you see here, the "Plug-in other into Netscape" button is selected, the other choices are grayed out. This means that a plug-in other than QuickView Plus is installed for the selected MIME type. When this is the case, you will not be able to change this MIME type to a different action because QVPMIME has no control over plug-ins that are not QuickView Plus's.

As suggested in the section on KeyView, you probably will not want to create external Web pages that make use of multiple MIME types in QuickView. It is too hard to know the way in which your users might have installed the plug-in. QuickView is, however, ideal for intranets, where software distribution and installation may be tightly controlled.

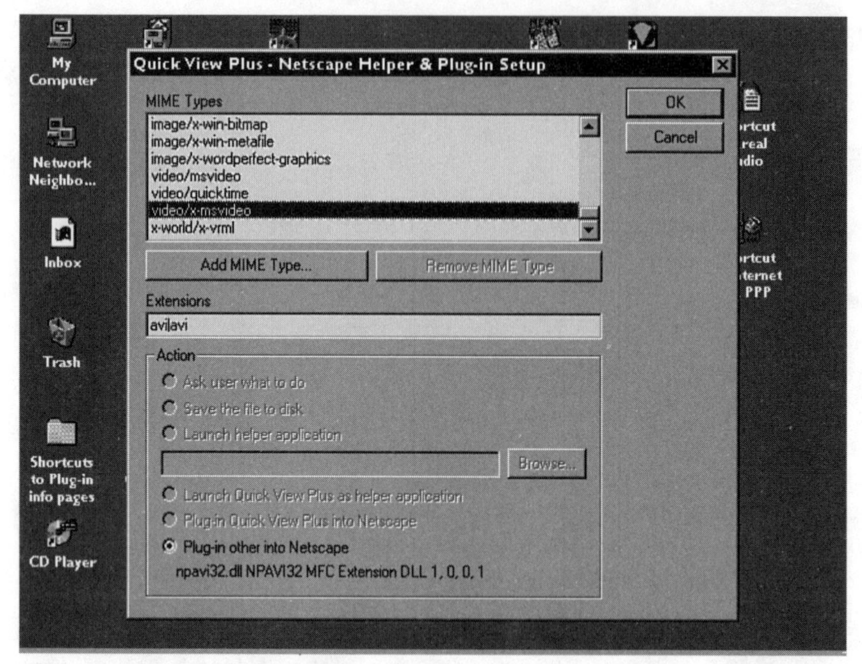

Figure 14–18 The QVPMIME control panel lets you control each MIME type associated with QuickView

If you do want to make files available externally or you just want to add all of QuickView's MIME types to the server on your intranet, it is not difficult to do. Edit your mime.types file (or the equivalent on your Web server) and include all the MIME types (and their associated extensions) listed in Table 14–5.

Another approach for intranet users is *removing* all of the MIME types except the ones that have nothing to do with QuickView Plus. Once you have done this, simply set up the default MIME type on your server to be application/x-quickviewplus instead of the default text/plain. The application/x-quickviewplus MIME type is installed by default when QuickView Plus plugs into Netscape. Thus, any file with an extension that is not explicitly mapped in mime.types can be viewed using the QuickView Plus plug-in.

This works for an intranet because QuickView Plus does not really care what the MIME type is; MIME types are just a way to get Navigator to run the QuickView Plus plug-in. Once the plug-in gets control, the file is identified by its content, not by the MIME type.

On an intranet, you can perhaps rely on the fact that every user will have a Windows machine. However, this technique is not recommended for Web servers that are accessed by the public at large, since their machines may not have a copy of QuickView Plus and—if they are Macs or UNIX boxes—may not even be capable of running it.

Lesson 2: Embedding QuickView Documents in Your Web Pages

Although INSO Corporation does not currently document any special EMBED attributes for the QuickView Plus plug-ins, they can be an excellent way of delivering information within a Web page. When you embed a file, QuickView Plus always displays it using the HEIGHT and WIDTH you've specified—if you omit these two attributes, Netscape is likely to crash.

The scroll bars occupy 18 pixels at the right and bottom of the image, so make sure to allow for them. Other attributes you can use, such as BORDER and ALIGN, are those common to every <EMBED> or <IMG> tag in Netscape.

Figure 14–19 shows a Web page with several different kinds of data embedded in it, including a PowerPoint file and an Excel spreadsheet. In each case QuickView gives it an interface appropriate to the type of data in question: for example, a list of files in a .ZIP file or, in contrast, rows and columns that you can move around in for an Excel spreadsheet.

Many of the QuickView plug-ins use a tabbed interface at the bottom of their windows that allows switching between slides, from worksheet to chart, or whatever is appropriate. When it it is relevant, you should leave room for these in your Web page design. Each instance of a plug-in also features a context menu: Right-click on it, and you can perform actions appropriate to the data type (saving files, zooming the window, and so on).

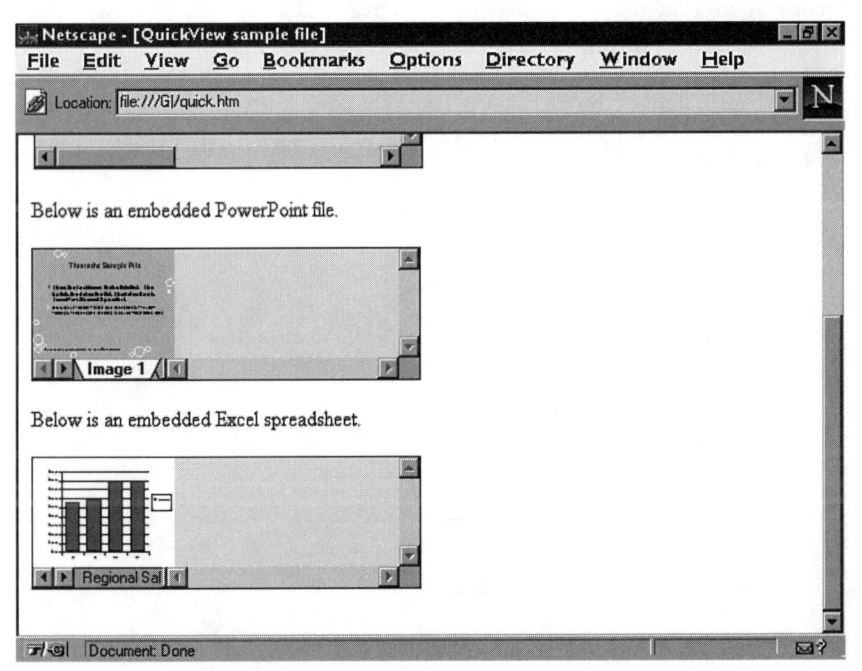

Figure 14–19 A Web page with different types of embedded data, all viewed courtesy of QuickView

This is a listing of the simple code that produced the Web page in Figure 14–19:

```
<HTML>
<TITLE>QuickView sample file</TITLE>
<BODY>
<b>Here is a QuickView test page.</b>
<hr>
Right-click on each thumbnail to see what you can do.<p>
Below is an embedded PowerPoint file.<p>
<EMBED SRC="sample.ppt" WIDTH=300 HEIGHT=100><p>
Below is an embedded Excel spreadsheet.<p>
<EMBED SRC="sample.xls" WIDTH=300 HEIGHT=100><p>
</body>
```

Though QuickView Plus might be—as in the past—mainly intended as a shell extension for Windows Explorer or Norton Navigator, it turns out to be tremendously useful as a set of plug-ins, too. Experiment further with each plug-in in the set, and you're likely to be surprised and delighted.

WHAT NOW?

This chapter covered document plug-ins, those designed to handle a specific type of document or documents. Obviously, there was some overlap in functionality between plug-ins in this chapter and those in previous chapters. What almost all have had in common so far, though, is that their appeal is broad. They have something to interest most users, and they lend themselves to tinkering by the average Web page designer.

In the next chapter you'll read about plug-ins that are a little more specialized. They didn't quite fit in the preceding chapters—perhaps because they require more expertise or because they don't really let you do any authoring. Whatever else they do, these plug-ins will once again show you the incredible power of Netscape as a working environment.

15

OTHER PLUG-INS

15

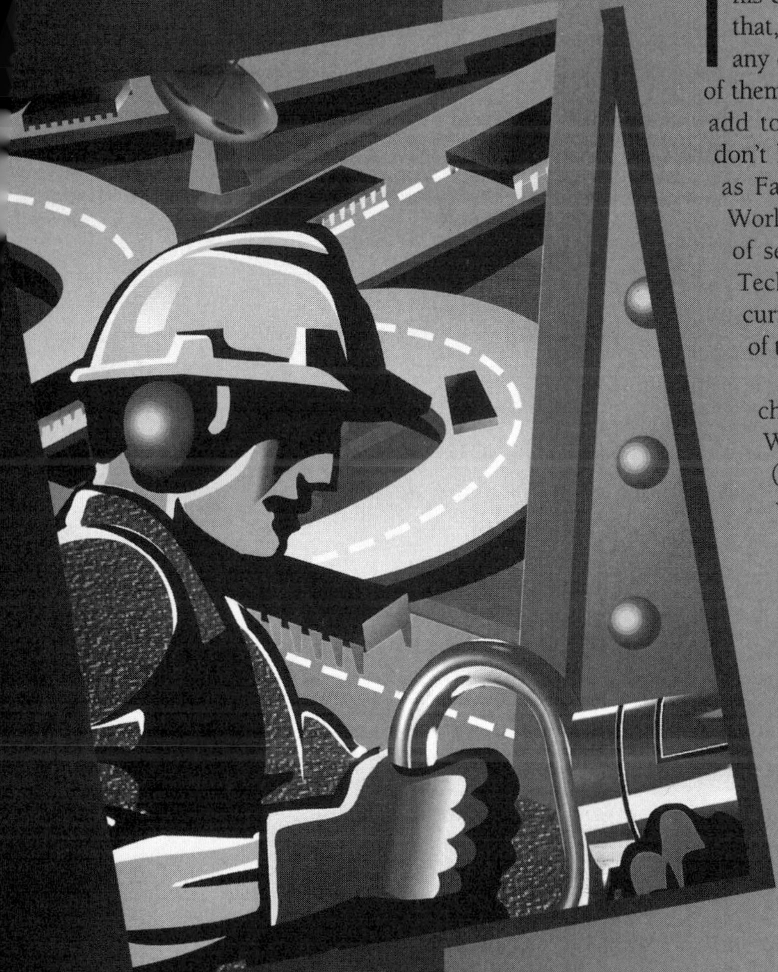

This chapter features an overview of plug-ins that, for various reasons, didn't quite fit in any of the chapters you've read so far. Some of them, such as Starfish Software's EarthTime, add to what Netscape can accomplish, but don't let you do any authoring. Others, such as Farallon's Look@Me or Galacticomm's Worldgroup, connect only to a specific type of server. And still others, such as Argus Technologies' Argus Map Viewer, face no current competition and thus are in a class of their own.

Because most of the plug-ins in this chapter are specialized—or don't allow a Webmaster to do any programming at all (e.g., EarthTime and PointCast)—it wasn't really practical to include the step-by-step instructions for installation and use that you've found in previous chapters. Don't think this means these plug-ins are any less "important" than any others.

This section also features a couple of late-breaking entries in the video and graphics categories. Though it would have been preferable to include these in earlier book chapters, they were released so close to press time that it simply wasn't possible. Rather than ignore these products, I've sneaked them in here. That way, you'll at least have access to as many plug-ins as possible.

You'll likely find at least one product in this chapter that you don't want to live without, and that you think I should've devoted a chapter to all on its own. (That's the beauty of plug-ins: They offer so much diversity that there's something for everyone.)

Some of these plug-ins *are* included on the CD-ROM that came with this book. To find out which ones, see Appendix A.

ARGUS MAP VIEWER

Available from *http://www.argusmap.com,* Argus Map Viewer is a plug-in for Windows that lets you interactively browse maps from within Netscape. Users can move around colorful vector-based maps. If they zoom in on an area, the map is automatically redrawn to display a greater level of detail matching the scale of view.

Information about selected, clickable objects on the maps can be viewed in a report. You can also be taken to a URL that has been hot-linked to any object on the map.

By using the separate Argus Map Author software, you can import geographic data purchased in GIS/Desktop Mapping data formats. You can also geocode your own census data or other information using a tool called Argus Geocoder.

Argus Map Author lets you create maps with multiple layers of information and levels of detail. You can also scan in existing maps and use them as a starting point. Of course, the program's drawing tools are designed to help you create typical map symbols and legends.

An especially interesting aspect of the program is that it can accept attribute data—census data, average vehicle speeds on certain roads, you name it—from any database program that has an ODBC interface. This includes Access, Oracle, Sybase, Gupta SQLBase, Paradox, and others.

Users of the Map Viewer plug-in will then see the data you've chosen, mapped in exactly the way you want it to be. Your source information is secure, since no user can access data other than what you've authorized them to see.

CARBON COPY/NET

Carbon Copy/NET from Microcom *(http://www.microcom.com)* is a development of Carbon Copy, the company's previous remote access tool. Instead of being a separate application, Carbon Copy/NET runs within Netscape's browser window.

You can access and control any other Windows PC in the world provided it, too, is running Carbon Copy or Carbon Copy/NET and you know its TCP/IP address. (Microcom has a demonstration PC you can connect to if you do not know any other users and you want to try out Carbon Copy/NET.)

Once connected to a remote PC, you can scroll around its desktop—which appears within your browser window—to access applications and documents. You can also press a hot key to switch between viewing the host PC's entire screen in your browser window, or to scroll around part of it at its original resolution.

The Carbon Copy/NET program does not permit file transfer, chat, or zooming to a full-screen window that appears outside Netscape's browser window. If you want these features, you need to purchase the full version of Carbon Copy.

CHIME

Available for both Windows and Macintosh computers, Chime (from MDL at *http://www.mdli.com/chemscape)* is a plug-in that lets you view chemical information on any Web page. It supports most of the popular display formats that scientists use, including MDL's Molfile, the Brookhaven Protein Databank (PDB) format, the Minnesota Supercomputer Center's Xmol XYZ format, and many others.

A planned enhancement, Chime Pro, will provide access to ISIS hosts including molecule, reaction, and Oracle databases. You'll be able to double-click on an embedded object, automatically placing the selected structure in the ISIS/Draw window.

Most of us remember 2D molecular diagrams from high-school chemistry. Chime, however, supports not only these but also animated, 3D images.

CINEWEB

Similar in function to plug-ins featured in Chapter 10, CineWeb from Digigami, Inc. (*http://www.digigami.com*) is a video plug-in for Windows 95/NT. Like Netscape's standard LiveVideo, it handles playback of .AVI files. It also plays QuickTime movies, provided you have installed Apple's QuickTime for Windows extensions.

However, CineWeb also offers compatibility with MPEG movies and even Autodesk Animator (.FLC) files. Unlike most of the other video plug-ins, it also allows movies to be used as image maps compatible with HTML's ISMAP and USEMAP commands.

CONCERTO

Concerto, from Alpha Software at *http://www.alphasoftware.com,* is an "intelligent form" plug-in for Windows Netscape. It uses a form description language (ASCII-based and similar to HTML in appearance) that lets you create multipart forms with a tabbed or wizard-style interface.

Without having to learn JavaScript, VisualBasic scripting, or ActiveX, you can create forms that perform client-side data validation. Thanks to Concerto's improved support for MAILTO: URLs, you'll no longer need a decoder to parse responses that users send you via e-mail.

COREL VISUAL CADD

In conjunction with the release of its Visual CADD drawing software, Corel is offering the new Visual CADD plug-in for Windows 95/NT versions of Netscape. Available at *http://www.corel.com/products/CAD/visualCADD/plug-ins.htm*, it supports several different CAD file formats. These include Visual CADD (.VCD), AutoCAD (.DWG and .DXF), and Generic CADD (.GCD).

Like similar plug-ins featured in Chapter 13, Visual CADD permits the Web page author to associate HTML links with different objects in a drawing. The plug-in also has features previously found only in a full-blown CAD program, including layer management, printing capabilities, database access, and the ability to save files locally.

CPC VIEW

Chapter 13 featured plug-ins that showcase a variety of different compression schemes, each seeking to make graphical images fit into as small a file size as possible. Now, here is news of yet another such plug-in: CPC View is a product from Cartesian Products Incorporated (*http://cartesianinc.com*), which concentrates on storing and delivering previously scanned documents.

As Cartesian Products points out, converting "legacy" documents for Web-accessible storage is not easy: Optical character recognition introduces errors or requires expensive post-editing, while documents take up too much space stored in TIFF format. The company's CPC (Cartesian Perceptual Compression) method claims to be optimized for document storage, providing compression that's an order of magnitude better than other methods.

With the CPC View plug-in, users of Netscape (Windows 95/NT only at present) can view CPC-compressed images over an intranet. The separate CPC Tool compression tool converts to CPC from TIFF, PBM, or Group III and Group IV fax.

CYBERAGE RAIDER

CyberAge Raider is a new plug-in for Windows 95/NT Netscape that's billed as providing a "Star Trek-like experience on your desktop." Once installed and invoked, it presents a viewer window within a Web page that shows stars and moving planets. You can navigate around the virtual space and click on planets representing various HTML links.

In the beta release of CyberAge Raider, the links presented were hard-coded into the program. However, CyberAge Communications (*www.miint.net:80/cyberage/*) plans to offer Web page authors a method for connecting the "planets" to links of their choice. Already present is a built-in "thesaurus" that restructures and submits a query to any search engine from a one-stop "launch pad."

DSM

Except for Talker (which uses voice synthesis), the audio plug-ins in Chapter 9 force the Web page author to choose between two basic types of sound. You can either record a sound in its entirety and embed it as a relatively large digital sample. Or, in the case of music, you can represent a sound as a MIDI file, storing just sequencing information. The latter makes for a much faster download, but gives you a lot less control over exactly what the user will hear.

Modules, long used in computer games, mix these two approaches. They are music files that combine a set of samples (digital recordings of the instruments to be used) with sequencing information, telling a player when to play which sample on which track at what pitch (optionally performing an effect such as vibrato). Thus, modules are different from pure sample files such as .WAV or .AU, which contain no sequencing information, and MIDI files, which do not include any custom samples/instruments.

The new DSM plug-in, currently available for Power PC Macintosh only, now provides a way to embed modules in Web pages. It supports these music files in basic .MOD format as well as enhanced ScreamTracker 3 (.S3M) versions and others. You can find more information at *http://www.risa.org/dsm*.

EARTHTIME

Starfish Software's EarthTime is not for you if you want to embed your own data and do your own programming. It's purely designed to entertain and inform.

When you load EarthTime, it takes over the Netscape browser window. An animated world map shows you daylight and darkness so you can plan the best time to make telephone calls. In addition, EarthTime shows you the current time in eight different time zones.

Naturally, EarthTime finds and uses an Internet time server to make sure your computer's clock is accurate. (This feature is not available on Windows NT.) Also built into the program are facts such as local telephone codes, local languages, and currencies.

While nothing about EarthTime is *EarthShaking,* it gives you yet another reason never to leave Netscape. Compatible with Windows 95 and NT systems only, it's available from *http://starfishsoftware.com*.

GOSCRIPT

LaserGo Incorporated (*http://www.lasergo.com*) has for years specialized in software-based emulation of PostScript. Now, the company brings its technology to the Windows 95 version of Netscape.

The new GoScript plug-in offers a black-and-white PostScript emulation, with 13 internal fonts that are similar to those built into standard PostScript printer fonts. You can embed PostScript files in your Web pages or—at least as useful—use Netscape to open .PS and .EPS files that have been previously stored on your hard drive. Since PostScript files are widely stored on the Internet (by UNIX users who take their PostScript printers for granted), the GoScript plug-in should be an extremely useful tool.

Note that the free evaluation version of the plug-in cannot print. For $199, you can upgrade to a version of the plug-in that prints PostScript documents to any Windows printer. It can also save PostScript files in a variety of bitmap file formats.

LOOK@ME

Farallon's Look@Me—currently available as a plug-in for Windows 95 (and as a helper app for other Netscape versions) from *http://www.farallon.com*—allows you to view the screen of any computer that's itself running Look@Me or Timbuktu Pro.

The computer you view needs to have its own IP address—operation over a LAN using IPX, which Timbuktu *does* support, is not yet available. It also needs to be not behind a firewall.

Like Carbon Copy/NET, Look@Me is more secure than you might think. No one can observe your computer if they don't know what its IP address is. Look@Me lets you watch only, not control the observed computer. Also, as with Carbon Copy/NET, you need to step up to the commercial sister application, Timbuktu Pro, if you want to transfer files from machine to machine.

HINDSITE

HindSite, a plug-in for Windows versions of Netscape, offers the unique ability to remember where you've been on the Web. Available in a limited edition from *http://www.isysdev.com,* it's ideal in situations where you saw something on the Web, but you can't remember where, and you didn't make a bookmark.

HindSite records the content of every Web page you visit, indexing and saving it for a time period you specify. It then lets you query this database with plain-English statements such as "Where did I see Nashville?" Or, you can display a structured tree outline of recently visited URLs.

Rather than relying upon the Netscape cache, or storing every page that you visited, HindSite indexes them as you work and stores only the URLs.

ICHAT

ichat is the first plug-in to integrate chat directly into Netscape. Available for Windows from *http://www.ichat.com,* it sounds as though it would be an IRC client. In fact, ichat is more interesting: It is specific to particular Web sites, which must be running the company's server software.

When users visit a chat-enabled Web page, the plug-in opens a frame in the lower part of the Netscape window. Within that frame, it displays a real-time, ongoing chat session among all the visitors to that Web page. You can enter the conversation just by typing.

An optional event moderation package configures ichat for "special guest appearances." Members of the audience can type questions to a moderator, and hence to the guest speaker, while Web users at large see only the speaker's replies.

JETFORM WEB FILLER

JetForm Web Filler is a trial plug-in designed specifically for users of the company's JetForm Filler software. You can download it from the company's Web site at *http://www.jetform.com.*

Once JetForm Web Filler has been installed into Netscape, you can use the browser to view, fill out, and print forms that appear within Web pages. The JetForm Web site boasts an extremely extensive library of forms for JetForm Web Filler users.

If you like what you see, you can purchase the complete JetForm Filler package. This lets you create forms, connect them to your databases, add logos, check spelling, and much more. Though naturally extremely useful to JetForm Filler users, JetForm Web Filler offers relatively little to others.

KOAN

The Koan plug-in for Windows 95/NT or Windows 3.x is dedicated to the notion that music on the Web doesn't have to be useful—it can be just for enjoyment. Koan can play MIDI files, or use MIDI equipment to play special koan music.

Koan music is named after the Zen word meaning a mystery or puzzle with no logical solution. It is computer-generated: Each time a Koan piece plays, it will have certain boundaries set by the author, outside which the music will not go. The music will be different each time it repeats, so a file that can play for up to eight hours can be stored in less than a few kilobytes. This makes the format much more compact than even MIDI.

If you want to experience this interesting type of music, you can download the Koan plug-in from *http://www.sseyo.com.* Like other audio plug-ins, the Koan plug-in plays embedded koan or MIDI files on the page currently loaded in your browser. If you want to play sound continuously as you move from page to page, you can use the Koan Web helper application instead.

Sseyo Ltd. offers the Koan Pro Authoring System, a way to create your own original koan files. Designed for generating new musical ideas, this is said to be ideal for making amazing music in the ambient genre (including techno) and for creating copyright free content for multimedia applications.

It can import MIDI phrases to be used in the piece and also use real sampled sounds to provide a "context" for a piece. It works with any sound card that supports general MIDI, but there is built-in special support for the Creative Labs AWE32, the Gravis Ultrasound/Ultrasound MAX, and the Roland SCC1.

MIDIPLUG

Yamaha's MIDIPLUG, available from *http://www.yamaha.co.jp/english/xg/html/mplug.html*, is billed as a dramatically new kind of MIDI plug-in. While Netscape 3.0 can play MIDI files via LiveAudio—and there are many other MIDI plug-ins, as reviewed in Chapter 9—these plug-ins all rely greatly on the MIDI playback capabilities of the user's hardware or operating system.

On the Mac, the waveform that produces the sound depends on QuickTime sounds, and on Windows, it depends on the FM tone generator of the sound board (usually a SoundBlaster or compatible) that is accessed through the MIDI Mapper.

On these systems, the general MIDI sounds and drum sets, etc., are not implemented completely—according to Yamaha—and the implementation of the various control changes, velocity, and program change data is incomplete. The result is that the playback of a song may not accurately reflect the original musical intent.

MIDIPLUG uses Yamaha's "Soft Synthesizer" technology, previously available only in Japan as part of the "Karaku" PC Karaoke product. The plug-in contains its own, software-based AWM2 (WaveTable) tone generator (22.1KHz 16 bit). MIDIPLUG fully implements general MIDI sounds and provides eight drum sets plus reverb. Versions are available for both Windows 95/NT and Power PC–based Macintoshes.

NAVIGATE WITH AN ACCENT

Accent Software's Navigate with an Accent wins the prize for the plug-in with the longest name! Apart from that, it will let you browse more new Web pages than any other plug-in. That's because it provides the first way to read Web pages written in Russian, Arabic, Greek, Japanese, Korean, and more than twenty-five other languages. Ordinarily these display as gibberish within Netscape Navigator unless you install one or more foreign versions of Windows.

Available in a 30-day evaluation version from *http://www.accentsoft.com/product/nwaaeng.htm*, Navigate with an Accent can automatically detect the language of many Web pages and display them properly. Even when the language of a Web page is not detected automatically, the plug-in will let you manually select the language of your choice.

NET-INSTALL

As has undoubtedly caught your attention by now, installing software from the Web isn't as easy as installing it from a local disk drive. Hunt for the right file; download a file to a temporary subdirectory, hoping there is room for it on your hard drive; uncompress the file to reveal a setup program; and then—finally—proceed as you would if you'd purchased shrink-wrapped software.

Those of us who live on the Web can perform this drill in our sleep. Sometimes, we do just that! However, most users are deterred by it all.

NET-Install is a plug-in linked to the first installation program designed specifically for installing software via the Web. It lets you place a small installation script, created by the NET-Install authoring utilities, in any Web page: When a user clicks on the relevant link, the NET-Install plug-in springs into action, downloading program files, checking the user's hard drive for space, prompting the user for a destination folder, and more.

NET-Install can perform all the actions that existing, diskette-based installation programs do. Installers can

- Incorporate custom graphics
- Search for installed software
- Modify AUTOEXEC.BAT, CONFIG.SYS, .INI files, and the Windows registry
- Uncompress installation files
- Display a progress bar during installation, and much more

NET-Install also allows for password- and serial-number protection (so you can use it to distribute software to only registered users even on a public Web site), and for installations that draw files from multiple directories, or even multiple servers. It also creates Program Manager groups or Start menu entries.

You can download the NET-Install plug-in free of charge from the 20/20 Software Web page at *http://www.twenty.com.* You can also download an evaluation version of the NET-Install Publishers Toolkit, which creates installation scripts and compresses data files. (This version limits installation files to access for only 30 days, and displays a nuisance message to the user during installation.)

NEURON

Neuron, from Asymetrix Corporation (*http://www.asymetrix.com*), is a plug-in that lets Internet users view presentations, kiosks, courseware, and other multimedia titles that were originally written using ToolBook 4.0. Unlike some other authoring programs, ToolBook already uses pages and hyperlinks. Therefore, it's relatively easy for authors to repurpose their applications for the Web.

Neuron supports both ToolBook (.TBK) files and external multimedia files, with a streaming-like functionality. Users can thus access either complete titles or just the portions they need.

POINTCAST NETWORK

Do you leave the Netscape window open even when you're not actively browsing the Web? If so, then PointCast has a plug-in for you. Its PointCast Network plug-in, available from *http://www.pointcast.com,* turns the browser window into a delivery vehicle for news headlines.

While you're connected to the Net, PointCast updates information in categories that you've chosen, such as News, Companies, Industries, Sports, Weather, and Lifestyle. Recently the company added "channels" that include

- Time-Warner, with content from *Time*, *People,* and *Money* magazines
- *Los Angeles Times*

- *Boston Globe*
- Business Wire
- Hambrecht and Quist Internet Stock Index, and the Weather Channel

And—oh, yes—this advertiser-supported service does display occasional commercial information. While PointCast information is displayed within Netscape, you can click on an advertisement (or any other links that might be highlighted) to jump to another Web site.

Unlike Web-site-based advertising, PointCast never interrupts your normal browsing! It only kicks in when your browser has been idle for a predetermined period.

POWERMEDIA

RadMedia's PowerMedia is a multimedia authoring program with the motto "author once, deliver anywhere." Available for Sun, SGI, HP, and IBM workstations, as well as Windows and Macintosh, and priced from $495 to about $2,500, it permits creating Web-centric applications on any of the supported systems and playing them back on any other.

Now, the PowerMedia Viewer plug-in makes Netscape one of the "supported systems." Download this from *http://www.radmedia.com* and you'll be able to view PowerMedia documents. The plug-in can display multiple PowerMedia applications and animations in a single Web page, or play a single one back in full-screen mode. There is also support for downloading a document from the Web and then playing it back later on a laptop.

PROJECT X

Apple's Project X—available for Power PC and 68K Macintoshes, with Windows support on the way soon—is a Netscape plug-in that demonstrates the company's new Meta Content Format. Somewhat similar to the CyberRaider plug-in mentioned above, this provides a representation of the Internet using 3D space.

You can move forward, backward and around this "Xspace" and open any of the links found by clicking on them. Better still, adding URLs or aliases to files on your local hard drive or network is a simple matter of moving them from your desktop using drag-and-drop.

As downloaded from *http://www.research.apple.com/go/projectx*, the plug-in includes a Meta Content Format representation of the Yahoo! hierarchy. You can add your own links to this or create an entirely new .MCF file—either for your own use or for visitors to your Web site.

SCRIPTACTIVE

As you may have read in Chapter 8, Microsoft Internet Explorer 3.0 offers a new technology known as ActiveX. ActiveX "controls" are similar to plug-ins: Both are downloadable software components that extend a browser's powers while remaining within the context of the Web page that spawned them.

Since ActiveX controls and plug-ins use an entirely different applications programming interface, however, Netscape is not normally compatible with the former. Now, however, the ScriptActive plug-in from NCompass Labs (*http://www.ncompasslabs.com*) gives Navigator the ability to run ActiveX controls (.OCX files) and scripts (.AXS files). ActiveX scripts may be written in VBScript or JScript (a JavaScript-compatible language).

Even so, Internet Explorer–style Web pages will need some modification to work with ScriptActive: Navigator does not recognize the <OBJECT> tag that is normally used to embed an ActiveX control. It uses the <EMBED> tag instead. (See Lesson 4 in Chapter 8 for a way around this problem.)

SUPERCEDE VM

SuperCede VM, from Asymetrix (*http://www.asymetrix.com/nettools/vm/vm.html*), is a plug-in for Windows 95/NT that is claimed to boost the performance of Java applets dramatically. Rated up to five times faster than the Java interpreter built into Netscape Navigator, SuperCede VM also offers client-side applet caching.

Unlike just-in-time compilers, where the interpreter selectively compiles functions, the SuperCede VM technology compiles all class files as they are downloaded from the server. The result, says Asymetrix, is an application that is fully compiled to machine code and therefore executes at C++ speeds.

Because the SuperCede VM generates relocatable code, an executable or dynamic link library (DLL) can be cached on the client machine until the applet is run again. When an end-user attempts to rerun the applet, SuperCede can check whether the cached version of the applet matches the version of the applet on the server. If the versions match, SuperCedeVM can simply run the cached DLL, avoiding the unnecessary overhead of downloading the applet again.

There is a small price to be paid for using SuperCede VM: You need to modify your Web pages slightly. Instead of referencing Java classes using paired <APPLET> tags and <PARAM> statemenents, you need to use an <EMBED> tag whose attributes provide both the path to the .class file and any desired parameters for it.

TCL/TK

Tcl/Tk (Tool Command Language/Tool Kit) is an interpreted language that has been popular in the UNIX community for building graphical user interfaces. Thanks to the Tcl/Tk plug-in from Sun (*http://sunlabs.com*), Tcl/Tk now runs on Windows and Macintosh as well. Once a script—which can allow for menus with multiple fonts, buttons, event handlers, and more—has been developed, it works within Netscape to provide a custom user interface.

For those who are concerned about security, Tcl/Tk offers a "padded cell" method of operation. A downloaded Tcl script cannot execute other programs, open files on your disk (except, optionally, in predefined directories), or find out information about your system.

TECHEXPLORER

IBM's techexplorer is a plug-in that processes a large subset of TEX/LATEX, the markup language often used for publishing in mathematics, education, and many of the sciences. TEX is a flexible and concise language. Because formatting takes place on the fly, source documents do not need to be too much larger than simple ASCII—they can be 1/4 the size of equivalent .PDF files.

The techexplorer plug-in is available for Windows 95 and NT from *http://www.ics.raleigh.ibm.com/ics/techexp.htm* and shows you TEX files within Netscape's browser window. Since it operates with TrueType fonts, unlike most other TEX products, you can easily customize the appearance of displayed documents.

IBM has added Internet-aware support for hypertext, images, sound, and video, though these things are naturally not part of the standard TEX format. Forthcoming enhancements to techexplorer include printing capability, and a drag-and-drop feature that will let you transfer mathematical expressions into external spreadsheets or math applications.

WEBBASIC

This plug-in supports and promotes WebBASIC, a new way of developing applets that operate within Netscape. By downloading the plug-in from *http://www.inetnow.net/~webbasic/webbasic.html*, you can interact with the company's sample applets, look at their source code, then learn how to obtain Amara's development products, WebBASIC Developer Bronze or WebBASIC Developer Gold.

WebBASIC was designed with the individual developer or small company in mind. Amara says the WebBASIC API allows the developer to create and manipulate objects with simple function calls, rather than having to learn concepts such as classes and inheritance (found in Java). WebBASIC applets are also lower-bandwidth than Java applets, the company says, because any graphics or sound they use are encrypted and compressed into a single file for travel over the Net, rather than requiring multiple server accesses.

WebBASIC also contrasts with Microsoft's relatively complex VBScript/ActiveX (OCX) technology. As Amara points out, the latter requires multiple .OCX files to be downloaded in advance before the user can browse a site with custom controls.

Choosing a programming tool will always be a personal decision—if your employers haven't already made the choice for you. However, the WebBASIC plug-in offers you a quick look at a whole new option.

WORLDGROUP

Galacticomm's Worldgroup plug-in, available for testing from *http://www.gcomm.com,* lets you place tags in HTML documents that access Worldgroup servers. When the plug-in finds such a tag, it opens up a (Telnet-style) connection to the specified server. This connection is persistent, so users will be able to keep interacting with Worldgroup applications even if they browse to a different Web page or close Netscape entirely.

The Worldgroup server software—offering client/server operation with full Windows functionality—runs on a 486 or Pentium computer, which can be your existing Web server or a separate one. Applications are available that let users fill out polls or questionnaires you devise, participate in threaded discussions, download files, teleconference, and more. Optional modules include a complete online shopping system, a credit card processing system, and fax-on-demand.

True to Galacticomm's original background as a developer of bulletin board software, the Worldgroup server also supports direct access via modem, ISDN, IPX/SPX, or X.25. You can even create a dial-up system that offers your users access out to the Internet via SLIP or PPP.

WHAT NOW?

With this chapter, you've reached the end of our review of available plug-ins. And one thing's for certain: There are plug-ins out there on the Internet as you read this that we somehow missed or—at least as likely—that didn't exist at all when this book went to press. The pace of today's software development and distribution makes a mockery of any author who would claim completeness. In the next chapter, therefore, I'll briefly review some of the ways you can use the Web to make sure you always have the *very latest* information about plug-ins.

16

FINDING NEW PLUG-INS

16

Software maintenance and upgrades have been of concern to MIS professionals since—well, since the power switch of the very first computer was flipped to "on." Those of us with microcomputers, however, have approached them with a fairly relaxed attitude. We've waited to see if we really want an upgrade, thinking that the bugs might be better worked out of the program in a few months. We've also been able to rest assured that when we decide to make the move, the software will be conveniently available all wrapped up in clear plastic on the shelves of our favorite computer store.

Even the hype that accompanied the release of Windows 95—which was, after all, merely an upgrade—didn't change the fact that for most people, upgrading their software was hardly an urgent matter. Now, though, the Web has done a couple of things to shatter this idyll: First, it has completely changed the distribution model. Software vendors no longer need stores to mediate between themselves and their customers. Freed from the costs and time constraints involved in copying diskettes, shipping boxes, and stocking shelves, they post upgrades and new releases on the Web as and when they feel like it.

With obvious advantages for the vendors, this also brings some benefits to us customers. For a start, it's easier to try out new programs free of charge, since "trialware" is easy to access. And, if we monitor a company's tech support site for patches and the like, we can now count on the fact that we're using the latest, hopefully most-debugged, versions of our favorite software applications.

The second thing that the wholesale move to the Net has done, though, is to make it *our responsibility* to see that we're using the most up-to-date version of our software. Maybe it shouldn't be our job, but it is.

Where new software releases were once hailed by the trade press and computer dealers, they go all but unmentioned today. Want to know if there's a new release of the software you use? You'll have to keep checking the company's Web site in order to find out. The only word for today's continuous cycle of patches, incremental improvements, and new features is *dribbleware*.

With its frequent releases of patches and new program code, Netscape is one of the worst offenders. (Of course, if you like getting your software hot off the press—and many of us do—you'll consider Netscape your best friend.) This company has helped redefine the word "beta" to mean...well, nobody knows exactly what it means anymore. Only one thing is for certain: If you're using a copy of Netscape, or any other software product today, that's labeled a "final release" or came out of shrink-wrap, you haven't got the latest version!

During the months in which this book was written, Navigator 3.0 went through multiple beta versions, then at last came out in its final form. In addition, most of the plug-ins the book covers were upgraded from alphas to betas, or from betas to "released" versions. Finally, more than a dozen—maybe more than two dozen—Netscape plug-ins were devised for the first time. (Just to add to the fun, three or four plug-ins even had their names changed.)

I've written this book with the conviction that there's still a need for something crafted from printer's ink and dead trees that you can hold in your hands to get an overview of what's going on. In a way, the constant turmoil and change on the Web makes having a tangible reference work all the more important. (But I would say that, wouldn't I?)

Combine the relentless competition in today's software industry, the inertia-less, Web-based distribution model, and the lead times still unavoidable in book publishing—and you'll see there's no possible way this book could feature *every* new plug-in. Nor, despite the valiant efforts of Dan Scherf at Waite Group Press, could the CD-ROM possibly contain the latest release of each plug-in stored there.

Instead, it's a case of live by the sword, die by the sword, or kinder words to that effect. Just as you use plug-ins *with* the Web, you are going to have to use the Web to get the latest information about plug-ins.

NETSCAPE'S PLUG-INS PAGE

Netscape's plug-ins page is both a boon and a source of annoyance. A boon, because it's your primary, most convenient source of information about available plug-ins. A source of annoyance, because Netscape Navigator will send you to it *every* time your browser encounters an embedded MIME type it doesn't know how to handle. (Unless, of course, a Web page's author foresaw this problem and used the PLUGINSPAGE attribute to direct you elsewhere.)

The Netscape plug-ins page is also a mixed blessing for third-party software vendors. Although it publicizes their efforts, it also puts them at a disadvantage when (if only temporarily) their product isn't listed.

At any rate, the plug-ins page gives you, the user, a pretty complete selection of the plug-ins that are available. It also provides brief information about what each plug-in can do, and then provides links to vendor background information or directly to the page from which you can download the plug-in.

Netscape's plug-ins page also lets you access developer information, in case you want to go into the business of creating your own plug-in. With other useful links, it also looks quite attractive—no small virtue in a Web site you'll be looking at so often.

The best way to call up Netscape's plug-ins page is to make the About Plug-ins menu choice from the Help menu or Apple menu. You'll see a screen like that shown in Figure 16-1.

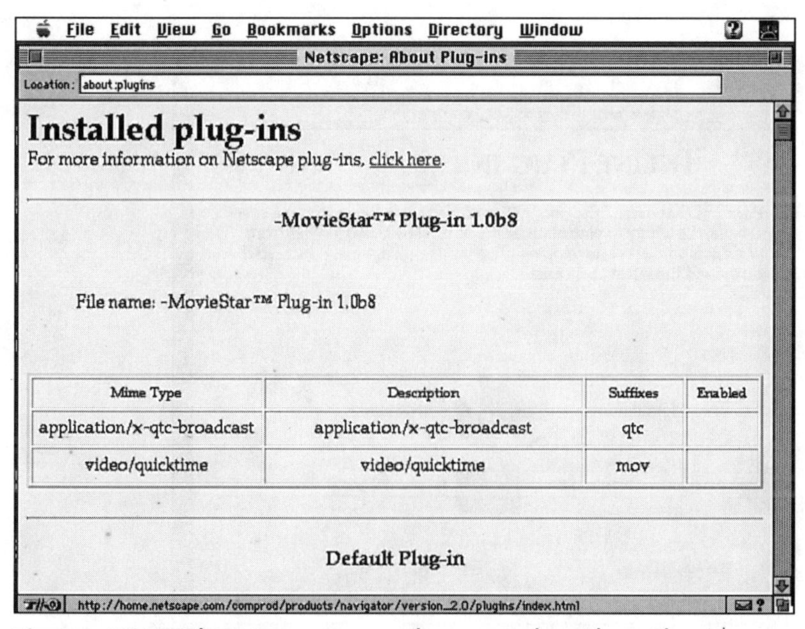

Figure 16–1 This page appears when you select About Plug-ins. Click on the link at the top to go to the plug-ins page

To go to the plug-ins list, click on the link that appears at the top of your screen. You'll see a page very similar to that shown in Figure 16-2. The URL for this page is coded into your version of Netscape Navigator, so, apart from the fact that it's a long one to type, you're best off keeping up-to-date by using About Plug-ins to call it up.

As you can see, the Menu is divided into sections for "3D and Animation," "Audio/Video," "Business and Utilities," "Image Viewers," "Presentations," and "What's New." While you might not completely agree with the company's choice of plug-ins to assign to each section—any more than you *completely* agreed with the chapter assignments in this book—the list does as good a job of dividing up the plug-ins universe as any.

Figure 16-3 shows the same Web page scrolled down to reveal links to developer information plus a list of "Cool Plug-ins."

BROWSERWATCH

Despite its advantages, Netscape's list of plug-ins is not the most complete, nor is it usually the first to list new plug-ins. That honor goes, instead, to Dave Garaffa's BrowserWatch site at *http://www.browserwatch.com.*

Figure 16-4 shows the main menu of BrowserWatch, which helpfully reminds you of who you are and what Netscape version you're running—in case you have forgotten either of those things. From this menu, you can access a variety of useful links, including news about new plug-ins and general browser-related gossip. (If Netscape has just posted, or is about to post, a new release of Navigator, this is where you'll read about it first.)

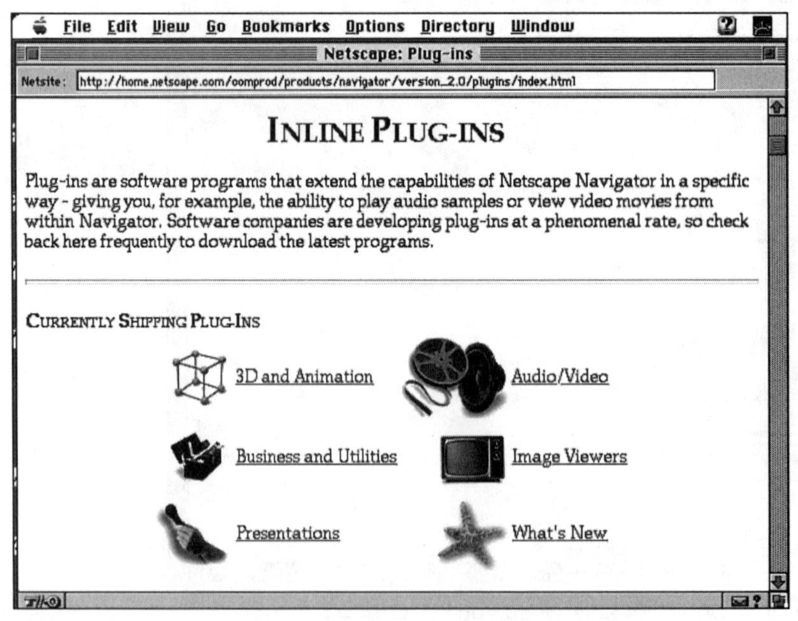

Figure 16–2 Netscape's main plug-ins list begins with this menu

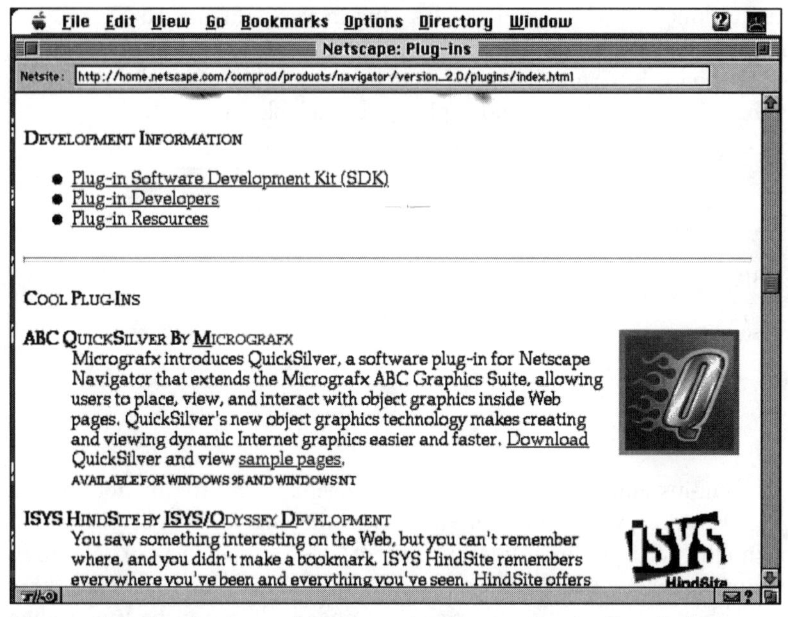

Figure 16–3 This part of Netscape's plug-ins page offers links to developer information

Figure 16–4 BrowserWatch's main menu

The most useful link here is BrowserWatch's Plug-In Plaza (Figure 16-5). You can choose an alphabetical list of every Netscape plug-in for both Mac and PC, or select Just MultiMedia, Just Graphics, Just Sound, Just Document, Just Productivity, or Just VRML. On each list, symbols tell you whether or not a plug-in is available for:

- Windows 95
- Windows 3.x
- Macintosh 68K
- Macintosh Power PC

OTHER LISTS

Netscape's list of plug-ins and BrowserWatch, taken together, let little or nothing fall between the cracks. However, you might want to consult other lists for special reasons.

One reason might be if you're a "platform bigot" so wedded to your Windows computer or to your Macintosh that you don't want to read about plug-ins for the other type of machine. Although this seems rather closed-minded, there can be times when you're in a hurry and just want to focus on the software you can use.

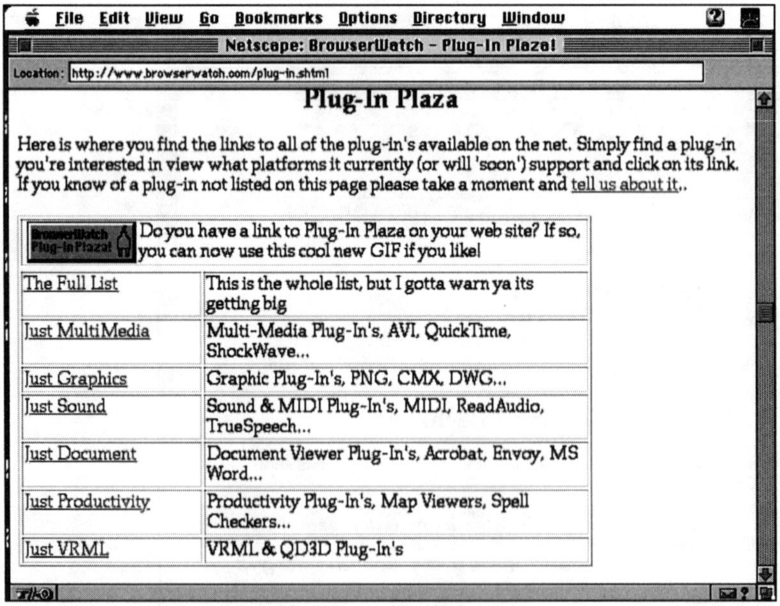

File Edit View Go Bookmarks Options Directory Window

Netscape: BrowserWatch - Plug-In Plaza!

Location: http://www.browserwatch.com/plug-in.shtml

Plug-In Plaza

Here is where you find the links to all of the plug-in's available on the net. Simply find a plug-in you're interested in view what platforms it currently (or will 'soon') support and click on its link. If you know of a plug-in not listed on this page please take a moment and tell us about it..

BrowserWatch Plug-In Plaza! Do you have a link to Plug-In Plaza on your web site? If so, you can now use this cool new GIF if you like!

The Full List	This is the whole list, but I gotta warn ya its getting big
Just MultiMedia	Multi-Media Plug-In's, AVI, QuickTime, ShockWave...
Just Graphics	Graphic Plug-In's, PNG, CMX, DWG...
Just Sound	Sound & MIDI Plug-In's, MIDI, ReadAudio, TrueSpeech...
Just Document	Document Viewer Plug-In's, Acrobat, Envoy, MS Word...
Just Productivity	Productivity Plug-In's, Map Viewers, Spell Checkers...
Just VRML	VRML & QD3D Plug-In's

Figure 16-5 BrowserWatch's Plug-In Plaza

Figure 16-6 shows the main page for TUCOWS, which stands for—now you know—The Ultimate Collection Of Winsock Software. Located, as seen here, at *http://www.texoma.com/mirror/tucows* and many other mirror sites worldwide, it concentrates on Windows Internet software of all types. TUCOWS has a special plug-ins area, too, as shown in Figure 16-7.

An advantage of TUCOWS and other "secondary" lists of plug-ins is that they often rate the programs and, more important, link to alternate sources for the software. If you find that a software vendor's own Web site is temporarily down or hard to reach from your location, you can check to see if the software is available from other servers. (A caveat, however: Since it takes time to update files on multiple servers, secondary lists often link to outdated versions of plug-ins. If you want to be sure you're getting the very latest version of any plug-in, go to the source.)

An alternative to TUCOWS, for those who prefer skulls to cows, is The Slaughterhouse at *http://www.magpage.com/~cwagner* (see Figure 16-8). This site features ratings, locally stored file archives, and descriptions of each plug-in it features. Actively maintained, this site sometimes lists plug-ins and other utilities before the more mainstream pages.

Figure 16-6 The TUCOWS main page, which explains why they adopted that down-home graphic

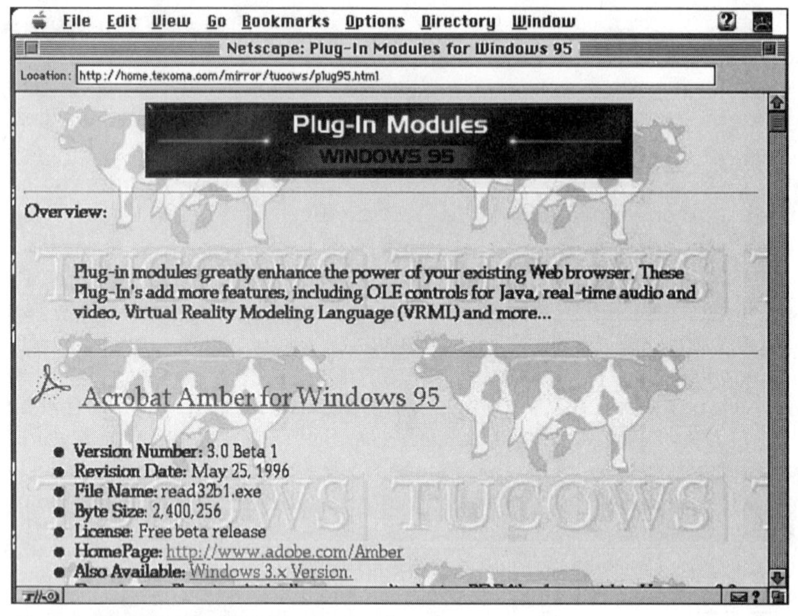

Figure 16-7 TUCOWS' plug-in list

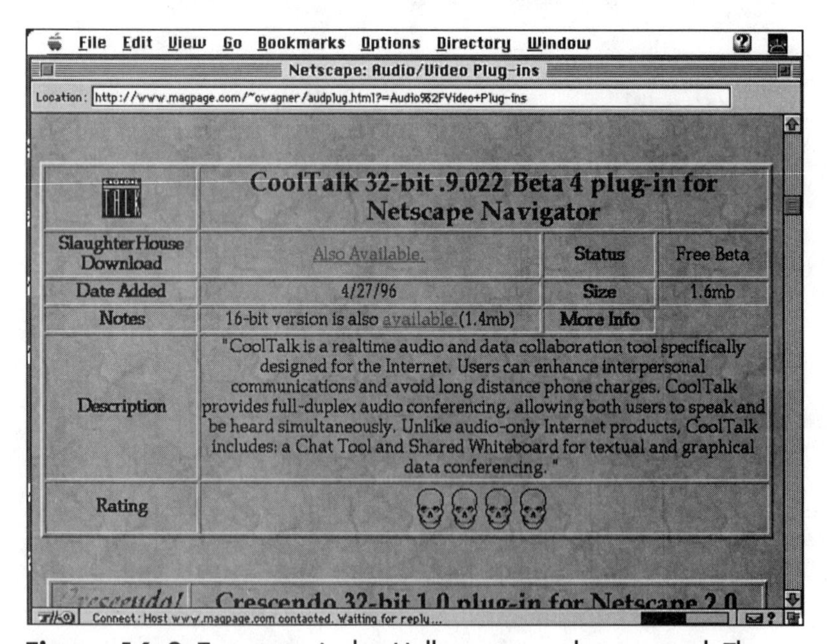

Figure 16-8 To put you in that Halloween mood year-round, The Slaughterhouse features skull ratings

Finally, if you're a Mac user who feels safest in the company of fellow travelers, you can access the *MacWeek* list of plug-ins at *http://www.zdnet.com/macweek/mw_1007/plugins.html* (Figure 16-9). Although becoming stale, this list is useful and is sure to be updated in due course.

SEARCHES

Perhaps you'd like to "cut out the middleman," or you're the sort of person who feels that information becomes too dated if it sits around in a list for more than a couple of days. If this describes you, then you might be happiest searching for Netscape plug-ins via one of the many popular search engines.

Just by entering some variation of "Netscape AND plug-in," you're sure to get more information than you ever dreamt of. Figure 16-10 shows the result of an Excite search *(http://www.excite.com)*.

Yahoo, with its library-like hierarchy of information, also offers plentiful information on plug-ins. Figure 16-11 shows an example of what you'll find by accessing Yahoo's *Computers and Internet:Internet:World Wide Web:Browsers:Netscape Navigator:Plug Ins* category.

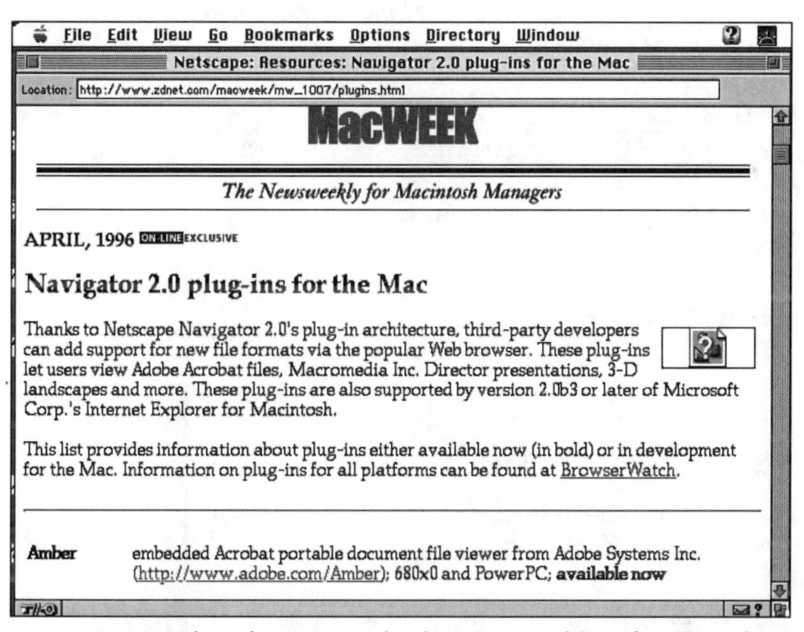

Figure 16-9 Though getting stale, this *MacWeek* list of Macintosh plug-ins is still useful

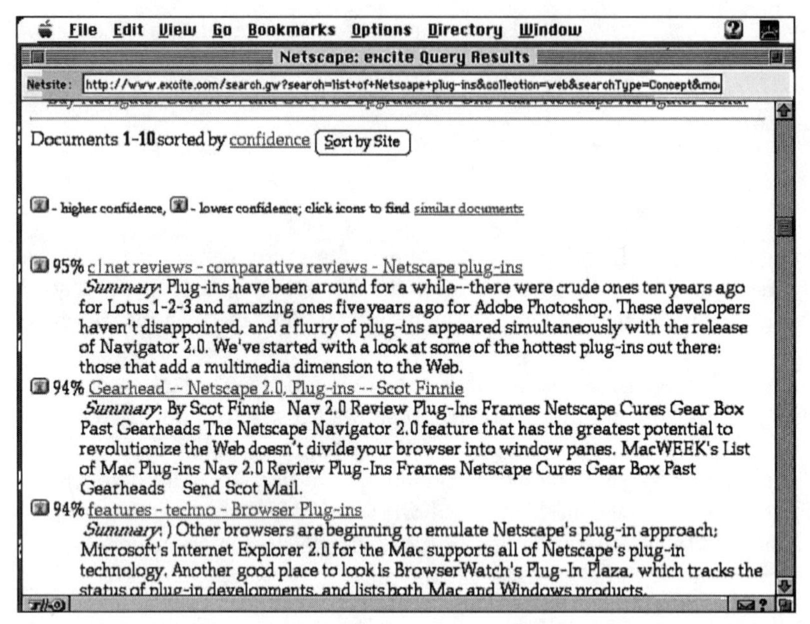

Figure 16–10 Using a search engine, you'll get more information about plug-ins than you ever dreamt of

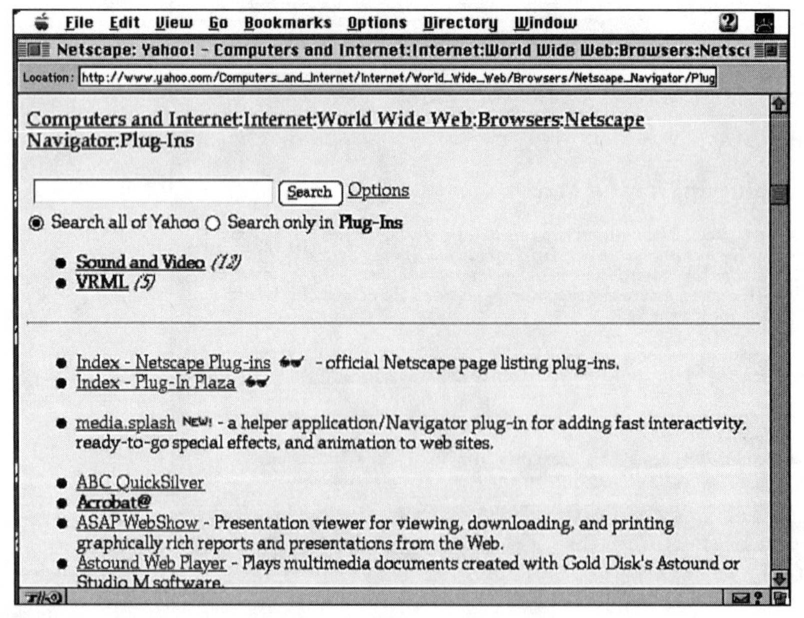

Figure 16–11 Yahoo has a category for most things, and plug-ins are no exception

WHAT NOW?

What do you mean "What Now?" If you're still here, thanks for reading this book. Now, it's time to put down this hunk of wood pulp and start exploring Netscape plug-ins.

In Appendix A, you'll find a list of the plug-ins that are on the CD-ROM and the subdirectories/folders you can use to access them. Windows users who are tired of looking in their plug-ins subdirectory and wondering which NP??????.DLL files are which will find a table in Appendix B that decodes most of them.

WHERE TO GET THE PLUG-INS FEATURED IN THIS BOOK

	Windows 95/NT	Windows 3.x	Macintosh	On the CD?	On the Web
Audio					
LiveAudio	X	X	X		comes with Navigator
Crescendo	X	X	X		www.liveupdate.com
Echospeech	X	X			www.echospeech.com
RapidTransit	X			X	www.fastman.com
RealAudio	X	X	X		www.realaudio.com
Talker			X	X	www.mvpsolutions.com
ToolVox	X	X		X	www.voxware.com
TrueSpeech	X	X		X	www.dspg.com
Video					
LiveVideo	X		X		comes with 32-bit Navigator
QuickTime	X	X	X		comes with Navigator
Action	X				www.open2u.com
ClearFusion	X			X	www.iterated.com
InterVU	X		X		www.intervu.com
MacZilla			X		www.maczilla.com
MovieStar	X	X	X	X	www.beingthere.com

continued on next page

continued from previous page

	Windows 95/NT	Windows 3.x	Macintosh	On the CD?	On the Web
VDOLive	X	X			www.vdolive.com
VivoActive	X				www.vivo.com
Presentation/Animation					
ASAP Web Show	X	X		X	www.spco.com
Astound	X				www.golddisk.com
Emblaze	X	X	X	X	www.geo.inter.net
FutureSplash	X	X	X		www.futurewave.com
mBED	X	X	X	X	www.mbed.com
Point Plus	X	X		X	www.net-scene.co.il
Shockwave for Authorware	X	X	X		www.macromedia.com
Shockwave for Director	X	X	X		www.macromedia.com
Sizzler	X	X	X	X	www.totallyhip.com
WebAnimator			X	X	www.deltapoint.com
VRML					
Live3D	X	X	X		Comes with Navigator
Topper	X				www.ktx.com
V•Realm	X				www.ids-net.com
VR Scout	X			X	www.chaco.com
WIRL	X			X	www.vream.com
Graphics					
ABC Quicksilver	X				www.micrografx.com
Corel CMX Viewer	X				www.corel.com
DWG/DXF Plug-in	X		X		www.softsource.com
SVF Plug-in	X			X	www.softsource.com
FIGleaf Inline	X				www.ct.ebt.com
Fractal Viewer	X				www.iterated.com
LightningStrike	X	X	X		www.infinop.com
Shockwave for FreeHand	X	X	X		www.macromedia.com
View Director	X	X			www.tmsinc.com
WebExpresso	X				www.dvcorp.com
Whip!	X				www.autodesk.com
Document Plug-ins					
Envoy	X	X	X	X	www.twcorp.com
Formula One/NET	X	X	X		www.visualcomp.com
KeyView	X	X		X	www.ftp.com
Quick View Plus	X	X			www.inso.com

	Windows 95/NT	Windows 3.x	Macintosh	On the CD?	On the Web
Other Plug-ins					
ActiveX	X			X	www.ncompasslabs.com
Argus Map Viewer	X			X	www.argusmap.com
Carbon Copy/NET	X	X		X	www.microcom.com
Chime	X	X	X		www.mdli.com/chemscape
CineWeb	X				www.digigami.com
Concerto	X				www.concerto.com
Corel Visual CADD	X				www.corel.com
CPC View	X				www.cartesianinc.com
CyberAge Raider	X				www.miint.net:80/cyberage
DSM			X		www.risa.org/dsm
EarthTime	X			X	starfishsoftware.com
GoScript	X				www.lasergo.com
Look@Me	X				www.farallon.com
HindSite	X			X	www.isysdev.com
ichat	X				www.ichat.com
JetForm Web Filler	X				www.jetform.com
Koan	X	X			www.sseyo.com
MIDIPLUG	X	X	X		www.yamaha.com
Navigate with an Accent	X				www.accentsoft.com
Net-Install	X				www.twenty.com
Neuron	X				www.asymetrix.com
PointCast Network	X				www.pointcast.com
PowerMedia	X			X	www.radmedia.com
Project X			X		www.research.apple.com/go/projectx
ScriptActive	X				www.ncompasslabs.com
SuperCede VM	X				www.asymetrix.com
TCL/TK	X	X	X		www.sunlabs.com
techexplorer	X				www.ics.raleigh.ibm.com
WebBASIC	X				www.inetnow.net/~webbasic
Worldgroup	X	X		X	www.galacticomm.com
Helper Applications					
Adobe Acrobat Reader 2.1	X	X	X	X	www.adobe.com
CoolEdit	X	X		X	www.syntrillium.com

continued on next page

continued from previous page

	Windows 95/NT	Windows 3.x	Macintosh	On the CD?	On the Web
MidiGate	X	X			www.prs.net
Pueblo	X	X		X	www.chaco.com
WebAnimator			X	X	www.deltapoint.com
WebPainter					www.totallyhip.com

B

FILE NAME DECODER FOR COMMON WINDOWS PLUG-INS

File(s) installed in Netscape Plug-ins directory	Plug-in
NPOKNETX.DLL	Topper
NP32ASW.DLL, NP16ASW.DLL	Shockwave for Authorware
NP32DSW.DLL, NP16DSW.DLL	Shockwave for Director
NP32FSW.DLL, NP16FSW.DLL	Shockwave for FreeHand
NP32MBED.DLL, NP16MBED.DLL	mBED
NP32VOX.DLL, NP16VOX.DLL	ToolVox
NPASAP32.DLL, NPASAP16.DLL	ASAP Web Show
NPAUDIO.DLL	LiveAudio
NPAVI32.DLL	LiveVideo
NPAWP02.DLL	Astound
NPBLZ32.DLL, NPBLZ16.DLL	Emblaze
NPCMX32.DLL	Corel CMX Viewer
NPCOD32.DLL, NPCOD16.DLL	LightiningStrike
NPCOOL32.DLL	CoolFusion
NPDSGNET.DLL	ABC Quicksilver
NPDWG32.DLL	DWG/DXF Plug-in
NPECHO32.DLL, NPECHO16.DLL	Echospeech
NPEVY7.DLL, NPEVY7S.DLL	Envoy

continued on next page

continued from previous page

File(s) installed in Netscape Plug-ins directory	Plug-in
NPF132.DLL, NPF116.DLL, WCF1DL32.DLL	Formula One/NET
NPFIF.DLL	Fractal Viewer
NPFIGLF.DLL	FIGleaf Inline
NPFST32.DLL	RapidTransit
NPIVMPG.DLL	InterVU
NPL3D32.DLL, NPL3D16.DLL	Live3D
NPMIDI32.DLL, NPMIDI16.DLL	Crescendo
NPMPG32.DLL	Action
NPPDF32.DLL, NPPDF16.DLL	Acrobat Reader
NPQ00032.DLL through NPQ04232.DLL or NPQ00016.DLL through NPQ04216.DLL	Quick View Plus
NPQTW32.DLL, NPQTW16.DLL	QuickTime
NPRA32.DLL, NPRA16.DLL	RealAudio
NPSCOUT.DLL	VR Scout
NPSLC32.DLL, NPSLC16.DLL	Point Plus
NPSPL32.DLL, NPSPL16.DLL	FutureSplash
NPSPR32.DLL, NPSPR16.DLL	Sizzler
NPSTAR32.DLL, NPSTAR16.DLL	MovieStar
NPSVF32.DLL	SVF Plug-in
NPTSP32.DLL, NPTSP16.DLL	TrueSpeech
NPVD32.DLL, NPVD16.DLL	View Director
NPVDO32.DLL, NPVDO16.DLL	VDOLive
NPVIV32.DLL	VivoActive
NPVREALM.DLL	V•Realm
NPWHP32.DLL	Whip!
NPWIRL.DLL, VRCJAVA1.DLL	WIRL
NPXPL32.DLL	WebExpresso
NPXV.DLL, NPKVX.DLL, NPKVX2.DLL	KeyView

INDEX

Symbols

A

B

C

D

E

F

G

H

I

J

K-L

N

O

P

Q

R

S

T

U-V

W

X-Z

ENVIRONMENTAL AWARENESS

Books have a substantial influence on the destruction of the forests of the Earth. For example, it takes 17 trees to produce one ton of paper. A first printing of 30,000 copies of a typical 480-page book consumes 108,000 pounds of paper, which will require 918 trees!

Waite Group Press™ is against the clear-cutting of forests and supports reforestation of the Pacific Northwest of the United States and Canada, where most of this paper comes from. As a publisher with several hundred thousand books sold each year, we feel an obligation to give back to the planet. We will therefore support organizations that seek to preserve the forests of planet Earth.

WAITE GROUP PRESS™

WEB PUBLISHER'S CONSTRUCTION KIT WITH VRML/LIVE 3D

David Fox and Philip Shaddock

Clear instructions on every aspect of VRML (Virtual Reality Modeling Language), including polygons, lines, points, cones, cylinders, spheres, text, manipulating 3D graphics, translation, transformation, light sources, materials, texture mapping, and camera angles. The CD includes 2 VRML browsers, a full-retail version of a 3D polygonal modeler, a save-disabled version of a professional NURBS modeler, conversion software, ready-to-use VRML code, and many ready-to-use 3D objects and textures.

Available now • 650 pages
ISBN: 1-57169-068-9
U.S. $39.99
1 CD-ROM

WEB DATABASE CONSTRUCTION KIT

Gunnit S. Khurana and Balbir S. Khurana

Explore real-life situations dealing with Web-based database publishing with this step-by-step guide. All the pieces of Web database publishing, covering the Microsoft Access database management system, HTML form support, and implementation of the Windows CGI standard through Visual Basic, are brought together. The CD-ROM contains example databases, applications, and shareware Web site software in the book.

Available now • 700 pages
ISBN: 1-57169-032-8
U.S. $49.99
1 CD-ROM

CGI PRIMER PLUS FOR WINDOWS

Mohammed J. Kabir

Start writing and serving CGI programs with *CGI Primer Plus for Windows*. You'll get extensive coverage of hot CGI topics like Netscape extensions, push/pull animation, Windows 95 Web servers, Perl 5, and HTML 3. With the accompanying CD-ROM you'll have all the software you need to start creating CGI programs, as well as ready-to-run applications of popular Web page features.

Available now • 950 pages
ISBN: 1-57169-025-5
U.S. $44.99
1 CD-ROM

Send for our unique catalog to get more information about these books as well as our other outstanding and award-winning titles.

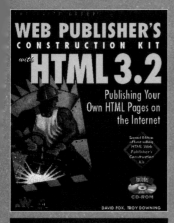

This is a legal agreement between you, the end user and purchaser, and The Waite Group®, Inc., and the authors of the programs contained in the disk. By opening the sealed disk package, you are agreeing to be bound by the terms of this Agreement. If you do not agree with the terms of this Agreement, promptly return the unopened disk package and the accompanying items (including the related book and other written material) to the place you obtained them for a refund.

SOFTWARE LICENSE

1. The Waite Group, Inc. grants you the right to use one copy of the enclosed software programs (the programs) on a single computer system (whether a single CPU, part of a licensed network, or a terminal connected to a single CPU). Each concurrent user of the program must have exclusive use of the related Waite Group, Inc. written materials.

2. The program, including the copyrights in each program, is owned by the respective author and the copyright in the entire work is owned by The Waite Group, Inc. and they are therefore protected under the copyright laws of the United States and other nations, under international treaties. You may make only one copy of the disk containing the programs exclusively for backup or archival purposes, or you may transfer the programs to one hard disk drive, using the original for backup or archival purposes. You may make no other copies of the programs, and you may make no copies of all or any part of the related Waite Group, Inc. written materials.

3. You may not rent or lease the programs, but you may transfer ownership of the programs and related written materials (including any and all updates and earlier versions) if you keep no copies of either, and if you make sure the transferee agrees to the terms of this license.

4. You may not decompile, reverse engineer, disassemble, copy, create a derivative work, or otherwise use the programs except as stated in this Agreement.

GOVERNING LAW

This Agreement is governed by the laws of the State of California.

LIMITED WARRANTY

The following warranties shall be effective for 90 days from the date of purchase: (i) The Waite Group, Inc. warrants the enclosed disk to be free of defects in materials and workmanship under normal use; and (ii) The Waite Group, Inc. warrants that the programs, unless modified by the purchaser, will substantially perform the functions described in the documentation provided by The Waite Group, Inc. when operated on the designated hardware and operating system. The Waite Group, Inc. does not warrant that the programs will meet purchaser's requirements or that operation of a program will be uninterrupted or error-free. The program warranty does not cover any program that has been altered or changed in any way by anyone other than The Waite Group, Inc. The Waite Group, Inc. is not responsible for problems caused by changes in the operating characteristics of computer hardware or computer operating systems that are made after the release of the programs, nor for problems in the interaction of the programs with each other or other software.

THESE WARRANTIES ARE EXCLUSIVE AND IN LIEU OF ALL OTHER WARRANTIES OF MERCHANTABILITY OR FITNESS FOR A PARTICULAR PURPOSE OR OF ANY OTHER WARRANTY, WHETHER EXPRESS OR IMPLIED.

EXCLUSIVE REMEDY

The Waite Group, Inc. will replace any defective disk without charge if the defective disk is returned to The Waite Group, Inc. within 90 days from date of purchase.

This is Purchaser's sole and exclusive remedy for any breach of warranty or claim for contract, tort, or damages.

LIMITATION OF LIABILITY

THE WAITE GROUP, INC. AND THE AUTHORS OF THE PROGRAMS SHALL NOT IN ANY CASE BE LIABLE FOR SPECIAL, INCIDENTAL, CONSEQUENTIAL, INDIRECT, OR OTHER SIMILAR DAMAGES ARISING FROM ANY BREACH OF THESE WARRANTIES EVEN IF THE WAITE GROUP, INC. OR ITS AGENT HAS BEEN ADVISED OF THE POSSIBILITY OF SUCH DAMAGES.

THE LIABILITY FOR DAMAGES OF THE WAITE GROUP, INC. AND THE AUTHORS OF THE PROGRAMS UNDER THIS AGREEMENT SHALL IN NO EVENT EXCEED THE PURCHASE PRICE PAID.

COMPLETE AGREEMENT

This Agreement constitutes the complete agreement between The Waite Group, Inc. and the authors of the programs, and you, the purchaser.

Some states do not allow the exclusion or limitation of implied warranties or liability for incidental or consequential damages, so the above exclusions or limitations may not apply to you. This limited warranty gives you specific legal rights; you may have others, which vary from state to state.

SATISFACTION REPORT CARD

Please fill out this card if you wish to know of future updates to *Web Publisher's Construction Kit with Netscape Plug-Ins* or to receive our catalog.

st Name: ______ Last Name: ______

reet Address: ______

ty: ______ State: ______ Zip: ______

mail Address ______

aytime Telephone: ( ) ______

Date product was acquired: Month Day Year Your Occupation:

Overall, how would you rate *Netscape Plug-Ins?*

☐ Excellent ☐ Very Good ☐ Good
☐ Fair ☐ Below Average ☐ Poor

What did you like MOST about this book? ______

What did you like LEAST about this book? ______

Please describe any problems you may have encountered with installing or using the disk: ______

How did you use this book (problem-solver, tutorial, reference...)?

What is your level of computer expertise?

☐ New ☐ Dabbler ☐ Hacker
☐ Power User ☐ Programmer ☐ Experienced Professional

What computer languages are you familiar with? ______

Please describe your computer hardware:

Computer ______ Hard disk ______
5.25" disk drives ______ 3.5" disk drives ______
Video card ______ Monitor ______
Printer ______ Peripherals ______
Sound board ______ CD-ROM ______

Where did you buy this book?

☐ Bookstore (name): ______
☐ Discount store (name): ______
☐ Computer store (name): ______
☐ Catalog (name): ______
☐ Direct from WGP ☐ Other ______

What price did you pay for this book? ______

What influenced your purchase of this book?

☐ Recommendation ☐ Advertisement
☐ Magazine review ☐ Store display
☐ Mailing ☐ Book's format
☐ Reputation of Waite Group Press ☐ Other

How many computer books do you buy each year? ______

How many other Waite Group books do you own? ______

What is your favorite Waite Group book? ______

Is there any program or subject you would like to see Waite Group Press cover in a similar approach? ______

Additional comments? ______

Please send to: **Waite Group Press
200 Tamal Plaza
Corte Madera, CA 94925**

☐ **Check here for a free Waite Group catalog**

SATISFACTION CARD

BEFORE YOU OPEN THE DISK OR CD-ROM PACKAGE ON THE FACING PAGE, CAREFULLY READ THE LICENSE AGREEMENT.

Opening this package indicates that you agree to abide by the license agreement found in the back of this book. If you do not agree with it, promptly return the unopened disk package (including the related book) to the place you obtained them for a refund.